TABLE OF CONTENTS

FRONT COVER William Stout **BACK COVER** Jordan Crane
PUBLISHER Fantagraphics Books, Inc. 7563 Lake City Way NE, Seattle, WA 98115
EDITOR IN CHIEF Gary Groth **ART DIRECTOR** Carrie Whitney **CONSULTING EDITOR** Michael Dean **ADDITIONAL COLORING** Rhea Patton
WEBMASTER Dirk Deppey **SCANMASTER** Paul Baresh **ADVERTISING** Matt Silvie **PUBLICITY** Eric Reynolds **CIRCULATION** Greg Zura **DUTCH UNCLE** Kim Thompson
All images and texts are copyright respective copyright holders.
First Fantagraphics Books edition: January, 2003
ISBN 1-56097-506-5
Printed in Korea through Print Vision.

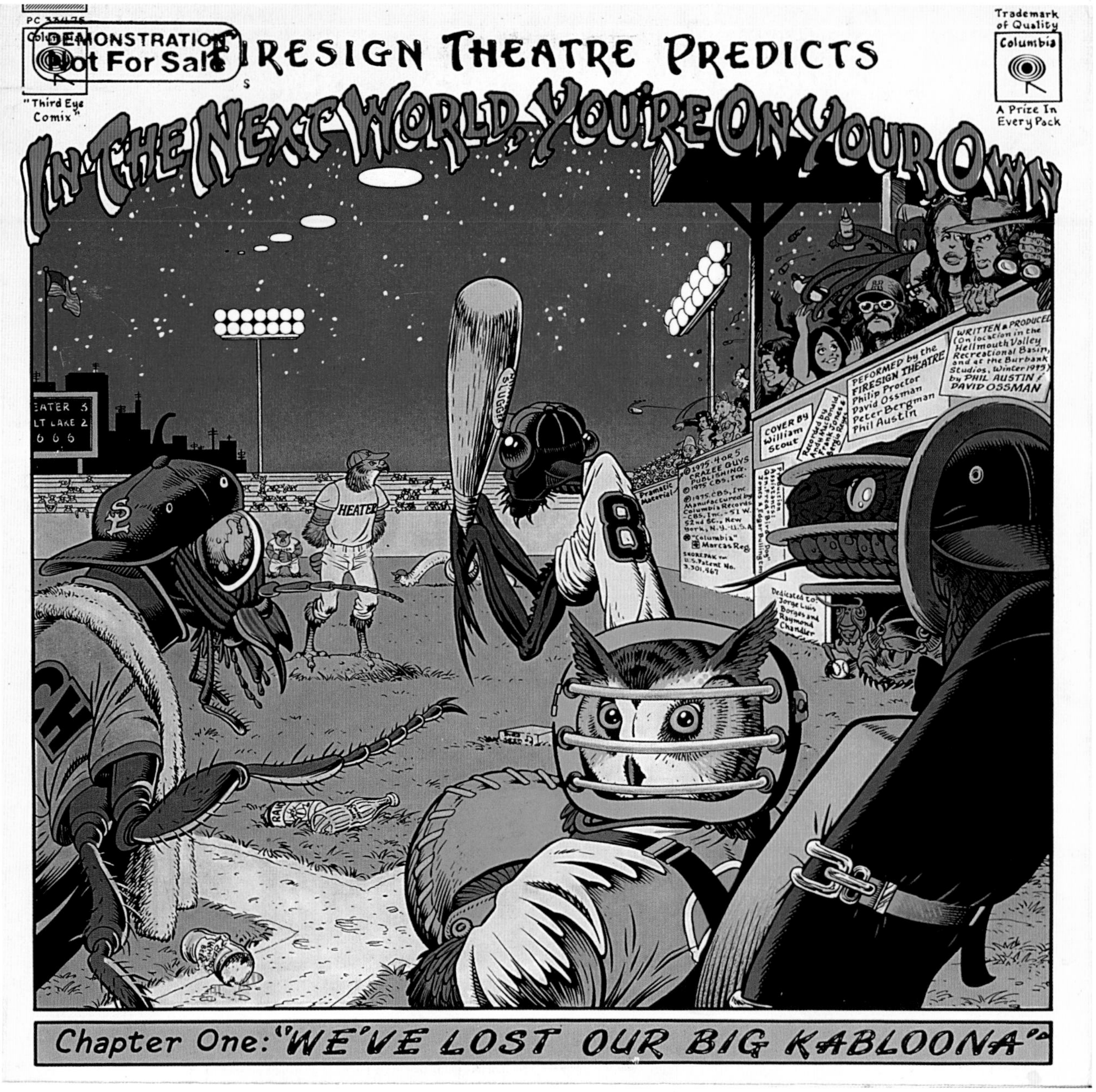
DEMONSTRATION Not For Sale
"Third Eye Comix"
FIRESIGN THEATRE PREDICTS
IN THE NEXT WORLD, YOU'RE ON YOUR OWN
Trademark of Quality
Columbia
A Prize In Every Pack
HEATER
WRITTEN & PRODUCED (On location in the Hellmouth Valley Recreational Basin, and at the Burbank Studios, Winter 1975) by PHIL AUSTIN & DAVID OSSMAN
PEFORMED by the FIRESIGN THEATRE Philip Proctor David Ossman Peter Bergman Phil Austin
COVER BY William Stout
Dramatic Material
©1975 4 OR 5 CRAZEE GUYS PUBLISHING
©1975 CBS, Inc.
℗1975 CBS, Inc Manufactured by Columbia Records - CBS, Inc. - 51 W. 52nd St., New York, N.Y. - U.S.A.
"Columbia" Marcas Reg.
Dedicated to: Jorge Luis Borges and Raymond Chandler
Chapter One: "WE'VE LOST OUR BIG KABLOONA"

WILLIAM STOUT

Poetry and Terror

by Kenneth R. Smith

"Movies are someone else's adventures. Wouldn't you rather spend those two hours having your own adventures?" It really stopped me. I thought about all that time I had spent in the dark living someone else's dreams and adventures. —Stout interviewed, reflecting on a remark by Nordy Roblin

Of the next-generation alumni who learned so much so avidly from E.C.'s rich lines of comics—Wrightson, Kaluta, Pound, Schultz, and numerous others—none has really reached into so many of the treasuries of artistic and illustrational traditions beyond comics as has William Stout. He truly has taken his good wherever he found it, in children's books, scientific and nature illustration, the pulp adventure and SF series, comics, animation, fine vintage-illustration, movie posters, album covers; and he has shown the acuteness of his hand and eye in every one of these fields. He has proved a multifarious designer and visionary at home in various media and genres, even as a conceptualist and planner for EuroDisney.

Like the Beatles' "white album," Stout's *The Dinosaurs: A Fantastic New View of a Lost Era* appeared in 1981 as a stylistic *tour de force,* bringing to bear on the saurians influences from Mucha, Frazetta, Rackham, Williamson, Moebius, Burian, Knight, and other masters of prehistorica and fantastica; and his new book in turn itself inspired Crichton's *Jurassic Park*. Stout's Argus-eyed work was such a labor of love and a groundbreaking conceptual and technical masterpiece as to gain him instant esteem as an artist's artist. Closely following this was his children's book, *The Little Blue Brontosaurus* (1984), revealing a sculptural and expressive gift for characterization that put him at once into the top fields of animation, as this ill-distributed, now all-too-scarce book became the basis for *The Land Before Time.*

Character-, set- and costume-design and storyboarding for four *Conan* movies and poster-work for *Wizards, Predator, More American Graffiti, Invaders from Mars, Masters of the Universe, Buck Rogers,* and other films or TV series continued to evidence his very supple sense of

This Page: Stout designed a double front cover for the Firesign Theatre's LP *In the Next World, You're On Your Own* with a different image on each side.

intriguing structure as well as nuanced coloring and realizable design of materiel for scenes to be constructed and shot. His fine-art fantasy work has in a way been even more wide-ranging than his commercial work, touching on the precious and opalescent watercolor effects of Sulamith Wulfing (with her poetic angels and fairies evident in part in his "Angel of the Moon"), the good-humored grotesquery of John Bauer (earthy little trolls and gnomes that remind one also of Brian Froud's sources), and the palpable gentleness of Edmund Dulac's dreamlike watercolors. But Stout has never affiliated himself single-mindedly with any source or style: his protean sense of approach has always obliged him to rethink a new way to recast classic themes. Frequently this takes the form of "stylistic quotations," borrowing some famous predecessor's eyes and hands more or less as an oblique homage. "Fairy Tales," for instance, Stout's Rackhamesque watercolor of a butterfly-nymph bringing a blush to a close-cuddling snail, is an excellent example of his puckish humor and marvelous filigree of natural detailing: there is no question that Rackham's poetic and dreamy stain-effects and woodsy grotesquery are the exactly right setting for this bit of whimsy.

Even his trees and ferns show remarkably original staging and rhythm.

Likewise, Stout's covers for underground comics like *Slow Death* and especially for alternative-press comic titles like *Alien Worlds* evoked the sure and voluptuous linework of Maurice Whitman from *Planet* and *Jungle Comics* — wonderfully luminous and painterly effects for the medium of comics, in which not just color but linework also is often rather perfunctory. Unlike the norm in most comics, Stout's work clearly shows painstaking studies to master anatomical form, not just for the human species but also for every natural creature he has represented: skeleton, musculature, scales, fur, pro-

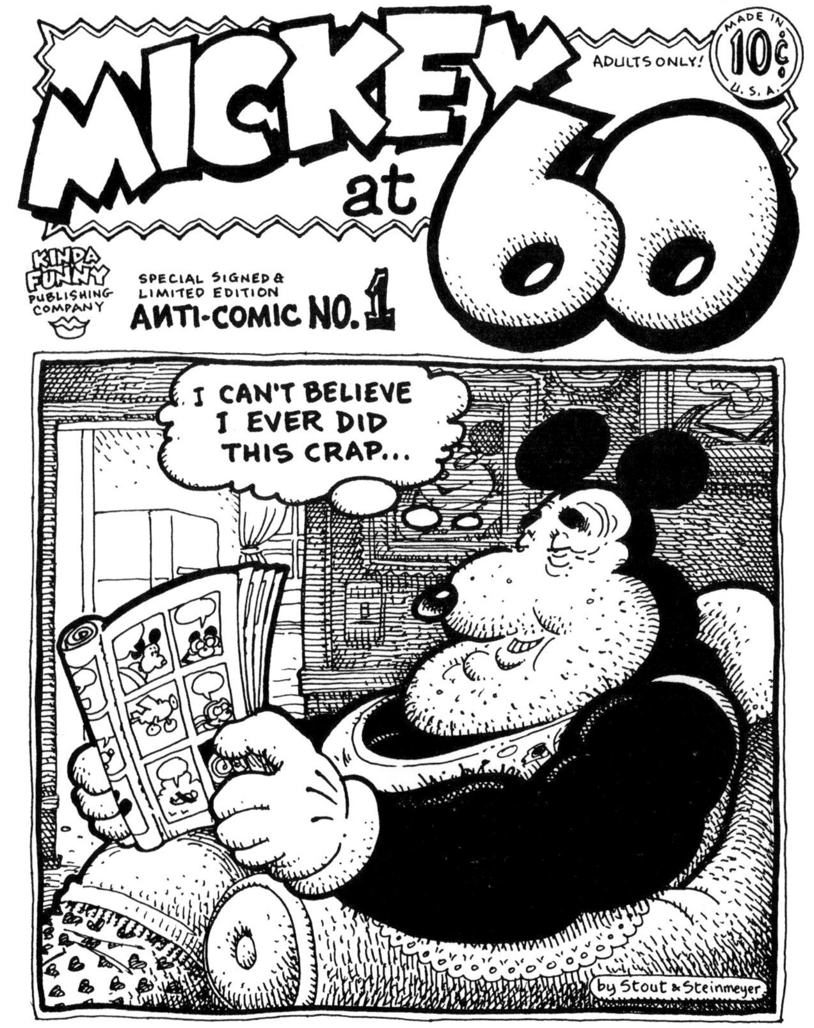
MICKEY at 60
ADULTS ONLY!
MADE IN 10¢ U.S.A.
KINDA FUNNY PUBLISHING COMPANY
SPECIAL SIGNED & LIMITED EDITION
ANTI-COMIC NO. 1
I CAN'T BELIEVE I EVER DID THIS CRAP...
by Stout & Steinmeyer

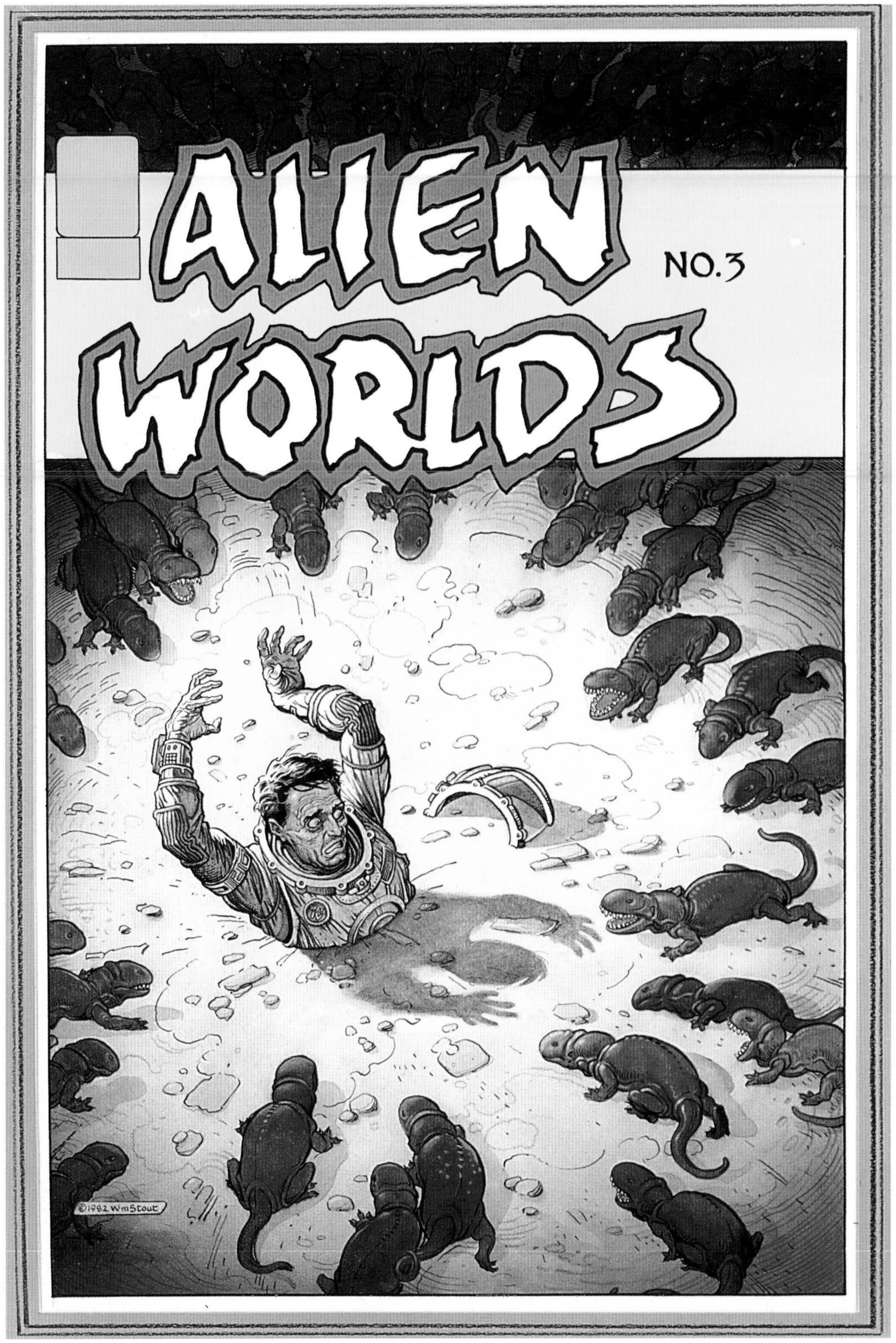
ALIEN WORLDS
NO.3
©1982 WmStout

portionality, all bear the authority of a seasoned and sympathetic eye. No less is true for his grasp of the entire natural setting of life, the flora and rockforms, the patterning of clouds far overhead. Trickles of water, the meandering line of a rivulet or the difficult perspective of a rock-bound waterhole, nail the authenticity of a scene even though one has to know the whole thing is sheer invention; even his trees and ferns show remarkably original staging and rhythm, as he inserts these things as virtual botanical portraits into a scene where they perform a subordinate role quite flawlessly. Stout's self-published series of *Convention Sketches* reveals a stupendous freshet of figures, creatures, poses, styles, all in all making him a more than worthy successor to the burgeoning imagination of fantasy art's Great Beginner, Roy Krenkel, a past master at setting the stage.

Stout has a wealth of technical finesse and stylistic repertory to draw upon, like a musical polymath who takes up whatever instrument may please him, to put it to virtuosic use. His realistic scenes of natural

This Page Left: "I've got a handwritten note from Michael Eisner stating that *Mickey at 60* is his favorite comic."

Right: The tech elements of this *Alien Worlds* cover convinced writer/director Dan O'Bannon that Stout was the man to production-design his *Return of the Living Dead.*

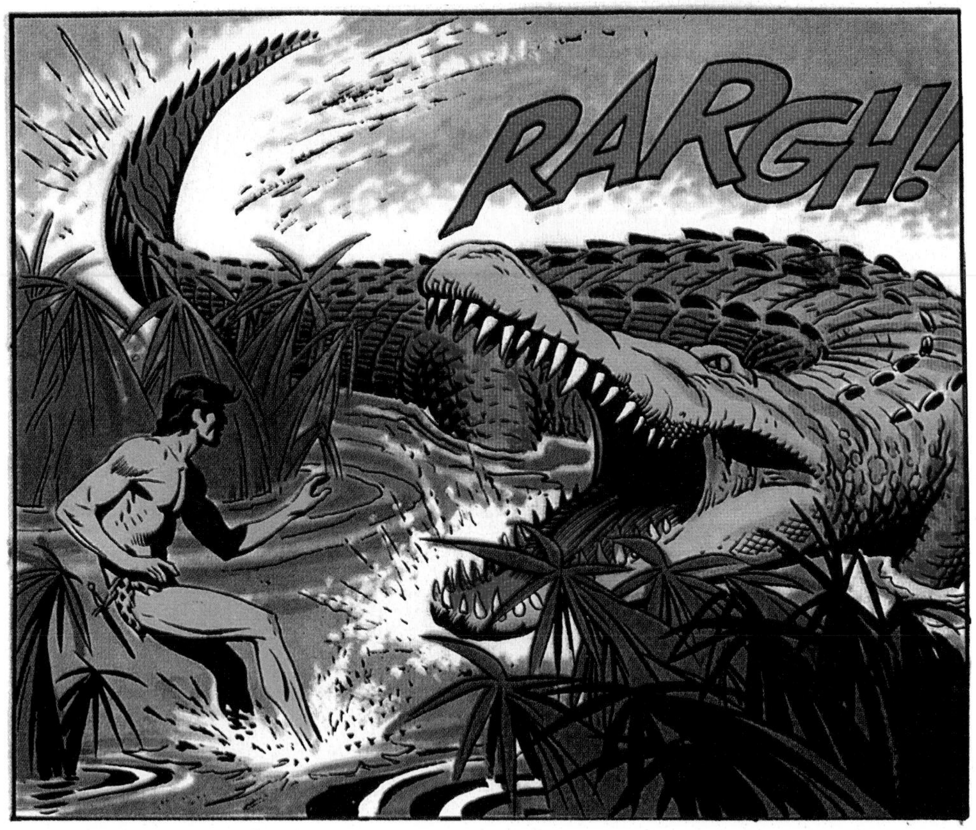
RARGH!

This Page: Stout inked and colored this panel from Russ Manning's *Tarzan in the Land that Time Forgot* graphic novel.

life — skuas for example, perching atop an outcropping of rock whose rash of speckling shows how it became over generations their own avian architecture, or his "Giant Petrel" nesting on its bed of shells (reminiscent of Durer's magnificent "Hare" in its khaki tones) or a pod of southern right whales ("Eroica," an ambitious 2x4' oil) — evoke the poignancy of nature in its isolation from man. Or, to reach to the other end of his spectrum of sensibility, even his satirical work, such as "The Evolution of a Mouse" or his Firesign Theater album covers, displays a flawlessly black-humored sense of form and timing or spacing. His self-collected portraits of the sad end of the overstuffed has-been Mouse, *Mickey at 60* — with the Disney icon enduring a proctological exam, and with five flawless variations on Edward Hopper's poetic delineations of banal modern life — resorbs a classic comic character into the cultural media of our considerably more cynical time. It is clear from Stout's comic dinosaur roughs that he drew a great deal of inspiration from Walt Kelly's marvelous characterizations, not just from *Pogo* but also from *The Glob*. Stout's fantasy work shows marvelous incursions of mood, humanizing perfectly what is less than human or other than human — "The Watcher," for instance, shows a troll sitting in his parka, wistfully studying in solitude the chimneysmoke from a remote human dwelling — and luminous idiosyncrasies, such as the peculiar crook in a swimming dragon's neck. Indeed, virtually every dragon that has left Stout's hand has perfectly captured the sullen and bilious temperament so typical of this hermitic species. If Stout is truly possessed, we can readily guess the species of the spirit.

Inkwork. Stout's earliest work, for the hot-rod subculture and underground LPs, was heavily influenced by comics, most of all by *Mad*'s singularly dense clash of icons and the byplay of counterpoint-commentary. For a time, in fact, he worked with Kurtzman and Elder on *Annie Fanny,* although the job bound his imagination in to much too mechanical strictures. His covers for the Firesign Theater's albums displayed a perfect mastery of such comic orchestration and a balance of semirealistic and caricatural rendering that was the equal of Wally Wood's or Howard Nostrand's. The black-and-white work Stout did for *The Dinosaurs* although bold and dramatic showed repeated influences from the sinuous forms of Art Nouveau, and sometimes recapitulated the epic style of classical illustration's most outstanding conduit to modern fantasy art, Roy Krenkel. No one of course could have synthesized these influences without also drawing upon Al Williamson's masterpiece in dinosauria, the utterly evocative and visionary retelling of Bradbury's "A Sound of Thunder" for *Weird Science-Fantasy* #25. But Stout's line is typically more bold or voluptuous, less spidery and poetic like Williamson's Vierge-, Coll- and Salinas-influenced touch.

There is no question that, just as dinosaurs have populated his best painted work, so too they have inspired his richest inkwork: his *Dinosaur Sketchbooks* contain not just richly detailed panoramic scenes but also splendid thumbnail sketches, preliminary poses with all the electric energy of the first glimmering of an idea presenting itself to his squinting mind's eye. Stout's extremely rough or provisional drawings often do not have the finesse or quavering micro-seismology of Krenkel's or Williamson's inquisitive penwork — needless to say, this kind of tentative work for which the pencil is more natural is absolutely forbidding for a penman, and few indeed are the Kleys or Colls who make such decisive and surgical strokes — but no matter, we are still privileged indeed to see such twilight-inklings of figures and forms that have not ventured all the way into the anteroom of full-glare consciousness.

In his self-published series of *Convention Sketches* Stout has shown a forthright indebtedness to Krenkel and Frazetta and the generally machismo-thematics of the more popular fantasy-art world. Stout's trees, ferns, toadstools, rock pinnacles, and other natural formations point back to those earlier hands and styles, but there is nothing in this repertory that he has not entirely digested into his own version. Stout's sense of spaciousness, of vignetted elements taken as the whole of a subject, are a touch he has in common not just with Krenkel but also with Moebius: an elegance of placement, a sublimity of distance and proportionality. Stout's quality of line may vary from a screen-wire hatchwork to a very fine integration of penstroke with the texture, fracture and stress of a subject. Clearly he has his own striking sense of dramaturgy for dragons and saurians and other fantasy-lore; his feminine anatomy has as a rule been less florid and hyperbolic than Frazetta's but always elegantly and effectively posed. In volumes 5-8 of his *Convention Sketches* Stout has offered a brief selection of Neruda's most iconic poems, translated by himself and illustrated to a perfect pitch. The projected book, *Stones of the Sky,* I will venture sight unseen to call a masterwork. The translator's deft wordings have a graphic tracery of their own and stand in an exquisite duet with the pictorials.

Clearly he has his own striking sense of dramaturgy for dragons and saurians and other fantasy-lore.

Paintings. Stout's earliest published color-work after his juvenilia for the digest *Coven 13*, his *Prehistoric Worlds* portfolio, was essentially tinted drawings, a method of conversion into color that was quite common then in fantasy art publications and of course remains so even now in comics. *The Dinosaurs* therefore revealed a whole palette of techniques, from wet-in-wet watercolors to viscous or stiff oils, that before then had no public evidence. His nature paintings have rightly earned him a place among our most accomplished realistic fine artists, being set on permanent display at the Houston Museum of Natural Science, the Museum of the Rockies, the Orton Geological Museum, and Walt Disney's Animal Kingdom. His sketches and paintings from his various trips to Antarctica were gathered into an exhibit, *Dinosaurs, Penguins and Whales,* that originated at the

Natural History Museum of Los Angeles County in 1991 and toured for three years afterward, as a 45-painting one-man show.

His dinosauria I believe are clearly his masterworks, showing epic conceptions of a finely evolved and detailed phase of the earth's life. He inveigles drama and mood into these prehistoric settings, often by bold spectra of colors but sometimes in spectacular strokes like the arch an Elasmosaur's neck makes as it darts for its minuscule prey. His "Spinosaurus aegyptiacus" won a Gold Medal from the Society of Illustrators recently. He has a great adeptness at putting just the inkling of an expression on the great saurians, an oblique and subtle (or winking) anthropomorphism that makes the creatures' alienness that much more piquant. His recent limited edition Iris-giclee prints of four dinosaur settings — "Riders on the Storm" and "Polar Predator" most outstandingly — display a consummate sense of orchestral color and poetically precise timing in gestures. Likewise with his portfolio of scenes from *The Wizard of Oz*, all fresh takes on the now-iconic Baum/Neill characters. *Oz* I have to say seems nonetheless far outclassed by the classical tenor of the dino-portfolio, as a pacific and esthetic vista on a violent era. It is sobering to

think how many CEOs and attorneys identify with the meat-rending tyrant-lizards in such paleozoic scenes; live by the talons, die by the talons.

The release of *The New Dinosaurs* at the end of 2000 showed decisively that Stout's vision of this epoch had become an authoritative registry for new work in this field of scientific research. Important new species simply could not seem real until Stout had put his visual imprint on them. His masterwork of two decades before could not thinkably be left without updating. The kind of genius for organic splendor and concretization that Zdenek Burian had brought to paleontology a generation ago — or Charles R. Knight before that — Stout was able to ply in an utterly cogent and animating way. Unlike Burian and Knight, Stout has competition galore in the current crop of paleo-illustrators — Sibbick, Henderson, Hallett, for instance — but still his work shines with iconic form, color and life. His millennial perspective on the evolution of life's fragile and exotic forms has naturally enough made him a fervent and engaged environmentalist, a field-researcher as well as a superb studio-talent. And this can hardly be underscored boldly enough: Not only has Stout been determined to delve into the understanding of experts in the fields of paleontology, paleobotany and ecology of Antarctica — to prepare himself thoroughly in an intellectual or scholarly way for the remarkable landscape of the South Pole, and even moreso for its physical rigors and extreme dangers — but he has also become an activist on behalf of environmentalism and political conscience. His remark about not being content to live out someone else's dreams is the logic of his personality, an audacious and authentic individual.

Stout has professed to be no genius: He has worked on projects with artists he considers genius-caliber, such as Moebius, and regards himself as merely a hardworking talent who puts in 12-hour days seven days a week and feels driven not just to keep himself busy but also to strike prudent deals and savvy contracts and keep an eagle-eye on the shape of his career. For most mere artisans who are merely industrious, even prodigious efforts do not yield anything remotely like the grandeur, grace and shock of lively forms that one sees in Stout's art. I am told by classical musicians that the public has been greatly oversold on the virtues of hard work and rehearsal: that a Heifetz or a Horowitz merely practiced enough to keep the edge keen, not as consumingly as someone still striving to arrive at his proper virtuosity. Bill Stout's abundance of superb work may just show that he has the kind of genius that is a slavedriver to itself, and does not like to let itself coast or glide. Someday, when a suitable artbook confirms and consolidates what his wondrous cluster of work has already shown in the format of trading cards, the fantasy-art public will learn to appreciate how some people may be the beneficiaries of other people's demons.

Quite apart from the rich gallery of Stout's work, he also holds in his possession a body of insights invaluable to other artists and illustrators — his diversified understanding, as a shapeshifting talent, of the very different cultures and personality-types that the "world" of art is now fractured into, in the fields of editorial or published illustration, commercial or advertising illustration, scientific or museum illustration, fine-art or gallery work, etc. Most young talents of course are aiming themselves toward regions of artistic practice about whose true working conditions they haven't got a clue. Stout has been there and has won the respect of all of them. His offhand remarks on the human realities of these different fields ought to be treasured, and expanded on. ★★★

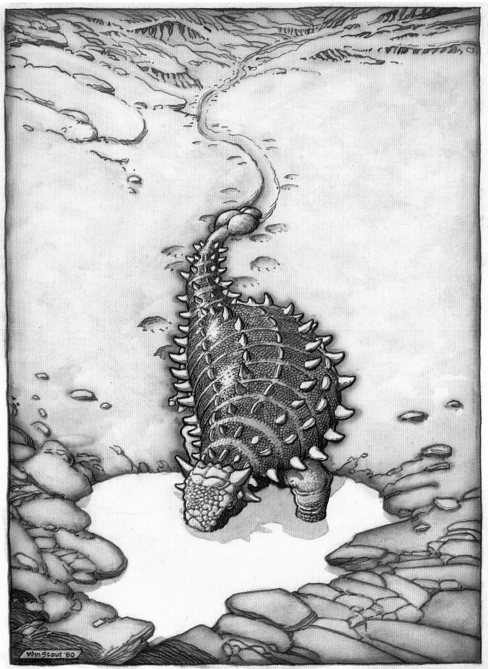

He has also become an activist on behalf of environmentalism and political conscience.

This Page: This was the first illustration Stout completed for his classic book *The Dinosaurs — A Fantastic New View of a Lost Era* (recently republished as *The New Dinosaurs*).

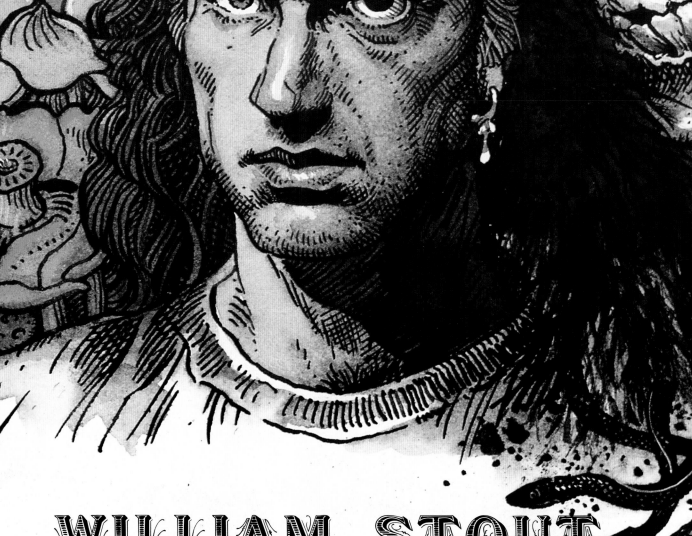

WILLIAM STOUT

It's a Wonderful Life
Interview by John Arcudi

ill Stout was born Sept. 18, 1949 in Salt Lake City while his parents were en route to their home in Los Angeles, the city in which he was raised, and where he still lives today.

Stout enjoyed drawing at a young age, encouraged by positive response from his parents, and especially a farsighted fifth grade teacher by the name of Elliot Wittenberg. Stout became a movie nut early on, encouraged again by his parents, who loved horror movies and musicals (Mom) and SF movies and Westerns (Dad); with such liberal tastes between his two parents, Stout was able to watch six to ten movies a week at the local theatres. His subsequent successful career as a movie poster artist was not exactly fortuitous.

His earliest influences were the illustrator William Scheele and comic book greats Gil Kane (*Atom* and *Green Lantern*) and Carmine Infantino (*Flash* and *Adam Strange*), whose work he would swipe when he started drawing his own comics at age 14.

In 1967, he entered the Chouinard Institute, also known as California Institute of the Arts (CalArts), where he majored in illustration. He felt lucky to be at CalArts because "they didn't push any one style on anyone. They were more focused on developing your individual potential as a unique artist." The animation department at CalArts was being taught by Disney's remaining Nine Old men. The environment, according to Stout, "was vital. To a kid who had grown up in a pretty cloistered, white bread conservative existence it was a taste of heaven."

When some left-leaning students asked him to draw a comic espousing their views, he drew his first comic, "Those Loveable

This Page: Cover half of this self-portrait to see either the Good Stout or the Dark Stout.

Peace-Nuts," in Charles Schulz's style. He started picking up freelance assignments while attending CalArts, including a stint doing illustrations and cover paintings for a fiction fanzine called *Coven 13* and an Edgar Rice Burroughs fanzine called *ERB-dom*. His drawings for the latter caught the eye of the legendary Russ Manning, who was drawing the Tarzan newspaper strip at the time and recruited Stout as his apprentice/assistant, where he "was inking, coloring, learning more about the importance of deadlines…" from 1971 to 1974-'75. Manning became a mentor to Stout, and even a father figure, and tutored him in the history of comics, turning him on to such artists as Hal Foster.

Eventually, Stout found his way to *Cycle-toons*, a motorcycle magazine. When the editor, Dennis Ellefson, saw Stout's portfolio he saw potential and assigned him a four-page comic on the spot. Stout wrote and drew comics for *Cycle-toons* for four years (1970-'73), learning on the job. (Ironically, Stout never rode or owned a motorcycle and drew them from model kits he bought at a toy store.)

Which brings us to Stout's next significant professional experience — working with Harvey Kurtzman on Playboy's *Little Annie Fanny* in 1972, at which point the interview officially begins.

[EDITOR'S NOTE: The original transcript to this interview ran 55,000 words. This was edited down, with great pain, to 35,000 words — still too long to run. But, Stout's careeer encompasses so many different areas — comics, commercial illustration, posters, design, and storyboarding for film, fine art, gallery paintings, murals — and Stout himself is such an articulate observer and engaging raconteur that we wanted to make as much of it available as possible. Our solution was to include discrete sections of the complete interview on the *Journal*'s Web site. Throughout the interview, you'll find a bar with an address and an icon directing you to an URL located on our Web site. For example, to read the first part of the interview that leads up to Stout's working with Harvey Kurtzman, go here: **http://www.tcj.com/ws03/stoutearly.html**]

ARCUDI: Around the same time as *Cycle-toons*, at one point you went off to New York to work with Kurtzman on *Little Annie Fanny* for *Playboy*. First of all, how did that come about? Second of all, why did that last so short?

STOUT: Well, I was in the middle of what I consider to be the peak of my *Cycle-toons* stuff. One of the reasons I was peaking was because I had just discovered the original *Mad* comics. I was especially enthralled with Kurtzman's work, Will Elder's work, and Wally Wood's work. I went nuts over this stuff. I wanted to do work like that more than anything. So I did a *Cycle-toons* story called "Motor-Psycho!" in which I aped Kurtzman's, Elder's and Wood's styles; three different styles all in one story. When it was published, I sent a copy off to Kurtzman. About a week or two later I got a letter back from Harvey asking me if I'd be interested in coming to New York and assisting him and Elder on *Little Annie Fanny*. It blew the top of my head off. I couldn't believe it. At that time there were three people I wanted to work with more than anything: one was Kurtzman, the other was Will Eisner; the third was Alex Toth.

I immediately called Kurtzman and said, "Yes. Of course!" That was quite an adventure. It was in 1972; they flew me out and I was initially put up in a hotel in Englewood, N. J., not far from where Willy [Elder] lived. I ultimately moved to Fort Lee, N. J., to my own apartment, which was right across the street from the George Washington Bridge. Just a walk across the bridge was Manhattan. It was an astounding time to be there. I was there for the very first EC Convention. Because of that, besides working with Kurtzman and Elder, I got to meet and become friends with Roy Krenkel, Al Williamson, and George Evans. I met Wally Wood for the first time.

ARCUDI: These were all names that you were familiar with because you had an early exposure to EC stuff?

STOUT: Yeah. Legendary names.

ARCUDI: When you were a kid, or a little bit older?

STOUT: The very first time I ever heard about EC's I think I was about 15 years old. There was a kid in my junior high who found out I collected comics. He asked, "Do you have any EC's?" I said, "Yeah. I got lots of D.C.'s." "No", he said, "EC's." I didn't know what he was talking about. I saw my first EC a year or two later. My friend Fred Romanek had some. They didn't make much of an impression at first because it

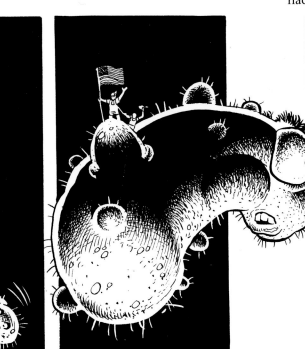

This I whispered, and an echo murmured back the word, "Lenore!" — merely this and nothing more.
Back into the chamber turning, all my soul within me burning
Soon again I heard a tapping something louder than before.

"Surely", said I, "surely that is something at my window lattice;
Let me see, then, what thereat is, and this mystery explore,—
Let my heart be still a moment, and this mystery explore;—
'Tis the wind and nothing more."

Top: Stout with Russ Manning (right). "Russ was a great father, a thorough professional and a patient mentor."

Bottom: "My complex adaptation of 'The Raven' owes more to Rick Griffin's trippy early '70s work in *Surfer* than to my usual EC influences."

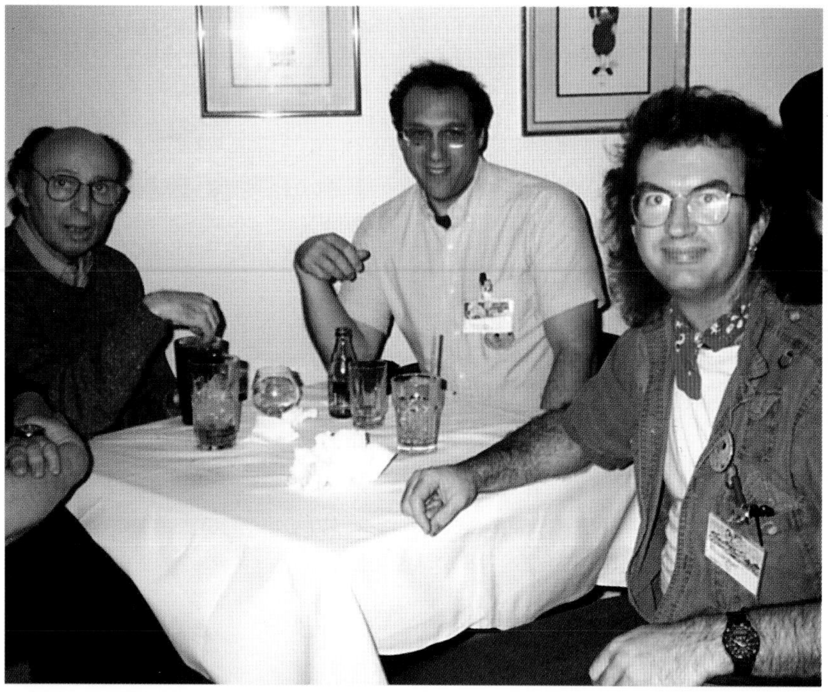

This Page: Harvey Kurtzman (left) and Stout (right). Stout: "Whenever Harvey ventured west we never failed to get together with each other to celebrate and commiserate."

was so not superhero, and that's what I was into – superheroes. But when I started drawing my own stuff, I fell under the influence of Frank Frazetta. I found out that Frazetta had done work for EC I went, "Really? God, Frazetta did comics? I'd love to see what that looked like!" I started to hunt them down. As I picked up the Frazetta EC comics, I was exposed to Al Williamson's stuff. And I couldn't ignore Wally Wood's stuff. I was like, Oh, my god. These guys are astounding! And so I got them all, all of the EC New Trends. Eventually, in a very short time, I amassed, through cash, but mostly through trade (trading art for comics) a complete collection of the EC New Trends, which I still have to this day.

The EC's were a huge influence on me. I was just consuming all of the Mad and all the Kurtzman stuff – everything! And here I was in New York with a chance to meet all of these guys. Jack Davis! Bill Gaines! Marie Severin! It seemed like everybody was there except Frazetta who I talked to on the phone. It was very, very exciting. Williamson, Krenkel and I especially became fast friends. I just love those two guys to pieces. Al invited me out to stay with him a little while and visit, which I did. I got to meet Reed Crandall, who was working in Al's studio. After that, every time I'd go to New York I'd look up Roy Krenkel and we'd get together.

ARCUDI: So what happened?

STOUT: My job on *Annie Fanny* wasn't the most creative job in the world. The job came about because Hefner wanted a greater output of *Annie* strips. Kurtzman and Elder used to have guys like Frank Frazetta, Arnold Roth and Jack Davis helping them put out more strips. That bothered Hefner, though, because he could always spot their individual styles; he wanted a consistent style and sheen to the strip. I was hired to speed up production of *Annie* without my work showing through. Kurtzman would pencil the strip, I would transfer his pencils to a board, and then using Kurtzman's color guides, I would watercolor the final strip, taking it to about a halfway finished point. Then I would hand it to Willy Elder; he would finish it. In that way, the strip had a very consistent look because it was Will Elder's style on the complete final sheen of the strip.

ARCUDI: You were doing a lot of the actual work, but very little creative work?

STOUT: There was almost no creative input on my part. In fact, I tried to put in some stuff and it really backfired. I can't believe how arrogant I was to think that I could come up with gags for Kurtzman and Elder. Here I was in my early 20s. Unbelievable. I'd hear the whir of Willy's electric eraser and just cringe. Oh, my god! Not only did my gag not work, but I was costing them time. I was supposed to be saving them time for pete's sake. After I had worked on two episodes it was clear to both Kurtzman and me that this was not the job for me. Kurtzman took me aside and said, "Bill, you're too creative for this. You're going to go on to do great stuff, but I can feel you champing at the bit to do your own stuff. This is not the job where you get to do that." I said, "I know." And we mutually agreed that I return to Los Angeles. We stayed best friends up until he passed away. Whenever Harvey came to L.A. on Playboy business he'd call me up and we'd get together and have dinner or visit the Playboy Mansion.

Kurtzman took me aside and said, "Bill, you're too creative for this. You're going to go on to do great stuff, but I can feel you champing at the bit to do your own stuff."

ARCUDI: It's interesting that Harvey didn't see that at the beginning when he saw your stuff. Obviously the reason he wanted you is because he saw that you were so good.

STOUT: Thank you, but I think he originally just saw a guy who was really good at aping styles, one of my fortés during the time in question. In fact, I got my first movie poster work because of that special ability of mine. It was for a film called *S*P*Y*S*. Rick Meyerowitz had done the poster, but had blown the caricatures of Elliott Gould and the girl, Zou Zou. He refused to correct it, so the poster came to L.A. They called me up; I think Robert Williams told the agency that I could duplicate anybody's style. One of Robert's friends, Dave Reneric, was one of the art directors at the ad agency. Dave called me and had me do a patch-over; then I did an exact Rick Meyerowitz version of Elliot Gould – but I made it look like Elliott Gould, and drew a new version of the girl that looked like the actress.

BOOTLEG ALBUM COVERS

ARCUDI: Before we get into the movie poster stuff, we have to talk about the bootleg records. How did that start?

STOUT: My favorite record store in Hollywood was a little shop called Record Paradise. I used to buy all of my records there. One of the things they carried in the store were bootleg record albums. Bootlegs, for those readers who don't know, were usually made thusly: A person would go to a rock concert, bring a little Sony tape recorder, record the concert, the next day go to a pressing plant and then press 500 copies of the concert based on those tapes. Pretty crappy sound quality, but it was a kind of cool souvenir remembrance of the concert. Initially, they were just sold on street corners. Initially, bootleg albums had white covers rubber-stamped with a title. Guys would have a bundle of them under their arms. "Hey, you want the new Led Zeppelin concert?" "Sure!" They were ten bucks. Soon, Record Paradise began carrying bootlegs. I had just been to a Led Zeppelin concert; I knew there was going to be a bootleg of it — someone had to have taped it! I was really looking forward to it. The record came in and I went, "Oh, man. This cover's so bad. The band deserves better than that. I wish they'd gotten me to do the cover." A guy tapped me on the shoulder and he said, "You wanna do bootleg covers?" I go, "Yeah." He handed me a little note-sized sheet of paper with a date, an address, and a time. He said, "Meet me there." Then he disappeared. He left the store. I thought, "Well, this guy's mysterious!" At 8:00 PM on a Friday night I stood at the corner of Franklin and Las Palmas – not the best neighborhood in the world, but not as dangerous as it is now. This coupe with smoked windows pulled up; the windows rolled down just a crack and some fingers pushed out a sheet of paper. I

NEIL YOUNG:
"B.B.C. BROADCAST"
A PIG-LOVERS SPECIAL!
c 1973 Wm Stout
All Rights Reserved 5-28
Dear Madge— Out on the Weekend! -Harry xxx
JOURNEY THROUGH THE PAST "Pigasaurus"
~ OLD MAN ~
HEART OF GOLD
Love in Mind
MONOLOGUE
TAKE MY WIFE... PLEASE!
SEE THE GIRL DANCE
DON'T LET IT BRING YOU DOWN!
A MAN NEEDS A MAID!
OH NO HE DOESN'T!
TRADE MARK OF QUALITY
TMQ 71072
P11

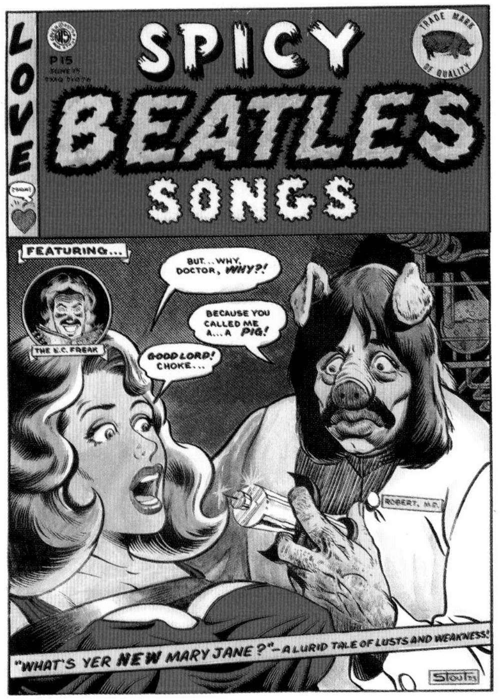

took the sheet of paper; it said, "Rolling Stones Winter Tour" followed by a list of songs. A voice inside said, "Same place. Same time. Two weeks." Then they drove away. I went, "Huh." I drove home and I drew my first bootleg cover. It was an homage to Robert Crumb's *Cheap Thrills* cover, with a comic illustration for each of the songs. I changed the title from *Winter Tour* to *All Meat Music*. I went back two weeks later, Friday, eight o'clock. The car drives up, the window cracks, and it's like mailing a letter. I stick the art through the slot and a $50 bill came out in its place; then they drove away.

I stick the art through the slot and a $50 bill came out in its place; then they drove away.

Eventually the bootleggers felt that they could trust me and I started to meet them face-to-face. We became good friends.

There was one bootleg I did for The Who, called "Who's Zoo" that John Entwistle, the bass player for The Who, saw.

ARCUDI: That's the Animal Crackers cover, right?

STOUT: Yeah. I made it look like an Animal Crackers box. John, when he looked at the tracks and thought, "Oh, my god. I didn't realize we had so much stuff that had never been collected on an album." So John put out *Odds and Sods*, a legitimate Who release of rarities and collectibles. Just a couple of years ago when The Who were about to re-release *Odds and Sods* on CD as a newly re-mastered version with bonus tracks, they asked for permission to use my Jack Kirby-style Who bootleg cover as the image on the CD's picture disk. I was like, "Whoa. Of course!"

ARCUDI: In spite of the fact that you were mimicking a lot of stuff, I think that cover especially, *Tales From The Who*, not the Kirby one, that's where you start to see the Stout style really start to gel.

STOUT: I think you might be right. Not so much in the earlier boots, except maybe the first. That other Who LP was drawn Kirby-style because I had just inked a Jack Kirby *Demon*. Usually you can tell what I was working on at the time with the bootleg covers, because they tended to reflect whatever I happened to be doing at the time.

JACK KIRBY AND EARLY COMIC BOOK INFLUENCES

ARCUDI: Obviously, before we move on you're going to have to elaborate about inking a Jack Kirby *Demon*.

STOUT: Mike Royer was Jack's inker at the time and was under a deadline crunch. He called me and asked if I'd help him out. I knew Mike because he was the inker previous to me with Russ Manning on the *Tarzan* strips. I jumped at the chance to ink Jack Kirby. I thought the experience would be great. I'd never seen Kirby's pencils, either; I was dying to see what he penciled like. I figured they'd be really loose, because I'd heard how fast he was. I drove over to Mike's house in Whittier where I set up in his studio. I inked side by side with Mike as we listened to tapes of old radio shows from Mike's collection. And was astounded to see that Jack pencils were really very tight. Everything was there; it was just beautiful, beautiful stuff. All I had to

LOVE
SPICY BEATLES SONGS
P15
TRADE MARK OF QUALITY
FEATURING...
THE E.C. FREAK
BUT... WHY, DOCTOR, WHY?!
BECAUSE YOU CALLED ME A... A PIG!
GOOD LORD! CHOKE...
ROBERT, M.D.
"WHAT'S YER NEW MARY JANE?"—A LURID TALE OF LUSTS AND WEAKNESS!

Yardbirds
MORE GOLDEN EGGS

Top: Upon seeing this bootleg in a Hollywood record shop, Neil Young picked it up and flung it across the store.

Bottom Left: Stout hand-colored one copy of this black-and-white EC horror-comics take-off cover for the Beatles bootleg LP *What's Yer New Mary Jane?*.

Bottom Middle: "Most of my *Dinosaur Dictionary* illustrations were ink on colored board with white highlights. I used chicken anatomy for the dinosaurs' musculature. It turned out years later that I wasn't too far off in doing so."

Bottom Right: This Yardbirds bootleg was the first semi-legitimate bootleg LP; Stout conducted an interview with Yardbirds lead singer Keith Relf, in which Relf commented on the bootleg's various Yardbirds rarities as they played — and the interview was included with the album as an insert.

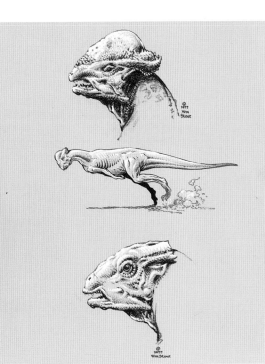

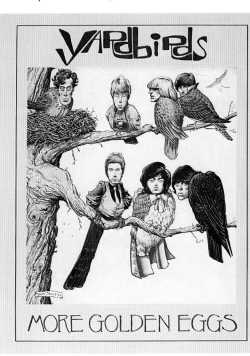

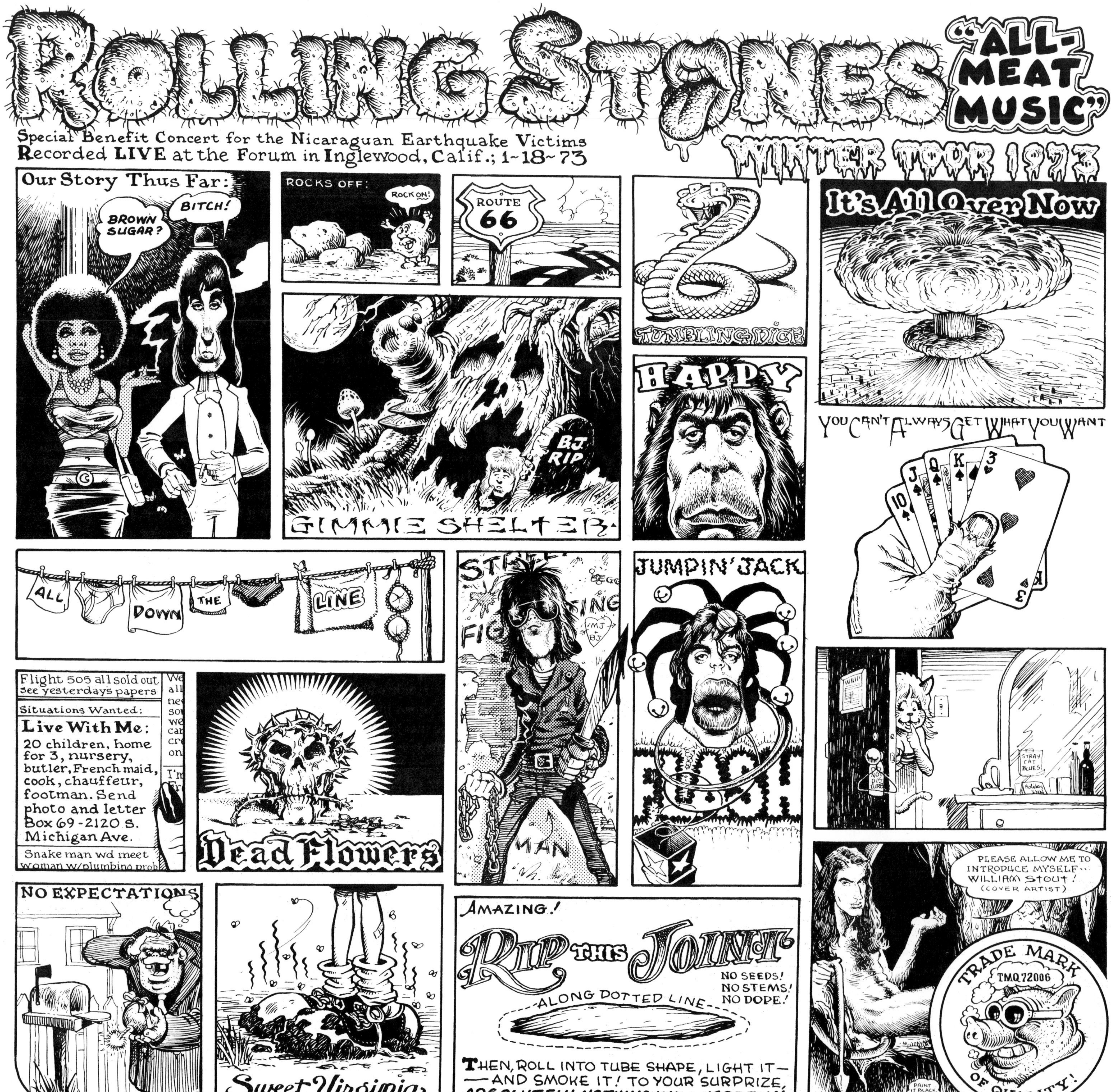

ROLLING STONES
"ALL-MEAT MUSIC"
Special Benefit Concert for the Nicaraguan Earthquake Victims
Recorded LIVE at the Forum in Inglewood, Calif.; 1~18~73
WINTER TOUR 1973
Our Story Thus Far:
BROWN SUGAR?
BITCH!
ROCKS OFF:
ROCK ON!
ROUTE 66
TUMBLING DICE
It's All Over Now
GIMME SHELTER
BJ RIP
HAPPY
YOU CAN'T ALWAYS GET WHAT YOU WANT
ALL DOWN THE LINE
JUMPIN' JACK
Flight 505 all sold out
see yesterday's papers
Situations Wanted:
Live With Me:
20 children, home for 3, nursery, butler, French maid, cook, chauffeur, footman. Send photo and letter Box 69 - 2120 S. Michigan Ave.
Snake man wd meet woman w/plumbing prob
Dead Flowers
STRAY CAT BLUES
DO NOT DISTURB
Holiday INN
NO EXPECTATIONS
Sweet Virginia
AMAZING!
RIP THIS JOINT
NO SEEDS! NO STEMS! NO DOPE!
ALONG DOTTED LINE
THEN, ROLL INTO TUBE SHAPE, LIGHT IT— —AND SMOKE IT! TO YOUR SURPRIZE, ABSOLUTELY NOTHING WILL HAPPEN!!
PLEASE ALLOW ME TO INTRODUCE MYSELF... WILLIAM STOUT! (COVER ARTIST)
TRADE MARK
TMQ 72006
OF QUALITY!
PAINT IT BLACK, YOU DEVIL!

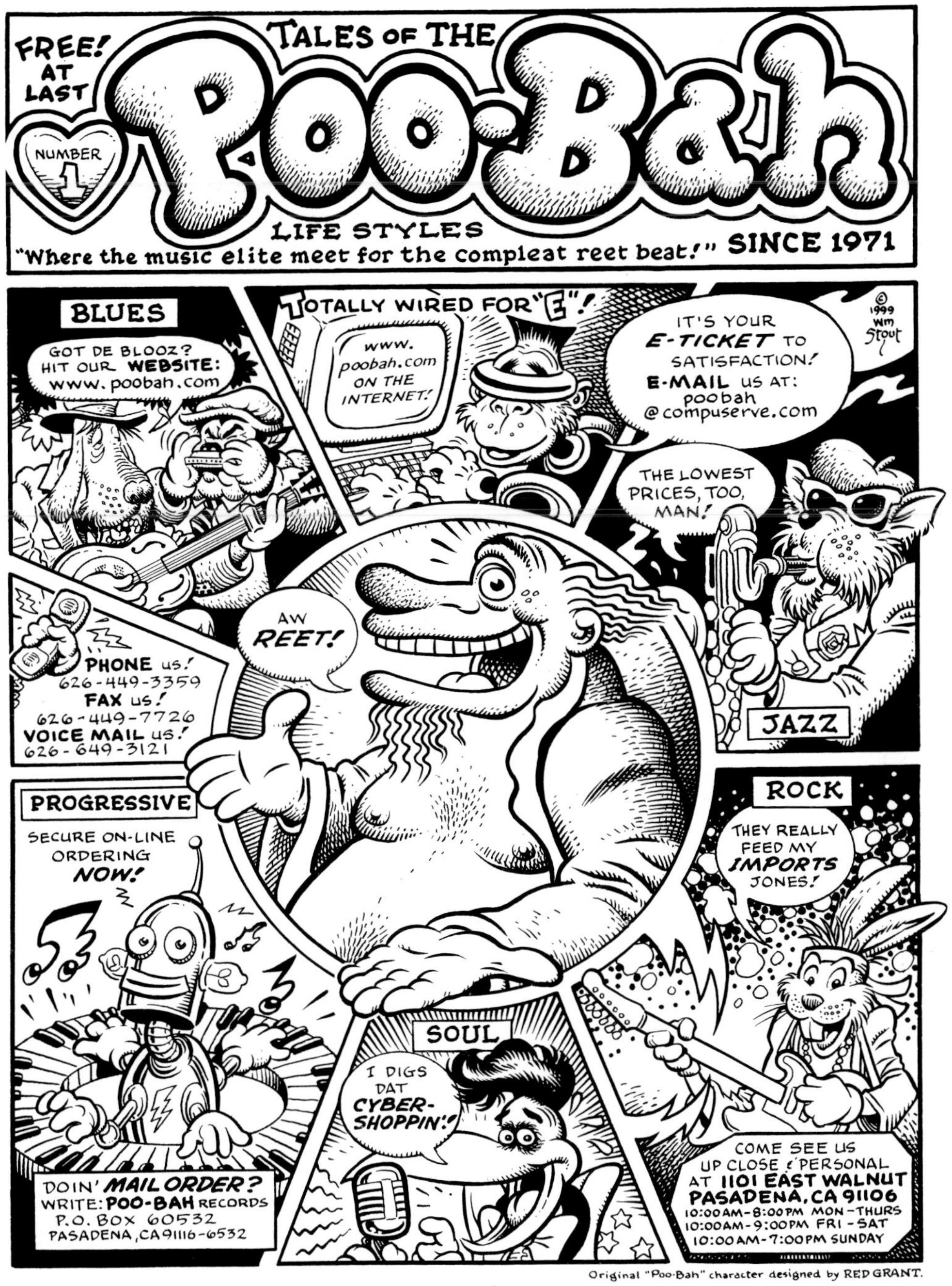
FREE! AT LAST
NUMBER 1
TALES OF THE
Poo-Bah
LIFE STYLES
"Where the music elite meet for the compleat reet beat!" SINCE 1971
BLUES
GOT DE BLOOZ? HIT OUR WEBSITE: www.poobah.com
TOTALLY WIRED FOR "E"!
www. poobah.com ON THE INTERNET!
© 1999 Wm Stout
IT'S YOUR E-TICKET TO SATISFACTION! E-MAIL US AT: poobah @compuserve.com
THE LOWEST PRICES, TOO, MAN!
AW REET!
JAZZ
PHONE US! 626-449-3359 FAX US! 626-449-7726 VOICE MAIL US! 626-649-3121
PROGRESSIVE
SECURE ON-LINE ORDERING NOW!
ROCK
THEY REALLY FEED MY IMPORTS JONES!
SOUL
I DIGS DAT CYBER-SHOPPIN'!
DOIN' MAIL ORDER? WRITE: POO-BAH RECORDS P.O. BOX 60532 PASADENA, CA 91116-6532
COME SEE US UP CLOSE & PERSONAL AT 1101 EAST WALNUT PASADENA, CA 91106
10:00AM-8:00PM MON-THURS 10:00AM-9:00PM FRI-SAT 10:00AM-7:00PM SUNDAY
Original "Poo-Bah" character designed by RED GRANT.

do was cover it with ink and that was it. Maybe use a ruler here and there. I learned a lot about storytelling looking at Jack's stuff; not so much from the action stuff, but in the way he handled his quiet passages. He was a real master at evoking a quiet, interesting psychological mood with his characters in a way that made them seem like real people. There's a quiet dignity to that work that I think speaks a lot about what Jack was like as a person. None of that stuff ever felt like it was just a job to him, from the reader's point of view. It all felt that he was personally and passionately involved.

Mike gave me a choice. I could either ink a *Demon* or a *Kamandi*. I chose the *Demon* because I like monsters. There also were fewer machines in *The Demon* than there were in *Kamandi*. I find drawing technical stuff slow and tedious. I'll do almost anything to avoid using a ruler. With *The Demon*, it was mostly organic stuff. If there was a castle, it was a crumbling castle. So *The Demon* was the obvious choice. I think it was *The Demon* #15. That was so cool getting to ink Jack's stuff. I had other involvement as well with Jack. I was doing a lot of advertising and package design at the time for Mattel. They called me in wanting me to do a whole batch of packaging for this new series of toys that were sort of superhero-esque. I looked at the style samples for the stuff they wanted me to do; basically they wanted me to ape Jack Kirby. Jack had recently moved to our neck of the woods from New York, actually up near my mom. I looked at this stuff and said, "Why don't you go to the source and just get the guy who created this entire style?" Just as a moral human being I couldn't take this kind of work from Jack. I knew that it was going to pay so much better than what Jack was making in comics. Why shouldn't Jack get the work? He originated that whole style. He should be getting some of the benefits from that. I said, "Here's Jack's number. Call Kirby and give him the job." The people at Mattel thought I was nuts. Jack was always really grateful for that, because it meant a huge boost in income for him. I felt great about it all – no regrets.

ARCUDI: Did you meet him through Mike Royer?

STOUT: No. I think the first time I met him was at a comic book convention where he appeared as a guest. It may have been a local L.A. convention, or it may have been the first San Diego convention. I know I got to know him at the very first San Diego ComicCon. We were two of their guests. The book had been published, so I figured it was finally okay to tell Jack that I had ghosted that issue for Mike. His only reaction was, "You must be good; I couldn't tell the difference." We both did like a chalk talk together. People asked us to draw stuff on these big drawing pads; we'd just do them on the spot. "Draw Thor!" And I'd say, "Oh, sure." It was weird – I'd never drawn Thor in my life, except when I was a teenager! I got to know Jack a little better back then because Jack and I were then both from Southern California, so we got invited to a lot of local conventions. We saw each other off and on at conventions, and occasionally at social outings. His wife Roz had a private birthday party for him for one of Jack's major landmark birthdays. I can't remember if it was the 60th or 70th. I stood up and spoke to Jack about what his work meant to me in my life and stuff.

It took me a while to warm up to Marvel because it was so radically different in its visual style.

ARCUDI: And you were still conservative.

STOUT: And I was a conservative. It was so different from everything I'd seen from D.C., which was really slick stuff. And here was this Steve Ditko guy drawing what I considered to be cartoons of people. And the Kirby stuff seemed unruly compared to the sublime sophistication of Infantino. But I began to look at them and to read them; it was Jack's and Steve's great stories that really sucked me in and made me appreciate the art. Soon I became a huge collector of all of this stuff. I just fell in love with that whole type of storytelling, with Jack's style and with Steve's style. They became huge influences on my work, augmenting what I'd learned from Kane and Infantino. I tried to combine the best of all of the

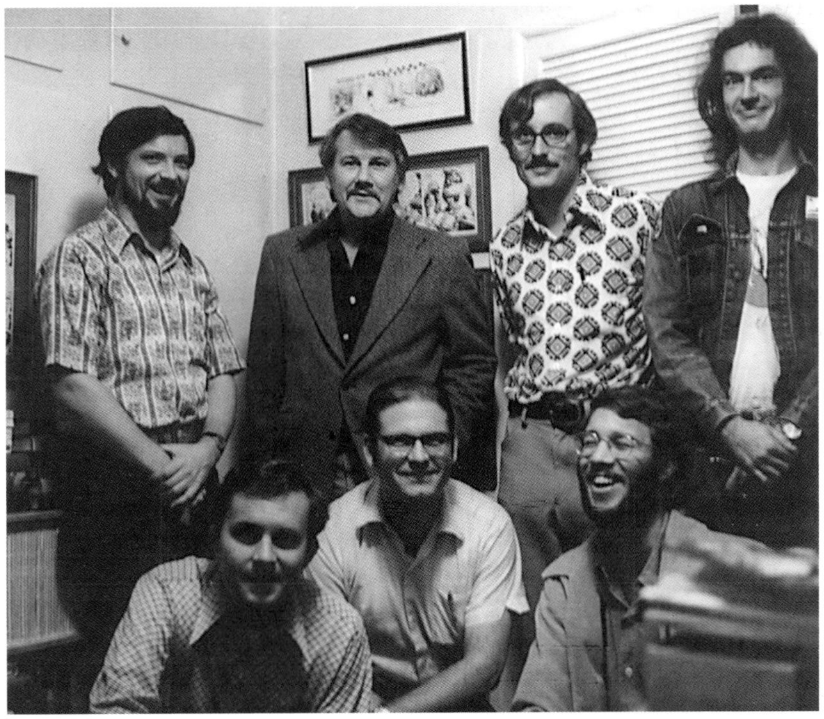

Opposite Page: Stout's first bootleg album cover is an homage to R. Crumb's *Cheap Thrills* cover.

Top Left: This ad sheet was recently drawn for Stout's favorite local record/CD shop, Poo-Bah Records.

Bottom Right: (Clockwise from upper left) Bob Foster, Alex Toth, unknown, Stout, John Pound, Fred Patten and Bill Spicer. Stout: "In the 1970s, there was an amazing amount of comics talent and knowledge in Los Angeles, about which the East Coast seemed completely clueless."

above, which was a really odd combo. I'm still trying to.

The thing I really loved about Ditko is that he drew the weirdest comic books that have ever been drawn. There were these "hot" artists later, not to take anything away from them, I'm thinking of Neal Adams and Frank Brunner in particular, who did these wild comic book pages where the panel borders would bend and twist so that if you stood back the whole page made a giant face or something. They would do everything they could to make their comics weird. But then here was Steve Ditko; he would work within a standard six-rectangular-panels-per-page comics format and do stuff ten times weirder than that other stuff that tried so hard to be weird! It was like Ditko was tapping directly into some God-knows-what portion of his inner spinal fibers to produce these mind-bending images that I don't think anybody has topped to this day.

ARCUDI: No. And that's interesting, because if you've ever met Steve, he's an ultra-conservative Libertarian.

STOUT: That kind of makes sense to me. Because if you look through history, you'll find that most of the real twisted or weird people had very conservative appearances or backgrounds. It's all about repression. I mean, look at Ted Bundy. Look at the Victorians; groups like the Hell Fire Club. Dick Cheney, Richard Ashcroft – totally sick.

ARCUDI: But you don't want to equate Steve Ditko with a Ted Bundy.

STOUT: Ditko, no. The others, yes. What I'm saying is that I think creativity is an avenue for the repressed

FIRESIGN THEATRE

ARCUDI: You moved then on to your relationship with the Firesign Theatre after the bootleg stuff.

STOUT: That came about at roughly the same time. A friend of mine, Dave Gibson, the guy who published the notorious Spirit bags, got permission from the Firesign Theatre to collect a series of Firesign newsletters called the Mixville Rocket and publish them all in one book. Dave asked me if I would do the cover. I drew a cover that to me epitomized visually what the Firesign Theatre meant to me aurally. I saw the Firesign Theatre as an aural version of Kurtzman's *Mad* comics. Instead of having eyeball kicks, they had all of these little, subtle, layered gags for your ear.

ARCUDI: You're going to have to explain "eyeball kicks."

STOUT: It's a Kurtzman expression. In the early *Mad* comics, you'd have your normal funny story going on. But in addition to the main story being told there would also be all of these little gags that both Wood and Elder would stick in the panels that had nothing or little to do with the story. Corny gags, funny signs, running gags, funny little characters and people commenting on what was going on. Elder, especially, was the master at this. Kurtzman called those "eyeball kicks." The effect of the eyeball kicks was that you could read the story once, and then you could read it again and catch something new. In fact, every time you read it you'd see something new because those guys packed each panel with so much stuff. So the Firesign Theatre was the first, and to my mind the only, comedy group that produced comedy for records that once you heard it the first time, you could go back a second time and a third time and a fourth time and get new stuff each time you listened to it because their material was so densely packed with comic information. It wasn't like listening to Cosby or even Richard Pryor. They're really funny the first time but you can't listen to their records five times in a row and find something new and funny revealed each time. I thought here's a chance to sort of reflect in art what I got from them.

ARCUDI: I guess maybe I should explain that Firesign Theatre was a comedy group.

STOUT: They were a comedy group based in Los Angeles, an outgrowth of an experimental radio show that was live from the Magic Mushroom, a Los Angeles rock nightclub. The show began as Peter Bergman's show. He pulled friends into it and it evolved into a four-man comedy group that produced record albums. They also did live performances, too, of some of their material. It was definitely a phenomenon of the pop culture of that generation, really extraordinary stuff. I did the cover for the *Mixville Rocket*. In doing so I got to meet the Firesign Theatre, sit in on some of their recording sessions and watch the process of how that stuff came about. I became friends with the guys. They loved my *Mixville Rocket* cover and asked me if I would do their next album cover, which was *In the Next World, You're on Your Own*. I did a double front cover for it, so it didn't matter which way the record was placed in the rack – each side was a front cover. I did it in that same style, just really packed with all kinds of comic information based upon all of the stuff that was in the album. That was my first exposure to Columbia Records and Nancy Donald, who was the art director at Columbia at the time. She started to give me other work because she really liked my Firesign cover. Because of that I got to do my first legitimate album cover work.

ARCUDI: Other work besides Firesign Theatre?

STOUT: Yeah. I did a cover for a group called Smash, for Capitol. The Beach Boys' *L. A. Album*. I did a lot of Columbia stuff where it didn't make it to the final pressing. I did one cover for a group called the Bliss Band, which Skunk Baxter (from Steely Dan and the Doobie Brothers) produced.

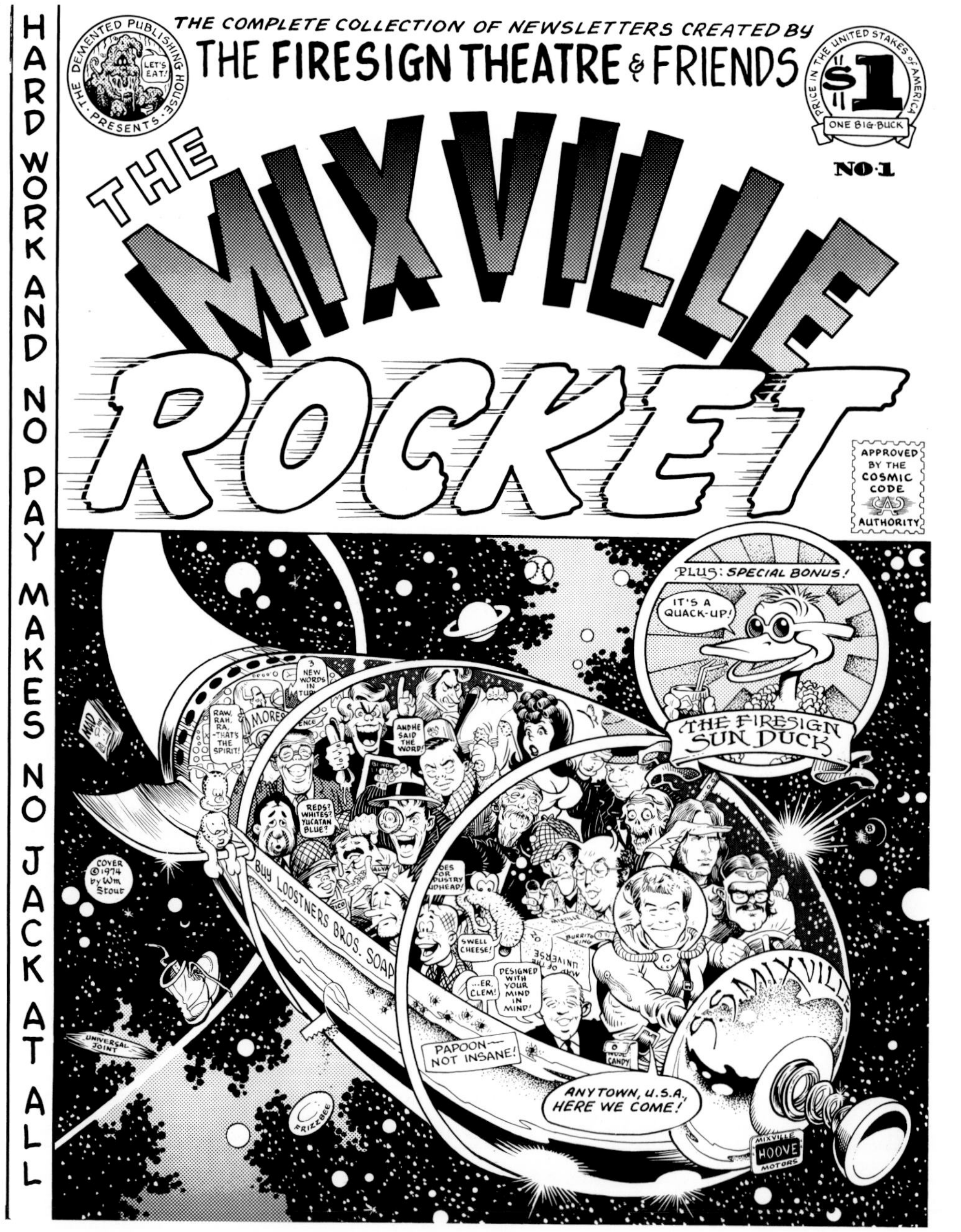

HARD WORK AND NO PAY MAKES NO JACK AT ALL
THE COMPLETE COLLECTION OF NEWSLETTERS CREATED BY
THE FIRESIGN THEATRE & FRIENDS
THE DEMENTED PUBLISHING HOUSE PRESENTS
LET'S EAT!
PRICE IN THE UNITED STATES OF AMERICA $1 ONE BIG BUCK
NO.1
THE MIXVILLE ROCKET
APPROVED BY THE COSMIC CODE AUTHORITY
PLUS: SPECIAL BONUS!
IT'S A QUACK-UP!
THE FIRESIGN SUN DUCK
RAW, RAH, RA, -THAT'S THE SPIRIT!
AND HE SAID THE WORD!
REDS? WHITES? YUCATAN BLUE?
COVER ©1974 by Wm Stout
BUY LOOSTNERS BROS. SOAP
SWELL CHEESE!
...ER, CLEM!
DESIGNED WITH YOUR MIND IN MIND!
MAP OF THE UNIVERSE
PAPOON— NOT INSANE!
ANYTOWN, U.S.A., HERE WE COME!
UNIVERSAL JOINT
FRIZZBEE
MIXVILLE HOOVE MOTORS

This Page: Stout's humorous visual complexity proved to be a perfect match for the Firesign Theatre's humorous aural complexity.

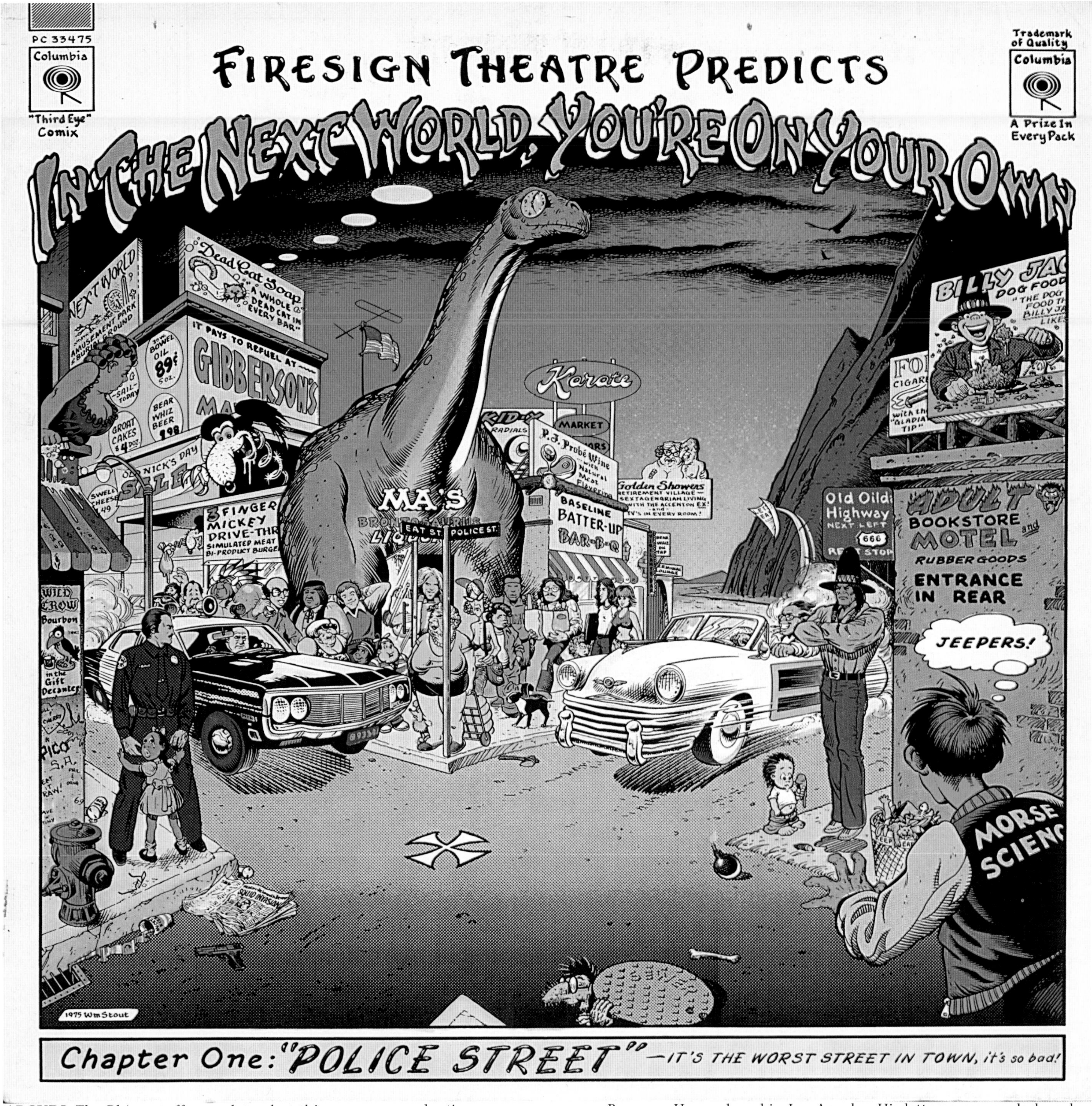
PC 33475
Columbia
"Third Eye" Comix
FIRESIGN THEATRE PREDICTS
Trademark of Quality
Columbia
A Prize In Every Pack
IN THE NEXT WORLD, YOU'RE ON YOUR OWN
Dead Cat Soap "A WHOLE DEAD CAT IN EVERY BAR"
IT PAYS TO REFUEL AT GIBBERSON'S
BOWEL OIL 89¢
BEAR WHIZ BEER
Karate
MARKET
Golden Showers
MA'S
EAT ST.
POLICE ST.
BASELINE BATTER-UP BAR-B-Q
Old Oildi Highway NEXT LEFT 666
ADULT BOOKSTORE and MOTEL
RUBBER GOODS
ENTRANCE IN REAR
JEEPERS!
MORSE SCIENC
1975 Wm Stout
Chapter One: "POLICE STREET" —IT'S THE WORST STREET IN TOWN, it's so bad!

This Page: Stout's work on the *Mixville Rocket* cover inspired the Firesign Theatre to hire Stout to work on their first film, *Everything You Know Is Wrong* and design this cover for their LP *In the Next World, You're On Your Own.*

ARCUDI: The Rhino stuff came later, but this seems as good a time as any to talk about it, especially since we can talk about your cover for that Beatles compilation with Mark David Chapman on the cover. Did the relationship that you had with Rhino grow out of that, or did it grow more organically out of later professional work?

STOUT: No. It came out of a completely different place. It somehow came out of my being a comics fan. Here's what happened: There was a guy who wrote regular letters to comics, and his name was Fred Bronson. He was based in Los Angeles. His letters were regularly published in the *Flash* and *Green Lantern* letters columns, mostly the Julie Schwartz books. It was an easy name to remember and kind of stuck in my brain. Cut to: five years later; I'm reading the *L.A. Free Press* or some local music magazine, and there was a really good article, review or letter in reference to the Yardbirds. It was signed Harold Bronson. By that time, I had forgotten "Fred" but I remembered "Bronson." I thought, "This is the same guy who was a comics fan. Hey, he's a

Yardbirds fan just like me!" So I wrote him a letter. It was a case of mistaken identity, but Harold Bronson, the Yardbirds fan, was happy to find another Yardbirds fan. We got together, we met and we hit it off. Harold was, at the time, working in the music industry in two functions. During the day he worked at Rhino Records, which was a very hip, funny record shop in Westwood. In the evening, he would do interviews and write reviews and articles for rock and roll music magazines. This was the hey-day of that occupation; for every new release the record companies would throw a gigantic spread, an enormous feast with all kinds of food and entertainment and stuff. Harold would invite me along because he knew I liked (and needed) to eat and loved free food. Eventually, I went along with Harold on some of the interviews as well, because a lot of the rock musicians wanted to start controlling the photographs of them that got out to the public. They wouldn't allow photographers at the interview sessions. I would come along and do drawings of the guys.
ARCUDI: Like a courtroom artist.
STOUT: Yeah. They thought that was really cool to see someone sit there with a blank piece of paper and minutes later during the course of the conversation there would be a drawing or picture of them. They thought that was great; they had no reason to object to that. So I got to meet a lot of different rock stars that way. The drawings would often be published along with Harold's interviews. Then Harold and his fellow co-worker at the Rhino Records store, Richard Foos, got an idea. They were frustrated musicians. They thought, "Wouldn't it be fun to put out our own record?" So they did it – and it sold out! They put out another – and it sold out, too! They did wacky stuff. One of very first things they did was a 45 of Led Zeppelin's *Whole Lotta Love*, except played on kazoos. Well, it was a local smash. That one sold out, too, and got a lot of airplay. This was so fun, so cool. When they did their first record, they called me up and said, "We want to put out a record and call our company Rhino Records. Could you do us a logo of a rhino to put on the record label?" So I did a cartoon rhino, which became the Rocky Rhino that everyone associates with Rhino Records, the very first Rocky Rhino. He was on the label of all their early records. And that was the acorn from which the mighty oak tree of Rhino Records, as we know it today, grew. I did a lot of their early covers since we were both heavily into music and humor. Rhino always had this sort of humorous, wise guy attitude toward the record industry; it was a natural that they would eventually sign on the Firesign Theatre. I had done some T-shirt designs for the Firesign, and we re-used some of the T-shirt designs for some of their the album covers. I also adapted the *Mixville Rocket* design into an album cover for their Firesign album *Lawyer's Hospital*. Firesign rewrote the word balloon dialogue for the cover of that one. That was how Rhino, and Firesign Theatre, and I all got reconnected.

This Page: This "Fear and Laughter" splash page combines Stout's art and Scott Shawl's Hunter S. Thompson-esque dialogue.

Opposite Page: This cover brought Stout and Rhino Records all sorts of death threats (and a front-page *Los Angeles Times* article, as well as coverage in *People* magazine), because Stout included John Lennon's assassin on the cover. Stout: "Hey, just like John, I've got this real dark sense of humor at times. I think that's healthy."

A NOTORIOUS BEATLES COVER

Stout drew the cover for an LP of songs about the Beatles and made the strategic error of including an image of Mark David Chapman in the illustration. This didn't turn out to be nearly as funny as Stout thought it would be. For the full scandalous story, go to: **http://www.tcj.com/ws03/stoutchap.html**

UNDERGROUND COMIX

ARCUDI: Before you started doing movie poster work, if I'm not mistaken you got back into doing some underground comix, right – like *Bicentennial Gross-Outs*?
STOUT: Since the *Peace Nuts*, there wasn't anything that I knew of that was called underground comix at the time. That was kind of a one-off

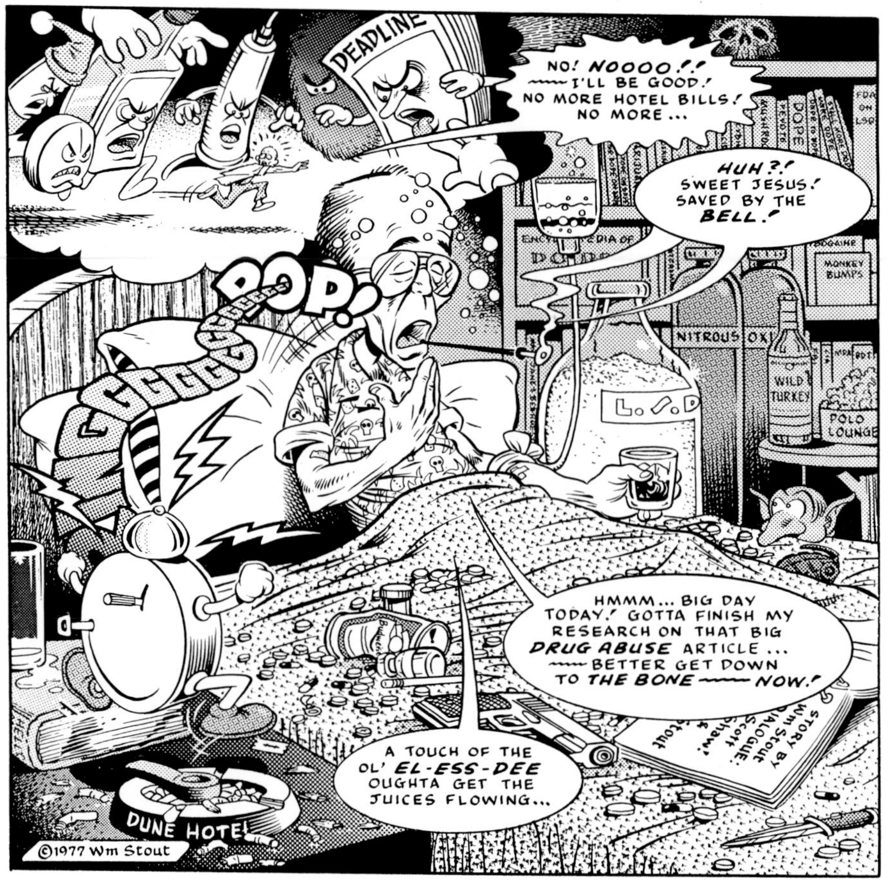
DEADLINE
NO! NOOOO!! —I'LL BE GOOD! NO MORE HOTEL BILLS! NO MORE...
HUH?! SWEET JESUS! SAVED BY THE BELL!
DOPE
MONKEY BUMPS
POP!
NITROUS OX
L.S.D
WILD TURKEY
POLO LOUNGE
HMMM... BIG DAY TODAY! GOTTA FINISH MY RESEARCH ON THAT BIG DRUG ABUSE ARTICLE ... —BETTER GET DOWN TO THE BONE — NOW!
STORY BY Wm STOUT DIALOGUE: Scott Shaw! & Stout
A TOUCH OF THE OL' EL-ESS-DEE OUGHTA GET THE JUICES FLOWING...
DUNE HOTEL
©1977 Wm Stout

thing. I just forgot about it after that. Then I met Jim Evans, who was art directing a rock festival I wanted to work on. I didn't get hired to do any of the work for the rock festival but Jim and I stayed in touch. He was the guy who introduced me to underground comics. I had never heard of them. Jim knew I was a big Rick Griffin fan. I loved Rick's stuff. He was an enormous influence on almost everyone in Southern California drawing cartoons in the '60s, because of the Murphy the Surfer strips he was doing for *Surfer* magazine. Everybody drew Murphy the Surfer on their notebooks. Everybody.
ARCUDI: What year was this?
STOUT: Murphy the Surfer stuff? That was the early '60s.
ARCUDI: When you met Jim Evans?
STOUT: That would have been late '60s/early '70s. I think I'd mentioned Rick's work to Jim because Jim was a surfer. I said, "Rick Griffin. I wonder what ever happened to that guy. I'd love to see his stuff." And Jim said, "Oh, man – you haven't seen his recent stuff?" Actually, I was aware that Rick was doing some rock posters, and I thought that stuff was great. But Jim said, "He's doing comics, too. He didn't stop doing Murphy the Surfer. His comics have really taken a different direction from the *Surfer* magazine days." I said, "Oh, really. I'd love to see what he's doing." So Jim brought over some of the early *Zap! Comix* with Rick's work. That was the first time I ever saw Crumb's stuff. I remember reading the Crumb story "Joe Blow." I read that story and I was forever changed. It was astounding; it was this moment of revelation – a real Eureka. It was, "Oh, my god! Comics are capable of anything!" That was an amazing revelation. They didn't have to be superheroes. They didn't have to be for kids. They could be anything that we wanted to make them. I got so excited by that; I just went nuts.

Of course I had to pick up as many of these "comix" as I could find. At the time, you couldn't just buy underground comics at a store. There was no way you could do that. I think a few of the porno shops sold them. The way I got them back then was this: my band and I found out there was a guy who had underground comics at his news rack. But none of the undergrounds were displayed on the rack. You had to walk up to the guy when there wasn't anybody around and

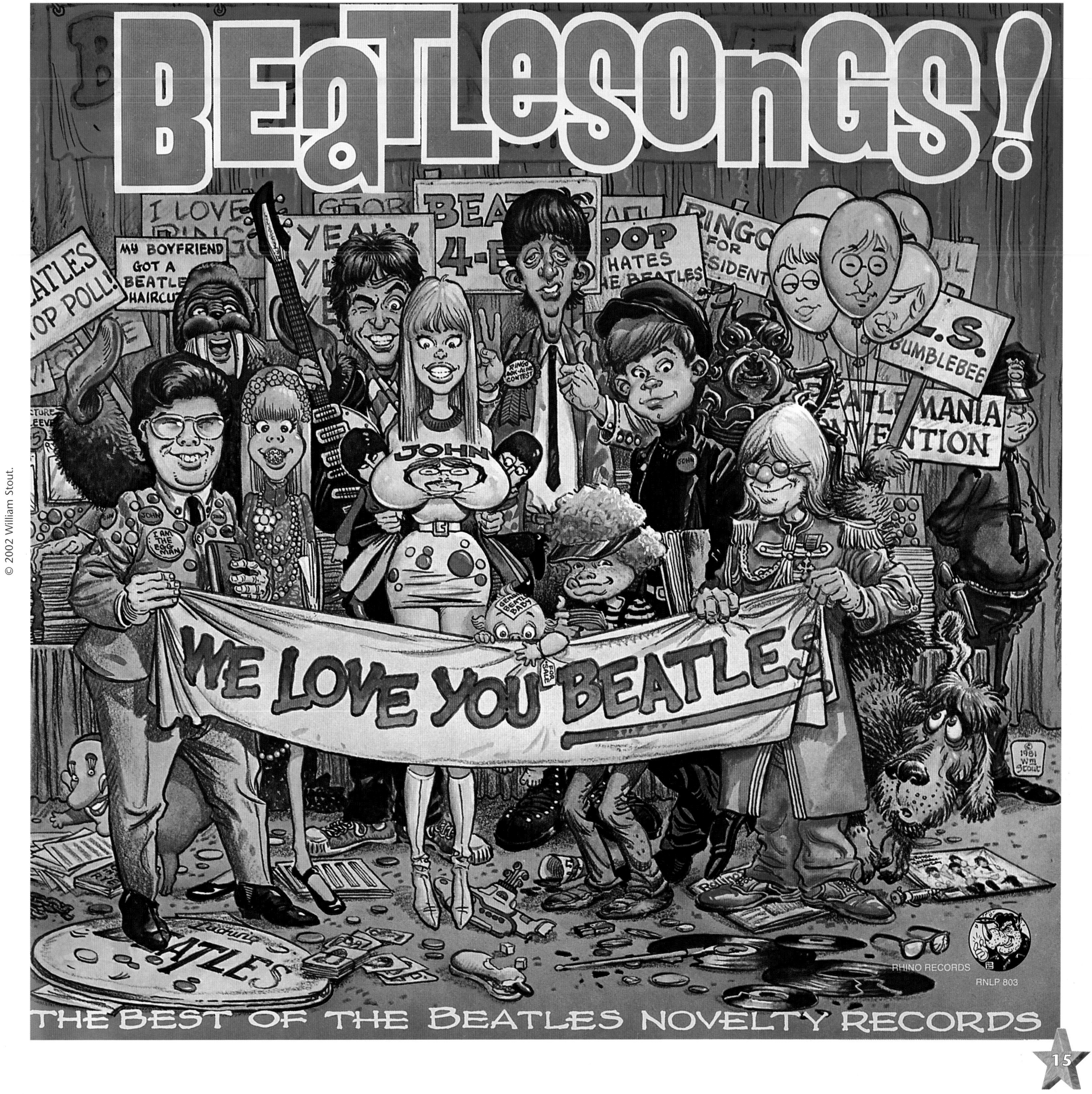
BEATLESONGS!
MY BOYFRIEND GOT A BEATLE
POP HATES
BUMBLEBEE
JOHN
WE LOVE YOU BEATLES
RHINO RECORDS
RNLP 803
THE BEST OF THE BEATLES NOVELTY RECORDS

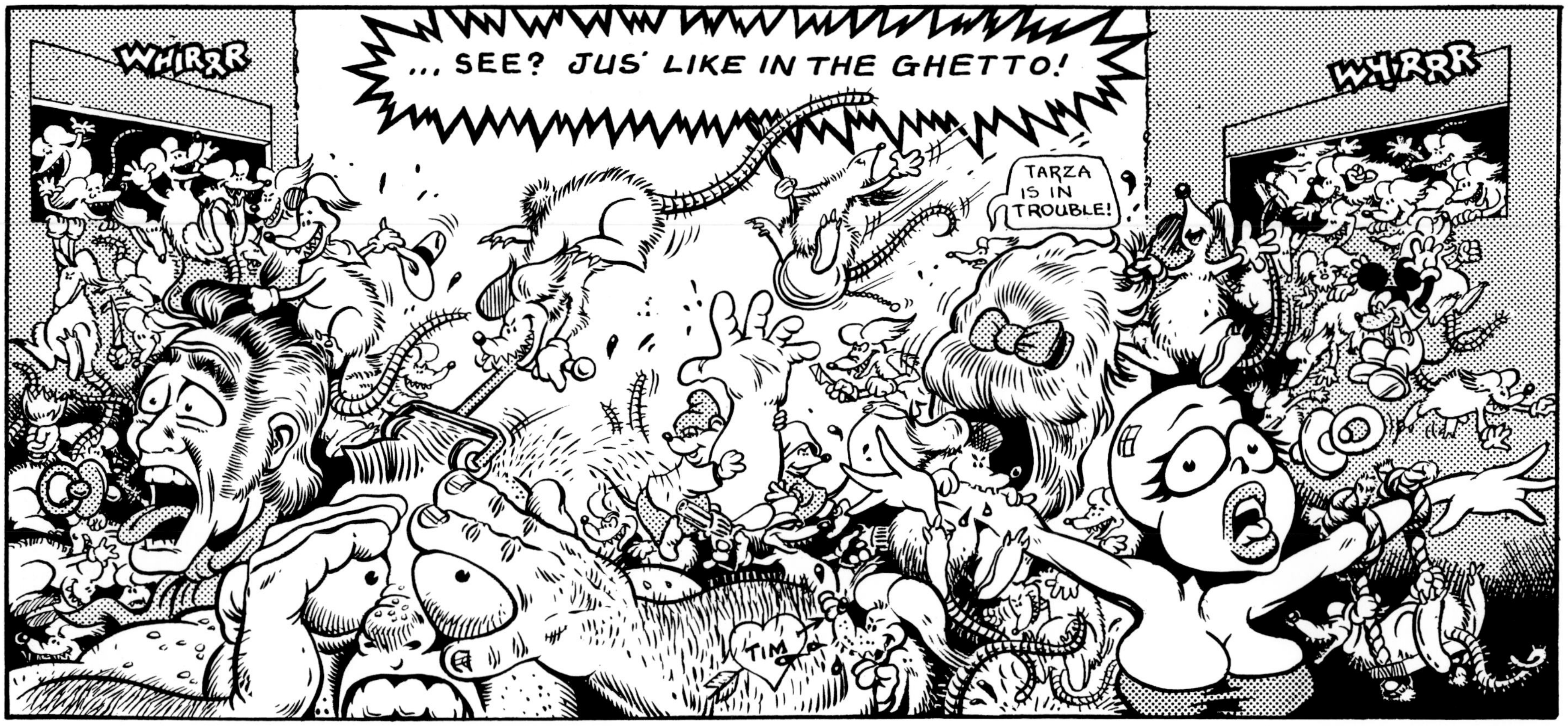
WHIRRR
... SEE? JUS' LIKE IN THE GHETTO!
TARZA IS IN TROUBLE!
WHIRRR
TIM

mention that you wanted to buy some underground comix. If you mentioned it when someone was there he'd yell at you and berate you. "Shut up!" He would look around furtively to make sure that no one was approaching, open up a little cabinet, and pull out the comix. You couldn't even look at them. You just had to buy them. I'd pass the money to him and he'd say, "Now get 'em out of here. Get 'em out of here. Don't let anybody see where you got 'em." So they really were underground. It was like he was selling dope or something. At the time, it was almost all Crumb's stuff, the early *Zap* comix and some of the *Furry Freak Brothers* comix. Really prime stuff. I knew I had to do that kind of work. So Jim Evans said, "I'm publishing an underground comic called the *Dying Dolphin*." It was an environmentally aware political comic about dolphins and saving the oceans. I jumped at the chance to contribute pages to Jim's book. It seemed like a good opportunity to get into the underground scene. Coincidentally, just a couple of days after Jim had introduced me to my first underground comics, he came over and said, "Hey. Let's go over to Cherokee Books and see what's up." Cherokee Books was a local bookstore in Hollywood. Upstairs was a legendary old comics department. We used to pore through there and try to find EC's or other good comics to buy. As we're walking up to the door of Cherokee Books, walking out of the shop is Robert Crumb, S. Clay Wilson, Robert Williams, Rick Griffin, Victor Moscoso, Spain Rodriguez... the entire *Zap* gang.

Jim knew these guys, so he introduced me. That was the very first time I met all of those guys. I happened to have with me my *Dying Dolphin* comic pages. They asked to see them. They looked at them and I got a whole variety of reactions. The nicest person, and the guy who is still one of the nicest people in the world of comics, was Spain Rodriguez. He went, "Cool. Just like Wally Wood. Wow, this is great." Later, I became good friends with Robert Williams, who lived locally. The rest of the guys were pretty much San Francisco/Bay area boys. I did my two pages for Jim Evans, and he couldn't use them. Because they were... In my mind, "underground" meant that you could do anything you want. My story included sex, naked women, dope and all kinds of stuff. That was not the direction of Jim's book, though, so he had the unpleasant task of telling me I couldn't be in it. I was disappointed but philosophical about it all and set the story aside. Either Robert Williams or George DiCaprio remembered it; one of those guys got it into a magazine called *Flash*.

ARCUDI: This is Leonardo DiCaprio's father?

STOUT: Yes. Leonardo DiCaprio's father used to distribute all of the underground comix in Los Angeles. He and I were really good friends.

I started to draw more underground stuff on my own. I took that two-pager that Jim rejected and used that to begin my own comic. I drew an entire comic book called *Juicy Comix*. I even did hand color separations for the covers and everything. I flew up to San Francisco. Like an idiot, I didn't call anybody first and make appointments. I thought, "Well, this is underground! I'll just show up! They'll love to see this stuff and they'll all want to publish it!" No. First of all, no one wanted to see me. They didn't know who I was. They were busy. I tracked the guy, Big Bob I think he was called, who owned Print Mint down at a party and showed him the pages. He just flipped. "How dare you bring business into my personal life?" He practically kicked my ass out on the sidewalk. But Last Gasp's Ron Turner was very kind about the whole thing. I think, like a lot of people in my life, like Harvey Kurtzman and Russ Manning, Ron saw past my socially inept enthusiasm to the person with a passion who really loved what he was doing. Ron said, "I don't have the budget or the space or the time to produce this right now. But I think it's really great work." We kept in touch. He kept me in mind for future projects and called me up when the next issue of *Slow Death* was being planned. I ended up doing a couple of covers for *Slow Death*. Ron especially knew about my passion for environmental politics, so the cover of *Slow Death* #8, a special Greenpeace issue, was earmarked for me. I contributed a couple of pages, as well. Then around 1976, the bicentennial year for the United States, Ron and George DiCaprio both approached me and said, "Remember that story you did on Disneyland?" I did a satire, an 11 or 13-page satire on Disneyland called "Reality Land" partly based upon my experiences working there. They said, "That would make a perfect story to go into a bicentennial book."

ARCUDI: This is the one you did for your own comic that ended up not getting published?

This Page: Stout's "RealityLand" from *Bicentennial Gross-Outs* was the result of too many summers and many holidays working at Disneyland, painting watercolor portraits in New Orleans Square. "I find this hard to look at now — too many in-jokes, pretty awful design and some real juvenile humor, but, hey — I was just a kid and I was learning."

STOUT: Right. I had planned it as the centerpiece for *Juicy Comix*. George DiCaprio, I think, had come up with the name *Bicentennial Gross-Outs*. George and I agreed to co-edit the book. I edited half of the book and he edited half of the book. Half of the book was my art plus I got Dennis Ellefson and Bill Wray each to do a piece. George got different people to do stories for his half of the book. The book also included a documentary story I had done about the Filipino massacre, something that's been censored from all of our history books. It's the story of when the United States went into the Philippines and massacred approximately two million men, women and children.

ARCUDI: The aboriginal Moro?

STOUT: Yes – we referred to that conflict as the Moro Wars. I was a big fan of Kurtzman's *Frontline Combat* and *Two-Fisted Tales* books. I thought, "Here's my chance to do my own true war story." This was something that had nested in the back of my head after reading a Gore Vidal state-of-the-union essay for *Esquire* in which he tangentially mentioned the Filipino Massacre. It caught my attention because I thought, "My god. I've never heard of anything like that. Ever." I couldn't find anything about it in the history books. And so it just sort of stayed in my mind for a while. I believe a month or two later I mentioned it to my lead guitar player who said, "You should talk to my landlord. His father was there – and he took photographs." I went, "Oh, my god." He said, "You have to be careful with the guy; he's a really hard-core conservative. He's worried that the commies are going to get their hands on this material." So I posed as a UCLA student writing a paper on the Philippines. I called him up and got permission to interview him. He wouldn't let me take the photos, obviously, but I got to take photos of the photos. I had a really good 35mm camera and I got really great photos of this stuff. This is astounding stuff. One photograph showed dozens of people in a pit they'd dug up just before they were executed. I have a "later" picture that shows the same tribes peoples' heads lined up on a log after their executions. The U. S. soldiers used the heads for barter. It was astounding that he had all of these photographs. With these pho-

The U. S. soldiers used the heads for barter.

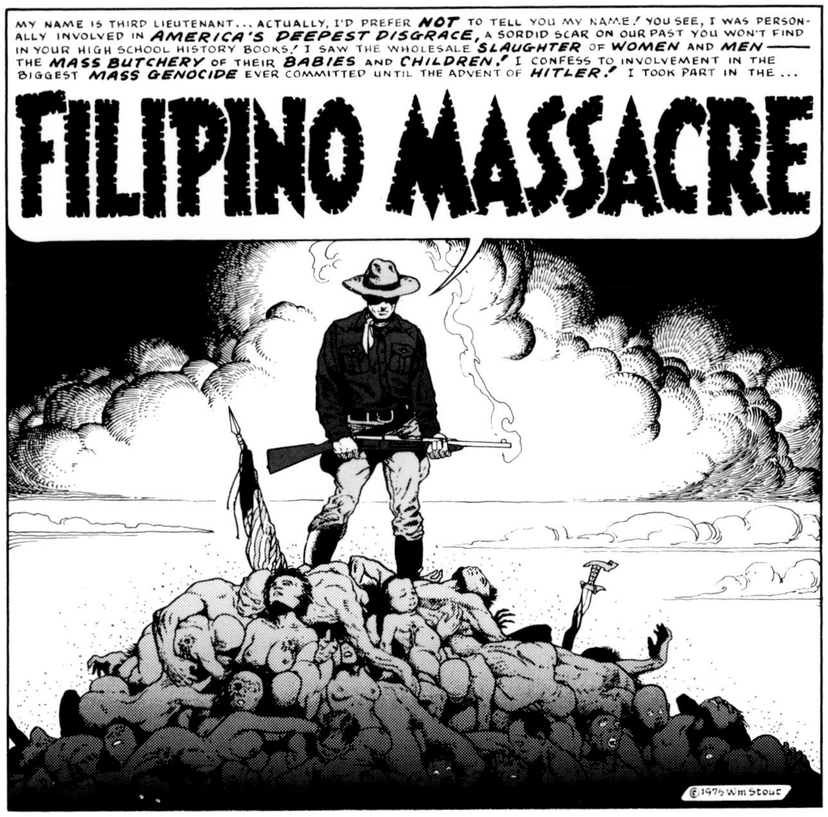
MY NAME IS THIRD LIEUTENANT... ACTUALLY, I'D PREFER NOT TO TELL YOU MY NAME! YOU SEE, I WAS PERSONALLY INVOLVED IN AMERICA'S DEEPEST DISGRACE, A SORDID SCAR ON OUR PAST YOU WON'T FIND IN YOUR HIGH SCHOOL HISTORY BOOKS! I SAW THE WHOLESALE SLAUGHTER OF WOMEN AND MEN — THE MASS BUTCHERY OF THEIR BABIES AND CHILDREN! I CONFESS TO INVOLVEMENT IN THE BIGGEST MASS GENOCIDE EVER COMMITTED UNTIL THE ADVENT OF HITLER! I TOOK PART IN THE...
FILIPINO MASSACRE
©1975 Wm Stout

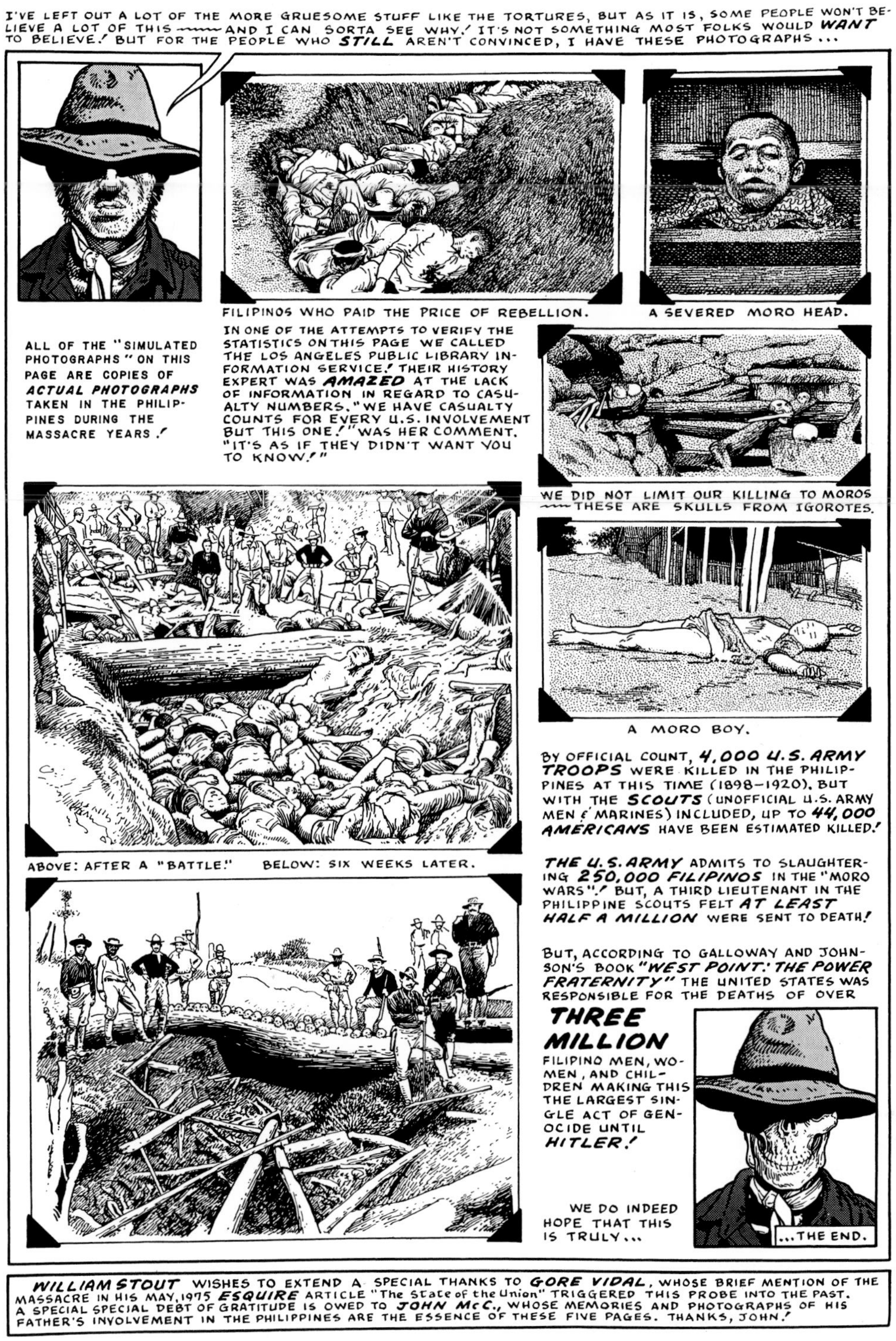
I'VE LEFT OUT A LOT OF THE MORE GRUESOME STUFF LIKE THE TORTURES, BUT AS IT IS, SOME PEOPLE WON'T BELIEVE A LOT OF THIS — AND I CAN SORTA SEE WHY! IT'S NOT SOMETHING MOST FOLKS WOULD WANT TO BELIEVE! BUT FOR THE PEOPLE WHO STILL AREN'T CONVINCED, I HAVE THESE PHOTOGRAPHS...
FILIPINOS WHO PAID THE PRICE OF REBELLION.
A SEVERED MORO HEAD.
ALL OF THE "SIMULATED PHOTOGRAPHS" ON THIS PAGE ARE COPIES OF ACTUAL PHOTOGRAPHS TAKEN IN THE PHILIPPINES DURING THE MASSACRE YEARS!
IN ONE OF THE ATTEMPTS TO VERIFY THE STATISTICS ON THIS PAGE WE CALLED THE LOS ANGELES PUBLIC LIBRARY INFORMATION SERVICE! THEIR HISTORY EXPERT WAS AMAZED AT THE LACK OF INFORMATION IN REGARD TO CASUALTY NUMBERS. "WE HAVE CASUALTY COUNTS FOR EVERY U.S. INVOLVEMENT BUT THIS ONE!" WAS HER COMMENT. "IT'S AS IF THEY DIDN'T WANT YOU TO KNOW!"
WE DID NOT LIMIT OUR KILLING TO MOROS — THESE ARE SKULLS FROM IGOROTES.
ABOVE: AFTER A "BATTLE!"
BELOW: SIX WEEKS LATER.
A MORO BOY.
BY OFFICIAL COUNT, 4,000 U.S. ARMY TROOPS WERE KILLED IN THE PHILIPPINES AT THIS TIME (1898–1920). BUT WITH THE SCOUTS (UNOFFICIAL U.S. ARMY MEN & MARINES) INCLUDED, UP TO 44,000 AMERICANS HAVE BEEN ESTIMATED KILLED!
THE U.S. ARMY ADMITS TO SLAUGHTERING 250,000 FILIPINOS IN THE "MORO WARS"! BUT, A THIRD LIEUTENANT IN THE PHILIPPINE SCOUTS FELT AT LEAST HALF A MILLION WERE SENT TO DEATH!
BUT, ACCORDING TO GALLOWAY AND JOHNSON'S BOOK "WEST POINT: THE POWER FRATERNITY" THE UNITED STATES WAS RESPONSIBLE FOR THE DEATHS OF OVER THREE MILLION FILIPINO MEN, WOMEN, AND CHILDREN MAKING THIS THE LARGEST SINGLE ACT OF GENOCIDE UNTIL HITLER!
WE DO INDEED HOPE THAT THIS IS TRULY...
...THE END.
WILLIAM STOUT WISHES TO EXTEND A SPECIAL THANKS TO GORE VIDAL, WHOSE BRIEF MENTION OF THE MASSACRE IN HIS MAY, 1975 ESQUIRE ARTICLE "The State of the Union" TRIGGERED THIS PROBE INTO THE PAST. A SPECIAL SPECIAL DEBT OF GRATITUDE IS OWED TO JOHN McC., WHOSE MEMORIES AND PHOTOGRAPHS OF HIS FATHER'S INVOLVEMENT IN THE PHILIPPINES ARE THE ESSENCE OF THESE FIVE PAGES. THANKS, JOHN!

tographs, I didn't just luck into a "smoking gun" – I was holding a smoking Howitzer! I turned it into a documentary story for *Bicentennial Gross-Outs* called "Filipino Massacre."

ARCUDI: You were the very first non-*Zap!* artist to do a comic book with the *Zap!* guys.

STOUT: I'm really proud of that work. I think it's some of the best comics work I ever did. In the late '60s/early '70s, the *Zap!* comic artists – Robert Crumb, Robert Williams, S. Clay Wilson...all of those guys got charged with pornography. They had drawn these small digest-sized comix that were considered pornographic. Janis Joplin testified on Crumb's behalf. They were acquitted because the judge and jury declared that these books had socially redeeming value in that they made you laugh. The *Zap!* guys were delighted not to go to prison, but they were kind of pissed off because they felt it removed some of their outlaw sheen. Their work had actually been officially justified by the Establishment; they chafed at that legitimacy. So S. Clay Wilson said, "Let's do a book that no one could possibly condone. Let's do a book on felching."

ARCUDI: I can't believe you're going to talk about this. Go ahead.

This Page: First and last page of "Filipino Massacre" from *Bicentennial Gross-Outs*. Stout combined the research and realism of Kurtzman's war comics with a modern documentary approach.

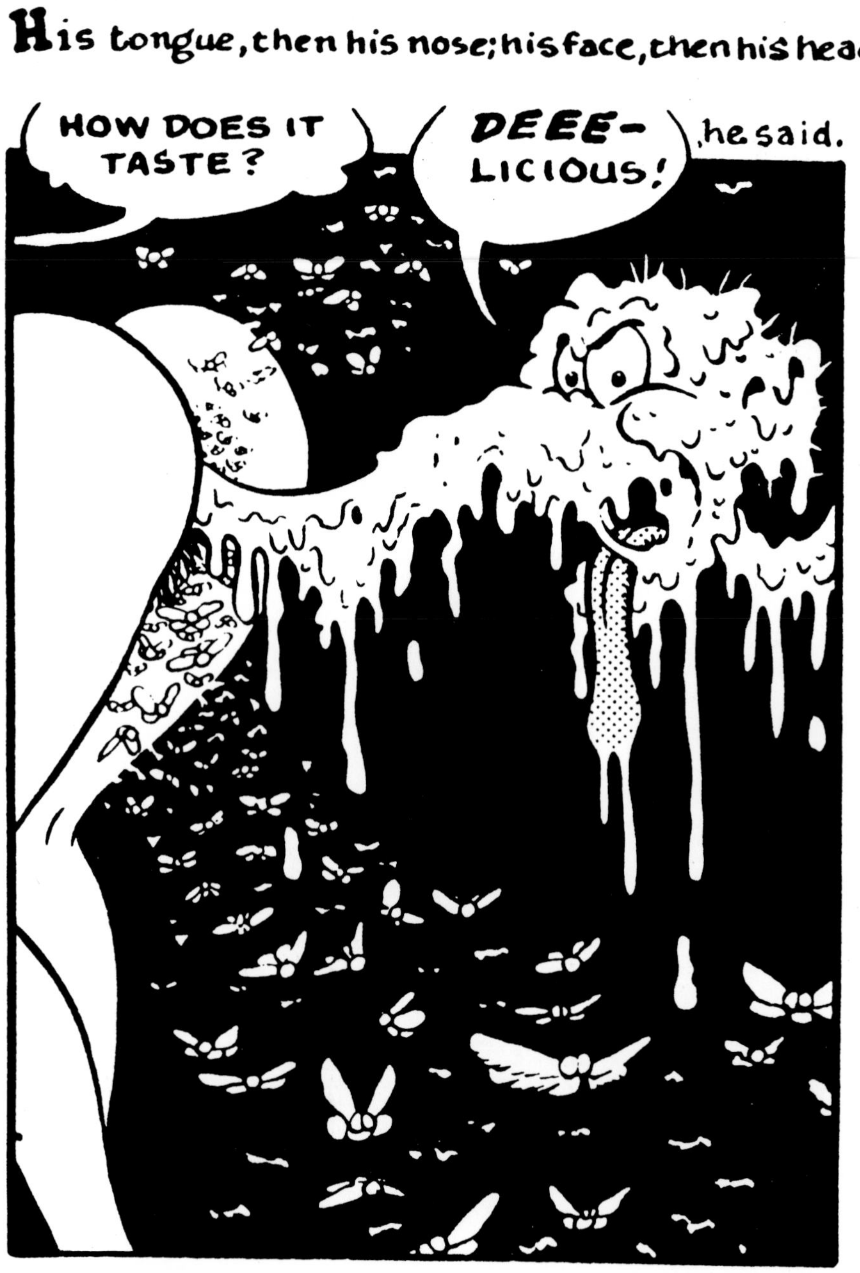
His tongue, then his nose; his face, then his head;
HOW DOES IT TASTE?
DEEE-LICIOUS!
he said.

This Page: "I think my story for *Felch* is one of my best underground works. I liked the absurdity of combining the innocence of Dr. Seuss-style rhymes with one of the most offensive-to-the-general-public sex practices I've ever encountered."

STOUT: The *Zap!* guys said, "Felching? What does that mean?" S. Clay explained. It's an arcane sexual practice that...I don't think we can really describe it here without getting Fantagraphics into enormous trouble. Let's just say that as soon as you hear what it is your typical reaction is either complete revulsion or you laugh your head off that anyone would do such a thing – although since the publication of that book I've had offers... All of the *Zap!* guys each agreed to contribute a story; Robert Williams contacted me to do a story as well. I wrote my story in a sort of Dr. Seuss style. I met my deadline right away, but some of the guys dragged their feet. By the time the book got published, the American public was so blasé about that stuff that it caused nary a ripple.
ARCUDI: I'm surprised to hear you refer to it as the best work you've ever done, because it's...
STOUT: No. I think it's one of the...
ARCUDI: OK. It's one of the best things you've ever done. And certainly, in terms of the writing, considering the subject matter it's hilarious. But it's fucking out there.
STOUT: It is out there. But I felt so honored to be in the company of those guys. Robert Williams was nice enough to say that my story was his favorite in the whole book, which was really sweet.
ARCUDI: The word "sweet" used to describe someone's reaction to a story about felching is a bit too much for me to wrap my head around.
STOUT: I was at a bar at Palmer Station in Antarctica, the only bar that the station has, and one of the guys was having a conversation with the woman running the bar. Suddenly he made reference to felching. Boy did I perk up. My eyes riveted to his; he saw my reaction and he knew: "Ah-HAH! A kindred spirit!" But that someone would even know that in Antarctica... Man, I think that says a lot about Antarctica and who goes there.

MOVIE POSTERS

ARCUDI: A little bit later you did movie poster work – *Wizards*, *Rock and Roll High School*. That came about, as you just said, because you were able to do those patches for that other poster.
STOUT: Actually, it was a slightly more intricate path than that. *S*P*Y*S* came about because I was able to duplicate styles. My second one sheet was my poster for the film *Wizards*. I had been working for an ad agency that had me doing comics-style stuff. They got a chance to compete for doing the poster for *Wizards*, so they called me up. I thought, "A poster for an animated film? Awesome! That sounds great to me." I was aware of Ralph Bakshi. I knew he'd done *Fritz the Cat*. I said, "Well, let's see the movie." And they said, "No. We're not going to show you the movie. You won't do as nice a poster if we show you the movie." Instead of showing me the film they got me a set of really crummy frame blow-ups of some of the characters. I said, "Wow. This is what I've got to work from?" They said, "This is what we want you to do. Do the movie poster as if it's your movie. Draw these characters as though they're your characters." I agreed, and that's how I drew the poster for *Wizards*. I was in this interesting movie circle at the time. I was doing work with Roger Corman, so I got to meet directors Joe Dante and Allan Arkush in their formative years. I knew a lot of the people doing a lot of the work for what was known later as the Brat Pack: John Milius, Steven Spielberg, Brian DePalma and George Lucas. I was good friends with Charlie Lippincott and Mick Garris. They had just been hired by George Lucas to oversee the merchandising of a new film that he was about to released called *Star Wars*. I went over to visit those guys; they were in this little office. It was the two of them plus Mick's wife at the time, Kelly; she was the receptionist/secretary. It was like being on the beach with three friends watching a tsunami heading your way. Three people to handle the entire merchandising for *Star Wars*!

They hired me to do the very first commercial merchandising, a series of twenty-two Coca-Cola cups for Burger King. George Lucas is a very loyal guy. Any time any cartoon work would come up, George would make a call and have me hired. *American Graffiti* was being re-released. George wanted a new ad campaign for *American Graffiti*. He insisted that the ad agency, that was reluctant to hire me because they'd never worked with me before, hire me to do a whole bunch of caricatures of the cast of *American Graffiti*, plus a new movie poster.
ARCUDI: What year was that?
STOUT: *Star Wars* came out in 1977, so the re-release of *American Graffiti* would have probably been in '78. That launched my movie poster career, which I was really eager to get into because at that time – it's not that way any more – movie posters were the highest paying job in illustration. It paid huge, huge dough. Suddenly I was right in the center of that world. I remember during one week in the late '70s looking in the *Los Angeles Times* and finding eight of my movie posters in the movie calendar section.
ARCUDI: That's pretty cool.
STOUT: It was awesome. I needed a pitchfork to count the dough.
ARCUDI: You told me this once before and I found this really interesting that when you worked on the *Rock and Roll High School* poster and other posters for Roger Corman, that you actually worked directly with Corman?

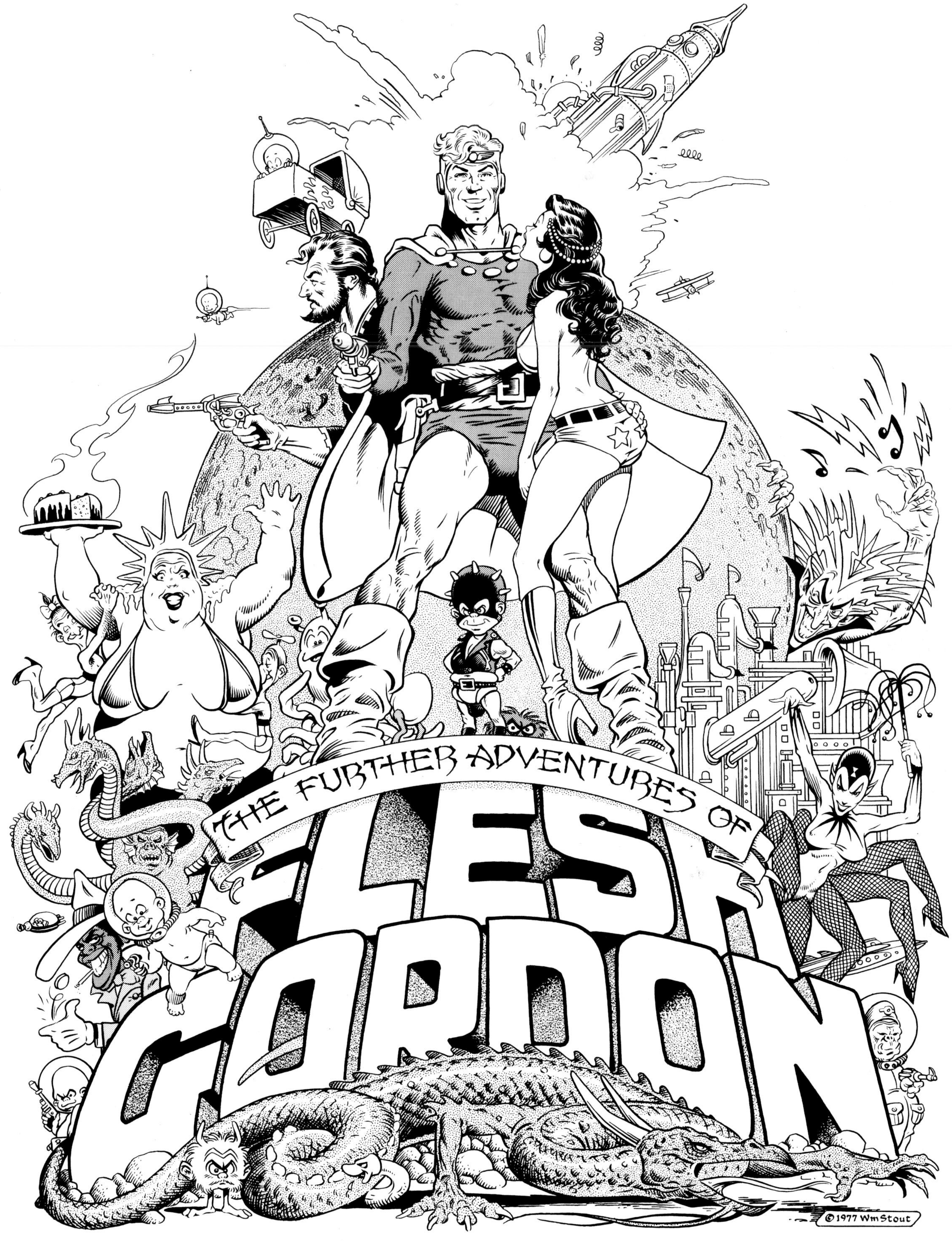
THE FURTHER ADVENTURES OF
FLESH GORDON
©1977 Wm Stout

This Page: "My poster for the sequel to *Flesh Gordon* was influenced a lot by Wally Wood's early *Mad* comic-book work."

STOUT: Yeah. I love Roger. He's an amazing guy. He was very up-front about everything, which was basically… "We're not going to pay you much, but you're going to get the chance to do what you want to do." That's how Coppola and Ronnie Howard and Martin Scorsese got to make their first movies. They didn't get paid much to direct, but they got the chance to make their movies. Plus, Roger did always pay. He didn't pay much, but you never got stiffed. His movie posters were the same way. He'd hire young people to do his posters. Obviously, they had to be competent. But traditionally, when I would do movie posters, the agency would have me do a whole series of roughs. I'd get so much per rough. From the roughs they'd select a couple of ideas to do as comps – comprehensives – sort of in between a rough and a finish. So

I'd do maybe more four or five comps. Then if they liked some of those comps, sometimes they'd have me do a color comp, which was like the poster in color but not quite as finished as a finish but more detailed than a rough. Eventually we'd go to a finish. I got to bill for each of those different steps. I always made more money from my roughs and comps than from my finishes. At that time I'd rather not do the finish. I had to work slower on a finish and there was the added pressure of it having to be perfect, whereas with the roughs and comps I could just bash 'em out. Roger Corman didn't want to spend that kind of money on a movie poster – so I would just show him a thumbnail sketch. He was very lucid visually; he could look at a thumbnail, completely understand it and go, "Yep. That's what I want. Go to finish." So he cut out all of those other steps, saving himself a ton of dough. Okay. So I didn't make all that much money from Roger, but there was a tremendous exhilaration in working with him. A lot of times, doing all of those steps for the other agencies resulted in a loss of energy and enthusiasm when it came time to do the finish – I'd already drawn the damn thing a dozen times! Going right from a rough to a finish, all of the energy was in the final illustration. I'm one of those guys who hates to draw the same drawing twice, which is why I never got into animation. So, yeah. Roger was great. From rough to finish and boom. And I got paid upon delivery. With Roger it was fun and I made a little

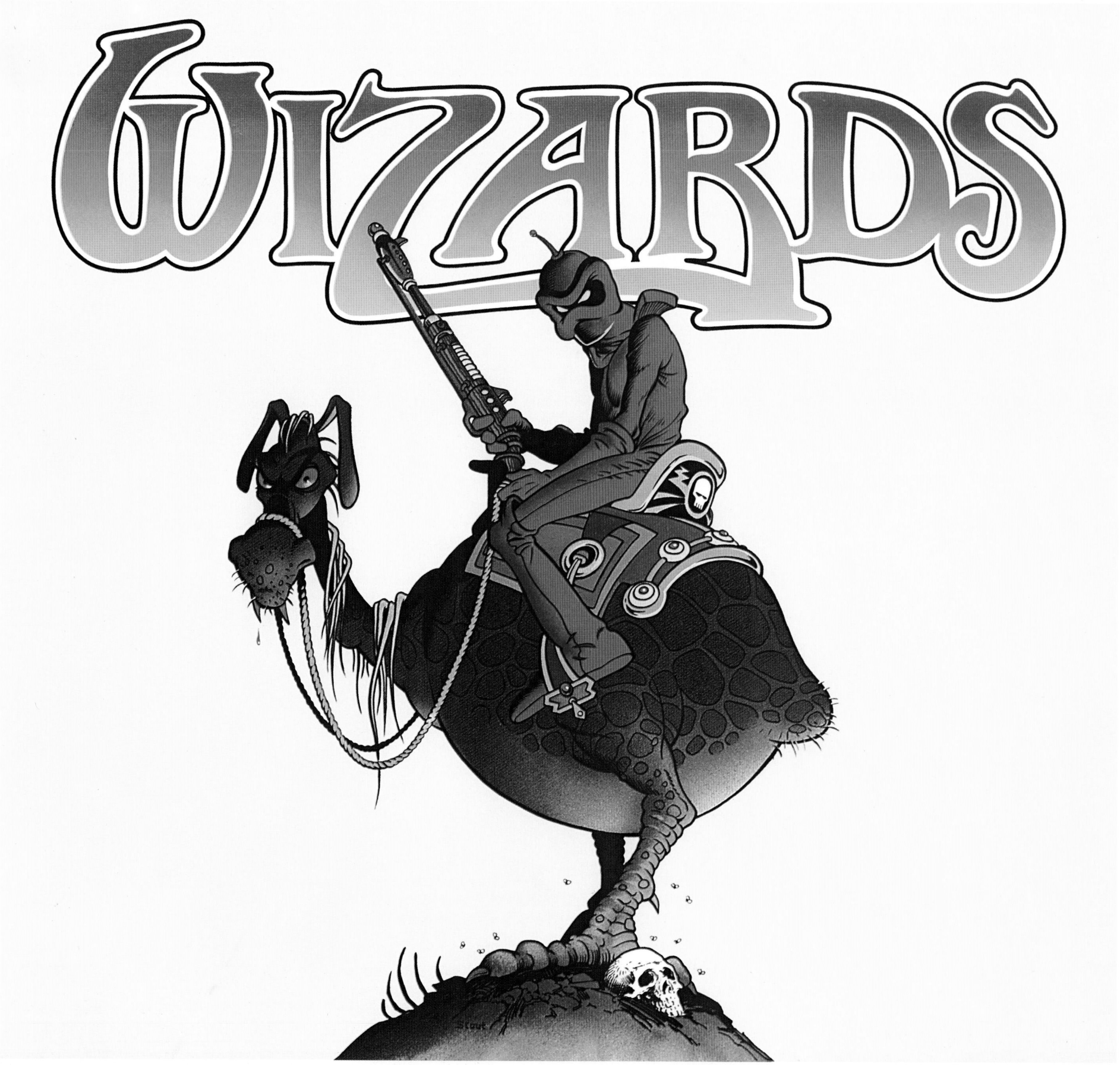
WIZARDS

This Page: This was the first published image for the film *Wizards*. It came inside the *Hollywood Reporter* as part of a special Twentieth-Century Fox insert (along with the first published image from *Star Wars*). The art nouveau lettering was changed for the film's teaser poster.

Would you buy a used secret from these men?
SUTHERLAND & GOULD
do to the C.I.A. what they did to the Army in M*A*S*H
as
S*P*Y*S
20th Century-Fox presents A ROBERT CHARTOFF-IRWIN WINKLER PRODUCTION
ELLIOTT GOULD and DONALD SUTHERLAND in S*P*Y*S
ZOUZOU · JOSS ACKLAND Produced by IRWIN WINKLER and ROBERT CHARTOFF Directed by IRVIN KERSHNER
Written by MALCOLM MARMORSTEIN and LAWRENCE J. COHEN & FRED FREEMAN Music-JERRY GOLDSMITH
TECHNICOLOR® PRINTS BY DELUXE®
PG PARENTAL GUIDANCE SUGGESTED
74/188
"SPYS"

money. With the others, it was work but I made a ton of money.

ARCUDI: Since you were making so much money doing these movie posters, did you pretty much abandon comics?

STOUT: It was a really easy decision to make. Let's see... Do I do this underground comic where, with all of the money spent on reference material, with all the research and work I put into it, I am basically making about five bucks a page; or do I do this movie poster where I'm making $200 an hour?

ARCUDI: You were a single guy then, though, right?

STOUT: Yep. I was a single guy, rent was a little over a hundred bucks a month in my rent-controlled apartment.

ARCUDI: You should have stuck with comics.

STOUT: I should have taken all of that money and invested it in real estate...

ARCUDI: Well, yeah. No kidding.

STOUT: ...instead of buying art books.

ARCUDI: So you seem to have been, at that point, working exclusively at movies, not a lot of comics work, really, in between '78 and now, really.

STOUT: Not a lot of comics work, but I still managed to do something in comics each year.

ARCUDI: Is that true?

STOUT: They may be hard to find, but that stuff turns up. I made a checklist recently of all my comics and comics-related work. I thought it would end up being about two or three pages of listings – the list ended up running over 60 pages! I never stopped drawing comics. There were long spaces between each endeavor. It's one of the reasons I kept doing covers – to keep my hand in comics. I did lots of covers for the undergrounds.

Comics as a mature national art form got co-opted.

ARCUDI: I was wondering if it had something to do with the disillusionment, because earlier you talked about how, when you saw your first underground comic you thought, "My God. You can do anything with underground comics." Did you think, "This is comics' coming of age? We're really going to see something happen." And then of course, that's not what happened.

STOUT: The blossoming of comics as a mature national art form got co-opted by the guys who were doing stuff for Marvel and D.C. They looked at underground comix and said, "Oh, we can do anything." So what did they do? The same old juvenile crap they had been doing but with tits and ass – extremely adolescent garbage; nothing adult

MONTY PYTHON'S
LIFE OF BRIAN

Top Left: Because of Stout's chameleonic ability to ape styles, Robert Williams recommended him for the job of redrawing Elliott Gould and Zou Zou for the S*P*Y*S movie poster after its original illustrator refused to make the changes.

Bottom Right: Stout drew this felt-marker piece before doing the final poster for *Life of Brian* in watercolor. This was the first of several advertising pieces done for Python movies by Stout.

She's got legs...
heart and head!

LINDA LOVELACE for PRESIDENT

IT'S THE FUNNIEST SEXIEST (GULP!) CAMPAIGN OF ALL TIME

SEE
HER
RAZZLE
THE
ELEPHANT
DAZZLE
THE
DONKEY!

starring LINDA LOVELACE and her CHEERLEADERS

with MICKEY DOLENZ • JOEY FORMAN
ROBERTA KENT • SCATMAN CROTHERS • MARTY INGELS
VAUGHN MEADER • JOE E. ROSS • LOUIS QUINN
EXECUTIVE PRODUCERS: WILLIAM B. SILBERKLEIT • ARTHUR MARKS
PRODUCERS: DAVID WINTERS • CHARLES STROUD
SCREENPLAY BY JACK S MARGOLIS   DIRECTED BY   CLAUDIO GUZMAN

This Page: "This gig was totally great! I got $400 cash for two hours' work. This was at a time when my rent was just 90 bucks a month."

about it at all. Insipidly puerile. People began to associate that with underground comix. They totally missed what was going on in the undergrounds, the main point of those books. Sure, a lot of undergrounds had sex, but there's always something thoughtful going on beneath the sex, some comment about us or our society – or really great humor. They weren't just jack-off books, which is what a lot of those New York idiots were doing.

ARCUDI: It seems to me that you really saw it as a way to put forth a political agenda.

STOUT: A way to put forth every agenda. Not just political, but a way to function and communicate graphically as a mature art medium in an adult way; to express adult concepts, ideas and dilemmas. That's what excites me about the alternative comics scene now. We're at a real crossroads here in the world of comics. Currently the numbers of the regular comics have dropped so low they're basically at the same level as the late '60s/early '70s underground books. There's virtually no difference from a numbers/business

> If an artist has a choice between expressing himself personally and drawing someone else's characters. Why on earth wouldn't they be doing their own stuff?

standpoint between the two. So if an artist has a choice between expressing himself personally with whatever he wants to do and working for Marvel or D.C. drawing someone else's characters – characters that the artist will never own – why on earth wouldn't they be doing their own stuff? There's no point in working for Marvel or D.C., really.

CREATOR RIGHTS

Stout believes that "there is more of an attack on creator's rights now than I've ever seen in my entire life." Go to:
http://www.tcj.com/ws03/stoutright.html

ART WITH A CAPITAL 'A'

STOUT: Marlon Brando said something that really opened my eyes in an interview for *Playboy* back in the early '60s. The interviewer commented about a particular movie being great art; Brando stopped him and said, and I'm paraphrasing here, "No. Come on. Movies aren't great art." The guy said, "What? No. What about...?" He named some movies that are generally considered to be really great films. Brando replied with something like, "No. Come on. Great art; we're talking a Beethoven symphony. Or Michelangelo's *Pieta*; Leonardo da Vinci and his paintings – Shakespeare's 'Hamlet'. Has there ever been a film that even comes close to that caliber of artistic achievement?" And he's absolutely right. Like I said – it's the movie business; not the movie arts. Brando talked about acting. He said, "Why would you ever revere an actor? It's not the actor who is great. It's the material. It's Shakespeare that's great. That's great art. Just because I can say his words well doesn't make me great." The actual greatness is in the words of Shakespeare. Those words are truly Great Art. Brando was discussing the relativity of quality and he's absolutely right. There's never been a movie that even comes close to being Great Art. There are great movies, terrific in relation to other movies. But in terms of the quality of greatness Brando was discussing, it hasn't happened yet. I think it may have to do with the nature of the medium...at least as it is today. I hasten to add that even with this awareness I've still never done less than my best work while making films.

ARCUDI: You think comics have the potential to be great art?

STOUT: Yep.

ARCUDI: To be the Sistine Chapel?

STOUT: Up with Mozart, the Sistine Chapel and all of that stuff Brando named. I think the potential is there much more than with motion pictures.

ARCUDI: Your assertion is that the best comics are made by a single cartoonist?

STOUT: I think overall, yes. There are real exceptions to that. When you get a writer as good as Alan Moore, you can team him with an artist and he's going to inspire that artist to do even better work than the artist normally does. I think in music, the Beatles together overall produced better stuff than they did apart. Sometimes the whole is greater than the sum of its parts. In film, that's much, much harder to accomplish, because it's not two guys making it.

ARCUDI: Or four loveable moptops.

STOUT: It often takes over a thousand guys to make a movie. On the movies I've worked on, I've had 1200 people working under me alone – just as the production designer. That doesn't even count the actors or the production staff, editing, camera or anybody else. The chances of the planet's aligning within those twelve hundred people and that everyone does their absolute best work to their ability and somehow it all pluses itself and creates a great film – you're more likely to win the lottery ten times consecutively. That's why seeing a good film always surprises me and seeing a great film completely amazes me. I know what the odds are against the filmmakers. On top of that, if you roll 50 sevens in a row and make a great film, that still doesn't mean you've made a successful film. It can still bomb at the box office. The success of your picture can be affected by something as uncontrollable as timing and the public mindset. Or the studio can botch the promotion – look at "Iron Giant."

ARCUDI: To put you on the spot, if comics can be great art is that what you're setting out to do with this superhero book?

STOUT: Certainly; that's my goal. I'm not saying that I'll accomplish that goal. I quite frankly don't think I come even remotely close to having Beethoven or Shakespeare potential. I'm just not that brilliant or deep. But I'll be damned if I'm not going to try.

ARCUDI: But are you slumming by using a superhero as your focal point?

STOUT: That's just a passion that I've had ever since I was a kid. There's an operatic, bigger than life, mythological aspect that the superhero genre has that I still find very appealing and certainly challenging to me as an artist and writer. Jack Kirby certainly understood that nature of superhero comics. Superhero comics get looked down upon, especially by the general public – but not comic fans. Obviously the fans have a great love of the genre. But is it possible to take a genre that is considered sort of silly and frivolous by the art literati and produce something that is substantial and speaks to the human condition and is of lasting value?

ARCUDI: At this point in your career, or at any point in your career over the last ten years or so, is there any temptation – because after all the bigger companies have some of the best toys, right? They've got Batman and they've got Superman. You said you started out with the Atom and the Flash, but is there any temptation to go in and play with those toys and say, "You own them, but I want to play?"

STOUT: Yes there is. I've agreed to do a Batman story.

I have no illusions about owning Batman. I know that DC or Time Warner owns Batman. There are other aspects, perks and rights for which I can negotiate, though. I've always liked Batman. I've never really done a mainstream popular superhero, so it will be a challenge. I'm going to do a black-and-white story; I think black and white is really appropriate for Batman. I'm not pretending that this is going to be "Great Art" with this one. I'm going to do an enjoyable Batman story, a real detective story.

ARCUDI: But you'll still approach it with the attitude of producing the best Batman story that you can produce

STOUT: Yeah. And I'm going to do it in a way that is different from any Batman story that I've ever seen; it will require reader participation and involvement.

I was knocked out by Frank Miller's *Dark Knight*. I thought he did a tremendous job of rethinking that character.

ARCUDI: It is Batman so it's Frank Miller. But you have no illusions about that being great art necessarily?

STOUT: Oh. God no. But I think *Dark Knight* was a major step toward us all getting there. I don't think *Dark Knight* is Shakespeare and I think Frank would agree with me that it's neither Shakespeare nor Mozart, but I think by rethinking the superhero genre as an adult he it pulled that genre up to the next level. He put us a step closer towards doing something that's more adult, more complex and more interesting within the superhero genre.

ARCUDI: Hmm. Okay. All right.

STOUT: You saw the public's reaction. When *Dark Knight* came out, for the first time people who had never entered a comic shop began venturing inside these shops saying, "I love this book. This is great. What do you have that's like it?" And of course there wasn't anything.

ARCUDI: Some would say in the 1980s that presumably the superhero book was coming of age, which is sort of an oxymoron. But right now, there seems to be a new opportunity to really break free from the idea that comics are for children. And the alternative market, some of the stuff is very exciting.

STOUT: Oh, it's really exciting. Not just the writing itself. It's the art, too. You don't have to draw the "Marvel Way." You can paint your strip. You can do it in wood blocks. You can do it as an etching. It doesn't matter. You can do it in any style. There are comics with a beautiful primitive style. There is stuff that's really elegantly drawn. There is stuff that harkens back to the '30s or the '20s. It's just completely open. In a sense, I think it is the fruit born from the underground comix movement's seeds.

ARCUDI: And in a way, I think the undergrounds were fruits born – especially some of the covers – of the EC seeds, in a lot of ways.

STOUT: Yep. Harvey Kurtzman's considered the father of the underground comics.

ARCUDI: In that way, he's a grandfather to what's happening right now. I'm thinking that something's going to happen to crunch this, though, because that seems to happen with every generation.

STOUT: Well, when I talk to people about it, I say, "Enjoy it while it lasts, because nothing good ever lasts." I'm a pretty optimistic person, but I'm realistic as well — no Golden Age ever lasts. It's that way with radio stations, with comics, with any sort of media.

ARCUDI: Do you have any favorites of the alternative stuff right now that you care to mention?

STOUT: Oh, man. Almost everything my kids show me. They're really selective. They don't show me anything but the very best stuff: *Barry Ween*, *Akiko*, *Bone*, *From Hell*, *Cave-In*, *Eightball* and *Jimmy Corrigan* – stuff like that.

FROM DESIGNING MOVIE POSTERS...

Stout got out of designing movie posters at "the perfect time." Go to:
http://www.tcj.com/ws03/stoutmovie.html

...TO DESIGNING MOVIES

ARCUDI: The work that you did for *Conan the Barbarian*... your storyboards were done in a comic book format. Did you get that job on the basis of your work in comics? Or was that another coincidence?

STOUT: Kind of/sort of. It was a series of coincidences. My friend Bob Greenberg was working for Ed Pressman, the original producer for *Conan*. Bob knew I was a big *Conan* fan. I loved all of the [Robert E.] Howard stories, and the Frazetta covers, and stuff. He said, "Man. You really gotta come by and see what Ron Cobb is doing on *Conan*." Ed had hired Ron to do presentation illustrations and production illustrations to visually define the film. This was before [John] Milius was attached to it, back when Oliver Stone was going to direct it. I said, "God, I'd love to – except, man, I've never been busier in advertising." I was doing so many movie posters it was just unbelievable. There was just no time to come up for air. Finally, I got a break – but I didn't go over to the *Conan* offices. Instead, I went to the ABA, which is the national book fair where every publisher in the United States gathers in one spot. It's a great place for illustrators to get work. You bring your

> I'm going to do it in a way that is different from any Batman story that I've ever seen; it will require reader participation and involvement.

portfolio and walk from booth to booth, show your work and get hired. I had my portfolio with me, and who should I run into but Ron Cobb himself. He said that I was his first choice of someone to work with on the film. I don't know how he was aware of my work, or whether it was just my portfolio that impressed him on the spot. But he said he had an arrangement with Milius, who by then was the director of the film, that whoever Ron hired John had veto power over and whoever John suggested for the art department, Ron had veto power over. So I had to show my stuff to John Milius. Ron asked me if I would come by the office and drop off my book. I said, "Sure. Sounds great." It sounded like fun. I was a huge admirer of Ron Cobb's work. He did most of the important underground political cartoons in the '60s for the *L.A. Free Press*. Amazing artist and an amazing mind. He invented the ecology symbol and donated it to the public domain.

I went in on a Friday. I was going to drop off my book, but Milius was actually there; I just handed it directly to him. I watched him look through it. He remembered the Harlan Ellison story I had illustrated for *Heavy Metal* called "Shattered Like A Glass Goblin". He had really liked that when it appeared in *Heavy Metal*. I also had my work from my recently published *Dragonslayers* portfolio with me, and he really liked that, too. He handed me all of my stuff back and started to walk out of the room. John's a really dramatic, charismatic guy. As he's walking out of the room, over his shoulder he grunted, "Hire him." Just like out of a western. I was directed to talk to Buzz Feitshans, the show's line producer. Our receptionist was Kathleen Kennedy, if you can imagine – a couple of years later she produced *E.T.*! I talked to Buzz who told me what they were going to be paying me to do the film's storyboards. I nearly fell off my chair laughing; it was about 10% of what I was making in advertising.

I'd been doing advertising for a while – for over 120 movies. I thought, "This might be fun for a couple of weeks." Well, the two weeks turned into two years. It was an interesting time to get into making motion pictures. John was just finishing his production duties on *1941*, which Spielberg directed. We were all sharing offices. Ron Cobb and I would work on *Conan* during the day, and then put down our pencils at 6 p.m., run across the hall to Steven's office and I'd watch them kick around ideas for *Raiders of the Lost Ark*. It was just one big exciting happy family there. We were in those offices for a good chunk of a year, maybe less. Then we moved to Dino DeLaurentiis' offices in Beverly Hills. That was a whole other experience meeting the DeLaurentiis family and dealing with them as producers. Then we took off for Zagreb, Yugoslavia. I began living in Zagreb, with the intention of making the film there. I started to learn Serbo-Croatian and made a lot of great Yugoslavian friends; I just loved the heck out of Zagreb. It was my first time living behind the Iron Curtain. I was startled to learn that this Communist country had a much greater freedom of the

We would work on *Conan* during the day, and then put down our pencils at 6 p.m., run across the hall to Steven's office and I'd watch them kick around ideas for *Raiders of the Lost Ark.*

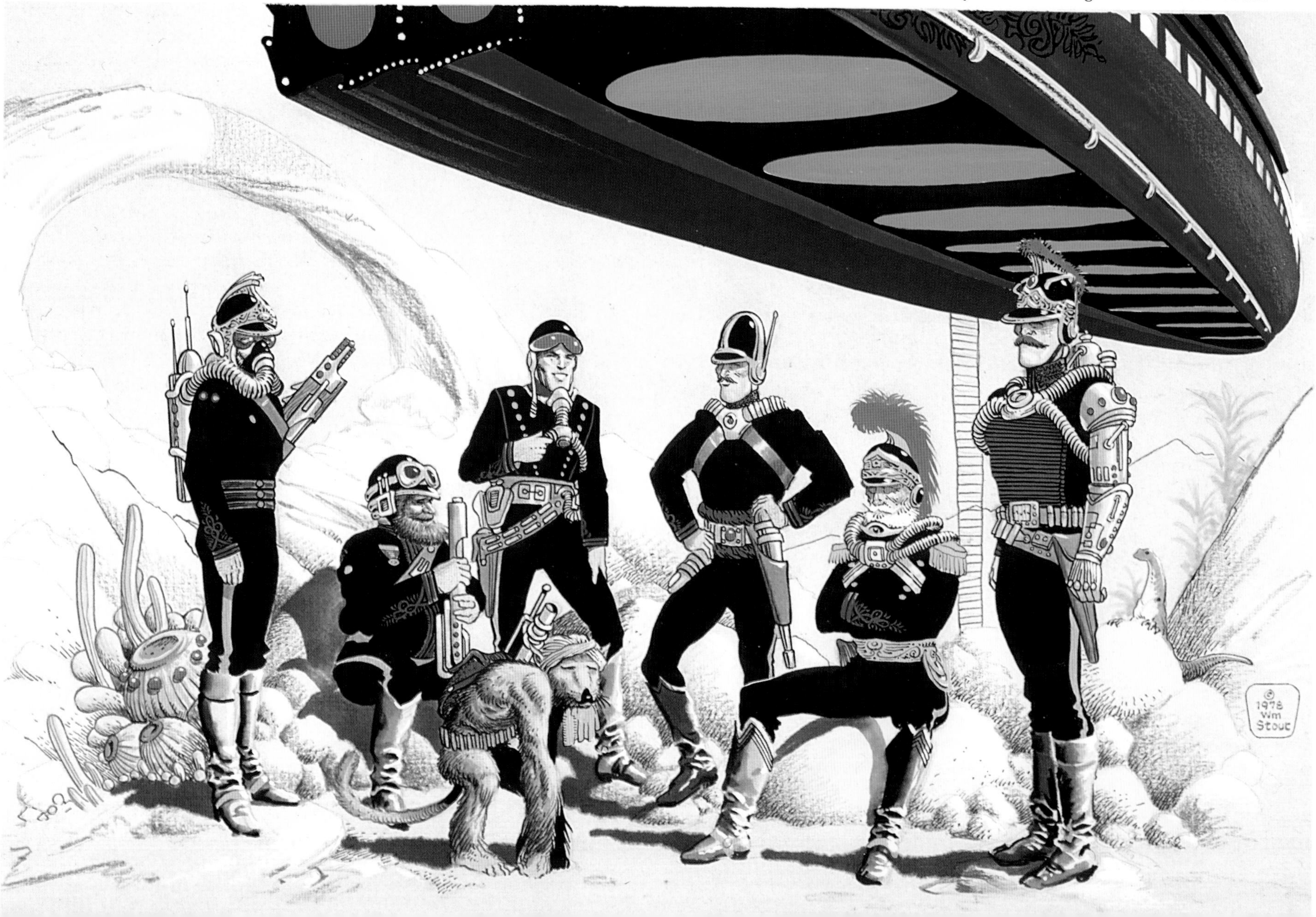
© 1978 Wm Stout

This Page: In 1977, Stout was hired as a key designer on *Buck Rogers*, which was initially planned to be a series of three feature films but ended up being a TV series. "*Buck Rogers* was my firrst studio film gig. It was a lot of fun, and I was given a lot of freedom. Ultimately, though, I blew this job by not giving it top priority and treating it like just another freelance gig. A hard lesson fortunately learned early in my film career."

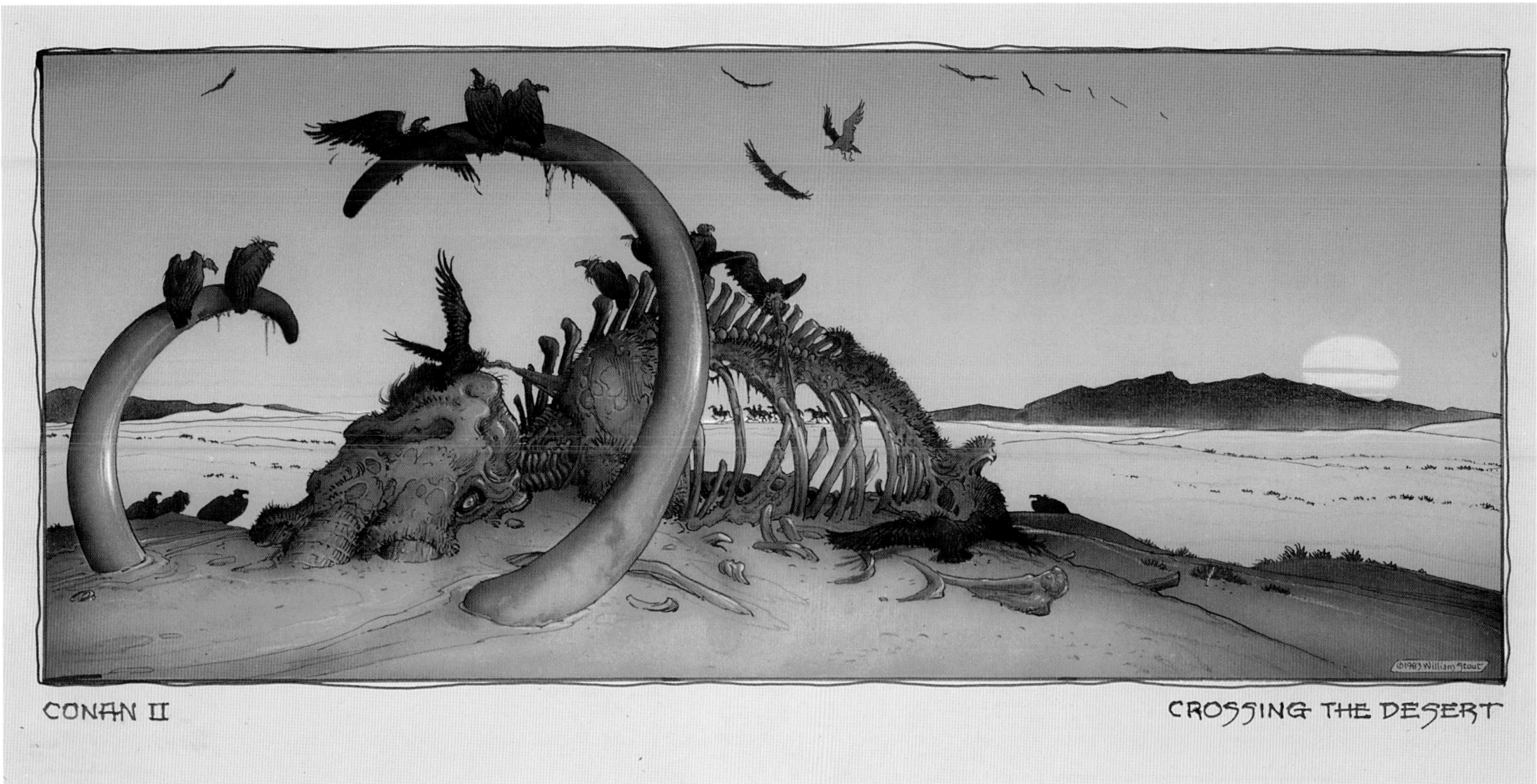
©1978 William Stout
CONAN II
CROSSING THE DESERT

press than in the United States. I could buy any American magazine on their newsstands: *Playboy*, *Time*, *Newsweek*, etc. – but also available was an equal array of Communist magazines; complete freedom of information. They did not fear a healthy marketplace of ideas and free discussion. My eyes were really opened to one of the great American myths that we've all been spoon fed since we were kids. As a staunch conservative, as a strong advocate of our Constitutional guaranteed free press, I was shocked. See how this all sort of relates to undergrounds? After several months the producers decided they couldn't make the movie in Zagreb – it became Spain instead. They gave me the choice of either coming with them to Spain and sitting around for a month while they set up our offices and things, or I could take that month and go without pay and spend it in Rome. I chose Rome. I knew eventually I was going to be in Spain, but I'd never been to Rome. I got to spend a month or two in Rome. Every morning the daughter of our set decorator would come by on her motor scooter; she'd pick me up and take me to a different art museum or a different park or a different Michelangelo sculpture. Then she'd take me back home where her mom would make me a nice Italian lunch. It was a pretty idyllic situation.

At the end of that time I went to live in Madrid to continue pre-production work on the film. I got very familiar with Madrid; I usually bopped over to the Prado each during lunch to look at paintings and pick up girls. About that time, something else reared its head. Before I had left for Yugoslavia, a friend of mine, Byron Preiss, who had published a lot of my work, was visiting my studio. I had just done a whole bunch of pictures for Don Glut's *Dinosaur Dictionary*. Don had asked me to do five pictures for his new *Dinosaur Dictionary*, because he wanted an illustration for every listing in the book; that five turned into about 40. So I had all of these dinosaur pictures. Byron was visiting and he said, "If you could do your own book on anything, what would you do?" My lightning response was, "I have no idea." He saw the stack of dinosaur pictures, and he said, "Well, would you like to do one on dinosaurs?" Thinking Byron was just being conversational, I said, "Oh, sure. That'd be fun." Well, a couple of months later Byron phones up and tells me we have a book deal – Bantam wants to do our dinosaur book. So I'm thinking, I can do this. I can design a motion picture and do a dinosaur book at the same time.

Because of *Conan* and *First Blood*, my film career was pretty much launched.

There I was, working on *Conan* during the day, and every other spare moment I was doing preliminary sketches for the illustrations for the dinosaur book. It soon became readily apparent to me that I was not going to be able to accomplish both the movie and the book and do both pieces justice. I announced to the production that I was going to have to leave the show to finish my dinosaur book. I said, "It's only going to take me a couple of months; I'll come back well before shooting." A couple months turned into two years once again. Shooting came and went. God, I got really desperate calls from overseas to come back to the film. But my attitude was – not the most professional attitude for a filmmaker – that this is Robert E. Howard's and John Milius's *Conan*, or even Ron Cobb's *Conan*, but this is my dinosaur book. So I stuck with and finished the book. Much to his faith and credit, after the book came out Buzz Feitshans hired me to do storyboards for *First Blood*. Because of *Conan* and *First Blood*, my film career was pretty much launched.

ARCUDI: You've worked on a lot of films that never got made. Probably the most famous one was the American *Godzilla*.

STOUT: That was in 1982 and '83. I spent close to two years on that one. That's another thing about the film business: for every project that goes past the initial okay point, maybe one percent gets to pro-

This Page: "This image is not in the script [for *Conan the Destroyer*]. The screenplay called for some traveling shots of Conan and his motley crew. I thought it would be cool and very Hyborian to have them in the distance and a rotting mammoth in the foreground to indicate the story's exoticness both in time and locale."

THE TRUNK DOOR FALLS AWAY BEHIND THE COPS' CARS.
THE COPS FAN OUT, APPROACHING ONE ON EACH SIDE.
JIM: "USE IT! WE'RE IN TROUBLE!" JIM HANDS NASH THE GUN FROM THE DASH.
NASH ROLLS DOWN THE WINDOW...
...LEANS OUT AND TAKES AIM.
POW!
"THE HITCHER"
Storyboards by William Stout '85

8 cont'd
JIM: "WHY ARE YOU LOOKING AT ME LIKE THAT?"
RYDER: "SCARE YA?"
JIM'S ATTENTION HAS BEEN DIVERTED...
THE WHITE VW BUG IS PARKED OFF TO THE SIDE OF THE ROAD, ALL ITS LIGHTS OFF.
JIM TAKES HIS FOOT OFF THE GAS, SLOWING DOWN ALONGSIDE THE CAR.
"THE HITCHER"
Storyboards by William Stout '85

duction. And out of those that go to production, only 10% of those ever make it to the theaters. There's no guarantee that even if your project does get lucky and green lit that anyone is going to see it, which can be pretty damn frustrating. There are also what I call the "X-factors" in making films. You can write the best script, hire the best director, do your best design work, but since film is such a collaborative process, there are any number of other links in the chain that can completely screw up the final product. You can do all of your best work and have it messed up by lousy editing, bad photography, a miscast actor or crappy music. This process of moviemaking is so difficult that when I see a good film to me it's like an absolute miracle. I know that somehow this thing was able to make it through this treacherous gauntlet to survive with its integrity somewhat intact. Then when I see pictures like *Brazil* or *Moulin Rouge*, which are not only great films but movies in which the people involved – primarily the director in those two cases – took so many risks at so many levels, I am literally moved to tears of joy and astonishment. I have an inkling as to what the filmmakers went through to achieve what they accomplished.

ARCUDI: Maybe this is a sore subject, but on *Godzilla* you did a redesign of the Godzilla character for your American version, right?

STOUT: Yes – *Godzilla* was a fabulous project. Fred Dekker had written this spectacular screenplay that read like a really good Spielberg film. Steve Miner, who had done the *Friday the 13th* movies, was producing and was also going to direct it. This was before he did *House, Soul Man* or *The Wonder Years*. He turned out to be a really fine director. This was my first film as a production designer. I was originally hired to do presentation paintings for the project. I did one big presentation painting and then Steve needed storyboards done to get a realistic effects budget. If you hand 10 effects companies the same script, they'll have 10 different ideas of what those effects are going to look like – and 10 different bids. But if you hand them storyboards, then we're all pretty much on the same page. So I began doing storyboards for the film. Around the time I was doing that, I got a visit from Mentor Huebner, one of the greatest storyboard artists who ever lived. He did a lot of the Hitchcock films [like] *North by Northwest*, just a spectacular guy; over 200 films to his credit. He looked at what I was doing and said, "These boards are so detailed – you know what you're doing here? You're really designing the film." I was drawing fairly large, detailed boards because of the nature of the film and because the boards were also part of Steve's presentation to the studios. I was designing all of the sets and drawing the set dressing, suggesting costumes and everything else. I thought about what Mentor said: "God, he's right." I approached Steve and asked him if I could be the production designer. He gave it some thought and he did his homework. He called people I'd worked with and came back to me and said, "Yes; if you hire a strong art director, you can be the film's production designer." I was really excited about that. I ended up storyboarding about 85% of the film; another 10% of the film was boarded by my studio mate Dave Stevens and his friend Doug Wildey, who I hired to help me out and speed things up. Rick Baker was on board to do the large robotic heads of *Godzilla*, Dave Allen was going to do the stop-motion animation. At the time, there wasn't any CGI to speak of – certainly nothing efficient or affordable. It was a first-class crew all of the way with a great script on top of it. The story had a lot of heart. Godzilla attacks San Francisco and ends up dying on Alcatraz. It's a wonderful story, but it was the right project at just the wrong time. Obviously, there were effects in almost every shot. Obviously it was going to be a very expensive film. So this expensive film was being pitched right at a time when there were four hugely expensive films that had just bombed dramatically – one of them being *Heaven's Gate*. The studios mistakenly lacked confidence in Steve as a director who could pull off a picture like this. You can't blame them; he didn't have the track record he's got today. It was a great project that should have been made but sadly never did.

He looked at what I was doing and said, "These boards are so detailed – you know what you're doing here? You're really designing the film."

This Page: "By the time I was working on *The Hitcher*, storyboards had become a lot more fun for me — it was like directing on paper! The action of *The Hitcher* so matches my storyboards that several French film critics think that I secretly directed the film. *Au contraire*; director Robert Harmon and I just shared the exact same vision and storytelling style."

Opposite Page: *Upper Cretaceous Antarctica*. "The most difficult things to research in this picture were not the animals: they were the prehistoric plants."

THE PRINCESS OF MARS FILM

In 1990 Stout was hired to work on the (potentially) disastrous *Princess of Mars* movie, an adaptation of Edgar Rice Burroughs' novel. The director was John McTiernan (*Die Hard, The Hunt For Red October, The Thomas Crown Affair*). Luckily, the movie was never made. Go to: **http://www.tcj.com/ws03/stoutmars.html**

A COMMITMENT TO DINOSAURS

ARCUDI: Let's backtrack a little to segue into this dinosaur thing and see if we can work Roy Krenkel into this, too. You had done a show of your prehistoric work in 1977, right?

STOUT: Yeah. That was my first one-man show. It consisted primarily of the pieces that I'd done for Don Glut's book, the revised *Dinosaur Dictionary*.

ARCUDI: I'm sure you had a lot of influences, but you said that you became pretty good friends with Krenkel, and he, of course, was a huge [Edgar Rice] Burroughs fan. I know that even at that time you were working to make your dinosaurs accurate. But how much of an impact did the way Krenkel staged some of this stuff have on the way you would stage your drawings? You know Roy's stuff... It's not just a dinosaur standing there. It's a whole dramatic scene.

STOUT: Through osmosis and careful study I picked up an enormous amount of information on how to both stage and design. Roy was really good at designing vignettes as well as full-picture scenes. I absorbed as much from him as I could. Another thing I was trying to absorb was the way that both Krenkel and Frazetta conveyed an atmosphere – that almost tangible romanticism of theirs. They really captured that rarified exoticism of Edgar Rice Burroughs and the slightly harsher decadent drama of Robert E. Howard in the way they portrayed things, designed things and presented things. Krenkel and Frazetta were sort of doorways to the past for me as well. I became so enamored of their work I needed to find out where it all came from. That led to an investigation of all of the different artists that influenced them who in turn became even bigger influences on me than both Krenkel and Frazetta. I became hugely affected by a lot of the great turn of the century artists and illustrators: Arthur Rackham, Edmund Dulac, Charles R. Knight, J. C. Leyendecker, [Norman] Rockwell, Dean Cornwell, N.C. Wyeth – all of the great turn of the century artists.

Krenkel and Frazetta were sort of doorways to the past for me.

ARCUDI: Now, you continued to do film work after you did *The Dinosaurs* book?

STOUT: The film business is hard to get into, but it's even harder to get out of unless you deliberately sabotage yourself by not showing up or doing horrible work and insulting people. Even then...

I found myself in a business that was both enticing and repulsive at the same time. Rod Stewart once described certain ex-wives or ex-girlfriends as being 51/49. The film business is like that. Fifty-one percent of it is the best time you'll ever have. Forty-nine percent is the absolute worst. The more distance there is between you and the girlfriend (or in my case, between me and the film business) the larger the 51% appears to loom, until you're thinking, "No. It was really more like 80/20 or 85/15." So you agree to take on another film, and the first day back you remember, it hits you, and you realize, "Damn! I forgot! Half the time spent over the next year or so on this project is going to be about the worst time I've ever had in my life."

ARCUDI: Let's return to your illustrations for the newly revised *Dinosaur Dictionary*. When you started doing that, you said it was

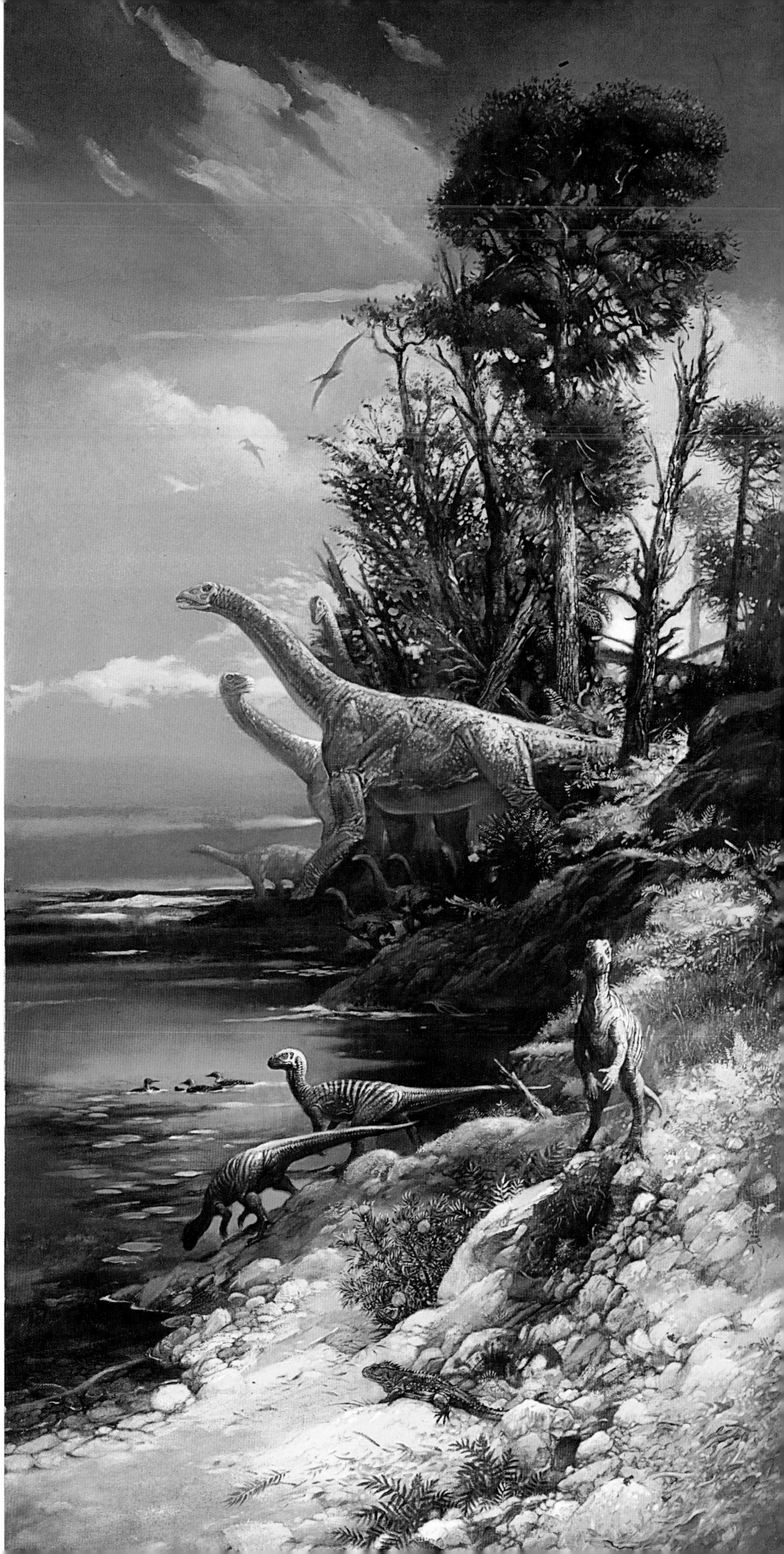

your mission to make this stuff as accurate as possible, to not just throw it off.

STOUT: I was going to be the first, and maybe the only person, to ever depict the dinosaurs that I was illustrating for Don's book. It dawned on me that because of that I had this enormous responsibility to the public to make it as accurate as possible. My picture might visually define that animal for quite a long time. I started to consult with the best paleontologists. I joined the Society of Vertebrate Paleontology in the late '70s so I could have access to all current information, which changes at an amazing rate. It especially started changing in the late '70s. As I drew the dinosaurs, I began to think about their settings. They needed to be accurate as well. That got me involved in researching paleobotany – prehistoric plants – and paleoecology. At the time I started doing this, around 1976-'77, very little was known about paleobotany, because plants and soft material fossilizes very poorly – if at all. There wasn't a whole lot known. However, at that time, there was an enormous breakthrough when the paleobotanists said, "You know what? Leaves don't preserve very well nor stems and all of that stuff; but pollen is small, hard and compact." So they started looking at microfossils; they found pollen all over the place. Suddenly, where they only had the sketchiest bits of information, whole forests were springing up. They discovered all kinds of plants that existed in prehistoric times by studying the pollen. I was the beneficiary of this knowledge. Suddenly I was able to foliate my dinosaur worlds with all of this new information.

ARCUDI: The interesting thing to me is that although you do see some dinosaurs cropping up earlier in your work, until *The Dinosaurs* prehistoric animals were just a small part of your overall career. Did you think you were going to end up having the kind of commitment to paleontological reconstruction in 1977 that has ended up consuming your life as it is right now?

STOUT: Not at all. That certainly was not my goal. I was a subscriber to what I call the "Pinball School of Career Planning" – I just bounced from job to job, project to project without any rhyme or reason or guiding direction other than I knew I wanted to do stuff that paid well. That's why I ended up doing movie posters, and why I ended up in film. Even though the film business didn't pay well initially, I saw that by pursuing a certain job niche within the industry, that of production designer, I would be making pretty decent money eventually. As far as a career doing dinosaurs, man, that was... The book initially started as just another freelance job for me – the *Dinosaur Dictionary*, and *The Dinosaurs: A Fantastic New View of A Lost Era*. I had no idea what an impact those books would have on my career.

ARCUDI: Well, and on you personally.

STOUT: And on me personally.

ARCUDI: You say it started as a job, but clearly that book is not just a job. I mean, you look at that stuff and clearly there's a lot of care and, let's say the word, "love" put into a lot of those pieces.

STOUT: When I say it started as a job, at that point in my career I was in a position where I could pick and choose pretty much any of the work that I cared to do. I was being inundated with offers of every kind of work every week, sometimes every day. I felt like a little king deciding which of the subjects to favor. I gave tons of work away to friends. So yes, the dinosaur stuff was a job. But it was also... The only jobs I chose to do at the time were the jobs that really excited me and that I was really passionate about. I did feel a responsibility but there was an excitement, too. I was the conduit to the public of all of this arcane knowledge that the scientists were discovering about dinosaurs that was only getting to the public, at that time, in little trickles and dribs and drabs. Here was a chance to put all of that new information – the fact that dinosaurs weren't stupid, that they weren't slow, that they were fairly intelligent, that they moved rapidly, that they possibly were warm-blooded – put all of this information into one book, one source for everyone. That got me really excited. I was in the right place at the right time and I had the opportunity to do it all in a very entertaining way.

ARCUDI: This was a huge undertaking, really. You were doing roughs initially to showboat the book, but then when it came down to drawing the stuff, you had to decide on all of the different techniques you wanted to use. Tell me about the thought process of why you chose to go with one style for this piece, another style for this piece, charcoal for that, watercolor for that.

STOUT: It was initially so that I wouldn't get bored. I had a fear that if I did everything the same style I'd be so sick of that style by the

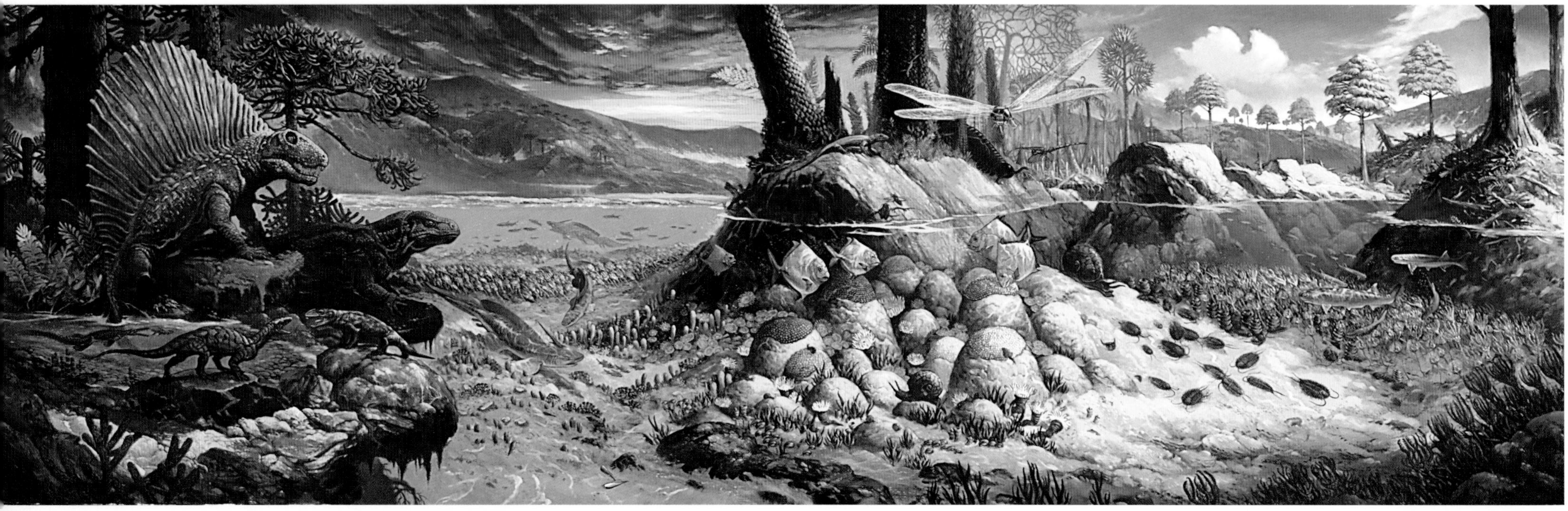

© 2002 William Stout.

This Page and Opposite: Stout arranged the elements in these two murals for the Houston Museum of Natural Science so that as you begin walking past them from right to left, you not only travel forward through different ages of prehistory, you witness a change in the time of day, as well, beginning at dawn and ending at sunset. "One of the most pleasurable jobs I've ever had."

I was the conduit to the public of all of this arcane knowledge that the scientists were discovering about dinosaurs.

end of the book that I'd never want to touch that style again and that I'd burn out before I'd finished the book. Plus, I was still somewhat in an experimental mode, and I had this huge passion for the turn-of-the-century children's book illustrators. One of my goals was to see if I could do illustrations in those styles. It helped to keep the project exciting for me, jumping from style to style to style. Let me try to do N.C. Wyeth here. Now I'll attempt Arthur Rackham. How about Edmund Dulac, or maybe the Detmold brothers. I figured if I kept everything interesting for me, it would have the same effect on the public, as well. They would look at this book and never get bored.

ARCUDI: Was it as capricious as you make it sound? For instance, you look at the two mating dinosaurs done more or less in a Mucha-esque style. Did you try to choose a style that would match the mood of the piece?

STOUT: Oh, certainly. And that comes from my training at Chouinard. I never ever tried to force one style or approach to solve everything. I always let the problem dictate the style and solution. I've done that all through my career, which is why there's such a variety to my work. The dinosaur book was the same way. For that particular piece you mentioned, the dinosaurs mating, I thought this could be really gross or coarse if done improperly; it had to be handled very delicately. So I went back to Mucha and I also went to Edward Detmold, who does stuff that is so light and so airy it looks like it can float off the page like a feather. I attempted to do that. In my own interpretation, as soon as I finished the picture I thought, Wow! I think I've done it. Of course, when I go back and compare my piece to the Detmold illustration that inspired it and my thing looks as ham-fisted as hell. But that's how you grow. You aim for 100 and you hit 70 or 80; maybe the next time you'll hit 85.

ARCUDI: It's interesting that you mention Detmold as an influence, because I think a lot of people have heard of Dulac and Rackham, but remarkably, for some reason, because the Detmold brothers were so good, they're names you never hear.

STOUT: They were astounding. Really, really tragic lives.

ARCUDI: In any event, *The Dinosaurs* was a huge undertaking. Just a little later you did at least the cover and the frontispiece for *The Little Blue Brontosaurus,* right?

One thing that has kept me from doing superhero comics is being associated with a character. I don't want to have to draw that character for the rest of my life.

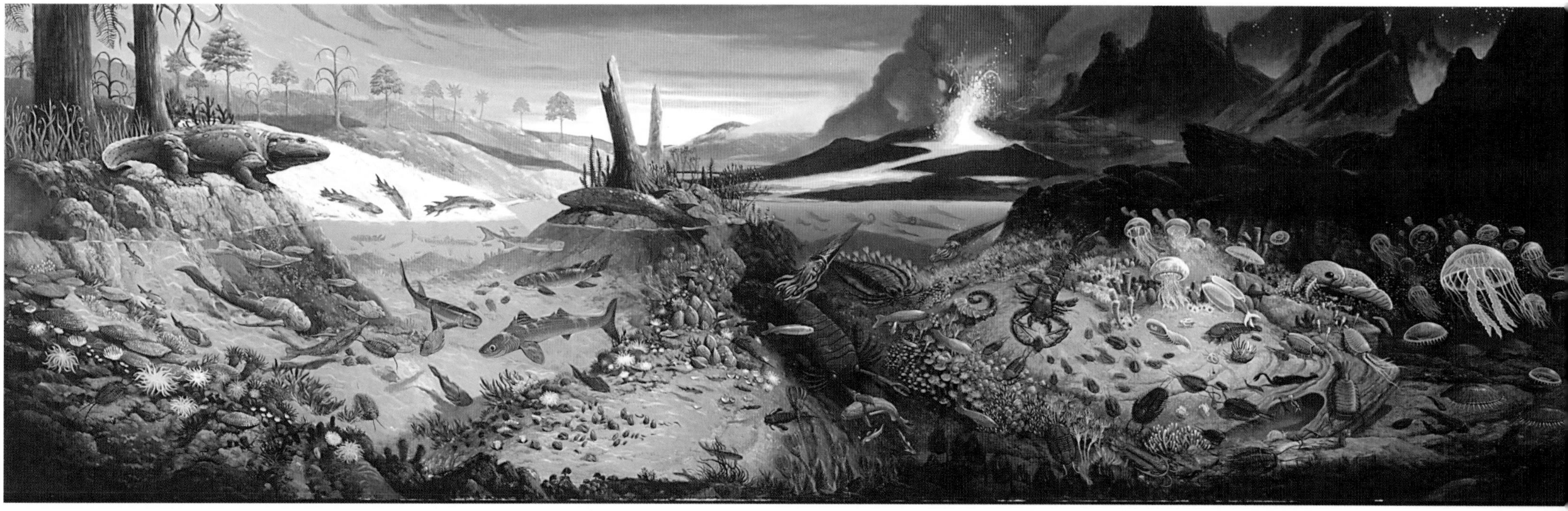

STOUT: For that one I did the cover, designed all of the characters, the frontispiece, the back cover, the endpapers, and then did the layouts for the whole rest of the book. The finished art from the layouts were painted by Don Morgan, who ghosted *Pogo* for Walt Kelly the last several years of the strip.

ARCUDI: Only you and Alex Toth, I think, have ever propounded that philosophy, saying that each problem deserves a different approach for a solution. Creative problems, if they were approached that way more frequently you'd have... I guess that's why there are so few geniuses in life. *Little Blue Brontosaurus* bears a not so...

STOUT: ...more than a passing resemblance to *The Land Before Time.*

SCREENWRITING AND WRITING

Stout was hired by Jim Henson to work on Henson's next feature after *Dark Crystal* and *Labyrinth* as a writer and designer. Stout discusses that and *Theodore Rex*, "the most nightmarish experience of my entire film career." Go to: **http://www.tcj.com/ws03/stoutscreen.html**

SUPERHEROES AND WORK-FOR-HIRE

STOUT: One of the things that has kept me from doing superhero comics is being associated with a character. I don't want to have to draw that character for the rest of my life. I see that happens at comic book conventions. I bet Bernie Wrightson's really sick of drawing Swamp Thing. I don't want to get into that rut. I've had the story idea for this superhero miniseries for many, many years now. That's one of the main things that's kept me from doing it. Whereas dinosaurs, there's such a diversity of dinosaurs and there's a richness to them. Plus, they keep discovering new dinos and new stuff about them. I don't really get too tired of drawing dinosaurs. For one, I don't do it all of the time. I recently illustrated Richard Matheson's first children's book: *Abu and the 7 Marvels*. That's out now. I just finished translating a book of Pablo Neruda poems: *Stones of The Sky*; I'm doing a mystical comics-style illustration for each of the poems as well.

ARCUDI: And that's what struck me odd when you said you're a big fan of superhero comics. Because I always got the sense that at no point in your career were you ever thinking, "I want to take over the *Fantastic*

Four." Is that accurate?

STOUT: That's really accurate. For one thing I know that Marvel wouldn't give me a piece of my version of the *Fantastic Four*. I love superhero comics and that whole thing, but I'm also a businessman. That's definitely one of the hats I wear. If I do something that enhances the value of something, I expect participation in that. I know I'm not going to be allowed to get that doing the *Fantastic Four* or *Spider-Man*.

ARCUDI: Just ask (well, you can't ask him any more) but just ask Jack.

STOUT: Great example.

ARCUDI: Who – you can see an argument for who actually created the Fantastic Four, but who elaborated upon and improved throughout a career on it.

STOUT: Did Jack get a piece of the Hulk TV show? No – he didn't. There's all kinds of properties that Jack was involved in the creation of that he was excluded from participating in their profits. Look at that recent issue of *Comic Book Artist*, with the big article on Tower. The Tower comics that Wally Wood created, the rights to all of his characters were purchased for two grand – and Wally wasn't even the guy who got the two grand! That makes me ill. That really makes me ill. Wood or Wood's estate should still own all that stuff.

ARCUDI: And Woody of all people, a man most outraged by interference and… The reason that *Heroes Incorporated* came into existence in the first place was to have a property that he had control over. Of course, it was unsuccessful for him. And even Tower came into being for that same reason. But a shit load of good that ever did him, unfortunately.

STOUT: I think guys like Wally Wood and Eisner and Kurtzman and John Stanley and Carl Barks should be officially considered national treasures. Guys like that should never have to wonder where their next buck is coming from for the rest of their lives.

ARCUDI: Well, at least Eisner doesn't. Eisner was a very good businessman. He made sure he kept a firm hold on *The Spirit*.

STOUT: Thank God for that. Because I've worked for so many years with the Hollywood sharks, I've picked up a lot of business savvy that I apply to my illustration and comic book work. I try to share that information with other artists and I freely share it, because I think the more that they are informed… They have a choice of whether to use that information or not, but if they don't know how they're being screwed or what their choices or opportunities are, then they're never going to get to exercise them one way or the other. At least when they make a bad decision that's based on good information they have only themselves to blame. They're not really being taken advantage of except by their own stupidity.

ARCUDI: A lot of these companies are giving equity in creative properties. I think that comes from people like Neal Adams. Maybe he was more antagonistic.

STOUT: Yeah. Neal definitely pushed the envelope. So did Frank Miller. I applaud those guys. But we should all be more like that. And it has little or nothing with the size of your reputation. At the business talks I give to artists people invariably say, "Well, you can ask for that. You can get your original art back. You can ask that because you're William Stout. You're famous." I go, "No. I was asking for that when I was a complete unknown; from the word go. When I was making four bucks an hour I still asked for and demanded that and if they wouldn't give it to me I'd walk." So it really has little to do with fame. Obviously, fame gives you more leverage. But even when I didn't have that leverage I was like that.

ARCUDI: You were one of the few guys who actually got his artwork

back from Disney.

STOUT: Yeah. I'm really proud of that particular negotiation and my other negotiations with The Mouse. I really like dealing with their attorneys. They've all been pretty decent, straight ahead people. It probably helps that we speak the same language and that I understand the problems of where their coming from and that I can come up with creative solutions to solve those problems and make both their life and the deal go through a little easier.

ARCUDI: I don't know how many other artists ever got any of their work back from Disney.

STOUT: I might have been the only one – I don't know. But they weren't going to get me to do the art in the first place if they wouldn't return my originals.

PAINTING ANTARCTICA

ARCUDI: You've had a commitment to the environment from at least the early '70s on and probably earlier on in your life, right? It ties somehow into this whole dinosaur thing, which has come to sort of possess your life.

STOUT: In some ways dinosaurs are a symbol of the environmental situation.

ARCUDI: Exactly, given the extinction theme. Those things sort of came together when you got the opportunity to go to Antarctica and embark on your latest all-consuming career project: depicting the history of life in Antarctica. Is it something that was symbolic in your mind and came together, or is it just coincidence that dinosaurs are a part of that, too?

STOUT: Here is how that all came about. In as many areas of disagreement I had with my father, there was one really valuable thing he passed on to me. My father had a great love of nature and of the outdoors. Every year he'd take my brothers and me up into the High Sierras. We'd go trout fishing and camp out. It gave me a great love of the wilderness, the land and its creatures. I've always been nuts about animals and nature anyway. When I was a teenager we really had our differences with each other, but I remember one time together with crystal clarity. My father never admitted to being wrong about anything. But this one time he said, "The one thing I feel really ashamed of is what my generation has done to the land and how we've left it for your generation." He said, "I'm deeply sorry about that." That had a real impact on me. I've always been aware of the land and the animals and the life that we lose each year. I've mainly contributed in the most typical way: writing checks to groups like Greenpeace, Defenders of Wildlife, the Environmental Defense Fund and the Nature Conservancy. I got a chance to go to Antarctica in 1989 as a tourist. One of the main reasons I wanted to go was that I discovered that the Antarctic Treaty was due to expire in 1991. It's an extraordinary treaty that came out of the International Geophysical Year of 1956-57. That was the year of international cooperation amongst the world's scientists. It was so successful that President Eisenhower wanted to come up with some way to continue this amazing international scientific cooperation; hence, the Antarctic Treaty. It basically states that no country owns Antarctica; all wildlife is protected; there is no commercial exploitation of the continent – no mining, no oil drilling; there's no nuclear waste storage there; There's no nuclear testing. It's one of the most extraordinary documents in world history. It went into effect in 1959. Once you're down there, it's really amazing; you see how artificial all of the conflicts are that are happening in the rest of the world. Because here's a place where thirty-nine nations, although they may be fighting north of the

Opposite Top:
Southern Cross. "Underwater depictions present their own special problems. If I crop the creatures, I often lose the sensation of their floating. (It's a lot like designing for 3-D comics.) I think this composition of male and female fin whales is very successful."

Opposite Bottom:
Kannemeyeria Vs. Cynognathus. "Sometimes I don't want a quiet, sublime depiction of Antarctic life — I want to go back to my roots. In this Antarctic scene, I've done just that, depicting several Triassic monsters in a Frazetta-like battle. Renowned big-cat-painter Guy Coheleach told me he loved this particular work when he visited my one-man show of Antarctic oil paintings."

The Tower comics that Wally Wood created, the rights to all of his characters were purchased for two grand – and Wally wasn't even the guy who got the two grand!

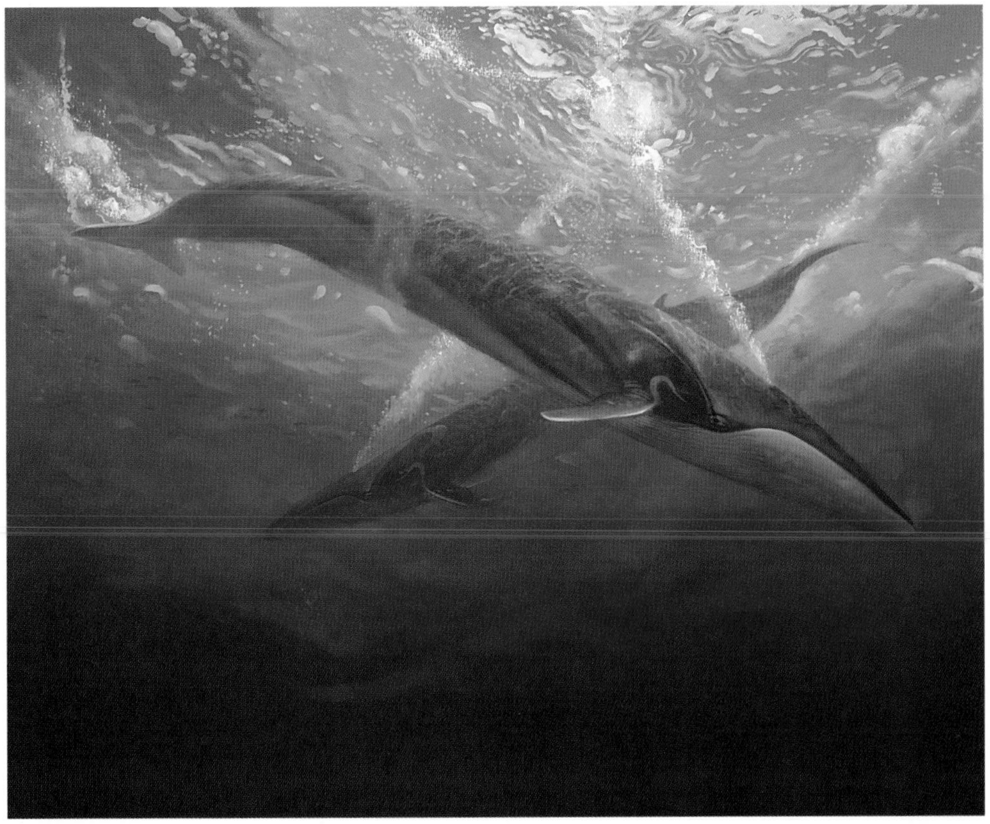

Southern Ocean, in Antarctica, everyone's cooperating just fine. You begin to see how the war situations, the battles and the conflicts are all artificially promoted and produced. This treaty was due to expire in '91, and ironically it was the Americans, the originators of this remarkable document, that were going to keep it from being re-signed. That's because George Bush was the president at the time. He's a Texas oilman; he wanted to keep the continent open for drilling.

ARCUDI: We have to make it clear that of course this is the first George Bush; King George the First.

STOUT: Dick Cheney's front man.

I thought, if I don't get down there soon, if they don't renew that treaty, I may never have a chance to go down there as a tourist. So I went down on a cruise ship with the American Museum of Natural History in 1989. I wasn't prepared for how spectacular this place was – the most spectacular place I've ever seen on the planet, and I've pretty much been all over the world. Now – not to dilute my noble intentions — there was another reason I wanted to see Antarctica that at least relates somewhat to our *Comics Journal* audience. I had read H.P. Lovecraft's book *At the Mountains of Madness.* The whole novel takes place in Antarctica. Lovecraft painted such a haunting and realistic picture of the place that I was just sucked right in. I compared his writing with maps of Antarctica and saw that he had used actual places. Intellectually I know that the guy never went there, but boy, he really did his homework. Because of him, Antarctica held this mystical quality that still haunts me today.

ARCUDI: What you're saying is that that mystical quality came through when you saw the reality of the place – its actual landscape?

STOUT: Absolutely. The place had an extremely profound effect on me. So profound that I thought I couldn't return home and face my kids without doing something to try and save that continent from despoiling and exploitation. While I was on the ship I found out about a group called The Antarctica Project (www.asoc.org). They're a low overhead umbrella organization helping to coordinate all of the activities of environmental groups like Greenpeace, the Environmental Defense Fund and the Nature Conservancy, to make Antarctica the first World Park. That idea of Antarctica being the first World Park really excited me. I thought, "What can I do on behalf of Antarctica, on behalf of the treaty?" I reasoned, quite rightly, I think, that one of the main reasons there was no public resistance to Bush's plan to drill and mine down there was that like almost everyone I talked to before going on the trip, the general public figured that it's nothing but a bunch of snow and ice down there. Why save it? My plan became a scheme to show Americans that Antarctica is much more than just snow and ice, that it is an incredibly beautiful part of the world with a spectacular array of wildlife, diverse species living in a variety of ecosystems.

ARCUDI: So you want to save it because it's pretty?

STOUT: It is beautiful and that's often the key to getting backing from the public. But if you investigate a little and do a little science homework you'll find that disruption of Antarctica and its ecosystems would be catastrophic to life on the rest of the planet. Sadly, that's not as sexy a message as saving seals with big sad eyes or whales or penguins. You've got to put on your political hat here. In doing so I thought I'd put together a show of paintings for the Natural History Museum of Los Angeles County depicting this diversity of wildlife in Antarctica and at least make people in southern California more aware of what we risk losing. Then my devious little promoter brain thought, "Now, to really make sure that everybody sees this show, I'll include the prehistoric life of Antarctica so that every kid with even a passing interest in dinosaurs will grab their parents and take them to this show." As soon as I got back from my first trip to Antarctica, I flew to Columbus, Ohio to the Byrd Polar Research Center at Ohio State and got a crash course in Antarctic paleontology from Dr. David Elliot. I noticed in studying prehistoric Antarctica, the same names kept coming up over and over again. There are just a special handful of people who do their studies down there. I contacted each of these scientists and became friends with them. To create reconstructions of prehistoric life in Antarctica, my process was to draw

If you investigate a little and do a little science homework, you'll find that disruption of Antarctica and its ecosystems would be catastrophic to life on the rest of the planet.

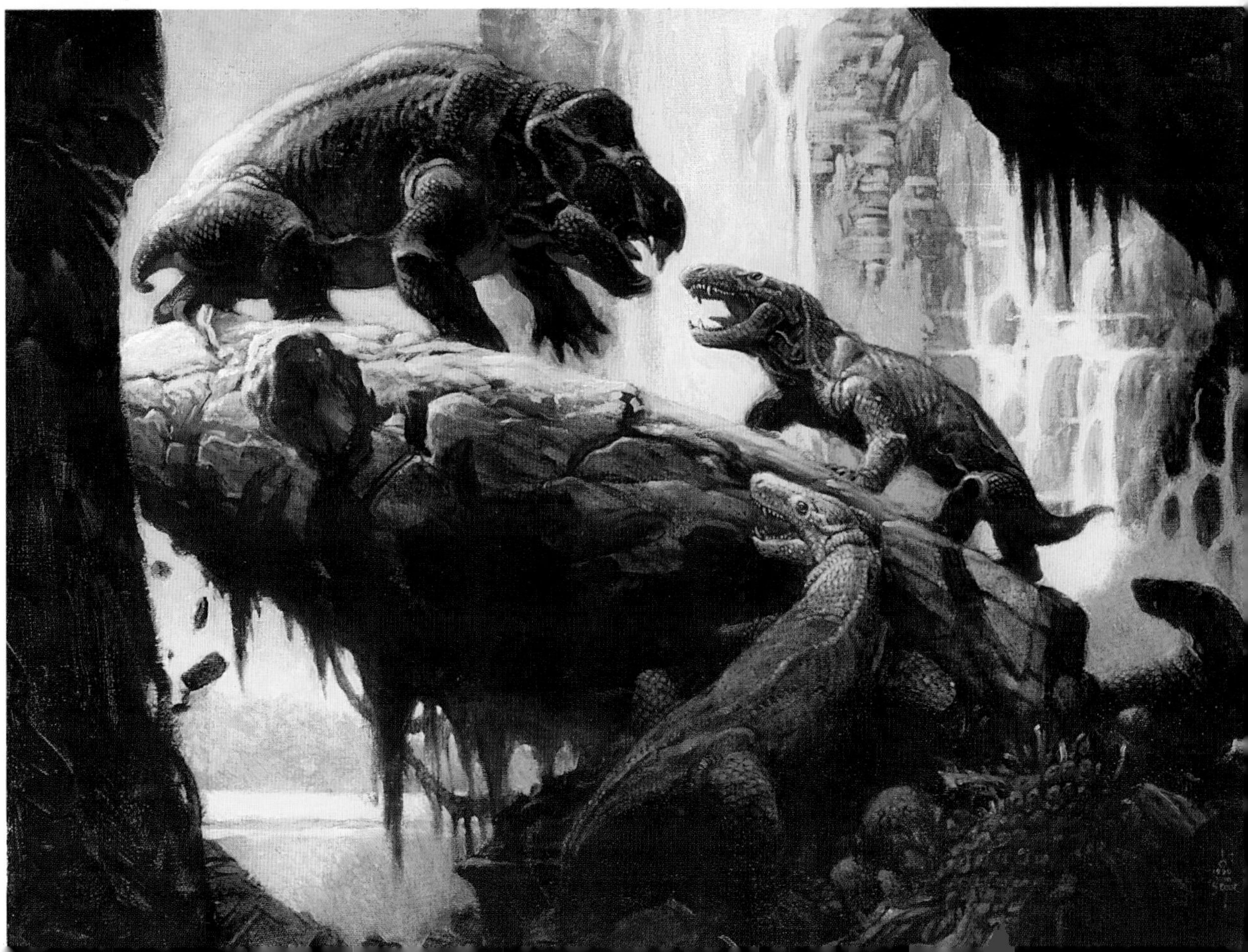

sketches of a particular creature, then contact the person who had actually found the fossilized animal and run the sketches and my ideas for the pictures past him or her, involving them in each step of the production of the painting so that it would be the most accurate piece possible. I did five large sample paintings and showed them to Dr. Craig Black, the director of the Natural History Museum of Los Angeles County. I got his okay and go ahead to do the complete show, 45 paintings, for the museum. They then indeed held the exhibition in Los Angeles. The Museum's Special Exhibits Department then traveled the show around the U. S. and the world for about seven years. It profoundly changed my life and the direction of my career. For those two and a half years it took me to paint the show, I pretty much dropped out of the entertainment business. Obviously this had a dramatic effect on my bank account. I was making less than 10% of what I was making prior to that, but I was never happier in my life than when I was doing these paintings. I really felt for the first time in my life that I had finally graduated from that Pinball School of Career Planning. I had a direction; I had finally come home. I felt these paintings were something I could do for the rest of my life and really be happy and satisfied. Other guys run out and buy Corvettes at that age. My midlife crisis resolved itself in a much more positive and productive way, a way that's completely in synch with my personal philosophy regarding the earth.

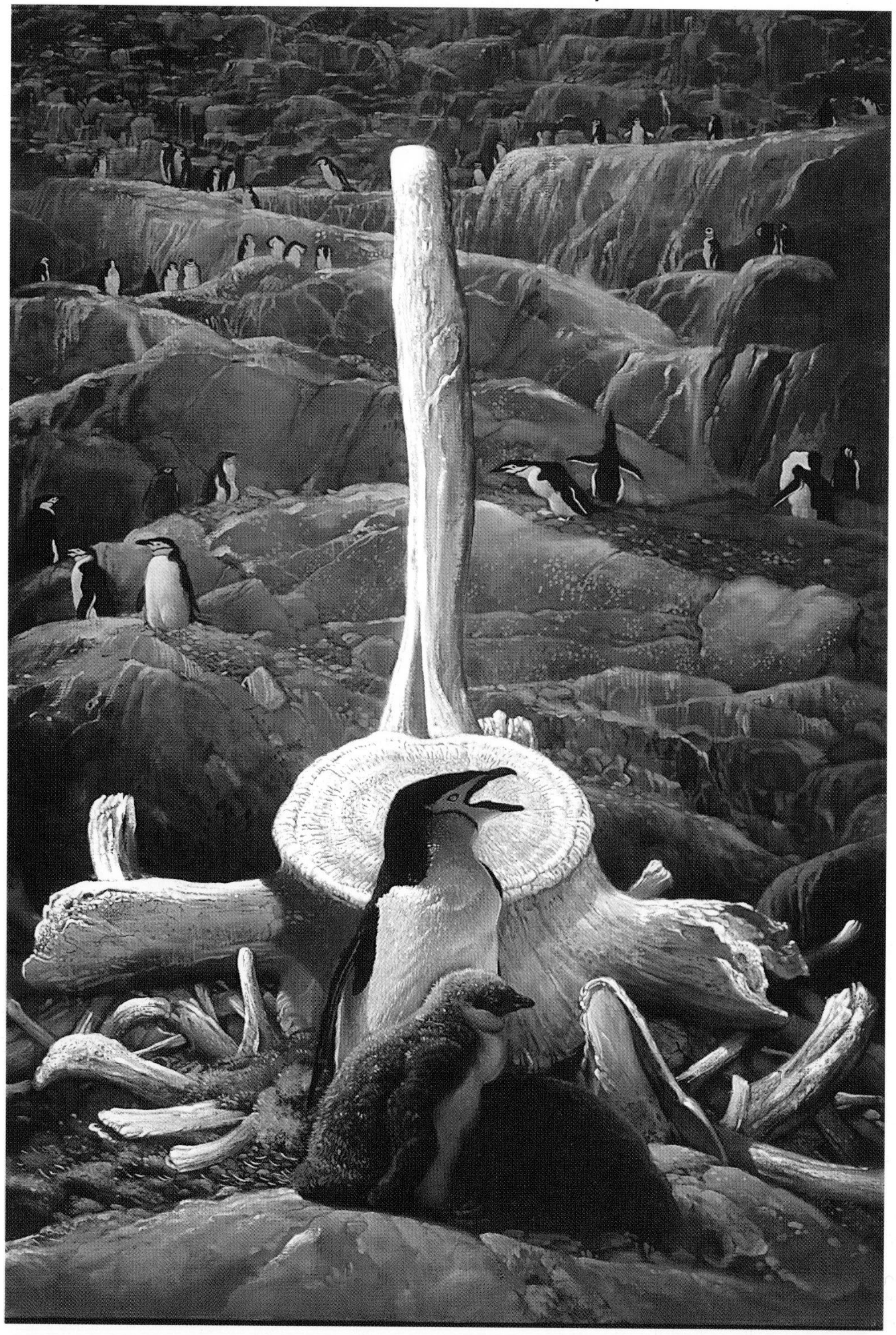

This Page: *Crucifix.* Several of Stout's field-study drawings found their way into this finished oil painting of a chinstrap penguin colony.

ARCUDI: Which is...?

STOUT: We have not inherited this planet from our parents; we are borrowing it from our grandchildren. That philosophy drives most of my politics, actions and decisions.

ARCUDI: The Antarctica project wasn't just that one show. Your dedication to that project didn't end with that one show. You went back to Antarctica again a few years later, right?

STOUT: As soon as I finished my first Antarctica show I knew I wasn't finished with that subject.

ARCUDI: We should mention the name of that show, shouldn't we?

STOUT: "Dinosaurs, Penguins and Whales: The Wildlife of Antarctica." As I finished that show it I felt like I'd come home; I was doing something that I really wanted to do a lot more of. I said to myself, "Why stop? Why not continue to paint on the same theme?" I got the idea of doing a book, which, when it's finished, will be the first visual history of life in Antarctica from prehistoric times to the present day; one hundred oil paintings and fifty drawings. It's never been done – and after all this work on it, now I know why! After I completed the first show I discovered that the National Science Foundation has a program called the Antarctic Artists and Writers program. It's a competetive grant program; every year the NSF picks one or two artists, writers, or photographers to go to Antarctica and live. The NSF gives them full support. What the artist, writer or photographer has to do in return is come back and produce something that conveys information about Antarctica to the public. That could be a book, a series of articles, an exhibition, a video, a comic book, a children's book. I was awarded that grant for the 1992/1993 Season. They gave me a year's advance notice, so I was able to really prepare for the trip. That lead-time was important because one of the things I had asked for in my grant was the chance to scuba dive underneath the Antarctic ice.

In Antarctica, diving visibility on a good day is 800 feet.

ARCUDI: Why did you want to do that?

STOUT: I felt that the scope of my book wouldn't be complete without showing the diversity of life on Antarctica's nutrient-rich shores. All of the Antarctic scientists I talked to said that it was the most spectacular diving in the world. Life under the ice is incredibly rich and diverse. I also found out that it indeed is the best diving in the world. In the Great Barrier Reef or in the Bahamas, on a good day visibility is 120 feet. In Antarctica diving visibility on a good day is 800 feet – clearer than the air I'm looking at right now in Pasadena. You don't feel so much like you're diving; it's more like you're flying. It's absolutely unbelievable.

ARCUDI: But it's really cold.

STOUT: It is cold: 28 degrees. Our more astute readers will say, "How can that be? 32 degrees is freezing."

ARCUDI: Salt water, right?

STOUT: Right. Salt water freezes at a lower temperature than fresh water. But you dress appropriately. To do dives under the ice I put on Patagonia extra heavy weight long underwear. On top of that I put on a Thermalite jumpsuit, sort of like an astronaut suit; after that I'd put

on my dry suit, which is the opposite of a wet suit. The wet suit uses your body heat and the water to keep you warm. Antarctica is too cold for that; you wear a dry suit. It allows you to do that cool James Bond thing – do a dive, come out of the water, unzip your suit and reveal your tuxedo.

ARCUDI: For all of the soirees at McMurdo Station.

STOUT: Party Central.

ARCUDI: We may have gotten ahead of ourselves but anyway you probably want to go back to the point where you started training for the scuba diving.

STOUT: The National Science Foundation told me that I had to contact James Stewart, not the actor, but the head of the dive program in Antarctica. He's a great old time diver. He created the dive-training program for the Navy SEALs, an amazing guy. He said in order for me to dive in Antarctica – and mind you, I'd never done any scuba diving in my life at that point – I'd have to get Open Water certification, Advanced Open Water certification, Medic First Aid certification, Rescue Diver certification, Dry Suit Diver certification, and Ice Diver certification. So thank God I had a year to do this; my very last dive to complete my certifications was made just two weeks before I left for Antarctica. It was really intensive training, especially when I became a rescue diver. That certification made me a really good diver.

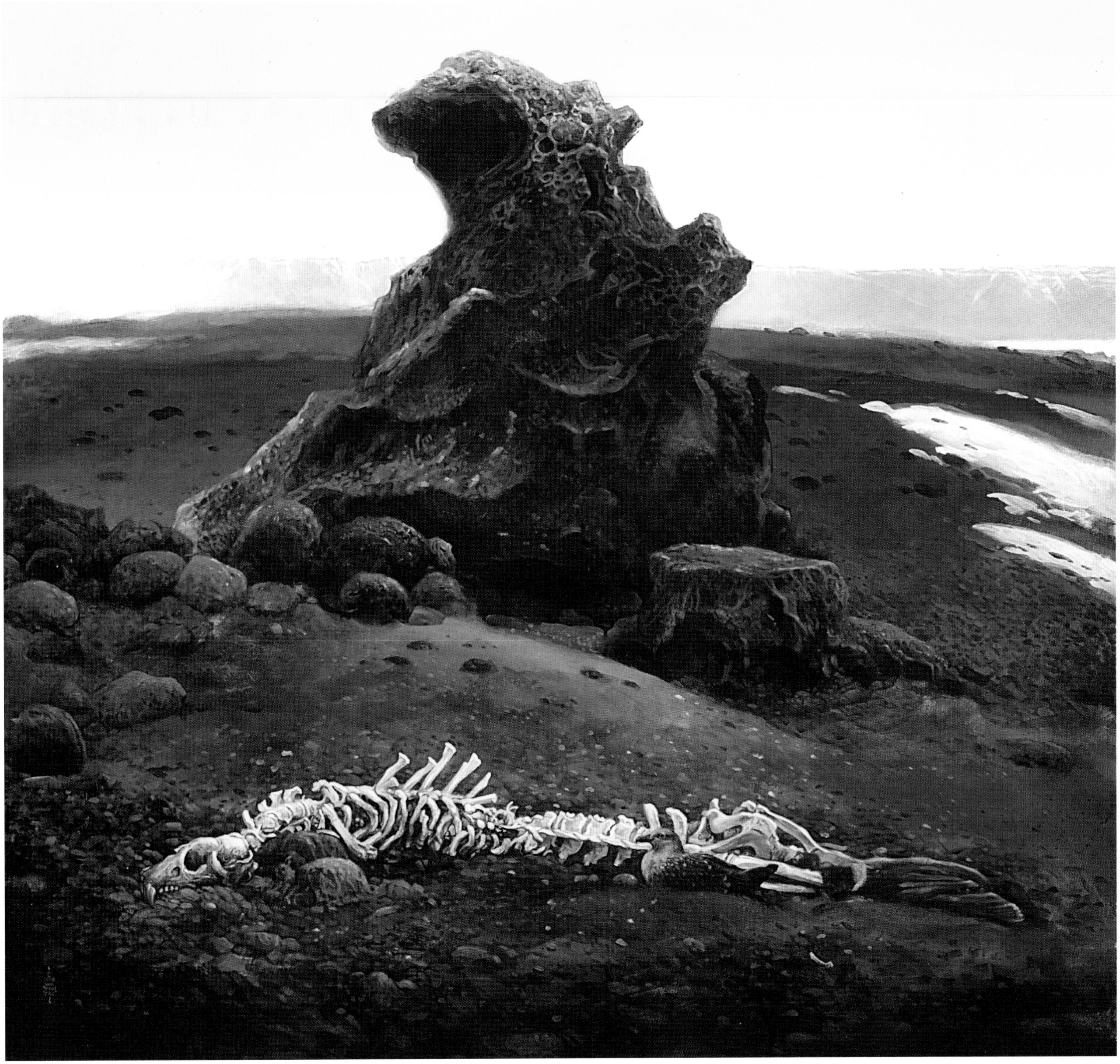

This Page: *Resurrection.* A skua nests inside a 90-year-old elephant seal skeleton/mummy left over from the ill-fated Robert Falcon Scott expedition. "One of my favorite paintings."

My first Antarctic dive is probably one of the most astounding memories of my entire life. I was sitting on the edge of the hole – they've cored out a hole with a big drill through the ice; the ice is 12 feet thick – and I'm looking down into the water. Because diving is ordinarily a stressful activity, ice diving in Antarctica is exponentially stressful. So as a diver, before your dive you don't do much of anything. You have dive tenders to check all of your equipment for you and put your equipment on you so you don't have to think about anything except for the dive, which is –

ARCUDI: ...Enough.

STOUT: I'm sitting there with my feet dangling in the water; I'm looking down and I make a remark that, "I thought our first dive was going to be a deep dive," because I can clearly see the bottom from where I'm sitting. The tenders asked, "How deep do you think that is?" I said, "Well, it looks like it's about 25 feet deep, 30 at the most." The tender said, "You're looking at a 100 feet bottom." The water was so crystal clear – it was just extraordinary. I get all of my stuff on and there's a rope called a "down line" that goes from the top of the hole down to the sea bottom. I start going down the rope through the ice. Intellectually I know this is not happening, but I swear to God that the tube I'm descending is getting narrower and narrower. I'm getting more claustrophobic going down this twelve-foot tube of ice. The sides of the tube are like milk glass, really extraordinary. I finally clear the bottom of the ice; this enormous vista opens up for me. I can see forever. The visibility is astounding. As I said, it felt like I was flying, hovering in thick air. There is so much to see; I'm trying to take it all in – I'm just on total sensory overload, just short-circuiting all over the place. I felt like the fetus baby in *2001: A Space Odyssey* on Jupiter, just trying to take all this stuff in. At the same time, this was a test-dive for me; I'm supposed to be diving responsibly and doing all of this stuff that the other diver on the bottom is telling me to do. And at the same time as that, my brain is completely shorting out from the input, from all of this spectacle. This goose egg-sized and egg-shaped creature floats past me. It's clear like a jellyfish; it's called a ctenophore. It's got rainbow track lights that are zipping up the sides of its body. I'm seeing this ten-foot jellyfish drifting by in all of its different colors. It was just unbelievable. At the same time, I'm thinking, "Oh, yeah. You're supposed to be following a particular instruction and function as a diver." It was absolutely exhilarating. I was surprised, too, by the cold. The things that get coldest first and fastest are your fingers because you've got an enormous amount of surface area surrounding your fingers. Just before you make your dive, the gloves are the last things that you put on. The tenders pour hot water in the gloves, you plunge your hands into this water, they snap the top of the gloves around your wrists and your gloves seal tight. You make the initial part of your dive with gloves full of hot water. The only area of you that is really exposed to the icy water directly is parts of your face, because you've got the mask over most of your face. You've got a hood over most of your head and the hood also covers your neck and the underside of your chin. Mostly, what are exposed are your lips and your cheeks. I thought that would be really painful, but in actuality I found it exhilarating. It felt like my skin was sizzling from the cold – not an unpleasant sensation at all; an extraordinary feeling, although in a very short time my lips were frozen numb. I couldn't feel my regulator – my breathing apparatus. Every once in a while I'd taste saltwater; I'd know that my breathing apparatus had drifted out of my mouth without my realizing it; I'd just mash it back in.

I did seven dives total down there. I feel really privileged. I am on the extremely short list of people who have scuba-dived in Antarctica [pause].

Long ago our readers must have thought, "What in the hell does this have to do with comics – or even movies?"

ARCUDI: Fair question.

STOUT: I think what we're talking about here is crucial to both comics fans and creators – and especially movie fans.

ARCUDI: How so?

STOUT: I used to be a huge movie fan; seriously, a bigger movie fan you'd never met. I was going on about some film to a friend of mine, Nordy Roblin. Nordy's an interesting guy in himself with an interesting family heritage. His grandfathers, Nordhoff (for whom he was named) and Hall wrote *Mutiny On The Bounty*; his uncles are Jon Hall, the star of John Ford's *Hurricane* and Conrad Hall, the Academy Award-winning cinematographer for *In Cold Blood* and *Butch Cassidy and the Sundance Kid*. Good genes. So Nordy cuts off my brief excited rant about some movie. He sneered at my anticipation of whatever cinematic event was forthcoming and said, "Movies are someone else's adventures. Wouldn't you rather spend those two hours having your own adventures?" It really stopped me. I thought about all that time I had spent in the dark living someone else's dreams and adventures. I decided to make it a point to start having my own adventures, living and creating my own compelling stories based upon my own life rather than wasting those two hours in the dark. Errol Flynn's autobiography *My Wicked, Wicked Ways* was an inspiration to live life to the fullest as well. And I've been doing that ever since. I've tried to pack three lives into one.

ARCUDI: Wake up, everybody! Get out of your parents' basements!

STOUT: Exactly! Do something you can call your own for Christ sakes. Live! Okay, the NSF trip to Antarctica: I was there for three months. For six weeks I was based at McMurdo Station, a U. S. station – the largest station in Antarctica. During the Antarctic summer, which is our winter, there are about 1200 people there, so it's like a small town. The other six weeks I was based at Palmer station, which is on the Antarctic Peninsula. There are only thirty-nine beds at Palmer so there are only thirty-nine people at that station. You can fly into McMurdo station, but the only way to get to Palmer station is by ship, because there's no place to land even a helicopter at Palmer. I took a research vessel down from Punta Arenas, Chile, down the coast of Chile, crossed the dreaded Drake Passage and sailed down the coast of the Antarctic Peninsula until we got to my drop-off point: Palmer station. Palmer station is the station most tourists visit because the Antarctic Peninsula is where you see the greatest abundance of life. It's warmer than the rest of continental Antarctica. I got certified as a Zodiac operator at Palmer so that I could man a Zodiac, a type of inflatable boat, and take it to a different island each day. I'd spend the entire day sketching and painting the wildlife. I did all of my ice dives at McMurdo; I did one shore dive at Palmer. At McMurdo I was transported to my ice dive locations in a Spryte, a box-like ice vehicle with tank treads. I drove my own Spryte over the sea ice to see a distant Weddell seal colony. If where I needed to go was farther than the range of a Spryte they'd put me on helicopter and hello me out to where I wanted to go. If it was too far for a helicopter they put me on a Twin Otter, a fixed wing plane, and fly me out. When I went to visit an Emperor penguin colony, I took a Twin Otter to get there.

I felt like the fetus baby in *2001: A Space Odyssey* on Jupiter, just trying to take all this stuff in.

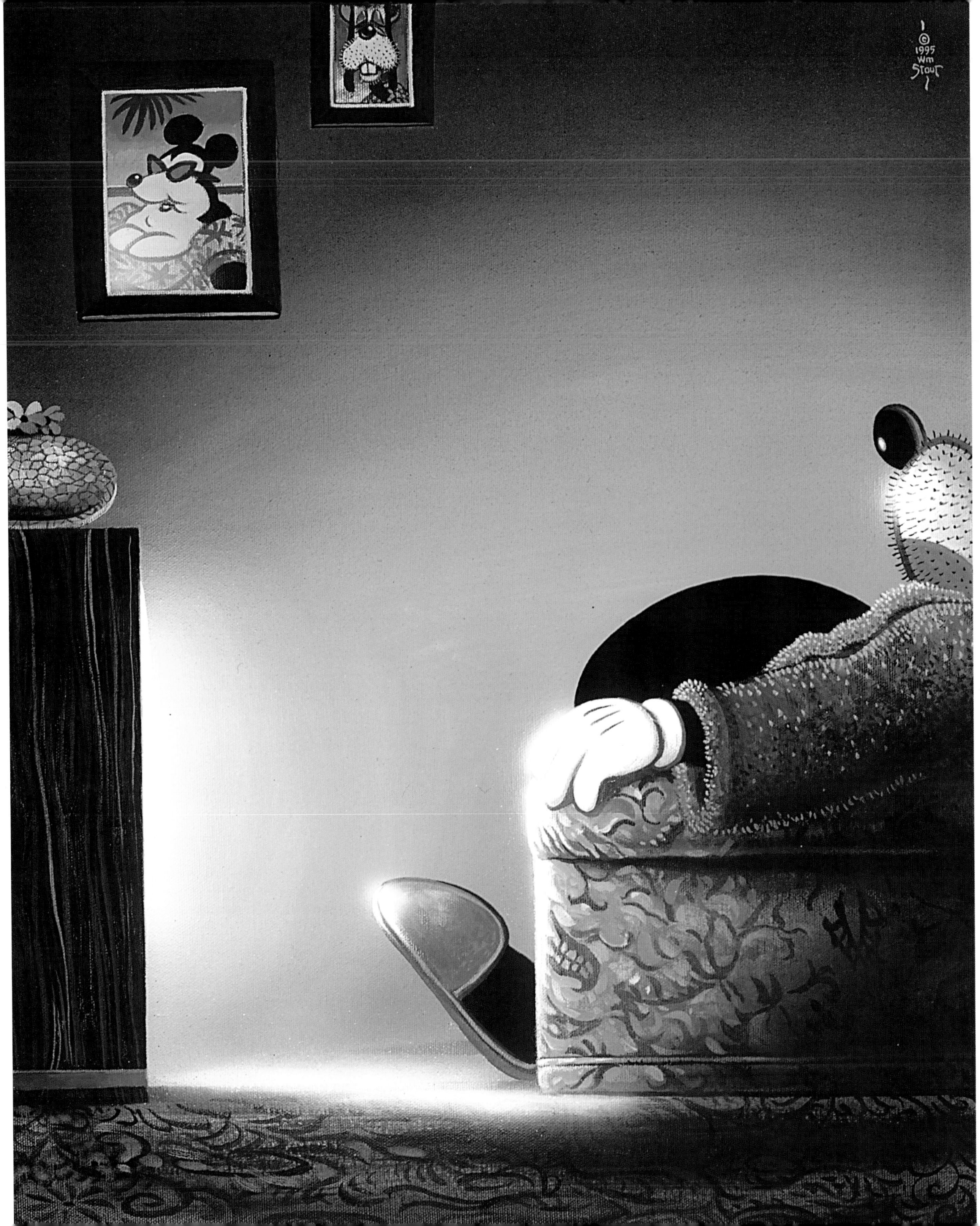
©
1995
Wm
Stout

This Page: Mickey feels shut out again at Oscar time in this Stout portrait of loneliness and despair.

STOUT AMONG THE PENGUINS

Stout recounts in some detail how he arrived at the Emperor penguin colony and had to build the trust of the academic who had been studying the penguins and who was in charge of the base camp – not to mention, the penguins themselves, before he could start drawing them. He also adds some historical background on how the penguins were almost wiped out by hunters in the 19th century. Go to:

http://www.tcj.com/ws03/stoutant.html

MICKEY AT 60

ARCUDI: On the flip side of that is *Mickey at 60* – isn't that really a reaction to what was going on at the time?

STOUT: Absolutely. It was a reaction to my own work in a sense. *Mickey at 60* came about when I was working as a full-time consultant for Walt Disney Imagineering, designing additions to Disneyland Anaheim, Tokyo Disneyland, Euro-Disneyland, and Walt Disney World in Florida. This happened to be during Mickey Mouse's 60th anniversary. We were being inundated with this *Mickey at 60* stuff. I stopped and thought one day, "What would Mickey really look like if he were 60? He hasn't done a picture in years; he's probably let himself go. Minnie's divorced him and is living off of her alimony in Miami." I did this drawing of this grotesque rat-like creature. He's unshaven and sulking in his own sort of miserable past glory. I showed it around and it got a big laugh, a big reaction at work. I thought, "Wouldn't it be fun to do a strip of this guy." So I did a three or four panel strip and I left the word balloons blank. The strip consisted of just Mickey's facial expressions changing. I passed the strip with the blank balloons to my friend Jim Steinmeyer, one of my best friends at Disney, a brilliant guy. He's probably the world's greatest authority on 18th and 19th century stage magic. He creates and designs magic tricks for a living: the major illusions for David Copperfield, all of Doug Henning's stuff, Siegfried and Roy, Lance Burton – Jim's the best; an extraordinary guy. He's also a very funny writer and a great caricaturist as well. He filled in the word balloons with some of the funniest dialogue I'd ever read. It just had me on the floor. I thought, "This is great." I drew some more strips and passed them to him and he wrote some more stuff in them. It was just as funny if not funnier than the stuff he'd originally written. People saw them and they wanted copies of them, so we Xeroxed copies and passed them around. We kept doing this because it was so much fun. It was the antithesis of everything that I was known for as an artist. People usually expect really slick, completely planned-out stuff with a really fine finish from me. I was always fascinated by Crumb's comics and sketchbook stuff. A lot of the stuff that he did wasn't penciled. He was inking it directly from his head. He did a lot of it actual size. It was just amazing to me. And it looked great, besides. So I made a promise to myself that I would draw these strips but I wouldn't pencil them. I would just go right to ink. I wouldn't even use rulers for the panel borders. That way it didn't seem like work. It was really liberating to be that free with my line. Because I wasn't actually writing them except for doing dramatic visual set-ups for each strip, the actual dialogue was being written by Jim Steinmeyer, this kept it really exciting and fresh for both of us. He never knew what I was going to draw, and I didn't know what he was going to write; it was entertaining and amusing and always a surprise to each of us.

After a while, I thought, "You know what? I think we have enough of these strips for a book. Wouldn't it be fun to... (harkening back to my underground stuff) ... publish a 'Mickey at 60' book and see the public's reaction." Again, I deliberately did really cheesy printing; it was Xerox printing on white paper with cardstock covers and a two staple binding. I called it an "anti-comic" because it was sort of the "anti-" of everything else I'd done in comics. There was a crudeness to it. We did a limited signed edition. I thought of it more as an art object like the artist books that Ed Ruscha did back in the `60s. For comics people who aren't familiar with Ed Ruscha, which is probably all of you out there, he was an important Los Angeles pop artist who did – and still does – extraordinary stuff. He worked in a realistic art manner with a great sense of humor. Probably his most famous piece is one that's not actually funny. It's a picture of the Hollywood sign at sunset. He would do stuff like render water pooling up on a slick surface and he would make the water spell out the

"What would Mickey really look like if he were 60? He hasn't done a picture in years; he's probably let himself go. Minnie's divorced him and is living off of her alimony in Miami."

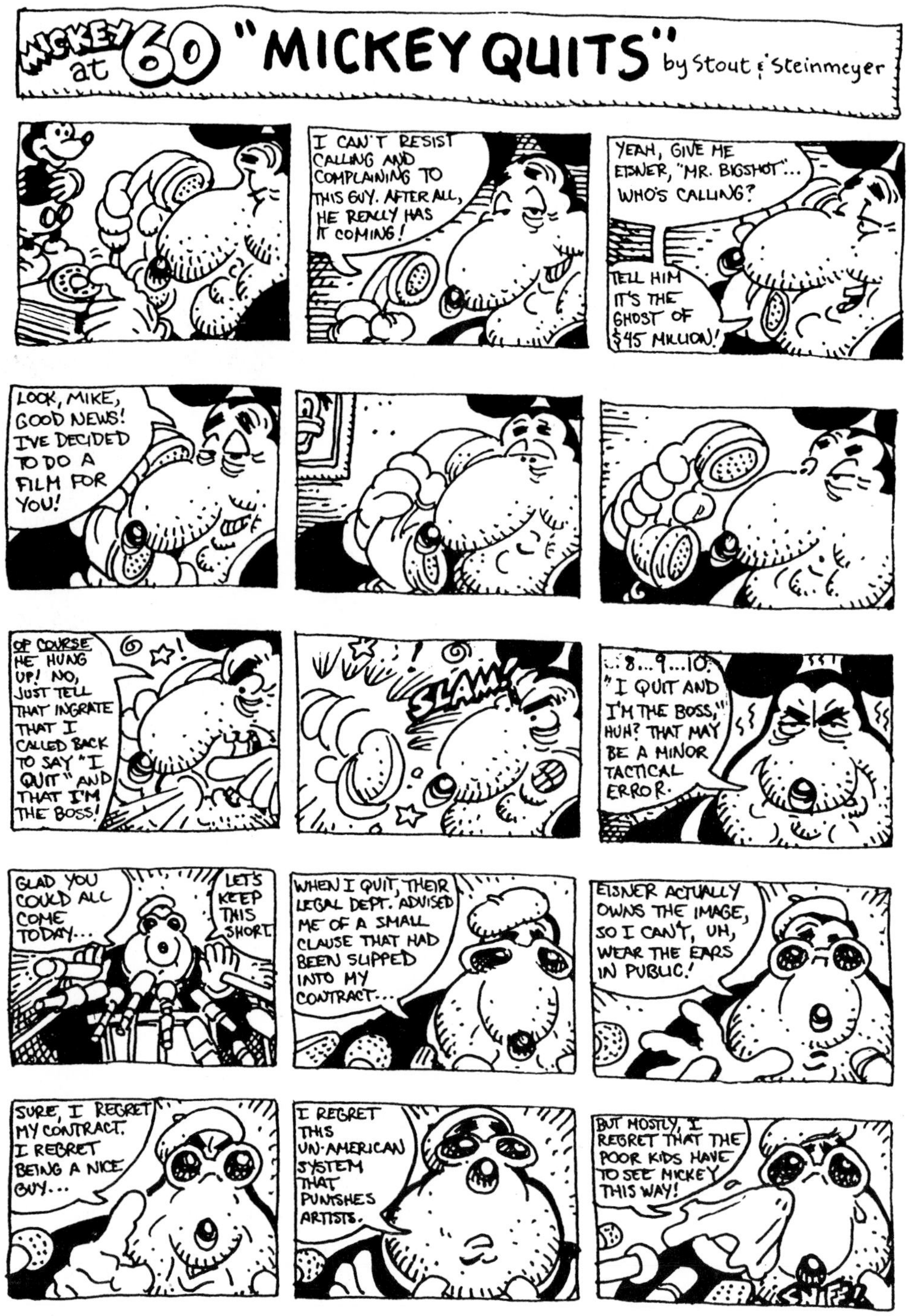
MICKEY at 60 "MICKEY QUITS" by Stout & Steinmeyer
I CAN'T RESIST CALLING AND COMPLAINING TO THIS GUY. AFTER ALL, HE REALLY HAS IT COMING!
YEAH, GIVE ME EISNER, "MR. BIGSHOT"... WHO'S CALLING?
TELL HIM IT'S THE GHOST OF $45 MILLION!
LOOK, MIKE, GOOD NEWS! I'VE DECIDED TO DO A FILM FOR YOU!
OF COURSE HE HUNG UP! NO, JUST TELL THAT INGRATE THAT I CALLED BACK TO SAY "I QUIT" AND THAT I'M THE BOSS!
SLAM!
...8...9...10. "I QUIT AND I'M THE BOSS," HUH? THAT MAY BE A MINOR TACTICAL ERROR.
GLAD YOU COULD ALL COME TODAY...
LET'S KEEP THIS SHORT.
WHEN I QUIT, THEIR LEGAL DEPT. ADVISED ME OF A SMALL CLAUSE THAT HAD BEEN SLIPPED INTO MY CONTRACT...
EISNER ACTUALLY OWNS THE IMAGE, SO I CAN'T, UH, WEAR THE EARS IN PUBLIC!
SURE, I REGRET MY CONTRACT. I REGRET BEING A NICE GUY...
I REGRET THIS UN-AMERICAN SYSTEM THAT PUNISHES ARTISTS.
BUT MOSTLY, I REGRET THAT THE POOR KIDS HAVE TO SEE MICKEY THIS WAY!
SNIFF!

This Page: "This story idea came from when a movie studio would not allow Clayton Moore to wear his Lone Ranger mask in public."

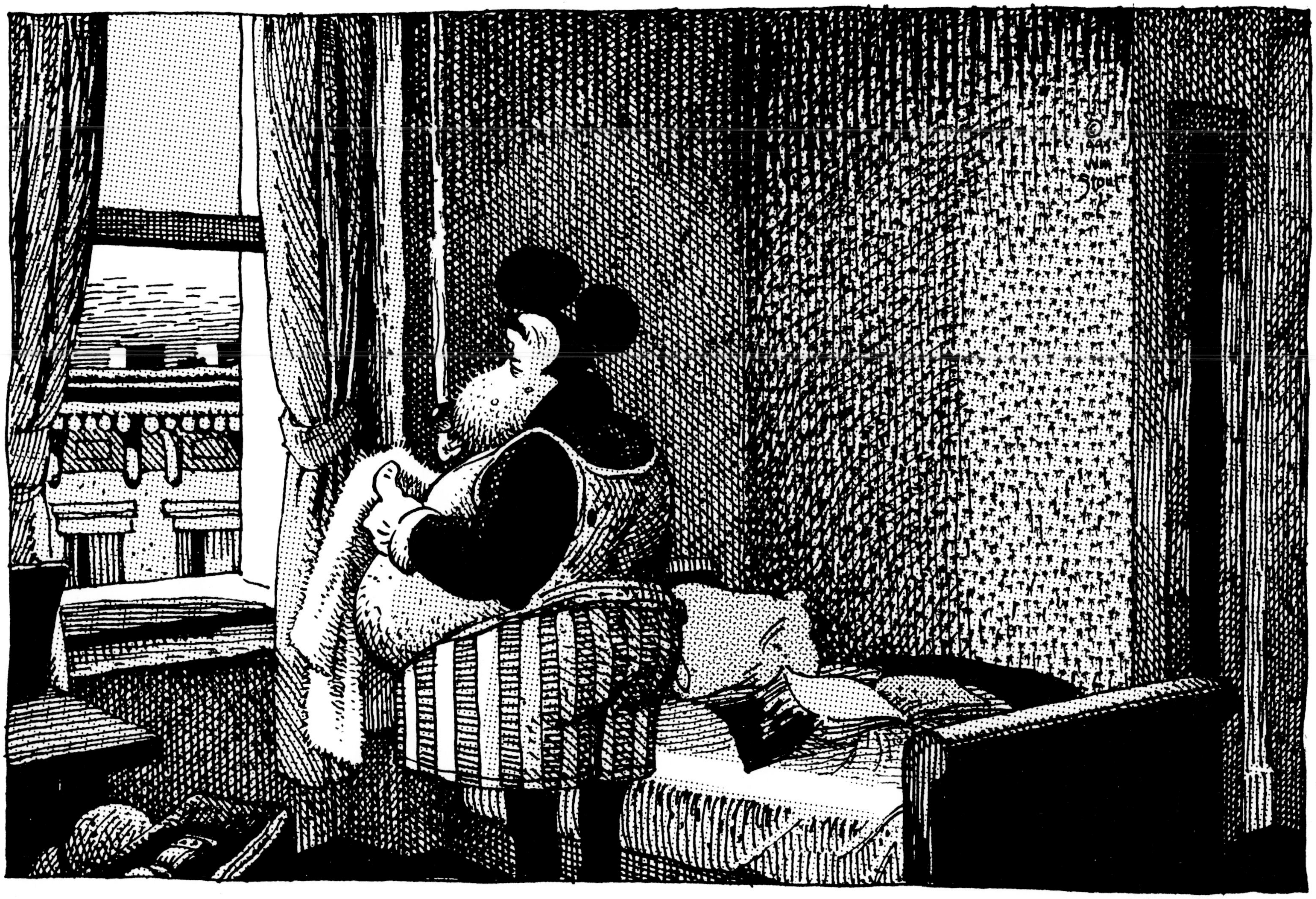

MORNING IN HOLLYWOOD

HOPPER VARIATION #5

letters "wet." Or he'd render all of these realistic-looking ants; they'd all be bunched together in clusters that spelled out "ants." Stuff like that. His work got appropriated by a lot of people, especially in advertising. Ed Ruscha used to do these cool little books of his photographs. He did one book where he photographed the entire length of the Sunset Strip and then made this book, *Sunset Strip*. The book was printed on one continuous sheet so that you could unfold the pages of the book and see the entire Sunset Strip. Another book was of places that were called Ed's. Another was just photographs of Los Angeles palm trees.

So I saw *Mickey at 60* as being an art object like that. We did 300 copies; it sold out in about two hours at Comic-Con in San Diego. It was unbelievably successful. We charged 15 bucks apiece for them and donated all of the money to the Crippled Children's Society. Since we were doing work at Disney, we didn't feel that it was right to make money from anything even slightly related to Disney.

I saw *Mickey at 60* as being an art object like that. We did 300 copies; it sold out in about two hours at Comic-Con in San Diego.

ARCUDI: Every strip, you do the art first and there was no discussion at any point about the direction any of these strips were going to go?

STOUT: There was discussion about the direction, but it was in the vaguest of terms. I would never dictate dialogue to Jim. For instance, I would say, "This is Mickey at a book signing, and no one's showing up for the signing. Or maybe one person shows up. On this page, he's in the progressive stages of having a heart attack." [Laughter] Not only is he having a heart attack – and this is something I didn't know of course, because I didn't write the dialogue – he's in the recovery room after the heart attack, and you discover through Jim's dialogue that Mickey's been given a heart transplant; he's been given the heart of the baboon from "The Lion King." Which of course sends him directly into another heart attack. We wouldn't tell each other what we were going to do. That was part of the fun of it.

ARCUDI: You were really dictating more the way the story was going

This Page: Stout drew a series of "Mickey at 60" portraits inspired by Edward Hopper.

than Jim, I guess by virtue of the art?

STOUT: Not neccessarily. There'd be a page and I'd say, "This is Mickey in Las Vegas." I wouldn't tell him any more than what he could conclude from the pictures – that Mickey's watching a stage show or he's working the slot machines. Because of Jim's Vegas experience, Jim suggested that Mickey play Keno in one strip.

ARCUDI: I know you weren't with Disney anymore, but when you did the second issue, did you do the strips in the same fashion?

STOUT: Yeah, the exact same way. It was a little more frustrating for me because I was really tempted to write. I really wanted to write some stuff of my own, but I thought, "No. I really want to keep that Jim's domain."

ARCUDI: Was that liberating in the sense of, "Hey, I don't have to do what everybody expects Bill Stout to do when I do this?"

STOUT: That was exactly the most liberating factor of it, discovering that I can do something kind of rough and crude and it's still effective as art; it doesn't have to be the ultimate in slickness. There was such a freedom to that.

It was also interesting to me what happened with the strip and where it went. Even though the very first drawing was, "O.K. What would Mickey Mouse look like if he were 60," almost immediately the strip had nothing to do with Mickey Mouse. It was really a satire of old Hollywood actors that both Jim and I had known; the life of these guys who were still mentally living in their days of former glory but who were now holed up in these squalid little bungalows, all bitter about the biz. It became a satire on show business, especially as Mick tries to get work and has to deal with the studios. At one point Disney takes away his ears. They won't let him wear the ears in public any more. [Interviewer laughs.]

ARCUDI: Have you done anything since? Have you allowed yourself that same freedom since then?

STOUT: Well, yeah, somewhat with my sketchbooks, although they seem to be getting tighter and tighter. One of the things I do now with some of the sketchbooks I've published is show my thumbnail drawings. I also show sketches that aren't necessarily finished sketches but that I think have a kernel of either a good design or a good idea; they're not necessarily all slick and finished. That's the sort of stuff I like to see from artists. I learn so much more from looking at sketches and drawings when I go to museums than from looking at the finished paintings. Because the finished painting – it's difficult to see how the artist thinks because all of his thinking is buried under the layers of paint and finish. The artist is actually trying to remove you from that in his finished work and to present the finished work as an entity on its own, whereas I'm more interested in the process of how the artist got to that finished piece. My Edgar Rice Burroughs and Monsters sketchbooks show that process. It shows stuff like, "I started out drawing Frankenstein this way, but I didn't like that so I redrew it that way. But I had a better idea the third time and that's the one I went with."

THE MEANING OF ART

ARCUDI: This might get too personal...

STOUT: Too personal? Not likely...This is already like a "Playboy" interview – but without references to my sex life.

ARCUDI: Okay. Talking about people who, through their style and their technique, usually remove the viewer from their technique, do you think that says anything about their personality or their view of art or their view of humanity, or what?

STOUT: I think it says a lot. And one of the things I love about comics is there is such a diversity in art styles right now and story-telling styles. I have different rules or demands upon different artists depending upon how they are trying to convey what they do. If for instance, an artist works in a realistic sort of turn of the century storybook style, a lá the Pre-Raphaelites, Arthur Rackham or Edmund Dulac or an early illustrator-influenced style like Williamson, Frazetta or Krenkel – I'm thinking of guys like Kaluta, Wrightson, Barry Windsor-Smith, and Charles Vess, etc. – I apply a different set of standards to those guys than I do to someone who works in a more expressionist style, like say Charles Burns, Daniel Clowes or Brian Ralph, the guy who did *Cave In*. Different rules apply because it's obvious that these first guys are trying to compete with the great illustrators of the past, so I'm going to be a lot more unforgiving when it comes to bad drawing. If you're going to jump into that rarified arena, you damn well better have the chops.

ARCUDI: To make this more personal, what does it say about you, then? Looking at the way you draw, what does that say about you as a) a person; b) an artist; c) a misanthrope. Do you think that the techniques you've developed say anything about you as an artist?

STOUT: I think it speaks volumes. For one, it says a lot about how I approach problem solving, which is letting the problem dictate the solution and style, what I call the "Chouinard method," as we discussed before. That has resulted in a remarkable diversity in my work. It has exposed me to more things in the art world than has your average comic artist. I get the feeling that people who like my work want me to experiment as much as I have. They seem to appreciate that I'm on this diverse artistic journey, and at least from what I can tell they seem to be delighted to come along. I think the joy for me and for my fans is the constant surprise of what I do. They – and I – never know what's going to come out of me. It's a double-edged sword, though. Because of that, for a lot of people it's really difficult to identify my work.

> One of the things I love about comics is there is such a diversity in art styles right now and storytelling styles.

FINE ART VS. ILLUSTRATION

ARCUDI: I think a lot of people look at landscapes and look at wildlife paintings and they don't have any trouble with applying the phrase "Fine Art" to what they're looking at. You paint as close to realism as a person can get. But I think people are really resistant to looking at a painting of a Trachodon eating marsh grass and calling that fine art.

STOUT: Incredibly resistant. In fact, they don't.

ARCUDI: Do you?

STOUT: I tell you I'm always laughing at myself, especially when I consider what I do as fine art. Within the huge realm of representational fine art there is this tiny slice of that pie called wildlife art – a speck on the butt of representational art. Actually, domestic animals are considered a proper theme for Fine Art. As soon as you paint wildlife, you're an illustrator. If you paint a cow, you're a Fine Artist. But if you paint a buffalo, you're an illustrator. Anyway, within that narrow slice of representational art called wildlife art, there is dinosaur art, which is a microscopic slice out of the wildlife pie. It's a footnote to an asterisk. But that's not enough. I do Antarctic dinosaurs, which is – well, you just can't get more obscure or find a smaller market for your work. If I were to set out wearing my commercial hat, saying, "You wanna paint wildlife. Okay, if you want to make money at this business, the one thing you don't do is 'dinosaurs.' And if you're going to do dinosaurs, for God's sake don't do Antarctic dinosaurs. At least do North American dinosaurs, where maybe there might be a small market amongst the U. S. museums." But I don't always think logically that way. I follow my heart and my heart led me to painting prehistoric and contemporary life in Antarctica. I don't consider that work illustration. Believe me, I know the difference. I have to say that I take an absolute Fine Art approach to whatever I do, illustration or fine art. But I draw a distinct line between illustration and fine art.

ARCUDI: So what's the difference?

STOUT: In a nutshell, in illustration you do the best art you can possibly do within the time allotted. There's always a deadline with illustration. With fine art, you do the best art that you can possibly do. Period. If that requires going back to the picture in a year and painting some more on it, then you do that. There is no deadline. You finish the picture and make it the best possible picture you can, if it takes a week, if it takes two years. In addition, there is usually a difference in depth. Fine art is deeper than illustration. It has to resonate for a long, long time. It stands on its own, regardless of whether you've read the text that goes with it or not.

ARCUDI: If you go back far enough, to someone like Van Eyck, The Annunciation, for instance, he really is illustrating something, and he probably had a deadline, but would anyone argue that that's not fine art?

STOUT: An even more popular example is Michelangelo's Sistine Chapel. It's a mural that tells the story of God's creation of man and other aspects of the Bible in pictures. Obviously on one level it's illustration – it's pictures telling a narrative story. But there's so much nuance, depth and heart and soul poured into that work that it transcends the mere fulfilling of a commercial job for the Pope.

ARCUDI: I don't want to beat this to death, but are you saying that it's the talent of a Michelangelo, a Van Eyck, a Bernini, a Da Vinci that makes their commercial work transcend commercial work and become Fine Art? Or has there just been a change in the perception because of the distance of time of what Fine Art is today? Do you really believe it's the talent that makes it transcend the commercial nature of the job?

STOUT: I think it's a mixture of both. I think the enormous vision those men had that took them beyond the mere fulfilling of an assignment had a lot to do with it. But also we have the benefit of history and hindsight. There were thousands of artists back then, and the artists we revere are the ones whose work had the staying power and stood the test of time. I'm sure there were thousands of guys doing the same subject matter for whom, to them, art was just a way to make a living, just a job. Their stuff was competent, especially by today's standards, but is now forgotten. History has a tendency to color things in different ways. I think there was no doubt in N. C. Wyeth's mind that he was an illustrator, up until the point where he wanted to change over into what he considered Fine Art. Yet there's something... Wyeth put so much of himself into his best illustrations, that to me, a lot of his illustrations, even though, yeah, he's illustrating a certain chapter from *Last of the Mohicans*, somehow the quality of the paint application, the design, the color, the subtlety of the way he expressed himself – to me, that takes that particular painting into the realm of Fine Art. There's another difference, though, between illustrators and fine artists. With Fine Artists, you judge them by their entire body of work. Illustrators, you judge by the best 25% of what they've done, discounting the rest for the time limits of deadline pressures, the limited scope of some of the work that was demanded by the job, the interference of art directors, and other things that may have affected the quality of the work. You

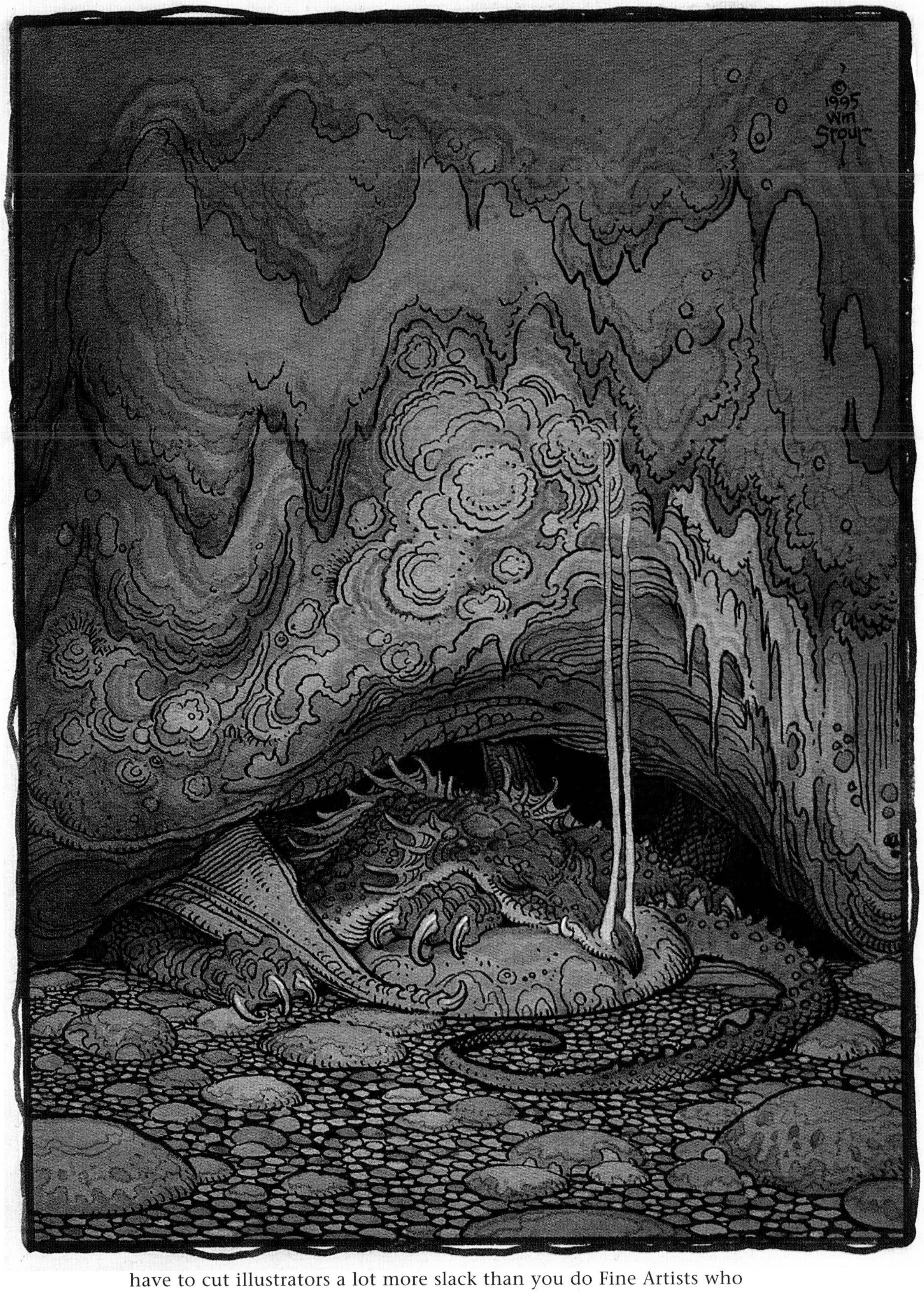
© 1995 Wm Stout

have to cut illustrators a lot more slack than you do Fine Artists who should be allowed no slack at all. Not everything that N. C. did was great. I've seen a lot of stuff that was pretty bad. But I don't know what was happening to him at the time. Maybe the magazine needed a painting in a day. That's certainly happened to me.

ARCUDI: And so, to make the obvious connection, Andrew Wyeth is certainly considered to be a Fine Artist by most people who know his work. Those people who know his and his father's work still consider Andrew Wyeth the "Finer" artist of the two painters in the sense that Andrew was painting "art-for-art's-sake," whereas N. C. Wyeth, even at his best, was just an illustrator. You agree, or disagree with that?

STOUT: I bristle at the phrase "just an illustrator." I think at least as much if not more high quality contemporary "fine art" has been produced by illustrators as has been produced by fine artists. On the

This Page: Stout eschews drama for design and linework in this depiction of a dragon snoozing.

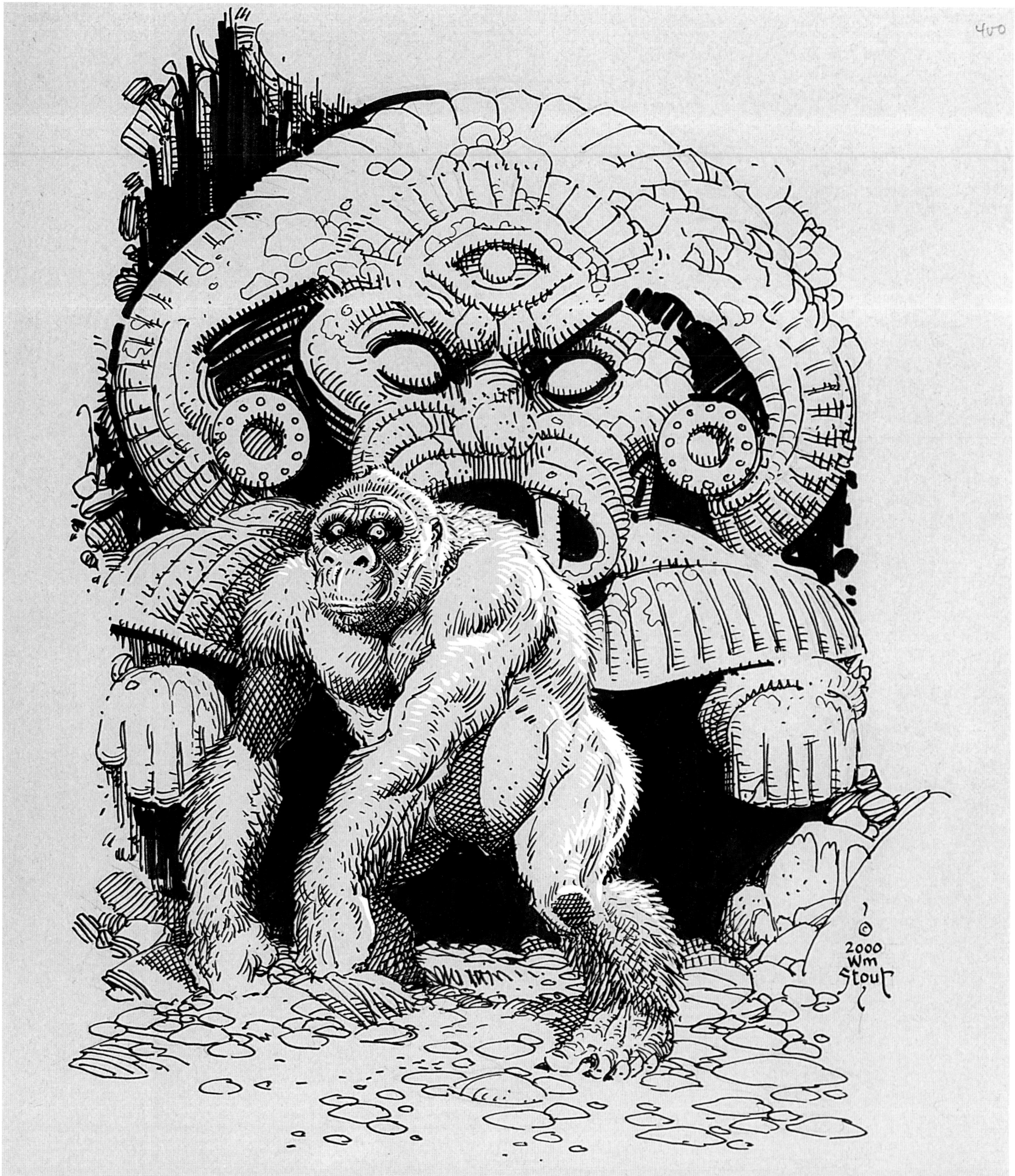
400
© 2000 Wm Stout

This Page: A convention sketchbook drawing of Son of Kong. "As lousy as it is, compared to *King Kong*, I nevertheless maintain a fondness for *Son of Kong*."

whole, though, I agree with what you said. Again, to compare Andrew and N. C., you have to compare the entire body of Andrew's work, because he is considered a Fine Artist, with the best 25 percent of N. C. Wyeth, and that's kind of unfair right there. N. C., because he was trained as an illustrator, had a different set of values and goals with his work, I don't mean moral values, but techniques, devices, and methods to convey his passions. For the most part, N. C.'s pictures couldn't be anywhere near as subtle as Andrew's – they wouldn't have satisfied the job. Most of N. C.'s work demanded an immediate impact with the public to sell a book or a product. So N. C. loses out there. A lot of times N. C. would try to advise Andrew to change something so that it would have a greater emotional impact. He wouldn't really get what Andrew was going for, that Andrew was not going for the greatest emotional impact, which is almost invariably what you do go for when you're doing illustration. You're trying to connect with your public in a forceful way. Andrew was going for something subtler, something softer, more contemplative, maybe more spiritual. His father didn't get that. So, yeah, Andrew really is a Fine Artist, and N. C.... I think some of his work is as good as any Fine Art that has been done, but essentially, he was an illustrator. But he was way more adventurous with color than Andrew has ever been. Which shows you how unimportant color can be in art.

INTER: Which of those two artists has had a greater impact on your work in Fine Art?

STOUT: Oh, without a doubt, N. C.; not that Andrew hasn't had an impact. I've taken a lot of stuff from him, but if you're going to learn color, you don't go to Andrew Wyeth to learn it. You go to N. C. to learn color. N.C. also is interesting to me, because he broke a lot of design rules. The big one that he broke is the one you hear over and over again: Never put the focus of your painting in the dead-center of the canvas, and he did that constantly – and pulled it off. It doesn't bother you. It looks just fine. Plus, N. C. had a great impact on Frazetta, and Frazetta was one of my main influences early in my career.

NATURAL HISTORY MURALS

ARCUDI: The next things I wanted to talk about are the Paleozoic Life murals you painted for the Houston Museum of Natural Science. How did that come about? It must have been really different for you; what was it like?

STOUT: The best! The Houston Museum of Natural Science was revamping their prehistoric hall; they needed two 27 feet long murals depicting the first life on earth leading up to the time of the dinosaurs.

ARCUDI: What made them aware of you?

STOUT: The curator who was in charge of the redesign of the exhibit called me up to get permission to use my Antarctic "Mosasaur and Loons" painting in their new exhibition. I never let an opportunity pass me by intentionally; I asked what was going on. He told me that they were redesigning the prehistoric hall at the museum. I asked them if there were any murals that needed to be painted and he said that there actually were two murals that they were taking bids on. I submitted samples and a bid, and they selected me to paint the murals. It took me nine months to paint both murals, and that was probably the happiest nine months I've ever had in my life. It was great on a number of levels. One reason was that I was painting art that was being permanently installed in a museum so that for decades people will be able to come and see my paintings in a fairly

respectable place. Two, it was my first experience painting large; it turned out to be an unexpectedly physical experience. I actually got a workout painting these paintings. In order to see them properly, I would paint a bit and then run across the yard to get the overview, and then run back. Plus, the size of the paintings was giving my arms a workout as well, just in covering that square footage of canvas. Since I was painting big for the first time, I was also learning; I found out that there are things that you don't do painting big but that you can get away with painting small. One of those things is intensity of color. What looks good small is far too intense and too much to take when it's gigantic. I went through a whole series of steps in painting the murals. I did several concept drawings and sent them to the museum for their approval. Then I did detailed color studies, small inch-to-a-foot oil painting versions of the paintings for the museum's approval before I went to full size.

ARCUDI: Was this based upon your usual system of problem solving, or is this because that's the way Zallinger did it for the Peabody Museum?

STOUT: When you're painting something that's 27 feet long and permanent, you want to make all your mistakes while it's still tiny. It's important to invest a lot of time in the preparatory stage so that by the time you get to the full-size paintings, everybody's on the same page. At the same time I'm rarely content to just do a job as given to me. I like to expand its depth to reach different levels. The basic job was to depict prehistoric plants and animals from point A to point B in timeline fashion. I thought, "Wouldn't it add to the psychological interest" – because these two paintings are each 27-feet long, a total of 54 feet, or more than five stories of painting – "if I painted this travel in time so that it also becomes a travel through the time of day, serving as a kind of visual metaphor?" I did just that. When you enter the hall and observe the beginning of the painting it's nighttime. As you progress in time the sun comes out and by the time you're at the middle of the mural it's noon; by the time you get to the end of the mural it's sunset. So there's a subconscious psychological transition from morning to evening going on while the prehistoric periods progress as well.

NOWHERE TO GO BUT CHINA

Is Stout really designing a dinosaur museum in Zigong, China? Yep. Read all about it at:

http://www.tcj.com/ws03/stoutchina.html

KEVIN COSTNER VS ANTARCTICA

ARCUDI: Does it ever surprise you that you've done as much as you have?

STOUT: Yeah. I just can't believe the amount of work I've produced.

ARCUDI: Is that impressive or depressing?

STOUT: I'm impressed. It's always been one of my goals to be really fast, to produce, to make money – why starve? Jack Davis was a real role model in that regard. It's never been a secret that I want to be successful in this business and I want to make money. I'm an American, for God's sake!

ARCUDI: I guess I just meant that it indicated a longer passage of time than you...

STOUT: I try not to even think about that, except that I consciously have to stay in shape to keep having all of the physical adventures that have become such a vital part of my life. Also, when I turned 50, I really did feel that I had an overview of life that I never had before,

> It's never been a secret that I want to be successful in this business and I want to make money. I'm an American, for God's sake!

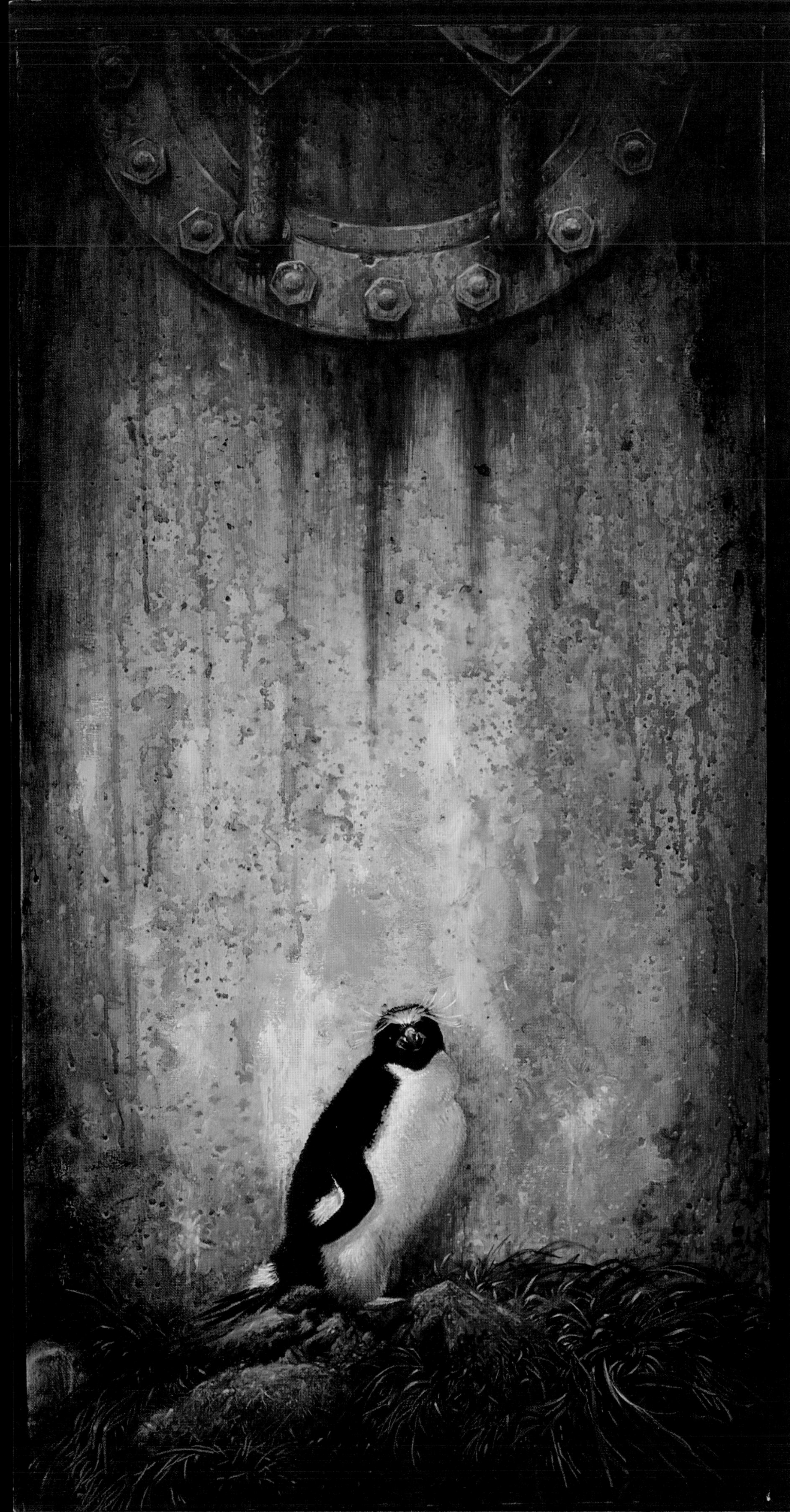

something I think is extremely beneficial to my art. This is why, now more than ever I want to do that comic story. I know I couldn't have written it as well ten years ago, without having this life experience, without having been a parent. Without traveling as much as I've done and exploring as many cultures and people.

ARCUDI: It's interesting. Most people, by the time they're 50, the last thing they want to do is write superhero stories. Now it's essentially the first thing that you want to do.

STOUT: Yeah. It could be total career suicide. God knows I've made those kinds of self-destructive choices before.

ARCUDI: You've managed, as it turns out.

STOUT: One of my dreams when I was working in the film business was to do a Western. I've always loved Westerns. Kevin Costner offered me a really great Western; I had to turn it down because I was right in the middle of my Antarctica show. I'm sure to this day people in the film business think I was totally insane for turning down *Dances with Wolves* in order to do "Dinosaurs, Penguins and Whales – The Wildlife of Antarctica".

ARCUDI: But that's not career suicide. It's not as if that hasn't paid off for you.

STOUT: I don't regret that choice for a second; I want to make that clear. I always knew that it would be Kevin Costner's *Dances with Wolves* – not Bill Stout's; but no one was ever going to take the "Dinosaurs, Penguins and Whales" show away from me. That was my show. I also knew that my show was going to be as good or as bad as I would make it, whereas with *Dances with Wolves*, there was no guarantee that it was going to be an Oscar winner when it started. I could have done my best work for two years and the film still could have turned out lousy.

FAMILY LIFE AND THE WORK ETHIC

In Antarctica anyway, you risk your life every day just by being there.

ARCUDI: You're away from your family for four months. It's work, but you're having fun.

STOUT: I'm working my butt off, but I'm also really having fun. I'm having great and exhilarating adventures. I'm risking my life. In Antarctica anyway, you risk your life every day just by being there. People have died just three yards from shelter they couldn't see during a whiteout; I ascended up a downline during one of my ice dives to discover there was no escape hole at the end of it – just a crack big enough for my fingers!

ARCUDI: Has that ever struck you ... Your family is going to read this, but did that ever strike you as irresponsible, if you're risking your life with a family and kids?

STOUT: It would be irresponsible if I was cavalier about it. When I say that I risk my life, those are really very calculated risks. I don't do things without a lot of thought beforehand. I don't intentionally put myself in a situation where the outcome is unknown or where the odds are pretty much guaranteed something fatal will happen.

ARCUDI: You did have fun. While it's happening, or soon thereafter, do you feel guilty about that? Having fun without your family around? Being away from them for so long?

STOUT: My observation is this: we're born alone and we die alone. We may have people around us, living with us, but they don't really know our innermost thoughts. And they do come and go; my oldest son is taking off for Yale at the end of this summer. Despite our love and best efforts, people die. The one constant in my life, and that might not even be a constant if my eyes or hands go, are my abilities as an artist, writer and problem solver. Life's aspects are going to all

change, rise, and fall. There is no guarantee in life other than that you're going to be with yourself the rest of your life. That's not selfish – that's reality.

ARCUDI: O.K. That's great for you, but does your wife, and the children — at least your oldest, probably — do they share that philosophy? Are they as forgiving of your exploits?

STOUT: They're very supportive for the most part; they know these things I do are a huge part of what makes me, me. I've had to promise no more four-month trips, though.

ARCUDI: That had to have had quite an impact.

STOUT: I have to limit it to two now. That's really understandable. I'll tell you, after being away for four months; coming back... it was like I was a stranger. And they were like strangers to me. It was bizarre.

ARCUDI: Your kids were both pretty young then, right?

STOUT: They were six and nine.

ARCUDI: So four months away, to a nine year old, that kid's like a foot taller when you got back.

STOUT: Plus he was really resentful that I'd been missing for all that time. It took us awhile to get close again, to get that trust back after what he perceived as a desertion. And it was a huge strain on my wife, too, because she'd just started medical school. That was really a tough one. But my wife and I are really supportive of each other. Obviously, our paths cross a lot because we're married to each other, but we do have separate lives. She used to be a successful actress; now she practices medicine. There are things that she needs to do. She needs to travel around the country and partake in medical courses called CME's to keep her medical credentials current. I take over the home front when she does that. My work requires me to travel a lot too, not just to paint but also to attend conventions around the country and to attend events like the annual meeting of the Society of Vertebrate Paleontology to keep current with my dinosaur information. Our relationship is really threatening to a lot of the people we meet through our kid's school.

ARCUDI: That you have to elaborate on.

STOUT: The wives feel very threatened that my wife allows me so much freedom and that I allow her so much freedom. They're more threatened by her allowing me freedom. They think it's insane; they like to keep a tight leash. But that says less about us than about their insecurities.

ARCUDI: And it's not as if you've only been married for six months. It seems to have worked out.

STOUT: Twenty years now.

ARCUDI: Let's get back to something else you said. You said that lots of creative people, artists, tend to be selfish.

STOUT: Uh huh. And that's not necessarily... I don't necessarily use that in a negative way. You certainly can use it as an excuse to be an asshole – Paul Gauguin, for example.

ARCUDI: Do you think that any artist who aspires to be something more than a hack can be anything but selfish?

STOUT: Oh, I know a lot of selfish hacks! But yeah, when I say selfish, I mean devoting an inordinate amount of time to oneself. I'm not talking about boorish behavior.

ARCUDI: Right, of course.

STOUT: Not necessarily, "Of course." I think a lot of artists through history have used their great talents or genius as an excuse for treating people really shabbily. I mean, I love Gauguin's paintings but God forbid – I would never have wanted to be a friend or even an

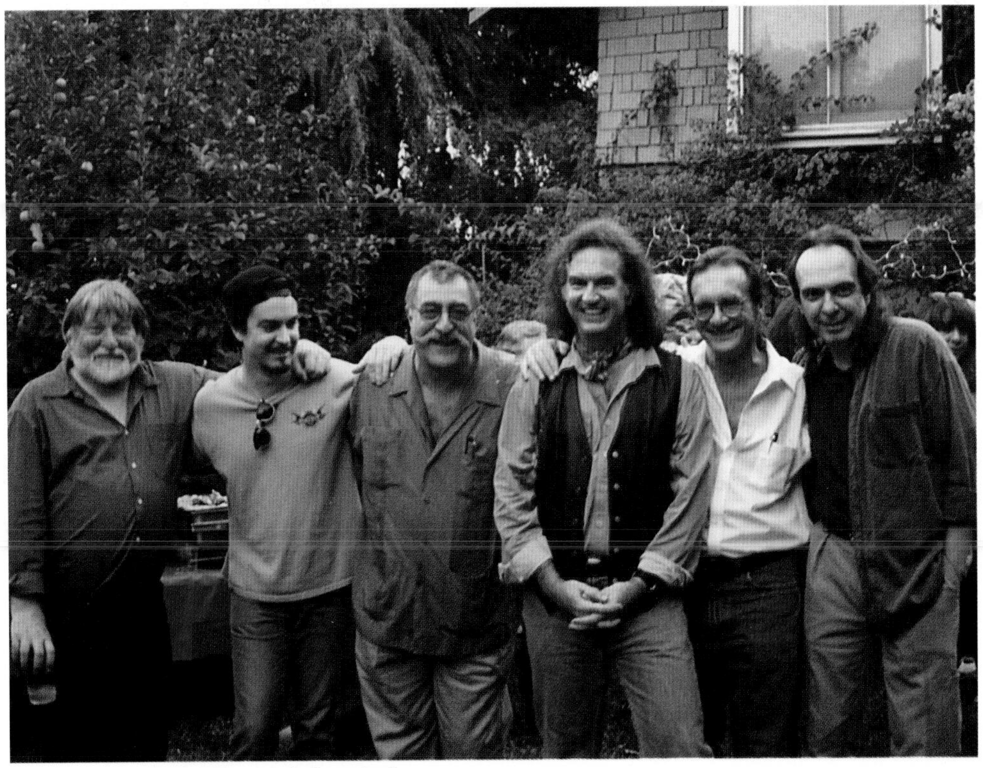

associate of that jerk.

ARCUDI: Which brings up another icon of American 20th century culture: Norman Rockwell. A guy who certainly portrayed the American way of life as ideal and idyllic, but...

STOUT: Yeah. He painted the most charming portraits of American life; these pictures visually reaffirmed what we thought of ourselves as a nation and as a people. And yet ironically, his life was the exact opposite. His son is very bitter about this. He says, "You know all of those paintings that my dad did depicting the family around the Thanksgiving table with the steaming turkey, those wonderfully cozy Christmas holiday paintings? We never had any of that. My dad was working on Thanksgiving. He was painting on Christmas. We never saw him." He had three marriages, two of which were completely disastrous. One wife was an alcoholic – certainly not a happy camper. As soon as one wife married Norman, he assumed that she would be the one to take over all of his business affairs, something she had never planned for or intended. She had a breakdown; they got divorced. Norman Rockwell brilliantly portrayed the ideal America yet his personal life was just the opposite. He went through many, many years – there was one five-year consecutive period I believe – of huge, deep, dark depressions. Here was a guy, arguably one of the most successful illustrators in the world, who was constantly terrified that his work was going to fall out of favor.

There are parallels between Rockwell and myself in our work philosophies. I know that I'm not a genius. I've worked with geniuses. Ron Cobb and Jean "Moebius" Giraud are both geniuses. I also know I'm not the best artist in the world. I can rattle off a whole list of guys inherently better than me. So my philosophy is that in order to compete with those talents out there who are geniuses, who are better than I am, I've got to work harder. So I do; I work really hard. I set really high creative standards for my work. "Good enough" is not in my vocabulary. There are people who can out-think, out-draw, and out-paint me. But there are damn few people who are gonna outwork me. And in the long run that becomes my answer to the competition. ★★★

My wife and I are really supportive of each other. Obviously, our paths cross a lot because we're married to each other, but we do have separate lives.

Opposite Page: The harsh past meets the optimistic present in this depiction of a macaroni penguin standing in front of a symbol of a penguin holocaust: a rusting boiler that was used to render the body oil from millions of penguins.

This Page: Stout's 50th birthday bash. Left to right: Ron Cobb, Dave Stevens, Sergio Aragonés, Stout, Bernie Wrightson and Bob Cabeen.

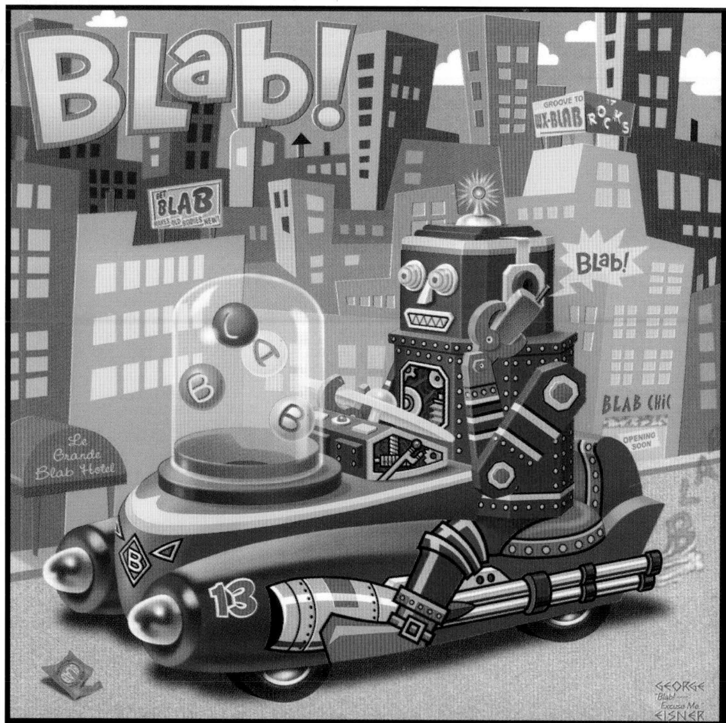
Blab!
GROOVE TO WX-BLAB ROCKS
THE BLAB
Blab!
BLAB CHIC
OPENING SOON
Le Grande Blab Hotel
13
GEORGE EISNER
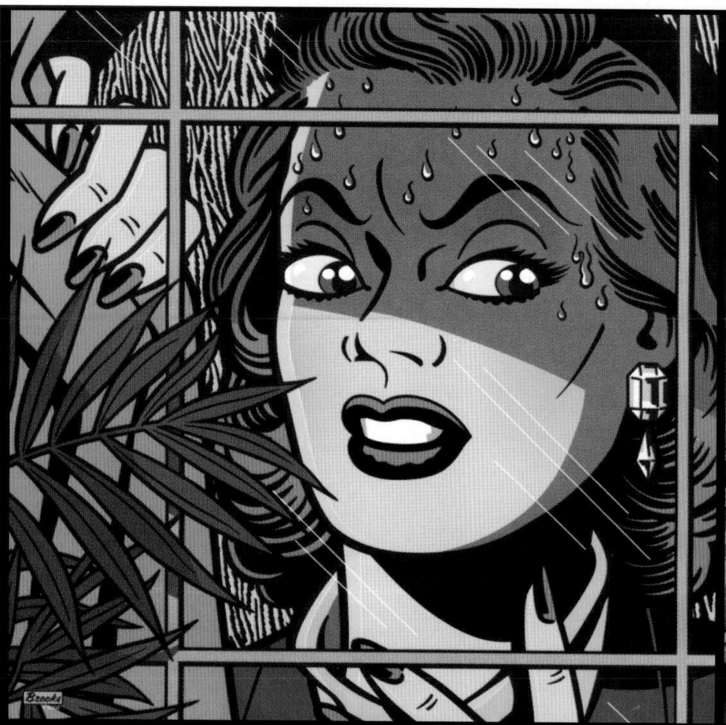
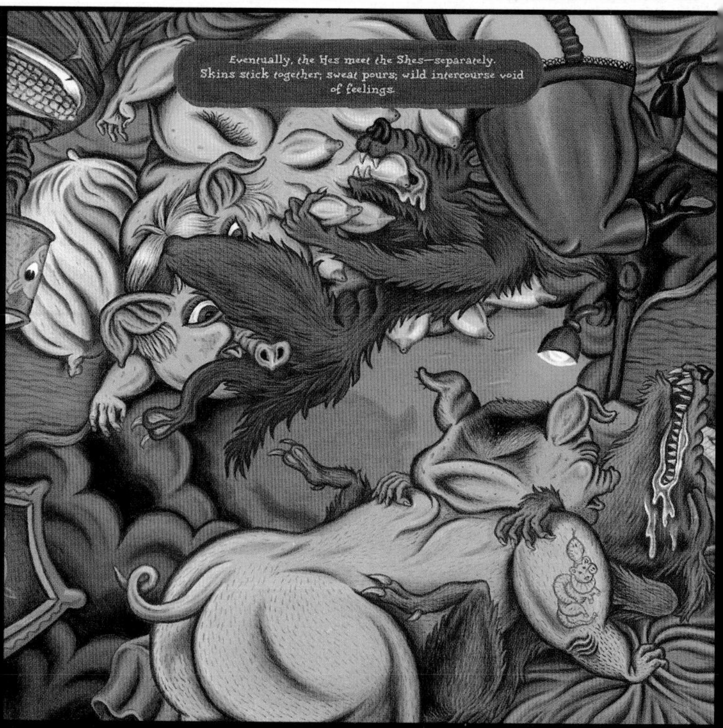
Eventually, the Hes meet the Shes—separately.
Skins stick together; sweat pours; wild intercourse void of feelings.
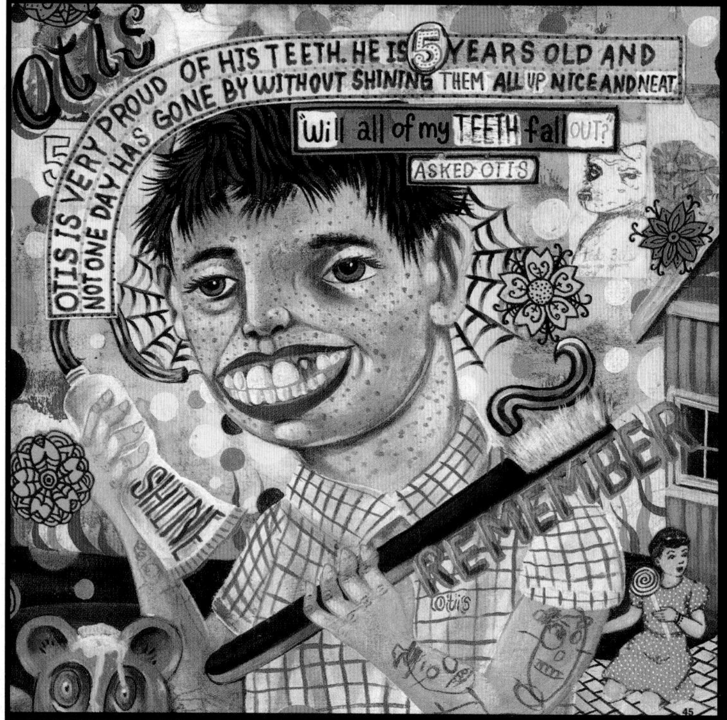
OTIS IS VERY PROUD OF HIS TEETH. HE IS 5 YEARS OLD AND NOT ONE DAY HAS GONE BY WITHOUT SHINING THEM ALL UP NICE AND NEAT.
Will all of my TEETH fall OUT?
ASKED OTIS
REMEMBER
SHINE
45
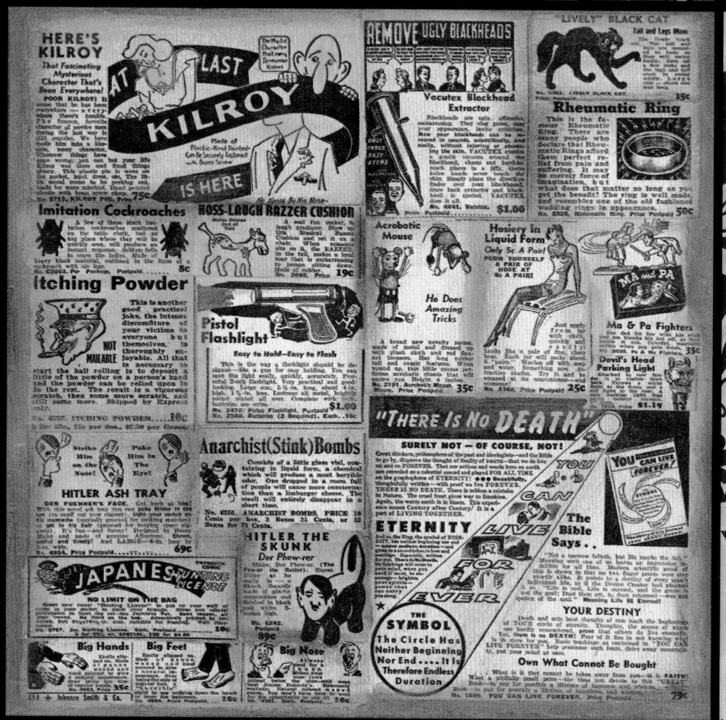
HERE'S KILROY
AT LAST KILROY IS HERE
REMOVE UGLY BLACKHEADS
Vacutex Blackhead Extractor
"LIVELY" BLACK CAT
Rheumatic Ring
HOSS-LAUGH RAZZER CUSHION
Imitation Cockroaches
Itching Powder
Pistol Flashlight
Acrobatic Mouse
Hosiery in Liquid Form
Ma & Pa Fighters
Devil's Head Parking Light
"THERE IS NO DEATH"
SURELY NOT — OF COURSE, NOT!
Anarchist(Stink)Bombs
HITLER ASH TRAY
HITLER THE SKUNK
ETERNITY
YOU CAN LIVE FOR EVER
The Bible Says...
YOUR DESTINY
Own What Cannot Be Bought
THE SYMBOL The Circle Has Neither Beginning Nor End.... It Is Therefore Endless Duration
JAPANESE
Big Hands
Big Feet
Big Nose
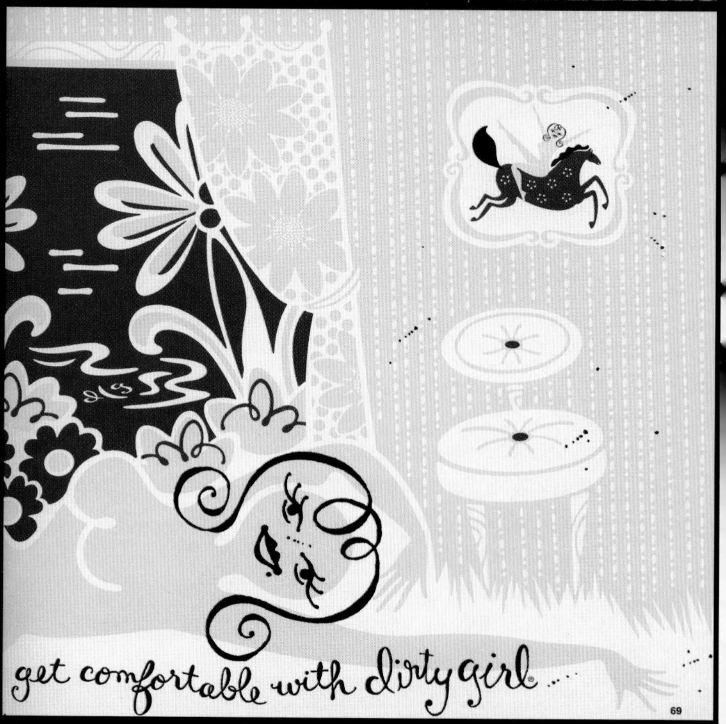
get comfortable with dirty girl....
69
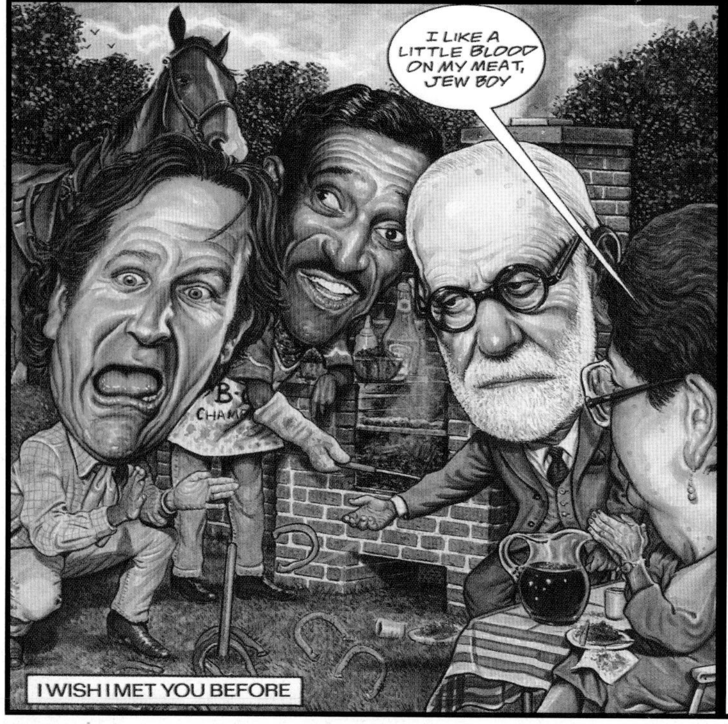
I LIKE A LITTLE BLOOD ON MY MEAT, JEW BOY
I WISH I MET YOU BEFORE
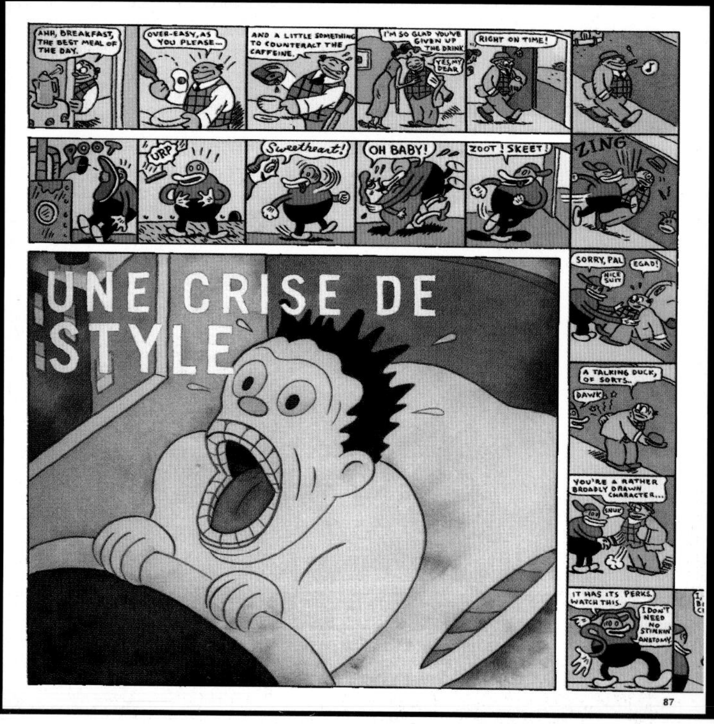
AHH, BREAKFAST, THE BEST MEAL OF THE DAY.
OVER-EASY, AS YOU PLEASE...
AND A LITTLE SOMETHING TO COUNTERACT THE CAFFEINE.
I'M SO GLAD YOU'VE GIVEN UP THE DRINK
RIGHT ON TIME!
POOT
URP
Sweetheart!
OH BABY!
ZOOT! SKEET!
ZING
UNE CRISE DE STYLE
SORRY, PAL
EGAD!
A TALKING DUCK, OF SORTS...
YOU'RE A RATHER BROADLY DRAWN CHARACTER...
IT HAS ITS PERKS, WATCH THIS.
I DON'T NEED NO STINKIN' ANATOMY!
87

ALL-NEW BLAB! 13

120 PAGES
10" SQUARE
$19.95
IN STORES NOW !

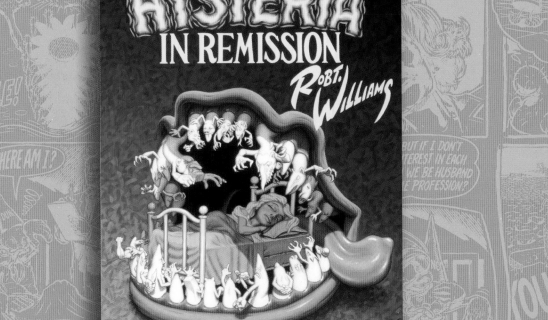

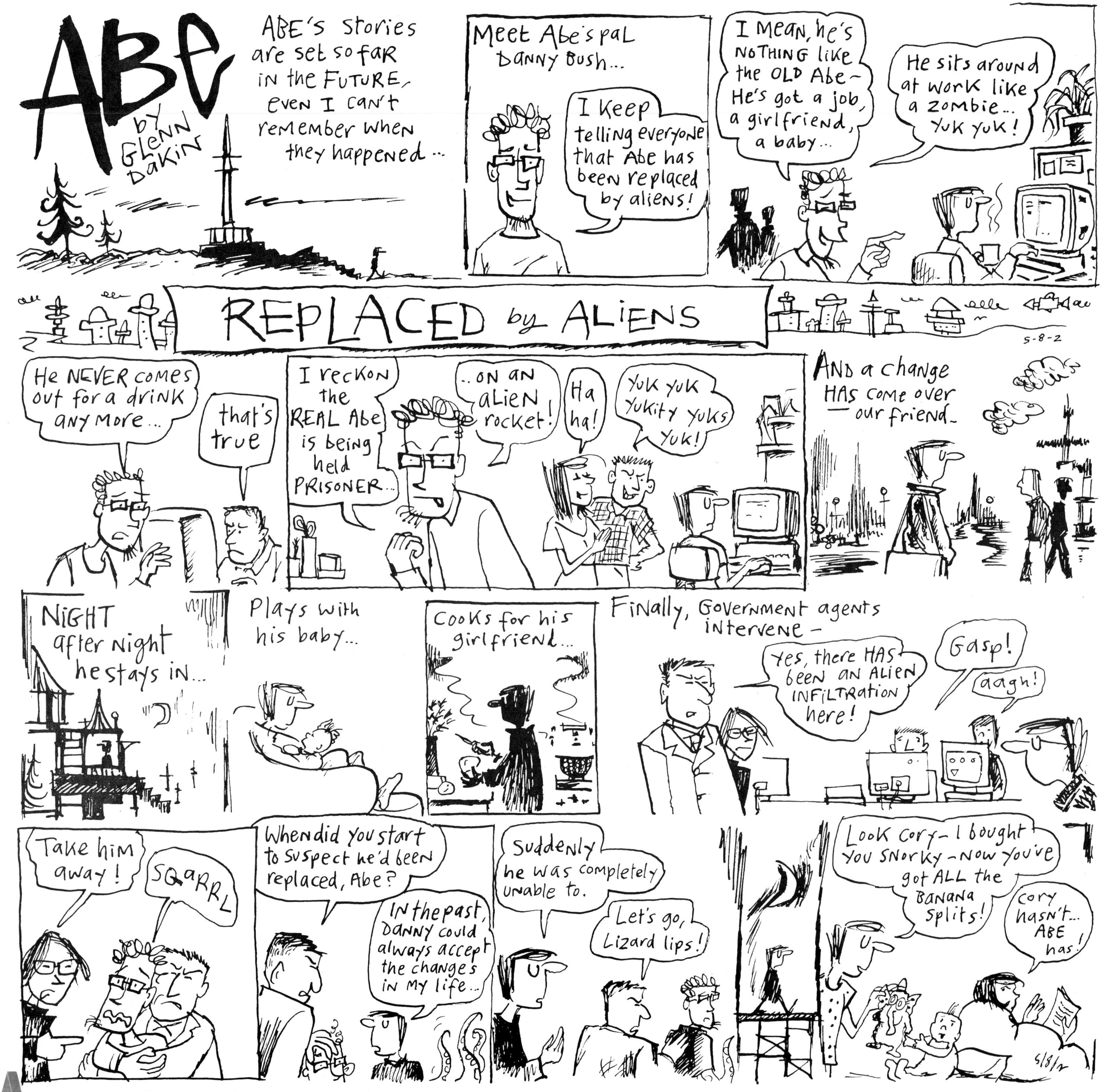

Abe
by Glenn Dakin
ABE'S stories are set so far in the FUTURE, even I can't remember when they happened...
Meet Abe's pal Danny Bush...
I keep telling everyone that Abe has been replaced by aliens!
I mean, he's NOTHING like the OLD Abe - He's got a job, a girlfriend, a baby...
He sits around at work like a zombie... Yuk yuk!
REPLACED by ALIENS
5-8-2
He NEVER comes out for a drink any more...
that's true
I reckon the REAL Abe is being held PRISONER...
..on an alien rocket!
Ha ha!
Yuk yuk yukity yuks yuk!
AND a change HAS come over our friend -
NIGHT after night he stays in...
Plays with his baby...
Cooks for his girlfriend...
Finally, Government agents intervene -
Yes, there HAS been an ALIEN INFILTRATION here!
Gasp!
aagh!
Take him away!
SQARRL
When did you start to suspect he'd been replaced, Abe?
In the past, DANNY could always accept the changes in my life...
Suddenly he was completely unable to.
Let's go, Lizard lips!
Look Cory - I bought you SNORKY - now you've got ALL the BANANA SPLITS!
Cory hasn't... ABE has!
5/8/2

This page: a new "Abe" by Glenn Dakin. © 2002 Glenn Dakin.

BRITAIN'S MAGAZINE OF INTERNATIONAL STORY-STRIPS
£1
MAGAZINE
NUMBER 6
QUARTERLY
ISSN 0266-1667
Alien ALAN MOORE
PASTA STRIPS
WOUND ME
LONDON PARIS NEW YORK
FLAME ON!
and a bit more!
STEVE BELL'S ANIMAL FARM!
SPAGHETTI FUMETTI • ITALIAN COMICS!
JOHN BAGNALL ★ EDDIE CAMPBELL ★ GLENN DAKIN ★ ANDY DOG ★ PHIL ELLIOTT ★ HUNT EMERSON ★ LAWRENCE GRAY ★ MIKE HAWTHORNE ★ RIAN HUGHES ★ SHAKY KANE ★ PHIL LASKEY ★ ED PINSENT ★ SAVAGE PENCIL ★ DAVE THORPE

Top: *Escape* #6 cover. © 2002 Andy Dog.

THE GREAT ESCAPE

With hindsight, Paul Gravett re-appraises the emergence and impact of *Escape* and the *Escape* Artists

by Paul Gravett with NEW strips from *Escape* artists

Can it really have begun only 20 years ago? It's hard to believe that spring 2003 marks the 20th anniversary of the first issue of *Escape*, the British comics magazine that Peter Stanbury and I co-edited 19 issues of until Autumn 1989. For six years, *Escape* helped to promote an evolving bunch of distinctive British creators, many of whom were quickly picked up by other comics publishers and by the UK music press, newspaper, magazines and galleries. Now is a good time to look back at how we came together and what some of the singular "*Escape* Artists" have achieved and are achieving still.

"*Escape* Artists" was nothing to do with Houdini or Steranko. It started out as a fun title for our Contributors' Notes column and was no more than a handy collective name. Obviously, the artists never "belonged" to *Escape* or to anyone, and they never saw themselves as a unified group. Most had art-school backgrounds, all had strongly individual approaches that largely ignored genre and formula and all were open to influences from within comics and from beyond. Cumulatively, their work appears as idiosyncratic and refreshing as ever and continues to motivate successive generations of cartoonists on both sides of the Atlantic.

Today, two decades after the birth of *Escape*, it seems so much easier and more natural to think and network globally, to look at the bigger picture. With e-mail we can make connections in the blink of a synapse. We can let the world and its Web sites flood into our home computer screens. In the American comics market, specialist stores, as well as many bookstores and libraries, fill their shelves with square-bound graphic novels that can earn literary awards and top the charts as Hollywood movies. Alternatively, you can bypass all the middlemen and deliver your paperless comics online direct to readers anywhere. Of course, physical gatherings of the clans, such as the Angoulême Festival in France or ICAF and SPX in Washington, are still vital and now truly international, bringing together people from all over the world, but the contacts they make there in the flesh can go on to develop virtually.

All this feels like living in some whiz-bang, sci-fi future out of one of Glenn Dakin's loopier *Abe* strips, when compared to just 20 years ago, pre-Internet, pre-manga (*Barefoot Gen* had barely begun), pre-*Maus*

WE COME ACROSS THE STRAND LIKE A LOG ON A DUCK-POND...
ECampbell
CITIBANK

(only the first chapters in *Raw*), pre-full-scale-British-Invasion (sparked by Alan Moore's *Swamp Thing* later in 1983). Back in those days, it was more low-tech, haphazard and, in a way, human. For instance, in Britain the comics community would write each other letters, usually by hand, and might meet up in each other's homes, or down the pub or at comic marts or the annual conventions. And through the miracle of modern xerography, almost anyone could photocopy their own comic, sometimes as few as ten copies, and try selling then in shops, at marts and, if you got it reviewed in one of the handful of fanzines, through the post.

It was Peter who hit on the perfect title, *Escape*, chosen not for "escapism" but for the idea of breaking out from the stifling conformity of the comics mainstream.

To go professional, the options in the UK in 1982 were limited. Pre-Vertigo, pre-*Watchmen*, the US publishers Marvel and DC had not yet come headhunting to Britain. The homegrown market, aside from children's weeklies, consisted of the American-influenced science fiction of *2000AD*, *Warrior*'s not-so-weird heroes and a few new pages in the Marvel UK line of reprints. As for more "adult" fare, Knockabout stayed true to the US-inspired underground humor tradition, and the more typically British rude, crude satire comic *Viz* was still in its early core stage and accepted few newcomers. The only openings for beginners were promised by *pssst!* magazine, which I will come to.

Around September 1982, Peter Stanbury and I moved into our first apartment together, where we decided that it would be fun to run a comics magazine. It was Peter who hit on the perfect title, *Escape*, chosen not for "escapism" but for the idea of breaking out from the stifling conformity of the comics mainstream. At the time, Peter had risen through the ranks at *Harpers & Queen*, a high-society, high-fashion women's glossy, and he knew everything about print design and production. He brought his love for drawing and storytelling and an essential layperson's perspective to temper my specialist zeal. I was less than a year into my first proper paid job in comics at *pssst!* magazine, the brave but misguided dream of a delightfully wacky and wealthy French couple, Serge and Henriette Boissevain, who were convinced that a British attempt at the sort of luxurious 'adult' monthly *bande dessinée* magazine that sold in France would make a fortune across the channel; instead, it nearly lost them theirs.

I had started at *pssst!* late in 1981 as their promotions man, touring England in the middle of winter with a beefy driver, Mick, and a punk assistant, Nick, on a double-decker London bus. Outside, its side windows were covered and painted with wild cartoon graphics, while inside, the seats downstairs had been removed to make a shop, and the seats upstairs were kept to form a cinema to screen a back-projected comics slide show for adults only. On the road, one of my duties was to seek out new artists and we found more than we could imagine. One of my discoveries when we hit Manchester's art college was curly-haired student Glenn Dakin, whose devilish cartooning on *Temptation* quickly made it into *pssst!* magazine.

In the end, after being hounded out of town by irate council officials and scraping ice off of the inside of the windows (mercifully we never had to sleep on the bus), it was a relief to be taken off the road for good. I got an ideal job back at the offices as traffic manager, coordinating artwork and interviewing potential contributors. There was a buzz to opening each day's submissions and presenting them to the weekly editorial meetings. I got to see loads of art and artists and I learnt a lot about magazines, both what to do and what not. Put together by committee, *pssst!* was a camel of a magazine, which was forced to close after ten issues, a victim of ill-considered editorial judgement and overlavish production costs.

While *Escape* owed a lot to the small-press explosion, it also partly grew out of the frustrations I felt at having no say about *pssst!* magazine's contents and seeing them reject such great material, including Eddie Campbell's life-affirming, autobiographical *Alec*. I had landed the promotions job at *pssst!* in the first place, because its main editor Mal Burns knew about my contacts within the UK small-press scene. Earlier still in 1981, I had started Fast Fiction (the name appropriated from a short-lived *Classics Illustrated* clone I found in an *Overstreet Price Guide*). Hardly anybody used to talk to each other at the bimonthly Saturday comic marts at Westminster Hall, London; all you'd hear were the plastic rustlings through a sea

TEMPTATION by Glenn Dakin
He's trying to keep me in suspense
It's some new idea to steal my soul off me.. He thinks he's getting me really curious by not saying anything
I can't stand the suspense.. but I can't let him realise it- it'll be a major moral victory for him.
I won't let him see that he's got me agitated.. the sneaky irritating beetle-faced RUNT
How do you like the nifty mind-reading helmet?
TEMPTATION

Top left: Panel by Eddie Campbell from *Escape* #6. © 2002 Eddie Campbell. **Bottom right:** "Temptation" by Glenn Dakin from *Escape* #5. © 2002 Glenn Dakin.

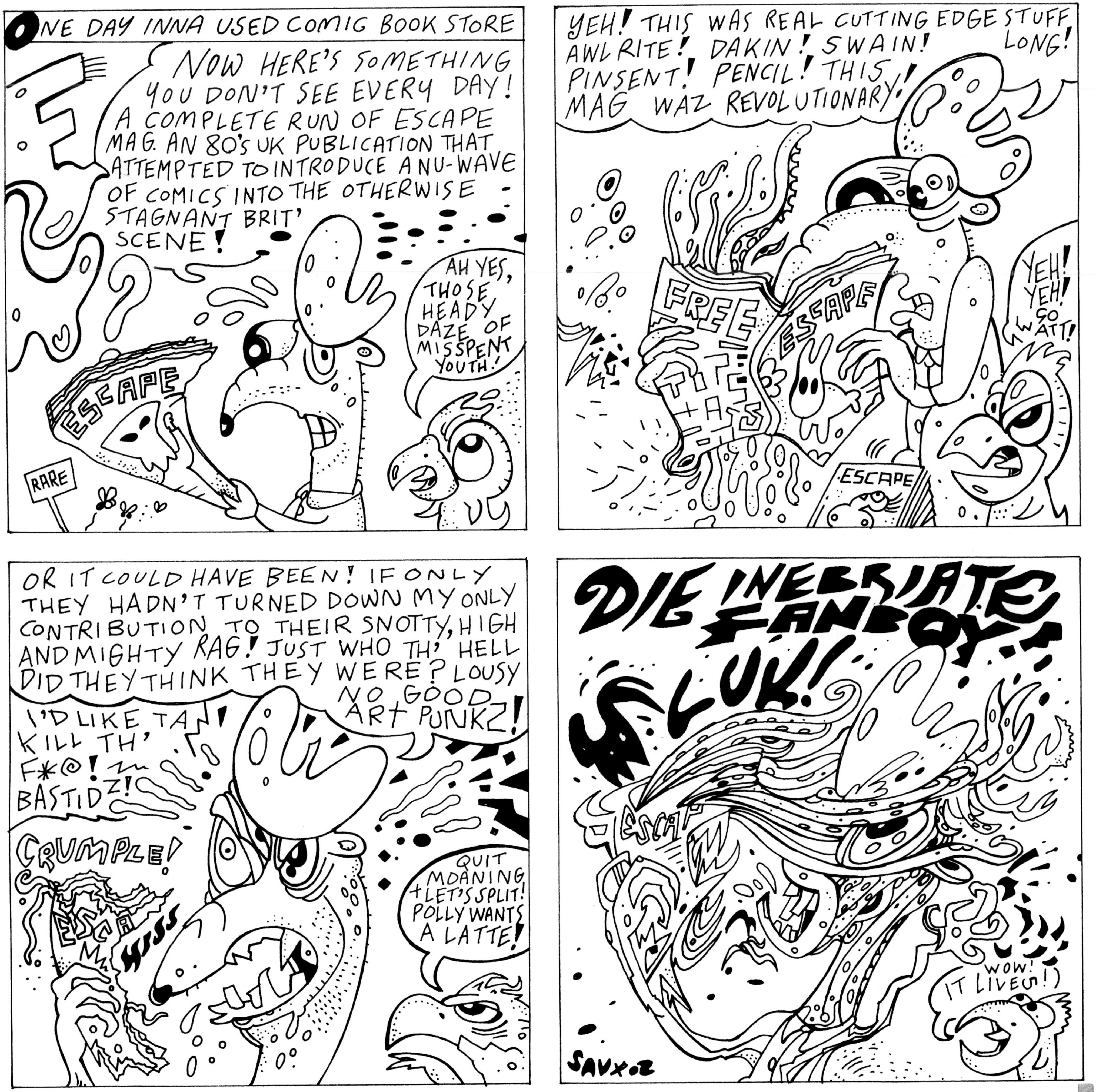
ONE DAY INNA USED COMIC BOOK STORE
NOW HERE'S SOMETHING YOU DON'T SEE EVERY DAY! A COMPLETE RUN OF ESCAPE MAG. AN 80'S UK PUBLICATION THAT ATTEMPTED TO INTRODUCE A NU-WAVE OF COMICS INTO THE OTHERWISE STAGNANT BRIT' SCENE!
AH YES, THOSE HEADY DAZE OF MISSPENT YOUTH!
ESCAPE
RARE
YEH! THIS WAS REAL CUTTING EDGE STUFF AWLRITE! DAKIN! SWAIN! LONG! PINSENT! PENCIL! THIS MAG WAZ REVOLUTIONARY!
YEH! YEH! GO WATT!
FREE
ESCAPE
ESCAPE
OR IT COULD HAVE BEEN! IF ONLY THEY HADN'T TURNED DOWN MY ONLY CONTRIBUTION TO THEIR SNOTTY, HIGH AND MIGHTY RAG! JUST WHO TH' HELL DID THEY THINK THEY WERE? LOUSY NO GOOD ART PUNKZ!
I'D LIKE TA KILL TH' F*@! BASTIDZ!
CRUMPLE!
ESCA
HISS
QUIT MOANING + LET'S SPLIT! POLLY WANTS A LATTE!
DIE INEBRIATED FANBOY!!
SLUK!
ESCAP
WOW! IT LIVES!
SAV×02

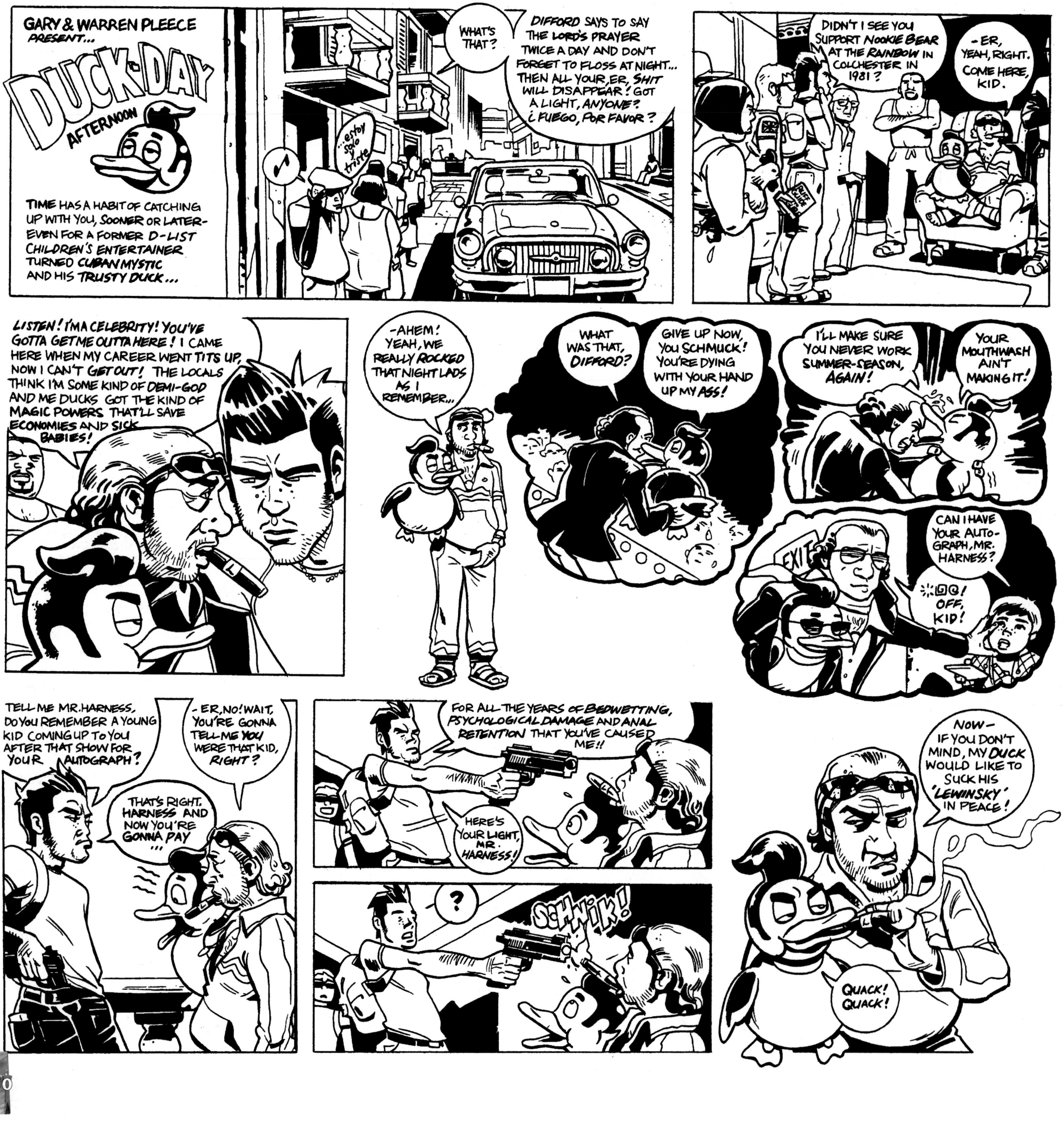
GARY & WARREN PLEECE PRESENT...
DUCK-DAY AFTERNOON
TIME HAS A HABIT OF CATCHING UP WITH YOU, SOONER OR LATER- EVEN FOR A FORMER D-LIST CHILDREN'S ENTERTAINER TURNED CUBAN MYSTIC AND HIS TRUSTY DUCK...
...estoy solo y triste
WHAT'S THAT?
DIFFORD SAYS TO SAY THE LORD'S PRAYER TWICE A DAY AND DON'T FORGET TO FLOSS AT NIGHT... THEN ALL YOUR, ER, SHIT WILL DISAPPEAR! GOT A LIGHT, ANYONE? ¿ FUEGO, POR FAVOR ?
DIDN'T I SEE YOU SUPPORT NOOKIE BEAR AT THE RAINBOW IN COLCHESTER IN 1981?
- ER, YEAH, RIGHT. COME HERE, KID.
LISTEN! I'M A CELEBRITY! YOU'VE GOTTA GET ME OUTTA HERE! I CAME HERE WHEN MY CAREER WENT TITS UP, NOW I CAN'T GET OUT! THE LOCALS THINK I'M SOME KIND OF DEMI-GOD AND ME DUCKS GOT THE KIND OF MAGIC POWERS THAT'LL SAVE ECONOMIES AND SICK BABIES!
-AHEM! YEAH, WE REALLY ROCKED THAT NIGHT LADS AS I REMEMBER...
WHAT WAS THAT, DIFFORD?
GIVE UP NOW, YOU SCHMUCK! YOU'RE DYING WITH YOUR HAND UP MY ASS!
I'LL MAKE SURE YOU NEVER WORK SUMMER-SEASON, AGAIN!
YOUR MOUTHWASH AIN'T MAKING IT!
EXIT
CAN I HAVE YOUR AUTO-GRAPH, MR. HARNESS?
OFF, KID!
TELL ME MR. HARNESS, DO YOU REMEMBER A YOUNG KID COMING UP TO YOU AFTER THAT SHOW FOR YOUR AUTOGRAPH?
- ER, NO! WAIT, YOU'RE GONNA TELL ME YOU WERE THAT KID, RIGHT?
THAT'S RIGHT. HARNESS AND NOW YOU'RE GONNA PAY ...
FOR ALL THE YEARS OF BEDWETTING, PSYCHOLOGICAL DAMAGE AND ANAL RETENTION THAT YOU'VE CAUSED ME!!
HERE'S YOUR LIGHT, MR. HARNESS!
?
SCHNIK!
NOW - IF YOU DON'T MIND, MY DUCK WOULD LIKE TO SUCK HIS 'LEWINSKY' IN PEACE!
QUACK! QUACK!

This page: "Duck Day Afternoon," a new piece by Warren and Gary Pleece. © 2002 Warren and Gary Pleece.

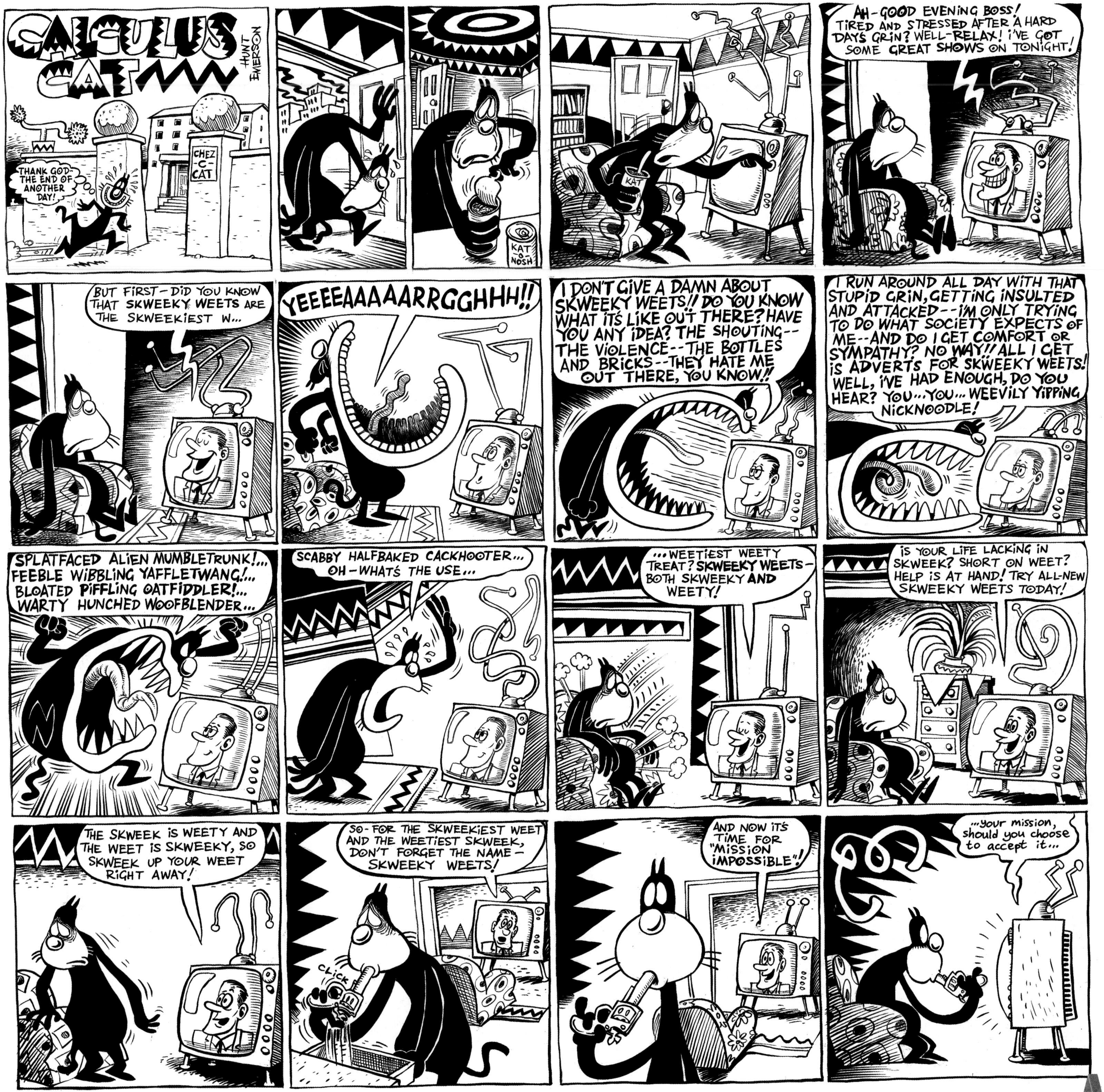
CALCULUS CAT
HUNT EMERSON
THANK GOD- THE END OF ANOTHER DAY!
CHEZ -C- CAT
KAT -O- NOSH
KAT
AH-GOOD EVENING BOSS! TIRED AND STRESSED AFTER A HARD DAYS GRIN? WELL-RELAX! I'VE GOT SOME GREAT SHOWS ON TONIGHT!
BUT FIRST- DID YOU KNOW THAT SKWEEKY WEETS ARE THE SKWEEKIEST W...
YEEEEAAAAARRGGHHH!!
I DON'T GIVE A DAMN ABOUT SKWEEKY WEETS!! DO YOU KNOW WHAT IT'S LIKE OUT THERE? HAVE YOU ANY IDEA? THE SHOUTING-- THE VIOLENCE--THE BOTTLES AND BRICKS--THEY HATE ME OUT THERE, YOU KNOW!!
I RUN AROUND ALL DAY WITH THAT STUPID GRIN, GETTING INSULTED AND ATTACKED--I'M ONLY TRYING TO DO WHAT SOCIETY EXPECTS OF ME--AND DO I GET COMFORT OR SYMPATHY? NO WAY!! ALL I GET IS ADVERTS FOR SKWEEKY WEETS! WELL, I'VE HAD ENOUGH, DO YOU HEAR? YOU...YOU... WEEVILY YIPPING NICKNOODLE!
SPLATFACED ALIEN MUMBLETRUNK!... FEEBLE WIBBLING YAFFLETWANG!... BLOATED PIFFLING OATFIDDLER!... WARTY HUNCHED WOOFBLENDER...
SCABBY HALFBAKED CACKHOOTER... OH-WHAT'S THE USE...
...WEETIEST WEETY TREAT? SKWEEKY WEETS- BOTH SKWEEKY AND WEETY!
IS YOUR LIFE LACKING IN SKWEEK? SHORT ON WEET? HELP IS AT HAND! TRY ALL-NEW SKWEEKY WEETS TODAY!
THE SKWEEK IS WEETY AND THE WEET IS SKWEEKY, SO SKWEEK UP YOUR WEET RIGHT AWAY!
SO-FOR THE SKWEEKIEST WEET AND THE WEETIEST SKWEEK, DON'T FORGET THE NAME- SKWEEKY WEETS!
CLICK
AND NOW IT'S TIME FOR "MISSION IMPOSSIBLE"!
...your mission, should you choose to accept it...

This page: a new "Calculus Cat" by Hunt Emerson. © 2002 Hunt Emerson.

SALVAGE AT SILVER CITY

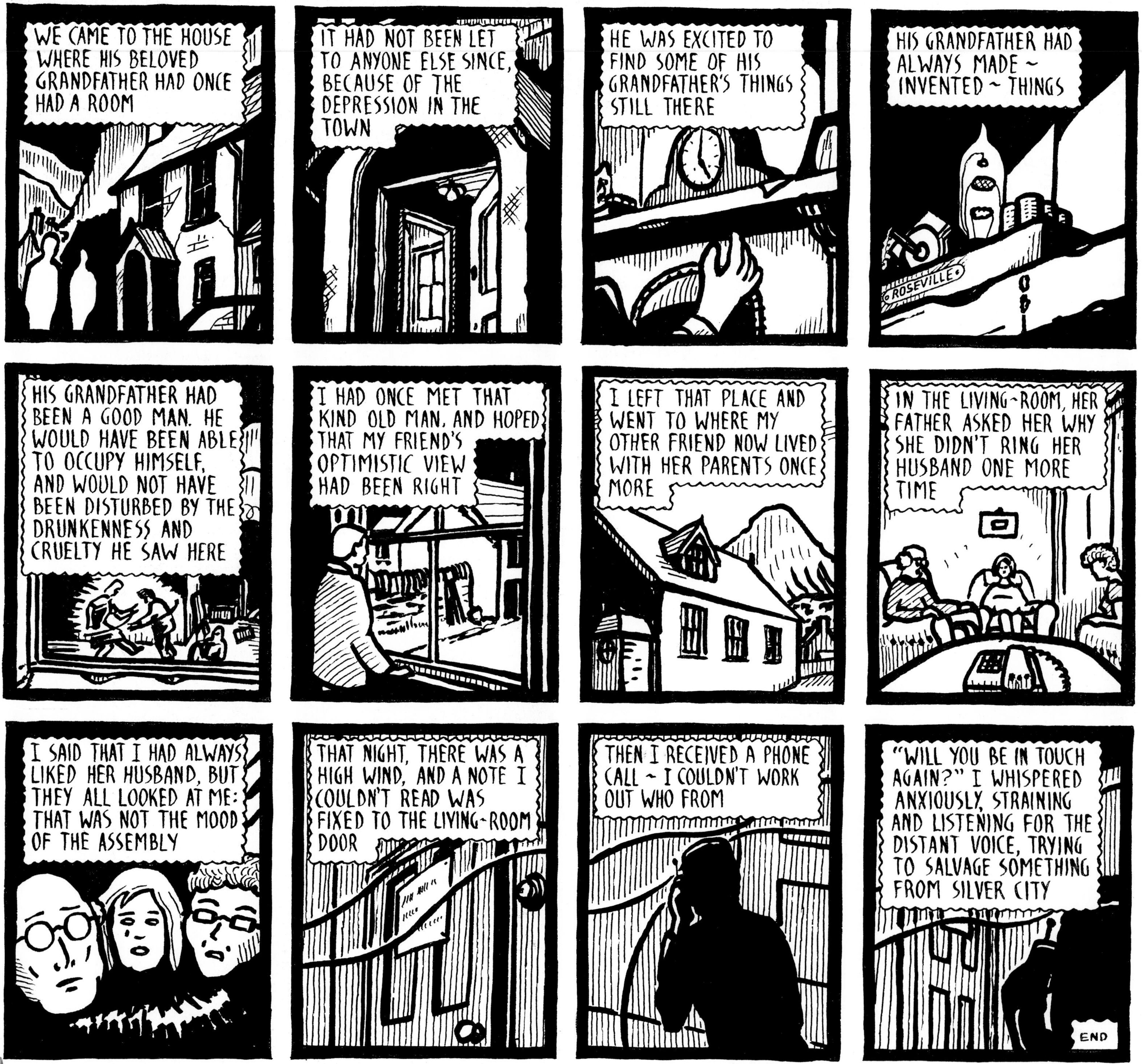
WE CAME TO THE HOUSE WHERE HIS BELOVED GRANDFATHER HAD ONCE HAD A ROOM
IT HAD NOT BEEN LET TO ANYONE ELSE SINCE, BECAUSE OF THE DEPRESSION IN THE TOWN
HE WAS EXCITED TO FIND SOME OF HIS GRANDFATHER'S THINGS STILL THERE
HIS GRANDFATHER HAD ALWAYS MADE ~ INVENTED ~ THINGS
ROSEVILLE
HIS GRANDFATHER HAD BEEN A GOOD MAN. HE WOULD HAVE BEEN ABLE TO OCCUPY HIMSELF, AND WOULD NOT HAVE BEEN DISTURBED BY THE DRUNKENNESS AND CRUELTY HE SAW HERE
I HAD ONCE MET THAT KIND OLD MAN, AND HOPED THAT MY FRIEND'S OPTIMISTIC VIEW HAD BEEN RIGHT
I LEFT THAT PLACE AND WENT TO WHERE MY OTHER FRIEND NOW LIVED WITH HER PARENTS ONCE MORE
IN THE LIVING~ROOM, HER FATHER ASKED HER WHY SHE DIDN'T RING HER HUSBAND ONE MORE TIME
I SAID THAT I HAD ALWAYS LIKED HER HUSBAND, BUT THEY ALL LOOKED AT ME: THAT WAS NOT THE MOOD OF THE ASSEMBLY
THAT NIGHT, THERE WAS A HIGH WIND, AND A NOTE I COULDN'T READ WAS FIXED TO THE LIVING~ROOM DOOR
THEN I RECEIVED A PHONE CALL ~ I COULDN'T WORK OUT WHO FROM
"WILL YOU BE IN TOUCH AGAIN?" I WHISPERED ANXIOUSLY, STRAINING AND LISTENING FOR THE DISTANT VOICE, TRYING TO SALVAGE SOMETHING FROM SILVER CITY
END

This page: "Salvage at Silver City," a new piece by Chris Reynolds. © 2002 Chris Reynolds.

ESCAPE
NUMBER 10
EAT YOUR HEART OUT AT JOE'S BAR
NEW COMICS REVIEWED
TINTIN
STEVE BELL
ALAN MOORE
2000 AD
40 pages of COMIC STRIPS
INTERVIEW
TEMPTATION
ESCAPE
Especial España
ESCAPE
THE HARD CORE OF THE BIG APPLE
MEAN STRIPS
NY
WISH YOU WERE HERE!
ESCAPE
French Sex
Cabaret Couture
Park Rendezvous
Cinema Dessine
Modern Jazz
Paris Souvenir
ESCAPE
ENGLISH ECCENTRICS

Top l-r: Covers to *Escape* #10 (José Munoz), #9 (Fernando Vicente), #13 (Charles Burns), #18 (Jean-Claude Gotting) and #19 (Steven Appleby). All © 2002 respective artists. **Bottom:** *Escape* advertisement by Phil Elliott. © 2002 Phil Elliott.

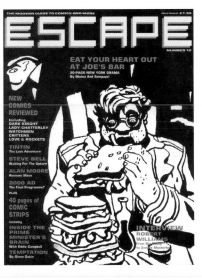

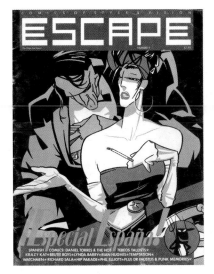

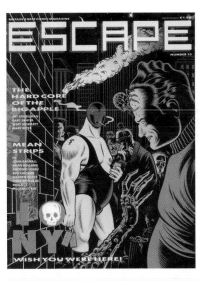

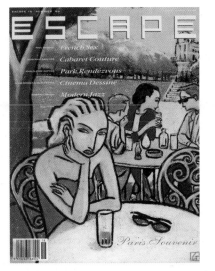

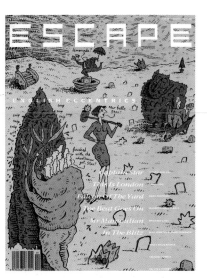

of comic boxes. I knew there must be some different comics out there, and all I really wanted to do was to meet the people creating them. I got their addresses and wrote inviting them to send in stock for the Fast Fiction stall at marts, the regular "Info Sheet" and mail-order service. By providing this encouragement, access to all and a regular meeting place, Fast Fiction brought together self-publishers from across the country into an ever-changing, do-it-yourself movement akin to the punk and indie music spirit.

Once I started working at *pssst!*, comic artists Phil Elliott and Ian Wieczorek, local Essex friends since my school days, had taken on the Fast Fiction service, with another school friend Alan Gaulton providing the transport. Phil and Ian soon wanted to publish their work in a Fast Fiction magazine and the first artist to join them had to be Eddie Campbell, another Essex boy down in nearby Southend-on-Sea, his 'Letratone' impressionism and seaside slice-of-life total revelations to us when we discovered his limited circulation zine *Flick*. I think it's safe now for me to confess that on Saturday mornings, I would moonlight with the three of them in the *pssst!* darkroom and reduce their pages for free on the chemical PMT (photo-mechanical transfer) machinery to print from. What's more, several artists in the first *Escape* had either made their debut, or were about to, in the pages of *pssst*, not only Glen Dakin, but also Paul Bignell, Rian Hughes, Paul Johnson and Shaky Kane. In a real sense, *Fast Fiction Magazine*, and *Escape* that followed, owed much of their beginnings to *pssst!* magazine.

Pssst!, however, was not a model for *Escape*. For those, Peter and I looked abroad, as much to Europe as to America. There is no denying the fundamental example set by Spiegelman and Mouly's *Raw* by bridging the American underground with its European counterparts. We knew that the *Escape* strips, largely by unknowns, needed context to be understood and some star names to help them sell. We wanted to interweave the strips with editorial features and "Snacks with the Stars" interviews (Clerc, Beyer, Swarte, Mariscal, Briggs, Burns, Moore, etc.), a recipe applied by BD anthologies like *Métal Hurlant*, *Charlie Mensuel, (À Suivre)* and *PLG* in France, and by American '70s forerunners *Arcade*, *Heavy Metal* and *Cascade Comix Monthly*. We settled, for the first seven issues of *Escape*, on a digest size — cheaper to print, handy for mailing and what most small-pressers were used to and suited to. Covers were wraparound, laboriously hand-separated by Peter until full-process color arrived from issue six. With nobody getting paid at the outset except the printers, Peter and I put in a couple of hundred pounds each to produce a thousand copies of the first issue, with the cover and lead strip drawn in his "UKBD" style by Phil Elliott. We were off.

Considering its modest quality, *Escape* #1 generated a crazily disproportionate amount of media interest, especially in the music and style press. We found readers, subscribers, retailers, distributors and, from the second number, much-needed advertisers. We also found more artists, through the Fast Fiction self-publishing channels mainly, including Jamie Hewlett, Philip Bond, Paul Grist and Dave McKean. But *Escape* was

Considering its modest quality, *Escape* #1 generated a crazily disproportionate amount of media intrest.

A TALE FROM GIMBLEY
EARLY ONE EVENING, AS I STOOD BY THE RIVER
I GLANCED UP TO THE BRIDGE....
STOP!!
DON'T JUMP!
WHY NOT? IT MATTERS LITTLE WHETHER I DIVE INTO THE MURKY DEPTHS OF THE RIVER OR RETURN TO MY DREARY BEDSIT..
IN FACT THE RIVER BED WOULD MAKE A FITTING RESTING PLACE FOR MY STRIFE-TORN BODY..
YOU WOULD THROW AWAY YOUR EXISTENCE IN THE SAME WAY THAT I RIP THE PAGES FROM THIS MAGAZINE? FLUNG INTO THE RIVER WITH NO SENSE OF PRIDE OR DIGNITY.. SURELY YOU ARE WORTH MORE THAN A FEW SCRAPS OF PAPER
MY SOLILOQUY WORKED..
MIND YOU.. IT COST ME MY ONLY COPY OF ESCAPE!..
THE END

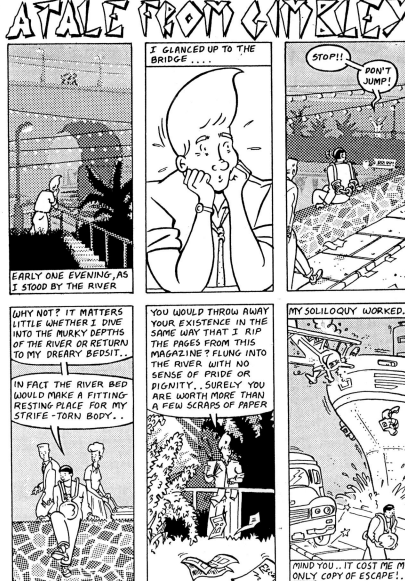

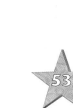

Chapter Six
The cycle of renewal in Art is pedalled by the periodic influx of stuff from somewhere else. That's why you need a Man at the Crossroads
HITHER
YON
INFLUENC
For three years he'll have been jabbering about what's going on in FRANCE. "La Ligne Claire" and all that.
One day they stop looking at all those Druillet monstrosities...
MINING ROBOTS! BUT CAN THEY STILL BE FUNCTIONING ?
© Druillet.
And decide that Hergé's the man to be with after all.
WOOU-HOUW-OU-OU-OU-WOOUUH!
Hergé 1948 ©Editions Casterman
The man at the Crossroads conveys it to Elliott and Elliott spends the rest of his life drawing 'clearlines'.
PERICLES THE PUNK WAS THROWING OUR PRECIOUS PORK PIES AT THE FLYING FISH ~
PLOP
PLOP
© Elliott '85
Serge Clerc will be one of the new French crop. In fact the NME will have been importing his little illustrations quite early
NME
WE POSE THE QUESTIONS AND QUESTION THE POSERS
© clerc
However, if you can read French, none of it is saying anything profound or memorable or even endearingly amusing on the level of Laurel and Hardy. It's just the next fashion.
48

always much more than merely the best of the UK small press. We found creators in all sorts of ways. From the UK underground press came relative veterans Hunt Emerson and Savage Pencil, who seemed to enjoy cutting loose in new directions in our pages. Myra Hancock was selling her spiky, spirited *Myra* magazines on Camden Lock market dressed like a punk match-girl or cinema usherette. Chris Long had just got back from Italy, where he had been contributing trendy *fumetti* to *Frigidaire* magazine. Later there was the thrill of "discovering" Carol Swain when she drew her first ever magical strip at an *Escape* workshop, and Warren Pleece exhibiting his mean and moody *noir* strips at his show.

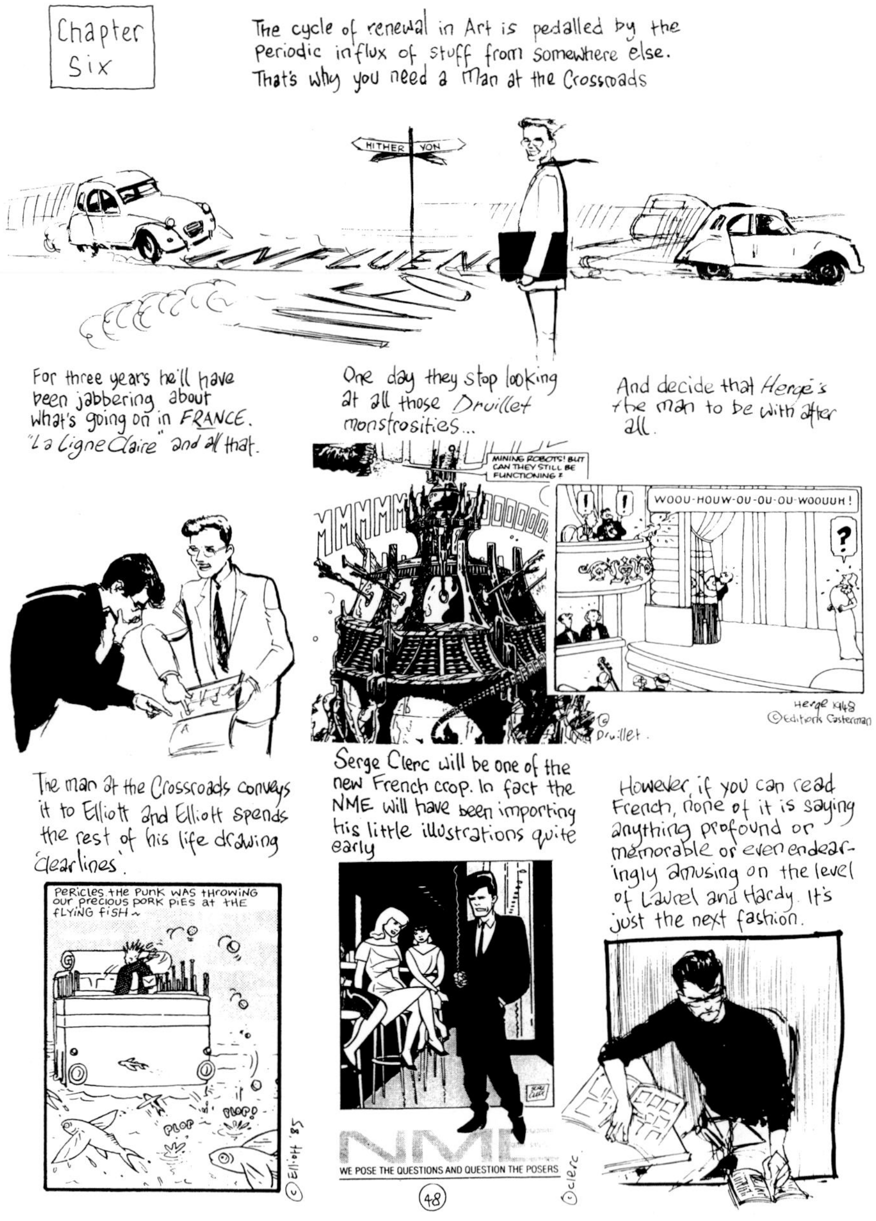

Rightly or wrongly, *Escape* was a living organism in restless evolution in format and contents. No issue was ever exactly like another. Inevitably, not every contributor liked everything in every issue. While we had some regulars for a time, there was a fairly rapid turnover partly due to our finding the next young guns to promote, making some artists feel overlooked or underappreciated. The turnover was also caused by artists moving to other projects and publishers. It was only human nature for Peter and me to feel nervous and reactive about these perceived threats to *Escape*'s identity. Knockabout started to pay *Escape* Artists to contribute to their eponymous comix, which helped persuade us that we had to start that too. *Escape* had always been run in an informal, gentleman's agreement manner, but when Fantagraphics insisted on tying cartoonists' strips in contracts, we felt pressured to try also, to a mixed response. Peter and I lived and breathed *Escape*, few people saw how much thought and work we poured into it. In the end, we came to realize that anyone could put artists from *Escape* into a magazine, but they didn't have the secret ingredient that defined *Escape*: our editorial vision.

I think there is a natural life cycle to that peculiar creature, the comics anthology. Like rock bands or marriages, they can't always last or stay the same. There is a tendency to start off with a core group and add to that gradually, often expanding the page count to the bursting point to accommodate them all. In *Escape*'s case, we kept on adding new artists, culminating in our bulging 'Bumper' issue seven. What often follows this is a total re-think, perhaps in the form of a shift in format, adding color or serials perhaps. With our eighth issue came the most controversial stage, a switch to American magazine format, reflecting our greater confidence in the contributors' skills, putting us more prominently on the racks and enabling us finally to translate work from Europe, reprint classics like *Krazy Kat* and show *Alec* upright as whole pages. There was also a change in *Escape*'s logo, from the scratchy italicized upper and lower case, Peter's writing in fountain pen, ascending hopefully to a crisp-edged graphic look, with extra prongs invented by Peter, all in bold capitals, horizontal, solid, confident. All but four of the 12 magazine-size covers were by non-British illustrators. These changes symbolized a long-expected shift away from *Escape*'s small-press origins.

With issue ten, after protracted negotiations, we were published squarebound by Titan Books, Britain's first graphic novel publisher of *Judge Dredd* and editions of DC Comics' hits, but with no magazine record. Try as they might, we resisted any attempts to dictate *Escape*'s contents, but it was not infrequently a bumpy ride. *Escape*'s newsstand sales were looking up with over 60% sell-through but confined to smaller London retailers. Titan was never behind our goal to get the magazine distributed more widely and nationally. To interest more non-comics readers, we began theming each issue. After two years and ten issues, we parted ways with #19, our last issue. Peter and I showed around a third incarnation of *Escape*, an upmarket monthly, bigger still with color and imported serials, which impressed several non-comics magazine publishers, but not enough to take the plunge. *Escape* did leave a void and I'm not the only one who thinks it has never quite been filled by subsequent Brit anthologies, however fine they were.

Rightly or wrongly, *Escape* was a living organism in restless evolution in format and contents.

Bottom: photograph of Bob Lynch, John Bagnall and Ed Pinsent. **Top:** page by Eddie Campbell from *Alec: How to be an Artist.* © 2002 Eddie Campbell.

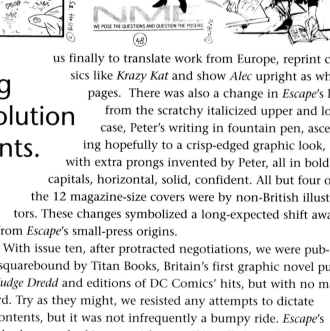

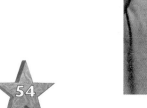

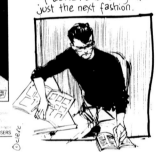

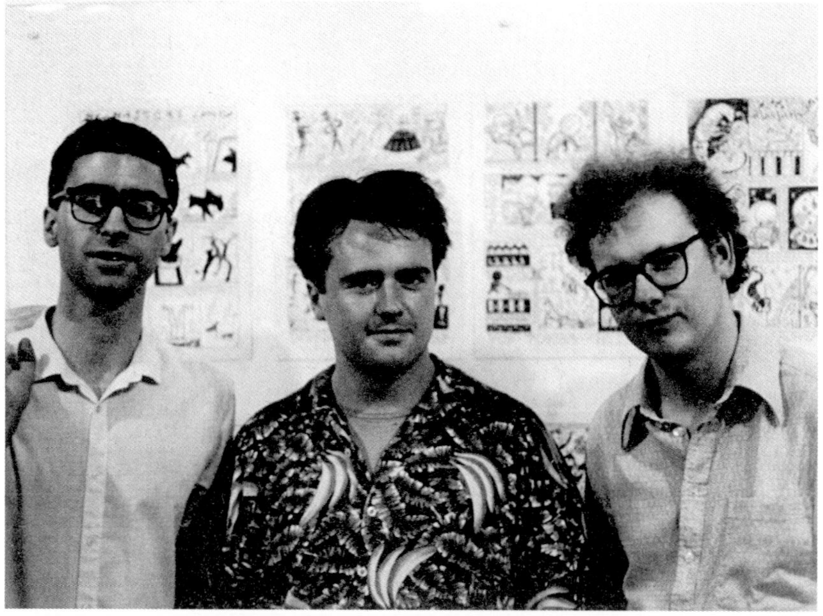

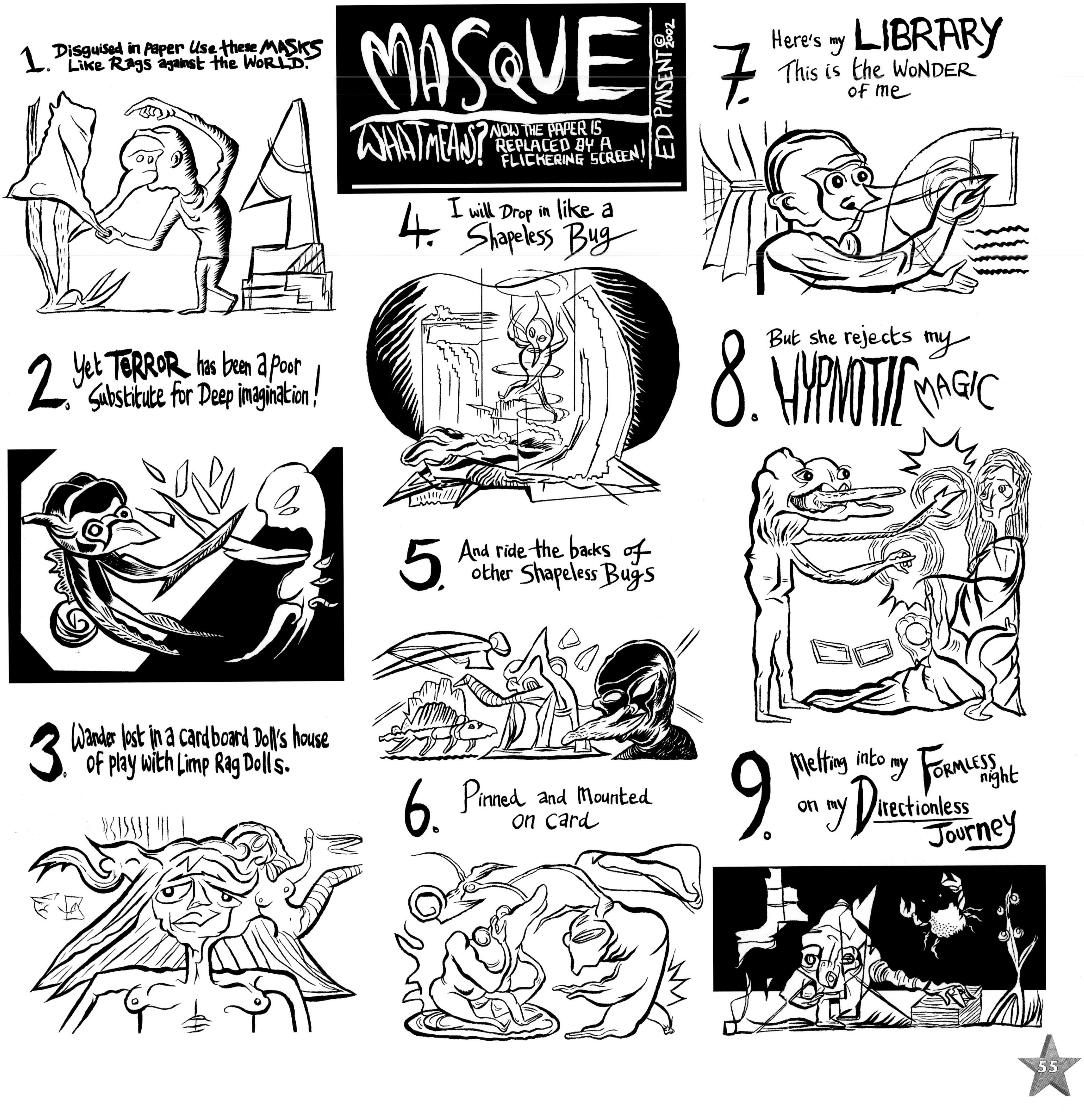
MASQUE
WHAT MEANS?
NOW THE PAPER IS REPLACED BY A FLICKERING SCREEN!
ED PINSENT © 2002
1. Disguised in Paper Use these MASKS Like Rags against the WORLD.
2. Yet TERROR has been a poor Substitute for Deep imagination!
3. Wander lost in a cardboard Doll's house of play with Limp Rag Dolls.
4. I will Drop in like a Shapeless Bug
5. And ride the backs of other Shapeless Bugs
6. Pinned and Mounted on card
7. Here's my LIBRARY This is the WONDER of me
8. But she rejects my HYPNOTIC MAGIC
9. Melting into my FORMLESS night on my Directionless Journey

This Page: "Masque," a new piece by Ed Pinsent. © 2002 Ed Pinsent.

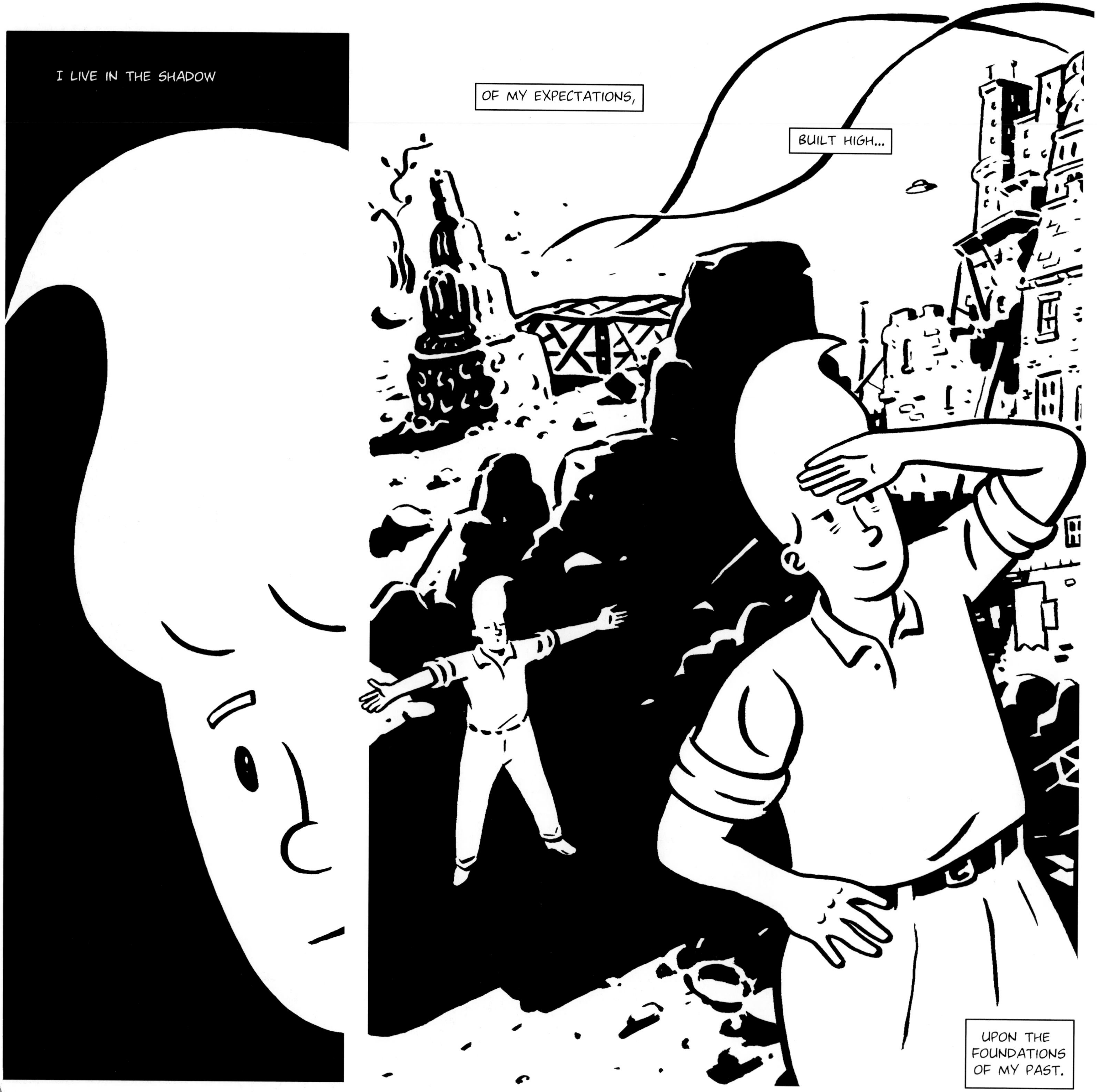
I LIVE IN THE SHADOW
OF MY EXPECTATIONS,
BUILT HIGH...
UPON THE FOUNDATIONS OF MY PAST.

This page: A new "Gimbley" by Phil Elliott. © 2002 Phil Elliott.

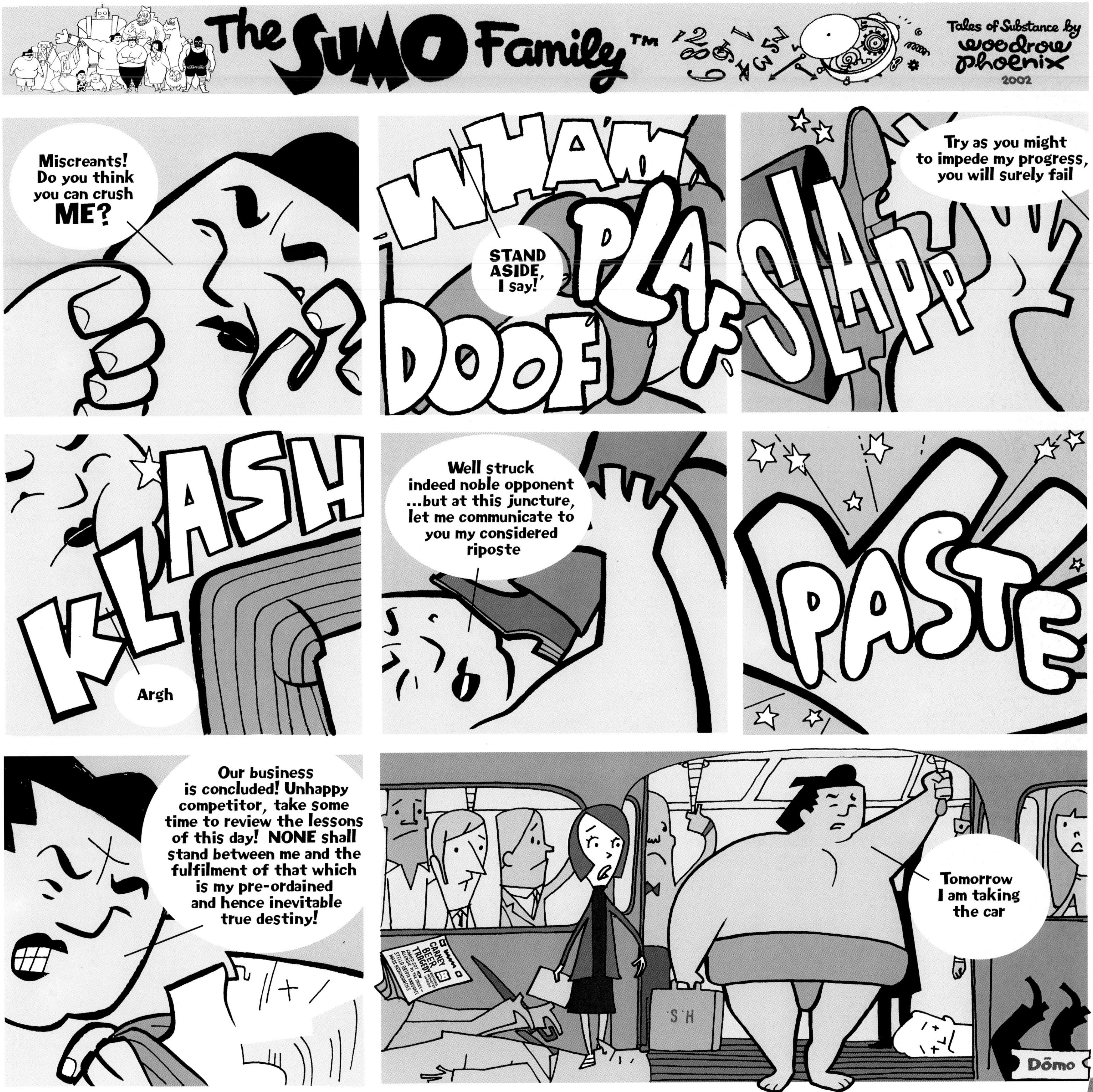
The SUMO Family™
Tales of Substance by woodrow phoenix 2002
Miscreants! Do you think you can crush ME?
WHAM
STAND ASIDE, I say!
DOOF
PLAF
SLAPP
Try as you might to impede my progress, you will surely fail
KLASH
Argh
Well struck indeed noble opponent ...but at this juncture, let me communicate to you my considered riposte
PASTE
Our business is concluded! Unhappy competitor, take some time to review the lessons of this day! NONE shall stand between me and the fulfilment of that which is my pre-ordained and hence inevitable true destiny!
CANNEY BEER TRAGEDY
H.S.
Tomorrow I am taking the car
Dōmo

This page: A new "The Sumo Family" by Woodrow Phoenix. © 2002 Woodrow Phoenix.

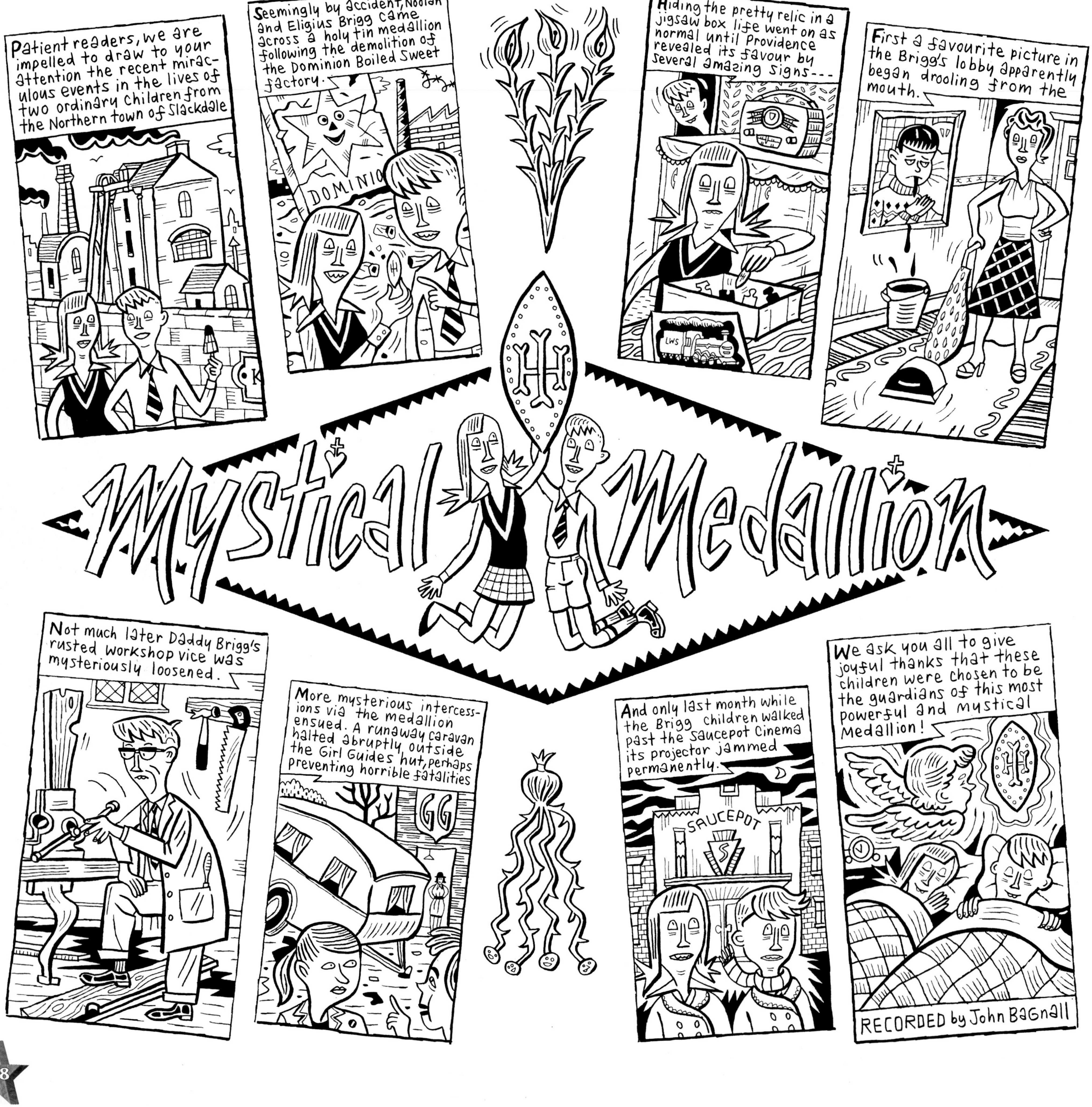
Patient readers, we are impelled to draw to your attention the recent miraculous events in the lives of two ordinary children from the Northern town of Slackdale
Seemingly by accident, Noolah and Eligius Brigg came across a holy tin medallion following the demolition of the Dominion Boiled Sweet factory.
DOMINIO
Hiding the pretty relic in a jigsaw box life went on as normal until Providence revealed its favour by several amazing signs---
LWS
First a favourite picture in the Brigg's lobby apparently began drooling from the mouth.
Mystical Medallion
Not much later Daddy Brigg's rusted workshop vice was mysteriously loosened.
More mysterious intercessions via the medallion ensued. A runaway caravan halted abruptly outside the Girl Guides hut, perhaps preventing horrible fatalities
GG
And only last month while the Brigg children walked past the Saucepot Cinema its projector jammed permanently.
SAUCEPOT
We ask you all to give joyful thanks that these children were chosen to be the guardians of this most powerful and mystical Medallion!
RECORDED by John BaGnall

This page: "Mystical Medallion," a new strip by John Bagnall. © 2002 John Bagnall.

Escape was also all about escaping the fetishistic fan-collector ghetto and reaching out to the rest of the population, the 'civilians' who might like comics but simply didn't know it yet. Peter and I always jumped at any chance to collaborate with other bodies to promote the *Escape* Artists, on art gallery shows, on seven-foot-high paintings for The Limelight nightclub, on supplements and catalogs for the Institute of Contemporary Arts "Comic Iconoclasm" and The French Institute's "The Black Island: Britain in *Bandes Dessinées*" and any opportunity for articles in the press or coverage on TV and radio. The social side was also important. *Escape* Artists would meet up at regular pub sessions after comic marts and through the month, joined by visitors in town like Ben Katchor or Dylan Horrocks, contacts from Europe and our latest newcomers. Friendships and dreams formed over a glass of beer. We laid on *Escape* parties, food and booze upstairs at a pub after conventions, teas and Christmas celebrations at our Munster Road home and studio. John Bagnall reminded me, "I remember on one visit laughing at Mark Robinson's wry comments that the UK scene was more vicar's tea party than the Haight-Ashbury revolution he'd just watched in a TV documentary on Robert Crumb!" *Escape* was post- but not anti-underground, more new wave and new romantic than punk, strongly pro-European but at the same time (at least initially) deliberately very English. Another reviewer criticized our first issue for being like a village cricket match.

I had failed to consider how painful the innocent raising of hopes could be.

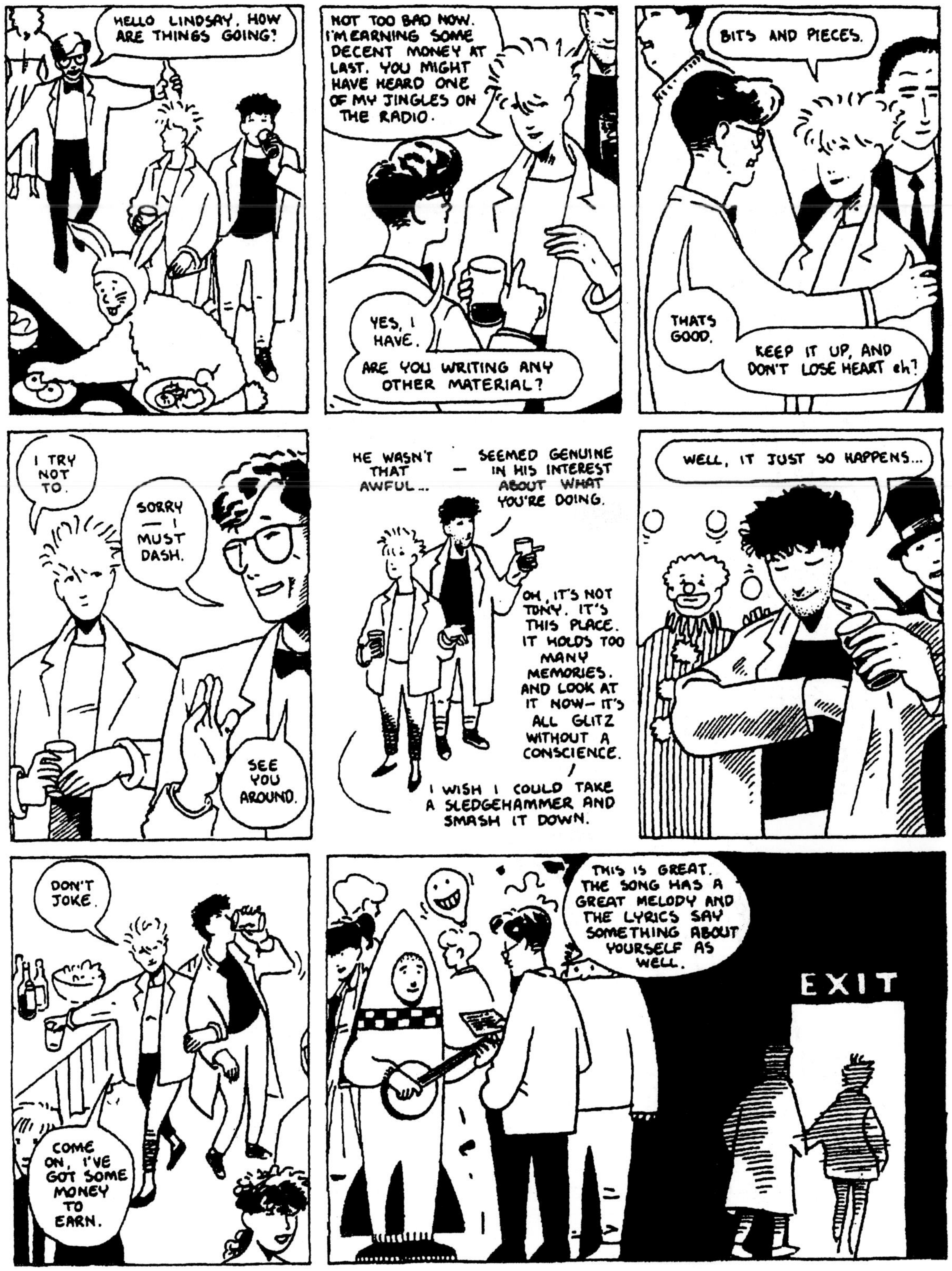
HELLO LINDSAY. HOW ARE THINGS GOING?
NOT TOO BAD NOW. I'M EARNING SOME DECENT MONEY AT LAST. YOU MIGHT HAVE HEARD ONE OF MY JINGLES ON THE RADIO.
YES, I HAVE.
ARE YOU WRITING ANY OTHER MATERIAL?
BITS AND PIECES.
THATS GOOD.
KEEP IT UP, AND DON'T LOSE HEART eh?
I TRY NOT TO.
SORRY — I MUST DASH.
SEE YOU AROUND.
HE WASN'T THAT AWFUL...
— SEEMED GENUINE IN HIS INTEREST ABOUT WHAT YOU'RE DOING.
OH, IT'S NOT TONY. IT'S THIS PLACE. IT HOLDS TOO MANY MEMORIES. AND LOOK AT IT NOW— IT'S ALL GLITZ WITHOUT A CONSCIENCE.
I WISH I COULD TAKE A SLEDGEHAMMER AND SMASH IT DOWN.
WELL, IT JUST SO HAPPENS...
DON'T JOKE.
COME ON, I'VE GOT SOME MONEY TO EARN.
THIS IS GREAT. THE SONG HAS A GREAT MELODY AND THE LYRICS SAY SOMETHING ABOUT YOURSELF AS WELL.
EXIT

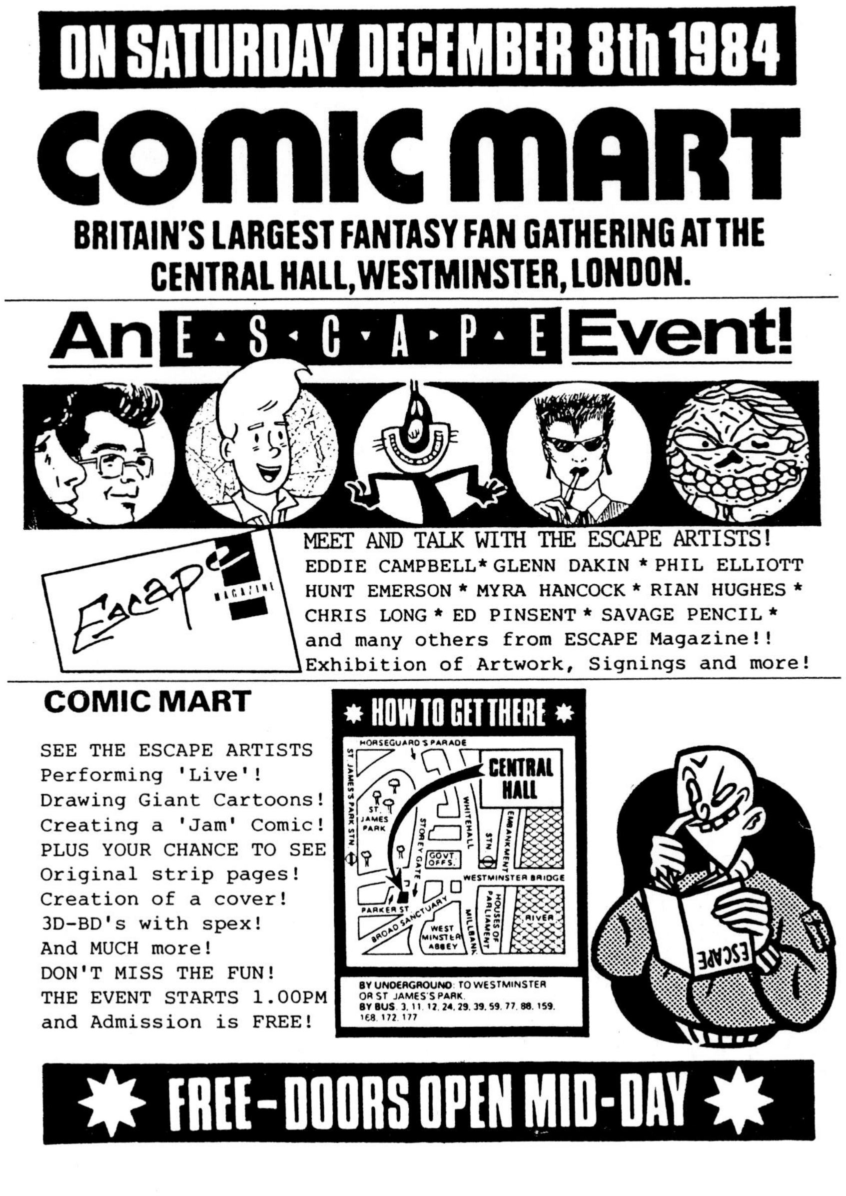
ON SATURDAY DECEMBER 8th 1984
COMIC MART
BRITAIN'S LARGEST FANTASY FAN GATHERING AT THE CENTRAL HALL, WESTMINSTER, LONDON.
An E·S·C·A·P·E Event!
Escape MAGAZINE
MEET AND TALK WITH THE ESCAPE ARTISTS!
EDDIE CAMPBELL* GLENN DAKIN * PHIL ELLIOTT
HUNT EMERSON * MYRA HANCOCK * RIAN HUGHES *
CHRIS LONG * ED PINSENT * SAVAGE PENCIL *
and many others from ESCAPE Magazine!!
Exhibition of Artwork, Signings and more!
COMIC MART
SEE THE ESCAPE ARTISTS
Performing 'Live'!
Drawing Giant Cartoons!
Creating a 'Jam' Comic!
PLUS YOUR CHANCE TO SEE
Original strip pages!
Creation of a cover!
3D-BD's with spex!
And MUCH more!
DON'T MISS THE FUN!
THE EVENT STARTS 1.00PM
and Admission is FREE!
HOW TO GET THERE
HORSEGUARDS PARADE
CENTRAL HALL
ST JAMES PARK
WESTMINSTER BRIDGE
PARKER ST
BROAD SANCTUARY
WEST MINSTER ABBEY
RIVER
BY UNDERGROUND: TO WESTMINSTER OR ST JAMES'S PARK.
BY BUS: 3, 11, 12, 24, 29, 39, 59, 77, 88, 159, 168, 172, 177
ESCAPE
FREE - DOORS OPEN MID-DAY

Top right: page from "Stagestruck," written by Phil Elliott and drawn by Paul Grist. © 2002 Phil Elliott and Paul Grist. **Bottom:** Flyer for Escape Artists Event, 1984. *Escape* © 2002 Paul Gravett and Peter Stanbury.

It would be a mistake to pretend that everything went smoothly and everyone got along. The way Glenn Dakin saw it, in *The Comics Journal* #238, October 2001, *Escape* "provided a focal point for people. People would meet up and discuss their dreams and ideas and get together as friends or have arguments and fall out and sometimes even if somebody annoys you or somebody didn't seem to have respect for your work, that would be enough to fill you with enough anger to go out there and try to prove them wrong." Eddie Campbell has transformed his experiences of *Escape* and that whole heady period into an unapologetically skewed diary cum self-help graphic novel, *Alec: How To Be An Artist*. It does capture those days, and I can't help feeling flattered by his mostly positive portrayals of me as The Man at the Crossroads, but everyone had his or her own perspective and personal history. With hindsight I am more aware of some of the expectations which, knowingly or not, *Escape* helped to raise in many people, not least in Peter and myself, and which could not

CAROL SWAIN

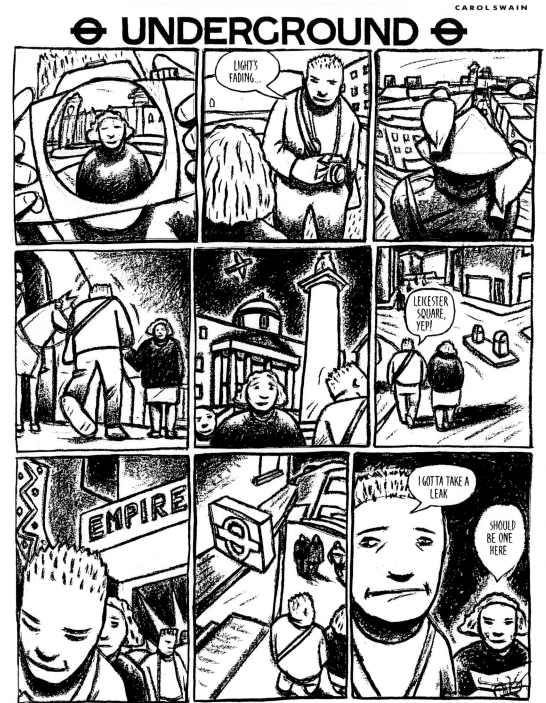

Speech bubbles in comic: "LIGHT'S FADING…" / "LEICESTER SQUARE, YEP!" / "I GOTTA TAKE A LEAK" / "SHOULD BE ONE HERE" / "EMPIRE"

Escape did have its critics and fallings out.

always come to fruition. Phil Elliott has written movingly about these ambivalent feelings in two stories drawn by Paul Grist. In "Stage Struck," I appear in a less flattering guise as "Tony," an energetic but flighty band promoter, always positive but always in search of new musical acts. Phil's alter ego is a woman singer-songwriter who feels hurt and disappointed and sees the field become "all glitz without a conscience." In the second story called "In Sight Of … ," a coda set a year later, Phil's songstress seems more reconciled and realistic, if less trusting, yet she remains drawn to the "tantalizing enticements" from publishers. This is a sensitive, sobering pair of pieces; I had failed to consider how painful the innocent raising of hopes could be.

Escape did have its critics and fallings out. As John Bagnall recently expressed to me, "To some readers at the time, *Escape* Artists were sometimes generalized as the school of strips 'where nothing happened,' but their approaches were actually much more disparate. As for the social scene, there was a loose sense of unity when we would meet up in London, though naturally not everyone got on well or were even huge fans of certain people's work." Even so, as Eddie Campbell commented in *Arkensword* #17/18 in 1986, "the whole small-press movement [was] the first real upheaval in this country of comics as a genuine Art — Art being to me a thing which is a lively part of life while commenting on

life — as opposed to comics as journalism-cartooning or comics as a collecting-hobby or comics as boys' power fantasies." Traditionalist comics readers and professionals were made uncomfortable by *Escape*'s pretension to raise the ambition of the medium and not define or confine it to chuckles, fantasy escapism or pimply rebellion. Comics is too strange a beast to be straitjacketed this way. Eddie Campbell recently wrote to me on this: "I remember what I liked about your *Escape* philosophy was that comics were culture and that they were of a particular sort, comics culture, a vision of the world cultivated through the best cartoons. A hip, alert, humorous, informed, aware, international view. We could assume that one who knew all the right comics would not be a political jerk, for instance. Nor would he or she be an Art jerk."

To give people a reminder, or a first taste, of the qualities of *Escape* Artists, a selection of brand new strips, limited to ten, have been commissioned for the Winter 2003 Special of *The Comics Journal*. For some, this unofficial *Escape* #19 1/2 was a surprise but welcome return to the drawing board and to characters they had not written in some time. Hunt Emerson brings his cheesy-grinning Calculus Cat back home again to his sole companion, the babbling boob tube, his animated angst as fevered as ever. To the lightness of Phil Elliott's Franco-Belgian roots — Hergé's clear line, Chaland's Atom Style — he has added darker, deeper shadows and symbols that fill the world of his quiffed everyman, Gimbley. Abe is now a husband and father, like Glenn Dakin himself, who blends his playful, fun-filled cartooning with his other register, a painterly wistfulness. John Bagnall has left behind his romance with Americana to subjects closer to home, to the spiritual foibles and family secrets of his home turf in the North of England, his drawing now bolder and more nuanced. Chris Reynolds conjures up again his subtly unnerving yet reserved atmosphere, and Los Bros Pleece, Warren and Gary, reunite at last for more of their biting chiaroscuro satire. Carol Swain's subdued players pulse in her charcoal soft focus, our gaze hovering threateningly all around them. Ed Pinsent disorientates and fascinates with his fractured creatures and clipped wording. Deranged yet surgically precise, Savage Pencil carves into his victims, while Woodrow Phoenix revives his Saturday morning TV absurdism, the charmingly non-PC Sumo Family.

Peter and I always had faith in these and the other *Escape* Artists that their work was valid, original and could find their audiences. By the time *Escape* came to an end, or soon after, many of the creators we had helped to get wider exposure found clients and outlets for their work. While some have since left comics for new careers, passions and family lives, many are still very much involved in today's comics-related culture, with new book collections, comics, even live-action film and TV animations forthcoming. Their emergence marked a sea change in British comics culture and gave a clear signal for others to be themselves, to find their voices and to sing the comics only they could sing. ★★★

Dedicated to my late friend Alan Gaulton.

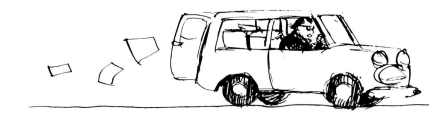

Top left: Page by Carol Swain from *Escape* #19. © 2002 Carol Swain. **Bottom right:** Panel of Alan Gaulton driving *Escape* from the printer by Eddie Campbell. © 2002 Eddie Campbell.

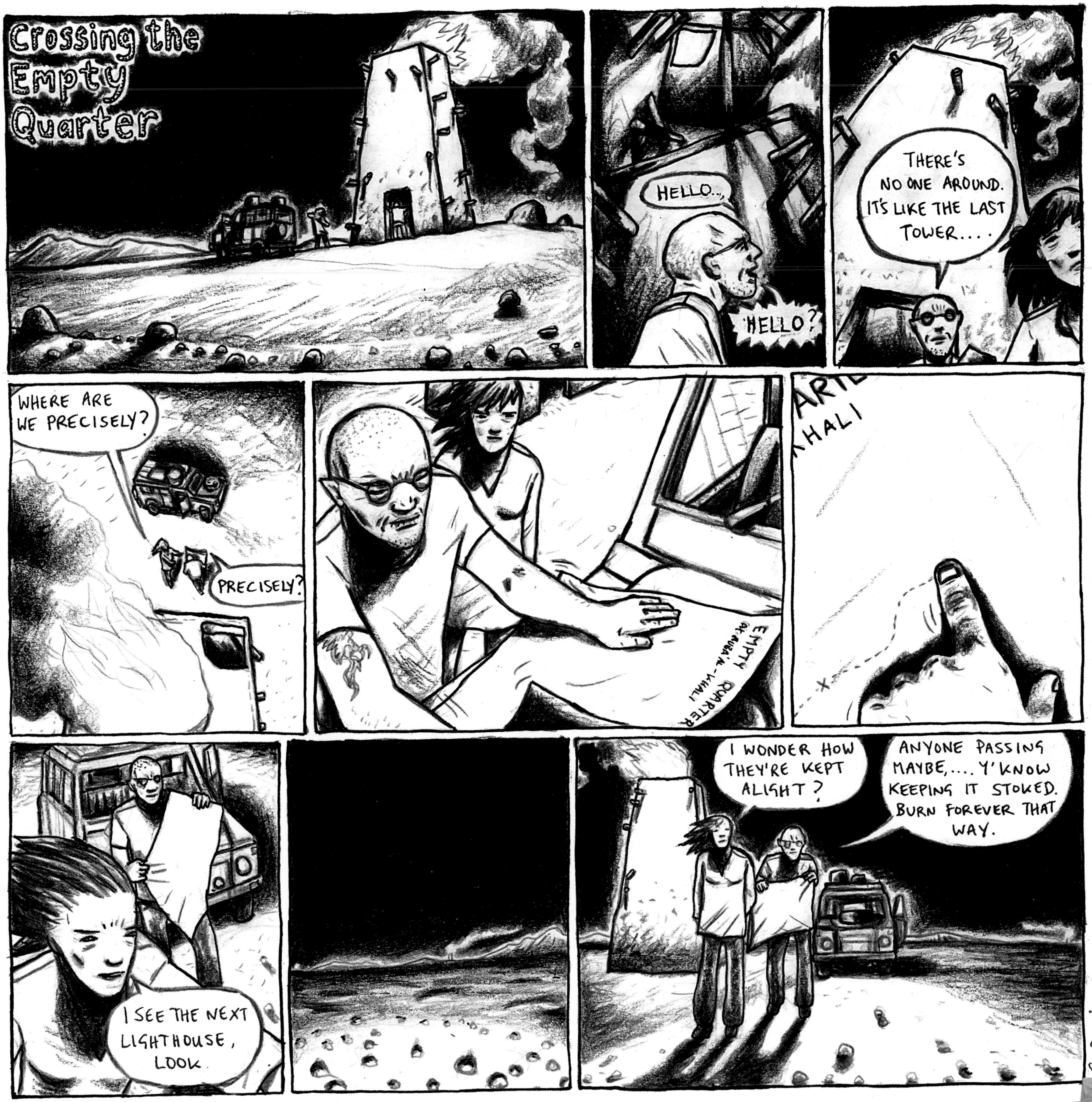
Crossing the Empty Quarter
HELLO..,
HELLO?
THERE'S NO ONE AROUND. IT'S LIKE THE LAST TOWER....
WHERE ARE WE PRECISELY?
PRECISELY?
EMPTY QUARTER
I SEE THE NEXT LIGHTHOUSE, LOOK.
I WONDER HOW THEY'RE KEPT ALIGHT?
ANYONE PASSING MAYBE,.... Y'KNOW KEEPING IT STOKED. BURN FOREVER THAT WAY.
C. Swain 2002

This Page: A new comic by Carol Swain.

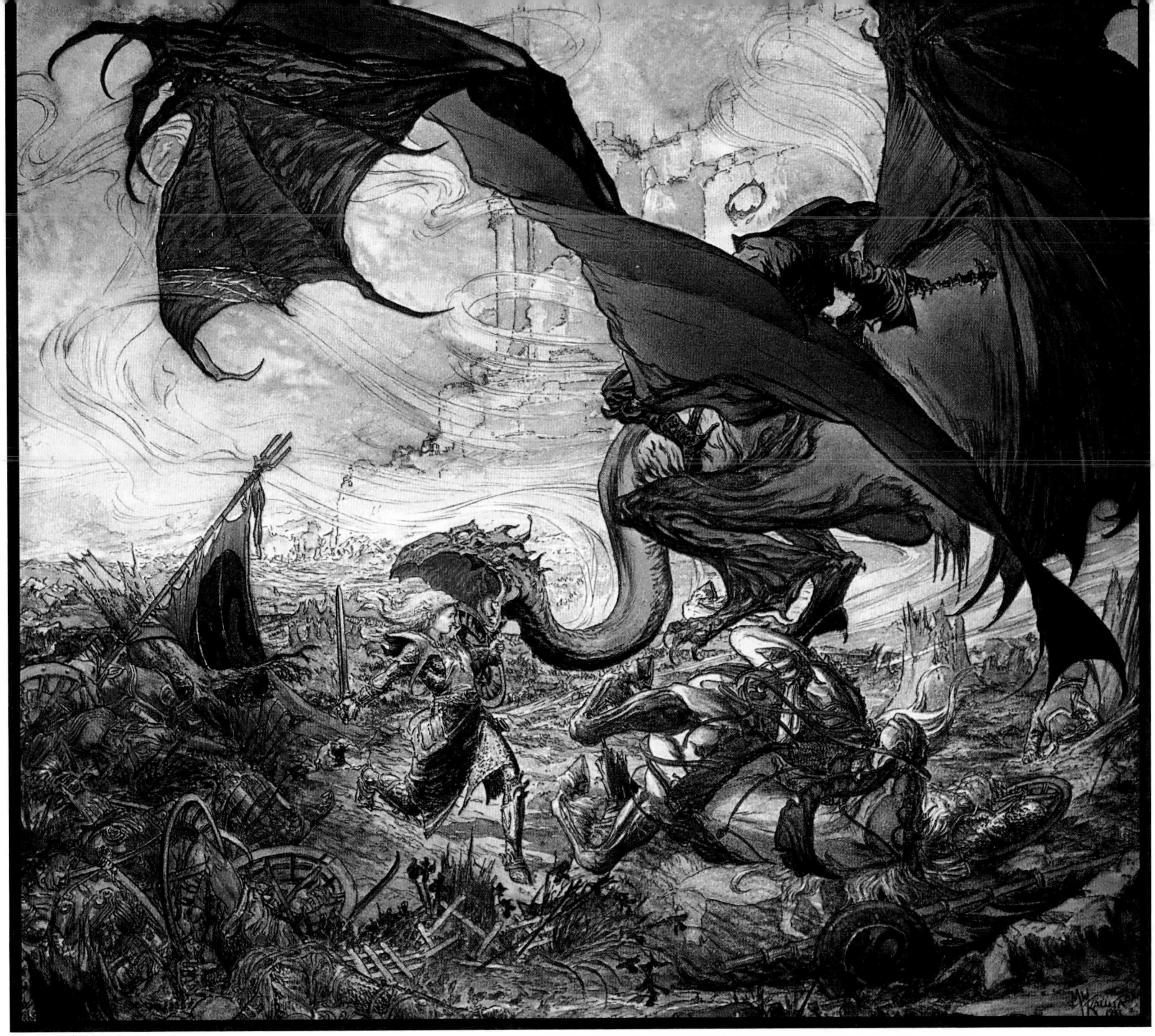

"Theoden Espies the Serpent Banner" from *Wings of Twilight: The Art of Michael Kaluta.* © 2002 Michael Kaluta.

BRAVE NOUVEAU WORLDS

Two New Books Showcase the Sublime Art of Michael Kaluta

by Kenneth Smith

I declare at the outset a bias or two: I not only am partial to Mike Kaluta's art but have found him for over three decades a simpatico artist and friend. With reviews even more than with realities, let the buyer beware. Reviews without bias are contradictions in terms.

Esthetes who delight in the ripening of a florid imagination have to find Mike Kaluta's career something rich and exotic. His earliest publication in fanzines like *Spa Fon* and *Squa Tront* gave only the bare outlines of the kinds of sources he loved and drew inspiration from — *Planet Comics,* the wonderful age of SF pulps, the elegant posters of Alphonse Mucha, Frazetta's *Famous Funnies* covers, the delirial panoramas of Roy Krenkel and Al Williamson collaborating in EC's *Weird Science* and *Weird Fantasy,* etc. Mike was readily embraced by DC as a superb splash-panelist, a brooding Art-Nouveau mind capable of instantly plunging the reader into a dense and ornate otherworldliness. He did some of his most astounding fine-art fantasy work for Christopher Enterprises' portfolios and prints, and his contributions to the art book *The Studio* — documenting his productivity together with Barry Smith, Bernie Wrightson and Jeff Jones — are truly for aficionados of fantasy art as much a part of American culture in that time as Woodstock or Crumb was. Tundra's little collection of Mike's sketchbook work, like Glimmer Graphics' little art book, was only so many hors d'oeuvres out of a vastly richer kitchen. His countless comic-book covers alone would make

"Jared and the Forest Elemental" from *Wings of Twilight: The Art of Michael Kaluta.* © 2002 Michael Kaluta.

an outstanding art book, and his graphic-novel and design work for the stage production *Starstruck* truly should have lodged his style in the pantheon of American illustrators. Kaluta has been an energy-geyser, a pipeline to the great forms and styles through which modern illustration and fantasy art evolved.

Some new riches have been unearthed — and high time it is — from Kaluta's cache of finely orchestrated work: this past year after a long drought we were treated to two excellent books, both rife with the material of his surreal imagination, and different enough that neither is superfluous or overshadowed.

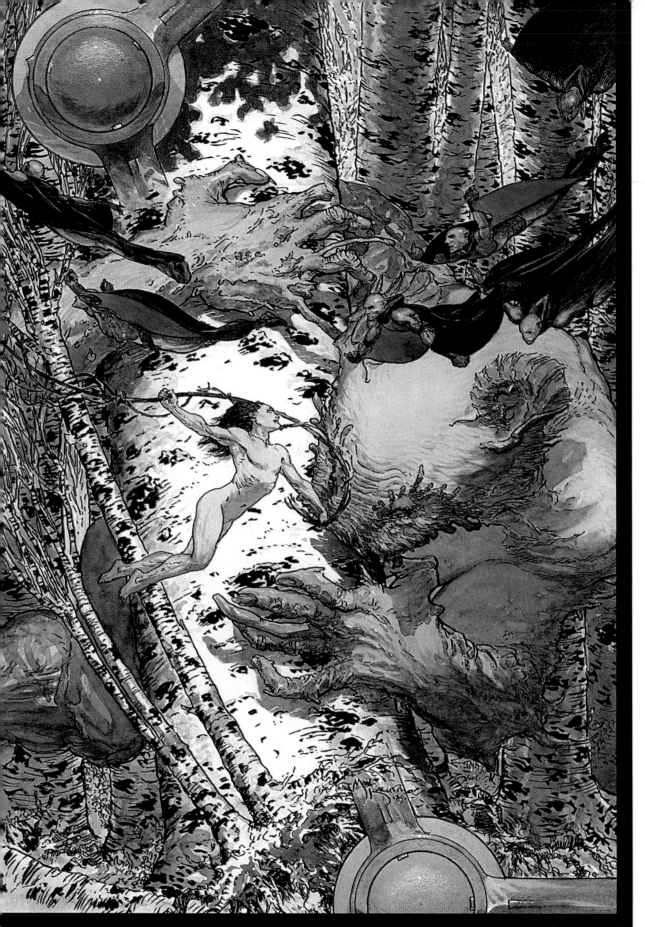

NBM has just issued *Wings of Twilight,* subtitled "The Art of Michael Kaluta," and Vanguard has produced *Echoes,* subtitled "The Drawings of Michael William Kaluta." NBM's volume is in a larger format, replete with finished art although it incorporates many intricate sketches, and aims to be truly an art book. Kaluta comes from the work-ethic school of art, and the detail he invests in many pieces is often mesmerizing. His fantasy art is intriguing and counterintuitive, flying in the face of whatever contemporary viewers may expect: he borrows many devices and forms from *Jugendstil* or art nouveau (but bends them generally to sinister effect), and others from Art Deco (but inlays these also with *noir*-grotesqueries that insinuate us into an often wicked or sly dreamworld). Mike is an artist who plainly has the courage of his confabulations, able to make the most *outré* subjects cogent and enveloping. Mike stresses the capaciousness of imagination that he developed as a Catholic youth, and in truth he brings an ardent quality of belief in the things he creates as rich and livable worlds, as concrete as the intersection of 45th Street and Seventh Avenue.

Some of Kaluta's pieces, like *Black Aria* (p. 13 of *Wings of Twilight),* have the classic and operatic tenor of Von Bayros' sublime plates from Dante. *The Dark Sphinx* (p. 22 of *Wings)* shows the kind of cleft dimensions — the windows into dreamworlds — that the French Decadents and surrealists explored. I believe it was Theodore Sturgeon who gave up on trying to describe the ineffable fruits of R. A. Lafferty's genius — all he could do was call these unique wonders of mythopoeia "lafferties." So too with Kaluta's exquisite *Stealer of Souls* (p. 34 of *Wings), In the Twinkling of an Eye* (p. 78), and *Veep 7 Vacationing on Aguatunusia*, all certainly quintessential kalutanesias, the products of a feverish kalutalobe.

"The Dark Sphinx" from *Wings of Twilight: The Art of Michael Kaluta*. © 2002 Michael Kaluta.

Kaluta cites something very sobering that Roy Krenkel observed: "The future is commonplace to the people living in it." Roy was a cosmopolitan and erudite imagination who sought out the exotic audacities of artists from Segrelles to Pogany, to Booth, Norman Lindsay, and beyond and if anyone has thought about the other side of that screen onto which we project our utmost hopes for beauty and transfigured life, it was indeed Roy. In every evolved or imagined world, whatever forms win out will inevitably make that world a mundane, even banal reality, no matter how rare it may look to the eyes of a stranger. Fantasy art is the search for those pristine fountains of forms that our dreadful and dull realities have not yet sullied. From the serene architectural fantasies of Franklin Booth, Roy grew the elegant fluted and classical futurist cities he passed on to Al Williamson's imagination. Kaluta's work is also grown over with his own architectural and enframing stylistics, but he is, like Al, now our only living link to that splendid Booth/Krenkel architectural dream, cities drawn out of the earth like crystal reeds grown in a cloistered, still cavern.

Just in what it sets out to cover, Vanguard's *Echoes* certainly has the stronger lot of sketches, faces, architecture, figures, and other energetic material. It was selected with a fine eye to illustrate the virtues of any artist applying him- or herself to a sketchbook, capturing visions at their peak of heat, before the rendering or "realizing" draftsmanly mind begins to make things too much like the inventory of commodities that belong in our day-to-day world. Not just in his futurism but in the elan of the figures he spills across the page, Mike proves himself a worthy successor to Krenkel, that musketeer of the grand gesture and statuesquely struck pose. We very nearly have two completely different vistas from his artistic mind in these two books.

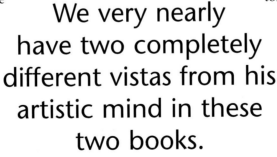

We very nearly have two completely different vistas from his artistic mind in these two books.

The production values in Vanguard's *Echoes* have an apparent edge over *Wings of Twilight,* although the art reproduced in the two books differs drastically and NBM's *Wings* is unmatched in its superb tapestry of Kaluta's paintings. Richness of tone in Vanguard's inks brings out something more like the luster and depth of glazed oil paintings (true also of the B&W work that predominates in *Echoes;* even pencil roughs seem varnished and resonant in this presentation). NBM's quality of inks is certainly true to the splendid watercolor renderings that predominate in its *Wings,* but Vanguard has pushed production standards a little further.

Decades ago art directors suggested to me the general theory (as they had been taught) of what commercial art demanded: it was necessary for an artist's work and style to be *iconic* or *archetypal.* When a job came to them that called for witty satire or folksy cartoonish effects or high-energy athletics or a nuanced portrait, the look of an artist's portfolio of work should be so distinctive and so perfectly right for the required effect that that work would serve not only as the instantly recognizable signature of that whole approach but also as the natural lens through which the art director could conceive how the piece ought to be strategized. In marketing, this strength or potency is known as "share of mind": Xerox,

Top: Concept drawing for proposed *G-Men* movie from *Echoes, The Drawings of Michael William Kaluta.* **Bottom:** Concept drawing for *Darkman* movie from *Echoes.* Both © 2002 Michael Kaluta.

Coke, Frigidaire, Scotch tape, etc. have spent billions on advertising to buy a *presumption,* a piece of the consumer's spontaneous intuitive mind, such that he is tacitly influenced to think of a whole genre of commodity in terms of their names — when we think of toilet paper or motor oil or steak seasonings, our consciousness runs effortlessly to those brand-names that have become archetypes or idiograms, paradigms for a whole generic type of thing.

For the artist this demands a wholehearted investment in his work, every production becoming saturated with his thoroughly original and thoroughly appropriate organic vision of how such art should be. And the reward for the artist is that he or she — his/her name and style — become the intimate terms in which appropriately conceived tasks will be cast, so to speak, the mother-tongue of imagination. The artist's name becomes synonymous with an entire mode of world, a proprietary dream-logic, the vocabulary or color-palette in which we couch a tone of feelings and for which we require those artists' labors to fulfill

our vague intimations. The challenge to such artists is that they must inveigle their work seductively, as virtually Platonic Ideas, into the minds of those who commission art.

Mike Kaluta's work in science-fantasy and comics has become one of those signature styles, like Frazetta, Giger, Raymond, Kley, Crumb and only a few others. It owns now a reserved parking space in our minds: It has its own dream-engine ready to be kick-started by a new piece of art from him. Over three decades he has produced such exquisite covers, splash pages and whole stories as have few other talents in our time, prolific and painstakingly filigreed work and all of it aromatic with the sense of wonder from the great age of pulps and SF digests. He remains a virtuoso at world-spinning, a Designated Creator for whole ranks of kalutoid creatures and persons.

— Mike is not such a close friend that I wouldn't give away one of his darker secrets, a dirty little fact that may well ruin him. Brace yourselves. Mike has, horror of horrors, an *aristocratic* sensibility: he has a taste for what is exemplary, for the finest work of the finest imaginations that preceded him, for the most daunting challenges in form and texture, for surpassing always the best work he himself has already done. For three decades now Mike Kaluta has had the audacity in our aristocrat-hating society to purvey work that is unfailingly subtle, devoid mostly of brawny heroes and buxom heroines; his work intrigues imaginations to be curious about the extraordinary, the cryptic and the sublime. He has kept his work and his career afloat without pandering to the barbaric elements in the market, and in these years that's saying something prodigious indeed.

There: I said it. Yahoos be damned. And even if Mike never speaks to me again, I outed him as an extraordinary imagination, one who works like a devout cloudbound trapper at capturing these singular dream-angels of the upper ether.

Books reviewed:
Wings of Twilight, The Art of Michael Kaluta (NBM, hardback, 2001, 80 pp., color and b&w, $24.95).
Echoes, The Drawings of Michael William Kaluta (Vanguard, hardback, 2000, 112+ pp., b&w, $27.95). ★★★

NEW FROM NBM

OUT NOW AND COMING SOON

DR. JEKYLL & MR. HYDE
Lorenzo Mattotti • Jerry Kramsky

At last, the return of one of the most influential comic artists of the last two decades! Mattotti (Fires), along with long-time collaborator Kramsky, creates a spectacular adaptation of the Robert Louis Stevenson classic of horror, emphasizing it as a psychological thriller.

At the height of his career, Dr. Jekyll pursues research on the duality of the soul. Secretly, he perfects a serum which he experiments with upon himself. Thus is he able to scientifically recreate the duality of the soul and bring to life, through extreme pain, the abominable Mr. Hyde. Powerless in front of the crimes committed by his alter ego, will Jekyll end up losing control of his destiny?

9x12, 64pp., full color hardcover: $15.95,
ISBN 1-56163-330-5

MATTOTTI & KRAMSKY
DR. JEKYLL & MR. HYDE
NBM Comics Lit

HOUSE OF JAVA, Vol.2
Mark Murphy

The newest collection of warm slice of life stories without the cynicism. Some melancholic, some hopeful, some humorous, all keenly and quietly observant. Main stories include 'Steven', exploring the blurry line between friendship and love between 2 comics fans, 'Tide Pools', where a visiting student encounters a girl with an itch to move on and out of her small town life but no gumption to go through with it, the particularly remarkable 'May 27th', which brings a student social worker face to face with delinquency brought on by lower class despair, and 'The Burial', with its aura of mystery, in which a terrible secret is literally unearthed leading to an insightful revelation. Collected from the comic book issues 1 through 4.

6x9, 96pp., B&W, clothbound, color jacket, $15.95, ISBN 1-56163-328-3

House of Java
NBM Comics Lit

NO PASARÁN!
Vol.2
VITTORIO GIARDINO
NBM Comics Lit

Max Friedman: NO PASARAN! VOLUME 2
Vittorio Giardino

The leftist forces are retreating north as Franco's army advances with the help of German and Italian aviation. Max Friedman approaches the front, posing as a photographer in a small group of foreign journalists. He flashes back to battles fought with his old comrade Guido Treves, who has gone missing and is the object of his mission. Amidst the ruin of war, Claire, the pretty Belgian reporter who got Max his press credentials, is developing a strong attraction to him, arousing the jealousy of her fellow reporter and would-be-boyfriend, Phil Lester. Caught in the middle of a retreat, Max and Claire get separated from the rest of their group. They have to cross a mountain pass and take shelter in a hut -- the romantic tension builds, but gets snuffed by the urgent need to press onward.

81/2x11, 48pp., full color trade pb.: $11.95
ISBN 1-56163-313-5

THE YELLOW·JAR
TWO·TALES·FROM·JAPANESE·TRADITION
PATRICK·ATANGAN
VOLUME I
NBM
WITH·INTRODUCTION·BY
P·CRAIG·RUSSELL

THE YELLOW JAR
Patrick Atangan

Introducing the delightfully precise and beautifully designed art of Patrick Atangan in a new series of adaptations of traditional Asian tales. This book, drawn in the ukiyo-e style (world of floating pictures), presents "The Yellow Jar" which centers around a simple fisherman and a beautiful maiden he takes as wife, after finding her in a magic jar. However, she is abducted by a demon warrior considerably more powerful than the simple fisherman. But the fisherman's resolve, even after many unsuccessful attempts to rescue her, does not flinch... In "Two Chrysanthemum Maidens", a monk is faced with two rather strange wild flowers in his carefully tended garden. They are wild and have planted themselves there at will. They are weeds but they are lovely like women.

81/2x61/2, 48pp., full color hardcover: $12.95
ISBN 1-56163-331-3

LI'L SANTA
Lewis Trondheim • Thierry Robin

You have no idea what Santa must go through, all the way up there at the North Pole, until you read this suspenseful, fully silent graphic novel! Besides the huge yearly job that faces him, the North Pole is no friendly place! Santa must use all his best cunning to make all the world's kids happy. A light, delightfully original album for Christmas that will amuse all ages.

81/2x11, 48pp., full color hardcover: $14.95
ISBN 1-56163-335-6

Thierry Robin
Lewis Trondheim
Li'l Santa
NBM

NBM, 555 8th Ave., Ste. 1202, New York, NY 10018, 1-800-886-1223

MC, VISA accepted, add $3 P&H for 1st item, $1 each additional. $1 per comic book.

www.nbmpublishing.com

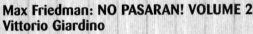

WITH YOUR CLUBS AND TRUCULENCE
"CLUB" - YOU CALL "CLUB"-
IT EXTENDS LIKE A STENCH FROM YOUR FILTHY SPIRITS!!!

This Page: From *New Hat*. © 2002 Tom Hart.

WORKING HARD

The Comics of Tom Hart

by Tom Spurgeon

In a field historically dominated by artwork that can stand alone as illustration, Tom Hart gives us comics where the words can be isolated as poetry. His comic-book novella *New Hat* (Black Eye, 1995) opens with one of the funniest and most provocative uses of the English language in the medium's history. Tied to a wooden post by a band of crude, muttering strong-arms, the poet Pardon Parcel screeches a hymn of protest and moral outrage for the ages. Hart's exquisite word choices and assured pacing propel the reader through the eight pages like a gunshot, the rhythms of individual lines echoing in one's ears for the remainder of the volume. The speech is both touching and deeply ridiculous, acting as an introduction to the larger work's values and as a subtle character moment whereby the unbowed protagonist reclaims for himself the lunatic joys of verse. It is virtuoso stagecraft, and demands to be read out loud.

> Strike me down!!
>
> With your clubs and truculence
> "Club" — you call "club"
> It extends like a stench from your filthy spirits!!!
>
> Loud and furious mules!
> Buck and whinny your indignation and subterfuge!!!
> Your "clubs" and your "clubs" —
> Beating tirelessly against what might
> possibly repose you…
>
> Bludgeon the still and resplendent
> Bludgeon the shrill and descendent…
> Bludgeon the curious, the composed
> Bludgeon the recollectant, and received
> Bludgeon it all!
>
> Bludgeon everything into the lifeless masses of meretricion you value with such demanding contumation
> Sequestering off your degrees of bombastic approbation into plackets of despite and repression
> Finally securing your assiduous fealty to the regressive repletion of your concerted condemnations
> Writhing, wallowing in the virulence of your caustic vagaries and caprices
> Locating, lastly, the steps of your stoic regard for the segregate and collusive
>
> Spade or spade? Club or club?
> Criminal! Criminal!
> "Criminal!" you declare in your emphysematic wheeze…
> And now you convoke your consternations
> Regale in your vituperations

And ache to render your final wicked blows…
You ask me —
In the depths of your ignorance
If I have a final request
Yes! I have a final request!

Do it fast and don't think about it all!

Such intensely fanciful writing is rare to the comics medium. On a first reading, Hart's skill with language recalls newspaper comic-strip masters like E.C. Segar (*Popeye*), Walt Kelly (*Pogo*) and George Herriman (*Krazy Kat*), each of whom gave idiosyncratic voice to their characters by grounding their speech in rough equivalents of regional dialect. But Hart is doing more than exploring specific aural peculiarities. Hart uses words to drive entire sequences, making some of his pages less about the juxtaposition of pictures than language broken across space. Hart upends the cinematic approach endorsed by the majority of cartoonists in favor of comics that draw equally from words and pictures, reviving ghosts of the medium's earliest decades, when fewer ideas about comics seemed certain and certain modes of storytelling had yet to be set in stone.

Yet much about Hart's work is modern. The closest popular cartooning equivalent to the opening suite of *New Hat* is Charles Schulz in full speechmaking mode, the word-intensive *Peanuts* Sundays featuring lengthy digressions by Linus, Schroeder or Charlie Brown. While Schulz's graceful line grounds his characters' aspirations in a way that makes their dialogue humane and slightly heartbreaking, Hart's cruder visual iconography gives his characters the energy and forcefulness that comes with impassioned conviction. Hart's comics force a reappraisal of the meaning of artistic craft in comics. While Schulz seems to have settled on his style deliberately and with a certain effect in mind, Hart appears to be drawing as well as he can with little choice in the styles available to him. But Hart's ability to render a world in ways that conform to high standards of illustration matters less than his drawing consistently and in a way that facilitates a range of emotional effect. His style may work for some as a rejection of the rigidities that come with an overemphasis on illustrator's craft, but seeing his art as primitive or playing the same role primitive work does in visual art misses the point. Hart recognizes — or his style has forced this recognition upon him — that drawing in comics plays more important roles than aesthetic. Hart's style has freed him to upset the hierarchy of standard narrative effects. The emphasis Hart gives language often casts the visual component of his comics as thematic or tonal support, a role for which his style is ideally suited. The only cartoonists of the last 25 years that came close to exploring this same fertile territory are the late fantasist Paul Ollswang (*Doofer*) and the collage artist and painter Ted Jouflas (*Scary!*). "I think Tom Hart's one of the sharpest formalists in comics," says Highwater Books Publisher Tom Devlin, "So sharp that his formalism is rarely noticeable." At age 33, Tom Hart walks in century-class artistic company. More than any cartoonist of his generation, Hart makes comics that celebrate and challenge his medium's rich foundation.

Hart's comics force a reappraisal of the meaning of artistic craft in comics.

Tom Hart was born in 1969 in the small town of Kingston, N.Y. Like many cartoonists born after 1960, he became obsessed as a child with every form of visual art except the 32-page superhero comic book that dominated spinner racks. "I grew up devouring comic strips, cartoon images, and funny illustrations," Hart says, citing greeting cards and the Al Feldstein-edited *Mad* magazine amongst a panoply of influences. His first meaningful encounter with comic books came at the age of 16. "A comic store opened up in Kingston just as my senior year high school was starting, and only a few months after reading about *Dark Knight Returns* and running into *Cerebus* and *Fish Police*, I think at a rural flea market." Hart made several false assumptions about the state of the comic book market. "I walked past a row of Wonder Woman/ Spider-Man, and thought it was cute that they still were presenting these old-time superhero comics. I went right to the very small shelf of black-and-white and dove in. I didn't realize 'til I started working there that those dopey superhero comics were the engines of these stores." Hart would eventually work at the store, beginning his education in the specifics of the form. "Looking back, this and later working at [comics shop] Zanadu in Seattle, I see that this was my extended comics history lesson, for which I am very grateful."

Hart's formal arts education consisted of a year at the School of Visual Arts (SVA) in New York City, which at the time of his attendance counted amongst its faculty such master formalists as Harvey Kurtzman (the original *Mad*) and Will Eisner (*The Spirit*). Hart says he had been locked into attending SVA since the 10th grade, but found the atmosphere disappoint-

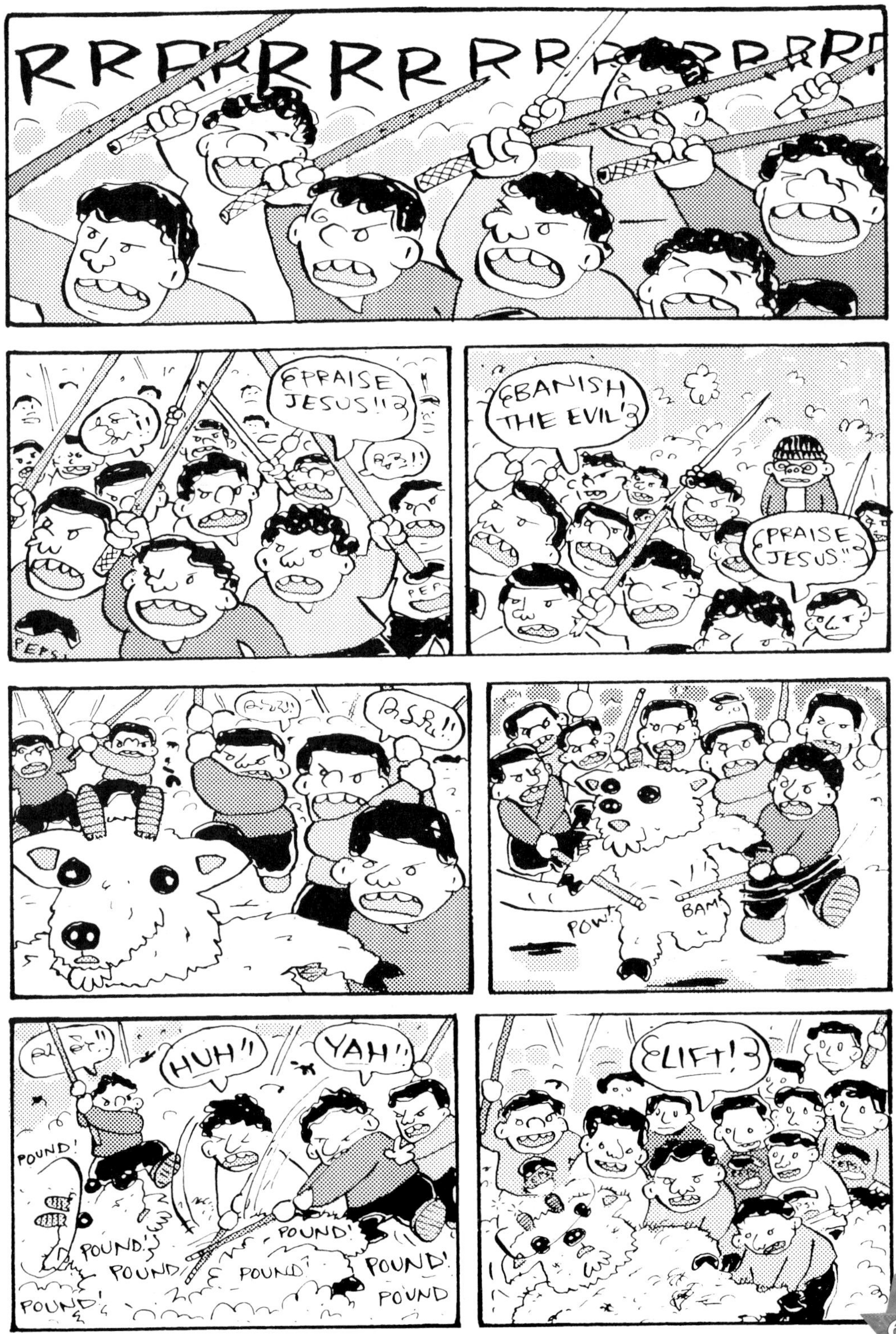
PRAISE JESUS!!
BANISH THE EVIL!
PRAISE JESUS!!
POW!
BAM!
HUH!!
YAH!!
POUND!
POUND!
POUND
POUND!
POUND!
POUND!
POUND
POUND!
LIFT!

This Page: From *Hutch Owen: Emerging Markets.* © 2002 Tom Hart.

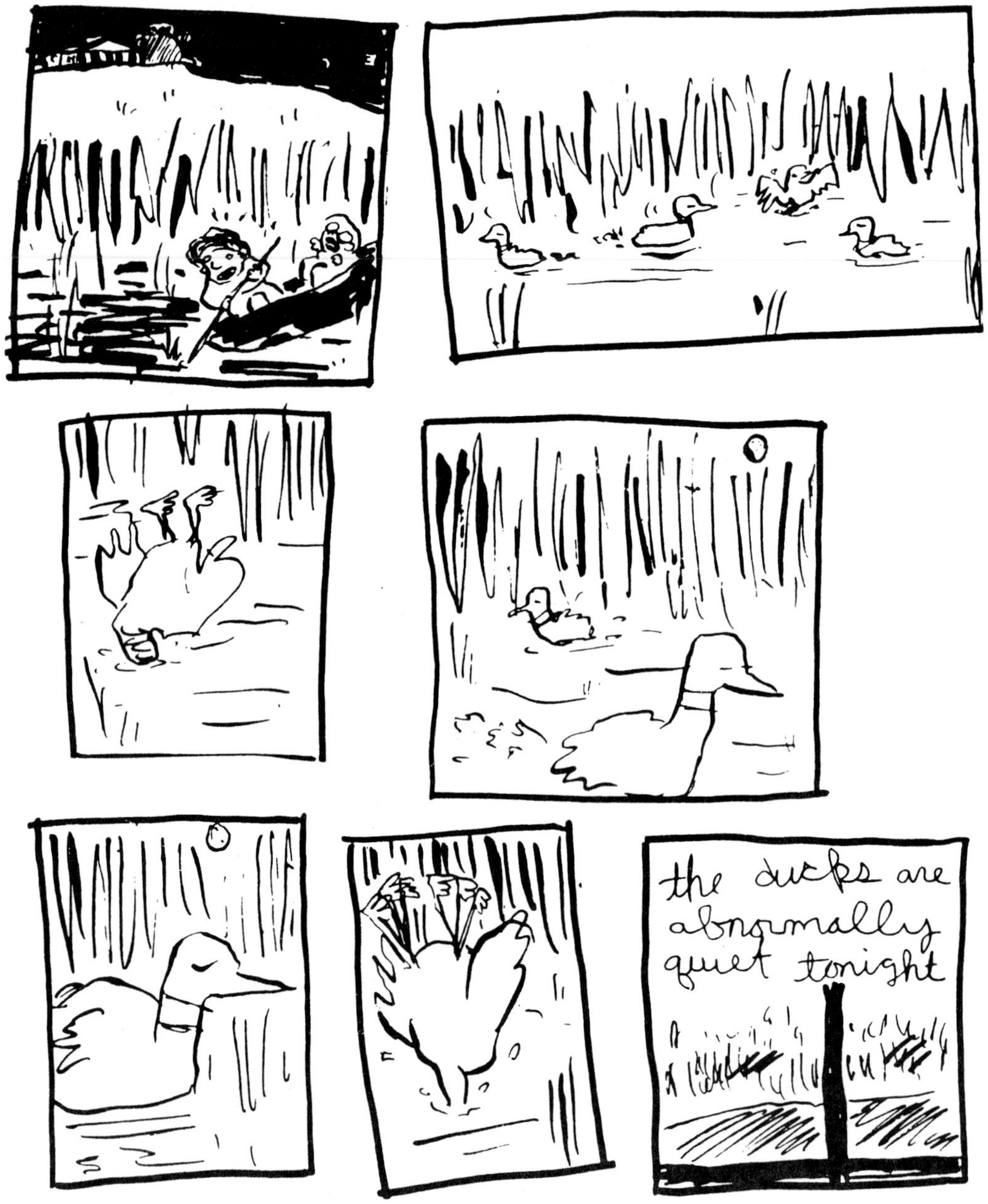
the ducks are abnormally quiet tonight

This Page: From the 24-hour comic *Maria.* © 2002 Tom Hart.

ing, his passion for the form far outstripping presiding student culture: "I used to bitch about SVA that what I wanted/expected out of college was *The Paper Chase*. Do you remember the TV show on CBS and then Showtime in the '80s with John Houseman as a truculent law professor? These kids stayed up *all night* discussing the issues and challenges raised in class the day before, time after time. And of course, it was art school, so it was pot and The Cure, and I was more befuddled than angry about it, though I was probably mad by the time I didn't sign up for a second year."

By this time Hart had made an important connection with a same-age peer, the comic book humorist Sam Henderson (*Magic Whistle*), one of many important professional relationships Hart would forge in the years to follow. Another friendship struck up around comics, this one with eventual collaborator Jon Lewis (*True Swamp*), led to Hart's relocation to Seattle and its burgeoning comics scene. As described by Hart and Lewis in 1997, the Seattle cartooning community of the early 1990s was split into three large groups: those associated with Fantagraphics Books, a group of "furry animal" artists centered around publisher Edd Vick, and a small faction of alternative cartoonists in the early stages of their artistic development, a group that included Hart.

In Seattle, Hart found the intellectual back-and-forth he had desired in art school. At various times, his immediate circle of peers included cartoonists such as Lewis, Ed Brubaker (*Lowlife*), James Sturm (*The Golem's Mighty Swing*), Megan Kelso (*Artichoke Tales*), Jennifer Daydreamer (*Jennifer Daydreamer*), K. Thor Jensen (*A Short, Happy Life*), David Lasky (*Boom Boom*), and Jason Lutes (*Berlin*). Several members of this group lived together in various combinations, and many of them met to discuss comics, solve problems, and to criticize each other's work. "We were always conscious to make it about the work and about development," says Hart, "because we all had this desire to be better artists, period. It wasn't social at all. Eventually we realized we had created a network of friends, but it seemed to me that mostly we were just feeding each others ravenous hunger to make art and express our visions."

Hart impressed his fellow cartoonists with the broad nature of his comic influences, his attention to the writing in comics, and the value he placed on artistic process. Hart advocated on behalf of such exercises as doing comics based on flashcards, or limiting a four-panel work to a few pre-selected elements. "The plan was that each of us would come up with comics exercises, and each time we would do one," Megan Kelso recalls. Lutes remembers Hart as a skilled critic. "I developed a great respect for Tom's insightful analysis. We would sometimes get into heated discussions about a particular aspect of the medium, like the size of a panel or the consideration of a page break, and each time I would come away feeling like I had learned a little more of this evolving language, or even contributed to its evolution by talking about it."

Hart continued making comics. Readers were able to mark Hart's development as a cartoonist through a series of mini-comics — self-published, Xeroxed booklets distributed in comic book shops and a smattering of book, magazine and music stores. Efforts like *Prince Frederick's Feet* (1991) and *Love Looks Left* (1994) are best remembered for Hart's raw visual style and the contrast the cartoonist explored between the endearing, romantic lyricism imbued in his characters and the underlying social criticism of the narratives through which they marched. Influences like Charles Schulz, small-press British cartoonist Glenn Dakin (*Abe*) and children's bookmaker Tove Jansson (*Moomintrolls*) were obvious but not overly intrusive.

Not surprisingly given his passions, Hart's best mini-comics could be linked to formal experimentation. Two of the most interesting are *Maria* (1994) and *The Most Powerful Gate* (1995), both 24-hour comics, a storytelling exercise made popular by cartoonist, author, and devoted comics formalist Scott McCloud (*Understanding Comics*). The free-form nature of such comics, designed to be completed in a single 24-hour period, forced Hart to tether his fanciful stories to rock-solid narrative fundamentals or risk not being understood at all. Both *Maria* and *Gate* contained wistful narration and the specter of unrequited love familiar to readers of Hart's previous comics. But this time the stories were told through difficult panel to panel transitions, natural imagery that served as a thematic commentary on the narratives.

Best of all, Hart's visual style was beginning to coalesce in such a way that his comics started to feature a recognizable look their own: simple and spare, but also vital and pulsating with energy. Hart's characters had always taken full advantage of comics' reliance on cartoon effects: their faces twisted and contorted around the words they spoke for emphasis, every line in service of the emotions on display. But by the end of his mini-comics run, Hart had stepped over the fine line between making raw, unsophisticated drawings and claiming for his comics a raw, unsophisticated visual world. Tom Hart's drawings had become Tom Hart drawings. That artistic hurdle passed, Hart's simplicity became a virtue. He was now working with a visual syntax that was versatile but universally approachable. "I don't have a lifelong love for comics,

He was now working with a visual syntax that was versatile but universally approachable.

and when comics are highly detailed and complex, I tend not to want to look at them," says Megan Kelso. "I loved Tom's comics for that reason. They were appealing without making you look cross-eyed."

As pleasurable as they were to read, nothing about Hart's mini-comics prepared readers for his first graphic novella, *Hutch Owen's Working Hard* (1994). Published through a comics art grant established by *Teenage Mutant Ninja Turtle* co-creator Peter Laird, *Hutch Owen* describes the title character's doomed struggle against a childhood rival turned corporation head honcho on a battlefield of slogans, competing memories, and a small boy's cobbled-together clubhouse. In some ways *Hutch Owen* functioned as a more fully realized version of Hart's mini-comics work. The character of Hutch Owen is a romantic loner who seems happier, smarter, and more fully alive than those around him, due in great part to living a life without economic or artistic compromise. And Hart's sense of humor is on full display, casting a welcome, slightly disreputable pall on the entire affair. At one point, Owen's straight-faced life lessons include exhorting his teen-age acolyte to masturbate constantly. "That semen fucks with your head — get it out of your system." The length of *Hutch Owen* allowed Hart to develop character-based humor with more significant payoffs. Owen and his corporate nemesis Wormer are extreme personalities, and many of the story's funniest moments come from their excessive enthusiasm. Wormer screams at and browbeats his corporate yes-men with a combination of Daffy Duck's logic and Roy Cohn's cruelty, while Owen stages proxies of arguments with handpuppets and drifts off into childhood reverie long enough for others to look on and stare. Any fan of Hart's earlier work would have been delighted by the richness of this material.

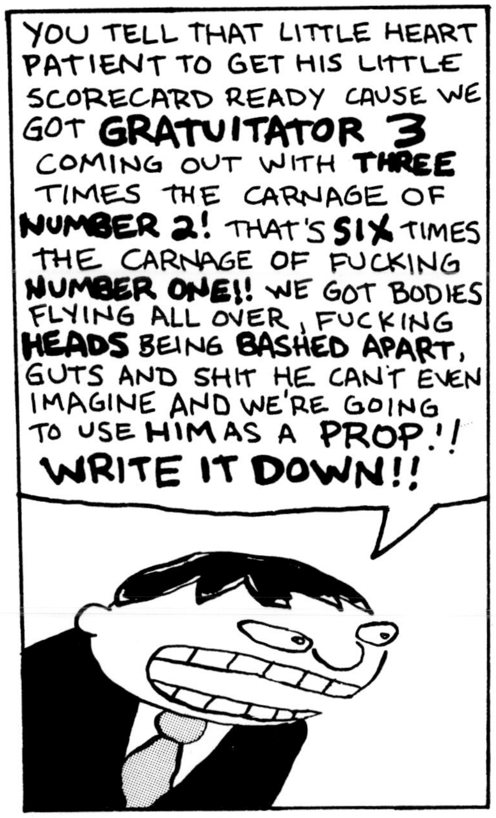
YOU TELL THAT LITTLE HEART PATIENT TO GET HIS LITTLE SCORECARD READY CAUSE WE GOT GRATUITATOR 3 COMING OUT WITH THREE TIMES THE CARNAGE OF NUMBER 2! THAT'S SIX TIMES THE CARNAGE OF FUCKING NUMBER ONE!! WE GOT BODIES FLYING ALL OVER, FUCKING HEADS BEING BASHED APART, GUTS AND SHIT HE CAN'T EVEN IMAGINE AND WE'RE GOING TO USE HIM AS A PROP.! WRITE IT DOWN!!

Taken solely as a manic comedy, *Hutch Owen's Working Hard* would have been a memorable standard format debut. But several scenes of pitch-perfect sociopolitical satire raise it to the level of that decade's best works. In his introduction to *The Collected Hutch Owen* (Top Shelf, 1999), the New Zealand cartoonist Dylan Horrocks celebrates the rarity of an American cartoonist with political insight and correctly identifies where Hart scores the most points. "This is a story about the way corporate power co-opts rebellious counter-cultures and movements, rendering them harmless — all in pursuit of profit." True, but Hart's contribution to social dialogue at that post-grunge, pre-WTO protest moment in American history wasn't simply pointing out the noxious marketing of Malcolm X or the lunacy of linking punk rock to an automobile purchase; everyone who didn't explicitly know that this was a false bill of goods felt it in his gut. What distinguished *Hutch Owen* is Hart's courage to repeat these arguments loudly and with moral conviction, refusing to make peace with the cynicism that mumbles its protests of cultural co-optation because to speak up might make one seem less cool. When, at the end of the story, Hutch Owen is soundly defeated by both the physical equipment knocking down the fort and by Worner marketing a protest videogame with Owen's likeness, it's both a savvy nod to the nature of the struggle (riot videogames are out there) and a knock at anyone whose belief in what Owen stood for was wrapped up in a fortuitous outcome.

Hart followed *Hutch Owen's Working Hard* with the shorter and more intensely lyrical *New Hat*. In addition to that work's extravagant use of language and controlled pacing, *New Hat* allows for a deeper rumination on the role of art and protest via overt manipulation of the narrative. The story progresses from Pardon Parcel's dramatic end to the seemingly meaningless war-related fatality of The President, a former leader turned earnest junior poet. Hart then jumps back in time to walk us through The President's decision to leave his office in search of greater meaning, and an uncomfortable confrontation he has with a cynical Parcel. Knowing what will happen to these characters infuses this initial confrontation with a great air of sadness. Given his violent end, it's difficult not to wince at Parcel's insistence that the greatest need in life is to have one's ass kicked, no matter how hilariously the scene plays as a misbegotten meeting between an artist and his hero. But the lingering effect by putting the destination first and journey second is to feel encouraged by the characters' search for a moral life. Hart says he believes in formal play in part because he believes it can lead "to new emotional territory." In *New Hat* the twists in narrative allow him to celebrate life's process in a way that calls attention to its frailty. The President is conflicted at book's end over the proper course his life should take; both he and the reader sense his death.

The next few years were marked by frustration. Hart began collaborating with close friend Jon Lewis on a comic series called *Pitch Unger* for the Japanese publisher Kodansha through their American Artists program, producing 160 pages of comics between 1996 and 1998. Lewis wrote and Hart drew, although both contributed to the visual breakdown of the page. The stories were divided between short fantasy comics (the lead character had a brother who was a fish) and longer, more realistic pieces. Despite keeping Lewis and Hart under close editorial control and paying for all of their work, Kodansha only used 28 pages and eventually killed the program. The inception of the project allowed Hart to quit a day job washing dishes. He even made plans to live off of Kodansha money in Morocco. But the reality is that neither the plans nor the comics came off as hoped. "This was always a source of immense frustration for us," says Hart, summarily. "I never believed this *Pitch* project worked."

Meanwhile, Hart's primary North American publisher, Black Eye, suspended publication on the serialization of Hart's graphic novel *The Sands* before its completion, promising a collection, but removing Hart's presence from the market until it was completed. A planned regular series called *Triple Dare* (Alternative Comics, 1998), to feature comics created under formal restraints by Hart, Lewis, and James Kochalka, took five years to produce the just-released second issue. The easiest place for many to find Hart after *New Hat* was through the tail end of his estimable run of self-published work, the mini-comics *The Ditch, The River...* (1996) and *Ramadan* (1997).

When *The Sands* was finally released in 1998 by Black Eye, shortly before that publisher closed its doors for good, Hart's artistic range had

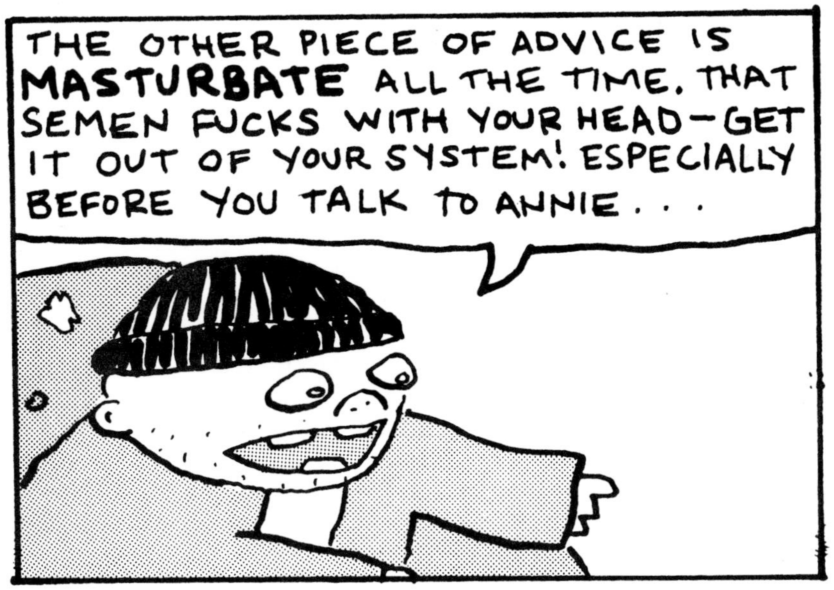
THE OTHER PIECE OF ADVICE IS MASTURBATE ALL THE TIME. THAT SEMEN FUCKS WITH YOUR HEAD—GET IT OUT OF YOUR SYSTEM! ESPECIALLY BEFORE YOU TALK TO ANNIE . . .

Top and Bottom: From *Hutch Owen's Working Hard*. © 2002 Tom Hart.

expanded exponentially. *The Sands* featured long meditations on the nature of love and devotion, and a bouncy, humorous secondary narrative about the teacher-student relationship between the protagonist Hawk Troy and a profane boy king. *The Sands* works most powerfully as a narrative about isolation and lack of direction. Troy not only lacks the moral compass of earlier Hart creations, he lacks for things to do to fill his time. Even his exact vocation remains indeterminate. Although Troy loves Margie enough to follow her to a foreign country in support of insect research, he seems to find little day-to-day solace in their relationship. Tenuous connections with locals contain undercurrents of contempt or disinterest. The achingly spare countryside Hart draws also seems to work against Troy making a meaningful connection. When Troy does manage to triumph over his ennui, through organizing a child's tea party or simply fantasizing about something exciting, it becomes difficult to resist seeing these small events as minor epiphanies in contrast to the emotional bruising that precedes and follows. A slightly fragmented narrative only increases the reader's sympathy for Troy's feelings of disorientation and loneliness. *The Sands* is an unsparing, emotionally honest work.

With *Banks/Eubanks* (Top Shelf, 1999), Hart began a cycle of stories that stand in contrast to, or act as commentaries upon, his earlier works. The life of protagonist Barney Banks revolves around his dog, a demeaning job, watching movies alone, and leering at women. In many ways, Banks recalls a "real world" Hutch Owen, and the opening scenes that depict the character's life in pathetic detail are as brutal and judiciously unsparing as any comics narrative in memory. The work's second half, where Banks undergoes a directionless adventure in a storm-threatened coastal town, proved a minor letdown. Unlike past works where trailing off into meaninglessness served to thwart narrative expectations, Banks stumbles through exactly the sort of non-event for which he seemed destined from page one.

Hart continued in self-reflexive mode that year by returning to his best-known character with the first of three stories that eventually saw print alongside *Hutch Owen's Working Hard* as the major trade paperback release *The Collected Hutch Owen* (Top Shelf, 2000). *Hutch Owen: Emerging Markets* is a mostly lifeless sequel to the original story, re-stating the original novella's critique of American culture by showing how its corporations export to and exploit their foreign markets. The visual iconography Hart assembled for the character and his world seemed as lively and energetic as the work done five years earlier. But despite some hints at a more deeply layered back story for Owen (Hutch's mother has made him uncomfortable around Christians) and a stage piece set at an exotic holiday celebration whose details feel observed rather than constructed from scratch, Hutch Owen's return found him saying little he hadn't enunciated earlier, more clearly and with greater force.

Hart on his online work: "It is a lot about distribution, and a lot about killing trees and wasting people's money and cluttering their houses with shit."

Hutch Owen: Stocks are Surging and *Hutch Owen: The Road to Self* were different beasts entirely, and marked another leap forward in Hart's artistic development. In these stories, Hart examines past assumptions through stories of greater narrative and thematic complexity, all without sacrificing the clarity of his vision. In the opening scenes of *Stocks are Surging*, Hart depicts a homeless Owen as cold, wet, and defeated. The sight disturbs, but by temporarily disabling Owen's rock-solid sense of himself, Hart is better able to make an unfiltered case why our mostly fallen world needs out-of-step iconoclasts like Hutch Owen. Owen's situation is so desperate and his resigned nature, when he takes a temporary job, so discouraging, that the cascade of brutal potshots Hart takes at modern moneymaking enervate like celebratory reaffirmations of the lead character's rightful place in the world. Owen is surrounded by so much stupidity — inane bus ads, casual displays of package-grabbing sexuality — the reader gains confidence that Owen can at least use the dimwitted bodies of his co-workers to climb out of his hole.

Hart surrounds Owen with supporting characters of unexpected nuance in *Stocks are Surging*, something he continues to even richer effect in *The Road to Self*. In that story, a lonely Owen comes to terms with an old girlfriend's big-money publishing gig in sublime passive-aggressive fashion. Hart's satirical ear allows him to brutally dissect the culture of this new milieu. He sums up everything you need to know about corporate creativity in one background exchange between cubicles:

"Will you send me that poopy e-mail?"

"Sure — do you have any Mylanta?"

But what nudges *Road to Self* into greatness is the protagonist's savagely conflicted reaction to the road not taken and the humor that springs forth from his attempts to have it both ways. Owen tries to write his own version of his ex-girlfriend's magazine, hopelessly attempts to cadge a freelance assignment, and in the end touchingly… admits? lies? confesses? that the story his ex wrote in a recent issue is really good. Hart says that his return to Hutch Owen is both an exploration of the connection such a character can create between audience and artist, and the fact that the stories seem better to him when Owen is present. *The Road to Self* serves as a positive affirmation of both theories. It is every bit as affecting and funny as the original novella.

Since 2000, the majority of Hart's new work has appeared in on-line venues, a move about which the cartoonist says, "It is a lot about distribution, and a lot about killing trees and wasting people's money and cluttering their houses with shit. I don't think it has changed anything I do artistically." Depending on how you look at it, *Hutch Owen: Aristotle* (topshelfcomix.com, 2001) is either a solid addition to the Hutch Owen canon or

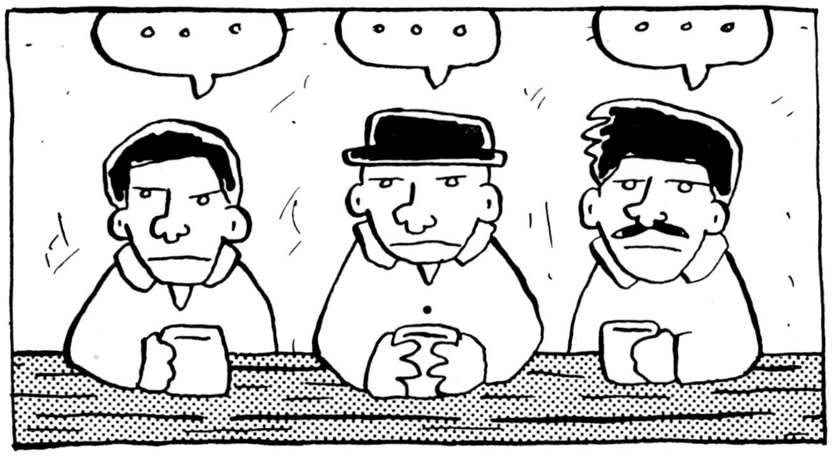

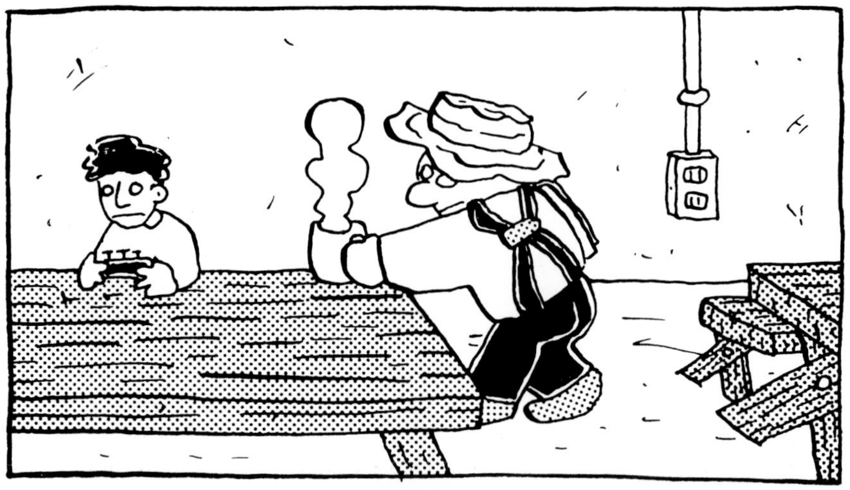

This Page: From *The Sands.* © 2002 Tom Hart.

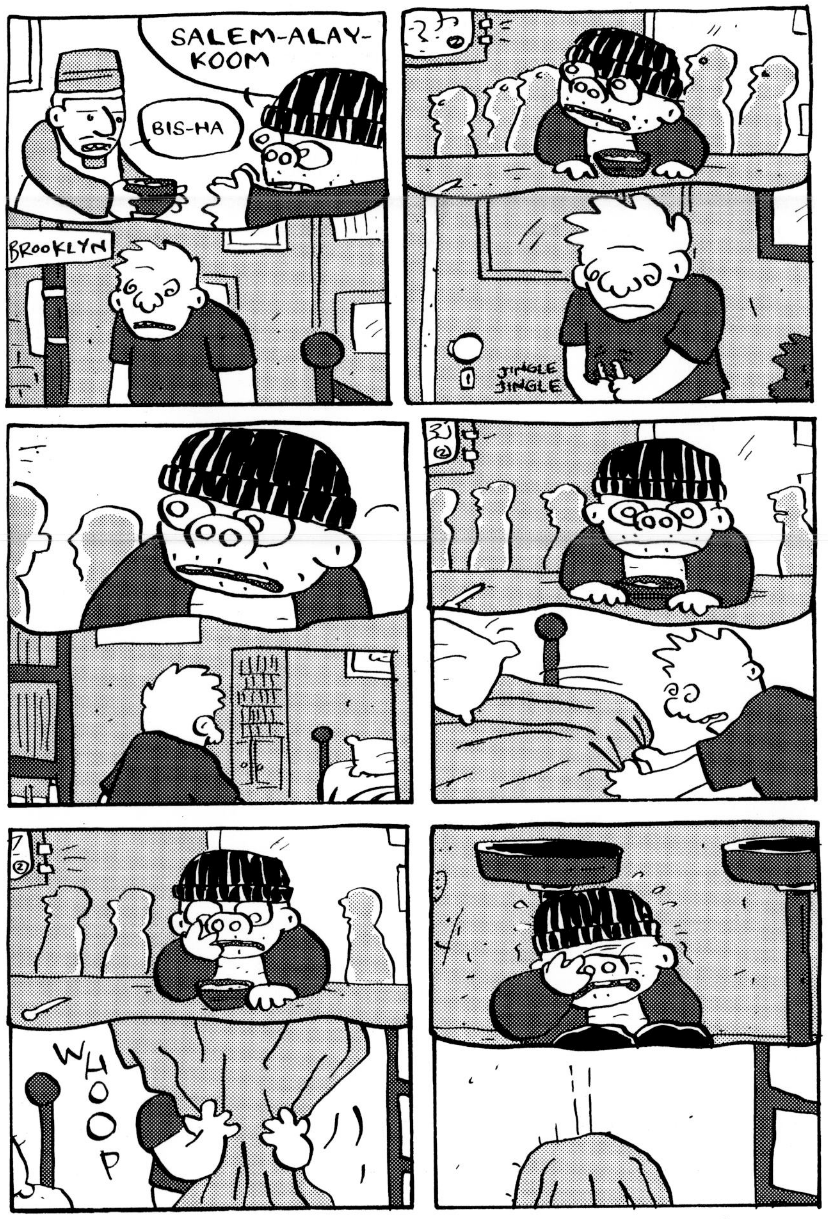
SALEM-ALAY-KOOM
BIS-HA
BROOKLYN
JINGLE JINGLE
WHOOP

This Page: From Hart's contribution to Alternative Comics' *9-11 Emergency Relief* benefit book. © 2002 Tom Hart.

the first sign that Hart is settling for less formally ambitious work in order to maintain a comics franchise. The coffee shop and corporate branding camp settings in *Aristotle* fail to measure up to the more archetypal settings of earlier Owen stories, at least in terms of offering interesting commentary on Owen's developing character. But Hart is still able to wring a few exquisite truths from the details: the wariness with which Owen's students treat him, the ease with which a computer-savvy geek takes over his discussion group, and the contrast between Owen's willfully innocent flirtation with capitalism and a loutish barista's cynical desire to make money so he can sue his record label. Hart's style seems perfectly suited to the computer screen. Driven by their verbal component, with simple shapes that communicate effectively and Hart's clear sense of design and pacing, on-line comics have in Hart a fine spokesman to help the tactile readership through the difficult transition from holding comics in one's lap to negotiating around them via the computer screen.

Tom Hart's current projects are the serials *Hutch Owen: Public Relations* (moderntales.com, 2002) and *Trunktown* (serializer.net, 2002), the latter a collaboration with the writer Shaenon Garrity on a site Hart edits. Both are important experiments in subscription model comics services, as well as opportunities to recognize the wide variety of work available on-line. Unlike most alternative cartoonists, whose creative control over each project often extends to the minute details of its package design, Hart is happy to share the creative burden of Trunktown with Garrity. He does so in part by necessity: "I love and need there to be a work that is all mine, where all the variables are provided, or at least enabled, by me, but to take on a second project and again handle all that needs to be handled in a comic — plotting, writing, laying out, penciling, etc. — I just can't do it. I'm not good enough, quick enough, fast enough on my feet." Hart also says a project like *Trunktown* allows him to work on the specific component skills. The Hutch Owen story is as solid as the one previous to it. But the art on *Trunktown*, a picaresque comedy in a mythical kingdom that unites past Hart characters with newer creations, is looser than anything Hart has done before, bursting with energy reminiscent of early cartoonists like Ham Fisher (*Mutt and Jeff*) and Roy Crane (*Wash Tubbs*). It reads like an odd love letter on yellow newsprint, a heavy dinner in an older relative's home where very little English is spoken, a 19th century blog.

At an age when many cartoonists are just beginning to assemble the skills necessary to create a recognizable idiom, Tom Hart can boast of hundreds of pages of quality work and at least two great novellas, both featuring the Hutch Owen character: *Working Hard* and *Road to Self*. Hart has also become an arts comics community fixture, following years of living in towns with lively comics scenes by settling down in New York with his wife Leela Corman, teaching at SVA and editing the art-comics friendly serializer.net. Teaching has taught Hart, as he puts it, to "put up or shut up" when it comes to his drawing, and his line has never looked more expressive or versatile than on pieces like *Public Relations* or the two-pager short "Zombies Loves Comics" that appeared in the anthology *Bogus Dead* (Jerome Gaynor, 2001). Blessed with an understanding of formal properties that is neither showy nor wasted on his page, Hart only has to live up to the expectations fostered by past work to continue being a cartoonist that entertains and occasionally demands us to ruminate on the nature of the medium. When you're rightfully claimed as both the paragon of comics simplicity and as an exemplar of the formally daring, one's artistic future is a wide-open page. Tom Hart will no doubt find beautiful language with which to fill it.

Selective Tom Hart Bibliography:
Trunktown, with Shaenon Garrity, On-Line Comic, Serializer.net, 2002.
Hutch Owen: Public Relations!, On-Line Comic, Modern Tales.com, 2002.
"Zombies Love Comics," *Bogus Dead*, 2002.
Hutch Owen: Aristotle, On-Line Comic, topshelfcomix.com, 2001.
"Kamandi — The Last Band on Earth!" with Nick Bertozzi, *Bizarro Comics*, DC, 2001.
The Collected Hutch Owen, Top Shelf Productions, 2000. Collection consisting of *Hutch Owen's Working Hard*, *Hutch Owen: Emerging Markets*, *Hutch Owen: Stocks are Surging* and *Hutch Owen: The Road to Self.*
"Pitch Unger: Island Story," On-Line comic, *USSCastrophe*, 2000.
Banks/Eubanks, Top Shelf, 1999
"Hutch Owen: Emerging Markets," *Mona* #1, Kitchen Sink Press, 1999.
The Sands, Black Eye Books, 1998.
"The Body Social," with Jon Lewis, *Oni Double Feature* #8-9, Oni Press, 1998.
"A Frequent Contributor," *Triple Dare* #1, Alternative Comics, 1998.
Pitch Unger, with Jon Lewis, Kodansha, 1996-1998 (largely unpublished).
"Devil Dinosaur & Moon Boy," *Coober Skeeber* #2, Highwater Press, 1997.
Ramadan, Self-Published Mini-Comic, 1997.
The Ditch, The River…, Self-Published Mini-Comic, 1996.
New Hat, Black Eye Books, 1995.
The Most Powerful Gate, Self-Published Mini-Comic, 1995.
Hutch Owen's Working Hard, Self-Published with aid of a Xeric Grant, 1994.
Maria, Self-Published Mini-Comic, 1994.
Love Looks Left, Self-Published Mini-Comic, 1994.
The Angry Criminal, Self-Published Mini-Comic, 1993.
Wodaabe Comics, Self-Published Mini-Comic, 1992.
Prince Fredrick's Feet, Self-Published Mini-Comic, 1991. ★★★

COMICS COUNTRY!

09
The Beguiling
08
Comicopia
05
Chicago Comics
03
Jim Hanley's Universe
06
Comic Relief
10
Quimby's
04
Big Planet Comics
07
Golden Apple
01
02
Alternate Reality Comics

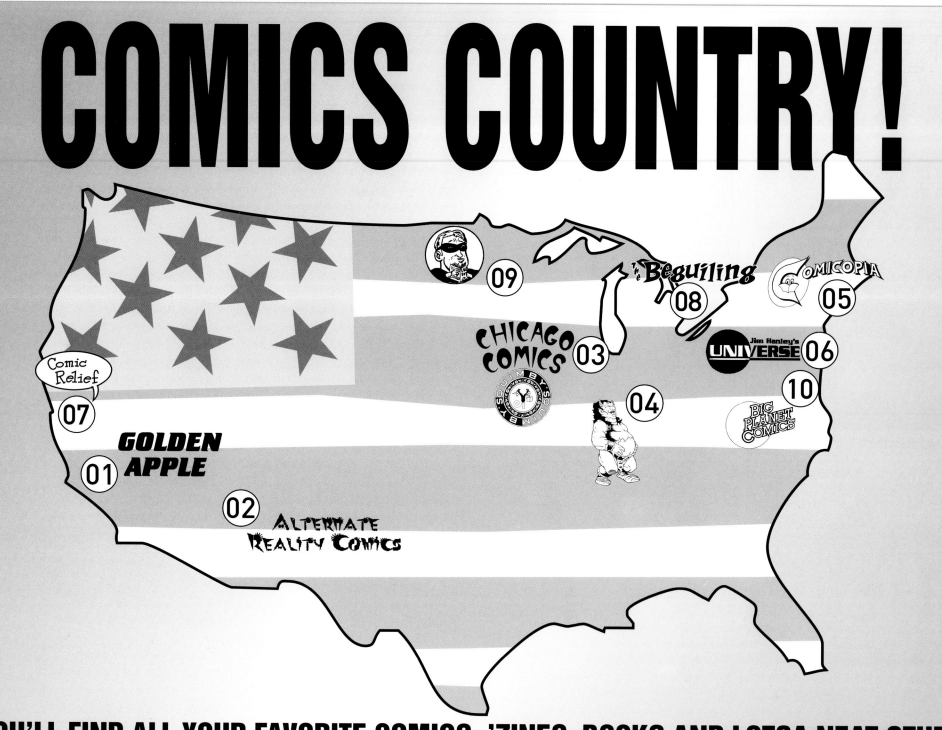

YOU'LL FIND ALL YOUR FAVORITE COMICS, 'ZINES, BOOKS AND LOTSA NEAT STUFF AT THESE WELL-STOCKED, HIGHLY RECOMMENDED SPECIALTY STORES.

01

Golden Apple
7711 Melrose Ave
Los Angeles CA 90046
tel: 323.658.6047
www.goldenapplecomics.com

02

Alternate Reality
4800 South Maryland Pkwy Ste D
Las Vegas NV 89119
tel: 702.736.3464

03

Chicago Comics
3244 N. Clark
Chicago IL 60657
tel: 773.528.1983

Quimby's
1854 W. North Ave.
Chicago, Ill 60622
tel: 773.342.0910

www.chicagocomics.com

04

The Laughing Ogre
4258 North High Street
Columbus OH 43214-3048
tel: 614.A.MR.OGRE
www.thelaughingogre.com

05

Comicopia
464 Commonwealth Ave
Boston MA 02215
tel: 617.266.4266
www.comicopia.com

06

Jim Hanley's Universe
4 W. 33rd Street
New York, NY 10001-3302
Tel. 212.268.7088

325 New Dorp Lane
Staten Island, NY 10306
tel: 718.351.6299

www.jhuniverse.com

07

Comic Relief
2138 University Ave.
Berkeley, CA 94704-1026
tel: 510.843.5002
www.comicrelief.net

08

The Beguiling
601 Markham St.
Toronto, Ontario
Canada, M6G 2L7
tel: 416.533.9168
www.beguiling.com

09

Big Brain
81 South Tenth Street
Minneapolis, MN 55403
tel: 612.338.4390

10

Big Planet Comics

4908 Fairmont Ave.
Bethesda, MD 20814
tel: 301.654.6856

426 Maple. Ave. East
Vienna, VA 22180
tel: 703.242.9412

3145 Dumbarton Ave.
Washington, DC 20007
tel: 202.342.1961

www.bigplanetcomics.com

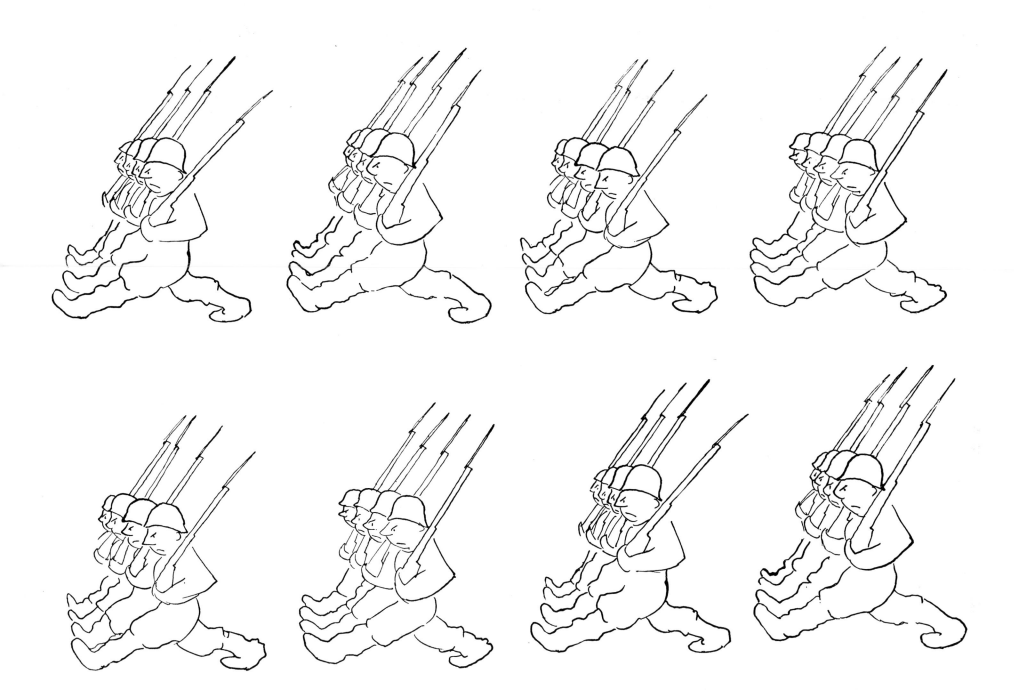

TRIBUTE TO JAMES THURBER

Before there was Justin Green, R. Crumb, Harvey Pekar, Chester Brown or Phoebe Gloeckner, there was James Thurber, the granddaddy of anxiety-ridden autobiographical cartoonists. (And not just a cartoonist, of course, but an essayist, short-story writer, and commentator.) Few cartoonists have been more eloquent in their humility than Thurber, or as witty about examining their own (and, by extension, our own) foibles. That his work is as funny and relevant today as when it was written is a sign of his unique ability to pare away excess detail to find the raw universal absurdity at the heart of private domesticity and everyday existence. It was a gift that was especially evident in the surreal minimalism of his cartoons.

Thurber grew up in Columbus, Ohio, but became a fixture in the New York literary scene and a prominent regular contributor to The New Yorker from 1927 until his death in 1961.

This is our woefully inadequate attempt at paying tribute to Thurber: a parodic homage done in the master's own style by today's closest equivalent to Thurber, Mr. Ivan Brunetti; an appreciation by Jesse Fuchs; and two pieces by Thurber himself, his picture story "The Race of Life" and his essay on himself and his art, "The Lady on the Bookcase." ★★★

THE THURBER Carnivore

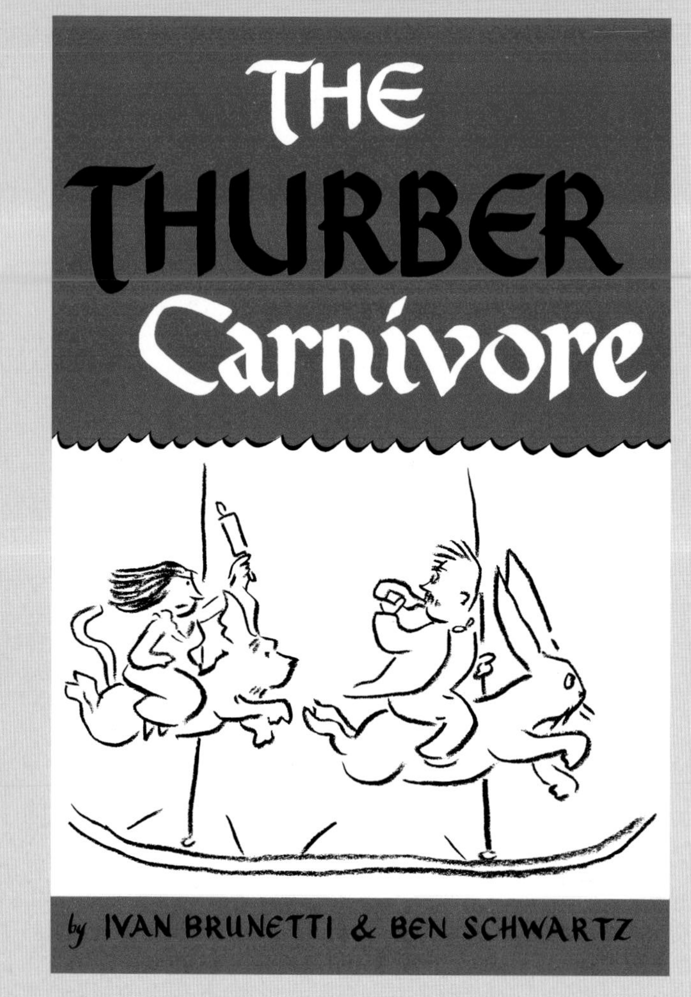

by IVAN BRUNETTI & BEN SCHWARTZ

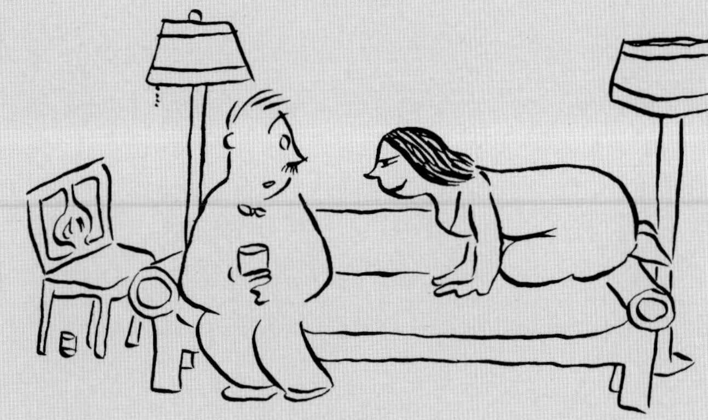

"You scare me."

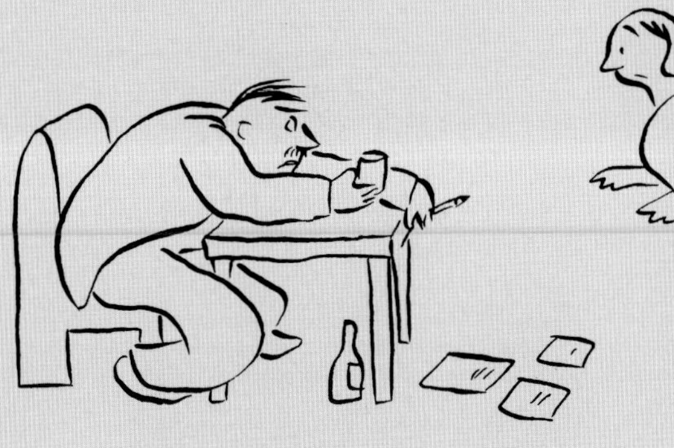

"Grief is of all the emotions the one under which I work best."

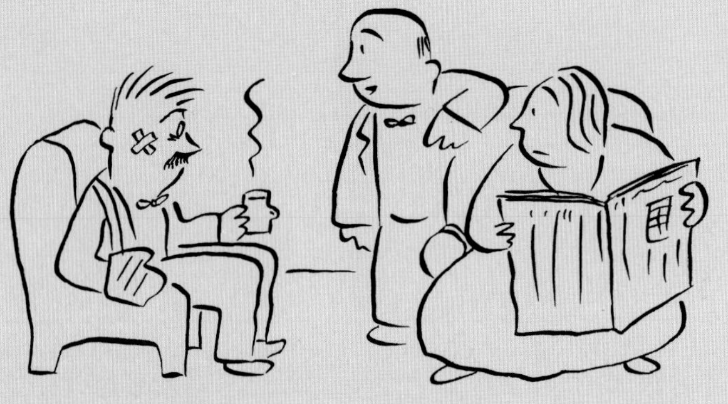

"By the way, your wife gave birth to a baby girl while you were out whoring last night."

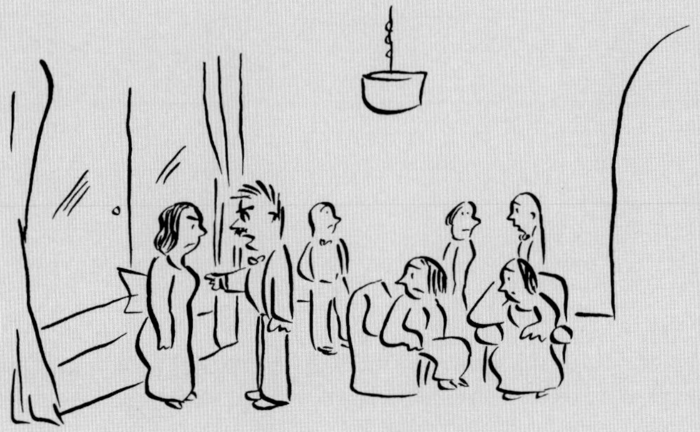

"The baby's from that chinless wonder you met on the beach."

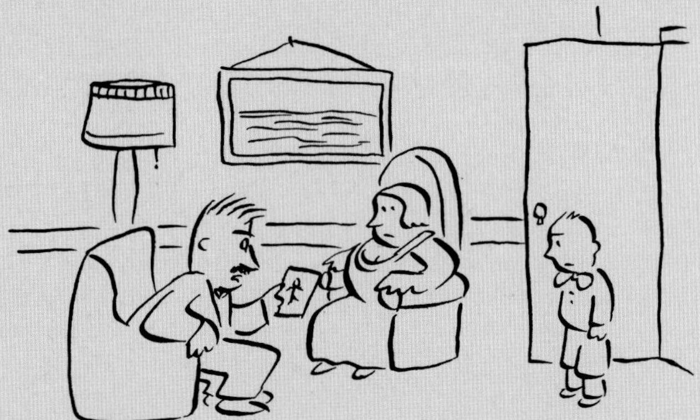

"Yes, your son can certainly draw as well as I can. The only trouble is he hasn't gone through as much."

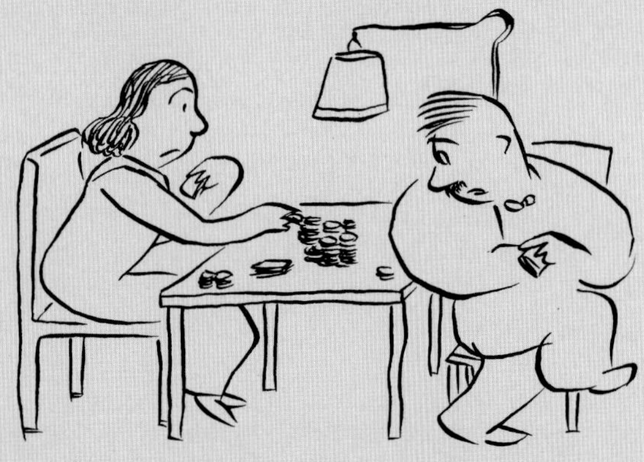

"I hate the modern world because it's made up of gadgets that whir and whine and whiz and shriek and sometimes explode."

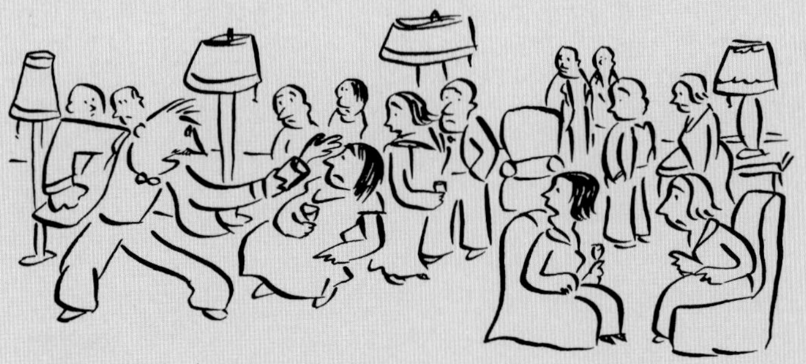

"Uh-oh... he's got 'the Thurbs' again."

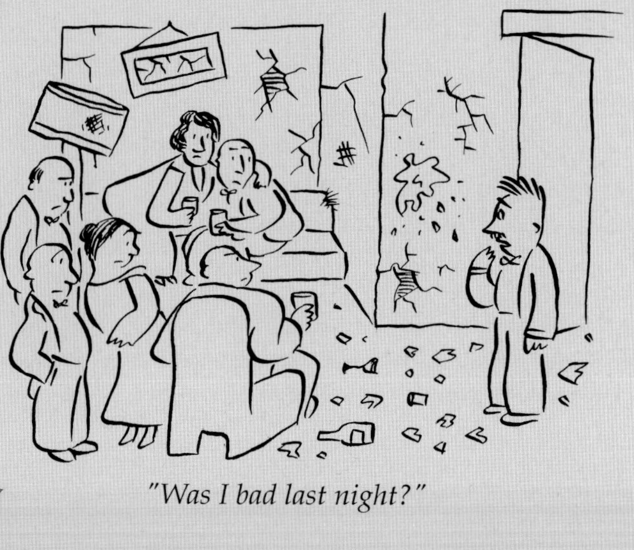

"Was I bad last night?"

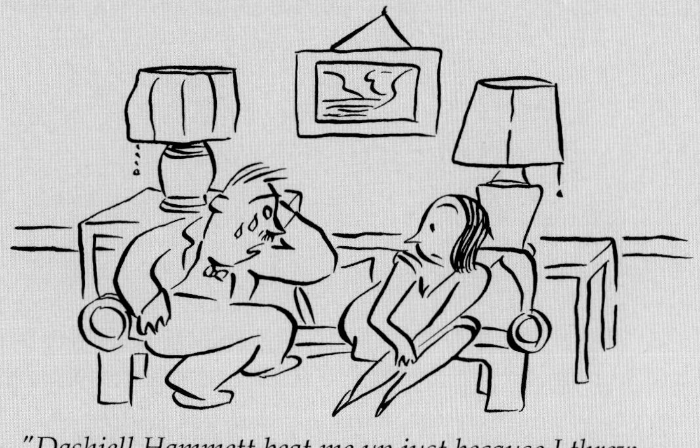

"Dashiell Hammett beat me up just because I threw a whiskey glass at Lillian Hellman's head."

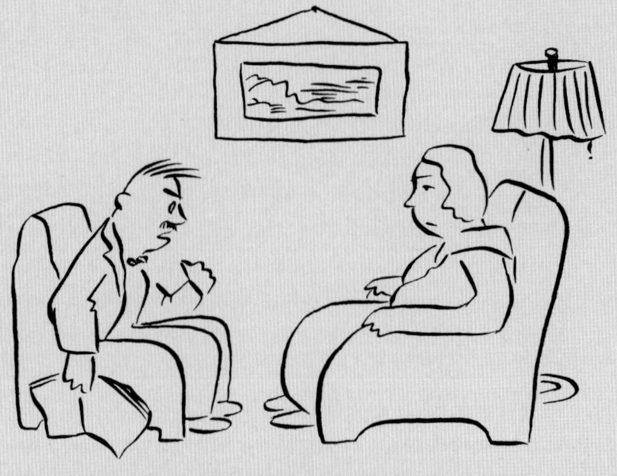

"Hemingway regarded me as a man!"

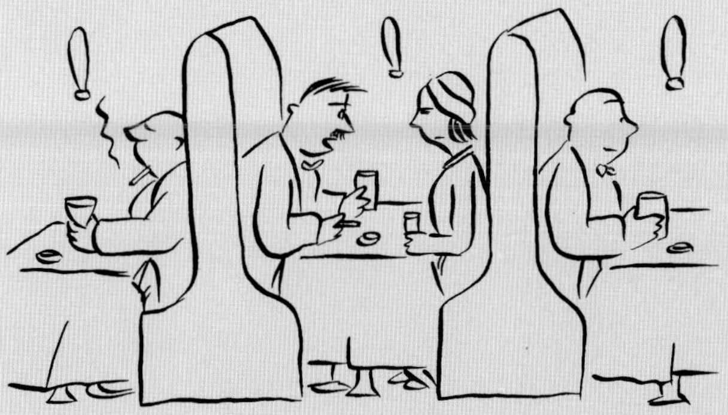

"It's too bad our love never ripened into friendship."

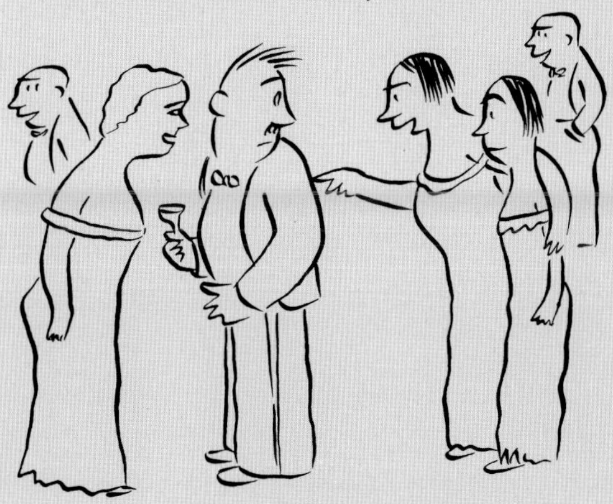

"He wasn't very good in the hay."

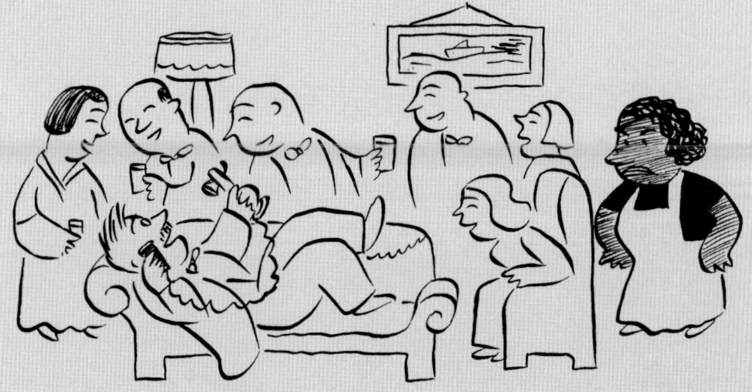

"Dis heah's Edith Rummum. Ah used wuck fo yo frens nex doah yo place a Sou Norwuck... Ah laundas."

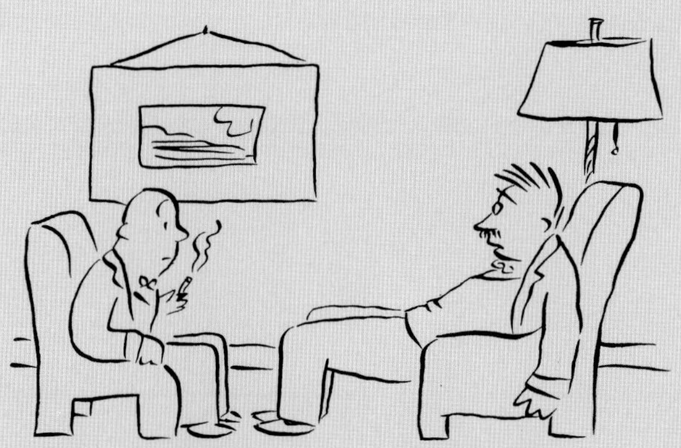

"I look like a slightly ill professor of botany who is also lost."

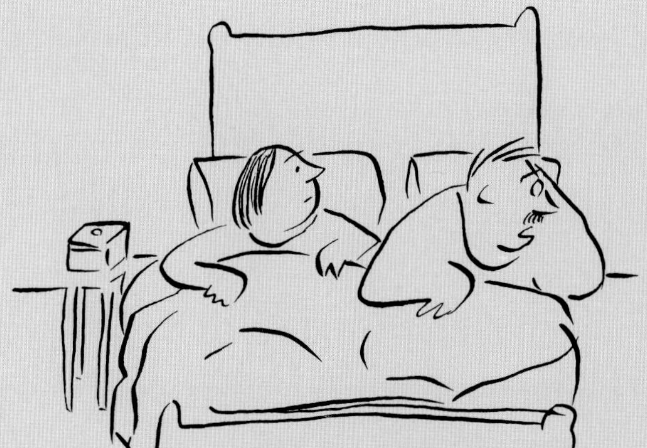

"Great... First I go blind; now I'm having erectionless ejaculations."

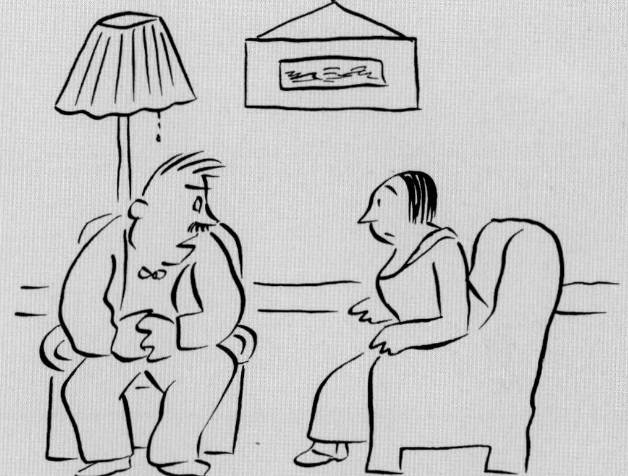

"I've wasted much of my life trying to think up new ways of killing you."

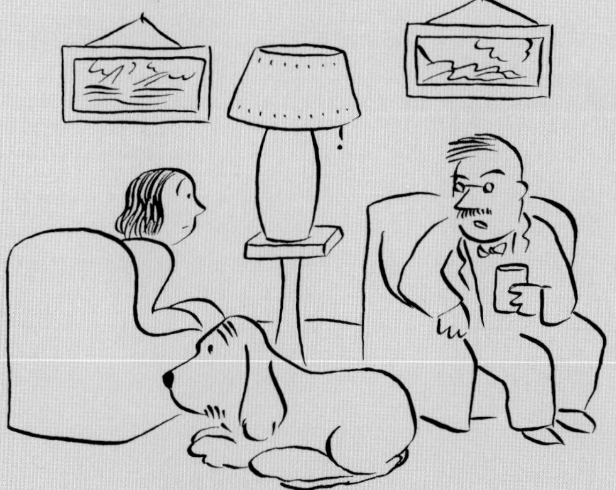

"People are not funny; they are vicious and horrible - and so is Life!"

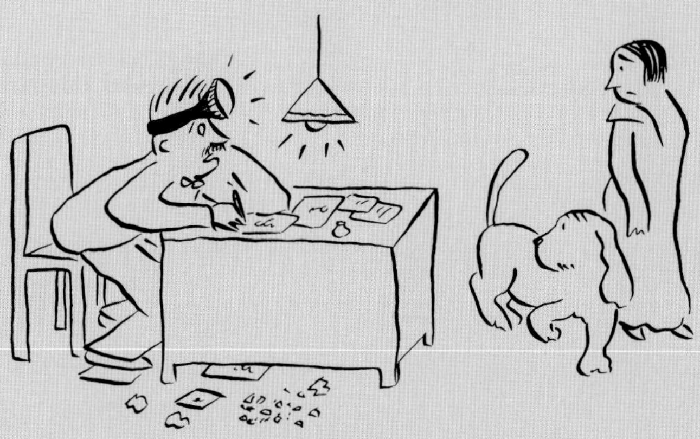

"I'm a welder from Mars."

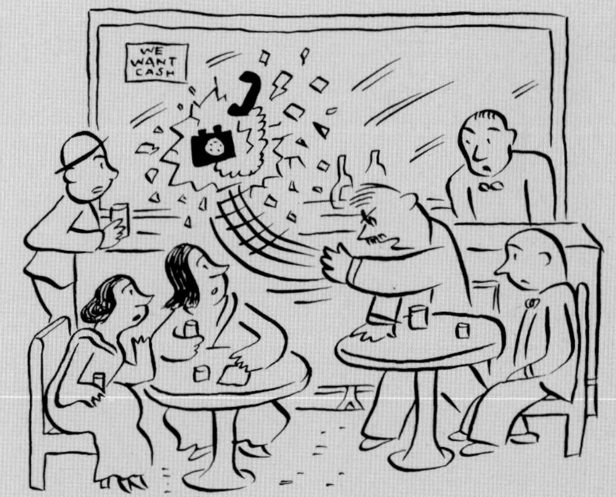
WE WANT CASH

"I don't care if you ARE from Columbus, Ohio... I am not signing your goddamned napkin!"

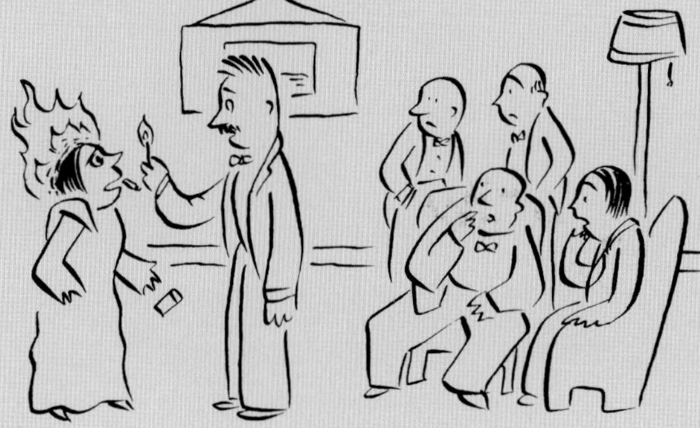

"I was shot at only once myself, by fraternity brothers during initiation. Their second shot got a blackbird in a cypress tree, which fell at my feet a fifth of a second before I fell at its - whoops, sorry."

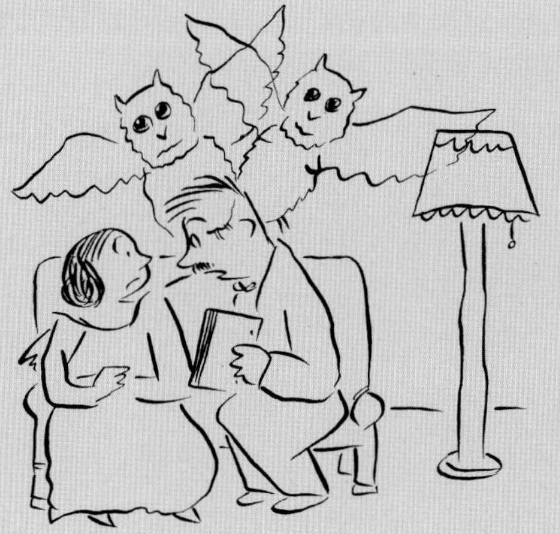

"This is my greatest book - 'Autobiography of a Mind' - in it, I describe my total recall, mental telepathy, ESP, and my ability to puncture beer cans with my thumbnails."

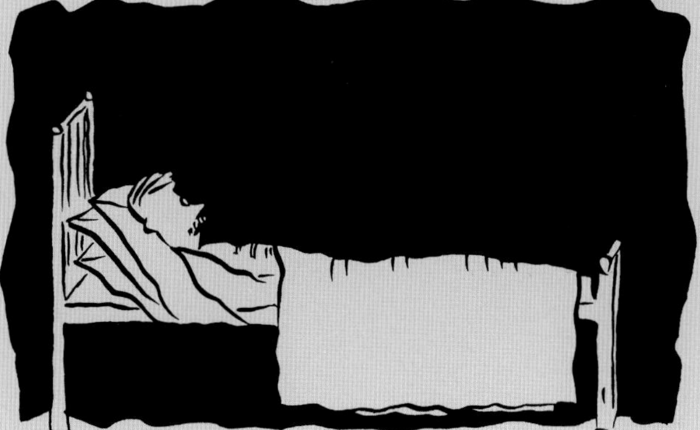

"God bless... God damn."

JAMES THURBER · 1934

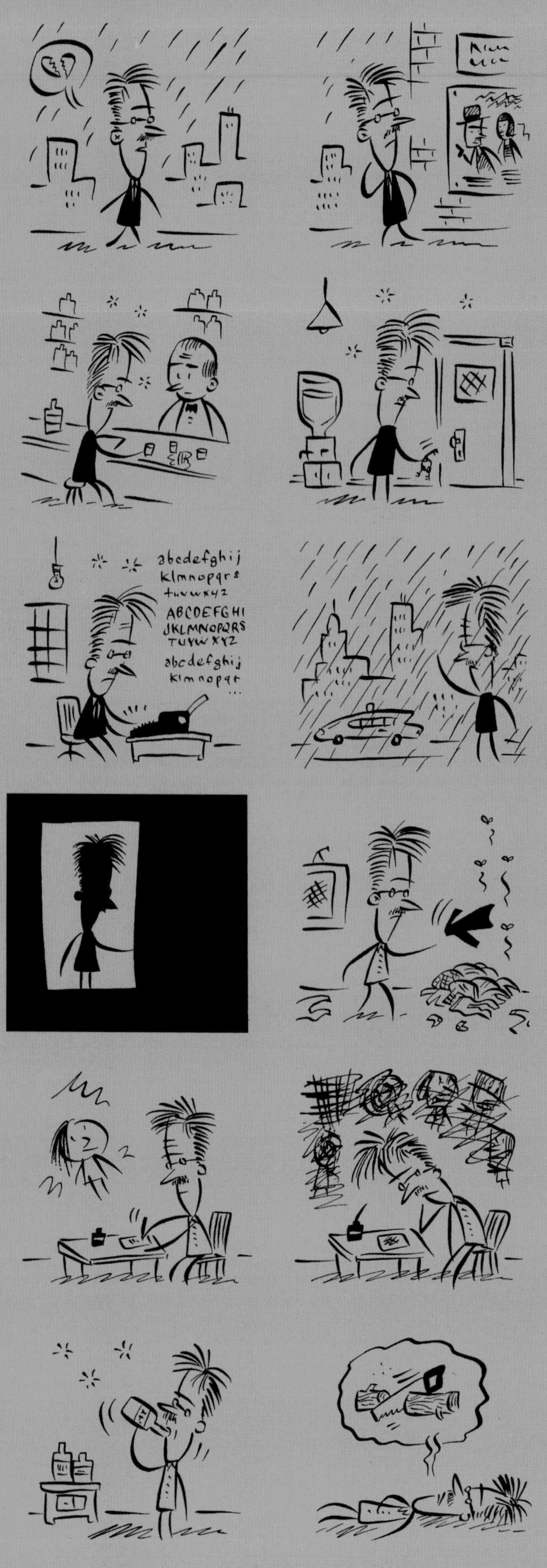

abcdefghij klmnopqrs tuvwxyz ABCDEFGHI JKLMNOPQRS TUVWXYZ abcdefghij klmnopqr ...

THE THURBER SCORECARD

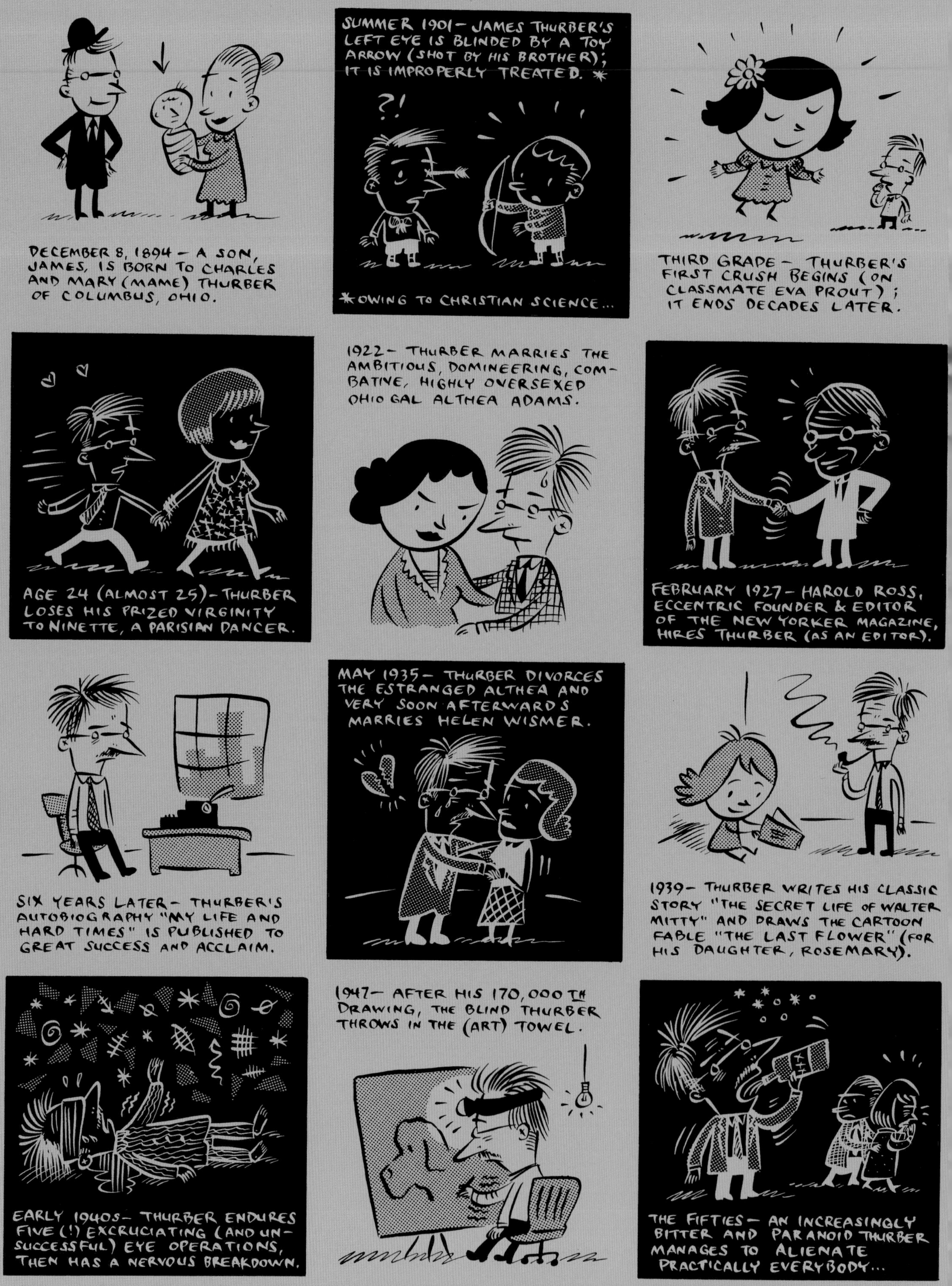

DECEMBER 8, 1894 – A SON, JAMES, IS BORN TO CHARLES AND MARY (MAME) THURBER OF COLUMBUS, OHIO.
SUMMER 1901 – JAMES THURBER'S LEFT EYE IS BLINDED BY A TOY ARROW (SHOT BY HIS BROTHER); IT IS IMPROPERLY TREATED. *
?!
* OWING TO CHRISTIAN SCIENCE...
THIRD GRADE – THURBER'S FIRST CRUSH BEGINS (ON CLASSMATE EVA PROUT); IT ENDS DECADES LATER.
AGE 24 (ALMOST 25) – THURBER LOSES HIS PRIZED VIRGINITY TO NINETTE, A PARISIAN DANCER.
1922 – THURBER MARRIES THE AMBITIOUS, DOMINEERING, COMBATIVE, HIGHLY OVERSEXED OHIO GAL ALTHEA ADAMS.
FEBRUARY 1927 – HAROLD ROSS, ECCENTRIC FOUNDER & EDITOR OF THE NEW YORKER MAGAZINE, HIRES THURBER (AS AN EDITOR).
SIX YEARS LATER – THURBER'S AUTOBIOGRAPHY "MY LIFE AND HARD TIMES" IS PUBLISHED TO GREAT SUCCESS AND ACCLAIM.
MAY 1935 – THURBER DIVORCES THE ESTRANGED ALTHEA AND VERY SOON AFTERWARDS MARRIES HELEN WISMER.
1939 – THURBER WRITES HIS CLASSIC STORY "THE SECRET LIFE OF WALTER MITTY" AND DRAWS THE CARTOON FABLE "THE LAST FLOWER" (FOR HIS DAUGHTER, ROSEMARY).
EARLY 1940S – THURBER ENDURES FIVE (!) EXCRUCIATING (AND UNSUCCESSFUL) EYE OPERATIONS, THEN HAS A NERVOUS BREAKDOWN.
1947 – AFTER HIS 170,000TH DRAWING, THE BLIND THURBER THROWS IN THE (ART) TOWEL.
THE FIFTIES – AN INCREASINGLY BITTER AND PARANOID THURBER MANAGES TO ALIENATE PRACTICALLY EVERYBODY...

THE NIGHT THE WRITER FELL

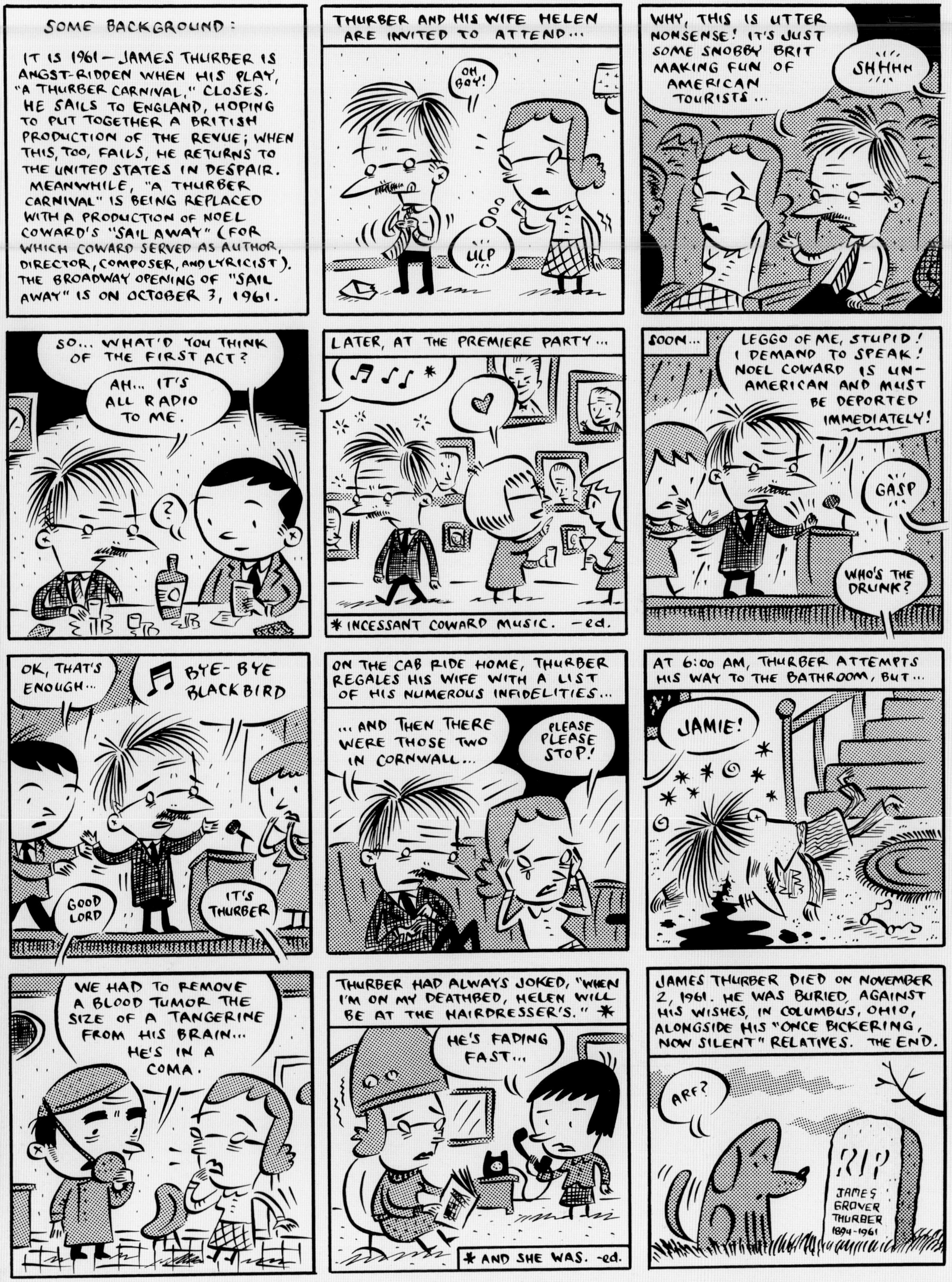
SOME BACKGROUND:
IT IS 1961 — JAMES THURBER IS ANGST-RIDDEN WHEN HIS PLAY, "A THURBER CARNIVAL," CLOSES. HE SAILS TO ENGLAND, HOPING TO PUT TOGETHER A BRITISH PRODUCTION OF THE REVUE; WHEN THIS, TOO, FAILS, HE RETURNS TO THE UNITED STATES IN DESPAIR. MEANWHILE, "A THURBER CARNIVAL" IS BEING REPLACED WITH A PRODUCTION OF NOEL COWARD'S "SAIL AWAY" (FOR WHICH COWARD SERVED AS AUTHOR, DIRECTOR, COMPOSER, AND LYRICIST). THE BROADWAY OPENING OF "SAIL AWAY" IS ON OCTOBER 3, 1961.
THURBER AND HIS WIFE HELEN ARE INVITED TO ATTEND...
OH BOY!
ULP
WHY, THIS IS UTTER NONSENSE! IT'S JUST SOME SNOBBY BRIT MAKING FUN OF AMERICAN TOURISTS...
SHHHH
SO... WHAT'D YOU THINK OF THE FIRST ACT?
AH... IT'S ALL RADIO TO ME.
?
LATER, AT THE PREMIERE PARTY...
♫ ♪♪ *
♥
* INCESSANT COWARD MUSIC. —ed.
SOON...
LEGGO OF ME, STUPID! I DEMAND TO SPEAK! NOEL COWARD IS UN-AMERICAN AND MUST BE DEPORTED IMMEDIATELY!
GASP
WHO'S THE DRUNK?
OK, THAT'S ENOUGH...
♫ BYE-BYE BLACKBIRD
GOOD LORD
IT'S THURBER
ON THE CAB RIDE HOME, THURBER REGALES HIS WIFE WITH A LIST OF HIS NUMEROUS INFIDELITIES...
...AND THEN THERE WERE THOSE TWO IN CORNWALL...
PLEASE PLEASE STOP!
AT 6:00 AM, THURBER ATTEMPTS HIS WAY TO THE BATHROOM, BUT...
JAMIE!
WE HAD TO REMOVE A BLOOD TUMOR THE SIZE OF A TANGERINE FROM HIS BRAIN... HE'S IN A COMA.
THURBER HAD ALWAYS JOKED, "WHEN I'M ON MY DEATHBED, HELEN WILL BE AT THE HAIRDRESSER'S." *
HE'S FADING FAST...
* AND SHE WAS. —ed.
JAMES THURBER DIED ON NOVEMBER 2, 1961. HE WAS BURIED, AGAINST HIS WISHES, IN COLUMBUS, OHIO, ALONGSIDE HIS "ONCE BICKERING, NOW SILENT" RELATIVES. THE END.
ARF?
RIP
JAMES GROVER THURBER 1894-1961

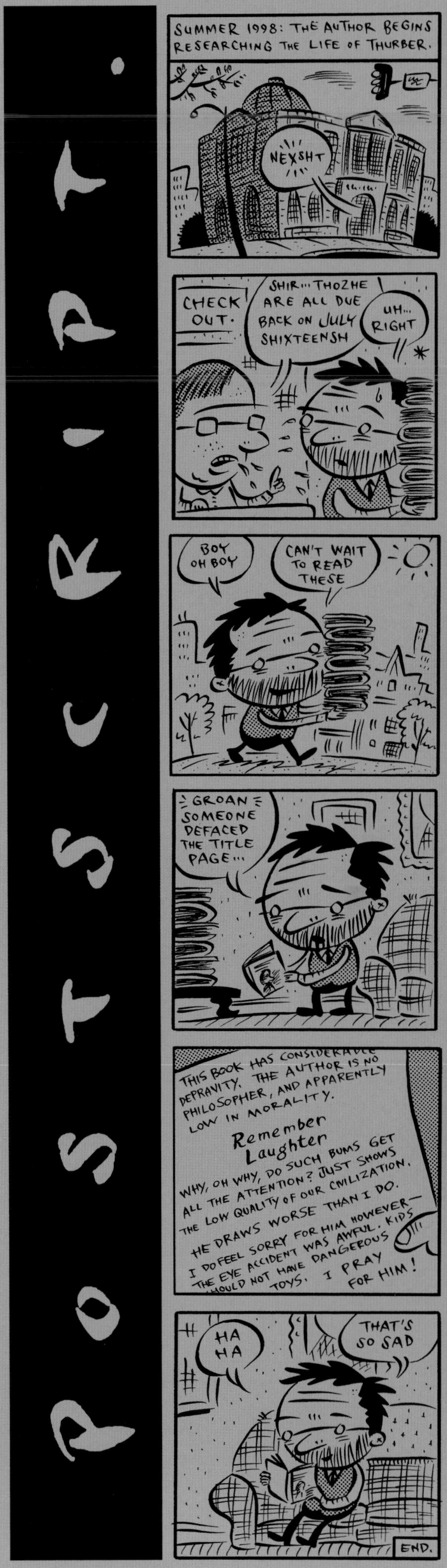
POSTSCRIPT.
SUMMER 1998: THE AUTHOR BEGINS RESEARCHING THE LIFE OF THURBER.
NEXSHT
CHECK OUT.
SHIR... THOZHE ARE ALL DUE BACK ON JULY SHIXTEENSH
UH... RIGHT
BOY OH BOY
CAN'T WAIT TO READ THESE
GROAN SOMEONE DEFACED THE TITLE PAGE...
THIS BOOK HAS CONSIDERABLE DEPRAVITY. THE AUTHOR IS NO PHILOSOPHER, AND APPARENTLY LOW IN MORALITY.
Remember Laughter
WHY, OH WHY, DO SUCH BUMS GET ALL THE ATTENTION? JUST SHOWS THE LOW QUALITY OF OUR CIVILIZATION.
HE DRAWS WORSE THAN I DO.
I DO FEEL SORRY FOR HIM HOWEVER — THE EYE ACCIDENT WAS AWFUL. KIDS HOULD NOT HAVE DANGEROUS TOYS. I PRAY FOR HIM!
HA HA
THAT'S SO SAD
END.

* I KEPT THESE BOOKS FOR OVER THREE YEARS. —ed.

The Race of Life

A Parable

This sequence of thirty-five drawings represents the life story of a man and his wife; or several days, a month, or a year in their life and in that of their child; or their alternately interflowing and diverging streams of consciousness over any given period. It seems to lend itself to a wide variety of interpretations. Anything may be read into it, or left out of it, without making a great deal of difference. Two or three previewers were brought up short by this picture or that — mainly the Enormous Rabbit — and went back and started over again from the beginning tempo of action. It is better to skip pictures, or tear them out, rather than to begin over again and try to fit them in with some preconceived idea of what is going on.

The Enormous Rabbit, which brought two engravers and a receptionist up short, perhaps calls for a few words of explanation. It can be an Uncrossed Bridge which seems, at first glance, to have been burned behind somebody, or it can be Chickens Counted Too Soon, or a ringing phone, or a thought in the night, or a faint hissing sound. More that likely it is an Unopened Telegram which when opened (see page ??, panel ??) proves not to contain the dreadful news one had expected but merely some such innocuous query as: "Did you find my silver-rimmed glasses in brown case after party Saturday?"

The snow in which the bloodhounds are caught may be either real snow or pieces of paper torn up. ★★★

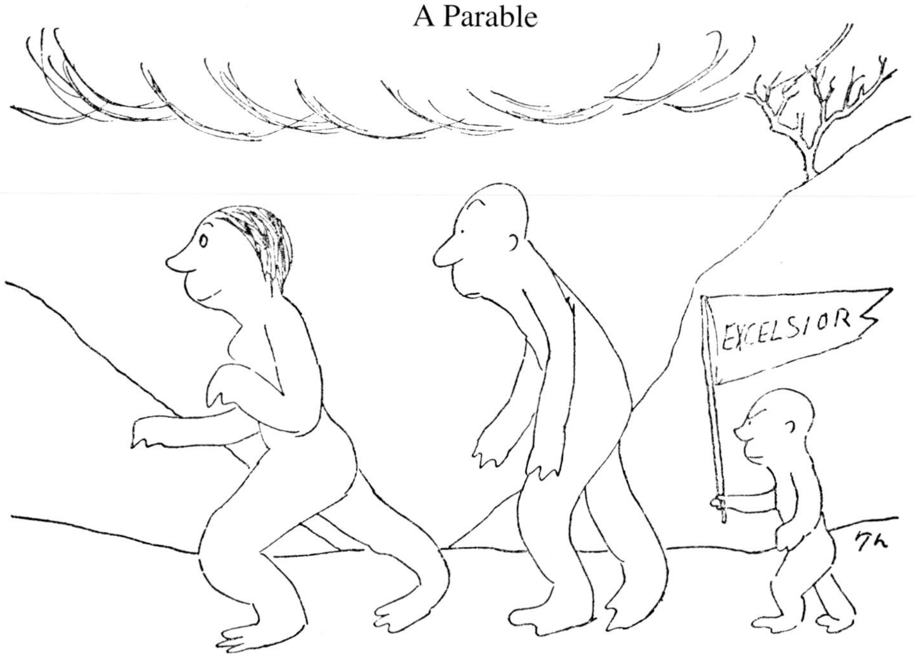
EXCELSIOR

The Start

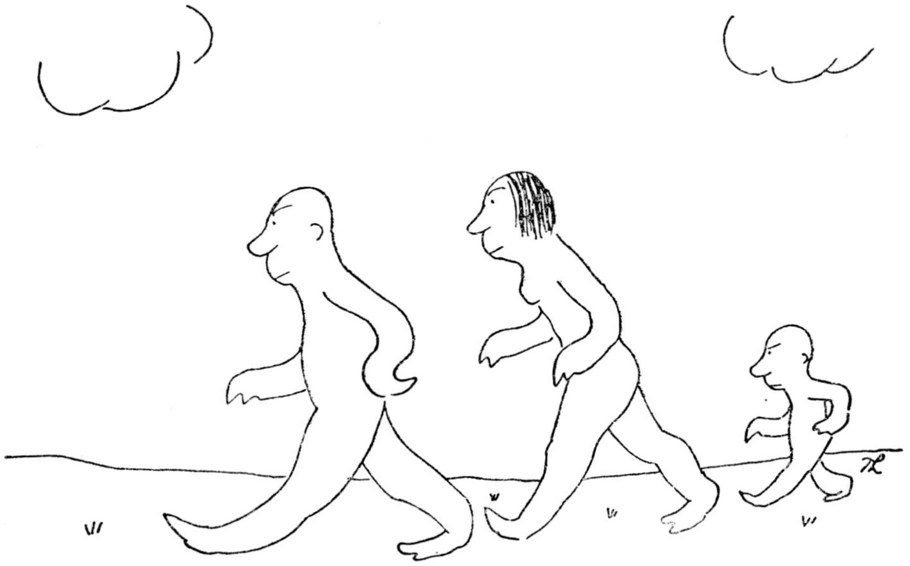

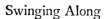

Swinging Along

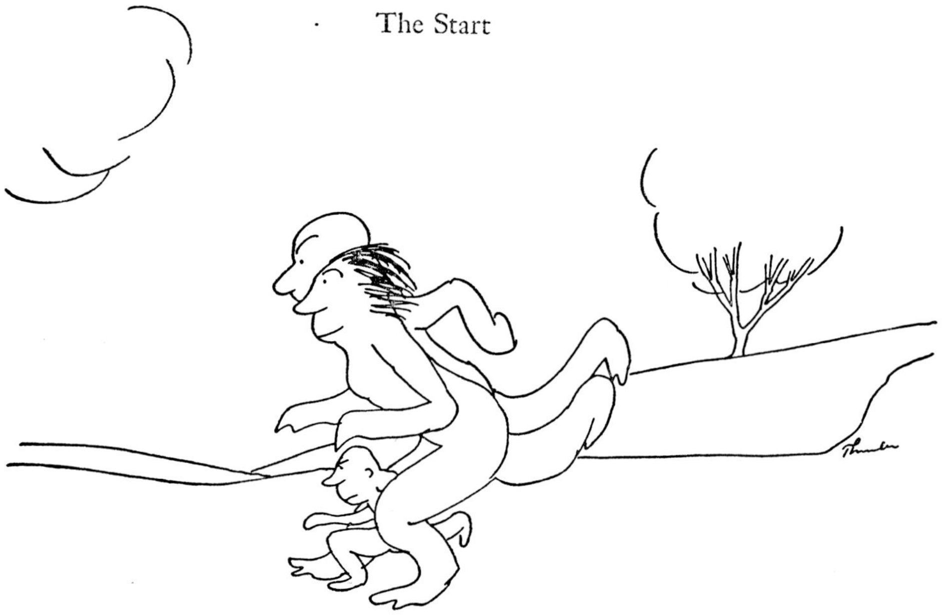

Neck and Neck

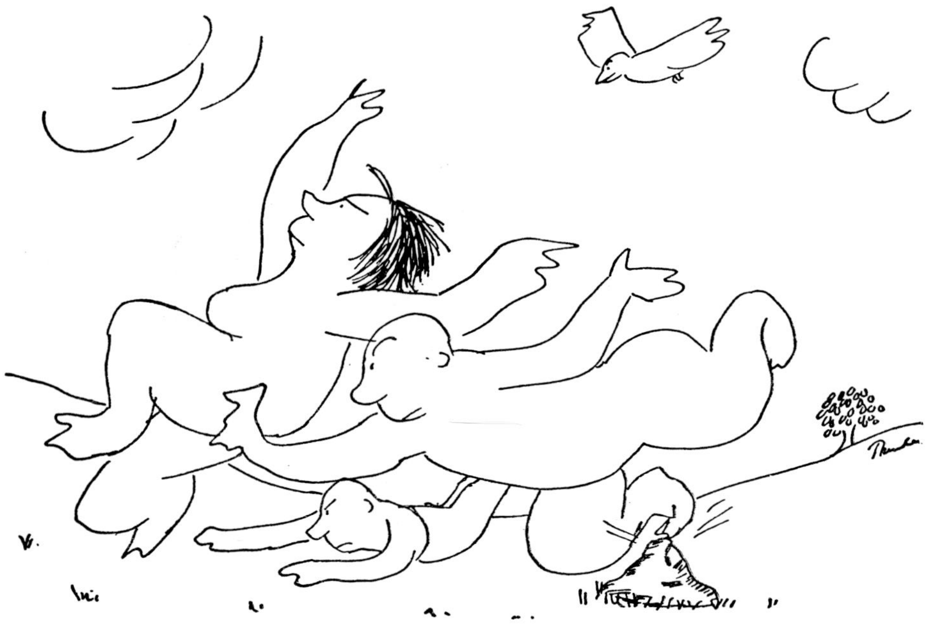

Accident

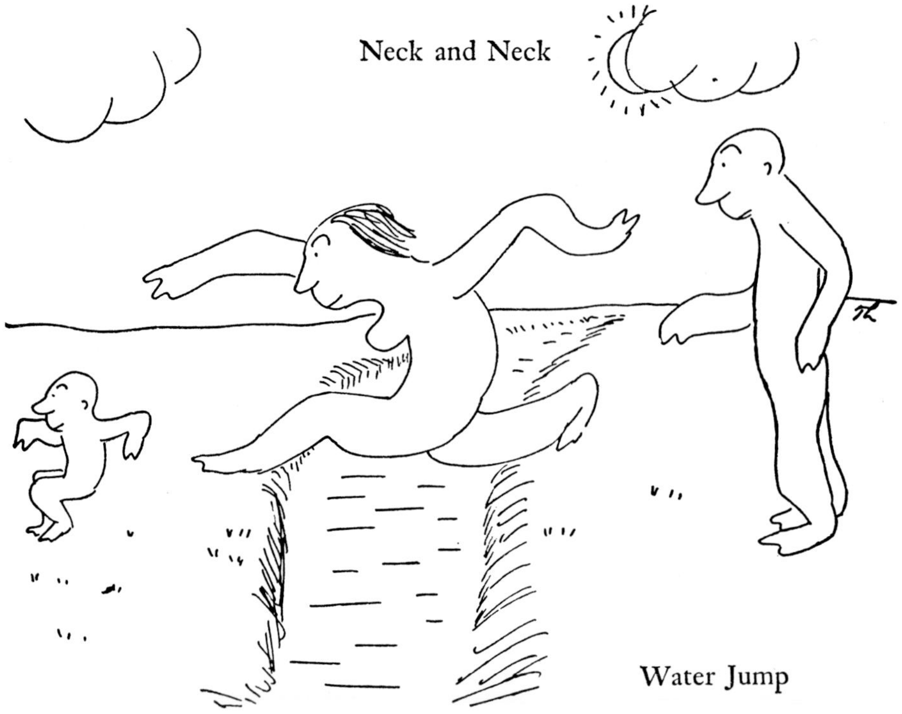

Water Jump

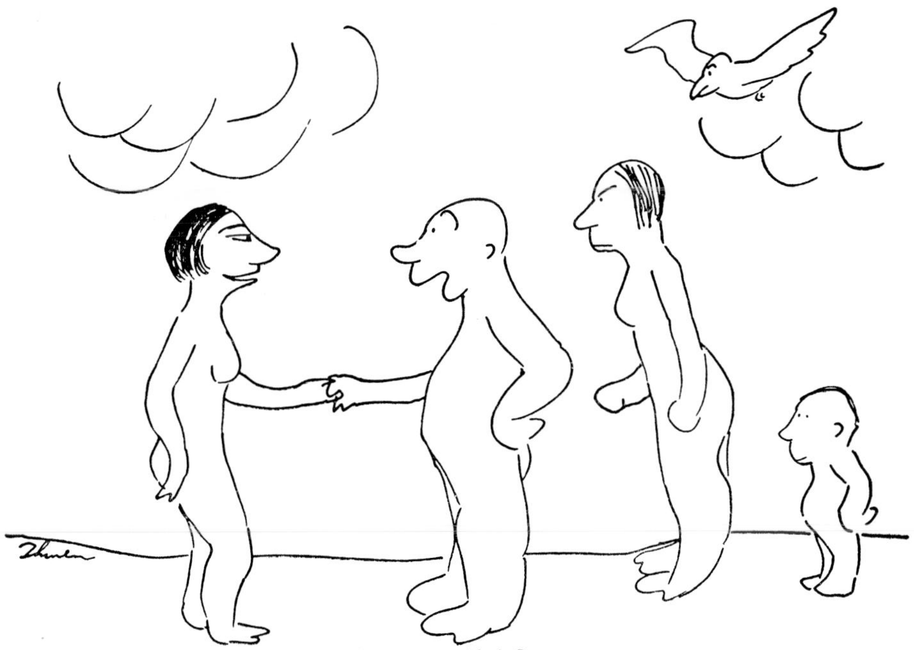

The Beautiful Stranger

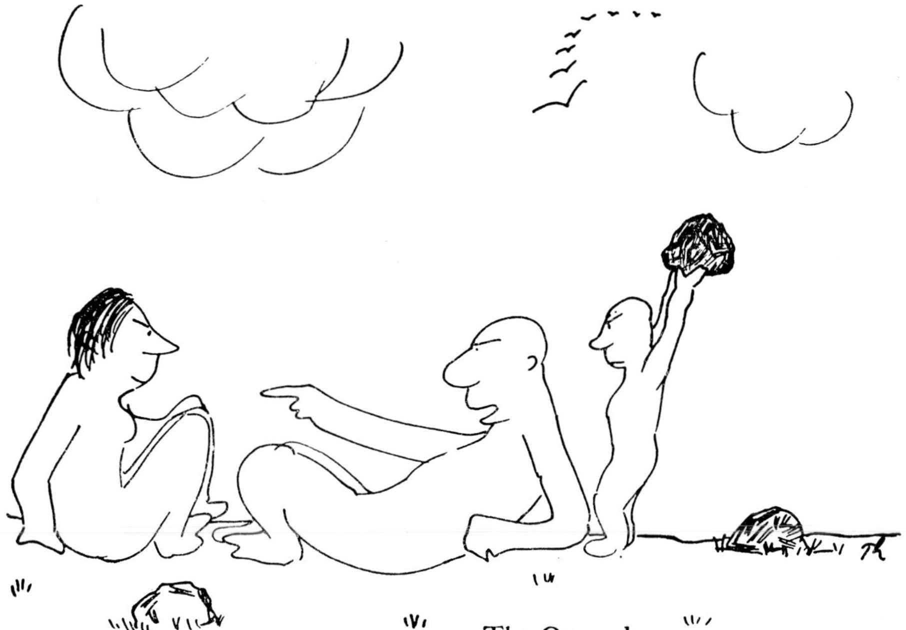

The Quarrel

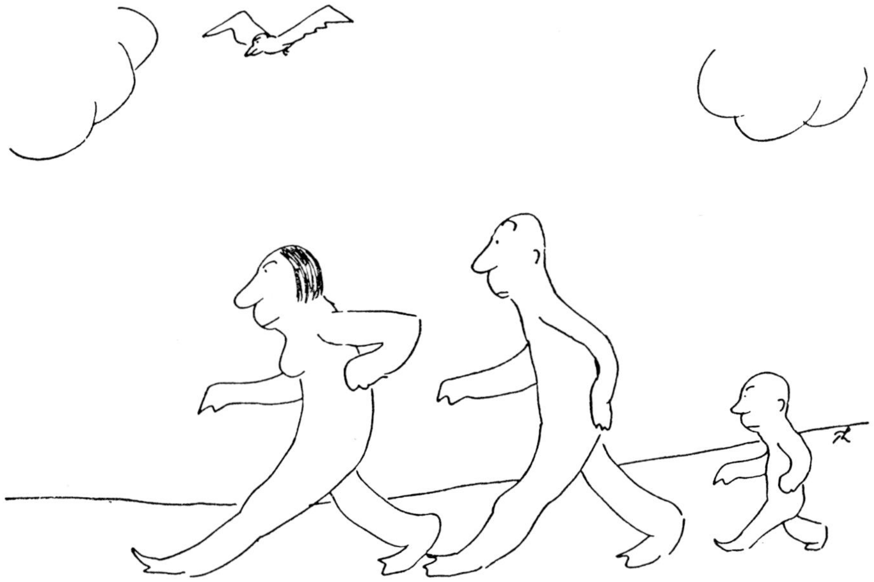

The Pacemaker

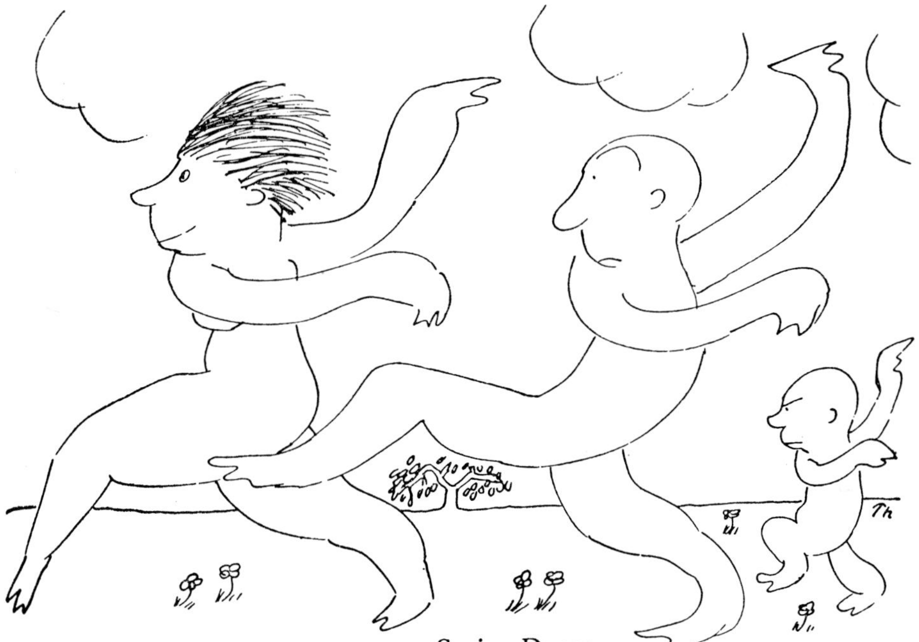

Spring Dance

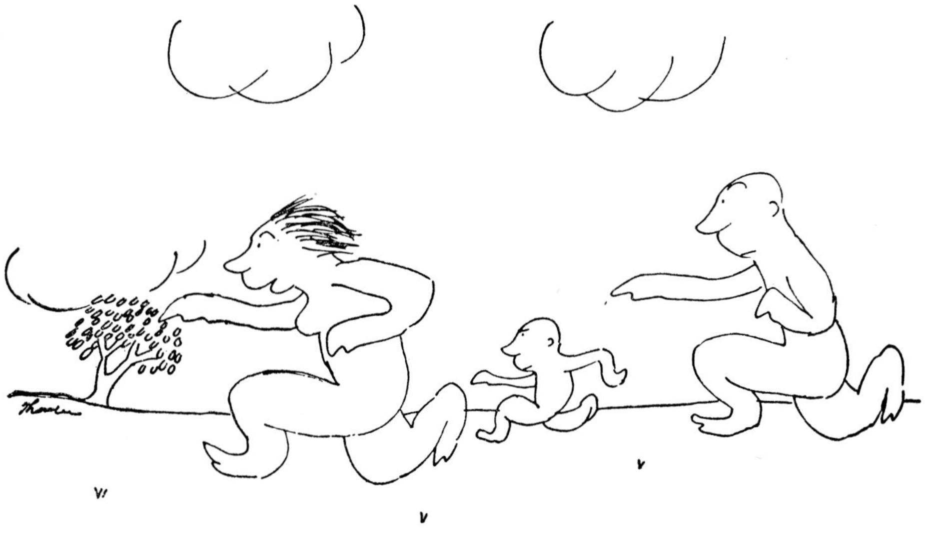

Faster

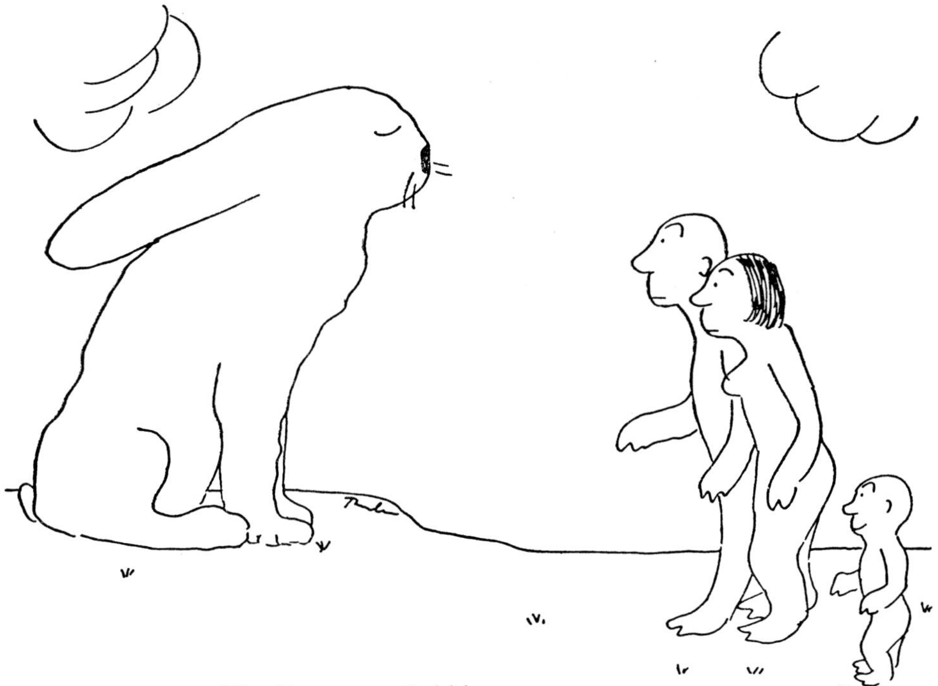

The Enormous Rabbit

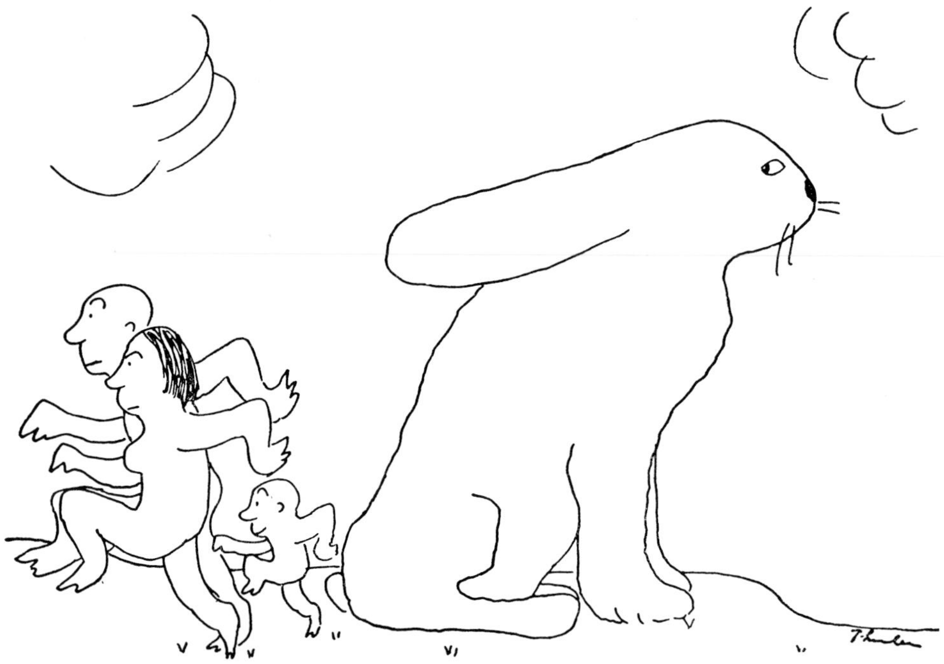

Escape

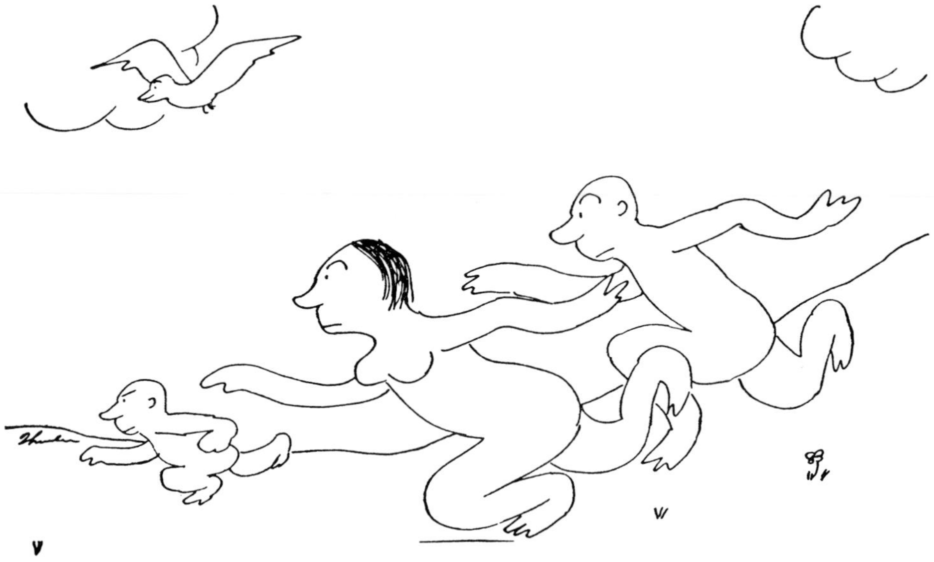

Top Speed

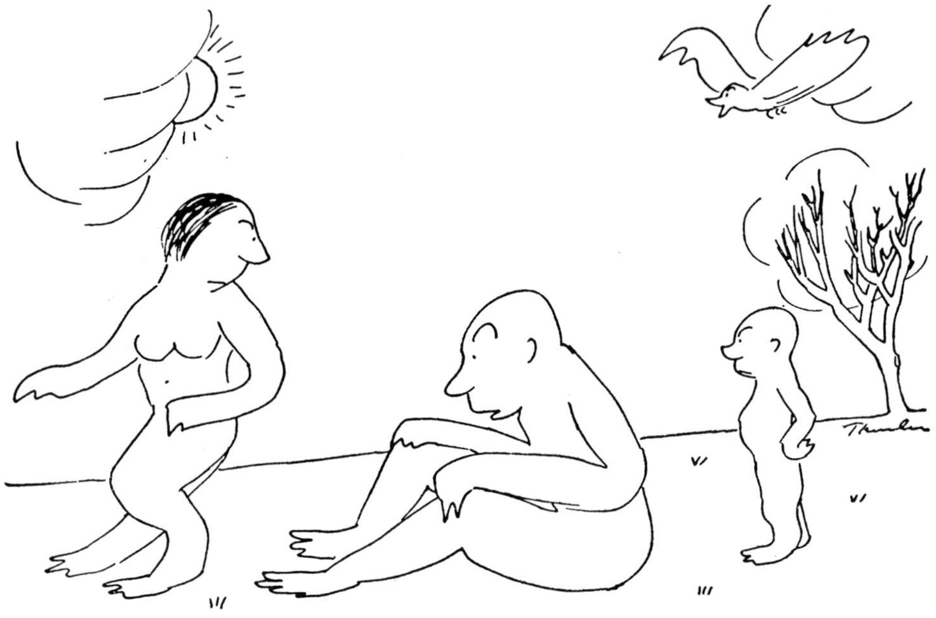

Winded

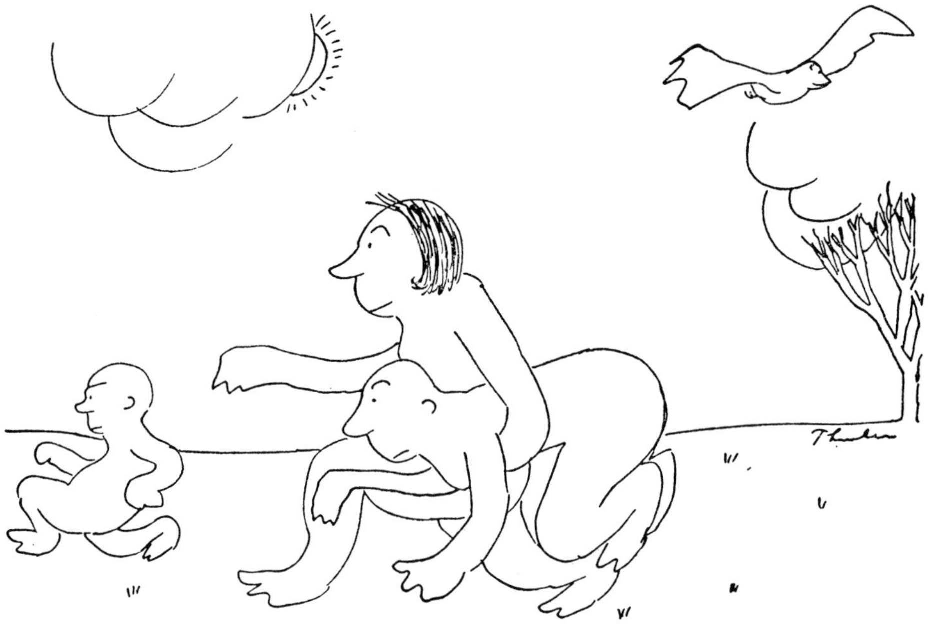

Quand Même

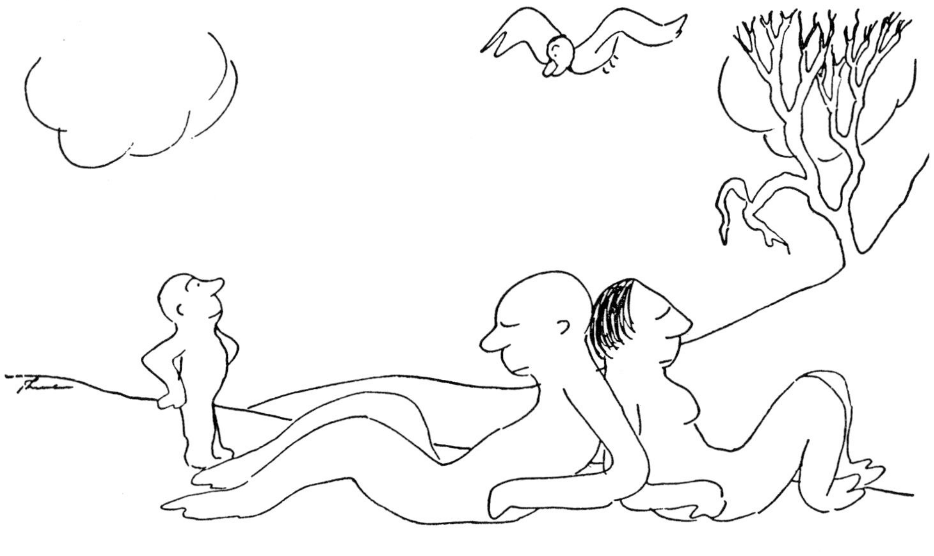

Breathing Spell

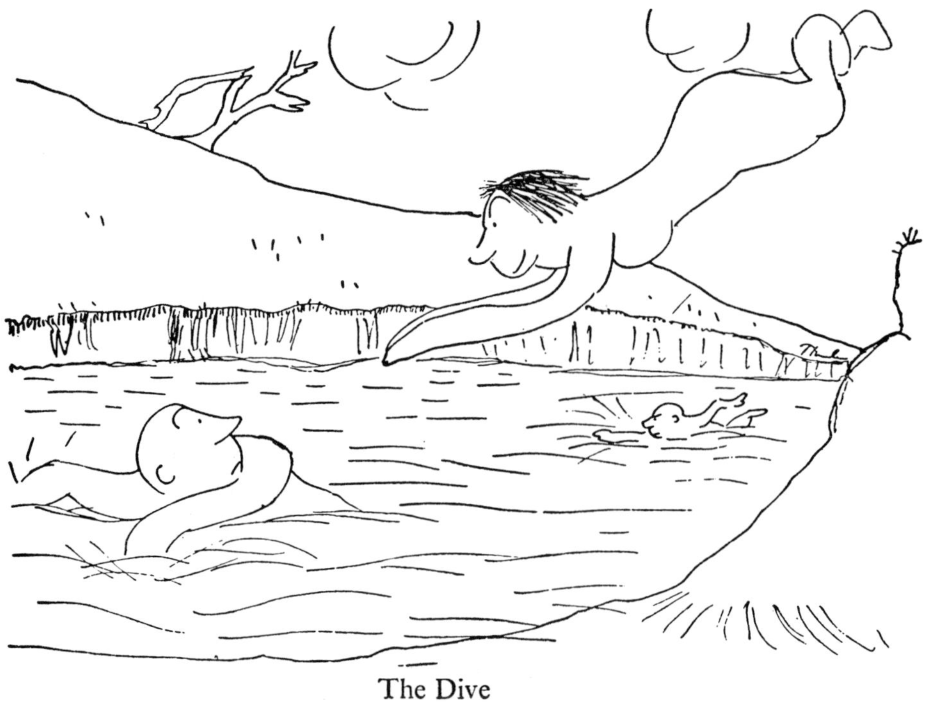

The Dive

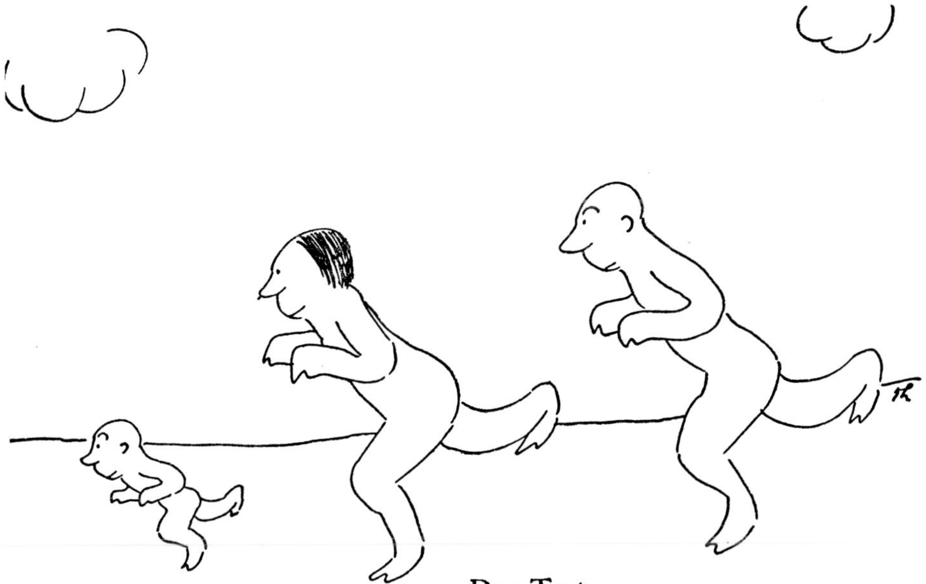

Dog Trot

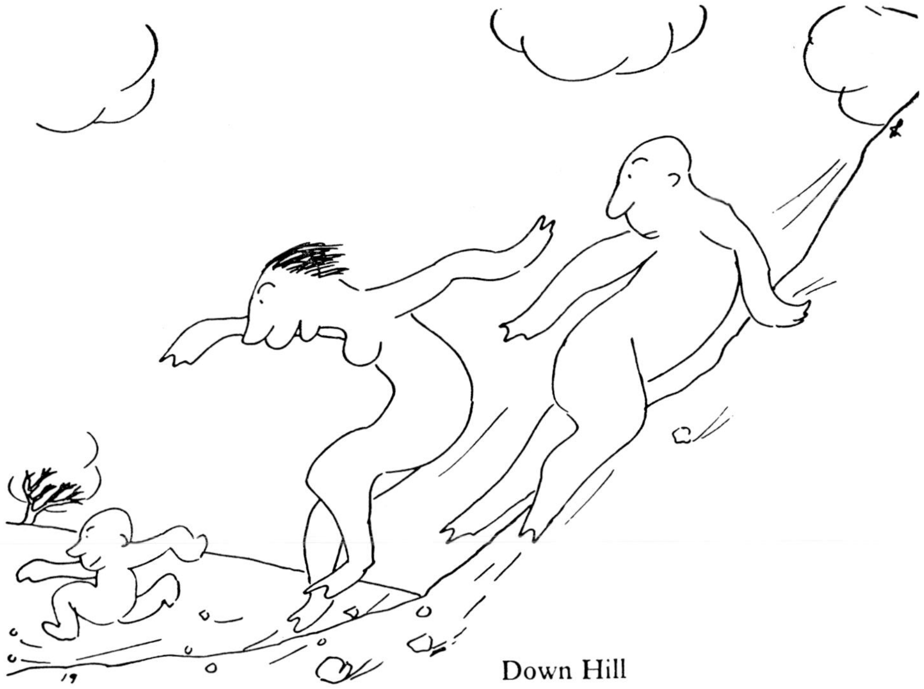

Down Hill

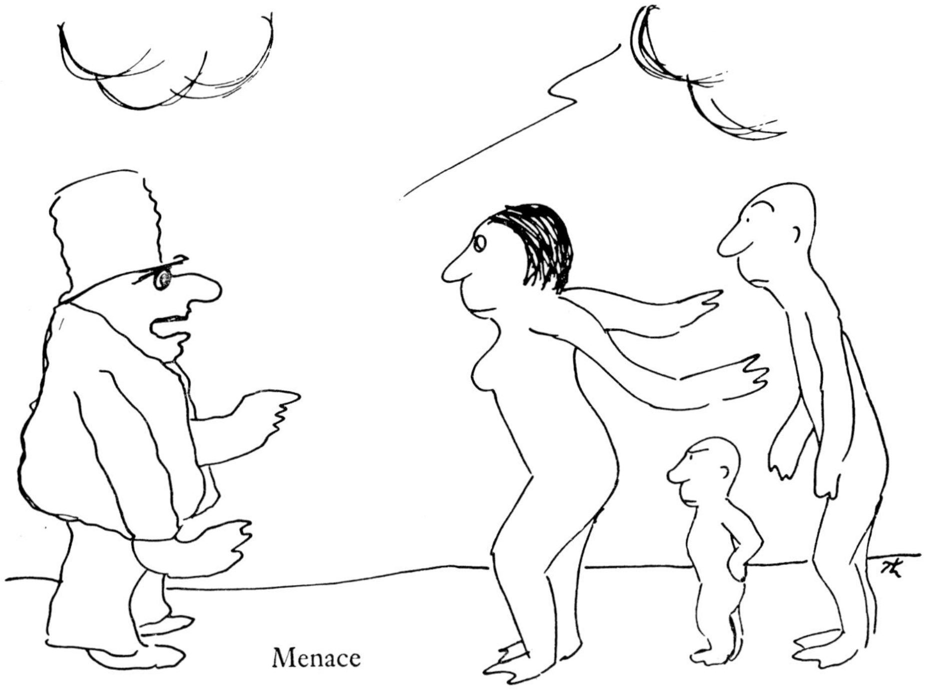

Menace

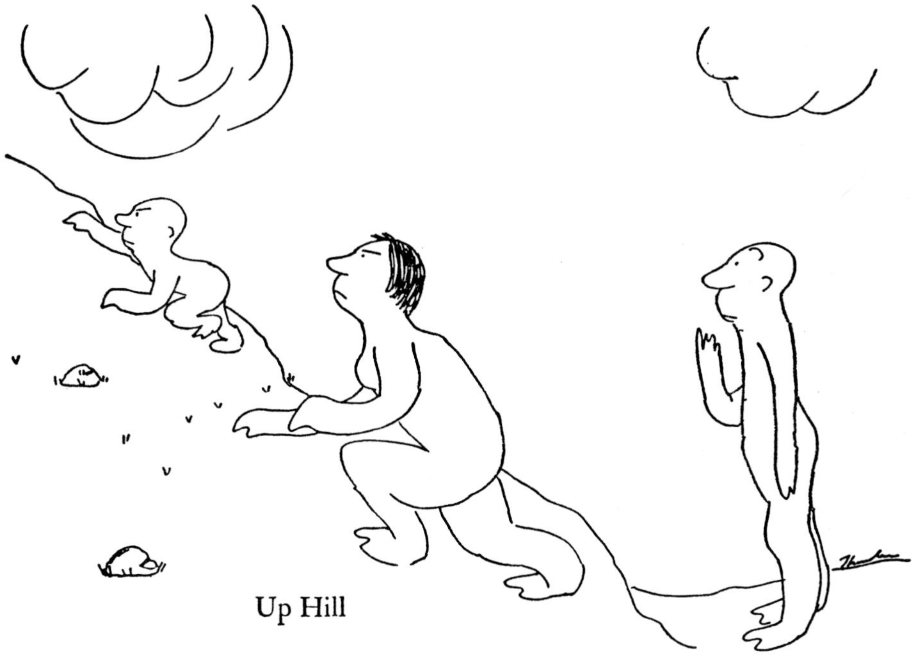

Up Hill

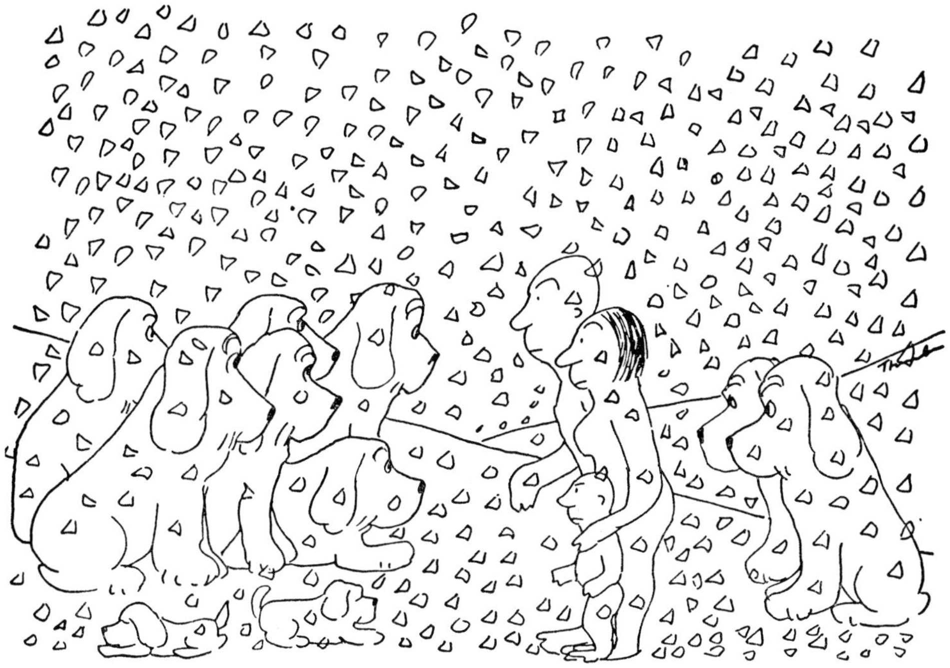

Dogs in the Blizzard

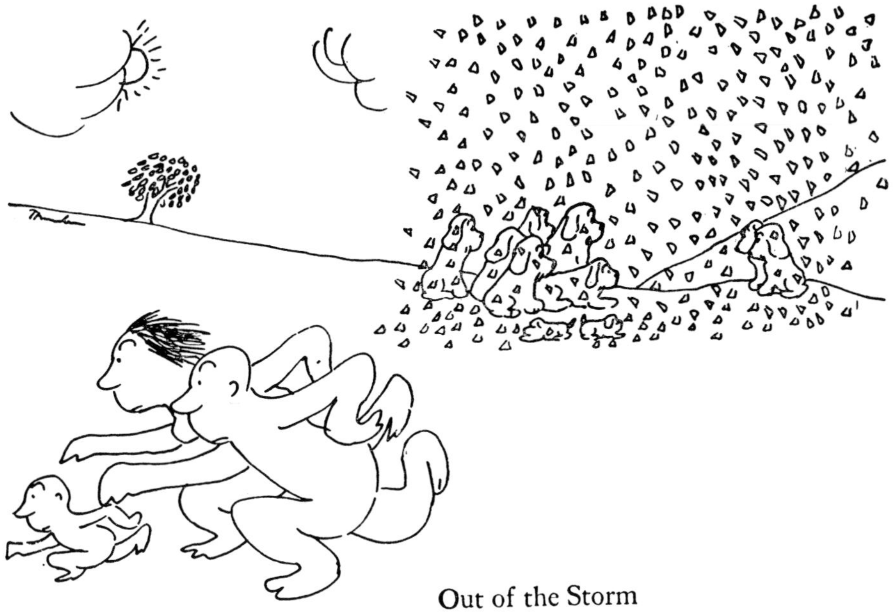

Out of the Storm

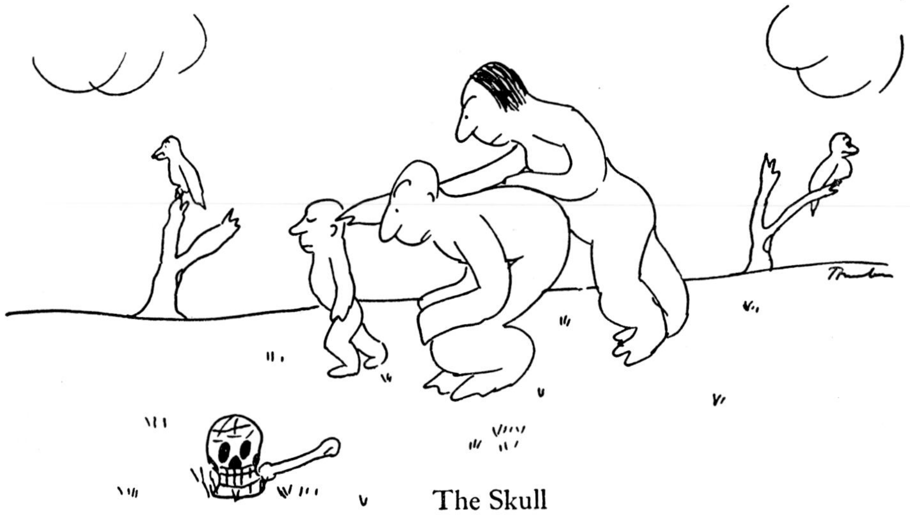
The Skull

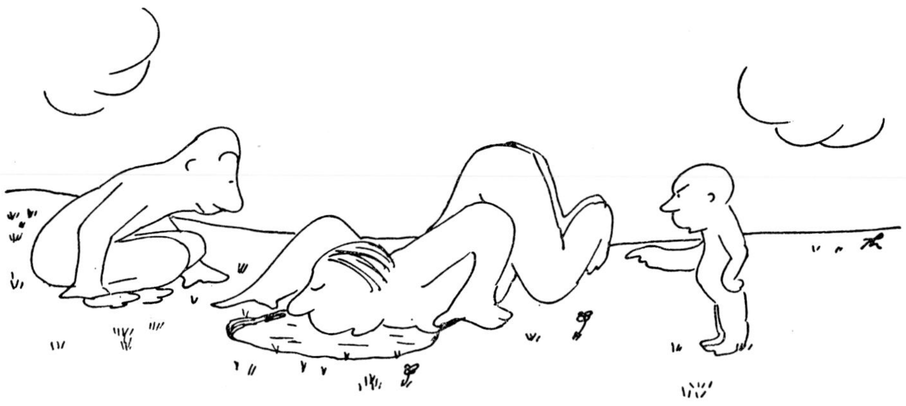
The Water Hole

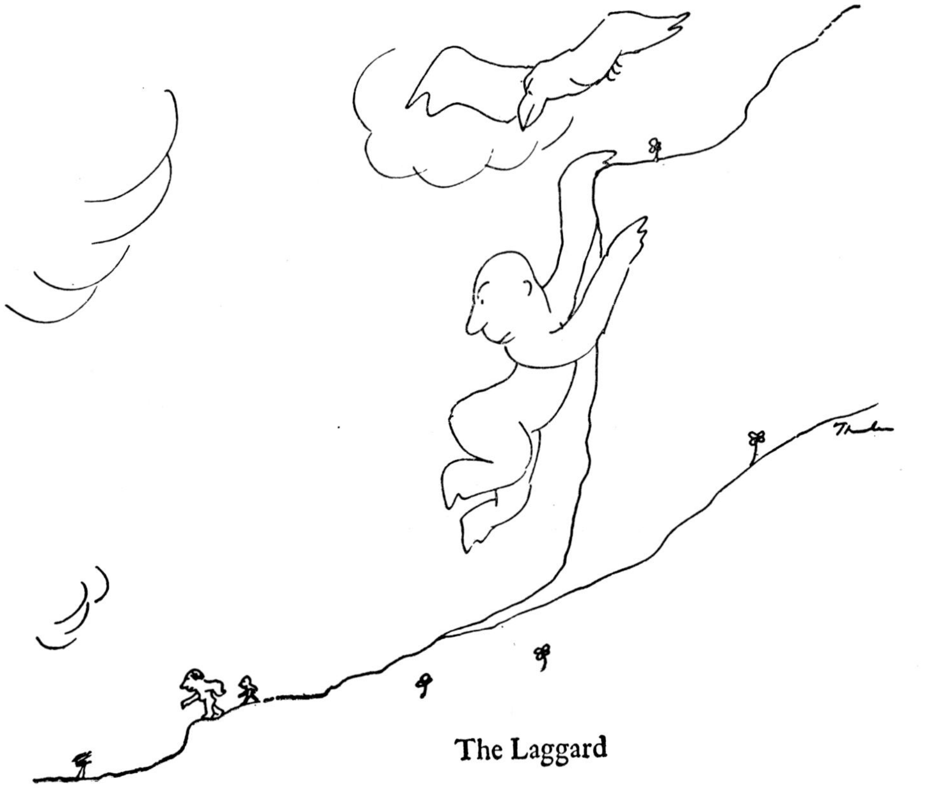
The Laggard

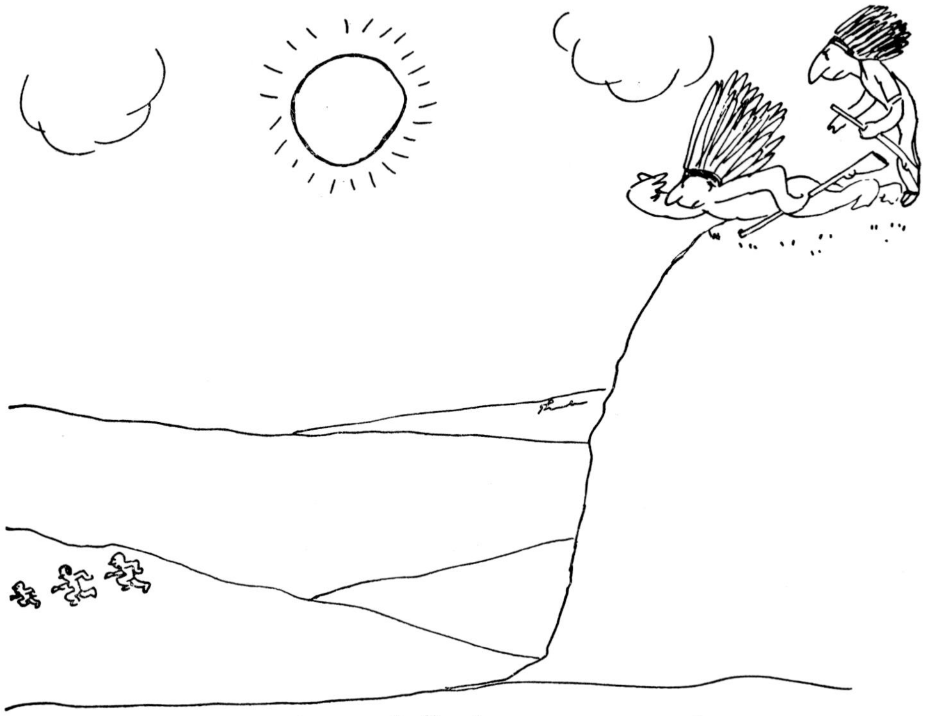
Indians!

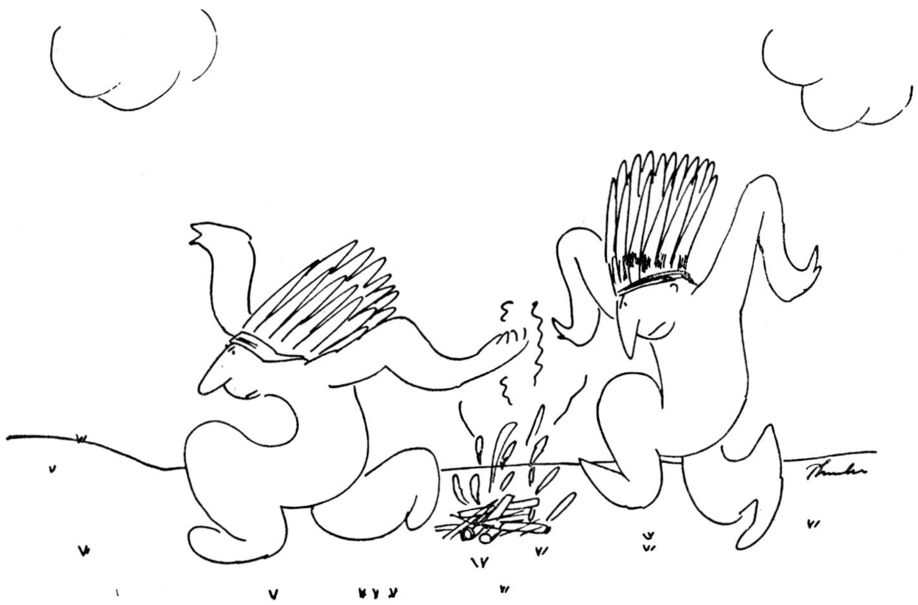
War Dance

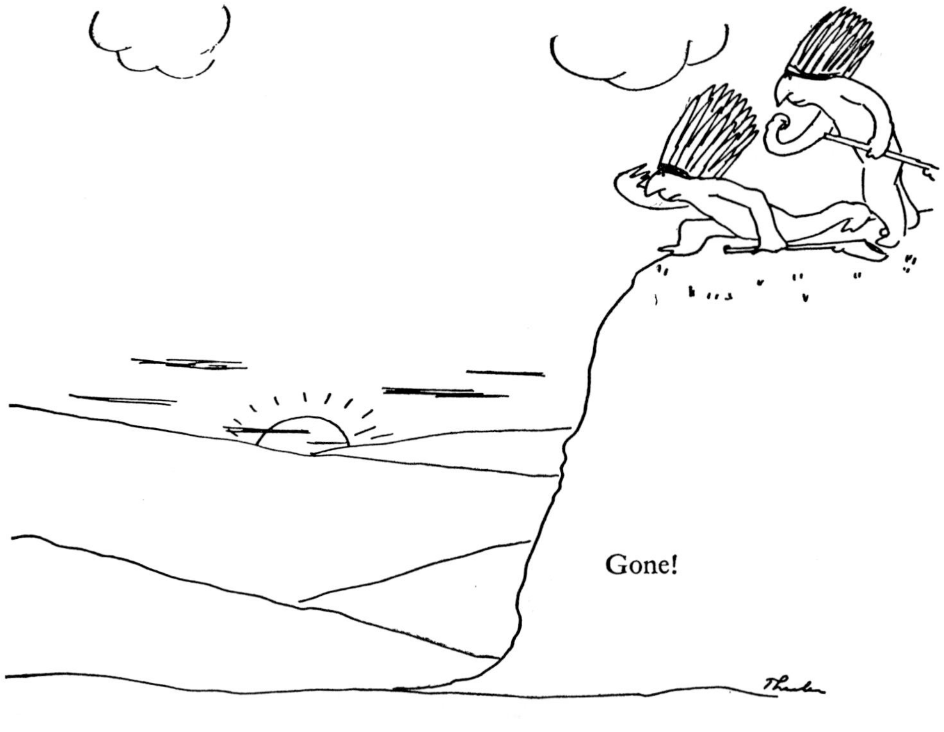
Gone!

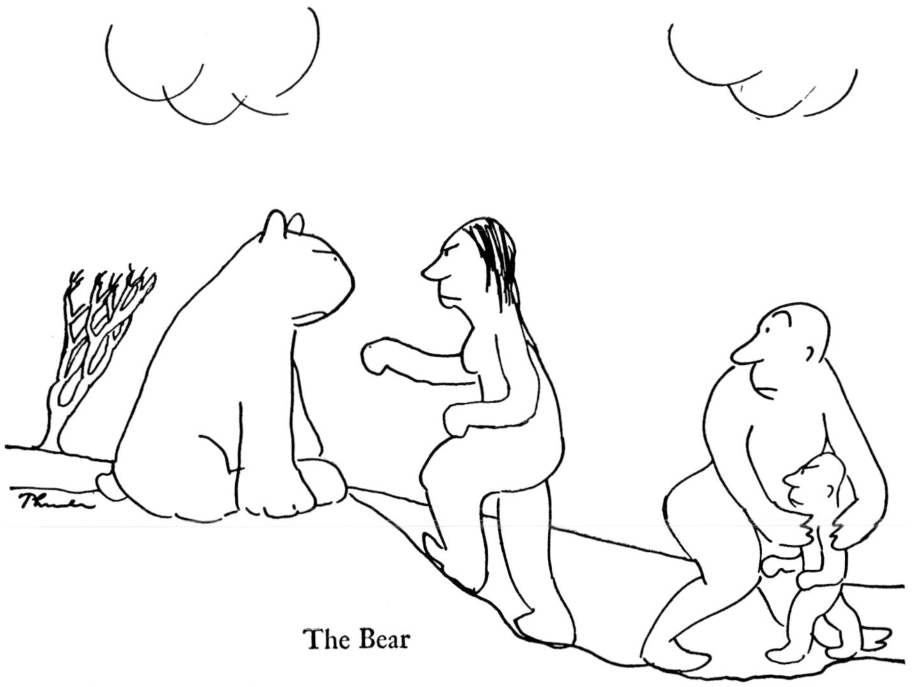

The Bear

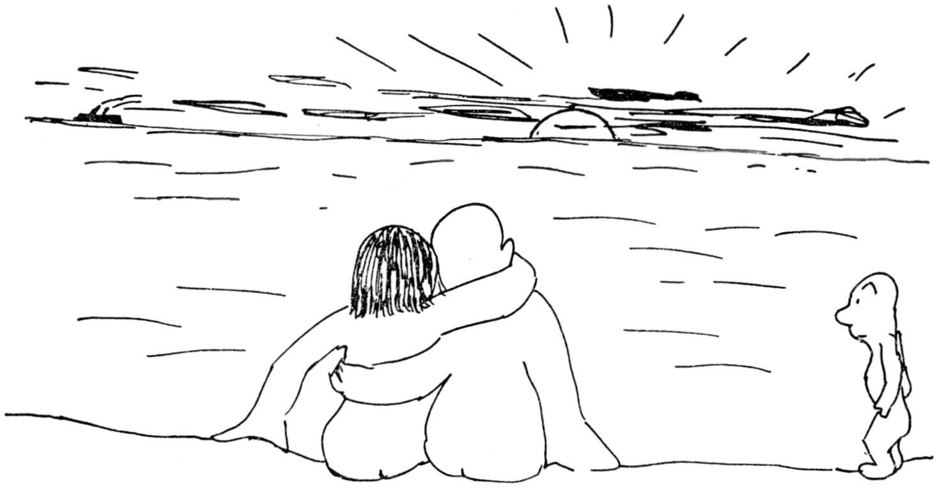

Sunset

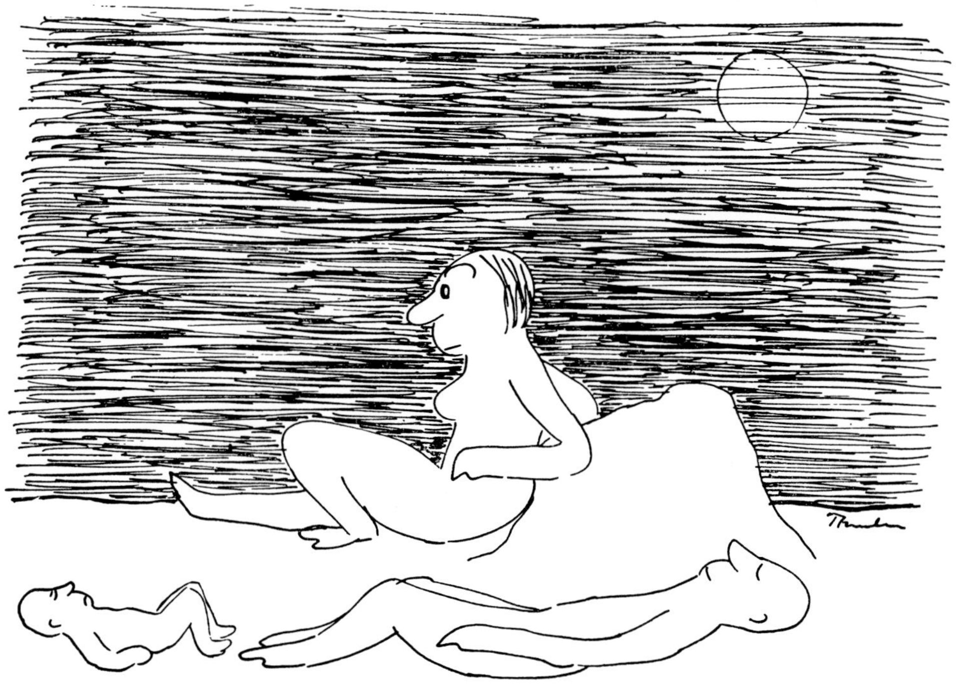

On Guard

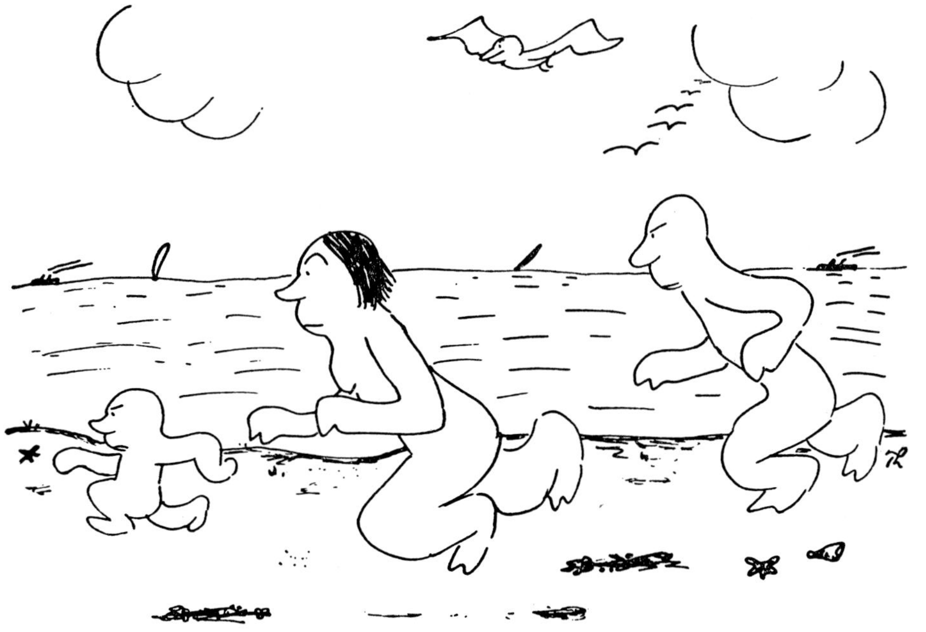

Dawn: Off Again

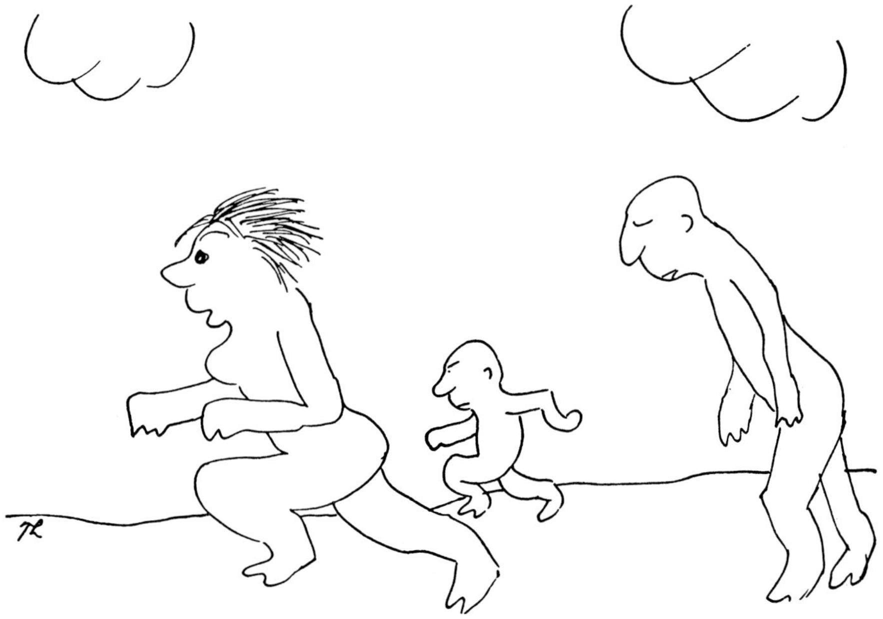

Final Sprint

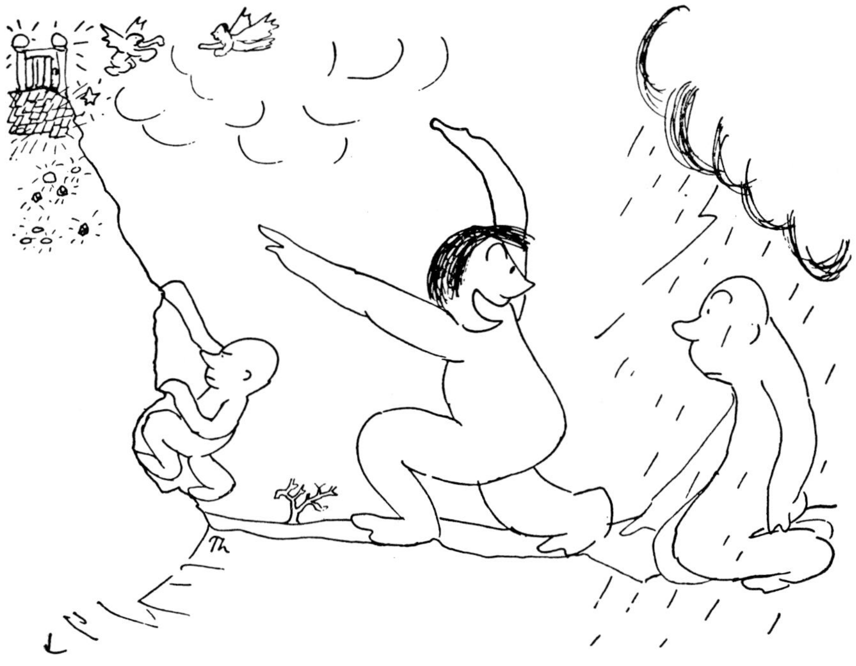

The Goal

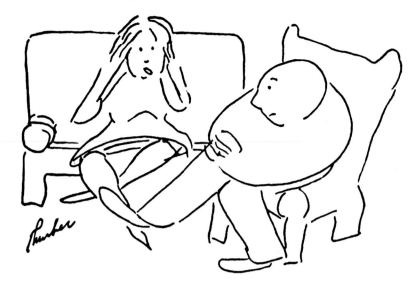

"With you I have known peace, Lida, and now you say you're going crazy."

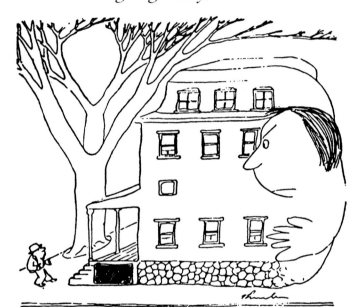

Home

THE LADY ON THE BOOKCASE

James Thurber on James Thurber

by James Thurber

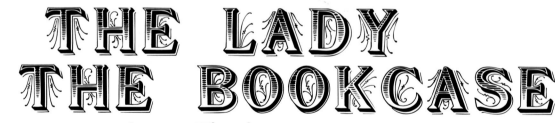

ONE DAY SOME 20 years ago an outraged cartoonist, four of whose drawings had been rejected in a clump by *The New Yorker,* stormed into the office of the late Harold Ross, editor of the magazine. "Why is it," demanded the cartoonist, "that you reject my work and publish drawings by a fifth-rate artist like Thurber?" Ross came quickly to my defense like the true friend and devoted employer he was. "You mean third-rate," he said quietly, but there was a warning glint in his steady gray eyes that caused the discomfited cartoonist to beat a hasty retreat.

With the exception of Ross, the interest of editors in what I draw has been rather more journalistic than critical. They want to know if it is true that I draw by moonlight, or under water, and when I say no, they lose interest until they hear the rumor that I found the drawings in an old trunk or that I do the captions while my nephew makes the sketches.

One day I was shoving some of my originals around on the floor (I didn't draw on the floor; I was just shoving the originals around) and they fell, or perhaps I pushed them, into five separate and indistinct categories. I have never wanted to write about my drawings, and I still don't want to, but it occurred to me that it might be a good idea to do it now, when everybody is busy with something else, and get it over quietly.

Category No. 1, then, which may be called the Unconscious or Stream of Nervousness Category, is represented by "With you I have known peace, Lida, and now you say you're going crazy" and the drawing entitled with simple dignity, "Home." These drawings were done while the artist was thinking of something else (or so he has been assured by experts) and

This page: Panels from *Thurber: Writings and Drawings.*

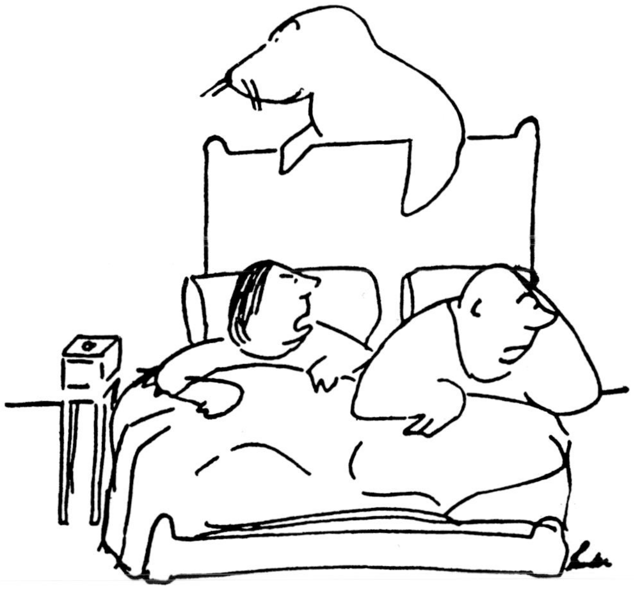

"All right, have it your way—you heard a seal bark."

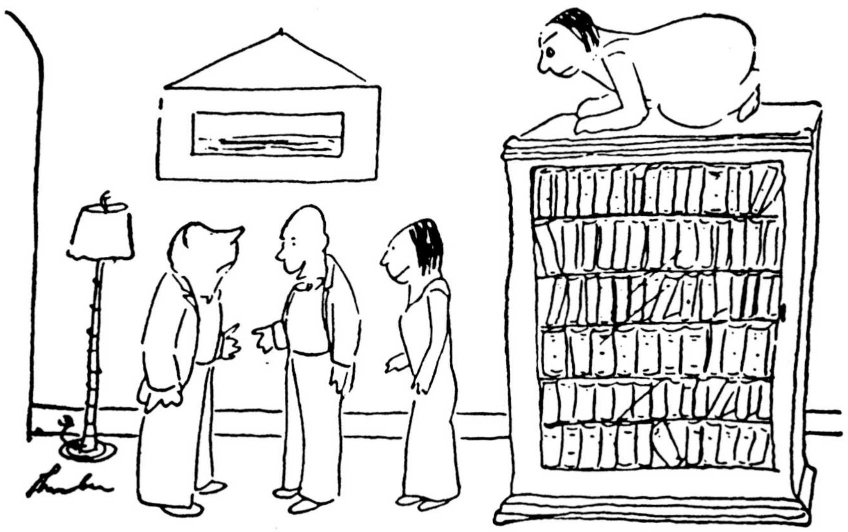

"That's my first wife up there, and this is the present *Mrs. Harris."*

This page: Panels from *Thurber: Writings and Drawings.*

hence his hand was guided by the Unconscious which, in turn, was more or less influenced by the Subconscious.

Students of Jung have instructed me that Lida and the House-Woman are representations of the *anima*, the female essence or directive which floats around in the ageless universal Subconscious of Man like a tadpole in a cistern. Less intellectual critics insist that the two ladies are actual persons I have consciously known. Between these two schools of thought lies a discouragingly large space of time extending roughly from 1,000,000 B.C. to the middle nineteen-thirties.

Whenever I try to trace the true identity of the House-Woman, I get to thinking of Mr. Jones. He appeared in my office one day 12 years ago, said he was Mr. Jones, and asked me to lend him "Home" for reproduction in an art magazine. I never saw the drawing again. Tall, well-dressed, kind of sad-looking chap, and as well spoken a gentleman as you would want to meet.

Category No. 2 brings us to Freud and another one of those discouragingly large spaces — namely, the space between the Concept of the Purely Accidental and the Theory of Haphazard Determination. Whether chance is capricious or we are all prisoners of pattern is too long and cloudy a subject to go into here. I shall consider each of the drawings in Category No. 2, explaining what happened and leaving the definition of the forces involved up to you. The seal on top of the bed, then ("All right, have it your way — you heard a seal bark"), started out to be a seal on a rock. The rock, in the process of being drawn, began to look like the head of a bed, so I made a bed out of it, put a man and wife in the bed, and stumbled onto the caption as easily and unexpectedly as the seal had stumbled into the bedroom.

The woman on top of the bookcase ("That's my first wife up there, and this is the *present* Mrs. Harris") was originally designed to be a woman crouched on the top step of a staircase, but since the tricks and conventions of perspective and planes sometimes fail me, the staircase assumed the shape of a bookcase and was finished as such, to the surprise and embarrassment of the first Mrs. Harris, the present Mrs. Harris, the male visitor, Mr. Harris and me. Before *The New Yorker* would print the drawing, they phoned me long distance to inquire whether the first Mrs. Harris was alive or dead or stuffed. I replied that my taxidermist had advised me that you cannot stuff a woman, and that my physician had informed me that a dead lady cannot support herself on all fours. This meant, I said, that the first Mrs. Harris was unquestionably alive.

The man riding on the other man's shoulders in the bar ("For the last time, you and your horsie get away from me and stay away!") was intended to be standing alongside the irate speaker, but I started his head up too

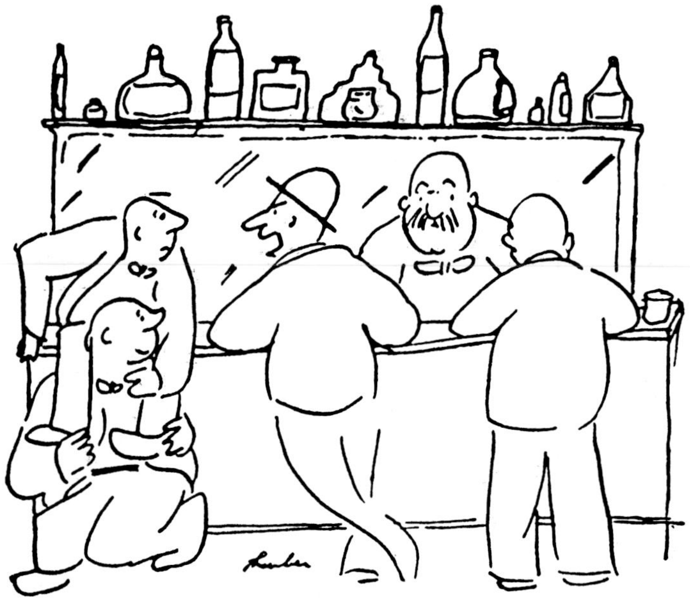

"For the last time, you and your horsie get away from me and stay away!"

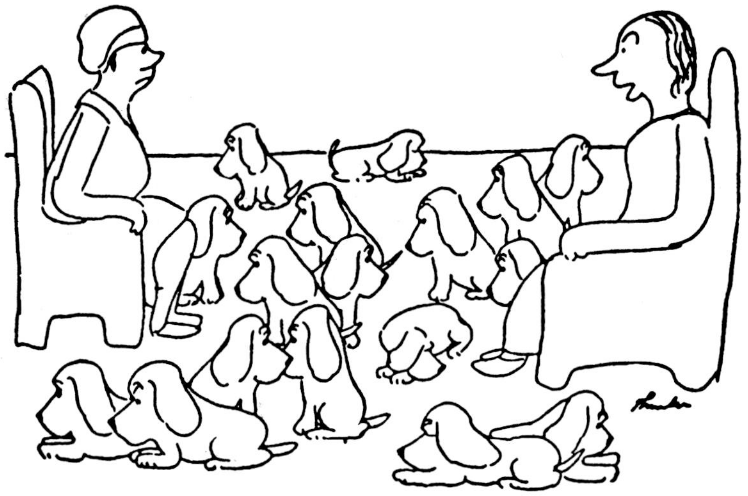

"The father belonged to some people who were driving through in a Packard."

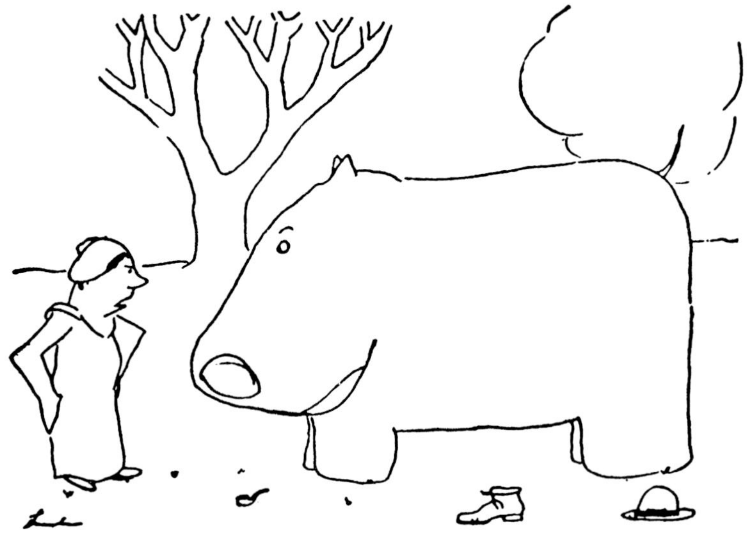

"What have you done with Dr. Millmoss?"

This page: Panels from *Thurber: Writings and Drawings.*

high and made it too small, so that he would have been nine feet tall if I had completed his body that way. It was but the work of 32 seconds to put him on another man's shoulders. As simple or, if you like, as complicated as that. The psychological factors which may be present here are, as I have indicated, elaborate and confused. Personally, I like Dr. Claude Thornway's theory of the Deliberate Accident or Conditioned Mistake.

The psychological factors which may be present here are, as I have indicated, elaborate and confused.

Category No. 3 is perhaps a variant of Category No. 2; indeed, they may even be identical. The dogs in "The father belonged to some people who were driving through in a Packard" were drawn in a captionless spot, and the interior with figures just sort of grew up around them. The hippopotamus in "What have you done with Dr. Millmoss?" was drawn to amuse my small daughter. Something about the creature's expression when he was completed convinced me that he had recently eaten a man. I added the hat and pipe and Mrs. Millmoss, and the caption followed easily enough. Incidentally, my daughter, who was 2 years old at the time, identified the beast immediately. "That's a hippotomanus," she said. *The New Yorker* was not so smart. They described the drawing for their files as follows: "Woman with strange animal." *The New Yorker* was 9 years old at the time.

Category No. 4 is represented by perhaps the best known of some 15 drawings belonging to this special grouping, which may be called the Contributed Idea Category. This drawing *("Touché!")* was originally done for *The New Yorker* by Carl Rose, caption and all. Mr. Rose is a realistic artist, and his gory scene distressed the editors, who hate violence. They asked Rose if he would let me have the idea, since there is obviously no blood to speak of in the people I draw. Rose graciously consented. No one who looks at *"Touché!"* believes that the man whose head is in the air is really dead. His opponent will hand it back to him with profuse apologies, and the discommoded fencer will replace it on his shoulders and say, "No harm done, forget it." Thus the old controversy as to whether death can be made funny is left just where it was before Carl Rose came along with his wonderful idea.

Category No. 5, our final one, can be called, believe it or not, the

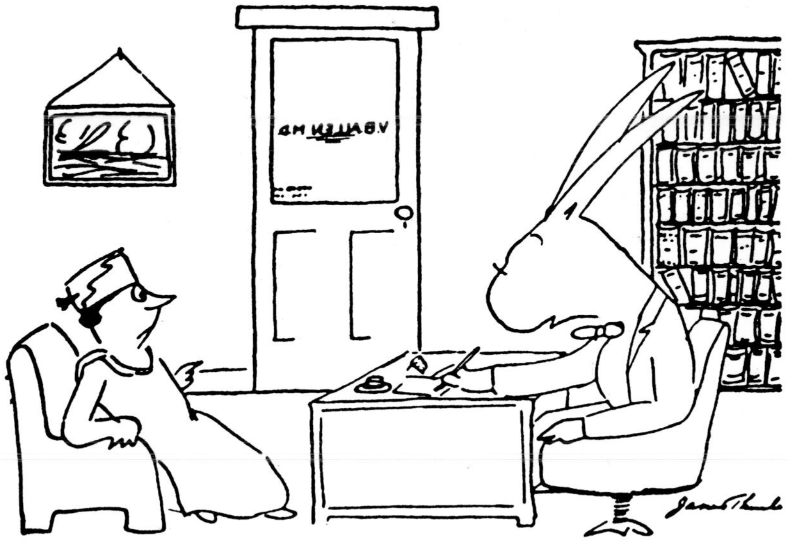

"You said a moment ago that everybody you look at seems to be a rabbit. Now just what do you mean by that, Mrs. Sprague?"

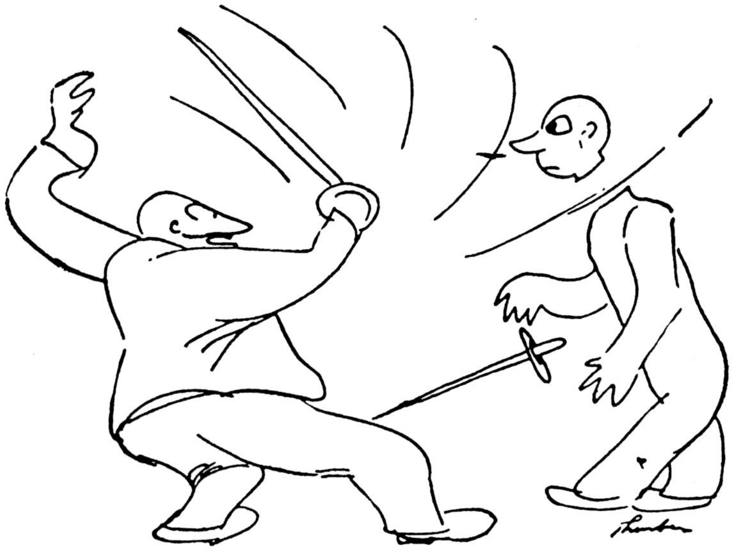

"Touché!"

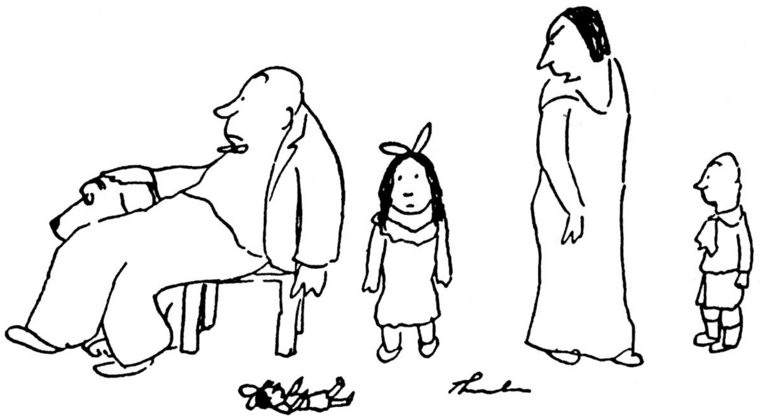

"Well, I'm disenchanted, too. We're all disenchanted."

This page: Panels from *Thurber: Writings and Drawings.*

Even though I used a heavy black crayon, the fine Ohio clarity of my work diminished.

Intentional or Thought-Up Category. The idea for each of these two drawings just came to me and I sat down and made a sketch to fit the prepared caption. Perhaps, in the case of "Well, I'm disenchanted, too. We're all disenchanted," another one of those Outside Forces played a part. That is, I may have overheard a husband say to his wife, on the street or at a party, "I'm disenchanted." I do not think this is true, however, in the case of the rabbit-headed doctor and his woman patient. I believe that scene and its caption came to me one night in bed. I *may* have got the idea in a doctor's office or a rabbit hutch, but I don't think so.

As my eyesight grew dimmer, the paper I drew on grew larger, and even though I used a heavy black crayon, the fine Ohio clarity of my work diminished. In one of my last drawings I had to make the eyes of a young lady so large that it was easy to arrive at the caption: "Where did you get those big brown eyes and that tiny mind?" Seven years ago I shifted to luminous white crayon on dead black paper, and then finally gave up drawing altogether for writing, meditation, and drinking.

Most of my originals have disappeared, mysteriously or otherwise. Thirty were never heard of again after a show in Los Angeles. Several pretty girls with big brown eyes and minds of various sizes have swiped a dozen or so of the scrawls, and a man I loved, now dead, told me one day he had taken seven drawings from my office desk to give to some friends of his in California. That is what became of Dr. Millmoss, among others. My favorite loss, however, occurred at the varnishing, or vanishing, of a show of my drawings in London in 1937. Seems that someone eased a portfolio of two dog drawings. I'm mighty proud of that, and I like to think that Scotland Yard was duly informed of the incident. Theft is an even higher form of praise than emulation, for it carries with it the risk of fine and imprisonment, or, in the case of my "work," at least a mild dressing down by the authorities.

If you should ever run across "Home" or "What have you done with Dr. Millmoss?" write to me, not to J. Edgar Hoover. We are equally busy, but he would only be puzzled, and possibly irked. So much for my drawings, wherever they are. ★★★

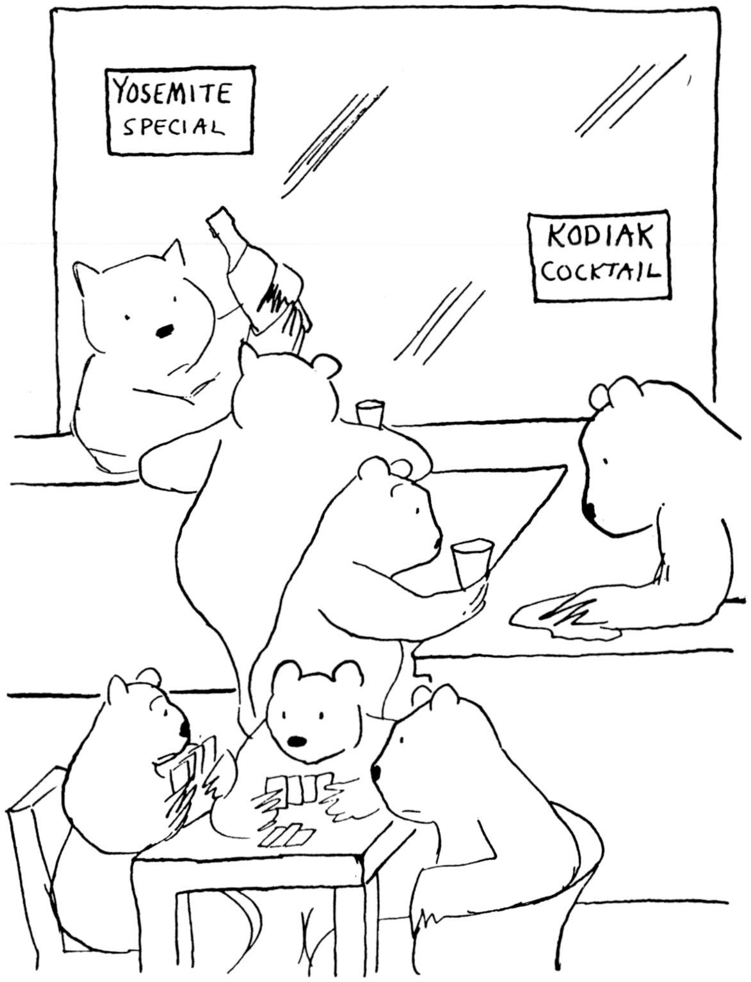
YOSEMITE SPECIAL
KODIAK COCKTAIL

JAMES THURBER

How to Succeed in Cartooning Without Really Trying

by Jesse Fuchs

In his time, Thurber wasn't just a popular and well-respected humorist, like Robert Benchley or Ring Lardner; he was a cultural icon, as recognizable a presence as Ernest Hemingway or Groucho Marx. Thurber's last drawing was a self-portrait for the cover of *Time* in 1951, an article in which T.S. Eliot, among others, praised his work to the point of canonization: "Unlike so much humor, it is not merely a criticism of manners — that is, of the superficial aspects of society at a given moment — but something more profound. His writings and also his illustrations are capable of surviving the immediate environment and time out of which they spring." His most famous short story, "The Secret Life of Walter Mitty," has been reprinted hundreds of times and became a Danny Kaye movie; Mitty himself became a cultural archetype, the handle of countless actual fighter pilots in WWII, the underlying mechanic of even more countless situation comedies, an entry in the dictionary, and Snoopy. Another short story, "You Could Look It Up," provided the inspiration for maverick owner Bill Veeck's most infamous act, sending midget Eddie Gaedel up to bat for the St. Louis Browns. By 1974, *Thurber: A Collection of Critical Essays*, could begin with the sentence "It is by now a truism to say that James Thurber is the greatest American humorist since Mark Twain," and go on to favorably compare Thurber's literary gifts to those of F. Scott Fitzgerald. And perhaps most tellingly, as noted by *New Yorker* founder Harold Ross, nearly every other basset hound he met was named either "James" or "Thurber."

Today you'd be more likely to run across one named "Fred," a sobering reflection on the evanescence of both fame and dogs. It's not that Thurber has vanished into the literary mist: his books are mostly in print, there are several excellent collections of his work, and he has a literary humor award named after him. But in terms of broader cultural influence, he's fallen off the map. More people can probably connect his name with Walter Mitty than can connect that of Al Capp with Sadie Hawkins, but not that many more, and I doubt there's a serious fan of cartooning under 40 in this country who could recognize Thurber's work but not R. Crumb's. By 1987, Charles Bukowski was referring in interviews to "the last best humorist ... a guy called James Thurber ... his humor was so great, they had to overlook it." At the Thurber House museum gift shop one can purchase a Thurber dog on a mug or a sweatshirt, but none of his cartoons are available as prints. Thurber did, by his biographer's reckoning, 170,000 drawings in his life, dashing them off willy-nilly at cocktail parties and giving them to any lady that caught his half-good eye. On eBay today, I found none for sale.

On an anecdotal scale, despite my status as a cartooning fan who

Top: Panel from *Thurber: Writings and Drawings.*

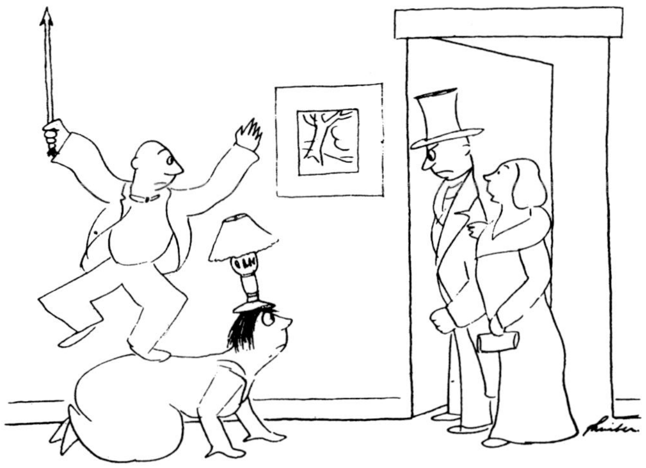

"I don't know them either, dear, but there may be some very simple explanation."

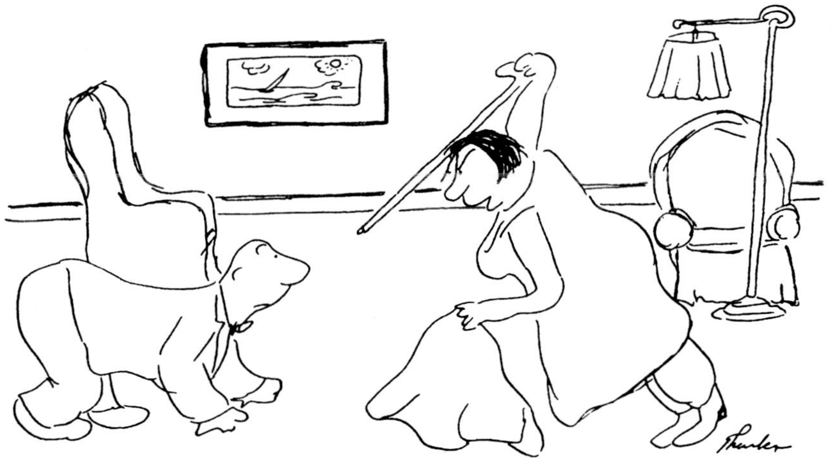

"Now I'm going to go in over your horns!"

has never had a serious girlfriend who didn't subscribe to *The New Yorker*, I never saw a cartoon of Thurber's until *The Comics Journal*, in its Top 100 list, ranked him as the greatest *New Yorker* cartoonist who wasn't Peter Arno. I looked at the drawing reprinted in the *Journal*, depicting the Woman's HQ in his series "The War Between Men and Women." It looked like something that was scrawled on a cocktail napkin by a half-blind alcoholic. Two out of three wasn't bad; I've since come to learn that he generally used typing paper. I've also come to learn that, if anything, he was ranked too low, if he can be ranked at all. Thurber's cartooning is the joker in the *New Yorker* deck, his scrawled line the orange that turns all their other cartoonists into apples, belonging to the heretofore undiscovered school of Not Thurber. It is anomalous, inexplicable, completely *sui generis*, and, unlike any of the kindergarteners to which it is sometimes compared, instantly recognizable as nobody's work but his own. It is inspired. It is pure genius.

II.

Drawing style aside, many of Thurber's cartoons fall into the recognizable template of the Generic *New Yorker* Gag Panel — a snapshot from a conversation, usually between members of *The New Yorker's* self-consciously urbane, upper-middle class demographic, in which the caption is a witty question or riposte. Thurber did more than his share of these, and his cartoons in this vein are as good as those of any other *New Yorker* cartoonist. The humor in the genre relies mostly on facial expression and posture — two things that Thurber was very good at even when his proportions and draftsmanship were wildly off, especially when involving his meek, bald Thurber Man and his broad, domineering Thurber Woman. But they're also relatively fungible; Thurber contributed some conversational zingers for other *New Yorker* artists to draw after he went fully blind, and if one of his older cartoons were to be re-drawn by one of the legion of current *New Yorker* cartoonists I can only think of as Not Roz Chast, it would survive the transition only moderately the worse for wear.

Thurber's interest in the subjective, fallible nature of perception runs through both his art and writing.

It's his more surreal, intuitive work that could have only come from his pen — his hallucinatory distortions, his unexplainable situations, his pantomime narratives. Thurber's interest in the subjective, fallible nature of perception runs through both his art and writing. In his writing, for obvious reasons, it runs towards the aural — decades before Sylvia Wright coined the term 'mondegreen,' Thurber was, in the words of Peter de Vries, "a connoisseur of misapprehension." Although much of this humor comes from his dubious inability to penetrate the accents of his black servants — he hears his maid call the icebox "doom shaped", and his groundskeeper say that he's going to go "hunt grotches in de voods" — he avoids outright racism through the phantasmagoric delight he takes in these incidents: "If you are susceptible to such things, it is not difficult to visualize grotches. They fluttered into my mind: ugly little creatures, about the size of whippoorwills, only covered with blood and honey and the scrapings of church bells."

In his cartoons, though, the inspiration for his most visually surreal work largely stemmed from his vision problems. While his childhood

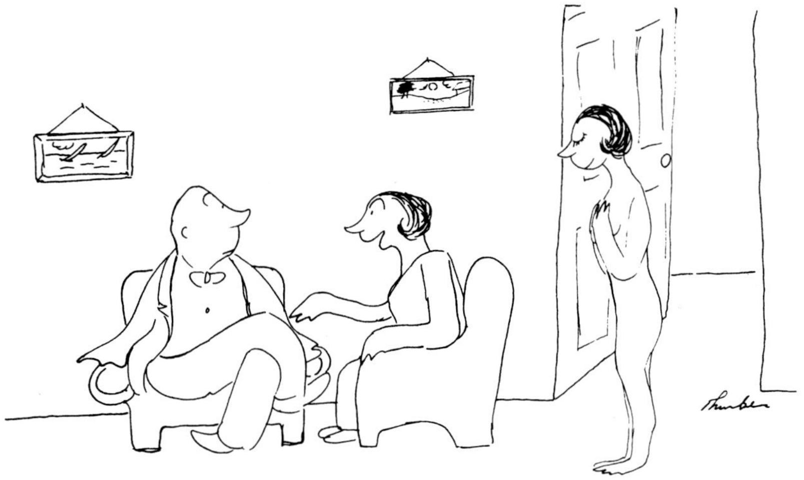

"A Penny For Your Thoughts, Mr. Griscom"

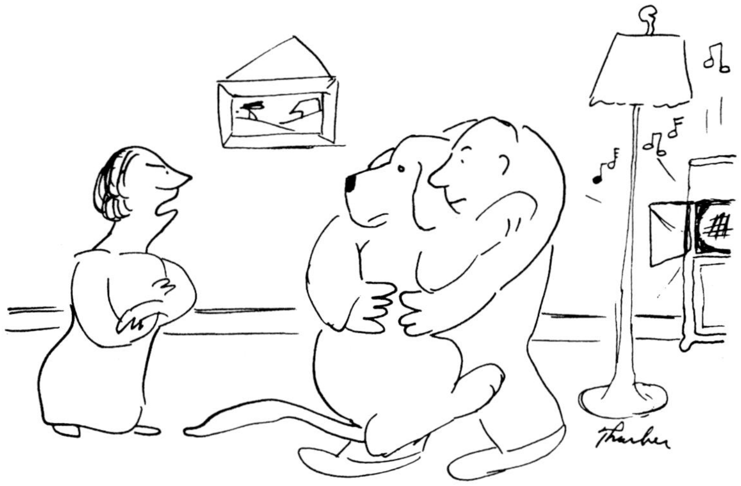

"Will You Be Good Enough to Dance This Outside?"

This page: Panels from *Thurber: Writings and Drawings.*

"He Claims Something Keeps Following Him, Doctor"

eye injury bedeviled him his entire life and eventually made him blind and crazy, he managed to see the silver lining of it, once writing in an essay about losing his glasses:

> "I saw the Cuban flag flying over a national bank, I saw a gay old lady with a gray parasol walk right through the side of a truck, I saw a cat roll across a street in a small striped barrel, I saw bridges rise lazily into the air, like balloons ... With three-fifth's vision or better, I suppose the Cuban flag would have been an American flag, the gay old lady a garbageman with a garbage can on his back, the cat a piece of butcher's paper blowing in the wind, the floating bridges smoke from tugs, hanging in the air. With perfect vision, one is inextricably trapped in the workaday world, a prisoner of reality, as lost in the commonplace America of 1937 as Alexander Selkirk was lost on his lonely island ... The kingdom of the partly blind is a little like Oz, a little like Wonderland, a little like Poictesme. Anything you can think, and a lot you never would think of, can happen there."

This explains why even his most hallucinatory creations — his rabbit-headed psychiatrist, his hieroglyphic little elves — have such conviction to them. In several senses, Thurber was drawing from life.

His most renowned cartoons, though, tend to be not so much visually as narratively surreal. This trait is also in his writing, to a less anarchic extent; *My Life and Hard Times*, an ostensible autobiography, is the ur-text of half the situation comedies ever made, and any *Seinfeld* or *Newsradio* fan will appreciate the clever, character-driven, plausibly ludicrous machinations that set up the book's funniest payoffs.

But in his drawings, the machinations are unseen; as Dorothy Parker put it, "Superbly he slaps aside preliminaries. He gives you a glimpse of the startling present and lets you go construct the astounding past. And if, somewhere in the process, you part with a certain amount of sanity, doubtless you are better off without it. There is too much sense in this world anyway." In these cartoons, everything depicted in the panel is consistent with the consensus laws of reality; there's no Newtonian edict that prevents a seal from hiding behind your bed, or an ex-wife from climbing atop your living room bookcase. It's just impossible to conceive of a possible permutation of those laws that would have allowed the depicted situation to occur, making them as incontrovertibly real yet irreducibly odd as a 1,000-digit prime number. And again, it's Thurber's offhand knack for expression that gives these cartoons their final twist; as with the Mona Lisa, the eternal mystery of that seal in the bedroom centers around its inscrutable smile. Though inadvertently, perhaps the final word on these cartoons was delivered by the great British painter Paul Nash — one of Thurber's most indefatigable champions — after meeting the inimitable Harold Ross for the first time. "He is like your skyscrapers. You cannot believe they exist. Yet, there they are."

III.

Finding parallels between artists is always dubious. Too often the search becomes an end in itself, reminiscent of those laundry lists of "startling coincidences" between Lincoln and Kennedy. But even on a physical level, Crumb and Thurber, with their gawkily handsome features, conservatively dapper attire, stooped posture, and grasshopper-like physique, bear an uncanny resemblance to one another. Their biographies also bear some striking resemblances. Both are from eccentric families, with an ostensibly more talented brother who wound up living at home his entire life. Both had a key experience that irrevocably

"He's Finally Got Me So That I Think I See It, Too"

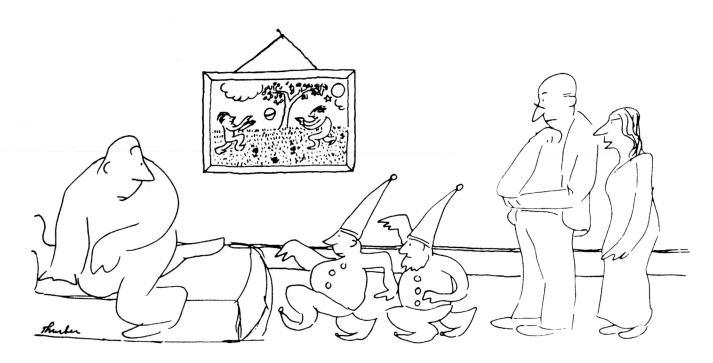

This page: Panels from *Thurber: Writings and Drawings.*

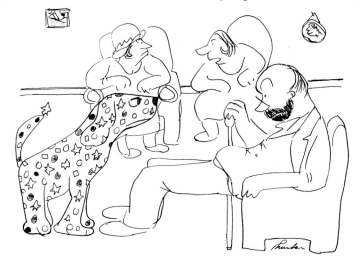

transformed their artistic vision; in Thurber's case, the eye injury, in Crumb's, a month-long acid trip. Each is easily the most highly esteemed practitioner in his field without a true magnum opus, a project neither one ever evidenced much interest in. If Crumb's *oeuvre* has a critical Achilles' heel, it's that he's never drawn a story that couldn't fit in a single comic book, while Thomas Wolfe, a man who never wrote a novel that didn't function better as a doorstop, once told Thurber that he didn't know what it was to be a writer. Neither one has a flagship recurring character in his work, with the possible exception of himself.

Both had their troubles with women — to be sure, a parallel that could be drawn between virtually any two male artists, and most female ones, but in their cases it forms the linchpin of their popular perception. Both, when young and sexually inexperienced, entered into unhappy first marriages with physically and emotionally dominating women. Both then had much happier second marriages to someone who, though more compatible, was also strikingly assertive and accomplished in a predominately male field. Both are arguably misogynist, or at least remarkably gynophobic — not an argument I'll get into here, but suffice to say both consistently depict 'romance' as incorrigibly adversarial, with the ironic twist of fearsome women usually bossing around the smaller, meeker men. Both are inarguably misanthropic — it's no coincidence that, like that other great misanthrope Kliban, their most popular cartoon creations are household pets, as the one thing that typical Garfield-loving Americans and misanthropes agree on is that animals are generally smarter and cuter than people. And, perhaps most importantly, both are uniquely compulsive drawers.

Historically, both Thurber and Crumb form key pivot points in their respective realms, producing astringently modern forms of humor in highly traditional if not outright folksy packages. Thurber's writing — self-deprecating, neurotic, ironic, overwhelmed by the modern world — marked a real sea change from the Will Rogers-ish rural sensibility that dominated American humor in the early part of the century. In this, Thurber was not terribly different from other humorists of the time such as Benchley and Perelman, but unlike those two, Thurber (at least at his peak) wasn't much for uncut whimsy or conspicuous cleverness. His style, when not a deliberate parody of some other writer or form, was virtually colorless. Sixty years before *The Onion* existed, Thurber was knocking them dead with a style that, while not quite as poker-faced, can only be described as deadpan small-town journalese.. ★★★

Historically, both Thurber and Crumb form key pivot points in their respective realms.

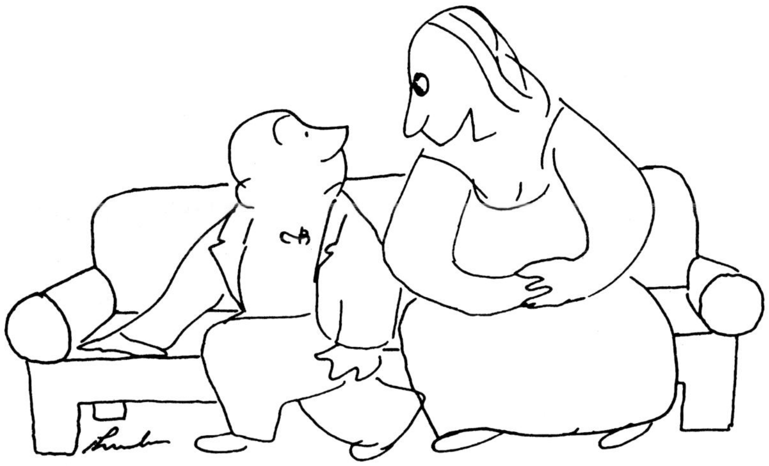

"If you can keep a secret, I'll tell you how my husband died."

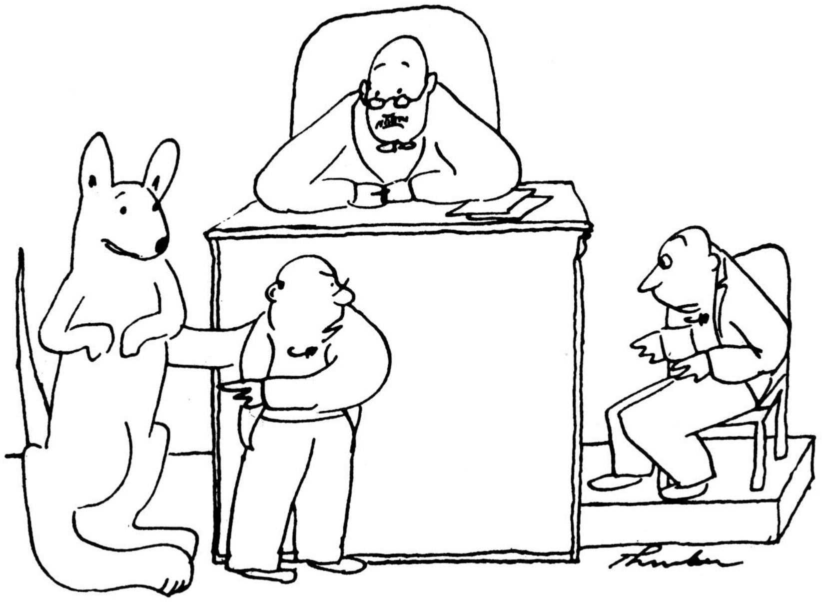

"Perhaps this will refresh your memory."

[1]Admittedly, Veeck half-facetiously denies the connection — as he says in his autobiography, *Veeck as in Wreck*, "I have frequently been accused of stealing the idea from a James Thurber short story ... sheer libel. I didn't steal the idea from Thurber, I stole it from John McGraw." But he admits that Thurber's story helped steer him clear of one possible disaster: "I remembered that the twist in the story was that the midget got ambitious, swung at the 3-0 pitch, and got thrown out at first base because it took him an hour and a half to run down the baseline. 'Eddie,' I said gently, 'I'm going to be up on the roof with a high-powered rifle watching every move you make. If you so much as look as if you're going to swing, I'm going to shoot you dead.' " Gaedel walked on four pitches, ending his career with an OBP of 1.000 and a batting average of 'undefined.'

[2]Even if you've never heard this term, you can probably figure it out from context, but if you haven't or are interested in the backstory, go to http://www.wordorigins.org/wordorm.htm

[3]The real-life castaway that inspired Defoe's *Robinson Crusoe*.

[4]A mythical medieval French province (the name is a compound of Poitiers and Angoulême) invented by proto-OuLiPo author James Cabell. Speaking of falling off the cultural map, Cabell easily bests Thurber as the most obscure writer of the 20th century who was at one time both critically revered — H.L. Mencken described him as "the only first-rate literary craftsman that the whole South can show" — and a household name, though the latter was mostly due to the first novel set in Poictesme, *Jurgen*, being brought up on obscenity charges.

[5]Which, as John Leavy once demonstrated in an article in *The Skeptical Inquirer*, can be found to an equal extent between such otherwise nondescript presidents as William McKinley and James Garfield, if you bother looking.

[6]When Thurber's wife, who was standing next to him, complained that her husband *was* a writer, Wolfe was genuinely surprised. "He is?" he asked. "Why, all I ever see is that stuff of his in *The New Yorker*."

[7]Aline Kominsky-Crumb, of course, is also an influential cartoonist; Thurber's wife, Helen, before their marriage, was the editor of several successful magazines, and was much admired by Harold Ross.

This page: Panels from *Thurber: Writings and Drawings*.

I DON'T KNOW WHAT TO WRITE. I DO THE SAME THING EVERY SUMMER — KEEP IT REAL! YOU KNOW?
LOOK, IT'S NOT THAT HARD ...
THINK ABOUT HOW MUCH HAPPENED THIS SUMMER. WE LEFT CHICAGO, MOVED HERE ...
A PAGE IS SO LONG ...
USE THIS ASSIGNMENT TO EXPRESS YOUR FRUSTRATION, YOUR OUTRAGE, YOUR ALIENATION!
WHO CARES IF I FAIL? (YAWN) THIS IS STUPID.
ONLY YOUR APATHY MANAGES TO ASTOUND ME MORE THAN YOUR LAZINESS.
WHATEVER, MAN ...

SO YOU DECIDED TO DO THE PAPER, HUH?
YEP. WANNA READ?
WELL, IT'S A FULL PAGE ...
I'M QUITE PROUD. I THINK IT'S GENIUS.
"GENIUS" IS HARDLY THE WORD I WOULD CHOOSE.
I KEPT IT REAL!!

Top: Strip from *The Boondocks* by Aaron McGruder. © 2002 Aaron McGruder.

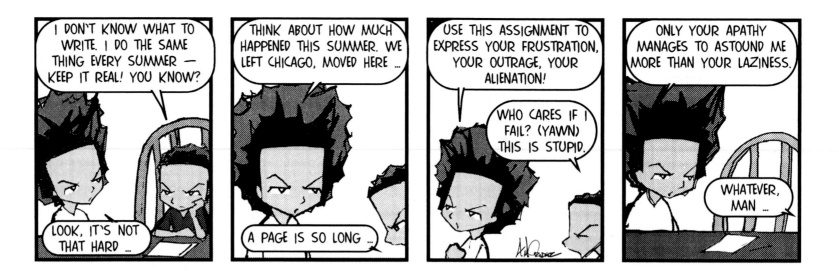

THE NEW SMARM

A Moribund Medium Finds a Purpose for Being

by Robert Fiore

Reading the comics page is not so much a pleasure these days as a reflex, like searching with your tongue for a missing tooth. The history of the newspaper strip can be divided into several eras. There's the Incunabula, which stretches from the dawn of time (or 1895) until about 1920; the Classic period that went from 1920 to the 1950s; Early Decadence, which stretches from the 1950s to about 1970; Late Decadence, which stretches from 1970 to the end of *Calvin & Hobbes*; and the present, or Posthumous era. So long as *Calvin & Hobbes* was on the page you could believe that comic strips of the first rank could still be made, and as long as that one treat was to be found there the mediocre-to-badness of most of the rest was easier to live with. When it disappeared the heart was cut out of the comics page, and the weaknesses of the other strips seemed to be thrown into relief. As in the old British soldier's song, the best have all gone before us, leaving only the dull behind, and here's to the next one to die. Except they don't. Once on the page a comic strip tends to remain on the page. It will cease publication only through seppuku, and then only if the Shogun allows it. This law of comic strip inertia makes a spot on the page a valuable commodity, so as long as there's someone to draw it and some *Dogpatch Gazette* willing to publish it, once a strip is in, it can continue indefinitely. (Actually, they tell me Dogpatch is being re-engineered as a suburb catering to the Southern Tech Corridor, under the name Dogpatche Estates. If you hurry, you can get a house where the Skunk Works used to be.)

Bereft of creative purpose, the modern newspaper strip has carved out a niche for itself as the last refuge of sweetness and light. In doing so the medium has taken a seeming disadvantage, that it is the only entertainment medium aimed at adults still working under significant content restrictions, and turned it to its advantage. This phase has produced at least one runaway hit in the form of Jerry Scott and Jim Borgman's *Zits*. I call it The New Smarm. To explain why it's a break from the previous era of the newspaper strip we'll have to go back to the beginning of the end.

The newspaper strip has for the past 50 years been suffering a slow death by smothering. In the classic era a daily strip would run all the way across a tabloid page, and a Sunday strip was granted a full page. An adventure storyline could run as long as a year. In the post World War II era newspaper editors in their infinite wisdom decided that more comic strips were better but more space devoted to comic strips was worse. They decided that the three words their readers least wished to see were "To Be Continued," and the length of storylines was significantly curtailed. The death of the adventure strip became a self-fulfilling prophecy. There is an interesting parallel between the development of the gag strip and the development of animated cartoons when full animation became financially impractical. In both, the phenomena that would eventually cripple them initially triggered a creative renaissance. In animated cartoons the UPA studio, faced with the constrictions of limited animation, forged a new style based on bold, abstract layouts, stylized characterization and sophisticated subject matter, dipping into the currents of modern art for inspiration. It made traditional animation look straight off the cob. Similarly, a new generation of cartoonists like Charles Schulz, Johnny Hart and Brant Parker, faced with space limitations, created a new minimalist style of comic strip which with their clean lines made existing strips, many drawn by aging cartoonists past of their prime or headed that way, look stodgy by comparison.

The trouble is that limitations are in the end limitations. Yes, minimalism is refreshing after a long baroque period, but if minimalism is decreed by circumstances, once it goes stale you don't have the option of going the other way. Animated cartoons didn't recover until they rediscovered Coolie labor. *Calvin & Hobbes* was neo-classical; Bill Watterson found a way to reincorporate detail in a limited space, but nobody followed his lead. The standard for modern newspaper comic style is not Schulz or Hart but Mort Walker, serviceable, "funny" but uninspired. The ultimate result is that the ability to draw becomes an optional attribute for the comic-strip cartoonist.

The dividing lines between the eras are murky and defined by style as much as time. *Pogo* and *Peanuts* started only three years apart, and yet the former is very much of the classic period while the latter is the flagship of Early Decadence. Late Decadence is marked by a slight but significant loosening in content restrictions. Sex and even drugs can be alluded to in several privileged strips, most notably the flagship of *this* era, *Doonesbury*. The panels have gotten as tiny as they can get, and then one size smaller still. A privileged few can get a little breathing room (*Doonesbury* again), amid howls of protest from editors about violations of their prerogatives, as if destroying the medium were an exercise in freedom of the press. The other significant trend is the rise of merchandising, the floodgates of which were opened by *Peanuts*. Numerous strips seem to exist primarily to be licensed into other products. The humor of Early and Late Decadence is sophisticated, sardonic and deflating. *Peanuts* is about defeat. *The Wizard of Id* cuts the days of old when knights were bold down to size and *Tumbleweeds* does the same for the myth of the frontier. *B.C.* reduces modern civilization to a tiny band surrounded by overwhelming forces. It is the humor of a society weary of bearing the responsibilities that began in their dreams. The New Smarm can hardly bear to face reality in any form. No one goes anywhere without a fairy godmother on their shoulder:

- In *Crankshaft*, a geezer's failing attempt to revive the local movie house is saved when he discovers a cache of valuable vintage movie posters in the attic.
- In *For Better or Worse*, the heroine's failing attempt to revive a children's book and toy store is saved when she finds a cache of valuable vintage toys in the basement.
- In *Frazz*, the title character is a successful songwriter who nevertheless retains his job as a school janitor because he likes kids so darn much. He rescues the school library by using his songwriter's riches to buy books.
- In *Jump Start* the hero had to sacrifice his much wished-for SUV to make the down payment on a house, but nevertheless wins the behemoth in a radio station contest.

Even the best of recent strips, Patrick O'Donnell's *Mutts*, is practically devoid of content and is redeemed only by O'Donnell's exquisite linework. It's like having the ghosts of Cliff Sterrett and Percy Crosby on the comics page. (This is not the same thing as having Cliff Sterrett and Percy Crosby on the comics page.) The flagship strip of our day however is *Zits*.

The new Smarm can hardly bear to face reality in any form.

Normally I don't hold with criticism based on popularity. It is an iron law of popular art thermodynamics that shit floats, and there's no point whining about what doesn't "deserve" its success. *Zits* is a special case. In itself, it's inoffensive; *Zits* is innocuous the way water is wet. Though its visual characterization is pedestrian it's not ugly to look at, and you could get a chuckle out of its gags once in a while if you hadn't been bored to paralysis. Its success is not hard to fathom. It is that rarest of things, and perhaps a unique thing, a strip about teen-agers and their parents that appeals to readers of both persuasions. Teen-age readers, I am guessing, are relieved to see themselves portrayed as something other than mentally defective drunks on the verge of shooting up the cafeteria. Their parents are relieved to be told that beneath the veneer of disaffection their children are innocents. What is truly appalling about *Zits* is that a large audience can look at an evocation of life in America so utterly vapid and actually see themselves in it.

Excuse me, I feel a tangent coming on.

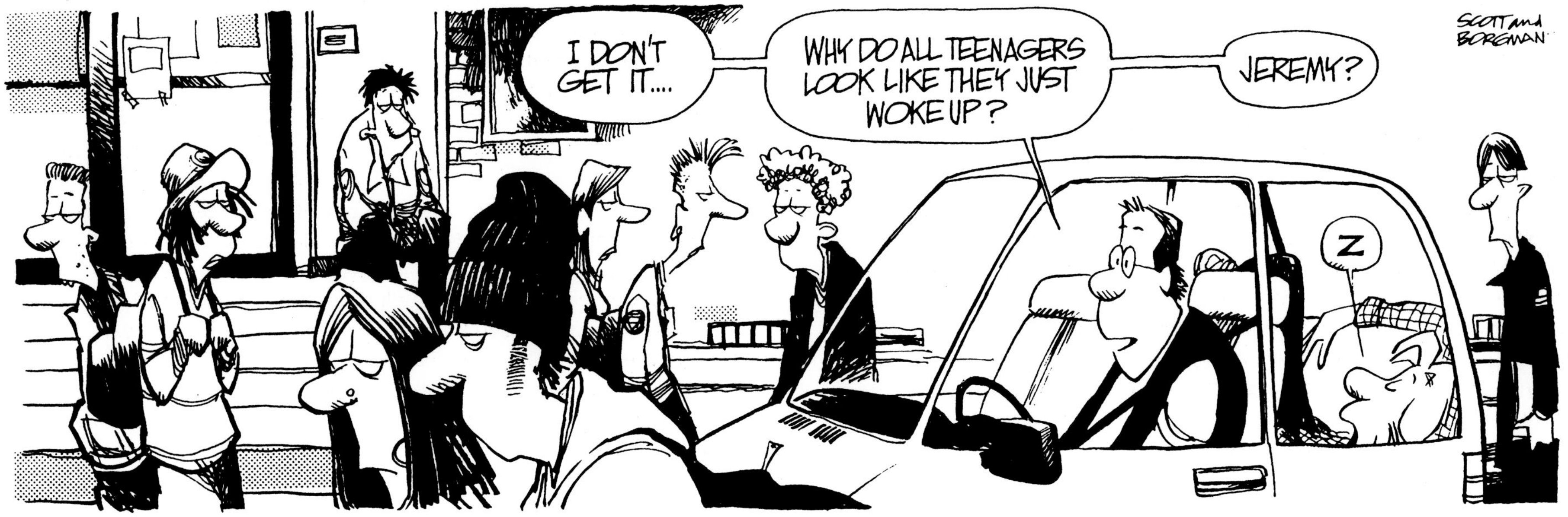
I DON'T GET IT....
WHY DO ALL TEENAGERS LOOK LIKE THEY JUST WOKE UP?
JEREMY?
SCOTT AND BORGMAN
Z

Bottom: Strip from *Zits Unzipped: Sketchbook Number 5* by Jerry Scott and Jim Borgman. © 2002 King Features Syndicate.

SCOTT and BORGMAN
11:35AM

People are weird. They think Beach Boys records are a myth and the movie *Chinatown* is the truth. You are more likely to see Chang without Eng than you are to see a reference to the Beach Boys without a qualifying reference to the myths of endless sunshine and Californian enjoyment they supposedly promulgate. To begin with, what "myth" of endless sunshine? In Southern California, the sun will shine until you get tired of it. After air pollution the biggest drawback to the climate is monotony. Secondly, allow me to break the news to you that the middle-class youth of Southern California do indeed go to the beach (where they might surf if so inclined), drive their own cars, and hang out with their friends. Whether California kids sitting on the patio were having any more fun than east coast kids sitting in the basement is an open question, but the claims the Beach Boys made were hardly extravagant. What is mythic about Beach Boys records, and what fills the listener with a skeptical yearning, is the picture they paint of a youth culture innocent of sex and drugs. However much enjoyment one might derive from sex and drugs, either or both will eventually make life complicated and earnest. The appeal of Norman Rockwell is similar. When Rockwell sat down at the easel to work he put on his spectacles and removed his testicles. All of his imagery has something of the eunuch about it. It's not feminine, but it's flabby, sleek, and lacking in aggressiveness.

The Beach Boys had conviction because they had the beliefs and assumptions of their entire society behind them. *Zits* and its readers are just kidding themselves. In a time when popular entertainment is for all intents and purposes a 24-hour commercial for sexual intercourse interspersed with murder you can see how people might want a respite, but this is ridiculous. The adolescents in *Zits* are so utterly devoid of libido it makes *Archie* comics look like *120 Days of Sodom*. It's not that kids are not basically "all right" or even innocent, it's just that they're all right and innocent in the way the kids in *South Park* are. Though the ages of the kids in that show are adjusted down for shock value and the situations are fanciful, I don't think anyone has ever captured how suburban kids act among themselves better than *South Park*. (The best of television animation these days is head and shoulders above anything on the comics page.) Middle-class kids get into things and they get ahead of themselves, but they're so well-insulated that they generally live to become more or less like their parents. And as for the parents in *Zits*, dear me. To think that this society has become so utterly dull and bourgeois that the parents in this strip could be considered accurate portraits of the readers and not vicious satire is — well, it doesn't bear thinking about. In the end it may be more accurate to say that *Zits* is what parents want to believe about their kids, and what their kids want their parents to believe about them too.

Why is this family strip in this family newspaper trying to make me hot for a clearly underaged girl?

Brooke McEldowney's *9 Chickweed Lane* is a strange little cheesecake strip about three generations of women (Juliet, a voluptuous college professor, Edda, her jailbait daughter, and her crabby and censorious mother whose name escapes me) eking out their post-divorce existences in a sylvan suburb. It exerts a strange fascination over me, though not for the normal cheesecake reasons (though Brooke McEldowney definitely has a gift). Rather I spend my days trying to fathom its cultural pretensions. Initially the question was simple: Why is this family strip in this family newspaper trying to make me hot for a clearly underage girl? (She has been advanced a little closer to the age of consent since.) Edda has since evolved into a kind of dream of culture and refinement. She plays classical piano, she dances the ballet, she reads good books (actually, she reads good books while practicing ballet), she's above the puerile pursuits of her peers. Juliet meanwhile fights a lonely battle for high standards with students who feel entitled to good grades and administrators who want to dumb things down for various pecuniary reasons. I don't doubt McEldowney's yearning for a life less tawdry is genuine, but it comes off a bit glib. Juliet and Edda want to have their beauty and disdain it too. That is, they seem to want the status this society confers to beauty while disapproving of a society that values beauty so highly. The professor's struggles come off fairly well because they can be dramatized. With the daughter, McEldowney uses his cultural touchstones the way a schlock novelist uses haute consumerist trademarks. Chopin, Jane Austen, ballet, they all seem like safe, undisputable symbols of class. You see in Edda none of the stumbling and overreaching or the trying on of new identities of a culturally ambitious adolescent. Like most straight men (let's assume) who

HALLMARKS OF FELINITY No. 141
I'M A CAT PERSON.
PEOPLE GIVE ME THE CREEPS.
Brooke
CATS GIVE ME THE CREEPS.
THE ABILITY TO ADAPT QUICKLY AS CIRCUMSTANCES WARRANT.
I'M A PEOPLE PERSON.
10-4 ©2002 Brooke McEldowney Dist. by UFS, Inc.

Top: Strip from *Zits Unzipped: Sketchbook Number 5* by Jerry Scott and Jim Borgman. © 2002 King Features Syndicate. **Bottom:** *9 Chickweed Lane* by Brooke McEldowney. © 2002 United Feature Syndicate.

SOMEBODY PUT MY CELL PHONE ON "VIBRATE."
LYNN

Top and bottom: Panels from *Family Business: A for Better or Worse Collection* by Lynn Johnston. © 2002 Lynn Johnston Productions.

identify with female characters in their work, McEldowney has a hard time allowing himself to see what a woman would find attractive in a man, and so Juliet's love interest seems a bit of a lump. As for Edda, well. Her best friend in parochial school is the extraordinarily geeky Amos, and one of the themes initially was how sad it was that this soul-mate wasn't attractive enough for her. McEldowney apparently decided that this attitude was unworthy of his paragon, so now it is understood that Edda and Amos will one day marry. (Pretty girl goes for the sterling inner qualities of ugly guy — this is the most well-regulated one-way street in popular entertainment.)

It's pretty to look at though, which these days is nothing to sneer at.

For Better or Worse is hardly new and doesn't really deserve to be relegated to the smarm category. While she is overly fond of what the situation comedy trade calls "squishy moments," Lynn Johnston has a good-faith commitment to showing everyday life in its complexity. She knows that she has to ration reality carefully, as is demonstrated by the furor when she killed off the family dog despite weeks of setting it up. I bring it up in this context because the subject of adolescent/post-adolescent sexuality reared its ugly head here as well. *For Better* follows the lives of a suburban family in real time, and it got to where the thing could not be put off any longer. Johnston wimped out with the older child Michael by having him elope with his high-school sweetheart, and with the older daughter Elizabeth entering university I'm sure she knew she wasn't going to get away with that sort of thing twice. I can't tell you how disappointed I was at the grace and finesse with which Johnston handled it. (Elizabeth is a serial monogomist and it is implicit but not directly stated that she will shack up.) I can't explain the black impulse that makes me want to see such a fundamentally decent person as Johnston embarrassed. I suppose what really grates is the way her characters seem to be insulated from the hardships of life, but there's a truth to that, as well. I don't know how many times I've heard the story (I tell a lie. Two or three times.) A middle class '60s radical abjures her class privileges to the extent that she (it always seems to be she) becomes an accessory to the murder of a policeman. Once the initial compensation runs out, the policeman's working class family is relegated to a life of near-destitution. Meanwhile, the radical, a fugitive from justice, hunted by the FBI, with no name, family or funds, is found to have wended her way back into the middle class complete with a nice house, husband, 2.5 children, active in the PTA, contributes to PBS, an exemplar of the contradictions of the system in a way she never had envisioned. Stripped of everything, including her name and identity, all she needed to do to be re-admitted, it would seem, was to show her ticket,which couldn't have been anything more than her manner. It's not that middle-class life is free of misfortune but that misfortune doesn't have the consequences it does elsewhere. You don't expect Johnston's characters to become fugitives from justice, but you do wonder if they're ever going to have a bad marriage or a drinking problem or a business that fails. Not that you normally expect that kind of thing from a comic strip not called *Mary Worth*, but Johnston is good enough at capturing the mundane details of life that it creates the expectation of a higher level of realism. Like the man said, all happy families are alike and, with three nuclear families on the horizon, that could be a lot of sameness. Johnston may have to engineer in some misery just for variety's sake. That would be something neither the majority of her readers or her editors would like very much. Though Johnston could surprise us, one expects to see Michael experriencing mild tribulations as a young father and Elizabeth experiencing mild tribulations as a young schoolteacher. For all its good faith, it would still be little more than another round of bland reassurance.

I can't explain the black impulse that makes me want to see such a fundamentally decent person as Johnston embarrassed.

The humor in Tom Batiuk and Chuck Ayers's *Crankshaft* is entirely synthetic. Rather than develop their premises through character over time, Batiuk/Ayers present their readers with stock situations and expect them to be found funny. Crankshaft, a cantankerous old school bus driver, is forever knocking over a Mr. Keesterman's mailbox, and we are expected to laugh at how mad old Keesterman gets when his property is wantonly

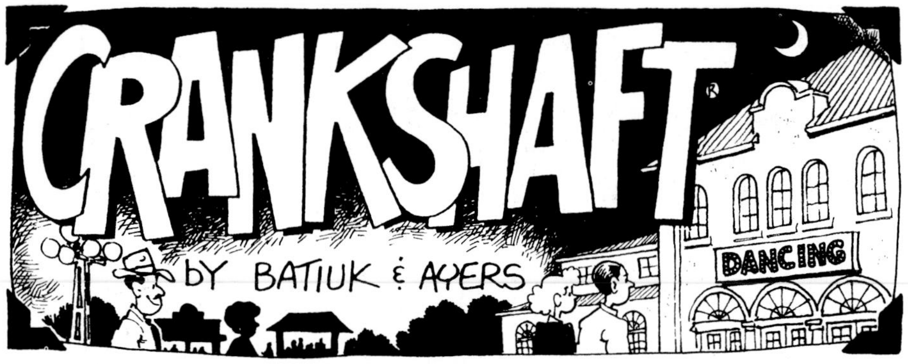
CRANKSHAFT
BY BATIUK & AYERS
DANCING

destroyed by the negligence of an incompetent public employee. Another bus driver, Lena, makes terrible coffee that all the other bus drivers must drink, and we are expected to laugh at this, because we all know how bad Lena's coffee is. As a positive counter-example, class, let's take a genuinely funny running gag, Charlie Brown trying to kick the football. To begin with, the idea of someone running at full throttle to kick a football only to fall on his back when it's snapped away is inherently funny. Lucy's mind games as she manipulates Charlie Brown into once again having faith in her are funny. The inevitable victory of hope over experience, as when a horseplayer continues to bet on a losing horse in order to validate his original error, that too is funny. Furthermore the humor arises out of character. Lucy will continue to be cruel until her cruelty catches up to her, which will be well after the time frame of the strip. Charlie Brown's faith is evidence of his goodness, but his gullibility is a weakness and a character flaw. Because we recognize these traits in ourselves and others, these characters achieve a reality that the characters in *Zits* and *Crankshaft* never approach. When we see the football gag coming again we're ready to laugh at it.

Crankshaft has been bad for a long time. What puts it in the Smarm category is its recent obsession with the Swing Era. Suddenly everybody in *Crankshaft* who could collect Social Security either had a chance to make the big leagues or play cornet with Bunny Berrigan or land the man of their dreams in those way-far-off days. Those days are so far off that all these characters would have to be in their 80s, but this fact is wished away through the magic of comics. This premise could be interesting if the stories were all bullshit, if these people were imagining the one that got away to add some romance to the dull lives they've led, but that would take a rather darker view of human nature than Batiuk and Ayers's. All they want to do is sink their readers into a pool of nostalgic rue.

Jef Mallett's *Frazz* is about suburban schoolchildren and their childish elders, and Michael Fry and T. Lewis's *Over the Hedge* is about animals living at the outskirts of yet another sylvan suburb. Actually, to say that a comic strip takes place in a suburb these days is almost redundant. A medium that started out overwhelmingly urban has become overwhelmingly suburban. It could be a reflection of where the cartoonists are these days, but is more likely a reflection of where the newspapers are. Where the urban newspaper of old presumed a world of crime, corruption and international crisis, the suburban newspaper serves a readership that wants to believe it has escaped all that, and the editors are happy to oblige. The escape becomes complete on the comics page.

What strips are there with an urban setting these days? There's *Jump Start*, *Sylvia* presumably, and *Cathy* could be. *Mutts* sometimes seems to be in the city, and sometimes in a small town. Not much beyond that. For that matter, it's very nearly redundant to say a strip is about kids or animals. You didn't expect syndicates to look at the success of *Calvin & Hobbes* and conclude it was due to good art and good writing, did you? You can now expect more strips about adolescents.

The funniest thing about *Over the Hedge* is how Fry once bragged that the syndicate had never tried to censor its content, as if there was anything to censor. *Frazz* isn't funny.

Huey is presented simultaneously as a parody of hotheaded and puritanical puritan excess and an exemplar of commitment and seriousness in a society too quick to compromise.

If *9 Chickweed Lane* is notable for its pretensions Aaron McGruder's *The Boondocks* is notable for its evasions. It's about Huey and Riley Freeman, two children of the inner city who have been evacuated to be raised by their grandfather in yet another sylvan suburb. Huey wants to be propaganda minister of the Black Panther party when he grows up and Riley wants to be Tupac Shakur, and neither is particularly concerned about where these paths of glory lead. Huey is presented simultaneously as a parody of hotheaded and puritanical puritan excess and an exemplar of commitment and seriousness in a society too quick to compromise. This ambiguity gives McGruder the opportunity to take a position without taking a position. Huey's point of view is not McGruder's but it's more McGruder's than not. Part of McGruder wants to embrace it all, but another part knows that life is more complex. Huey sees the state of the inner city not as a case of poverty but as a sociopolitical struggle where black people are their truest selves. To Riley, who's too young to see the consequences, it's a gaudy land of adventure and riches. Huey looks at thug culture and Riley's entrancement with it the way an old time Panther would have looked at pimp culture of the 1970s, as a conspiracy of fate or the power structure (or both) to frustrate political progress. The grandfather's rectitude and kindness are respected by Huey and McGruder (and, with some bristling, by Riley), but

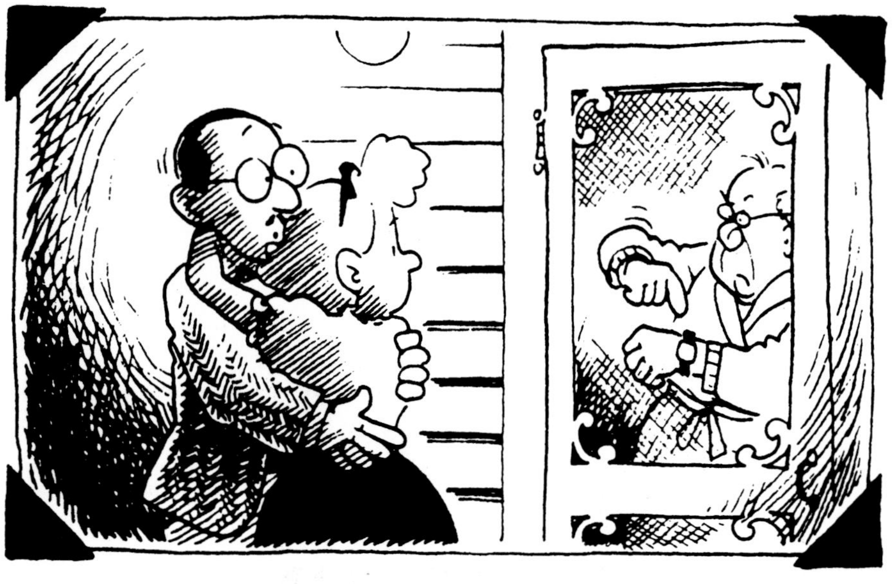

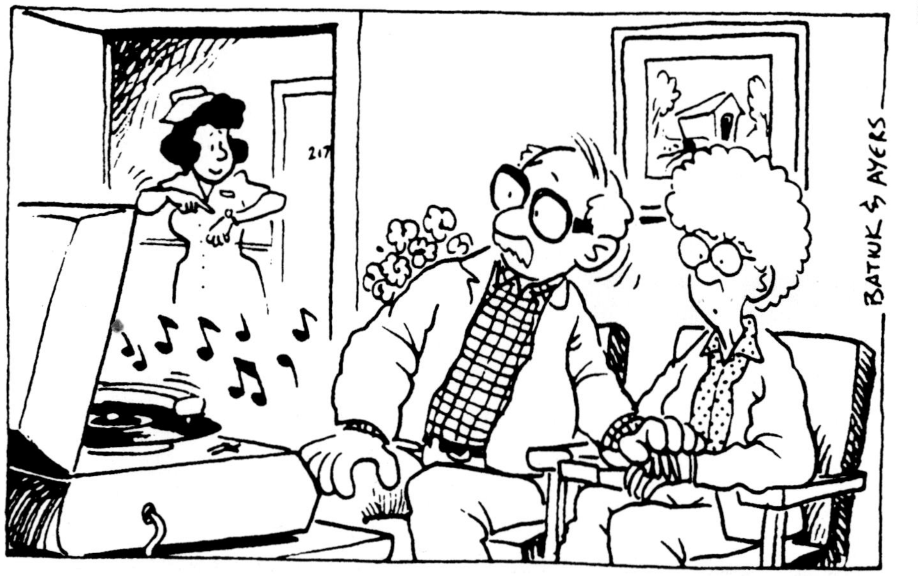
BATIUK & AYERS

Top and bottom: Panels from *Safe Return Home* by Tom Batiuk and Chuck Ayers. © 2002 Mediagraphics.

are seen ultimately as an accommodation rather than an answer. Because there's no sector of society that's both materially successful and primarily black, success is seen as a peril to identity. Where I live every so often there will be a cycle of handwringing articles about black flight to the suburbs and the potential dilution of political power. What these articles really demonstrate is how slow and fitful racial progress has been: so slow and fitful that people have forgotten that this is the way it's supposed to work. The racist assumption was that once black people dominated a neighborhood, it was spoiled for everyone else, and the process of upwardly-mobile-group-leaves-the-crappy-to-the-next ends with them. Now some black people at least can have the novel experience of looking back and seeing someone on the ladder behind them. I don't think it's so much that McGruder can't stand prosperity as that he distrusts it. In McGruder's scheme, Riley represents an infantile stage of development and Huey, a step along the right road but still incomplete, with the wise, vigorous and powerful adult stage still to be discovered. Ultimately I believe McGruder's ambivalence is less a result of coyness than of the knowledge that he doesn't know the answer any better than anyone else does. As a comic strip it's OK, and sometimes better than that. The artwork is no more than serviceable (each character is issued one expression and sticks with it), but it's early in McGruder's career and he could improve considerably.

The rest of the comics page is basically the same as it was ten years ago, except ten years more tired. One exception is *Classic Peanuts*, which is just old strips. Given 20 years of sustained brilliance to choose from, the editors in their wisdom have instead chosen to utilize the other 30. Schulz was the Tennessee Williams of the comic strip, an artist who dominated his field but whose career outlived his genius. By the time these "classics" had appeared, the comic inventiveness that had given us the Great Pumpkin, Lucy's psychiatry stand, the kite-eating tree and Snoopy's early Walter Mitty adventures had grown stale and labored. Regarding Charlie Brown, the strip just went soft. Schulz must have come to feel sorry for the kid, so he let him be a winner for a change. In one episode he is a marbles shark, avenging the weak. In an episode being reprinted as I write this, the girl Charlie Brown longs for now likes him back. Her pet name for him is "Brownie Charles," and if this doesn't make Tonstant Weader fwow up, then Tonstant Weader has a stomach of drop-forged steel. Looking back on what I've written on *Peanuts* over the years, I suppose I've been more antagonistic towards it than was warranted. I fear part of the reason is that Charlie Brown's personality is a little too close to mine for comfort. Schulz was a cartoonist the way Williams was a writer, and neither was any more eager to cease practicing their art than he was to stop breathing. With the

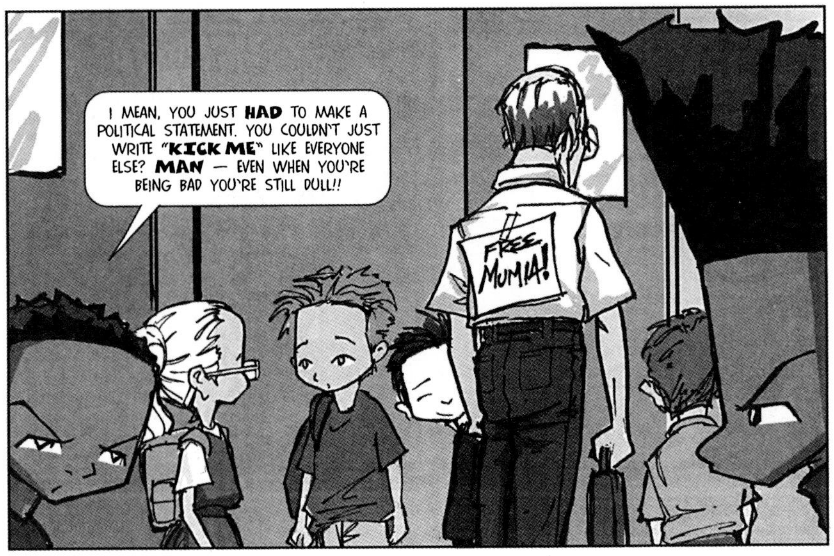
I MEAN, YOU JUST HAD TO MAKE A POLITICAL STATEMENT. YOU COULDN'T JUST WRITE "KICK ME" LIKE EVERYONE ELSE? MAN — EVEN WHEN YOU'RE BEING BAD YOU'RE STILL DULL!!
FREE MUMIA!

Bottom: Strip from *The Boondocks* by Aaron McGruder. © 2002 Aaron McGruder. **Top:** Panels from *Dilbert: A Treasury of Sunday Strips: Version 00* by Scott Adams. © 2002 United Feature Syndicate.

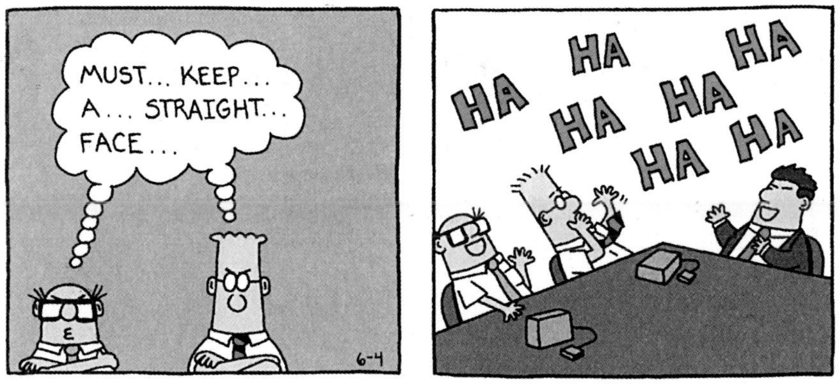
MUST... KEEP... A... STRAIGHT... FACE...
HA HA HA HA HA HA HA

exception of Berke Breathed, the cartoonists who did quit when their strips were past their prime have not proven adept at opening second acts. The last 30 years of his career will not tarnish the achievement of the first 20. It just won't enhance it.

In *B.C.* Johnny Hart prayed for the conversion of the Jews once too often, and it was dropped from my paper. I suspect that some time previous he had decided to compromise with his editors by keeping his Christian Right looniness out of *The Wizard of Id*, and that remains. Dropping *B.C.* and keeping *Id*, I wonder how many times this has been repeated across the country? When they're not nutty, they're dull as ditchwater anyway.

[Adams] and McGruder are about the only people on the comics page that really get angry at anything and, in the age of the New Smarm, that's enough to distinguish you.

Doonesbury may not be any less good than it was ten years ago, but I'm bored with it.

A couple of soap-opera strips persist. God knows why.

The best thing on the comics page is by acclamation the worst drawn strip in the history of comics. It is true that what Scott Adams engages in on *Dilbert* is not so much drawing as a simulation of drawing, but he remains a superior gag writer. Adams had the good fortune to start a business strip at a time when the business world was about to be swept up in a long parade of management fads, and so for a while the strip wrote itself. As that trend has gone into abeyance, Adams has not been immune to the ten-years-more-tired rule, but so far he retains some bite. He and McGruder are about the only people on the comics page that really get angry at anything and, in the age of the New Smarm, that's enough to distinguish you.

The market economy is so productive that it creates a kind of artificial benevolence. It's not until you make yourself useless to the system that you learn just how indifferent to your well-being it is. A similar phenomenon applies to commercial entertainment. A set of circumstances will periodically occur that makes the commercial sphere conducive to creative endeavor, and the popular arts will flourish. However, art is not the object of the exercise, and when circumstances turn against art there will be no one in the apparatus to speak for it. At the end of the 1950s, the Broadway musical had developed to the point that one more step along that line of development would require that it become a serious art form. The people who backed musicals had no interest in subsidizing that kind of thing and so it died on the vine. It continued for a while on inertia and talent left over from better times, but now it's akin to a circus act. The pop music form that replaced show tunes came to demand that all musicians conform themselves to what had been popular previously. Now it consists of a raft of synthetic acts eager to do whatever their handlers tell them, and their handlers wonder why they don't command the public affection and loyalty of yesterday's acts. It's certainly not out of the question that another Bill Watterson or Gary Larson will emerge to breathe a little life into the comics page, but it's hard to imagine anything is going to happen to reverse the trends that have sucked the life out of it. An art form that lives by the sword of profit will die by it. ★★★

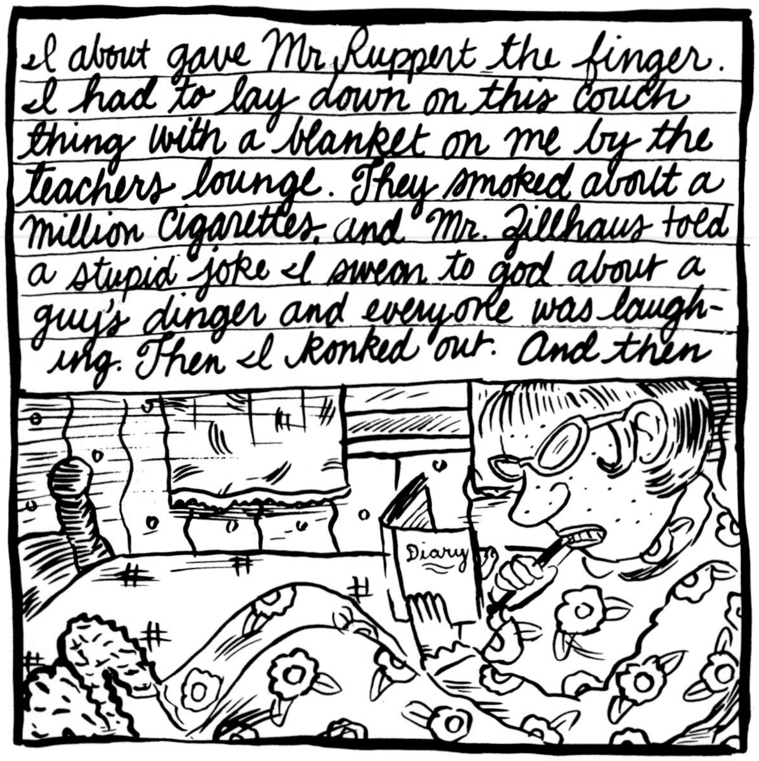
I about gave Mr. Ruppert the finger. I had to lay down on this couch thing with a blanket on me by the teachers lounge. They smoked about a million cigarettes and Mr. Zillhaus told a stupid joke I swear to god about a guy's dinger and everyone was laughing. Then I konked out. And then
Diary

Top: Panel from *Come Over Come Over* by Lynda Barry. © 2002 Lynda Barry.

A CHILD'S GARDEN OF DETRITUS

The Cartoon Chronicles of Lynda Barry

by Donald Phelps

SHOW AND TELL

Besides the numerous convulsive alliances (siblings, cousins, amorous couples, school chums) that are scrutinized by Lynda Barry's five category-defying cartoon narrative presentations and all-out spectacles, her work engages a perpetual, often fiercely competitive partnership: image and text. In the present generation of American cartoons, the contentious marriage has been adjusted and at best revitalized by the emergence of the cartoon strip as *correspondence*. "Biography" is now an acknowledged category. However, in Stan Mack's vignettes from the steam rooms of the advertising industry, or the serpentine excursions of Jim Woodring, one sees autobio broadened into psychodrama or public meditation. Such are the progeny of those 1950 innovaters, Jules Feiffer (whose stand-up cartoon sequences widen their sights within the first year beyond satire on pre-Woody Allen psychopiffle) and Charles Schulz, whose *Peanuts* delivered an elegant variation on kidspeak, and forecast the TV phenomenon of "talking heads."

Throughout the ensuing decades, the texts of certain major (if not uniformly famous) cartoon strips introduced reflection on the nature of the language employed, on its substance – a signal difference from loquacious comic strips of the '20s and '30s, like Sidney Smith's *The Gumps*, or Harold Gray's *Little Orphan Annie*, in which the dialogues and monologues sometimes distend their balloons to resemble a mid-Victorian air regatta. Their concern, however, was almost entirely with the dramatic goings-on of the story. Until recently, there remained largely untouched any attention by comic strips to the possible soundings of text as literature. One hears little, in today's litcrit marketplaces, of either "tone" or "texture" at any literary level; both have often seem consigned to that possibly terminal detention camp Elitism.

"Tone" might be defined as the vocal resonance, the extra-specific significance of language; "texture," the sensuous autonomy of language: the value, the peculiar coloration, that distinguishes artistic precision from mere specificity. Both may be observed emerging, albeit irregularly, in cartoon work from America's last five decades. Both may be found *a fortiori*, in the 1980s-'90s work of Lynda Barry.

THE SWINGING SHEPHERDESS

In roving burlesque manuals like the 1983 *Big Ideas* and *Leaving Mr. Wrong*, Lynda Barry is seen shlepperdessing an ungainly (and ungainful) cast of players on an expedition of surveillance and scavenging. Her terrain is the present generation's over-abundant spillage of bargain-basement bromides, popular myths straggling in from the expiring new age; an unstinting ever-present treasure trove of junk wisdom, scattered from the retail outlets of magazine ads and quizzes, TV ads and talking-head wisdom bees. All such are set forth by Barry, not with the nostril-pinched scorn of some uptown counterrarts; but with a ripe sense of drollery and its chief component: a prankish curiosity (that sneaker-footed cousin of wonder). Also on hand is an equally vagrant, yet ever-hovering empathy; sugarfree, but warm and dry.

She dispenses sad little vignettes of women trying to impress closure on some blatantly wrong Mister; trying to control weight in the face of a visit from a friend bearing a freshly baked pie; sparring with the temptation to gobble Ayds as though they were capsules of salvation. Their struggles mainly give rise to nightmares of a glutton's Hell, in which the Devil sentences them to monitor and devour endless doughnuts.

The drawing suggests the maladroit earnestness, the frantic gawkishness of

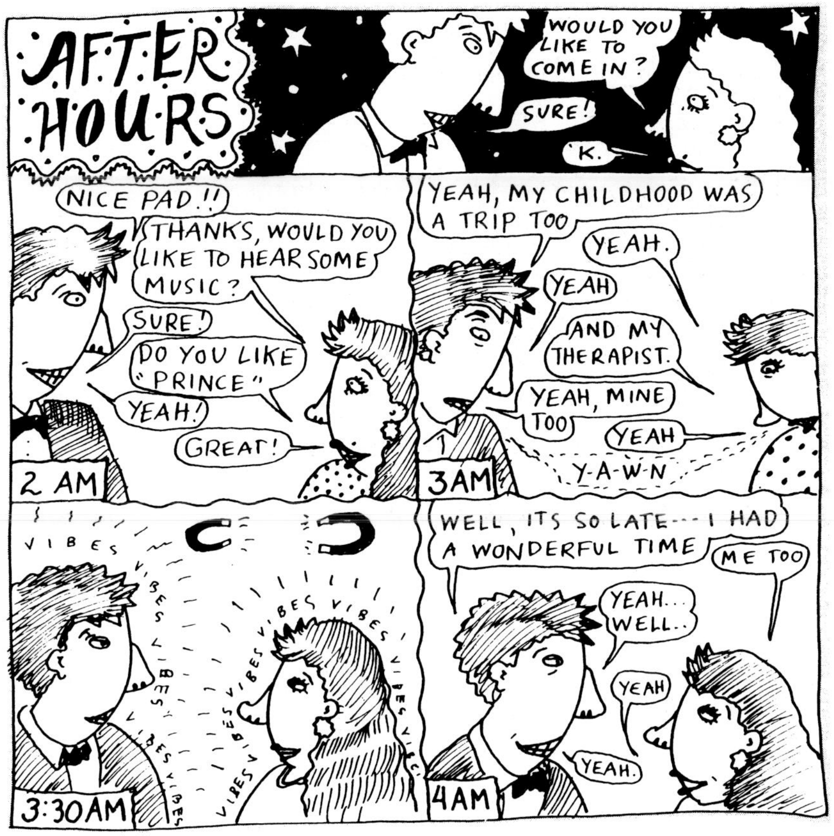

AFTER HOURS
WOULD YOU LIKE TO COME IN?
SURE!
K.
NICE PAD!!
THANKS, WOULD YOU LIKE TO HEAR SOME MUSIC?
SURE!
DO YOU LIKE "PRINCE"
YEAH!
GREAT!
2 AM
YEAH, MY CHILDHOOD WAS A TRIP TOO
YEAH.
YEAH
AND MY THERAPIST.
YEAH, MINE TOO
YEAH
Y-A-W-N
3AM
VIBES
3:30AM
WELL, ITS SO LATE--- I HAD A WONDERFUL TIME
ME TOO
YEAH... WELL..
YEAH
YEAH.
4AM

Top: Panel from *Big Ideas* by Lynda Barry. © 2002 Lynda Barry.

young children's drawing; true, between the early '80s work, and the latter accounts of Marlys the girl impresario, the sweaty cachet of childhood is never entirely absent. But the lines in *Big Ideas* are wire-taut and unyielding. Most of her personae (usually seen in profile) suggest a bilious marriage of imitation Picasso and Art Deco, each at its respective worst; without the wriggling litheness that will mark Marlys, her family and chums. Those earlier bodies seem to have been posture-trained in jammed telephone booths. The bolster-like torsos of man and woman are canted toward each other; their beaky noses suggest a resemblance to infant birds seeking food.

More than anything else, these figures suggest human diagrams, ventriloquist's dummies for Barry's ever present managerial text. The text is the true star and the unifying force of the mock-didactic *Leaving Mr. Wrong*, and the mock-inspirational *Big Ideas*. Sometimes neatly printed, often written in laboriously dainty schoolgirl calligraphy, the text inundates and at times overruns the panels (when there are any). Like some familiar mold, it infiltrates the no-frills housing space, often squeezed into what seems like any available corner.

Sometimes neatly printed, often written in laboriously dainty schoolgirl calligraphy, the text inundates and at times overruns the panels.

The texts are borne along at times by first-person narratives: a young miss on New Year's Day anticipates a *wunderjahr* with fervid hope. Her sole visitor (in signature Barry fashion) is a burglar, who breaks in merely to deliver his own lament about his thwarted life ambition to be a filling station attendant. The burglar's *De Profundis* occupies most of the panel space, leaving room only for fractional glimpses of his bowed head, and the attentive profile of his auditor. Elsewhere, Barry, a self-confessed Capricorn native, lays down endless symmetrical columns of Dos and Don't s for meeting, keeping, or shedding a man; dietary recommendations (two pages feature displays of "Basic Food Groups," including Chocolates, Fast Foods, Cool Gratifications, and Beverages); all illustrated with carefully labeled samples. Their range may be noted in the Beverage segment: a shot glass labeled "Filthy Roadhouse," a bottle tersely marked "Brewski" and a garden hose.

The texts don't override, but emphasize the domination of whiteness, which contributes to the overtone of cockeyed classicism. Even the occasional bedtime scenes are sharply demarcated; the sleepers' ovoid heads in clean relief against a rectangle of no-nonsense black sky. This linear tautness will change with the chronicles of Marlys. It changes even here, in a vignette entitled "Chuckie and Harry": a younger and (slightly but significantly) older brother enacting the litanies of pre-sleep squabbling. ("I wouldn't talk, Chump." "So who says I'm talkin' to *you*, Scrub.") Barry's juggling of dialogue balloons competes with Segar's *Thimble Theatre*. Moreover, her drawing of Chuckie and Harry invokes a warm, shaggy, deeply shaded bedtime; the bodies, beneath blankets, are fully dimensioned. The same densely sketched intimacy follows in a segment called "Phobia-Phobia," dealing with schoolday terrors.

Such "exceptions" to Barry's style offer (as usual in such cases) a sense of its true capacity. Her overtone is an affable pedantry, its deadpan patience proof against the incongruities or absurdities of its content. It recalls somewhat those vagarious, faltering, yet dauntless lectures delivered in the printed essays and numerous short movies of Robert Benchley.

He, like Barry, took side excursions into his childhood. Barry's preoccupation with domestic props like dishware and makeup appliance, recalls Benchley's usually calamitous sorties among typewriters and electric shavers; they share a decent reverence (nonsectarian) for food. Barry, who recounts the health problems of her pet turtle Gamora, might have willingly illustrated Benchley's "The Sex Life of the Polyp." (The very early sound films show Benchley with a white doll-like face, beady eyes and dainty moustache; which, with his puppet-like obsequious gestures, seem to propose him for Barry's company.)

Of course, a chasm of history separates them. Benchley, the suburban home-owner, yields to the bedrock reality of Barry's rootless teetering fringe dwellers. Benchley's chuckle has died with him. The vaulting realities of loneliness, addiction, and disconsolate daydreams all outreach Uncle Bob's usually self-generated quandaries involving home repairs or dieting. Yet, the current of sturdy cheer in Barry's graphic journals suggests a private heirloom of gallantry from a man who kept sometimes uneasy house for his most private troubles.

Barry's bright eye is never averted from her sparrows. Those preposterously

THE MARLYS SCHOOL OF CHARM!
LET'S DO "HOW TO SIT IN A CHAIR".
OH. MY GUEST TODAY IS THE HAIRY BEING. HE WILL HELP ON THE DEMONSTRATION PARTS.
WELCOME, HAIRY BEING. NOW, ARE YOU MYTHOLOGICAL OR WHAT?
I'D SAY I WAS MORE PRIMITIVE.
WELL THAT'S LOVELY. LET'S GET STARTED!
NOW, OK, WHAT YOU HAVE TO DO FIRST IS SIT DOWN ON THE CHAIR GRACEFULLY. DON'T STICK YOUR REAR END OUT! LOWER IT DOWN!
WRONG!
RIGHT!
OK. NOW SIT WITH YOUR WEIGHT ON THE FRONT OF THE CHAIR, PUT YOUR HANDS ON THE CHAIR AND SLIDE YOUR HAIRY BEHIND BACKWARDS.
SLIDE IT!
DON'T TWITCH IT!
THEN, SIT STRAIGHT NOT ALL HUNCHY! KEEP ONE FOOT BEHIND THE OTHER FOR EXTRA ELEGANCE!
WRONG!
THIS WAY SHOWS FAT WADS!
FANTASTIC!
IT'S SLENDERIZING!
NO WADS!
WELL DONE, HAIRY BEING!
I REALLY ENJOYED IT.
ME TOO.
WELL THAT'S OUR SHOW! HAPPY AND BEAUTIFUL SITTING, EVERYBODY!
L Y N D A B A R R Y 99

incapable looking figures are drawn with a deliberate dry gravity, a muted, hovering pessimism that hangs around like an unsightly retainer.

And still another layer activates, lightens and sweetens her work: the recurrently perceptible shimmer of wonder; reminding us that her thrust is in truth neither the sheer chipper cynicism of Stan Mack, nor the file-rough satire of George Grosz (cited in a quoted testimonial to her work). Barry's theme as maintained and extended through her style is the foraging search of the starvling human imagination, accompanied by its little brother Hope, through the dreck-strewn fields of current popular culture.

In this regard, her text and pictures not only supplement each other, but join in a style that, like the best artistic styles, can encompass experience in its variety. Her comedy sometimes recalls to me the arid, grainy, achy look of B. Kliban's work in the '60s and '70s. Kliban's definitive forte was his mock iconography in single panels like that of the Virgin Mary seen by an automobile. Barry shares Kliban's cockeyed regard for popular objects of reverence (sliqhtly fewer these days) and awe (only too plentiful and misdirected). A lonely lady hears chiding messages from her cigarette lighter (labeled "Capricorn"). Barry's take on a supermarket tabloid feature ("Now It Can Be Told: The Dead Are Trying To Reach Us!") lists uncanny phenomena: "Missing Caps on Your Toothpaste Tubes," "A Sock Is Missing After Doing the Laundry." In these pages, Barry is not a fantasist; but she acutely understands fantasy hunger, and the way pedestrian fripperies like the above may furnish flower boxes for meager but comforting blooms. (Benchley *would* have chortled at that last one.)

BABES UP IN ARMS

Marlys Mullen, the polycreative heroine and embodied Zeitgeist of three Barry collections, enriches and amplifies the bleak comic map set forth in earlier Barry works. Marlys' showcase volume, *The Greatest of Marlys,* is flanked by two others: *Come Over, Come Over* recounts the views, strivings and crystalizing reflections of Marlys' 14-year-old sister Maybonne. *The Freddie Stories* chronicle the demon-beset days and nights of the Mullen sisters' 14-year-old brother. Be it noted: Freddie's demons, unlike the canons of stereotypical teenage fiction, are not solely evoked by his sisters. They are numerous, persistent and alarming.

The two adjoining books enlarge and vitalize the wunderkind excursions of Marlys; furnishing supplementary perspectives ("perspectives" summarizes a major theme of all three books: the saga of the Mullens). Indeed, the trilogy offers a nurturing earth for the comedy of Marlys, which, with its scars and ridges, provides the terrain for a deeper and more resonant comedy.

Marlys is the undoubted center of the triptych.

Yet, Marlys is the undoubted center of the triptych. Her presence blossoms like a sunflower from the cover of her own volume. Her figure, in red and yellow diagonal-striped dress, performs a dance of welcome: rubbery, ever mobile limbs swinging; her braids bouncing in the air like friendly snakes; she is surrounded by inserts, blazing like a Busby Berkeley meteor storm, of her siblings, and of (Arna and Albert Arneson) her cousins and next-door neighbors. It should be noted that many of Marlys' stories are told by Cousin Arna: Marlys herself is barely at the threshold of introspection. But hers is the cavorting muse of creativity. Her resilience (plus the extraordinary bulk of information conveyed through the girls' narratives)

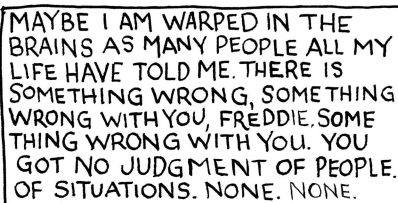

MAYBE I AM WARPED IN THE BRAINS AS MANY PEOPLE ALL MY LIFE HAVE TOLD ME. THERE IS SOMETHING WRONG, SOMETHING WRONG WITH YOU, FREDDIE. SOME THING WRONG WITH YOU. YOU GOT NO JUDGMENT OF PEOPLE. OF SITUATIONS. NONE. NONE.
HEL-LO DEAD BOY...
3

Top: Panel from *The Greatest of Marlys* by Lynda Barry. **Bottom:** Page from *The Freddie Stories* by Lynda Barry. Both © 2002 Lynda Barry.

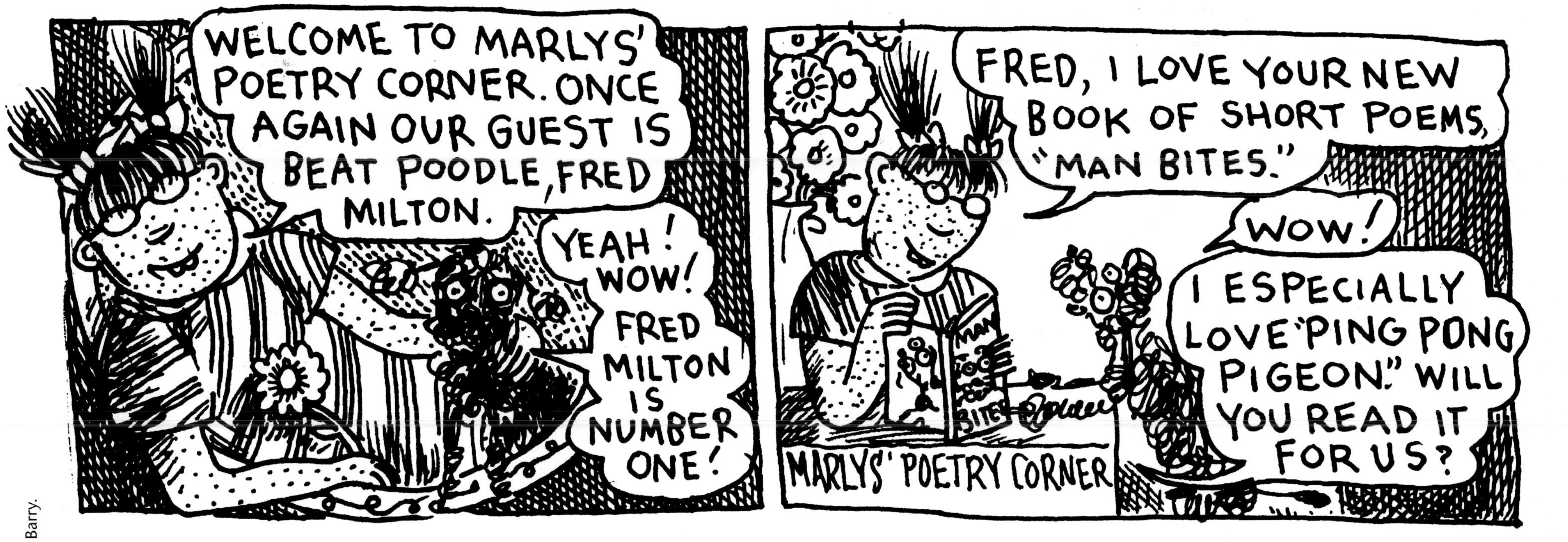
WELCOME TO MARLYS' POETRY CORNER. ONCE AGAIN OUR GUEST IS BEAT POODLE, FRED MILTON.
YEAH! WOW! FRED MILTON IS NUMBER ONE!
FRED, I LOVE YOUR NEW BOOK OF SHORT POEMS, "MAN BITES."
WOW!
I ESPECIALLY LOVE "PING PONG PIGEON." WILL YOU READ IT FOR US?
MARLYS' POETRY CORNER

Top and bottom: Panels from *The Greatest of Marlys* by Lynda Barry. © 2002 Lynda Barry.

reminds me of that fine Irish novelist Roddy Doyle's beleaguered young hero Paddy Clark (*Paddy Clark Ha Ha Ha*). However, Marlys' mimicry and zestful adaptation of advice columns and schlock-movie synopses echo with a more tickling resonance, not only Barry's earlier work. They also shimmer with the remembered image of Penrod Schofield, Booth Tarkington's jimson weed. Like the memorable and too little remembered Penrod, Marlys gets her juvenile high from the popular prints. Penrod honored the fiddle music of pulp detective magazines by writing stories of his own. Counter to yet another dictum of pop teenage fustian, he and Marlys are burgeoning artists, rather than mere fantasists; more than juvenile Walter Mittys and Alice Adamses.

Perhaps the most heartening and challenging evolution in Barry's work here displayed is the multiplied scope and vigor of her style. The tightsphinctered lines and miniature fripperies of earlier books have given place to a writhing, rampant line, accompanied by raw shading and recurrent darkness. The effect is of an unceremonious, often mauling vigor. Barry resorts to distortion and foreshortening as freely as in her earlier urban comedies; here, however, the effect is of a squirming, rippling current of potential change. As the episodes progress Barry incorporates some of her more whimsical penchants in the children's seeking out and befriending of eccentrics, fringe-dwellers, human oddities whether by nature's cruelty or election. (I recall one of Marlys' display pages as recreating the contents of a *Believe It Or Not* book by Bob Ripley. I can remember the original book.) The hallucinatory and near-autistic Freddie finds a corridor of peace in friendship with an autistic girl, from the "special class" to which he has been assigned. Even Arnold Arneson, the feral-faced and weasel-spirited brother of Anna, finds love with a harelipped girl (he reenacts their kiss and his ambivalent spasms with a hand-puppet rabbit). Marlys herself records interviews with the original Cyclops, and a hairy, faceless prehistoric man. She also documents the New Year's resolutions of socially unacceptable insects, including ants, termites and the ubiquitous cockroaches. These later episodes suggest Barry not backtracking, but newly encountering her own fantasy tropes. A frequent interviewee of Marlys in the later episodes is Fred Milton, a beat poet poodle: as assemblage of corkscrew ringlets, who utters sporadic exclamations of approval or disfavor in what seems to be the speech of a recent East Indian immigrant.

I have barely mentioned Barry's mastery and manifest love of language, consistently on view in the children's frantic makeshifts, their bubbling hyperboles, the vaulting rebirth of cliches. All serve to propel the embracing beauty of Barry's accuracy in a pedestrian epic of evolving spirit. I consign my epigraph to Maybonne: "It's mainly about how life can magically turn cruddy then beautiful—and then back to cruddy again, then it just keeps on evolutionizing you."

I seem to remember when that might have been a pretty good description of the novel. ★★★

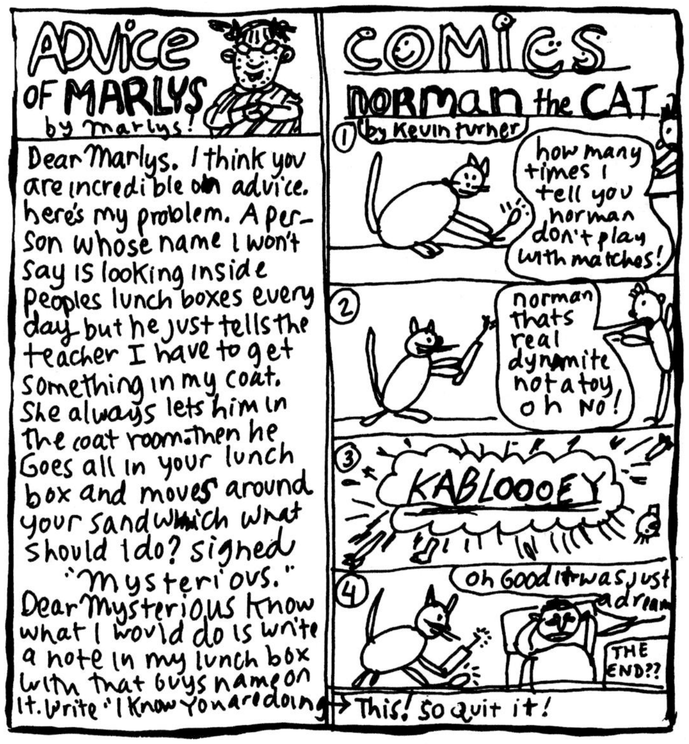
ADVICE OF MARLYS
by marlys!
Dear Marlys. I think you are incredible on advice. here's my problem. A person whose name I won't say is looking inside peoples lunch boxes every day but he just tells the teacher I have to get something in my coat. She always lets him in the coat room. Then he Goes all in your lunch box and moves around your sandwhich what should I do? signed "Mysterious." Dear Mysterious Know what I would do is write a note in my lunch box with that guys name on it. Write "I Know You are doing → This! so quit it!
COMICS
norman the CAT
by Kevin turner
how many times I tell you norman don't play with matches!
norman thats real dynamite not a toy oh No!
KABLOOOEY
oh Good it was just a dream
THE END??

CARTOONISTS ON PATRIOTISM

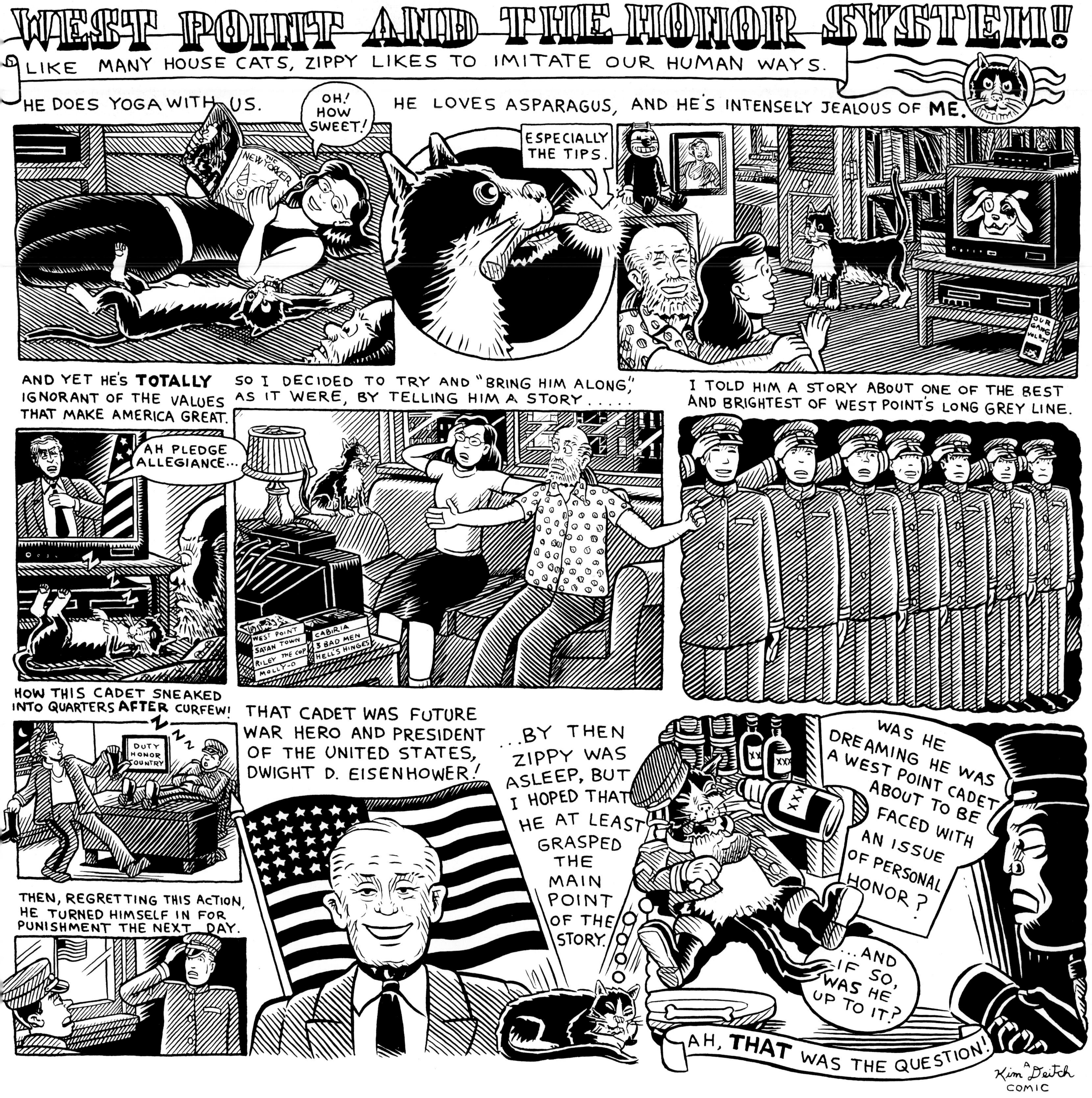
WEST POINT AND THE HONOR SYSTEM!
LIKE MANY HOUSE CATS, ZIPPY LIKES TO IMITATE OUR HUMAN WAYS.
HE DOES YOGA WITH US.
OH! HOW SWEET!
THE NEW YORKER
HE LOVES ASPARAGUS, AND HE'S INTENSELY JEALOUS OF ME.
ESPECIALLY THE TIPS.
AND YET HE'S TOTALLY IGNORANT OF THE VALUES THAT MAKE AMERICA GREAT.
AH PLEDGE ALLEGIANCE...
Z Z Z
SO I DECIDED TO TRY AND "BRING HIM ALONG," AS IT WERE, BY TELLING HIM A STORY.....
WEST POINT
SATAN TOWN
RILEY THE COP
MOLLY-O
CABIRIA
3 BAD MEN
HELL'S HINGES
I TOLD HIM A STORY ABOUT ONE OF THE BEST AND BRIGHTEST OF WEST POINT'S LONG GREY LINE.
HOW THIS CADET SNEAKED INTO QUARTERS AFTER CURFEW!
Z Z
DUTY HONOR COUNTRY
THEN, REGRETTING THIS ACTION, HE TURNED HIMSELF IN FOR PUNISHMENT THE NEXT DAY.
THAT CADET WAS FUTURE WAR HERO AND PRESIDENT OF THE UNITED STATES, DWIGHT D. EISENHOWER!
...BY THEN ZIPPY WAS ASLEEP, BUT I HOPED THAT HE AT LEAST GRASPED THE MAIN POINT OF THE STORY.
XXX
WAS HE DREAMING HE WAS A WEST POINT CADET ABOUT TO BE FACED WITH AN ISSUE OF PERSONAL HONOR?
...AND IF SO, WAS HE UP TO IT?
AH, THAT WAS THE QUESTION!
Kim A Deitch COMIC

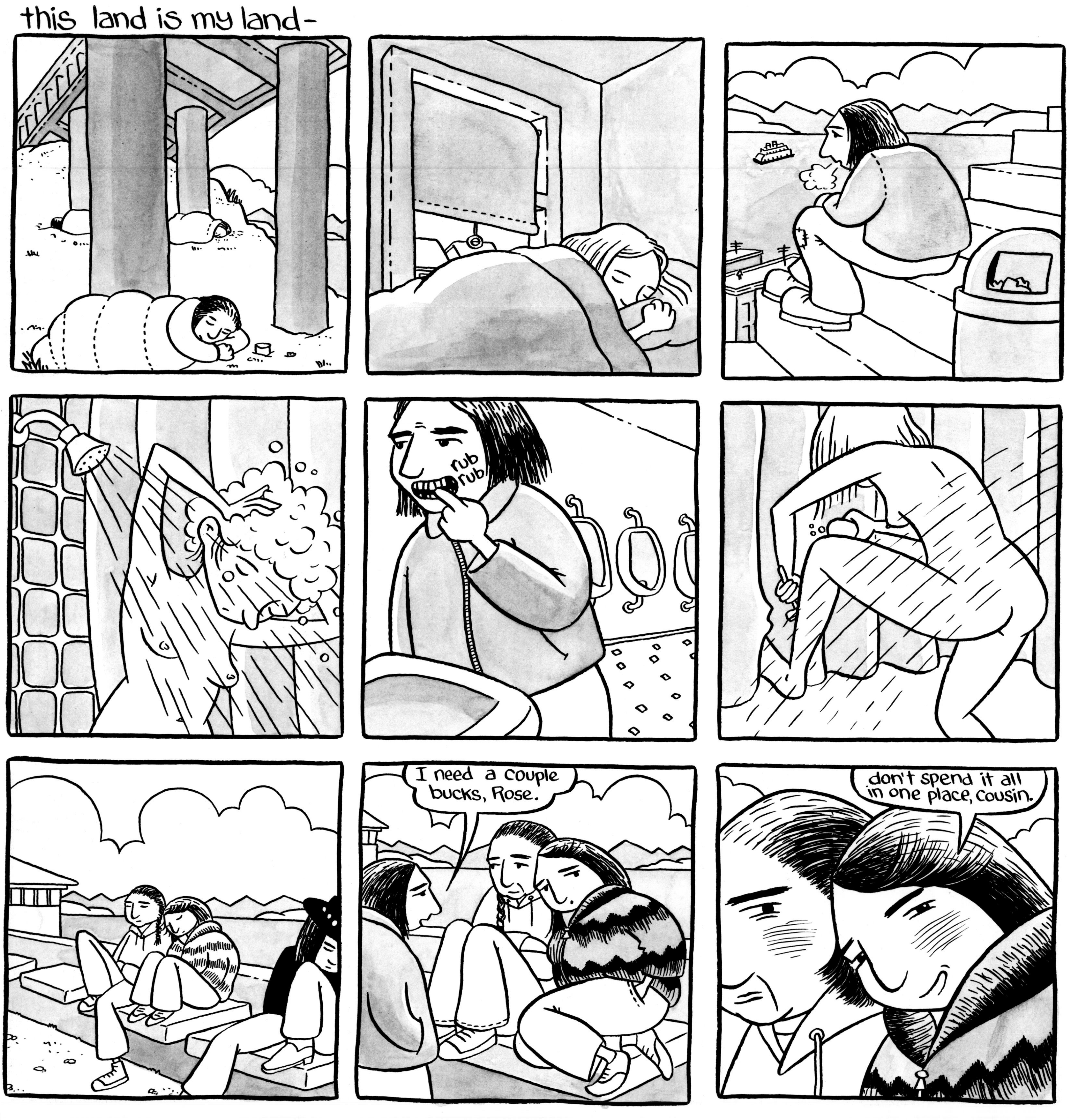
this land is my land-
rub rub
I need a couple bucks, Rose.
don't spend it all in one place, cousin.

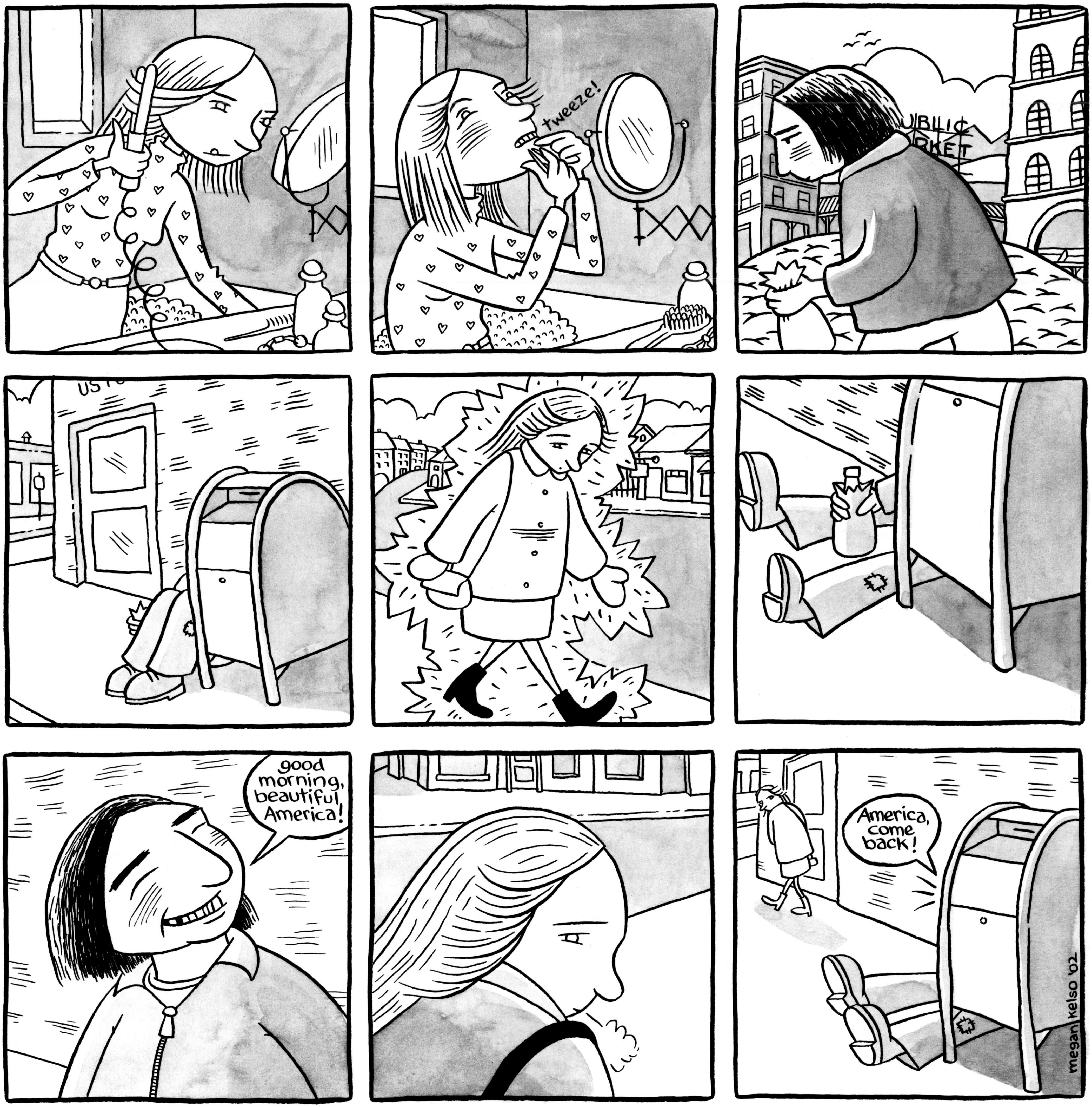
tweeze!
good morning, beautiful America!
America, come back!
megan kelso '02

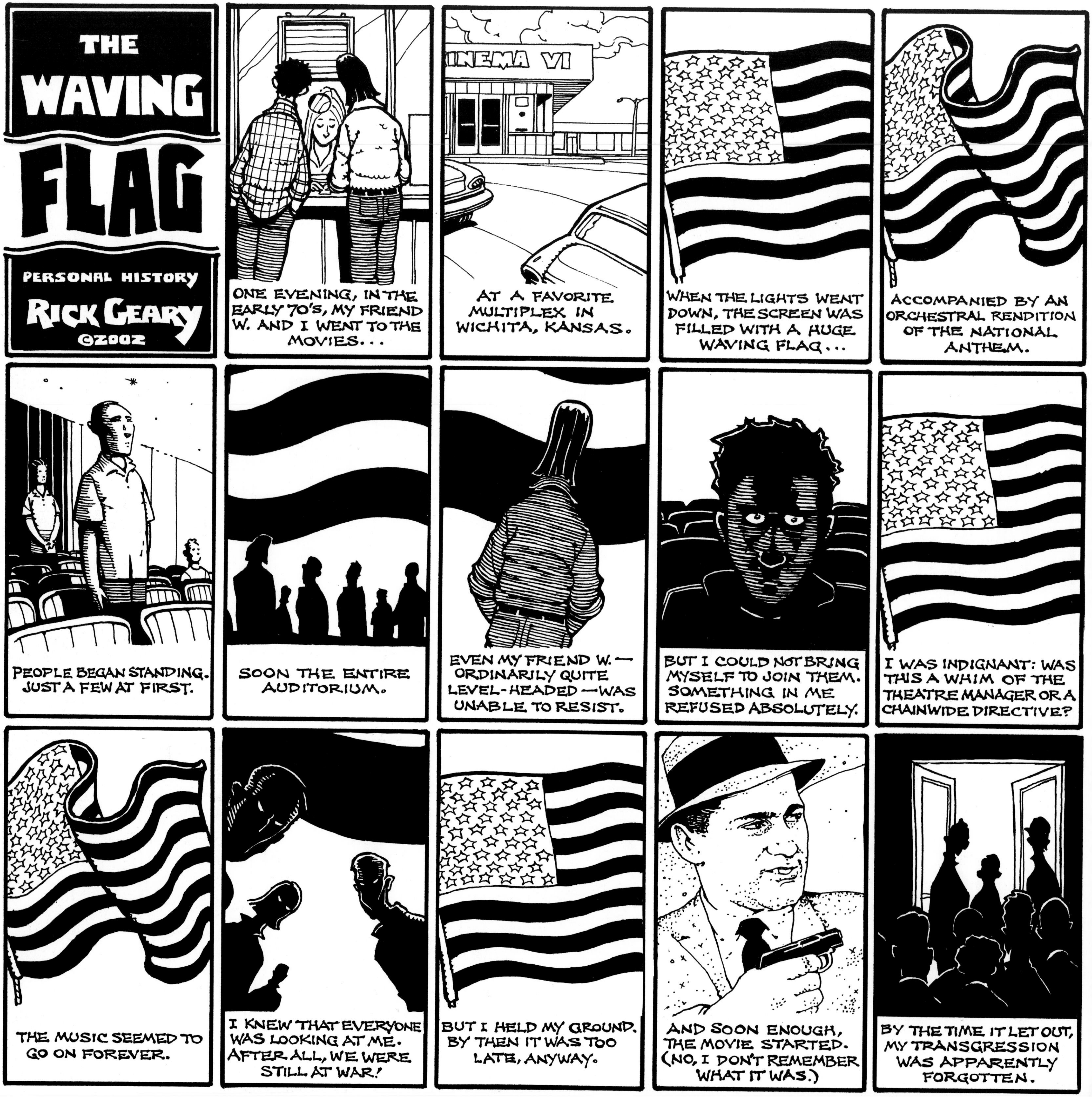
THE WAVING FLAG
PERSONAL HISTORY
RICK GEARY
©2002
ONE EVENING, IN THE EARLY 70'S, MY FRIEND W. AND I WENT TO THE MOVIES...
INEMA VI
AT A FAVORITE MULTIPLEX IN WICHITA, KANSAS.
WHEN THE LIGHTS WENT DOWN, THE SCREEN WAS FILLED WITH A HUGE WAVING FLAG...
ACCOMPANIED BY AN ORCHESTRAL RENDITION OF THE NATIONAL ANTHEM.
PEOPLE BEGAN STANDING. JUST A FEW AT FIRST.
SOON THE ENTIRE AUDITORIUM.
EVEN MY FRIEND W.— ORDINARILY QUITE LEVEL-HEADED —WAS UNABLE TO RESIST.
BUT I COULD NOT BRING MYSELF TO JOIN THEM. SOMETHING IN ME REFUSED ABSOLUTELY.
I WAS INDIGNANT: WAS THIS A WHIM OF THE THEATRE MANAGER OR A CHAINWIDE DIRECTIVE?
THE MUSIC SEEMED TO GO ON FOREVER.
I KNEW THAT EVERYONE WAS LOOKING AT ME. AFTER ALL, WE WERE STILL AT WAR!
BUT I HELD MY GROUND. BY THEN IT WAS TOO LATE, ANYWAY.
AND SOON ENOUGH, THE MOVIE STARTED. (NO, I DON'T REMEMBER WHAT IT WAS.)
BY THE TIME IT LET OUT, MY TRANSGRESSION WAS APPARENTLY FORGOTTEN.

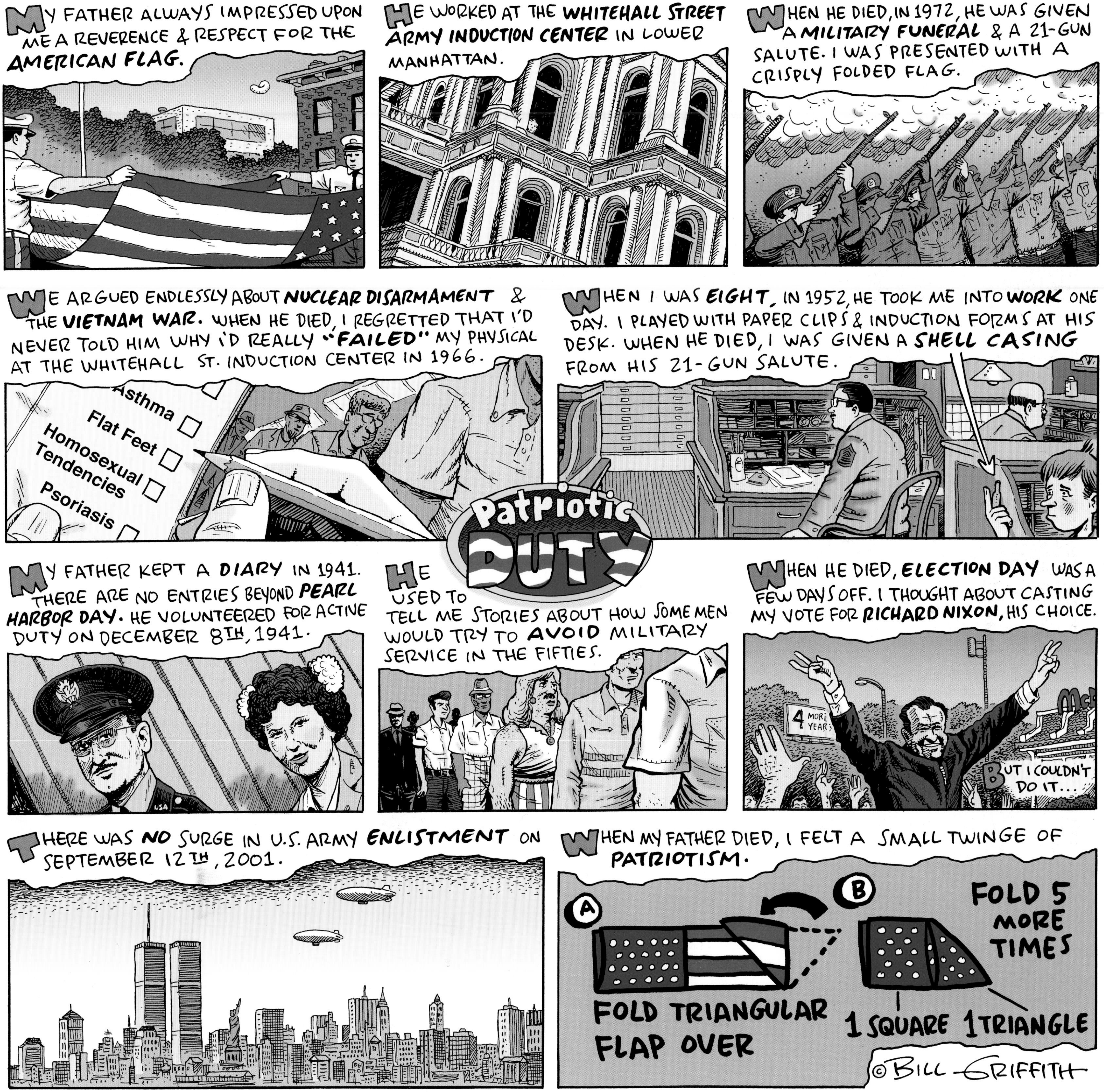

MY FATHER ALWAYS IMPRESSED UPON ME A REVERENCE & RESPECT FOR THE AMERICAN FLAG.
HE WORKED AT THE WHITEHALL STREET ARMY INDUCTION CENTER IN LOWER MANHATTAN.
WHEN HE DIED, IN 1972, HE WAS GIVEN A MILITARY FUNERAL & A 21-GUN SALUTE. I WAS PRESENTED WITH A CRISPLY FOLDED FLAG.
WE ARGUED ENDLESSLY ABOUT NUCLEAR DISARMAMENT & THE VIETNAM WAR. WHEN HE DIED, I REGRETTED THAT I'D NEVER TOLD HIM WHY I'D REALLY "FAILED" MY PHYSICAL AT THE WHITEHALL ST. INDUCTION CENTER IN 1966.
Asthma
Flat Feet
Homosexual Tendencies
Psoriasis
WHEN I WAS EIGHT, IN 1952, HE TOOK ME INTO WORK ONE DAY. I PLAYED WITH PAPER CLIPS & INDUCTION FORMS AT HIS DESK. WHEN HE DIED, I WAS GIVEN A SHELL CASING FROM HIS 21-GUN SALUTE.
Patriotic DUTY
MY FATHER KEPT A DIARY IN 1941. THERE ARE NO ENTRIES BEYOND PEARL HARBOR DAY. HE VOLUNTEERED FOR ACTIVE DUTY ON DECEMBER 8TH, 1941.
HE USED TO TELL ME STORIES ABOUT HOW SOME MEN WOULD TRY TO AVOID MILITARY SERVICE IN THE FIFTIES.
WHEN HE DIED, ELECTION DAY WAS A FEW DAYS OFF. I THOUGHT ABOUT CASTING MY VOTE FOR RICHARD NIXON, HIS CHOICE.
4 MORE YEARS
BUT I COULDN'T DO IT...
THERE WAS NO SURGE IN U.S. ARMY ENLISTMENT ON SEPTEMBER 12TH, 2001.
WHEN MY FATHER DIED, I FELT A SMALL TWINGE OF PATRIOTISM.
A
B
FOLD 5 MORE TIMES
FOLD TRIANGULAR FLAP OVER
1 SQUARE
1 TRIANGLE
©BILL GRIFFITH

"SIR BOLD" IS A STRIP I ABANDONED YEARS AGO. BUT IN THE CURRENT CLIMATE...

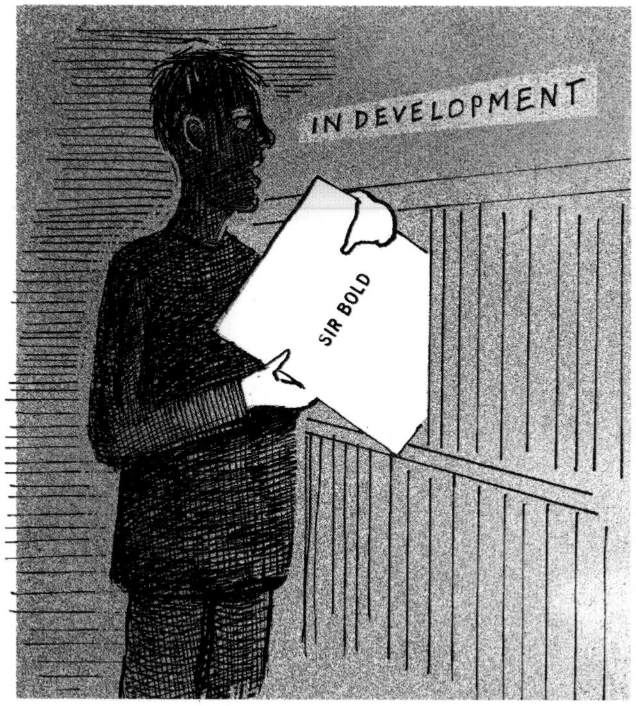
IN DEVELOPMENT
SIR BOLD

... MAYBE I SHOULD DUST IT OFF. PATRIOTISM IS TOPICAL AGAIN. SIR BOLD COULD EXPLORE THE THEME FROM UNFAMILIAR ANGLES.

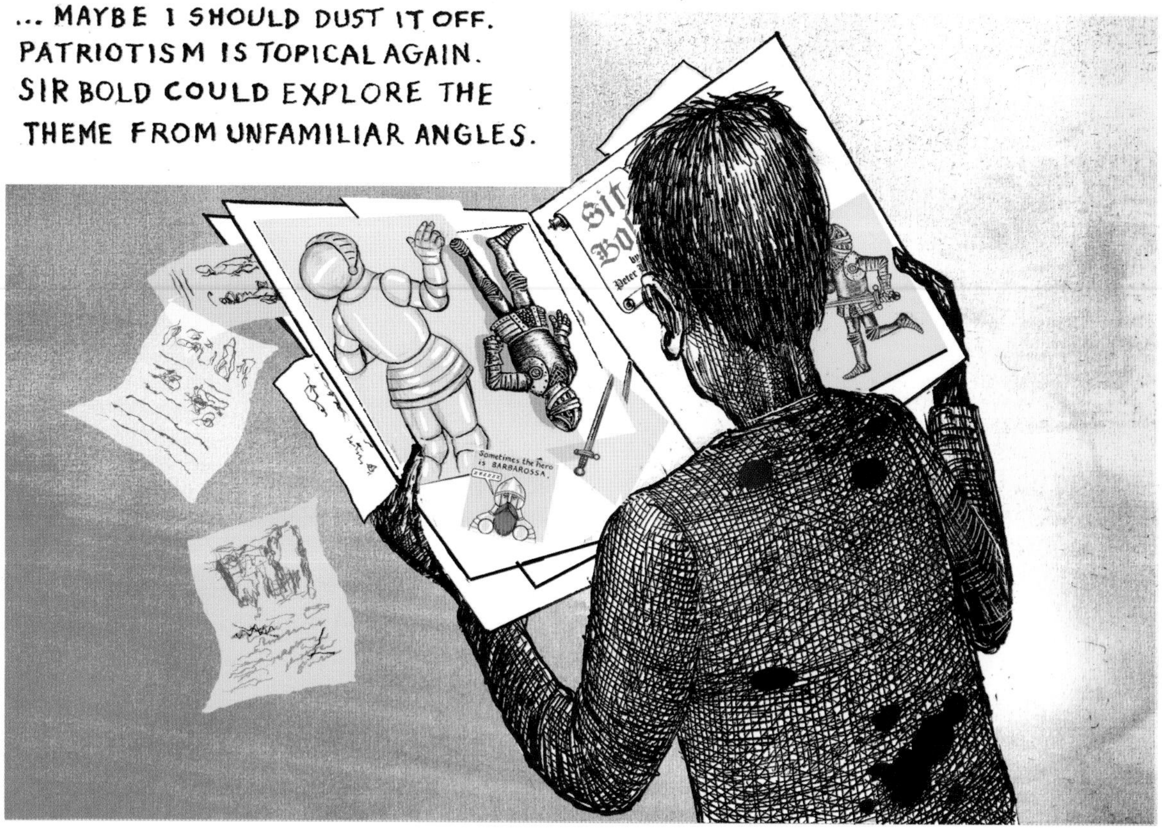

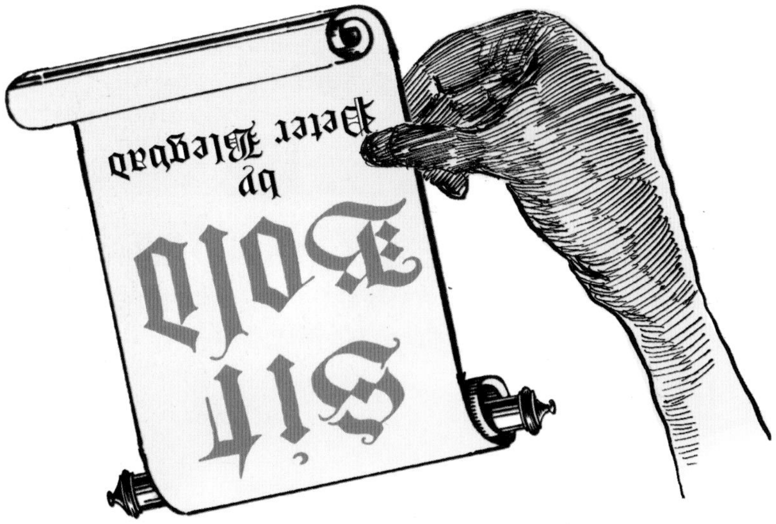
Sir Bold
by
Peter Blegvad

MANY LEGENDS TELL OF A SLEEPING HERO WHO WILL COME TO THE RESCUE IN THE NATION'S DARKEST HOUR.

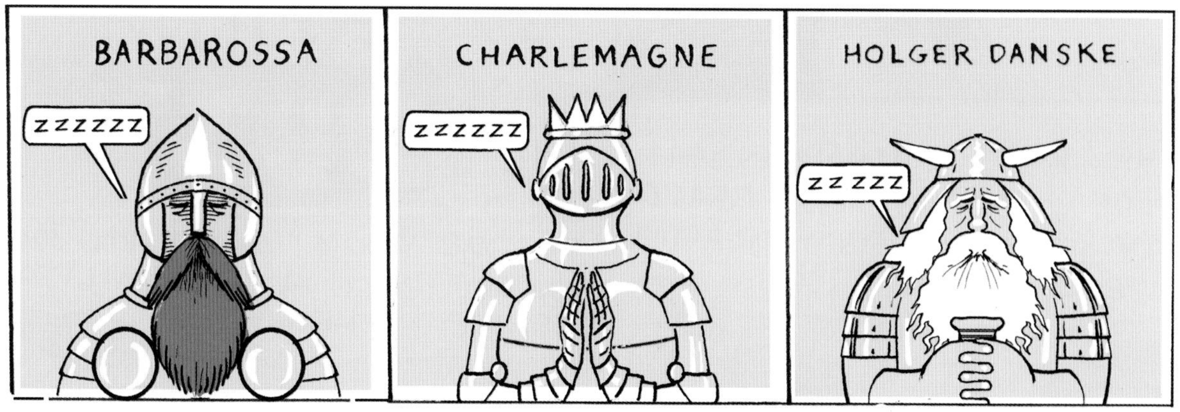
BARBAROSSA
ZZZZZZ
CHARLEMAGNE
ZZZZZZ
HOLGER DANSKE
ZZZZZ

SIR BOLD, PATRIOT OF THE FATHERLAND, IS A HERO OF THIS ILK. FOR SEVEN CENTURIES, UNDER THE HILL, UNDER A SPELL, HE AWAITS THE CALL TO ARMS.

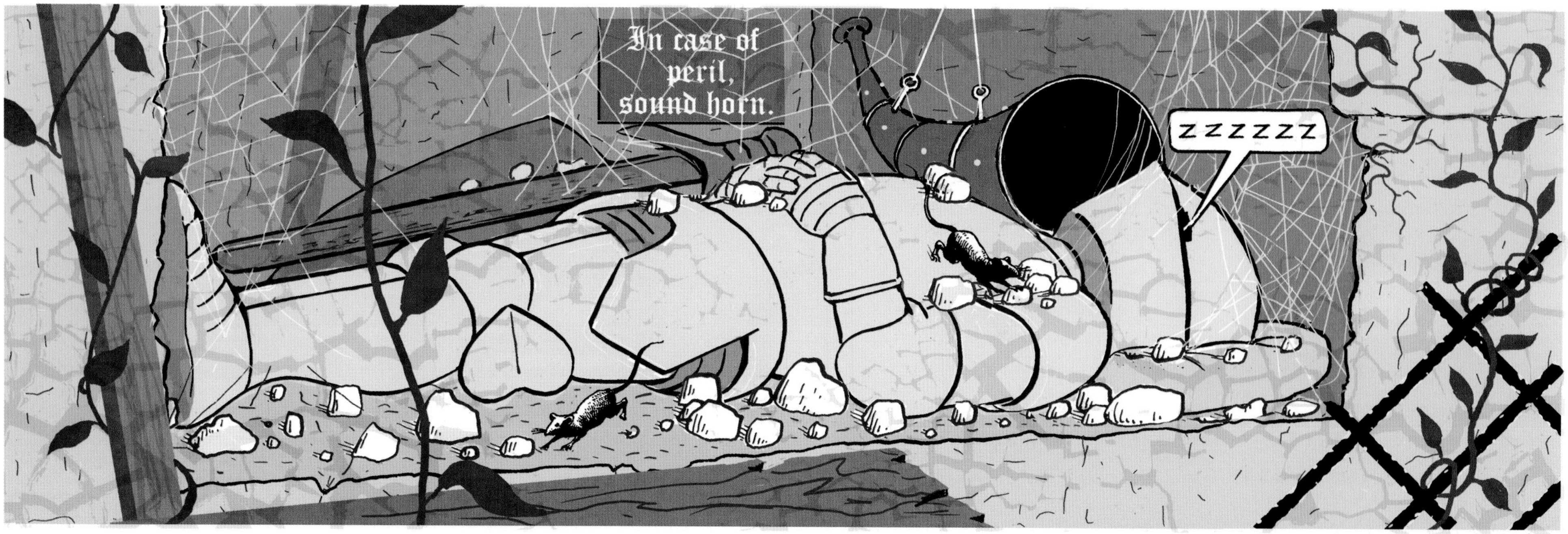
In case of peril, sound horn.
ZZZZZZ

E SPIRIT OF PATRIOTISM IS SLOW TO RISE.
HONK!
ZZZZZ
BUT, ONCE ROUSED, ...
SIR BOLD'S P.O.V.
yawn...
... LET THE FOE BEWARE!
T WHO OR WHAT *IS* THE FOE? THE YEAR IS 50. A FOREIGN ENTERTAINMENT GIANT HAS ANSFORMED THE FATHERLAND INTO A THEME-RK.
Welcome to Fatherlandland!
Knyghtes
Ladyes
ye Tyckettes
SIR BOLD HAS FOUGHT GIANTS BEFORE.
BUT THE FOREIGN ENTERTAINMENT GIANT'S PEN PROVES MIGHTIER THAN BOLD'S SWORD.
SIR BOLD ENDS UP INKING A THREE-PICTURE DEAL.
WITHIN WEEKS "SIR BOLD" MERCHANDISE IS IN THE STORES.
HIS FIRST FILM IS A SMASH.
In BOLD BLOOD
HIS SECOND, "BOLDER", ...
You're not there!
Oh, but I am, *right* here, Else!
...SHOWS THE TENDER SIDE OF BOLD.
Ahhh
You must be way down in your legs, then, 'cos you're not up here. *Mmm.* You smell so ***old.***
Are you eating Else, Sir Bold?
IT DOES LESS WELL.
CLANK!
No, Pip, I don't eat.
You're a ***spirit***, right?
My dad says you don't exist.

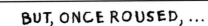

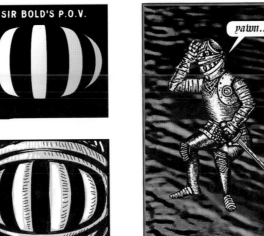

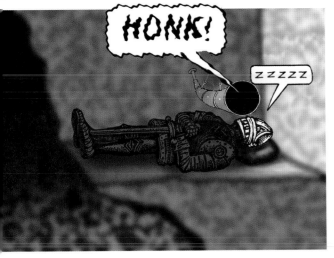

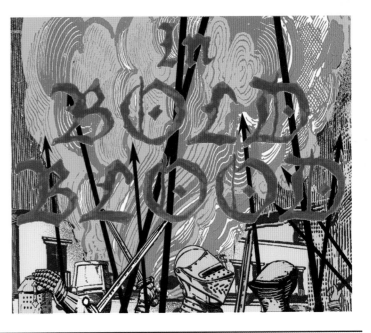

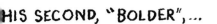

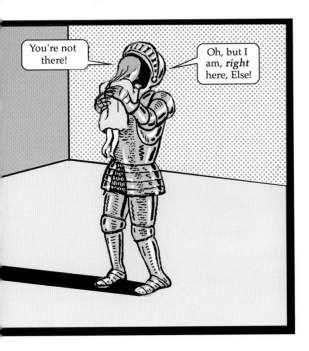

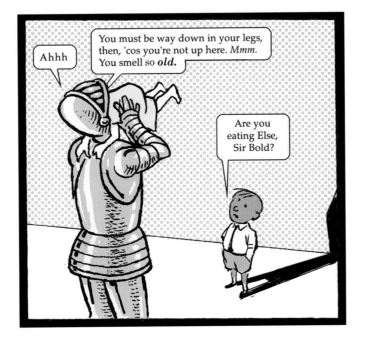

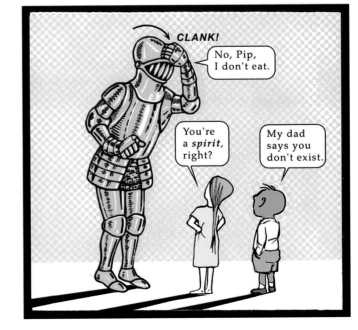

AUDIENCES OBJECT TO BOLD'S ABRUPT CONVERSION.

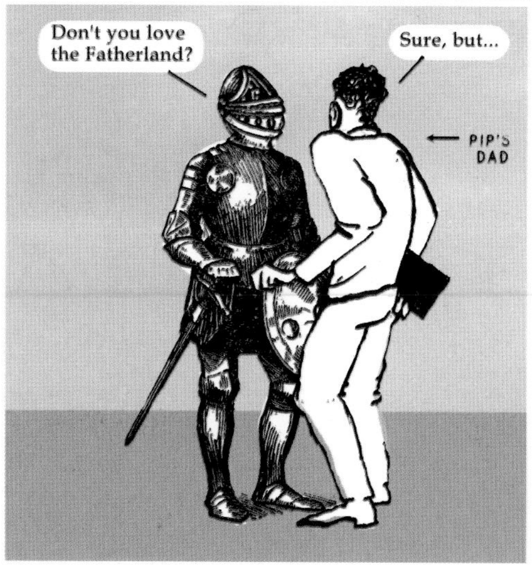
Don't you love the Fatherland?
Sure, but...
PIP'S DAD

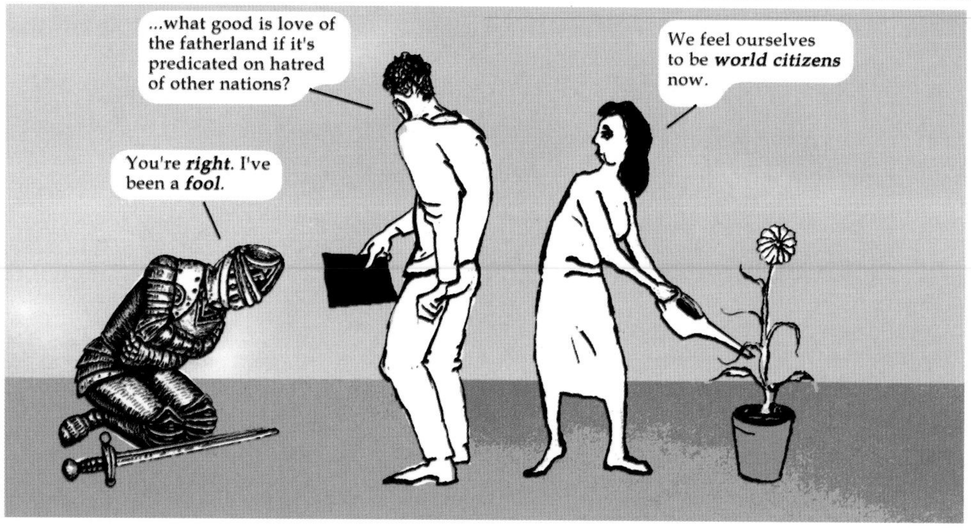
...what good is love of the fatherland if it's predicated on hatred of other nations?
You're *right*. I've been a *fool*.
We feel ourselves to be ***world citizens*** now.

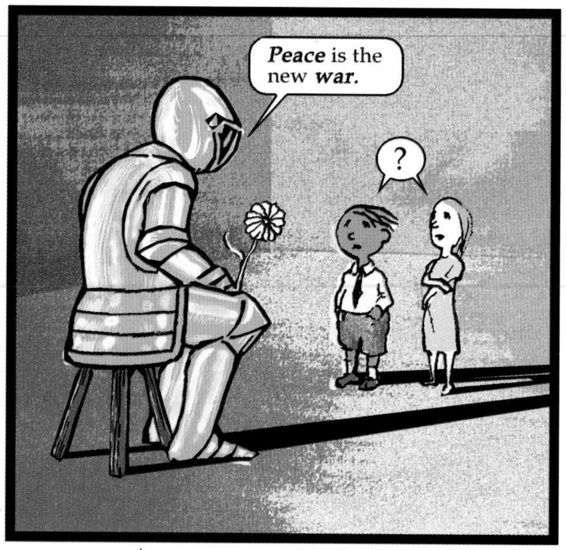
Peace is the new ***war.***
?

IN HIS THIRD FILM, "BOLDEST", BOLD DOES BATTLE WITH HIMSELF.

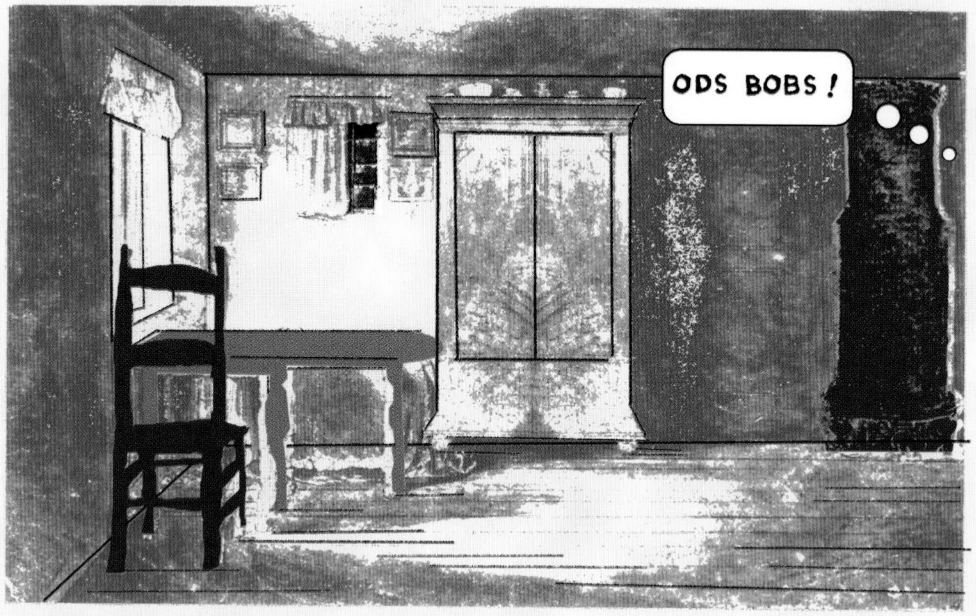
ODS BOBS!

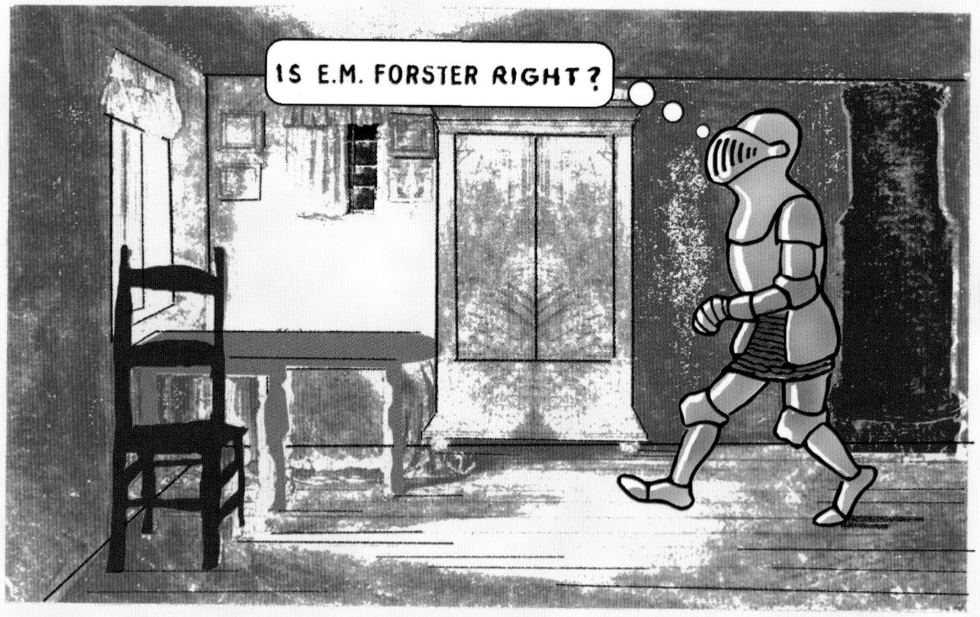
IS E.M. FORSTER RIGHT?

SIR BOLD'S CONTRACT IS NOT RENEWED.

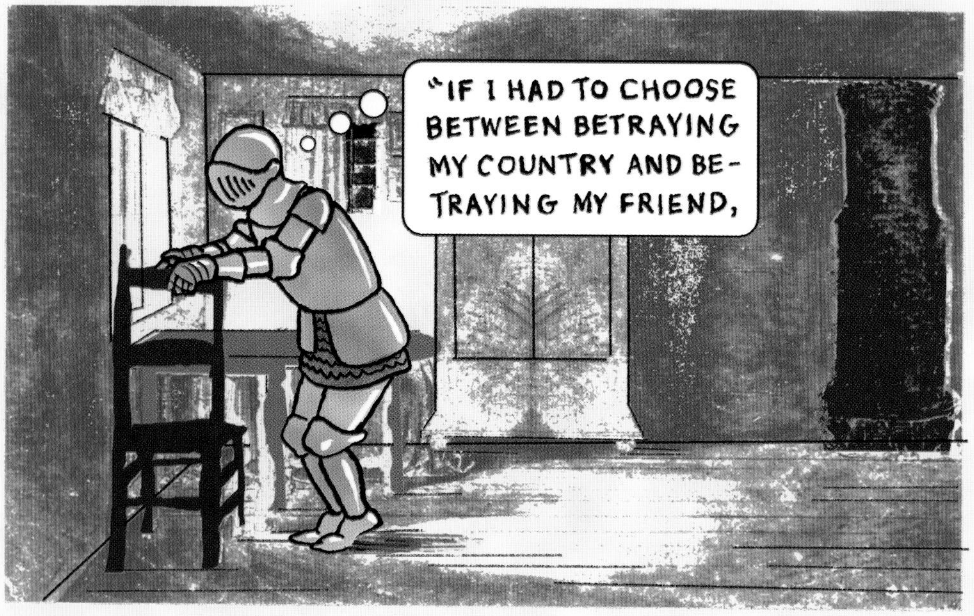
"IF I HAD TO CHOOSE BETWEEN BETRAYING MY COUNTRY AND BETRAYING MY FRIEND,

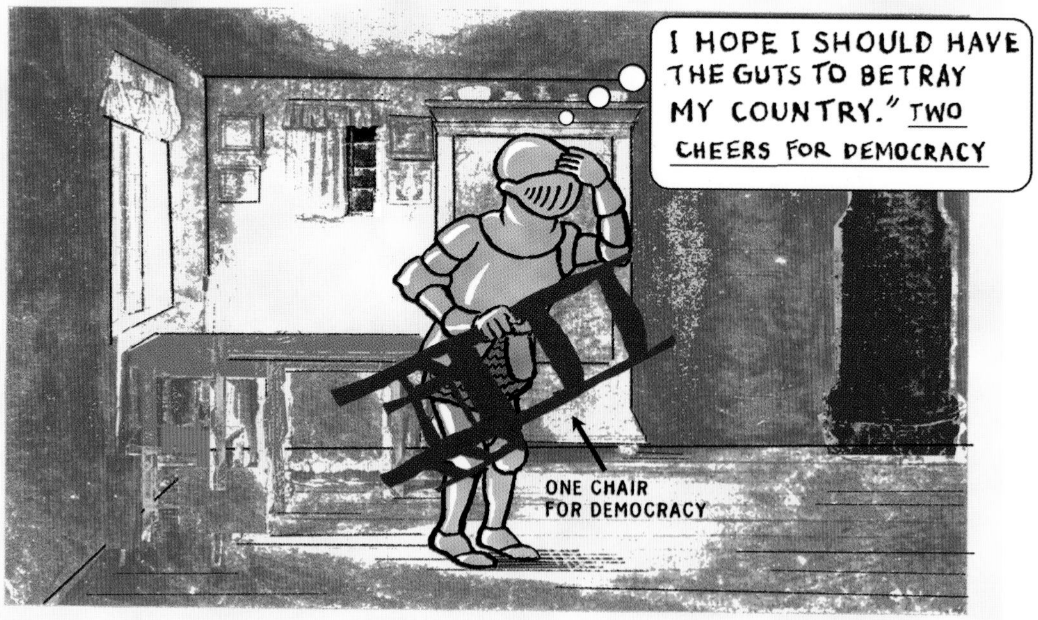
I HOPE I SHOULD HAVE THE GUTS TO BETRAY MY COUNTRY." TWO CHEERS FOR DEMOCRACY
ONE CHAIR FOR DEMOCRACY

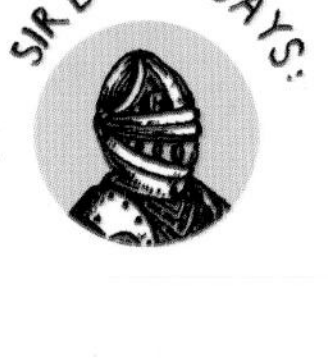
SIR BOLD SAYS:

HARK! THE HORN SOUNDS! *SLEEPERS AWAKE!*

PEACE

14th C. EMBLEM
HELMET USED AS HIVE.
"OUT OF THE STRONG
CAME FORTH SWEETNESS."

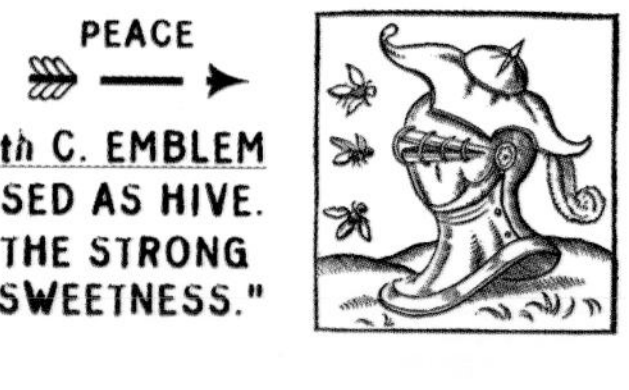

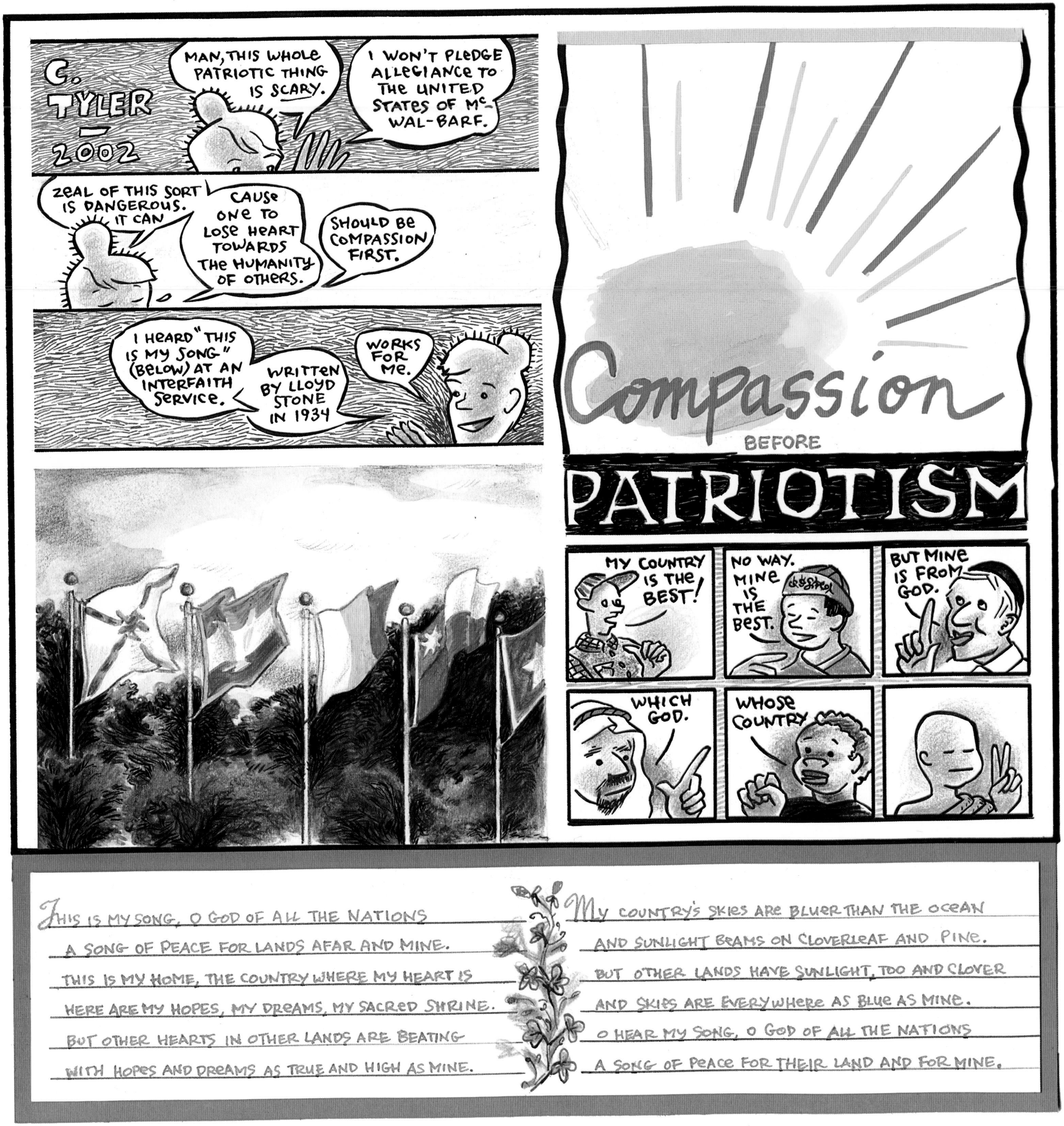

C. TYLER — 2002
MAN, THIS WHOLE PATRIOTIC THING IS SCARY.
I WON'T PLEDGE ALLEGIANCE TO THE UNITED STATES OF Mc WAL-BARF.
ZEAL OF THIS SORT IS DANGEROUS. IT CAN
CAUSE ONE TO LOSE HEART TOWARDS THE HUMANITY OF OTHERS.
SHOULD BE COMPASSION FIRST.
I HEARD "THIS IS MY SONG" (BELOW) AT AN INTERFAITH SERVICE.
WRITTEN BY LLOYD STONE IN 1934
WORKS FOR ME.
Compassion
BEFORE
PATRIOTISM
MY COUNTRY IS THE BEST!
NO WAY. MINE IS THE BEST.
BUT MINE IS FROM GOD.
WHICH GOD.
WHOSE COUNTRY
THIS IS MY SONG, O GOD OF ALL THE NATIONS
A SONG OF PEACE FOR LANDS AFAR AND MINE.
THIS IS MY HOME, THE COUNTRY WHERE MY HEART IS
HERE ARE MY HOPES, MY DREAMS, MY SACRED SHRINE.
BUT OTHER HEARTS IN OTHER LANDS ARE BEATING
WITH HOPES AND DREAMS AS TRUE AND HIGH AS MINE.
MY COUNTRY'S SKIES ARE BLUER THAN THE OCEAN
AND SUNLIGHT BEAMS ON CLOVERLEAF AND PINE.
BUT OTHER LANDS HAVE SUNLIGHT, TOO AND CLOVER
AND SKIES ARE EVERYWHERE AS BLUE AS MINE.
O HEAR MY SONG, O GOD OF ALL THE NATIONS
A SONG OF PEACE FOR THEIR LAND AND FOR MINE.

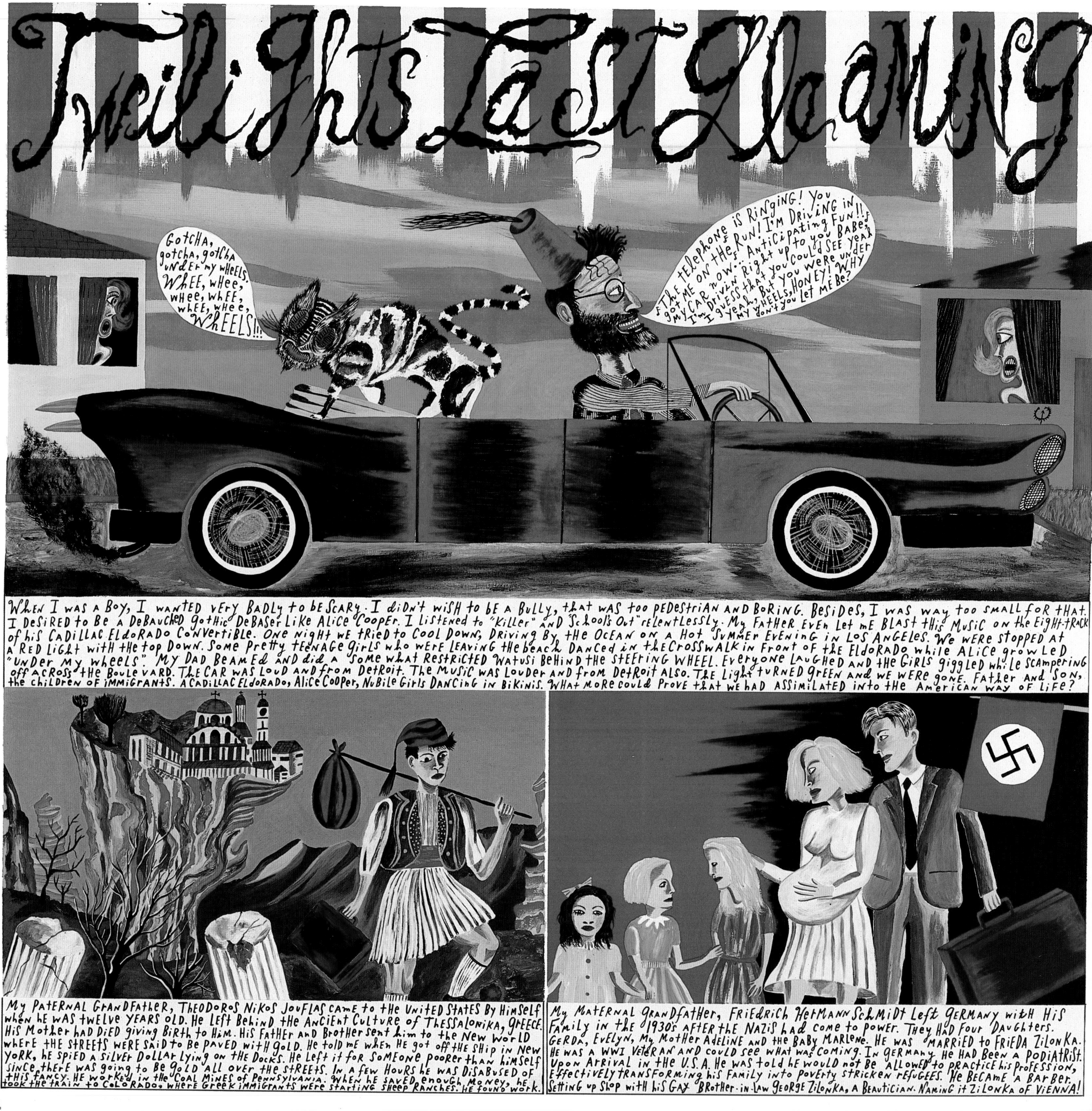
Twilight's Last Gleaming
Gotcha, gotcha, gotcha under my wheels. Whee, whee, whee, whee, whee, whee, Wheels!!!
♪ The telephone is ringing! You got me on the run! I'm driving in my car now... Anticipating fun!! ♪ I'm drivin right up to you babe, I guess that you could see yeah yeah, but you were under my wheels, honey! Why don't you let me be?
When I was a boy, I wanted very badly to be scary. I didn't wish to be a bully, that was too pedestrian and boring. Besides, I was way too small for that. I desired to be a debauched gothic debaser like Alice Cooper. I listened to "Killer" and "School's Out" relentlessly. My father even let me blast this music on the eight-track of his Cadillac Eldorado convertible. One night we tried to cool down, driving by the ocean on a hot summer evening in Los Angeles. We were stopped at a red light with the top down. Some pretty teenage girls who were leaving the beach danced in the crosswalk in front of the Eldorado while Alice growled "Under My Wheels". My dad beamed and did a somewhat restricted Watusi behind the steering wheel. Everyone laughed and the girls giggled while scampering off across the boulevard. The car was loud and from Detroit. The music was louder and from Detroit also. The light turned green and we were gone. Father and son, the children of immigrants. A Cadillac Eldorado, Alice Cooper, nubile girls dancing in bikinis. What more could prove that we had assimilated into the American way of life?
My paternal grandfather, Theodoros Nikos Jouflas came to the United States by himself when he was twelve years old. He left behind the ancient culture of Thessalonika, Greece. His mother had died giving birth to him. His father and brother sent him to the New World where the streets were said to be paved with gold. He told me when he got off the ship in New York, he spied a silver dollar lying on the docks. He left it for someone poorer than himself since there was going to be gold all over the streets. In a few hours he was disabused of this fancy. He worked in the coal mines of Pennsylvania. When he saved enough money, he took the train to Colorado, where Greek immigrants were starting sheep ranches. He found work.
My maternal grandfather, Friedrich Hermann Schmidt left Germany with his family in the 1930's after the Nazis had come to power. They had four daughters. Gerda, Evelyn, my mother Adeline and the baby Marlene. He was married to Frieda Zilonka. He was a WWI veteran and could see what was coming. In Germany he had been a podiatrist. Upon arrival in the U.S.A. he was told he would not be allowed to practice his profession, effectively transforming his family into poverty stricken refugees. He became a barber. Setting up shop with his gay brother-in-law George Zilonka, a beautician. Naming it Zilonka of Vienna!

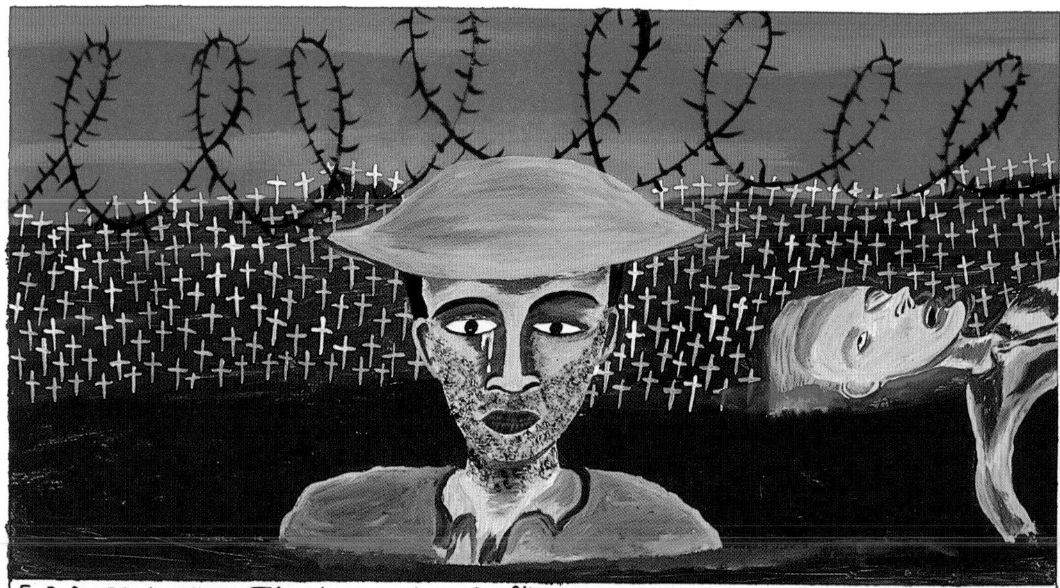

For several years, Theo had worked as a shepherd in the mountains of Colorado and Utah, on sheep ranches run by Greek immigrants. He had become a citizen of the United States, and was a happy and proud young man. When World War One started, like many recent immigrants he was promptly drafted. He was sent back to Europe to fight and live in a trench. A hero, he was decorated with medals.

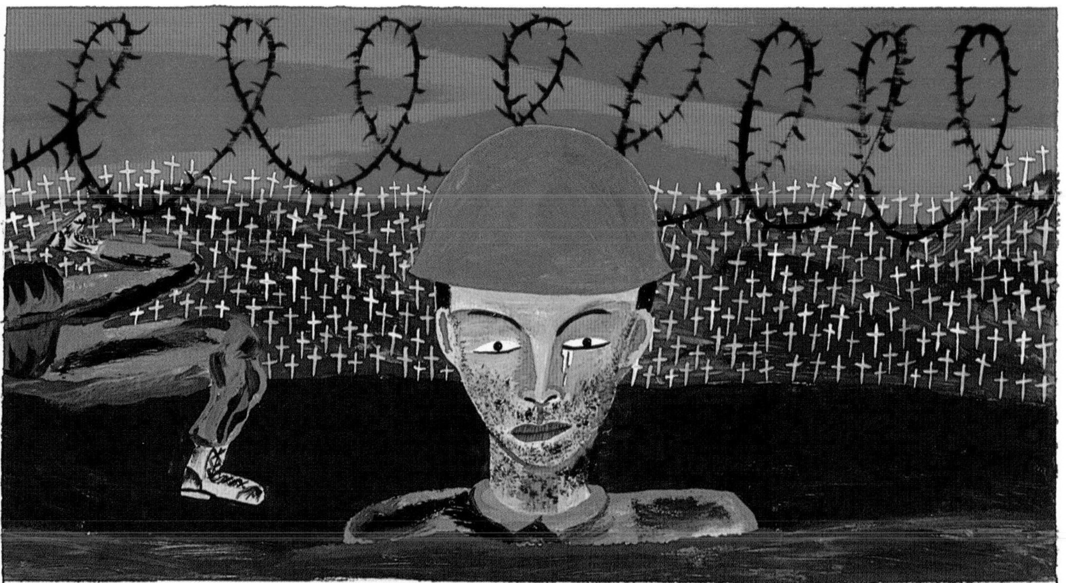

Friedrich was also a happy and proud young man. When World War One broke out, he also happened to have found himself drafted, into the service of the Kaiser. A hero, he was decorated with medals, something that would haunt him later. Thus it was that both of my grandfathers turned into cannon fodder, to dance with Death, that debutante slattern at a cotillion of mayhem. Someday, they would be friends.

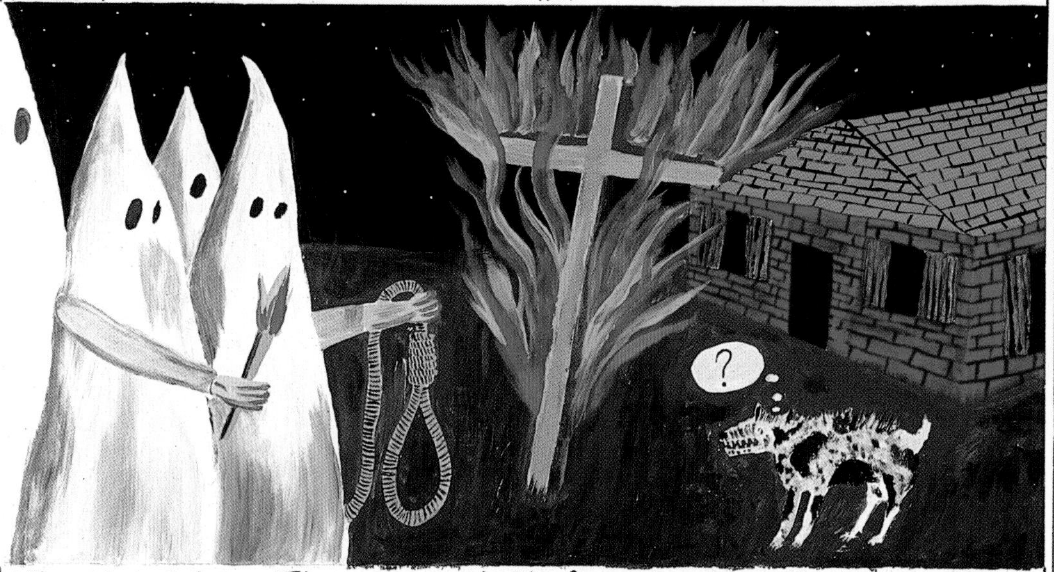
?

After the war ended, Theo returned to the Rocky Mountains. He married a Greek immigrant named Anastasia Pappas. They had four sons, Geo, my father Nikos, Peter and Milton. They started their own ranch, eventually becoming successful. During the Depression, this was a source of deep rage and resentment for bigots. The KKK would come and burn crosses. In Steamboat Springs Greeks were lynched.

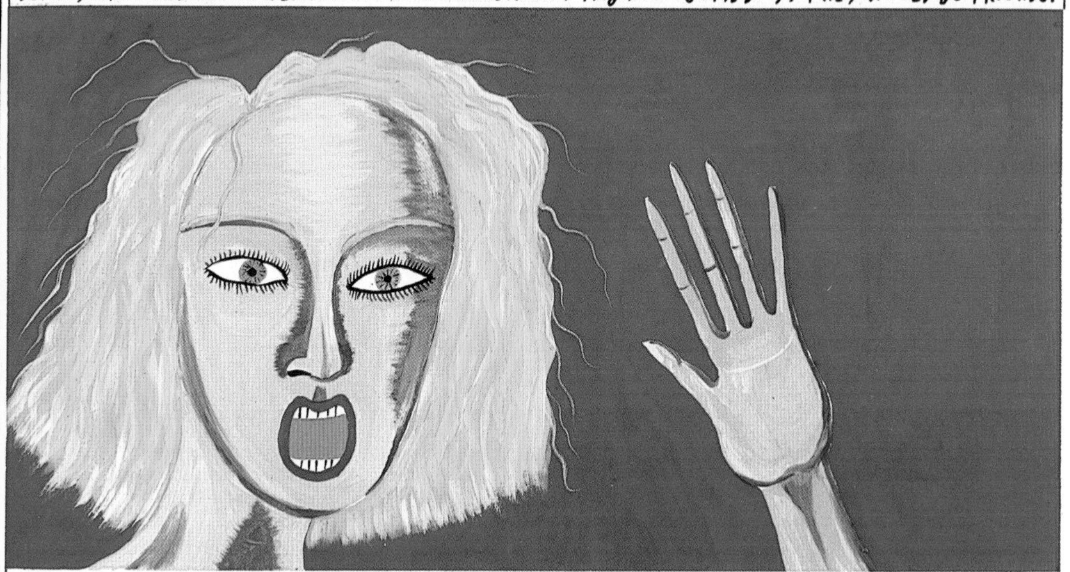

When the United States entered the Second World War, things got a lot worse for Friedrich and family. Zilonka of Vienna was vandalised. The children had rocks thrown at them as they walked to school. Because he was a WWI veteran, the F.B.I. repeatedly made surprise searches of their home. Worst of all, Prinzie the German Shepherd, was poisoned with ground glass that someone fed him with hamburger.

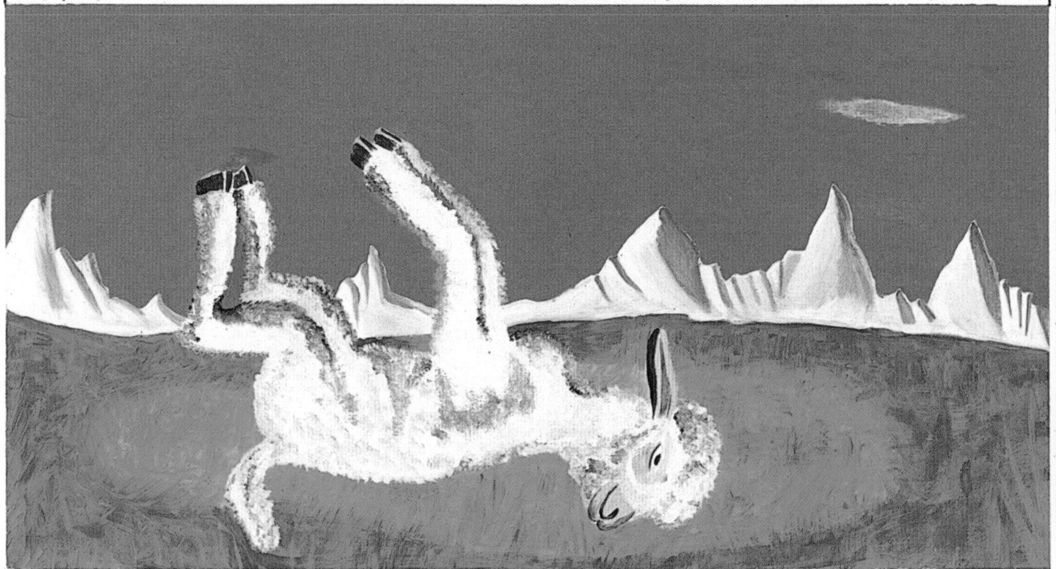

In the 1960's, Theo, now old, had his flocks at the winter range in Skull Valley, Utah. Fifty miles away lay an Army base known as Dugway Proving Ground. Pilots were secretly testing nerve gas. A flyover experiment went very wrong. All of the sheep were killed by chemical weapons. Thousands of them! To this day, the Army continues to deny responsibility. Classified documents prove otherwise.

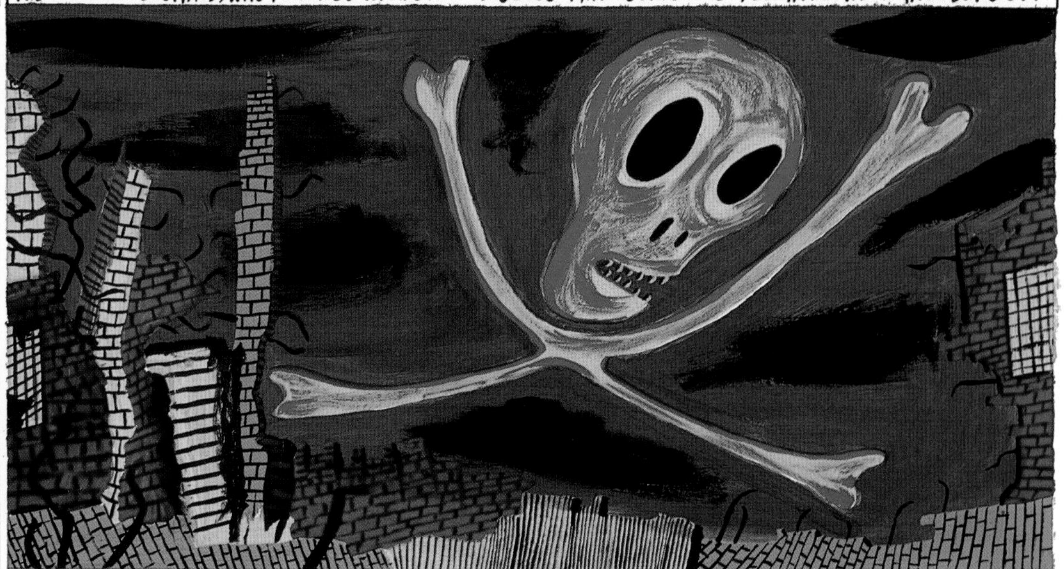

When World War Two was over, the city that Friedrich had fled with his family was destroyed. He had made the right decision. Bombs had rained for so long they became the weather. Dust, rubble, fire, mud, broken glass and corpses all had to be cleaned up. Death had come to beat the doors asunder. Like a drunk at the very best of Halloween parties, he just wasn't quite ready to go home.

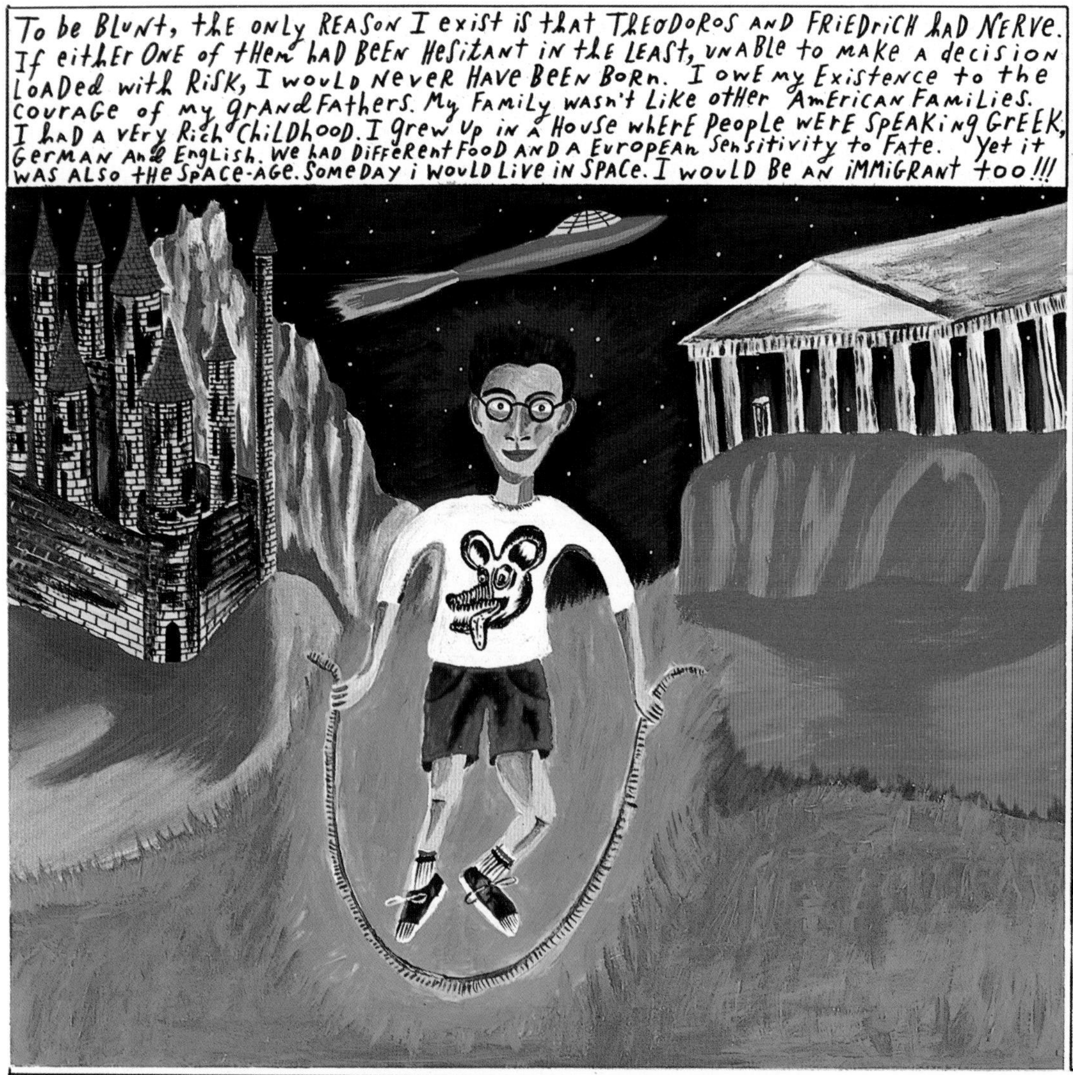
To be blunt, the only reason I exist is that Theodoros and Friedrich had nerve. If either one of them had been hesitant in the least, unable to make a decision loaded with risk, I would never have been born. I owe my existence to the courage of my grandfathers. My family wasn't like other American families. I had a very rich childhood. I grew up in a house where people were speaking Greek, German and English. We had different food and a European sensitivity to fate. Yet it was also the space-age. Someday i would live in space. I would be an immigrant too!!!

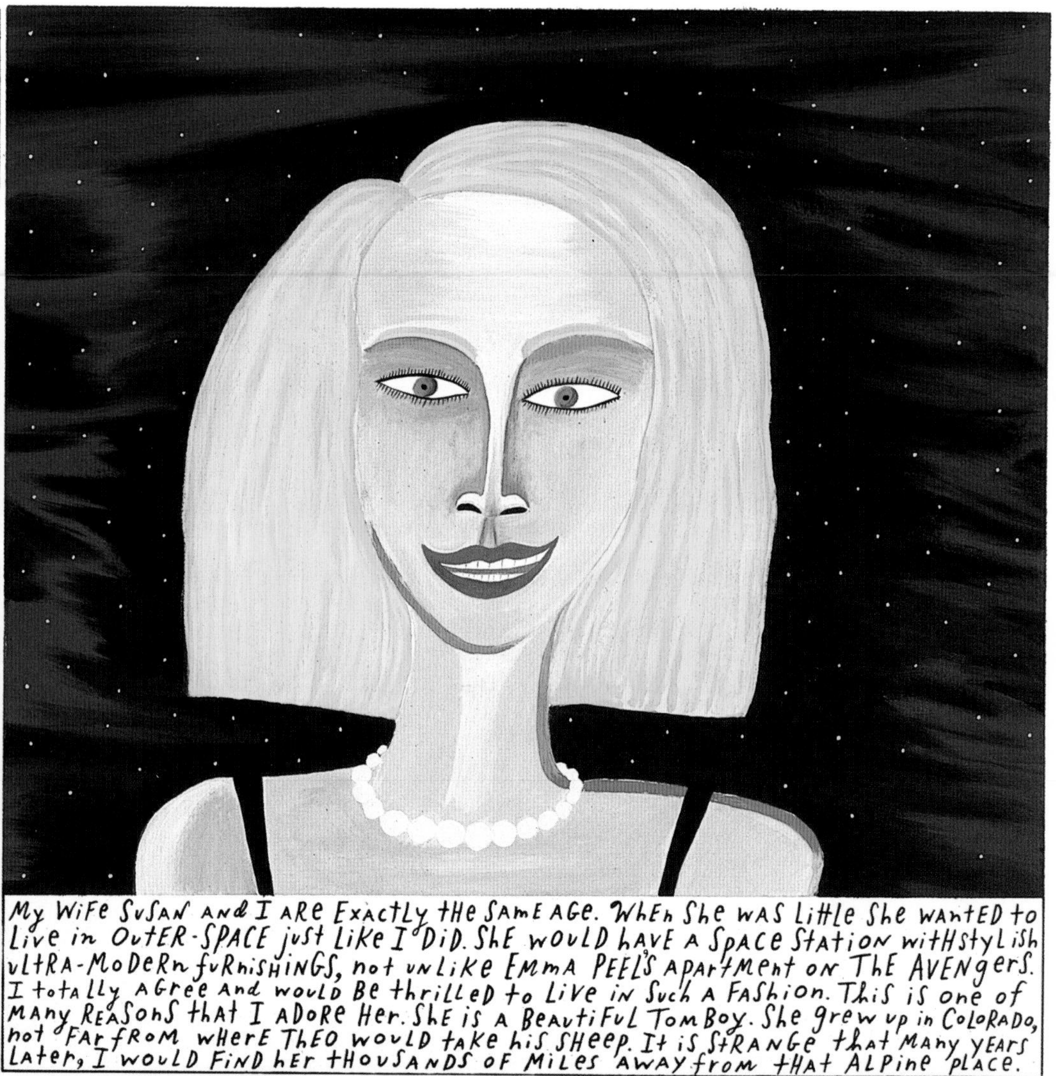
My wife Susan and I are exactly the same age. When she was little she wanted to live in outer-space just like I did. She would have a space station with stylish ultra-modern furnishings, not unlike Emma Peel's apartment on The Avengers. I totally agree and would be thrilled to live in such a fashion. This is one of many reasons that I adore her. She is a beautiful tomboy. She grew up in Colorado, not far from where Theo would take his sheep. It is strange that many years later, I would find her thousands of miles away from that alpine place.

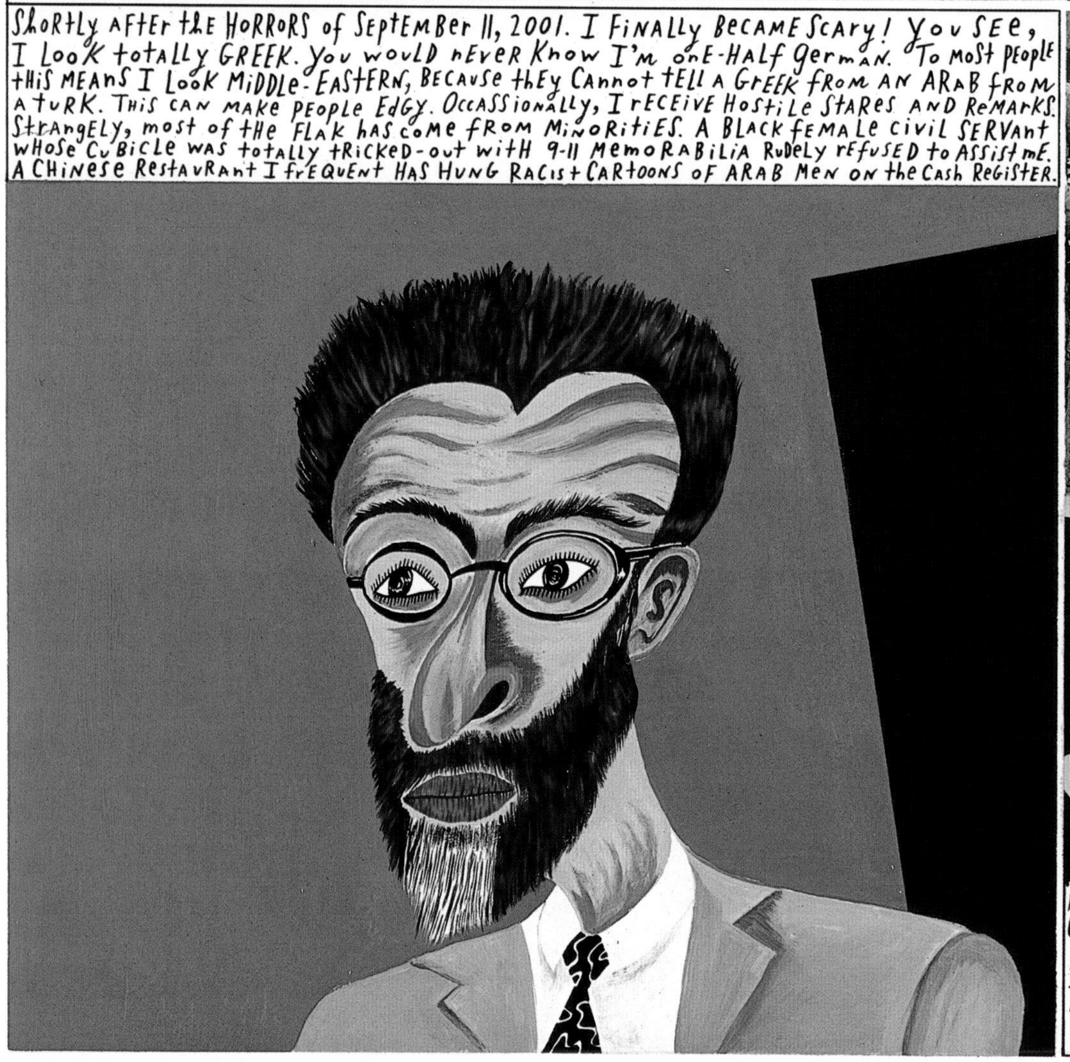
Shortly after the horrors of September 11, 2001. I finally became scary! You see, I look totally Greek. You would never know I'm one-half German. To most people this means I look Middle-Eastern, because they cannot tell a Greek from an Arab from a Turk. This can make people edgy. Occassionally, I receive hostile stares and remarks. Strangely, most of the flak has come from minorities. A black female civil servant whose cubicle was totally tricked-out with 9-11 memorabilia rudely refused to assist me. A Chinese restaurant I frequent has hung racist cartoons of Arab men on the cash register.

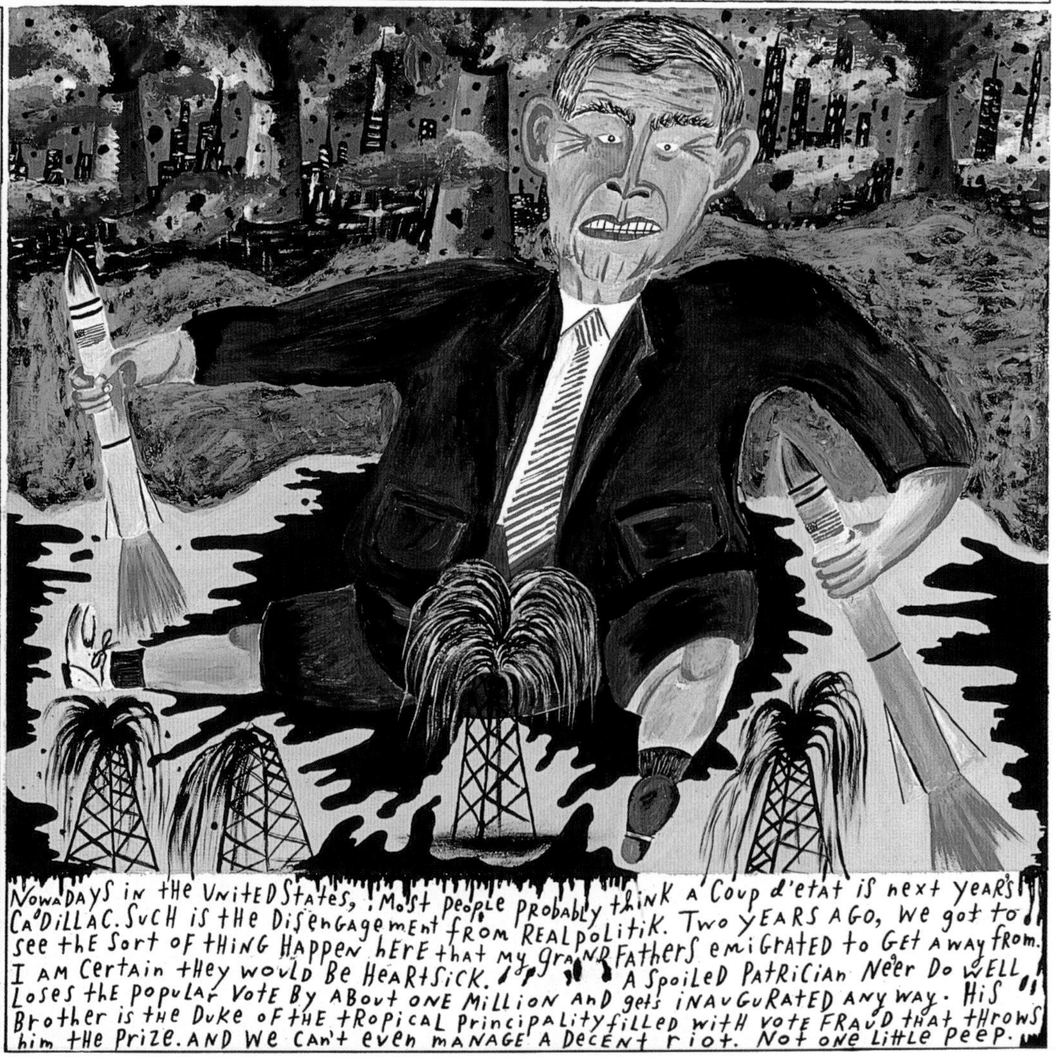
Nowadays in the United States, most people probably think a coup d'etat is next year's Cadillac. Such is the disengagement from realpolitik. Two years ago, we got to see the sort of thing happen here that my grandfathers emigrated to get away from. I am certain they would be heartsick. A spoiled patrician ne'er do well loses the popular vote by about one million and gets inaugurated anyway. His brother is the Duke of the tropical principality filled with vote fraud that throws him the prize. And we can't even manage a decent riot. Not one little peep.

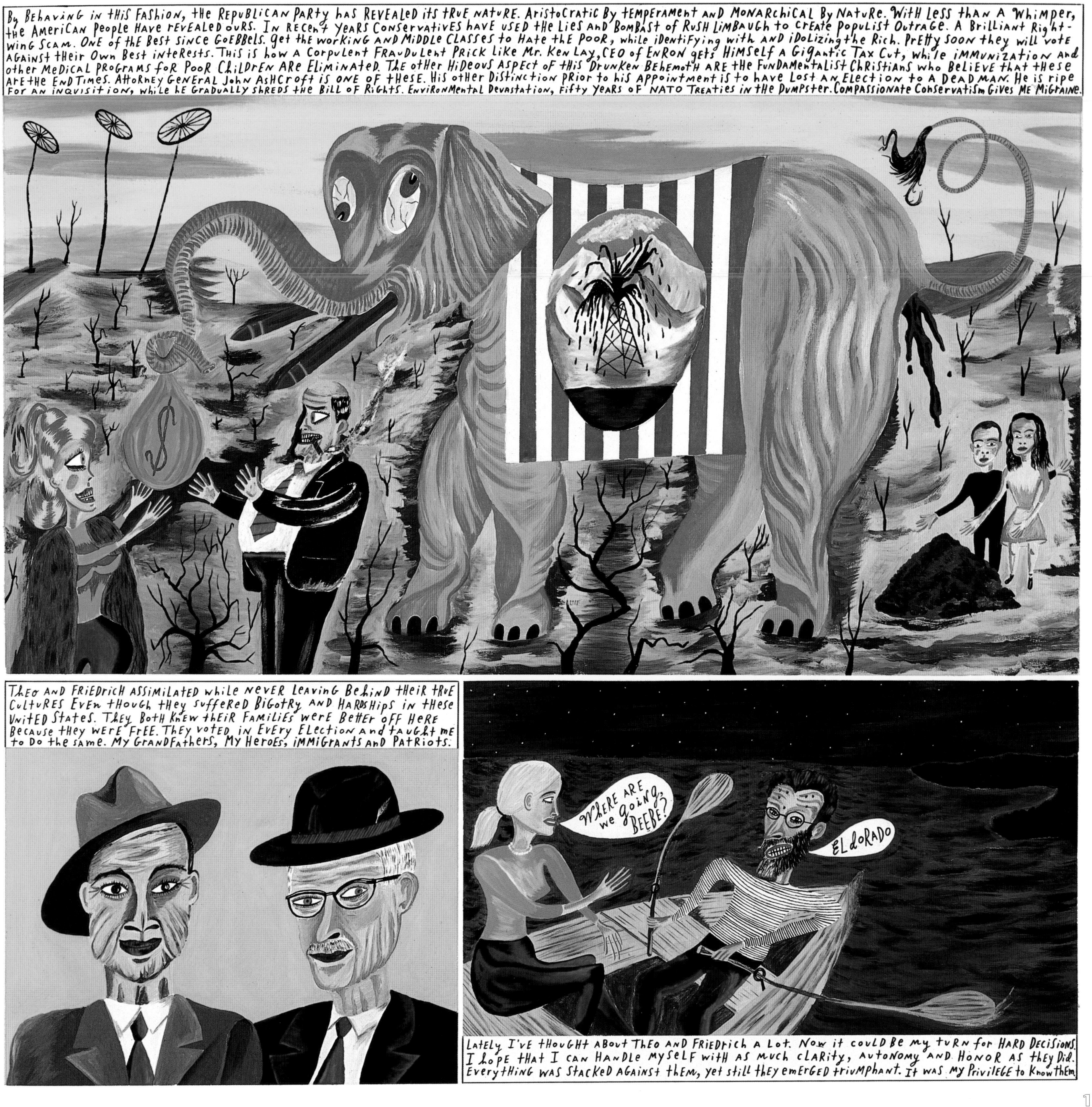
By behaving in this fashion, the Republican Party has revealed its true nature. Aristocratic by temperament and monarchical by nature. With less than a whimper, the American people have revealed ours. In recent years conservatives have used the lies and bombast of Rush Limbaugh to create populist outrage. A brilliant right-wing scam. One of the best since Goebbels. Get the working and middle classes to hate the poor, while identifying with and idolizing the rich. Pretty soon they will vote against their own best interests. This is how a corpulent fraudulent prick like Mr. Ken Lay, CEO of Enron gets himself a gigantic tax cut, while immunization and other medical programs for poor children are eliminated. The other hideous aspect of this drunken behemoth are the fundamentalist Christians who believe that these are the end times. Attorney General John Ashcroft is one of these. His other distinction prior to his appointment is to have lost an election to a dead man. He is ripe for an inquisition, while he gradually shreds the Bill of Rights. Environmental devastation, fifty years of NATO treaties in the dumpster. Compassionate conservatism gives me migraine.
Theo and Friedrich assimilated while never leaving behind their true cultures even though they suffered bigotry and hardships in these United States. They both knew their families were better off here because they were free. They voted in every election and taught me to do the same. My grandfathers, my heroes, immigrants and patriots.
Where are we going, Beebe?
El Dorado
Lately I've thought about Theo and Friedrich a lot. Now it could be my turn for hard decisions. I hope that I can handle myself with as much clarity, autonomy and honor as they did. Everything was stacked against them, yet still they emerged triumphant. It was my privilege to know them.

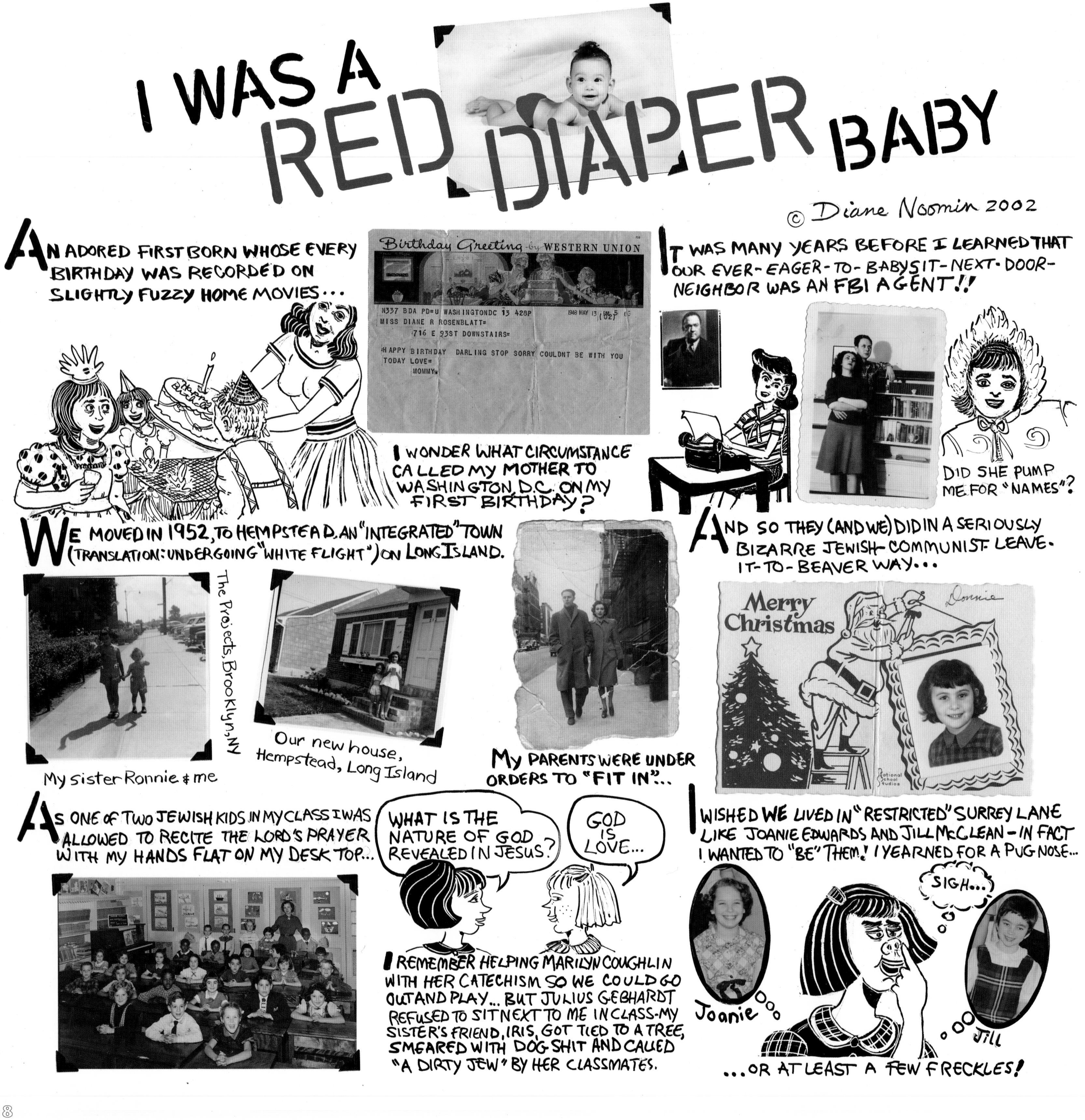
I WAS A RED DIAPER BABY
© Diane Noomin 2002
AN ADORED FIRSTBORN WHOSE EVERY BIRTHDAY WAS RECORDED ON SLIGHTLY FUZZY HOME MOVIES...
Birthday Greeting by WESTERN UNION
N337 BDA PD=U WASHINGTONDC 13 428P 1948 MAY 13 PM 5 05
MISS DIANE R ROSENBLATT=
716 E 93ST DOWNSTAIRS=
HAPPY BIRTHDAY DARLING STOP SORRY COULDNT BE WITH YOU TODAY LOVE=
MOMMY.
I WONDER WHAT CIRCUMSTANCE CALLED MY MOTHER TO WASHINGTON, D.C. ON MY FIRST BIRTHDAY?
IT WAS MANY YEARS BEFORE I LEARNED THAT OUR EVER-EAGER-TO-BABYSIT-NEXT-DOOR-NEIGHBOR WAS AN FBI AGENT!!
DID SHE PUMP ME FOR "NAMES"?
WE MOVED IN 1952, TO HEMPSTEAD, AN "INTEGRATED" TOWN (TRANSLATION: UNDERGOING "WHITE FLIGHT") ON LONG ISLAND.
The Projects, Brooklyn, NY
My sister Ronnie & me
Our new house, Hempstead, Long Island
MY PARENTS WERE UNDER ORDERS TO "FIT IN"...
AND SO THEY (AND WE) DID IN A SERIOUSLY BIZARRE JEWISH-COMMUNIST-LEAVE-IT-TO-BEAVER WAY...
Merry Christmas
Donnie
National School Studios
AS ONE OF TWO JEWISH KIDS IN MY CLASS I WAS ALLOWED TO RECITE THE LORD'S PRAYER WITH MY HANDS FLAT ON MY DESK TOP...
WHAT IS THE NATURE OF GOD REVEALED IN JESUS?
GOD IS LOVE...
I REMEMBER HELPING MARILYN COUGHLIN WITH HER CATECHISM SO WE COULD GO OUT AND PLAY... BUT JULIUS GEBHARDT REFUSED TO SIT NEXT TO ME IN CLASS-MY SISTER'S FRIEND, IRIS, GOT TIED TO A TREE, SMEARED WITH DOG SHIT AND CALLED "A DIRTY JEW" BY HER CLASSMATES.
I WISHED WE LIVED IN "RESTRICTED" SURREY LANE LIKE JOANIE EDWARDS AND JILL McCLEAN-IN FACT I WANTED TO "BE" THEM! I YEARNED FOR A PUG NOSE...
SIGH...
Joanie
Jill
...OR AT LEAST A FEW FRECKLES!

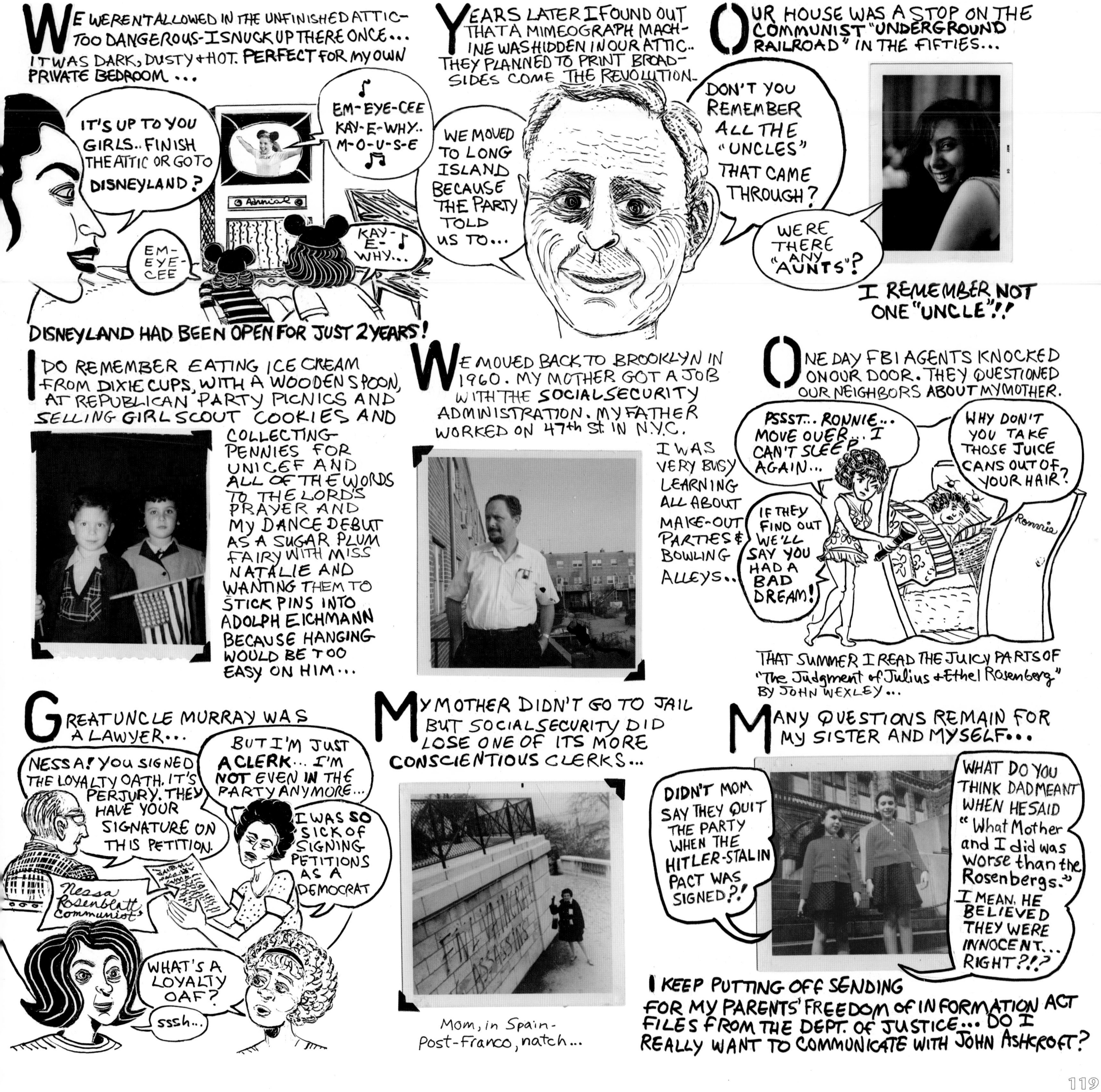
WE WEREN'T ALLOWED IN THE UNFINISHED ATTIC- TOO DANGEROUS-I SNUCK UP THERE ONCE... IT WAS DARK, DUSTY + HOT. PERFECT FOR MY OWN PRIVATE BEDROOM...
IT'S UP TO YOU GIRLS.. FINISH THE ATTIC OR GO TO DISNEYLAND?
EM-EYE-CEE KAY-E-WHY.. M-O-U-S-E
Admiral
EM-EYE-CEE
KAY-E-WHY...
DISNEYLAND HAD BEEN OPEN FOR JUST 2 YEARS!
YEARS LATER I FOUND OUT THAT A MIMEOGRAPH MACHINE WAS HIDDEN IN OUR ATTIC.. THEY PLANNED TO PRINT BROADSIDES COME THE REVOLUTION.
WE MOVED TO LONG ISLAND BECAUSE THE PARTY TOLD US TO...
OUR HOUSE WAS A STOP ON THE COMMUNIST "UNDERGROUND RAILROAD" IN THE FIFTIES...
DON'T YOU REMEMBER ALL THE "UNCLES" THAT CAME THROUGH?
WERE THERE ANY "AUNTS"?
I REMEMBER NOT ONE "UNCLE"!!
I DO REMEMBER EATING ICE CREAM FROM DIXIE CUPS, WITH A WOODEN SPOON, AT REPUBLICAN PARTY PICNICS AND SELLING GIRL SCOUT COOKIES AND COLLECTING PENNIES FOR UNICEF AND ALL OF THE WORDS TO THE LORD'S PRAYER AND MY DANCE DEBUT AS A SUGAR PLUM FAIRY WITH MISS NATALIE AND WANTING THEM TO STICK PINS INTO ADOLPH EICHMANN BECAUSE HANGING WOULD BE TOO EASY ON HIM...
WE MOVED BACK TO BROOKLYN IN 1960. MY MOTHER GOT A JOB WITH THE SOCIAL SECURITY ADMINISTRATION. MY FATHER WORKED ON 47th St. IN N.Y.C.
I WAS VERY BUSY LEARNING ALL ABOUT MAKE-OUT PARTIES & BOWLING ALLEYS..
ONE DAY FBI AGENTS KNOCKED ON OUR DOOR. THEY QUESTIONED OUR NEIGHBORS ABOUT MY MOTHER.
PSSST.. RONNIE... MOVE OVER... I CAN'T SLEEP AGAIN...
WHY DON'T YOU TAKE THOSE JUICE CANS OUT OF YOUR HAIR?
IF THEY FIND OUT WE'LL SAY YOU HAD A BAD DREAM!
Ronnie
THAT SUMMER I READ THE JUICY PARTS OF "The Judgment of Julius + Ethel Rosenberg" BY JOHN WEXLEY...
GREAT UNCLE MURRAY WAS A LAWYER...
NESSA! YOU SIGNED THE LOYALTY OATH. IT'S PERJURY. THEY HAVE YOUR SIGNATURE ON THIS PETITION.
BUT I'M JUST A CLERK... I'M NOT EVEN IN THE PARTY ANYMORE...
I WAS SO SICK OF SIGNING PETITIONS AS A DEMOCRAT
Nessa Rosenblatt Communist
WHAT'S A LOYALTY OAF?
sssh...
MY MOTHER DIDN'T GO TO JAIL BUT SOCIAL SECURITY DID LOSE ONE OF ITS MORE CONSCIENTIOUS CLERKS...
Mom, in Spain- Post-Franco, natch...
MANY QUESTIONS REMAIN FOR MY SISTER AND MYSELF...
DIDN'T MOM SAY THEY QUIT THE PARTY WHEN THE HITLER-STALIN PACT WAS SIGNED?!
WHAT DO YOU THINK DAD MEANT WHEN HE SAID "What Mother and I did was worse than the Rosenbergs." I MEAN, HE BELIEVED THEY WERE INNOCENT... RIGHT?!?
I KEEP PUTTING OFF SENDING FOR MY PARENTS' FREEDOM OF INFORMATION ACT FILES FROM THE DEPT. OF JUSTICE... DO I REALLY WANT TO COMMUNICATE WITH JOHN ASHCROFT?

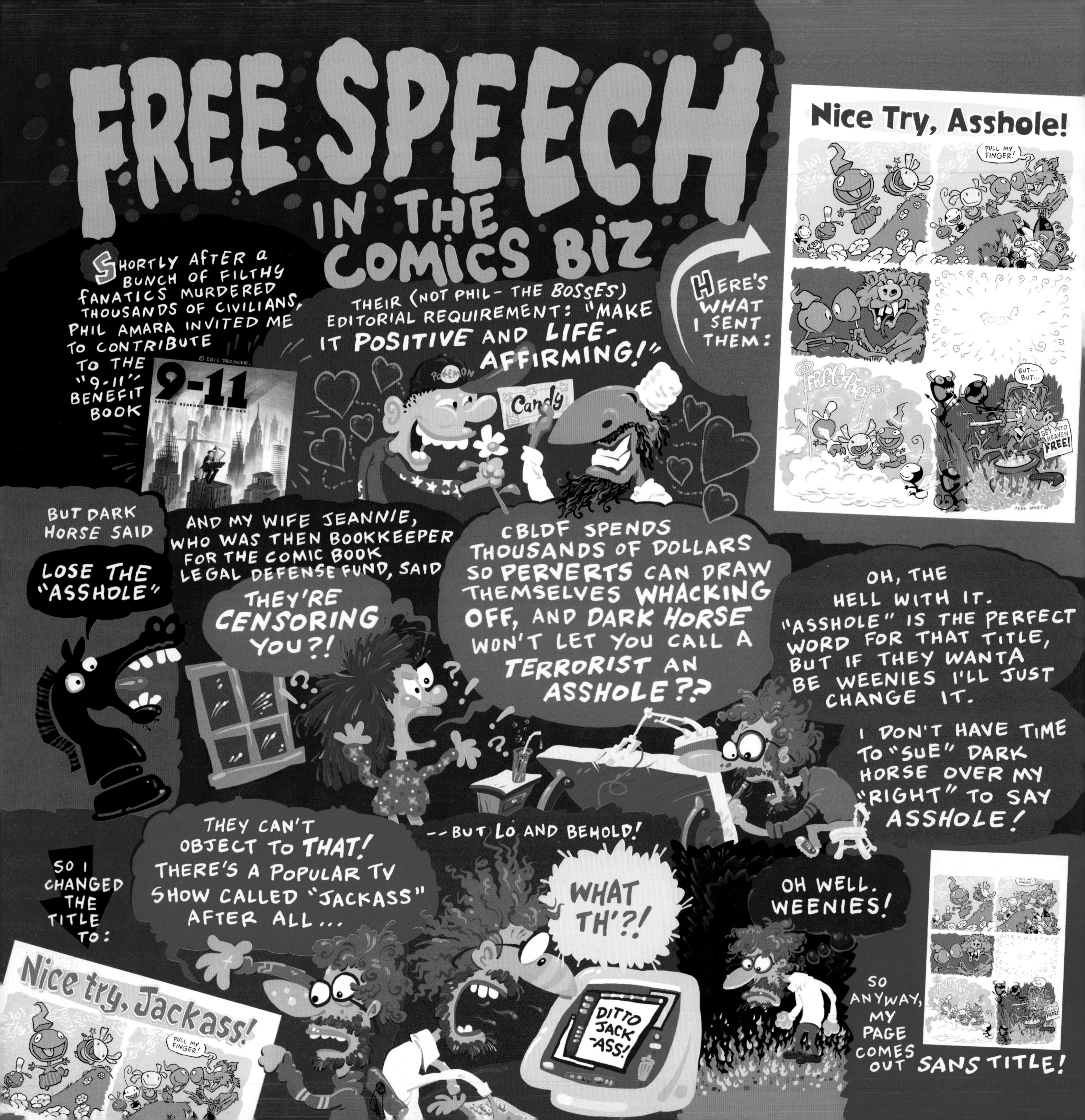
FREE SPEECH IN THE COMICS BIZ
SHORTLY AFTER a BUNCH OF FILTHY FANATICS MURDERED THOUSANDS OF CIVILIANS, PHIL AMARA INVITED ME TO CONTRIBUTE TO THE "9-11" BENEFIT BOOK
© ERIC DROOKER
9-11
ARTISTS RESPOND • VOLUME ONE
THEIR (NOT PHIL- THE BOSSES) EDITORIAL REQUIREMENT: "MAKE IT POSITIVE AND LIFE-AFFIRMING!"
POKEMON
Candy
HERE'S WHAT I SENT THEM:
Nice Try, Asshole!
PULL MY FINGER!
POOF
FREE PIE
BUT... BUT...
GET INTO HEAVEN FREE!
MARK MARTIN
BUT DARK HORSE SAID
LOSE THE "ASSHOLE"
AND MY WIFE JEANNIE, WHO WAS THEN BOOKKEEPER FOR THE COMIC BOOK LEGAL DEFENSE FUND, SAID
THEY'RE CENSORING YOU?!
CBLDF SPENDS THOUSANDS OF DOLLARS SO PERVERTS CAN DRAW THEMSELVES WHACKING OFF, AND DARK HORSE WON'T LET YOU CALL A TERRORIST AN ASSHOLE??
OH, THE HELL WITH IT. "ASSHOLE" IS THE PERFECT WORD FOR THAT TITLE, BUT IF THEY WANTA BE WEENIES I'LL JUST CHANGE IT.
I DON'T HAVE TIME TO "SUE" DARK HORSE OVER MY "RIGHT" TO SAY ASSHOLE!
SO I CHANGED THE TITLE TO:
Nice try, Jackass!
PULL MY FINGER!
THEY CAN'T OBJECT TO THAT! THERE'S A POPULAR TV SHOW CALLED "JACKASS" AFTER ALL...
--BUT LO AND BEHOLD!
WHAT TH'?!
DITTO JACK-ASS!
OH WELL. WEENIES!
SO ANYWAY, MY PAGE COMES OUT SANS TITLE!

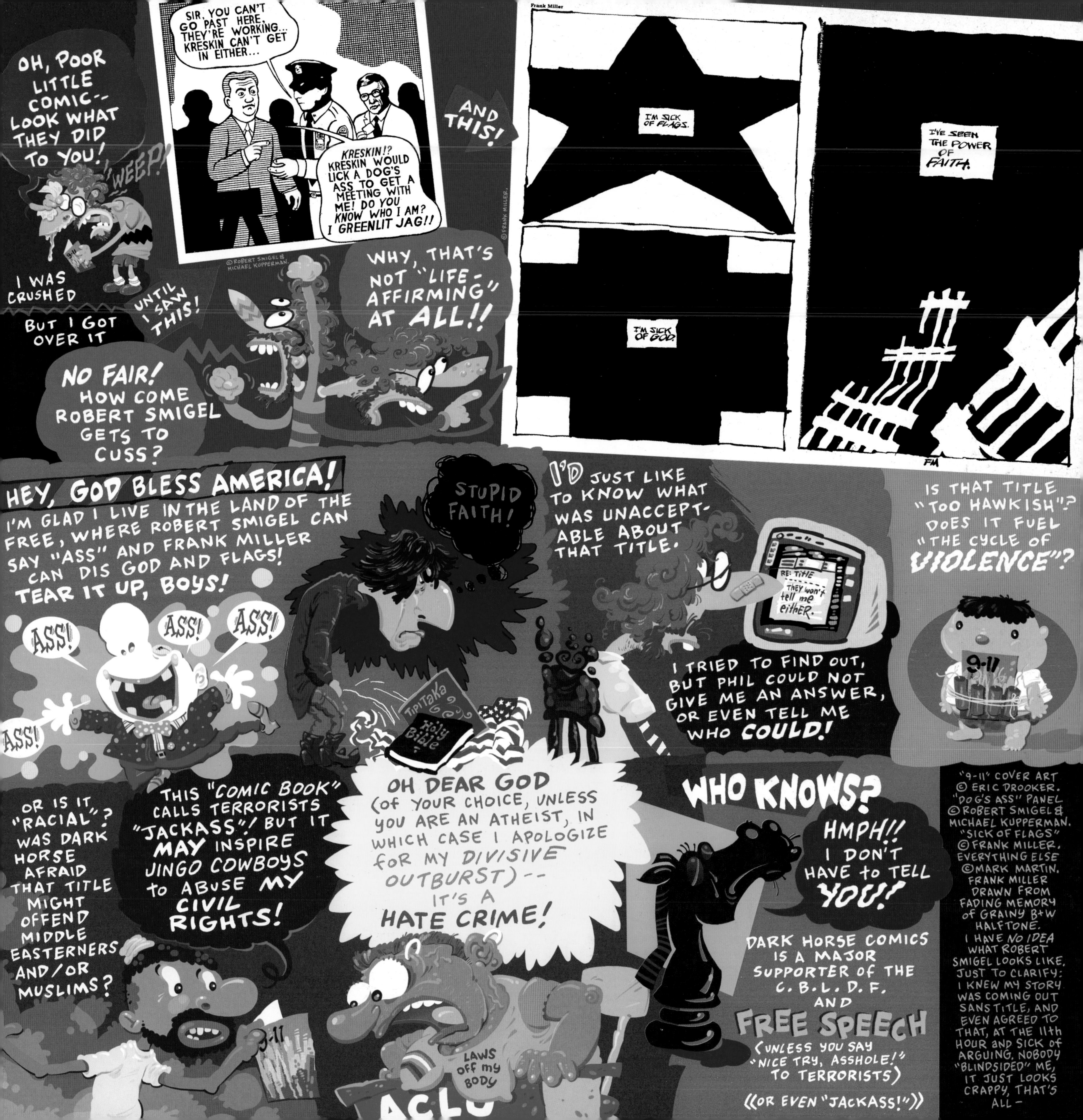
OH, POOR LITTLE COMIC-- LOOK WHAT THEY DID TO YOU!
WEEP!
I WAS CRUSHED
BUT I GOT OVER IT
SIR, YOU CAN'T GO PAST HERE. THEY'RE WORKING... KRESKIN CAN'T GET IN EITHER...
KRESKIN!? KRESKIN WOULD LICK A DOG'S ASS TO GET A MEETING WITH ME! DO YOU KNOW WHO I AM? I GREENLIT JAG!!
© ROBERT SMIGEL & MICHAEL KUPPERMAN.
© FRANK MILLER.
AND THIS!
UNTIL I SAW THIS!
WHY, THAT'S NOT "LIFE-AFFIRMING" AT ALL!!
NO FAIR! HOW COME ROBERT SMIGEL GETS TO CUSS?
Frank Miller
I'M SICK OF FLAGS.
I'VE SEEN THE POWER OF FAITH.
I'M SICK OF GOD.
FM
HEY, GOD BLESS AMERICA!
I'M GLAD I LIVE IN THE LAND OF THE FREE, WHERE ROBERT SMIGEL CAN SAY "ASS" AND FRANK MILLER CAN DIS GOD AND FLAGS! TEAR IT UP, BOYS!
ASS!
ASS!
ASS!
ASS!
STUPID FAITH!
TIPITAKA
Holy Bible
I'D JUST LIKE TO KNOW WHAT WAS UNACCEPTABLE ABOUT THAT TITLE.
RE: TITLE
They won't tell me either.
I TRIED TO FIND OUT, BUT PHIL COULD NOT GIVE ME AN ANSWER, OR EVEN TELL ME WHO COULD!
IS THAT TITLE "TOO HAWKISH"? DOES IT FUEL "THE CYCLE OF VIOLENCE"?
9-11
OR IS IT "RACIAL"? WAS DARK HORSE AFRAID THAT TITLE MIGHT OFFEND MIDDLE EASTERNERS AND/OR MUSLIMS?
THIS "COMIC BOOK" CALLS TERRORISTS "JACKASS"! BUT IT MAY INSPIRE JINGO COWBOYS TO ABUSE MY CIVIL RIGHTS!
9-11
OH DEAR GOD (of YOUR CHOICE, UNLESS YOU ARE AN ATHEIST, IN WHICH CASE I APOLOGIZE for MY DIVISIVE OUTBURST) -- IT'S A HATE CRIME!
LAWS OFF MY BODY
ACLU
WHO KNOWS?
HMPH!! I DON'T HAVE to TELL YOU!
DARK HORSE COMICS IS A MAJOR SUPPORTER OF THE C.B.L.D.F. AND FREE SPEECH (UNLESS YOU SAY "NICE TRY, ASSHOLE!" TO TERRORISTS)
((OR EVEN "JACKASS!"))
"9-11" COVER ART © ERIC DROOKER. "DOG'S ASS" PANEL © ROBERT SMIGEL & MICHAEL KUPPERMAN. "SICK OF FLAGS" © FRANK MILLER. EVERYTHING ELSE © MARK MARTIN. FRANK MILLER DRAWN FROM FADING MEMORY OF GRAINY B+W HALFTONE. I HAVE NO IDEA WHAT ROBERT SMIGEL LOOKS LIKE. JUST TO CLARIFY: I KNEW MY STORY WAS COMING OUT SANS TITLE, AND EVEN AGREED TO THAT, AT THE 11th HOUR AND SICK OF ARGUING. NOBODY "BLINDSIDED" ME, IT JUST LOOKS CRAPPY, THAT'S ALL -

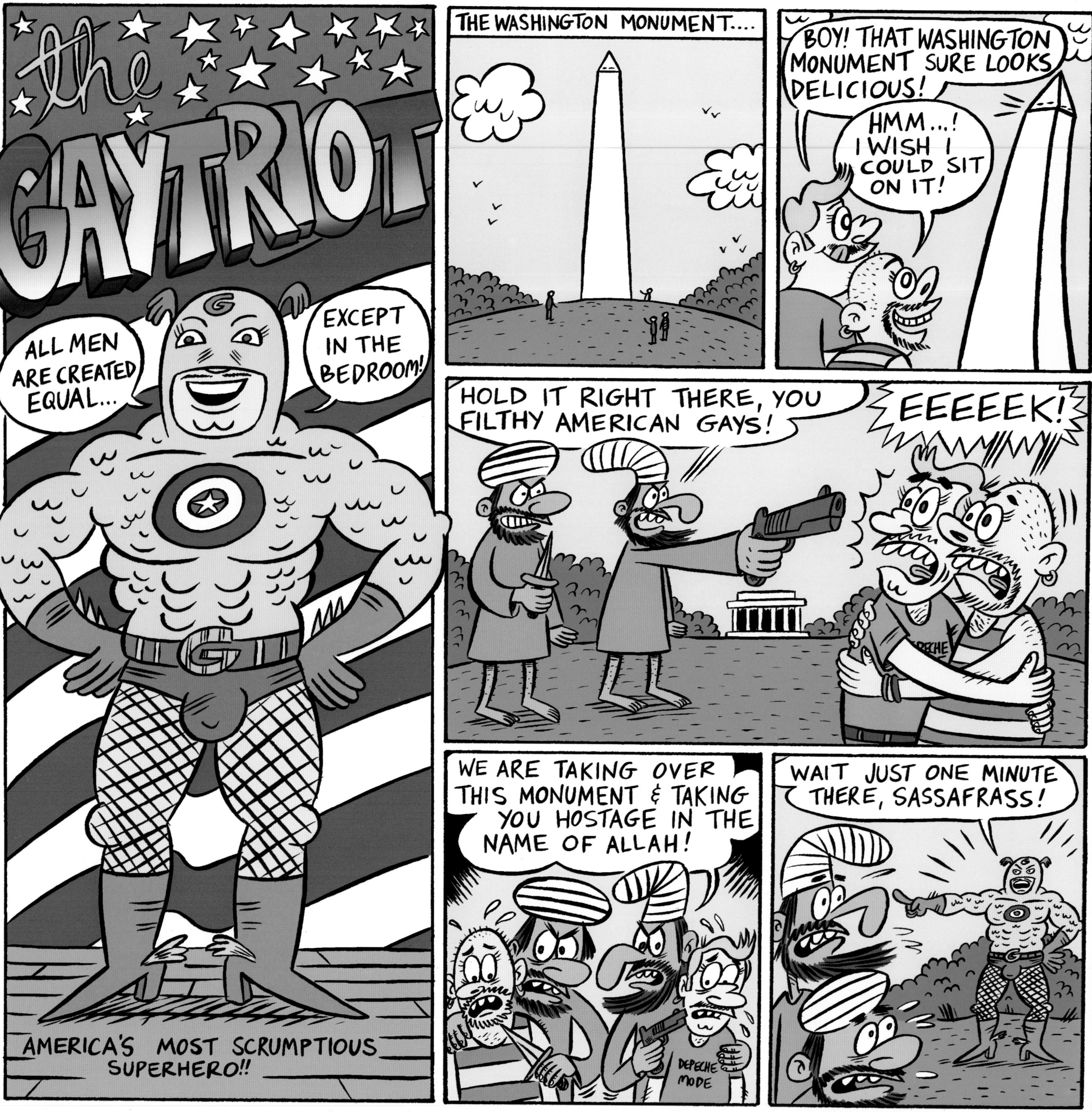
the
GAYTRIOT
ALL MEN ARE CREATED EQUAL...
EXCEPT IN THE BEDROOM!
AMERICA'S MOST SCRUMPTIOUS SUPERHERO!!
THE WASHINGTON MONUMENT....
BOY! THAT WASHINGTON MONUMENT SURE LOOKS DELICIOUS!
HMM...! I WISH I COULD SIT ON IT!
HOLD IT RIGHT THERE, YOU FILTHY AMERICAN GAYS!
EEEEEK!
WE ARE TAKING OVER THIS MONUMENT & TAKING YOU HOSTAGE IN THE NAME OF ALLAH!
DEPECHE MODE
WAIT JUST ONE MINUTE THERE, SASSAFRASS!

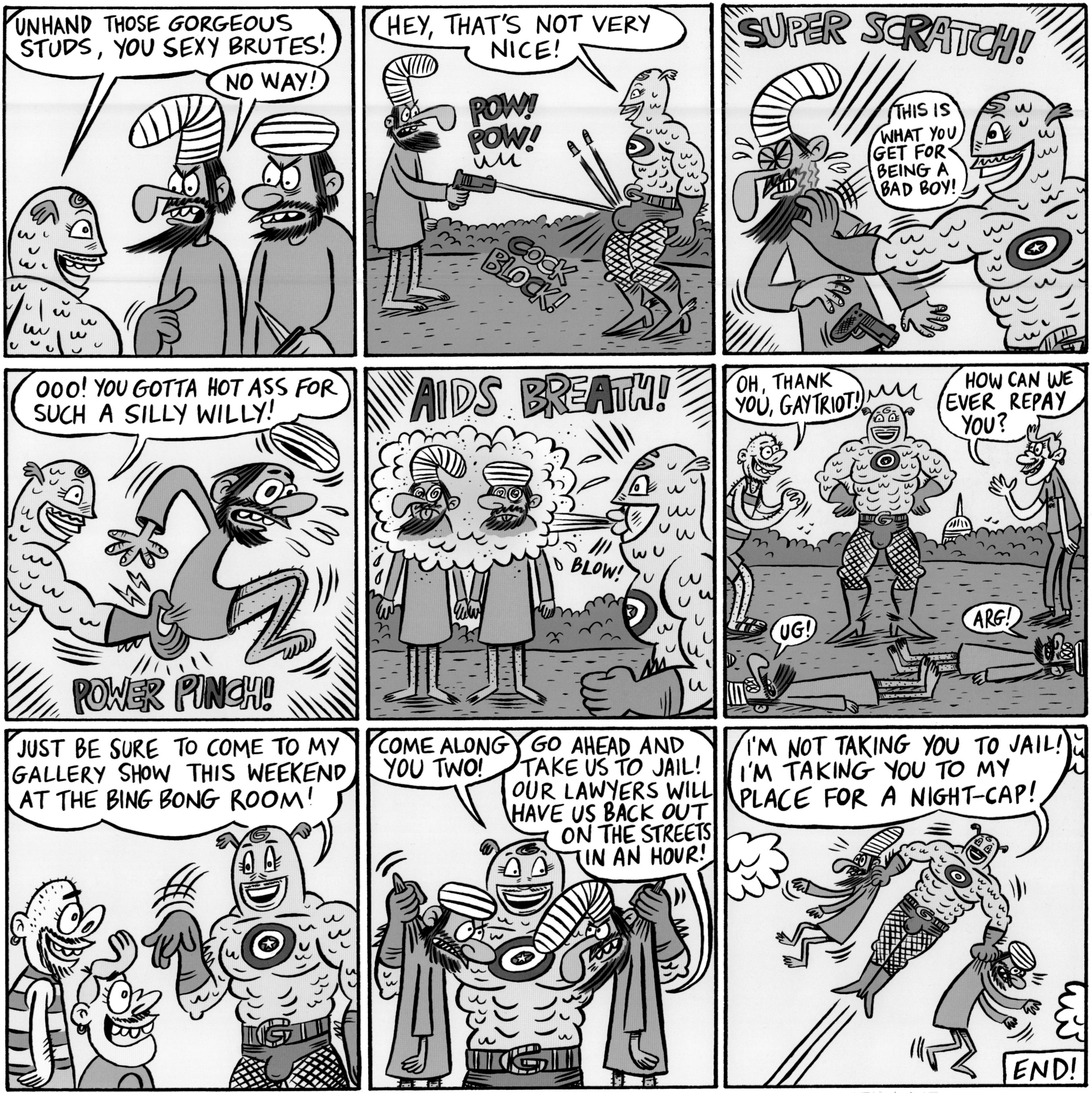
UNHAND THOSE GORGEOUS STUDS, YOU SEXY BRUTES!
NO WAY!
HEY, THAT'S NOT VERY NICE!
POW! POW!
COCK BLOCK!
SUPER SCRATCH!
THIS IS WHAT YOU GET FOR BEING A BAD BOY!
OOO! YOU GOTTA HOT ASS FOR SUCH A SILLY WILLY!
POWER PINCH!
AIDS BREATH!
BLOW!
OH, THANK YOU, GAYTRIOT!
HOW CAN WE EVER REPAY YOU?
UG!
ARG!
JUST BE SURE TO COME TO MY GALLERY SHOW THIS WEEKEND AT THE BING BONG ROOM!
COME ALONG YOU TWO!
GO AHEAD AND TAKE US TO JAIL! OUR LAWYERS WILL HAVE US BACK OUT ON THE STREETS IN AN HOUR!
I'M NOT TAKING YOU TO JAIL! I'M TAKING YOU TO MY PLACE FOR A NIGHT-CAP!
END!

JOHNNYR.COM

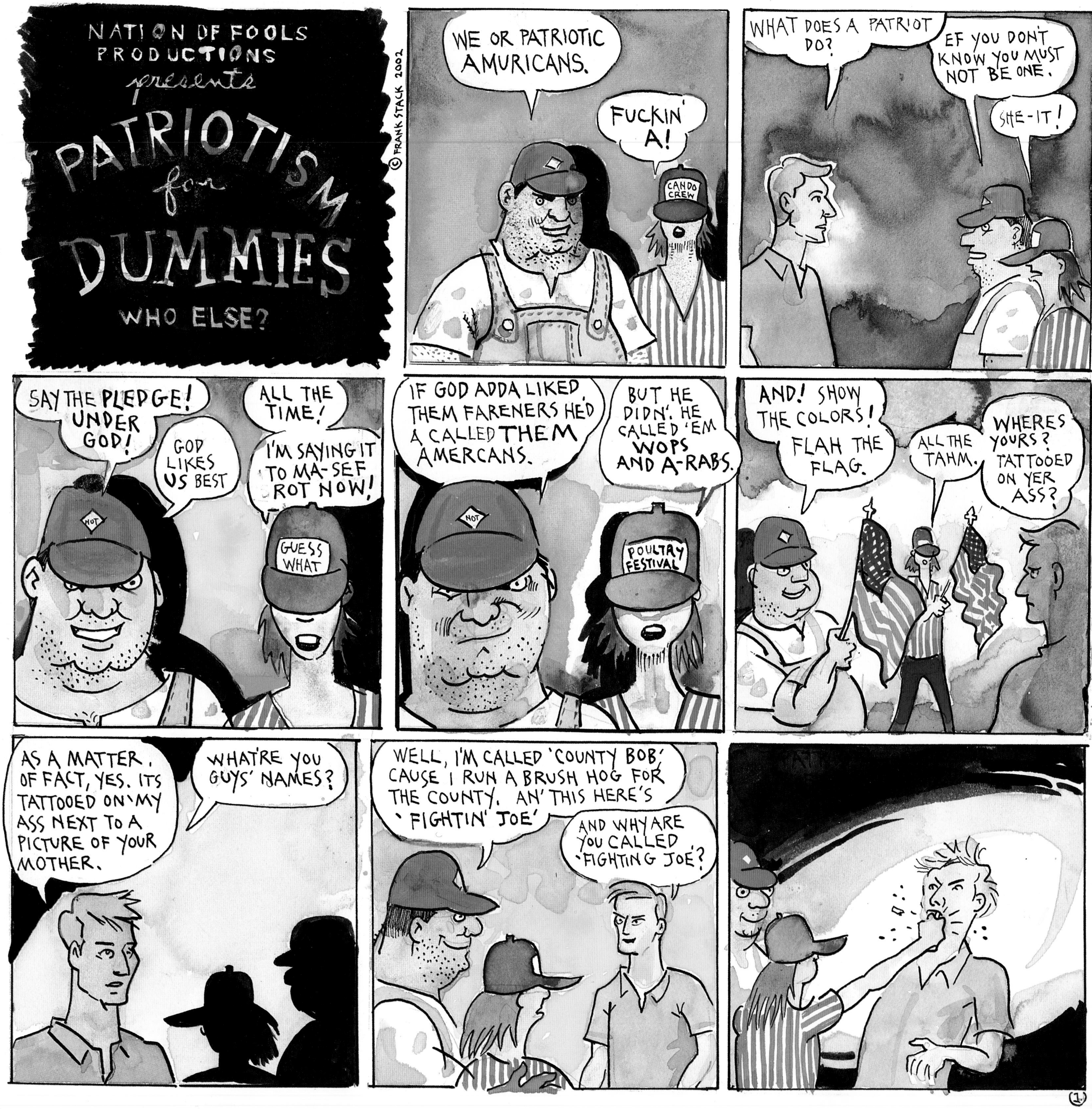
NATION OF FOOLS PRODUCTIONS
presents
PATRIOTISM for DUMMIES
WHO ELSE?
© FRANK STACK 2002
WE OR PATRIOTIC AMURICANS.
FUCKIN' A!
CAN DO CREW
WHAT DOES A PATRIOT DO?
EF YOU DON'T KNOW YOU MUST NOT BE ONE.
SHE-IT!
SAY THE PLEDGE! UNDER GOD!
GOD LIKES US BEST
ALL THE TIME!
I'M SAYING IT TO MA-SEF ROT NOW!
NOT
GUESS WHAT
IF GOD ADDA LIKED THEM FARENERS HE'D A CALLED THEM AMERCANS.
BUT HE DIDN'. HE CALLED 'EM WOPS AND A-RABS.
NOT
POULTRY FESTIVAL
AND! SHOW THE COLORS! FLAH THE FLAG.
ALL THE TAHM.
WHERES YOURS? TATTOOED ON YER ASS?
AS A MATTER OF FACT, YES. ITS TATTOOED ON MY ASS NEXT TO A PICTURE OF YOUR MOTHER.
WHAT'RE YOU GUYS' NAMES?
WELL, I'M CALLED 'COUNTY BOB' CAUSE I RUN A BRUSH HOG FOR THE COUNTY. AN' THIS HERE'S 'FIGHTIN' JOE'
AND WHY ARE YOU CALLED 'FIGHTING JOE'?
1

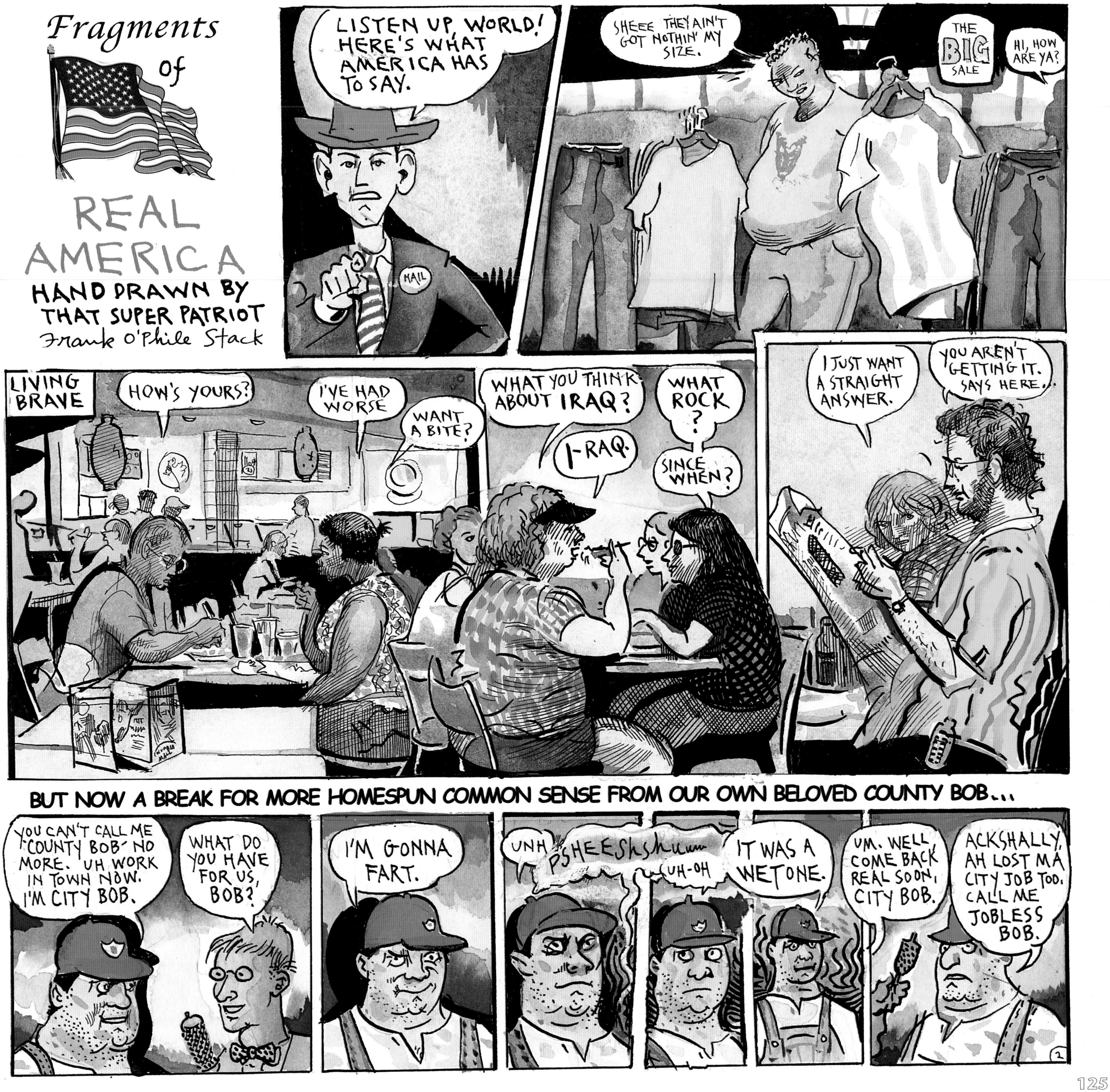
Fragments of
REAL AMERICA
HAND DRAWN BY THAT SUPER PATRIOT
Frank O'Phile Stack
LISTEN UP, WORLD! HERE'S WHAT AMERICA HAS TO SAY.
HAIL
SHEEE THEY AIN'T GOT NOTHIN' MY SIZE.
THE BIG SALE
HI, HOW ARE YA?
LIVING BRAVE
HOW'S YOURS?
I'VE HAD WORSE
WANT A BITE?
WHAT YOU THINK ABOUT IRAQ?
I-RAQ.
WHAT ROCK?
SINCE WHEN?
I JUST WANT A STRAIGHT ANSWER.
YOU AREN'T GETTING IT. SAYS HERE...
BUT NOW A BREAK FOR MORE HOMESPUN COMMON SENSE FROM OUR OWN BELOVED COUNTY BOB...
YOU CAN'T CALL ME "COUNTY BOB" NO MORE. UH WORK IN TOWN NOW. I'M CITY BOB.
WHAT DO YOU HAVE FOR US, BOB?
I'M GONNA FART.
UNH
PSHEEShShuuu
UH-OH
IT WAS A WET ONE.
UM. WELL COME BACK REAL SOON, CITY BOB.
ACKSHALLY, AH LOST MA CITY JOB TOO. CALL ME JOBLESS BOB.

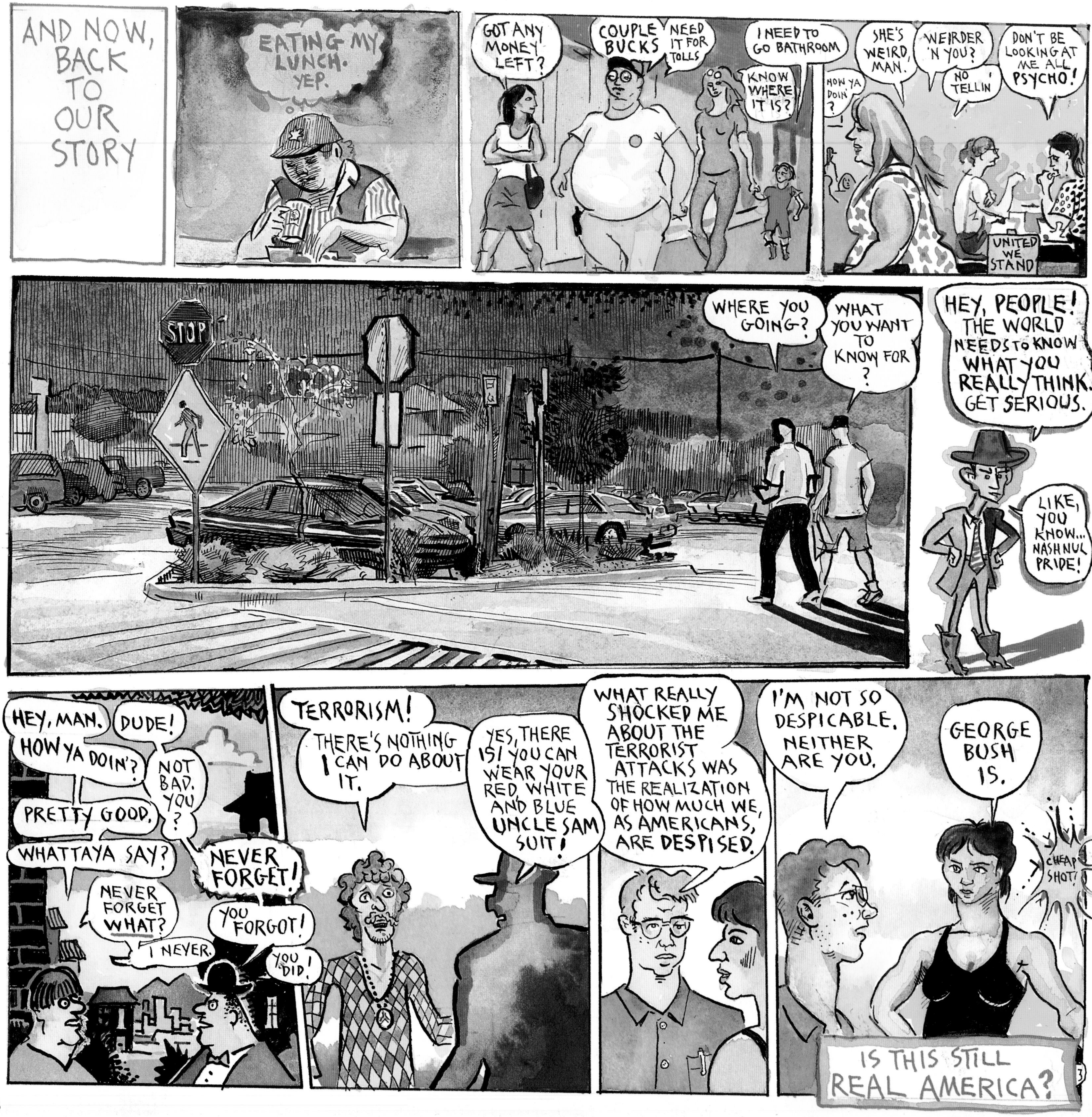
AND NOW, BACK TO OUR STORY
EATING MY LUNCH. YEP.
GOT ANY MONEY LEFT?
COUPLE BUCKS
NEED IT FOR TOLLS
I NEED TO GO BATHROOM
KNOW WHERE IT IS?
HOW YA DOIN'?
SHE'S WEIRD, MAN.
WEIRDER 'N YOU?
NO TELLIN'
DON'T BE LOOKING AT ME ALL PSYCHO!
UNITED WE STAND
STOP
WHERE YOU GOING?
WHAT YOU WANT TO KNOW FOR?
HEY, PEOPLE! THE WORLD NEEDS TO KNOW WHAT YOU REALLY THINK. GET SERIOUS.
LIKE, YOU KNOW... NASHNUL PRIDE!
HEY, MAN.
DUDE!
HOW YA DOIN'?
NOT BAD. YOU?
PRETTY GOOD.
WHATTAYA SAY?
NEVER FORGET!
NEVER FORGET WHAT?
YOU FORGOT!
I NEVER.
YOU DID!
TERRORISM!
THERE'S NOTHING I CAN DO ABOUT IT.
YES, THERE IS! YOU CAN WEAR YOUR RED, WHITE AND BLUE UNCLE SAM SUIT!
WHAT REALLY SHOCKED ME ABOUT THE TERRORIST ATTACKS WAS THE REALIZATION OF HOW MUCH WE, AS AMERICANS, ARE DESPISED.
I'M NOT SO DESPICABLE. NEITHER ARE YOU.
GEORGE BUSH IS.
CHEAP SHOT!
IS THIS STILL REAL AMERICA?
3

"GEE, I'D SURE LIKE TO HAVE A REAL COUNTRY LIKE YOURS!"™

BY WILFRED SANTIAGO
mrkalkan@hotmail.com

CANADIAN C.E.O.

"WITH PATRIOTEX 500® IT'S QUICK 'N' EASY!"
-SAYS UNCLE BUSH

It's a well known fact that you can't have a great Nation without lies, manipulations or oppression. Pledge to the flag, control the masses with **PATRIOTEX®500** with the highest level of patriotism acceptable. No more unpatriotic, disloyal insubordinates. Plunge into any military operation with unconditional support from the bewildered herd. NO QUESTIONS ASKED!

BE THE ENVY OF YOUR ALLIES!

Help create new markets, get away with murder...literally! Let your country be the standard with which lesser nations are ranked. When it comes to mass manipulation, besides religion, **nothing** is more effective than patriotism. **PATRIOTEX®** CAN HELP.

BEFORE

AFTER

"I used to question our policies. I was marginalized. I lost all my friends. Guilt, fear & hopelessness took me to the brink of suicide; now I don't give a fuck what we do to what country. Like a good American, everything I need fits in my fridge. U.S.A. #1! Thank you PATRIOTEX 500!"

..Trina Padilla El Paso, Texas*

*Trina's results typical

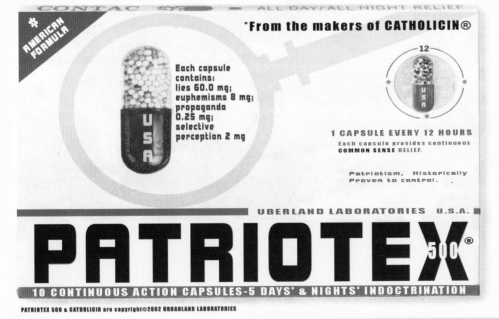

AMERICAN FORMULA

*From the makers of CATHOLICIN®

CONTAC — ALL DAY/ALL NIGHT RELIEF

Each capsule contains:
lies 60.0 mg;
euphemisms 8 mg;
propaganda 0.25 mg;
selective perception 2 mg

12

1 CAPSULE EVERY 12 HOURS

Each capsule provides continuous COMMON SENSE RELIEF.

Patriotism, Historically Proven to control.

UBERLAND LABORATORIES U.S.A.

PATRIOTEX ®500
10 CONTINUOUS ACTION CAPSULES-5 DAYS' & NIGHTS' INDOCTRINATION

PATRIOTEX 500 & CATHOLICIN are copyright©2002 URBANLAND LABORATORIES

OVER 600 "TINY PILLS" WITH THE COLORS OF YOUR COUNTRY'S FLAG HELP THE PUBLIC ACCEPT THE MYTHOLOGY ABOUT THE NOBILITY OF YOUR WARS AND THEIR MOTIVE.

Patriotism is just a swallow away™

copyright©2002 FOR THE LOVE OF KEVORKIAN INK.

WWW.UBERLAND.COM

ow available in British Formula. **Possible side effects**: xenophobia, self-indulgence, arrogance, amnesia, racism. **This product contains bullshit and may** ause other countries to hate yours if used improperly.

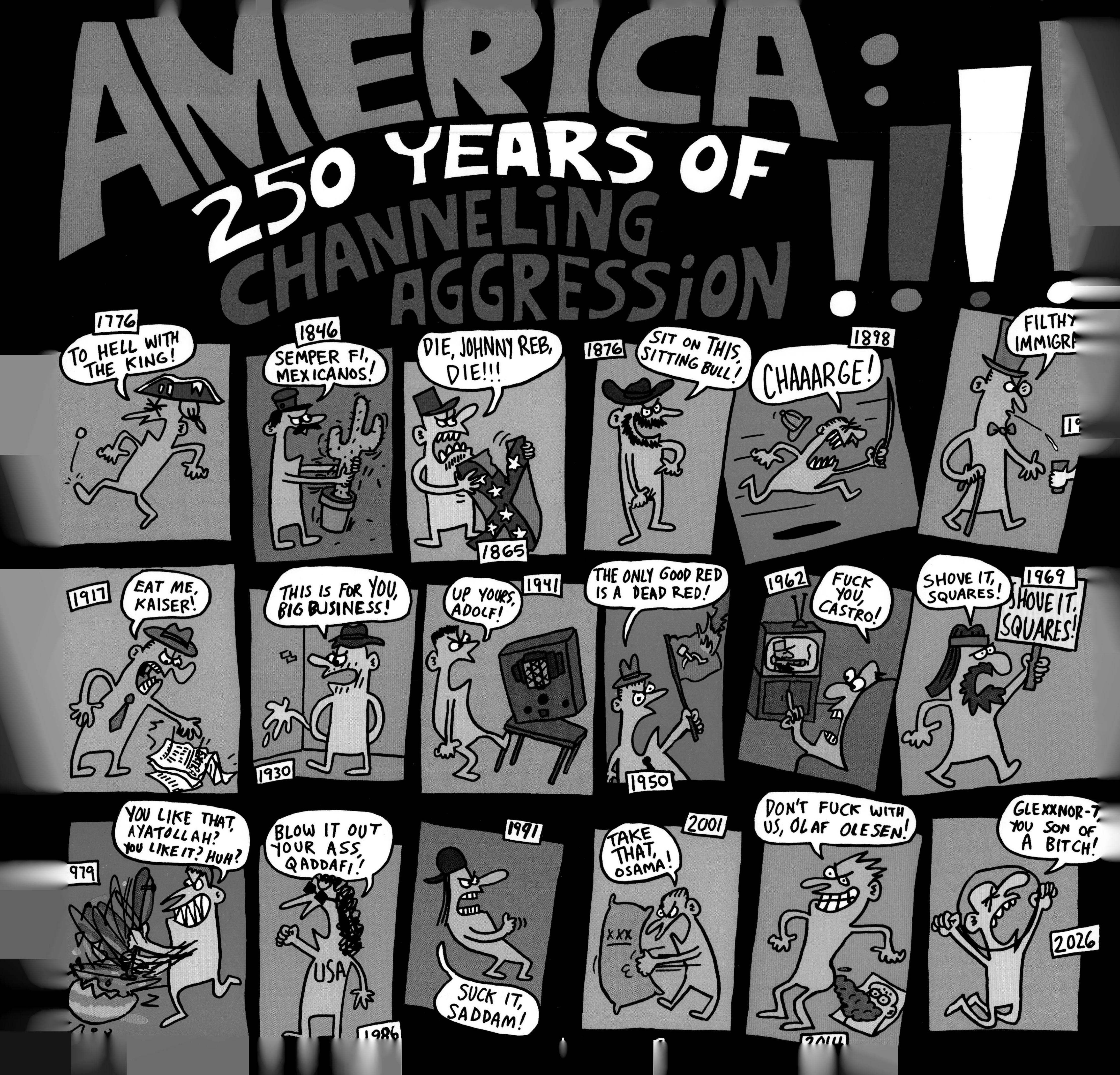
AMERICA: 250 YEARS OF CHANNELING AGGRESSION!!!
1776
TO HELL WITH THE KING!
1846
SEMPER FI, MEXICANOS!
DIE, JOHNNY REB, DIE!!!
1865
1876
SIT ON THIS, SITTING BULL!
1898
CHAAARGE!
FILTHY IMMIGRA
1917
EAT ME, KAISER!
THIS IS FOR YOU, BIG BUSINESS!
1930
1941
UP YOURS, ADOLF!
THE ONLY GOOD RED IS A DEAD RED!
1950
1962
FUCK YOU, CASTRO!
SHOVE IT, SQUARES!
1969
SHOVE IT, SQUARES!
979
YOU LIKE THAT, AYATOLLAH? YOU LIKE IT? HUH?
BLOW IT OUT YOUR ASS, QADDAFI!
USA
1991
SUCK IT, SADDAM!
2001
TAKE THAT, OSAMA!
XXX
DON'T FUCK WITH US, OLAF OLESEN!
GLEXXNOR-7, YOU SON OF A BITCH!
2026

A COMPARISON OF THE ANATOMICAL STRUCTURES PALPABLE *PER ANUM* IN MALE SUBJECTS CHOSEN FROM RANDOMLY SELECTED GLOBAL POPULATIONS

Principal Investigator:
Phoebe Gloeckner, M.D., Ph.D., Mid-Island Teaching Hospital, Department of Urology, Amityville, New York.

Subjects of study:
Four subjects were chosen, one each from the following countries: China, United States, Iraq, and Israel.

Subjects fulfilled the following criteria:

a. Each subject was male, between 30-35 years of age.

b. Each subject was in general good health at the time of the examination.

c. Each subject was of average height and weight.

d. Each subject held an upper-level military or civil service position.

e. Each subject had demonstrated allegiance to his respective national government.

Participating Institutions:

China: Beijing Vista Clinic, Beijing. Specialist Clinic in Urology.

United States: Methodist Medical Center, Dallas, Texas, Dept. of Urology.

Iraq: Al Qadissiya Hospital, Baghdad, Dept. of General Medicine.

Israel: Hadassah Ein Karem Medical Organization, Jerusalem, Dept. of Urology.

Conclusion:

Our Digital Rectal Exam (DRE) results showed no significant anatomical differences between patriotic males from randomly chosen global populations.

PROCEDURE

Digital Rectal Exam (DRE): A physician examines pelvic structures by inserting his or her gloved and lubricated finger into the anus (fig. 1).

The subject may be examined in the genupectoral or "knee-chest" position (fig. 2), exaggerated lithotomy (fig. 3), or lateral prone position (fig. 4). Any position with the body dependent causes the intestines to gravitate towards the diaphragm, relieves pressure upon the sigmoid, and permits the rectum to dilate upon the admission of the practitioner's digit.

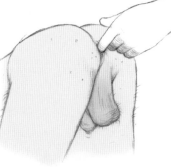

Figure 1.

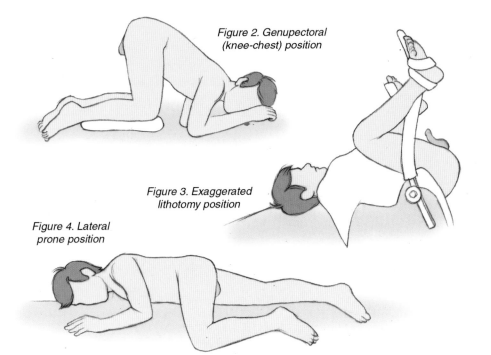

Figure 2. Genupectoral (knee-chest) position

Figure 3. Exaggerated lithotomy position

Figure 4. Lateral prone position

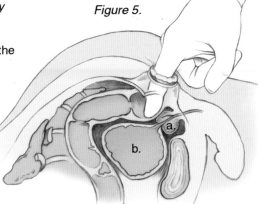

Subject A: *33-year-old national security adjudant, China (fig. 5)*

Figure 5.

Parasagittal section, palpation through the anterior rectal wall.

Structures felt on examination:
a. Prostate (anterior)
b. Urinary bladder

Also noted:
internal hemorrhoidal veins

Subject B: *30-year-old transportation team manager, United States (fig. 6)*

Figure 6.

Parasagittal section, palpation through the anterior rectal wall.

Structures felt on examination:
a. Prostate (anterior)
b. Urinary bladder

Also noted:
rectal fistula

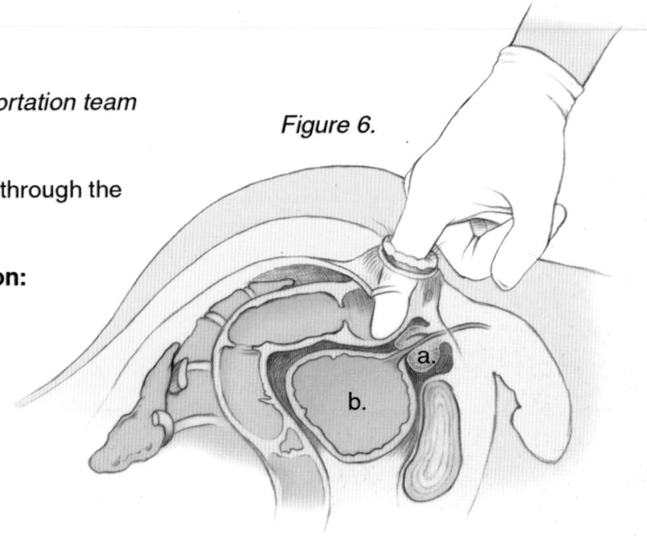

Subject C: *31-year-old charge-d'affaires, Iraq (fig. 7)*

Figure 7.

Parasagittal section, palpation through the anterior rectal wall.

Structures felt on examination:
a. Prostate (anterior)
b. Urinary bladder

Also noted: perianal warts

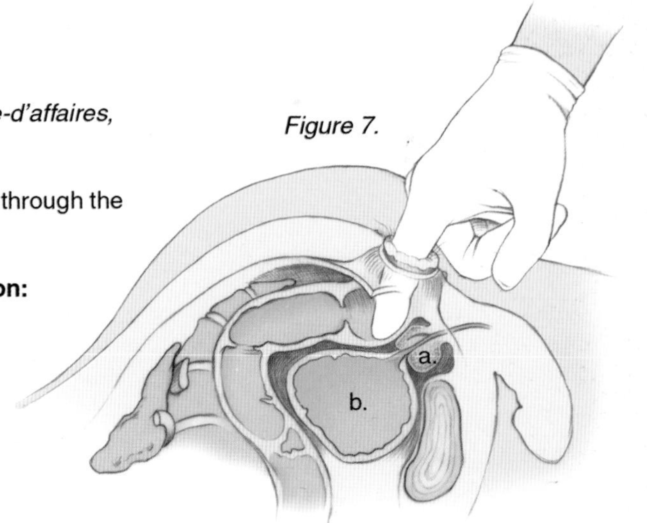

Subject D: *34-year-old munitions engineer, Israel (fig 8.)*

Figure 8.

Parasagittal section, palpation through the anterior rectal wall.

Structures felt on examination:
a. Prostate (anterior)
b. Urinary bladder

Also noted:
fecal mass (posterior)

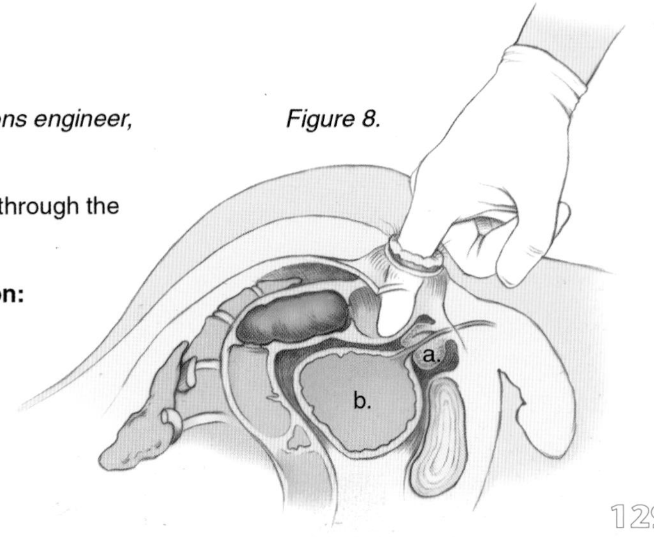

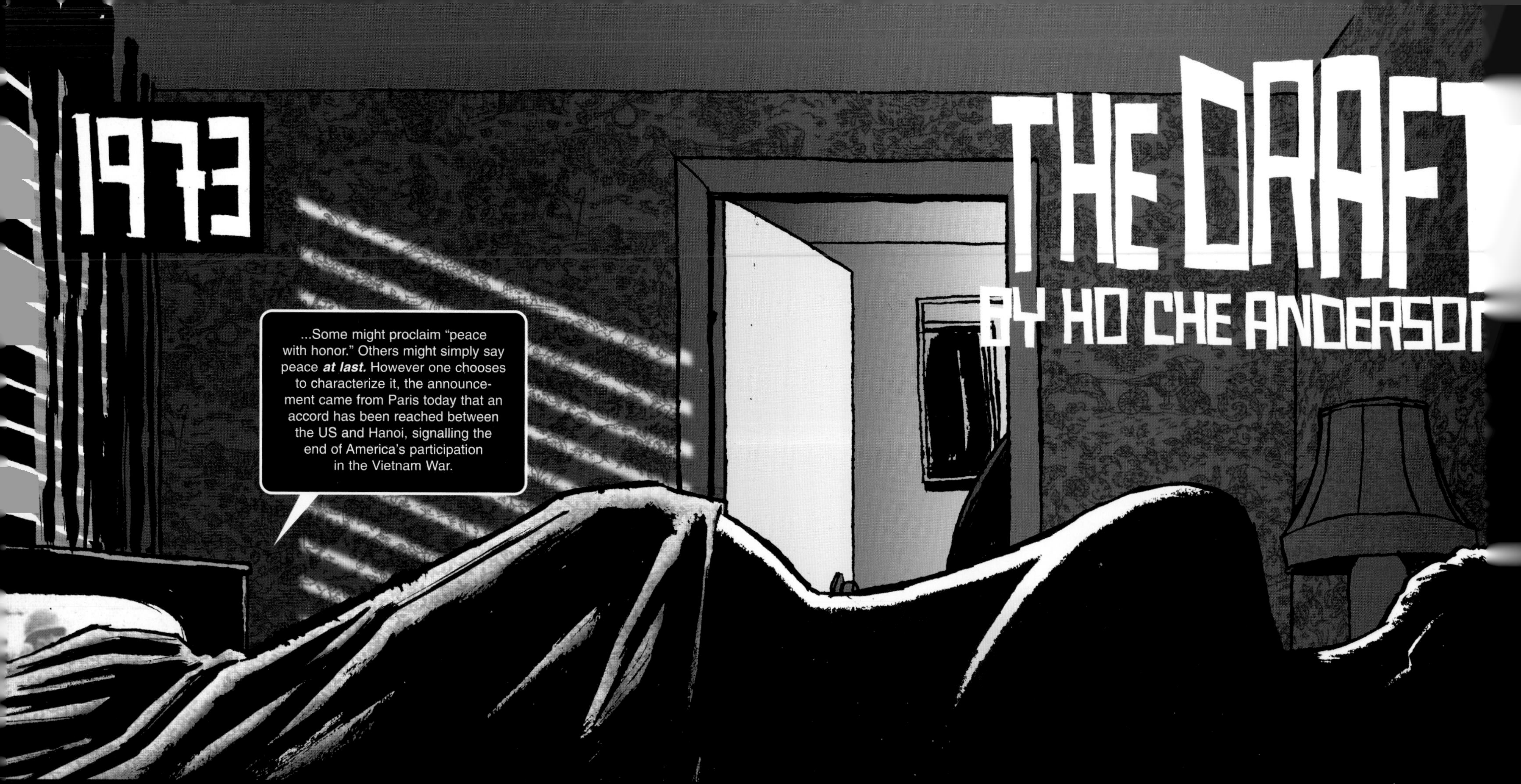
1973
THE DRAFT
BY HO CHE ANDERSO
...Some might proclaim "peace with honor." Others might simply say peace ***at last.*** However one chooses to characterize it, the announcement came from Paris today that an accord has been reached between the US and Hanoi, signalling the end of America's participation in the Vietnam War.

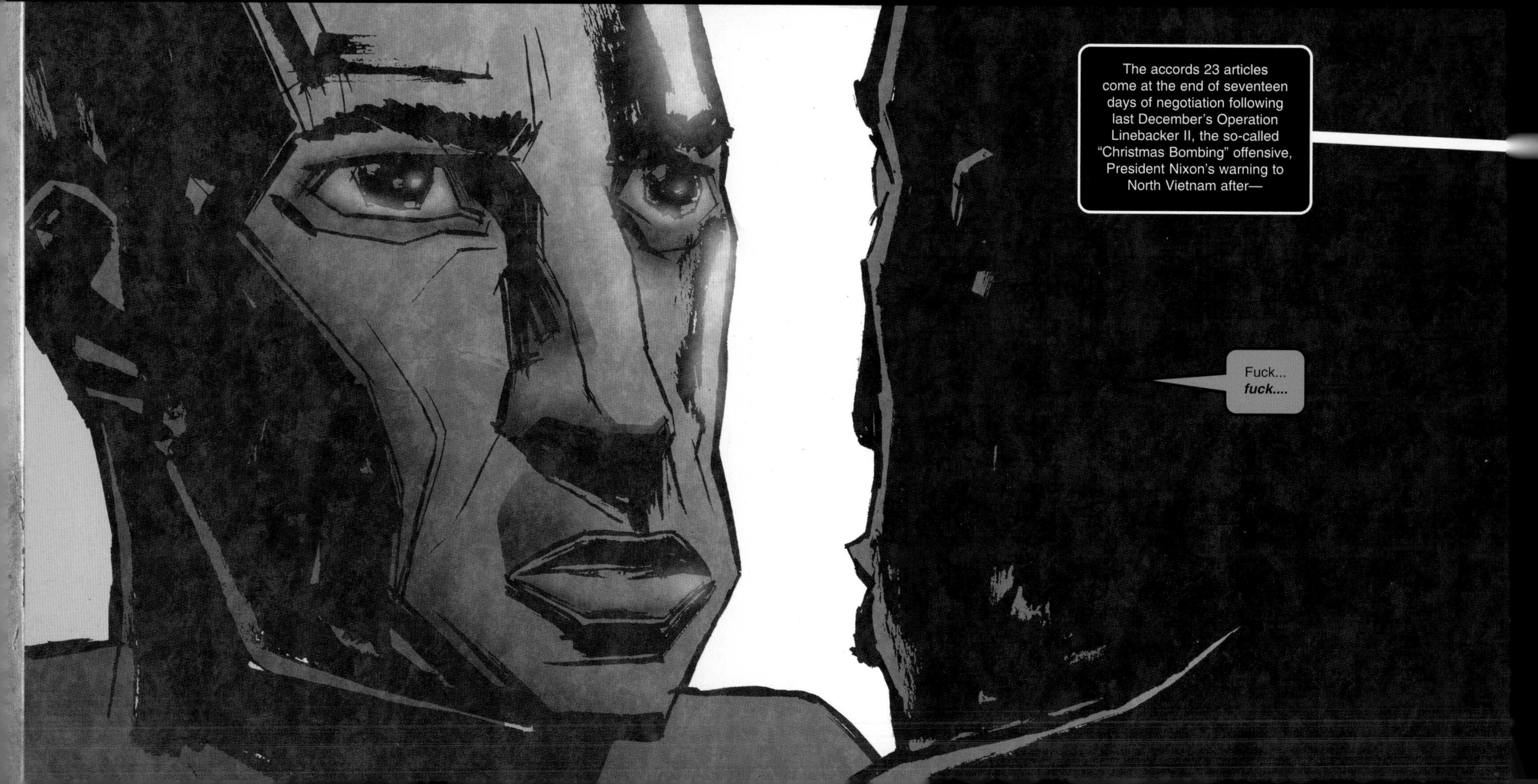
The accords 23 articles come at the end of seventeen days of negotiation following last December's Operation Linebacker II, the so-called "Christmas Bombing" offensive, President Nixon's warning to North Vietnam after—
Fuck... ***fuck....***

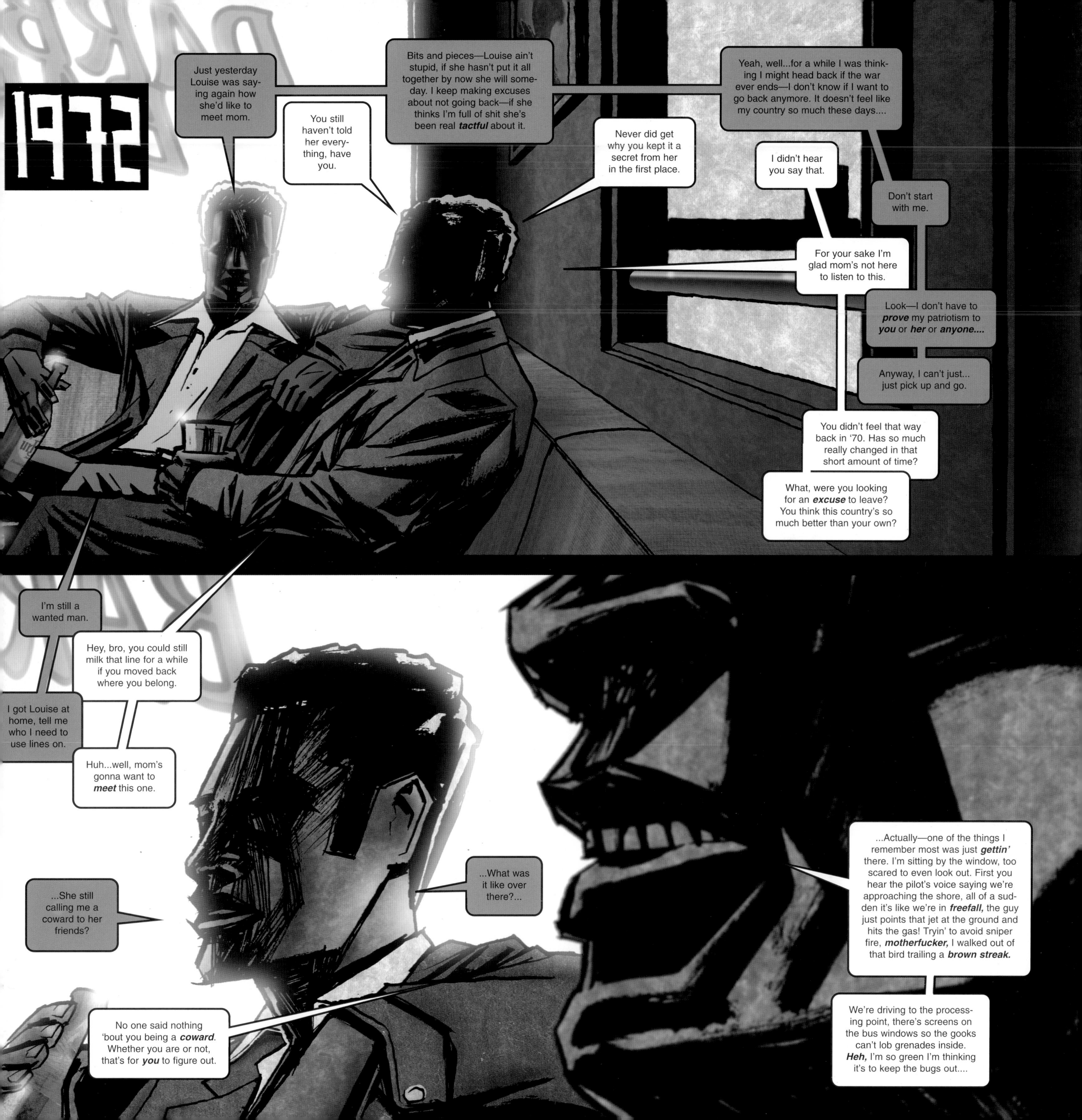
1973
Just yesterday Louise was saying again how she'd like to meet mom.
You still haven't told her everything, have you.
Bits and pieces—Louise ain't stupid, if she hasn't put it all together by now she will someday. I keep making excuses about not going back—if she thinks I'm full of shit she's been real ***tactful*** about it.
Never did get why you kept it a secret from her in the first place.
Yeah, well...for a while I was thinking I might head back if the war ever ends—I don't know if I want to go back anymore. It doesn't feel like my country so much these days....
I didn't hear you say that.
Don't start with me.
For your sake I'm glad mom's not here to listen to this.
Look—I don't have to ***prove*** my patriotism to ***you*** or ***her*** or ***anyone....***
Anyway, I can't just... just pick up and go.
You didn't feel that way back in '70. Has so much really changed in that short amount of time?
What, were you looking for an ***excuse*** to leave? You think this country's so much better than your own?
I'm still a wanted man.
Hey, bro, you could still milk that line for a while if you moved back where you belong.
I got Louise at home, tell me who I need to use lines on.
Huh...well, mom's gonna want to ***meet*** this one.
...She still calling me a coward to her friends?
No one said nothing 'bout you being a ***coward***. Whether you are or not, that's for ***you*** to figure out.
...What was it like over there?...
...Actually—one of the things I remember most was just ***gettin'*** there. I'm sitting by the window, too scared to even look out. First you hear the pilot's voice saying we're approaching the shore, all of a sudden it's like we're in ***freefall,*** the guy just points that jet at the ground and hits the gas! Tryin' to avoid sniper fire, ***motherfucker,*** I walked out of that bird trailing a ***brown streak.***
We're driving to the processing point, there's screens on the bus windows so the gooks can't lob grenades inside. ***Heh,*** I'm so green I'm thinking it's to keep the bugs out....

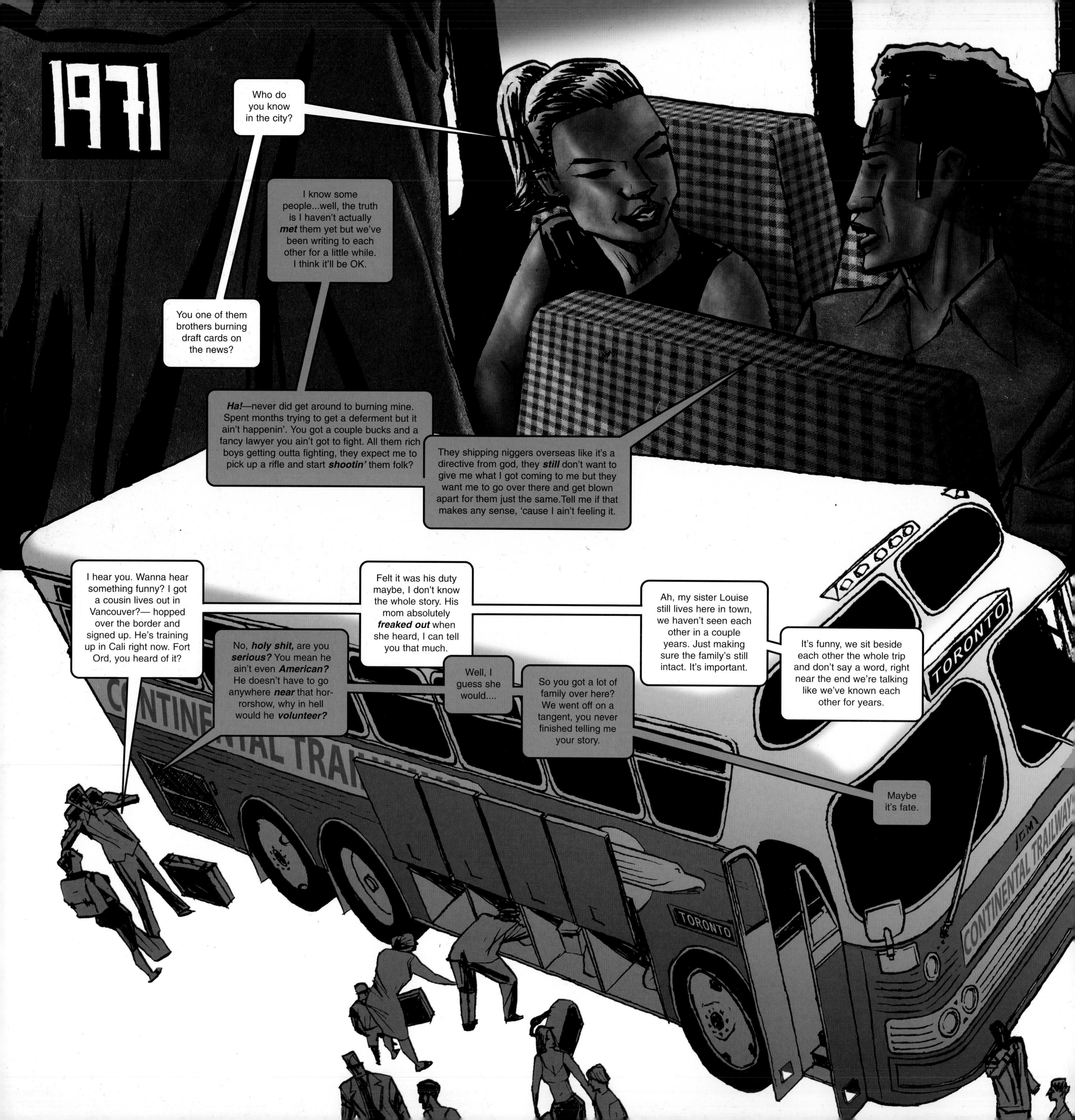
1971
Who do you know in the city?
I know some people...well, the truth is I haven't actually *met* them yet but we've been writing to each other for a little while. I think it'll be OK.
You one of them brothers burning draft cards on the news?
Ha!—never did get around to burning mine. Spent months trying to get a deferment but it ain't happenin'. You got a couple bucks and a fancy lawyer you ain't got to fight. All them rich boys getting outta fighting, they expect me to pick up a rifle and start *shootin'* them folk?
They shipping niggers overseas like it's a directive from god, they *still* don't want to give me what I got coming to me but they want me to go over there and get blown apart for them just the same.Tell me if that makes any sense, 'cause I ain't feeling it.
I hear you. Wanna hear something funny? I got a cousin lives out in Vancouver?— hopped over the border and signed up. He's training up in Cali right now. Fort Ord, you heard of it?
No, *holy shit,* are you *serious?* You mean he ain't even *American?* He doesn't have to go anywhere *near* that hor-rorshow, why in hell would he *volunteer?*
Felt it was his duty maybe, I don't know the whole story. His mom absolutely *freaked out* when she heard, I can tell you that much.
Well, I guess she would....
So you got a lot of family over here? We went off on a tangent, you never finished telling me your story.
Ah, my sister Louise still lives here in town, we haven't seen each other in a couple years. Just making sure the family's still intact. It's important.
It's funny, we sit beside each other the whole trip and don't say a word, right near the end we're talking like we've known each other for years.
Maybe it's fate.
CONTINENTAL TRAILWAYS
TORONTO
TORONTO
TORONTO
CONTINENTAL TRAILWAYS

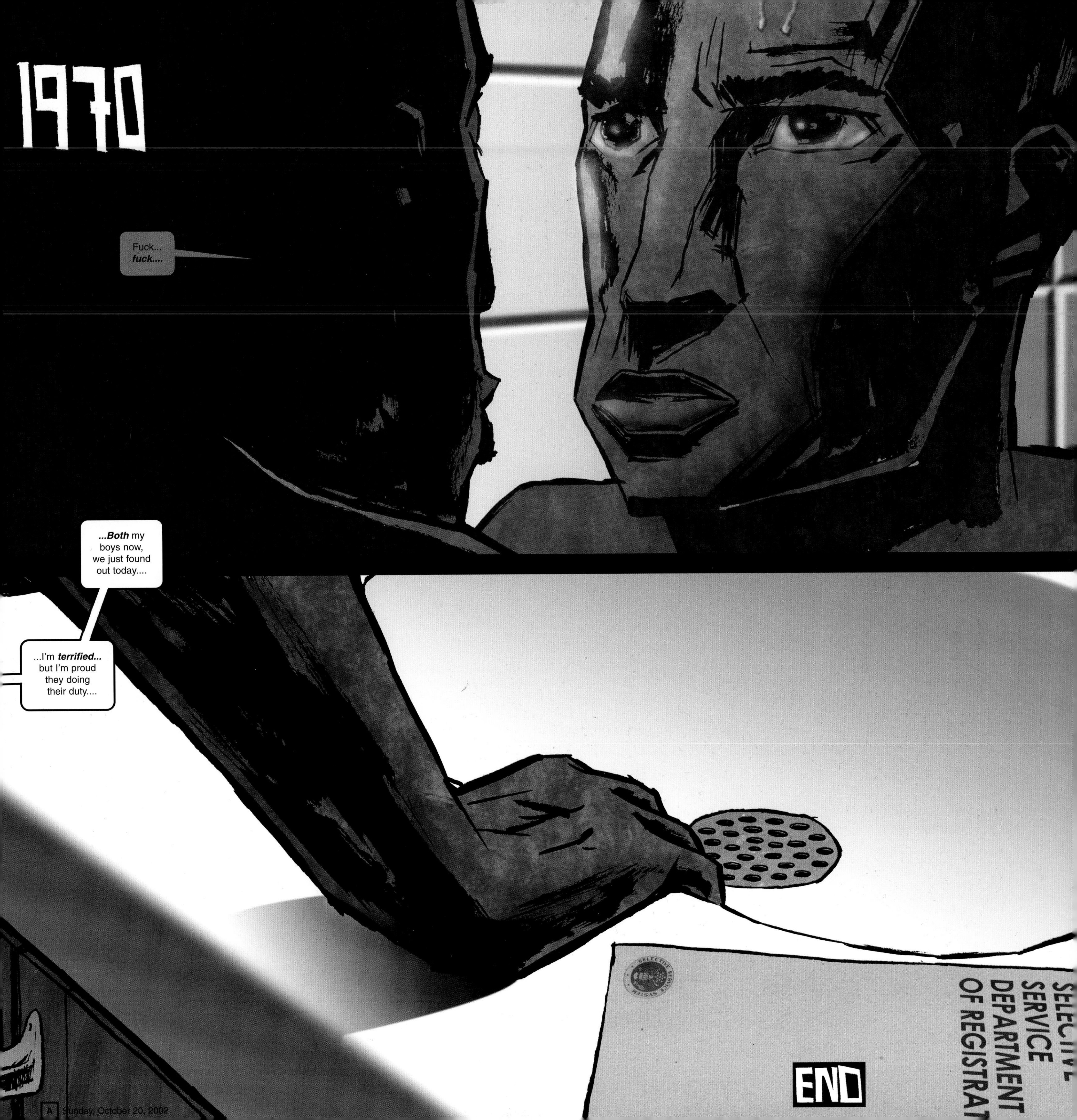
1970
Fuck... *fuck....*
...Both my boys now, we just found out today....
...I'm *terrified...* but I'm proud they doing their duty....
SERVICE
DEPARTMENT
END
Sunday, October 20, 2002

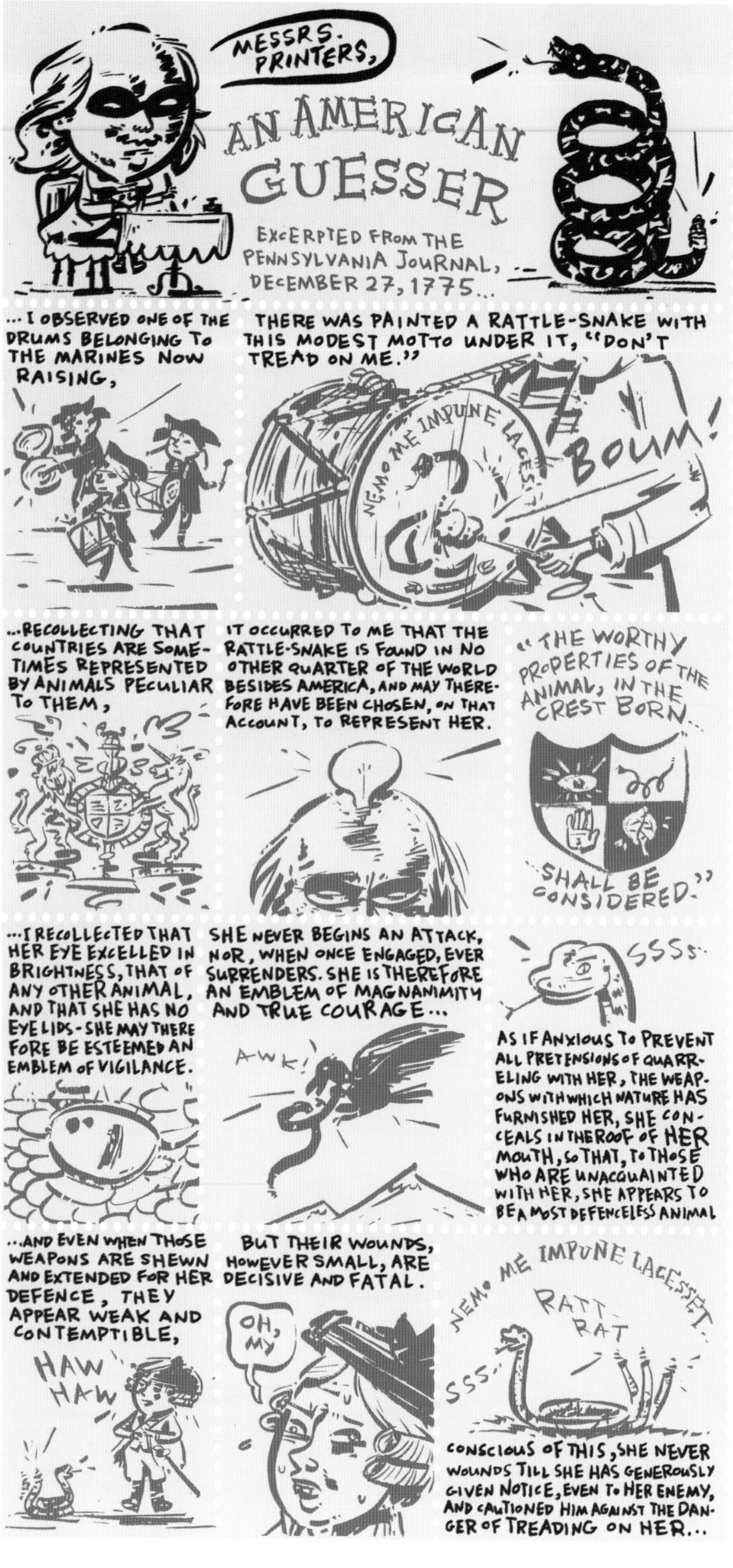
MESSRS. PRINTERS,
AN AMERICAN GUESSER
EXCERPTED FROM THE PENNSYLVANIA JOURNAL, DECEMBER 27, 1775...
...I OBSERVED ONE OF THE DRUMS BELONGING TO THE MARINES NOW RAISING,
THERE WAS PAINTED A RATTLE-SNAKE WITH THIS MODEST MOTTO UNDER IT, "DON'T TREAD ON ME."
NEMO ME IMPUNE LACES
BOUM!
...RECOLLECTING THAT COUNTRIES ARE SOMETIMES REPRESENTED BY ANIMALS PECULIAR TO THEM,
IT OCCURRED TO ME THAT THE RATTLE-SNAKE IS FOUND IN NO OTHER QUARTER OF THE WORLD BESIDES AMERICA, AND MAY THEREFORE HAVE BEEN CHOSEN, ON THAT ACCOUNT, TO REPRESENT HER.
"THE WORTHY PROPERTIES OF THE ANIMAL, IN THE CREST BORN...
SHALL BE CONSIDERED."
...I RECOLLECTED THAT HER EYE EXCELLED IN BRIGHTNESS, THAT OF ANY OTHER ANIMAL, AND THAT SHE HAS NO EYE LIDS - SHE MAY THEREFORE BE ESTEEMED AN EMBLEM OF VIGILANCE.
SHE NEVER BEGINS AN ATTACK, NOR, WHEN ONCE ENGAGED, EVER SURRENDERS. SHE IS THEREFORE AN EMBLEM OF MAGNANIMITY AND TRUE COURAGE...
AWK!
SSSS
AS IF ANXIOUS TO PREVENT ALL PRETENSIONS OF QUARRELING WITH HER, THE WEAPONS WITH WHICH NATURE HAS FURNISHED HER, SHE CONCEALS IN THE ROOF OF HER MOUTH, SO THAT, TO THOSE WHO ARE UNACQUAINTED WITH HER, SHE APPEARS TO BE A MOST DEFENCELESS ANIMAL
...AND EVEN WHEN THOSE WEAPONS ARE SHEWN AND EXTENDED FOR HER DEFENCE, THEY APPEAR WEAK AND CONTEMPTIBLE,
HAW HAW
BUT THEIR WOUNDS, HOWEVER SMALL, ARE DECISIVE AND FATAL.
OH, MY
NEMO ME IMPUNE LACESSET.
RATT RAT
SSS..
CONSCIOUS OF THIS, SHE NEVER WOUNDS TILL SHE HAS GENEROUSLY GIVEN NOTICE, EVEN TO HER ENEMY, AND CAUTIONED HIM AGAINST THE DANGER OF TREADING ON HER...

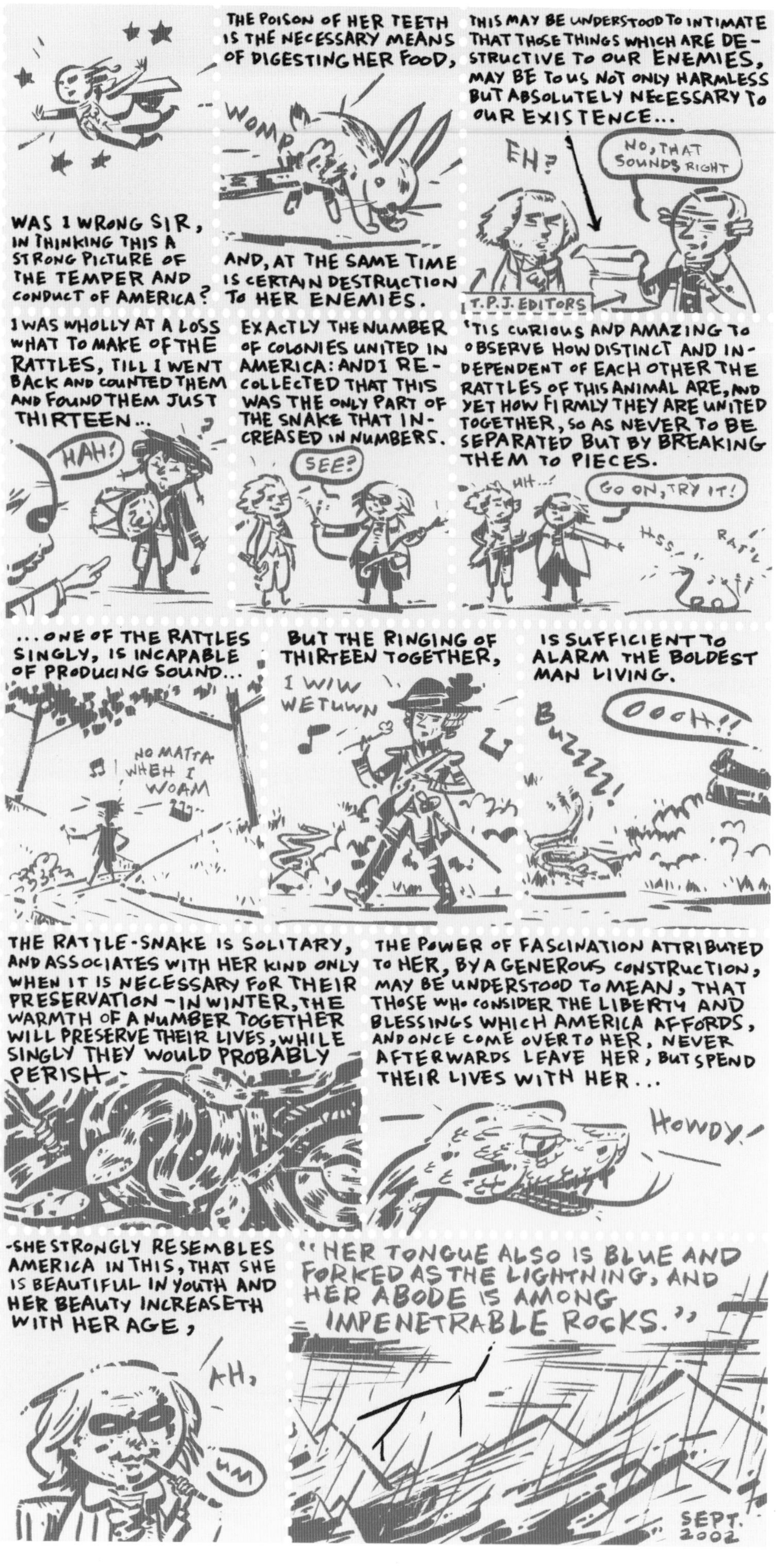
WAS I WRONG SIR, IN THINKING THIS A STRONG PICTURE OF THE TEMPER AND CONDUCT OF AMERICA?
THE POISON OF HER TEETH IS THE NECESSARY MEANS OF DIGESTING HER FOOD,
WOMP
AND, AT THE SAME TIME IS CERTAIN DESTRUCTION TO HER ENEMIES.
THIS MAY BE UNDERSTOOD TO INTIMATE THAT THOSE THINGS WHICH ARE DESTRUCTIVE TO OUR ENEMIES, MAY BE TO US NOT ONLY HARMLESS BUT ABSOLUTELY NECESSARY TO OUR EXISTENCE...
EH?
NO, THAT SOUNDS RIGHT
T.P.J. EDITORS
I WAS WHOLLY AT A LOSS WHAT TO MAKE OF THE RATTLES, TILL I WENT BACK AND COUNTED THEM AND FOUND THEM JUST THIRTEEN...
HAH!
EXACTLY THE NUMBER OF COLONIES UNITED IN AMERICA: AND I RECOLLECTED THAT THIS WAS THE ONLY PART OF THE SNAKE THAT INCREASED IN NUMBERS.
SEE?
'TIS CURIOUS AND AMAZING TO OBSERVE HOW DISTINCT AND INDEPENDENT OF EACH OTHER THE RATTLES OF THIS ANIMAL ARE, AND YET HOW FIRMLY THEY ARE UNITED TOGETHER, SO AS NEVER TO BE SEPARATED BUT BY BREAKING THEM TO PIECES.
UH..!
GO ON, TRY IT!
HSS..
RAT'L
...ONE OF THE RATTLES SINGLY, IS INCAPABLE OF PRODUCING SOUND...
NO MATTA WHEH I WOAM
BUT THE RINGING OF THIRTEEN TOGETHER,
I WIW WETUWN
IS SUFFICIENT TO ALARM THE BOLDEST MAN LIVING.
BUZZZZ!
OOOH!!
THE RATTLE-SNAKE IS SOLITARY, AND ASSOCIATES WITH HER KIND ONLY WHEN IT IS NECESSARY FOR THEIR PRESERVATION - IN WINTER, THE WARMTH OF A NUMBER TOGETHER WILL PRESERVE THEIR LIVES, WHILE SINGLY THEY WOULD PROBABLY PERISH.
THE POWER OF FASCINATION ATTRIBUTED TO HER, BY A GENEROUS CONSTRUCTION, MAY BE UNDERSTOOD TO MEAN, THAT THOSE WHO CONSIDER THE LIBERTY AND BLESSINGS WHICH AMERICA AFFORDS, AND ONCE COME OVER TO HER, NEVER AFTERWARDS LEAVE HER, BUT SPEND THEIR LIVES WITH HER...
HOWDY.
-SHE STRONGLY RESEMBLES AMERICA IN THIS, THAT SHE IS BEAUTIFUL IN YOUTH AND HER BEAUTY INCREASETH WITH HER AGE,
AH,
UM
"HER TONGUE ALSO IS BLUE AND FORKED AS THE LIGHTNING, AND HER ABODE IS AMONG IMPENETRABLE ROCKS."
SEPT. 2002

Jubilee

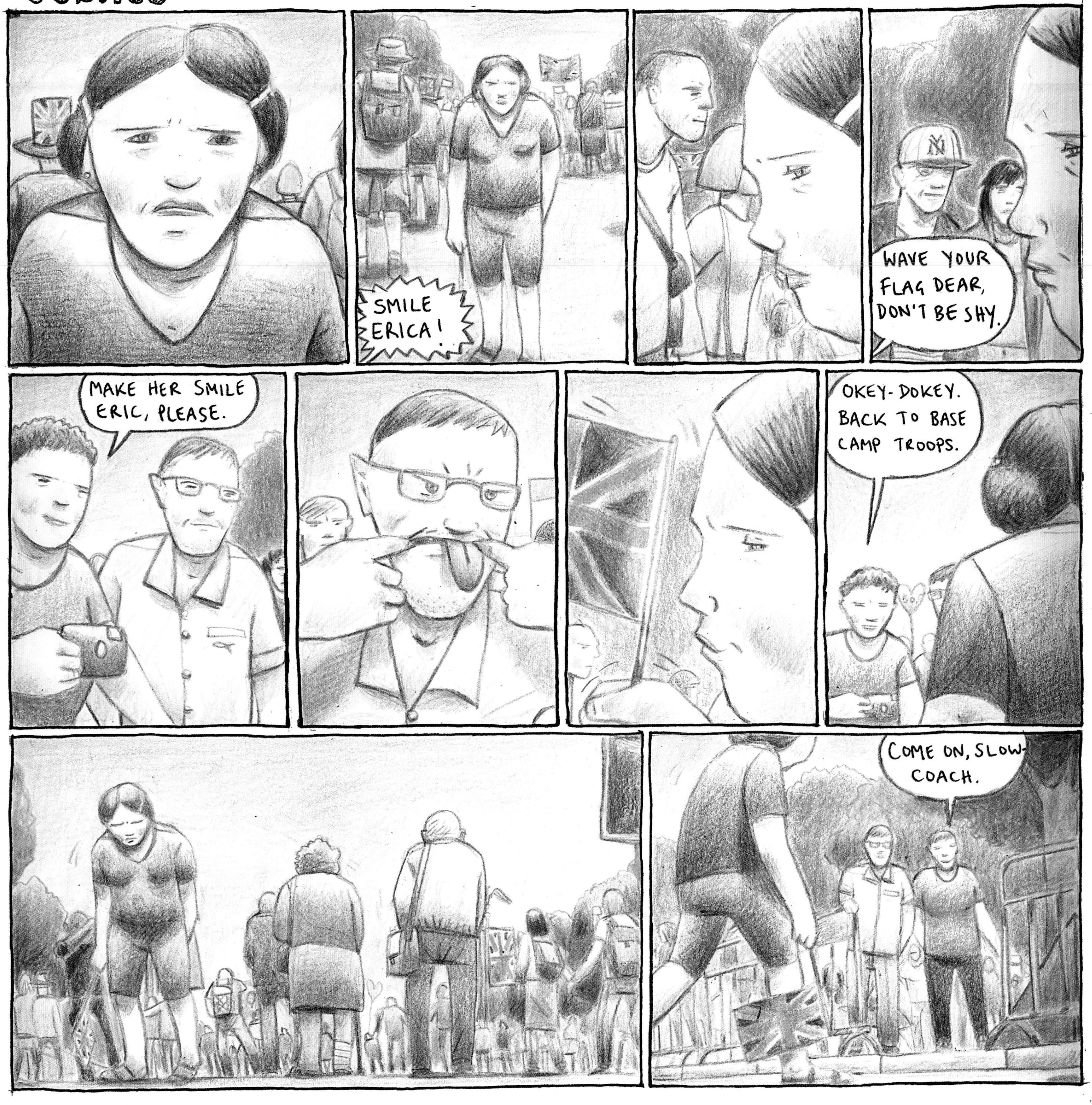
SMILE ERICA!
WAVE YOUR FLAG DEAR, DON'T BE SHY.
MAKE HER SMILE ERIC, PLEASE.
OKEY-DOKEY. BACK TO BASE CAMP TROOPS.
COME ON, SLOW-COACH.

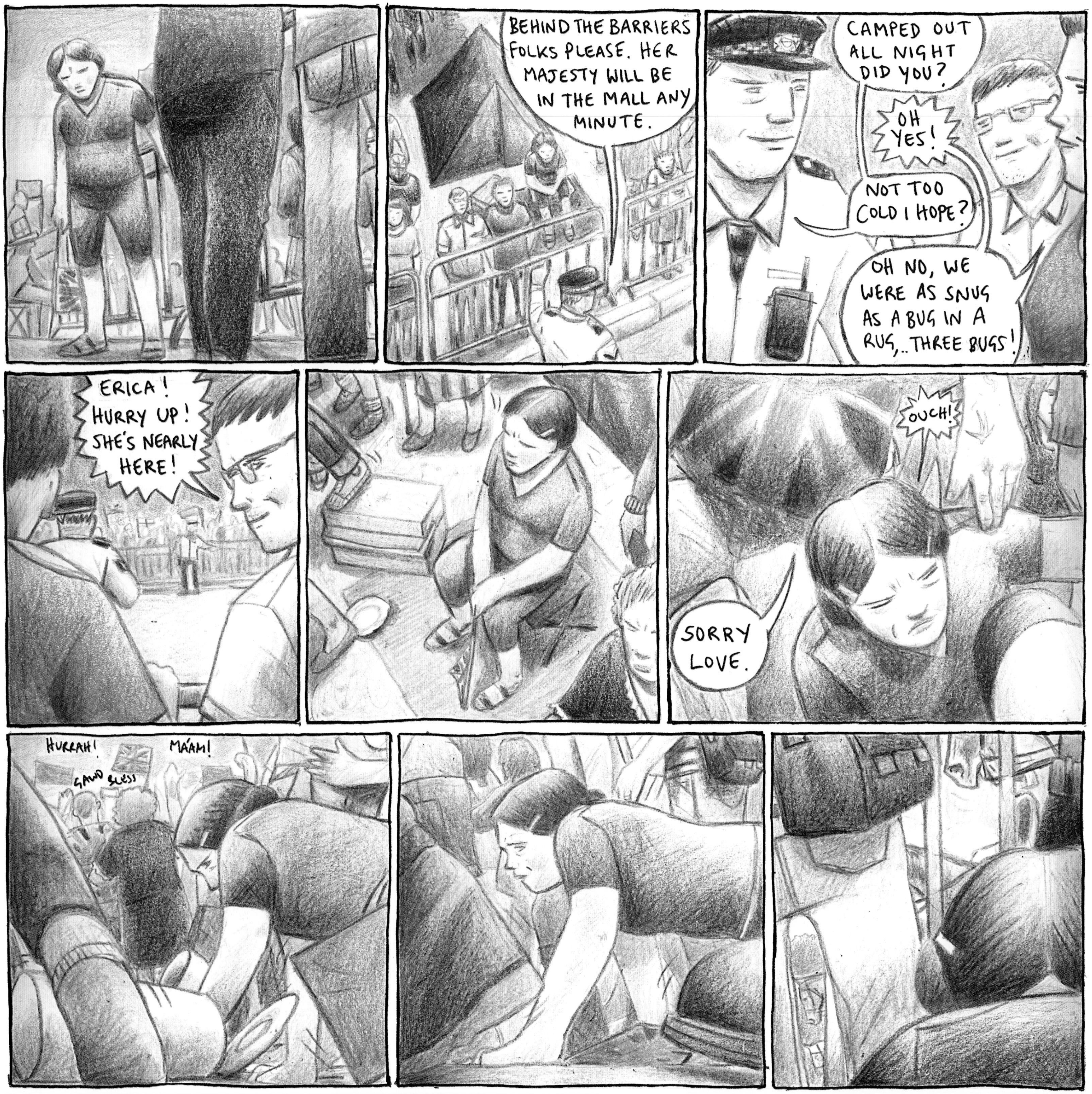
BEHIND THE BARRIERS FOLKS PLEASE. HER MAJESTY WILL BE IN THE MALL ANY MINUTE.
CAMPED OUT ALL NIGHT DID YOU?
OH YES!
NOT TOO COLD I HOPE?
OH NO, WE WERE AS SNUG AS A BUG IN A RUG,.. THREE BUGS!
ERICA! HURRY UP! SHE'S NEARLY HERE!
OUCH!
SORRY LOVE.
HURRAH!
MA'AM!
GAWD BLESS

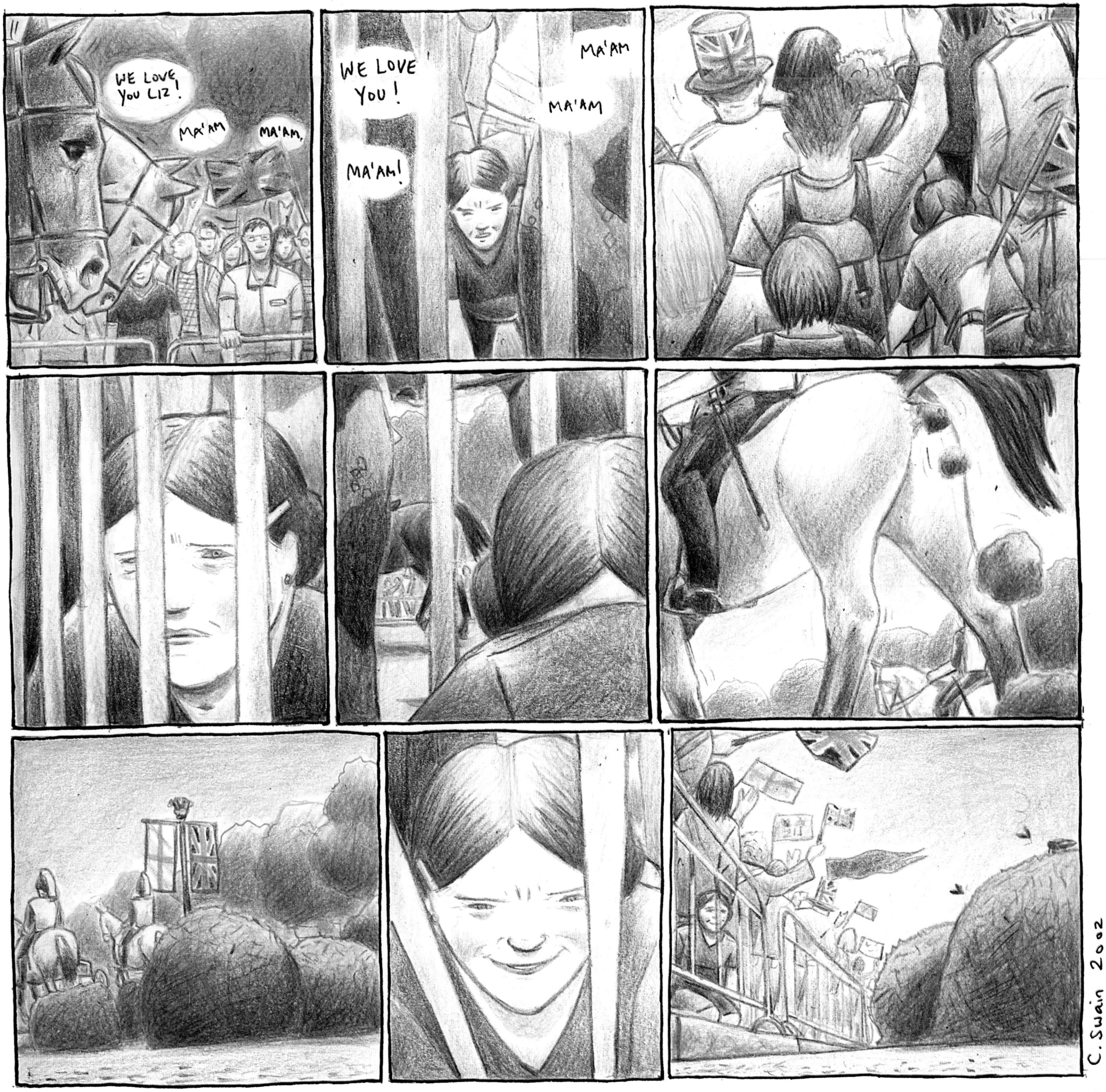
WE LOVE YOU LIZ!
MA'AM
MA'AM,
WE LOVE YOU!
MA'AM
MA'AM
MA'AM!
C. Swain 2002

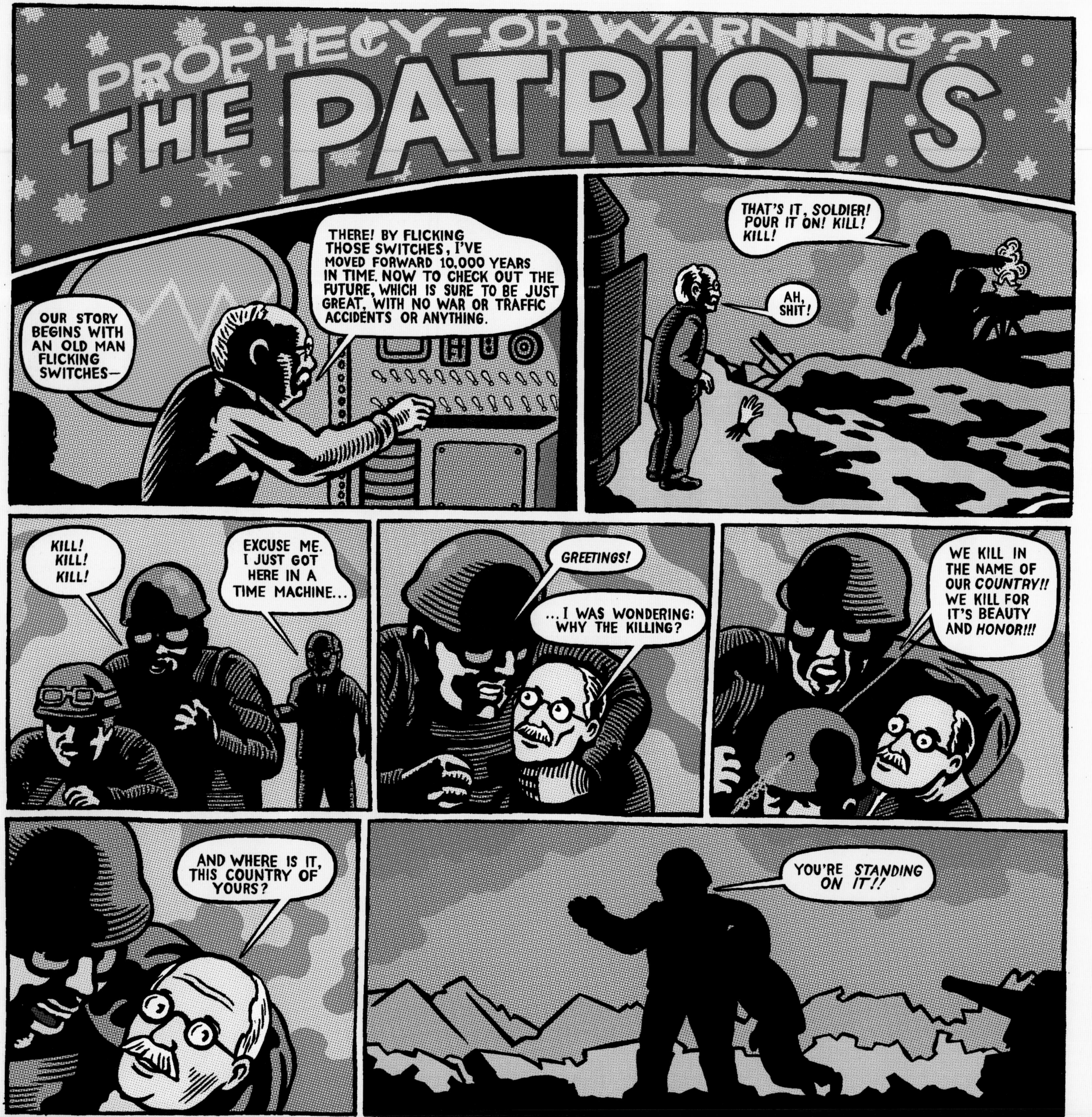
PROPHECY—OR WARNING?
THE PATRIOTS
OUR STORY BEGINS WITH AN OLD MAN FLICKING SWITCHES—
THERE! BY FLICKING THOSE SWITCHES, I'VE MOVED FORWARD 10,000 YEARS IN TIME. NOW TO CHECK OUT THE FUTURE, WHICH IS SURE TO BE JUST GREAT, WITH NO WAR OR TRAFFIC ACCIDENTS OR ANYTHING.
THAT'S IT, SOLDIER! POUR IT ON! KILL! KILL!
AH, SHIT!
KILL! KILL! KILL!
EXCUSE ME. I JUST GOT HERE IN A TIME MACHINE...
GREETINGS!
...I WAS WONDERING: WHY THE KILLING?
WE KILL IN THE NAME OF OUR *COUNTRY!!* WE KILL FOR IT'S BEAUTY AND *HONOR!!!*
AND WHERE IS IT, THIS COUNTRY OF YOURS?
YOU'RE *STANDING ON IT!!*

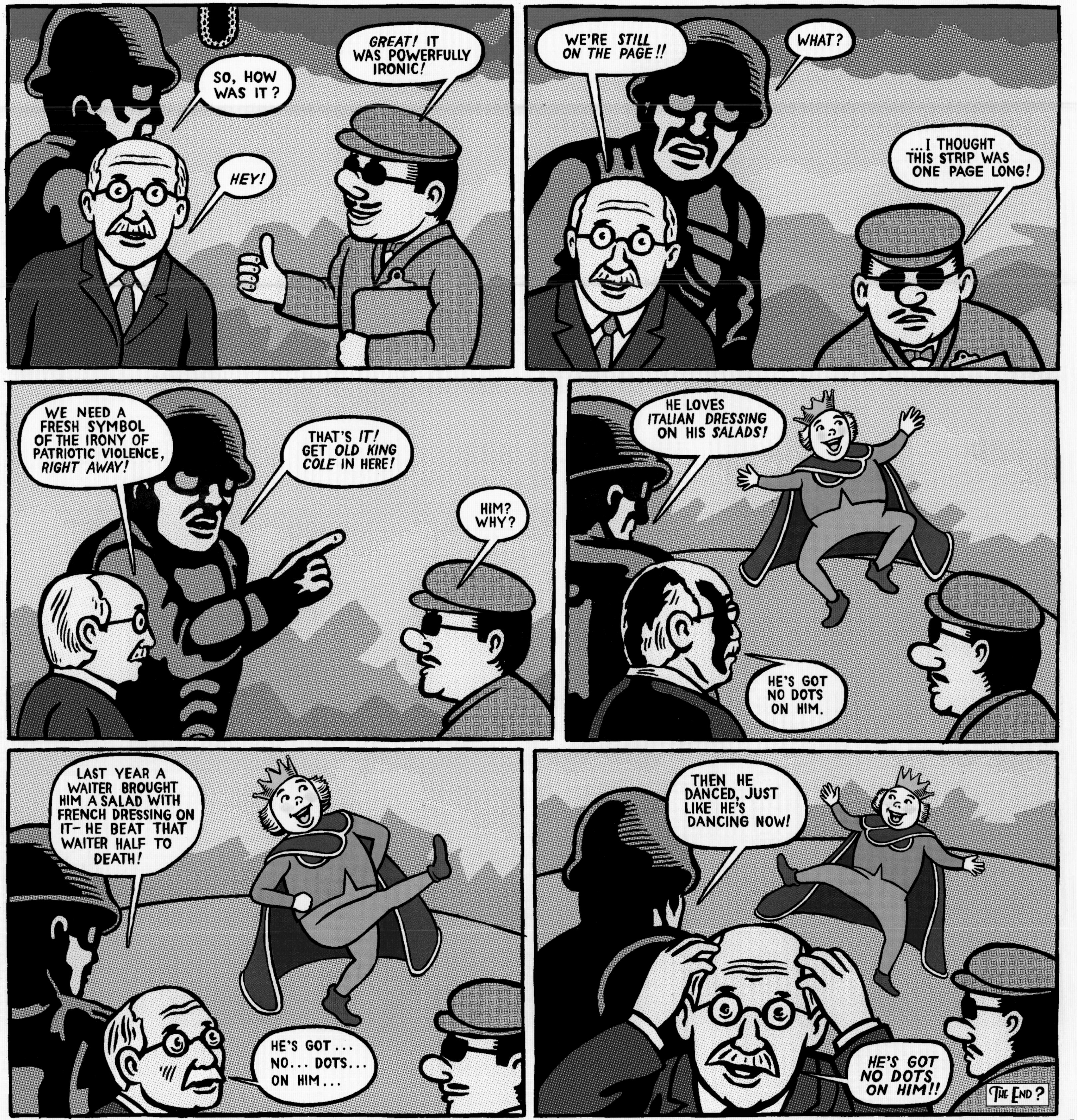
SO, HOW WAS IT?
GREAT! IT WAS POWERFULLY IRONIC!
HEY!
WE'RE STILL ON THE PAGE!!
WHAT?
...I THOUGHT THIS STRIP WAS ONE PAGE LONG!
WE NEED A FRESH SYMBOL OF THE IRONY OF PATRIOTIC VIOLENCE, RIGHT AWAY!
THAT'S IT! GET OLD KING COLE IN HERE!
HIM? WHY?
HE LOVES ITALIAN DRESSING ON HIS SALADS!
HE'S GOT NO DOTS ON HIM.
LAST YEAR A WAITER BROUGHT HIM A SALAD WITH FRENCH DRESSING ON IT- HE BEAT THAT WAITER HALF TO DEATH!
HE'S GOT... NO... DOTS... ON HIM...
THEN HE DANCED, JUST LIKE HE'S DANCING NOW!
HE'S GOT NO DOTS ON HIM!!
THE END?

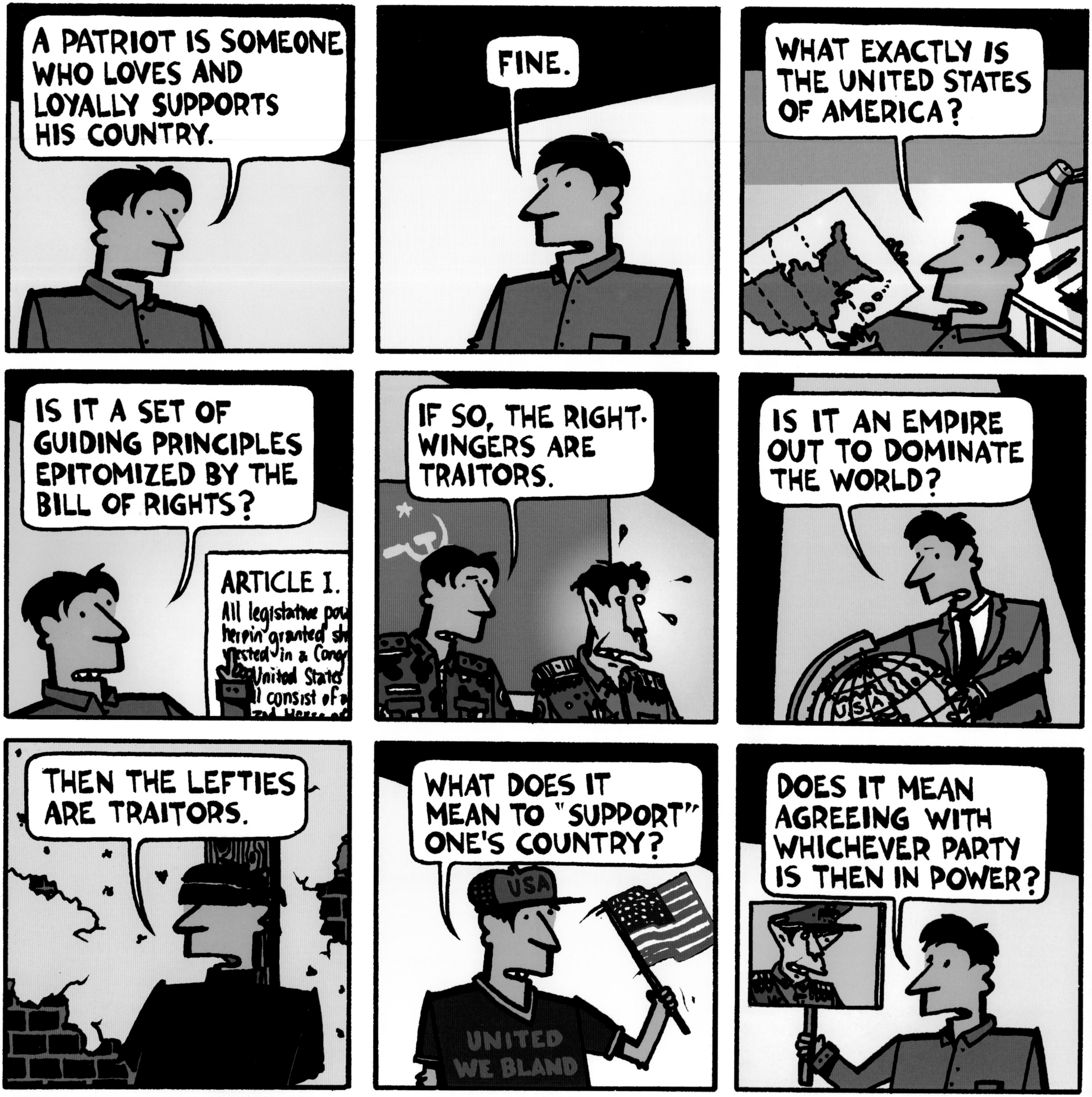
A PATRIOT IS SOMEONE WHO LOVES AND LOYALLY SUPPORTS HIS COUNTRY.
FINE.
WHAT EXACTLY IS THE UNITED STATES OF AMERICA?
IS IT A SET OF GUIDING PRINCIPLES EPITOMIZED BY THE BILL OF RIGHTS?
ARTICLE I.
IF SO, THE RIGHT-WINGERS ARE TRAITORS.
IS IT AN EMPIRE OUT TO DOMINATE THE WORLD?
USA
THEN THE LEFTIES ARE TRAITORS.
WHAT DOES IT MEAN TO "SUPPORT" ONE'S COUNTRY?
USA
UNITED WE BLAND
DOES IT MEAN AGREEING WITH WHICHEVER PARTY IS THEN IN POWER?

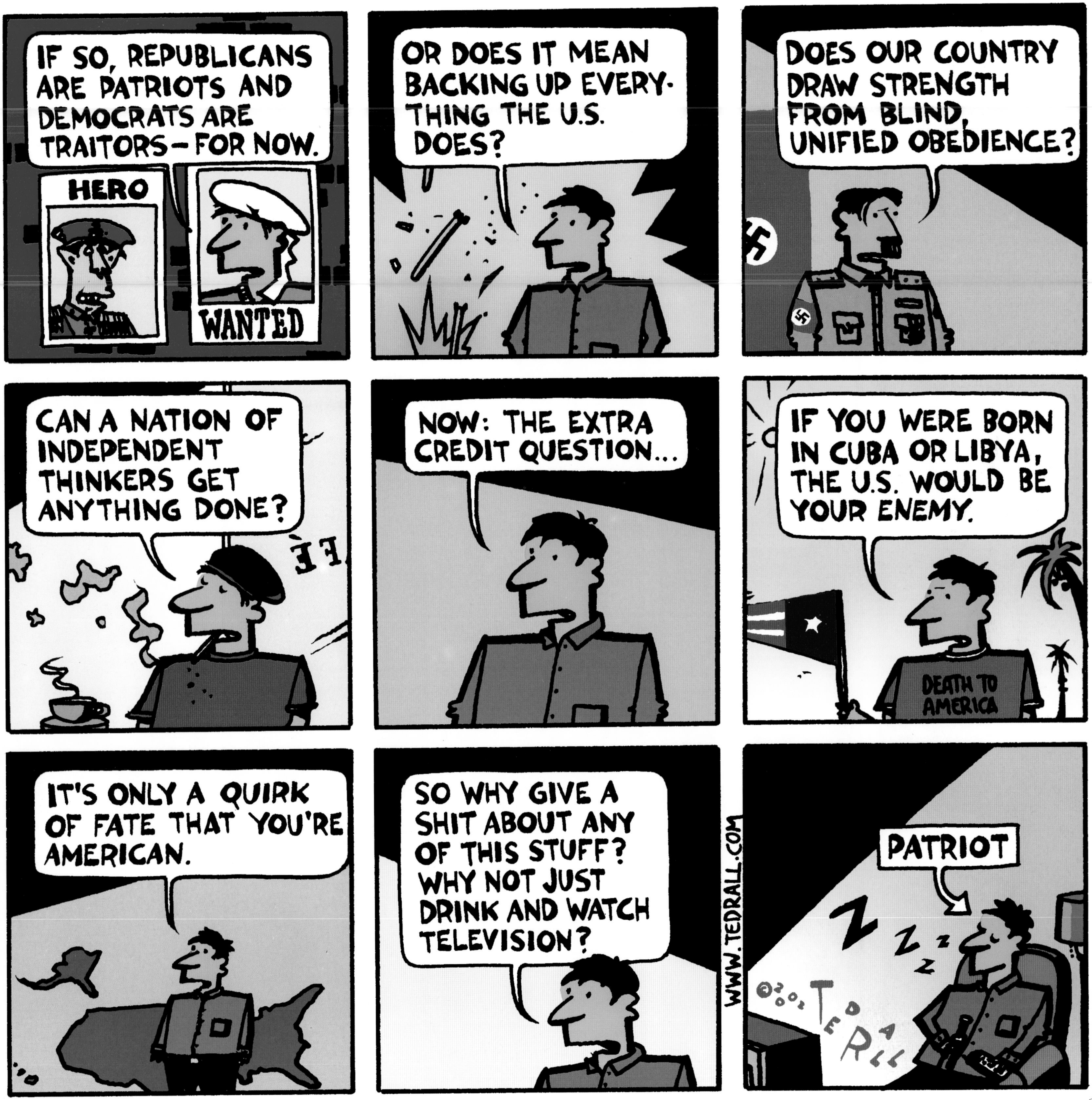
IF SO, REPUBLICANS ARE PATRIOTS AND DEMOCRATS ARE TRAITORS—FOR NOW.
HERO
WANTED
OR DOES IT MEAN BACKING UP EVERY-THING THE U.S. DOES?
DOES OUR COUNTRY DRAW STRENGTH FROM BLIND, UNIFIED OBEDIENCE?
CAN A NATION OF INDEPENDENT THINKERS GET ANYTHING DONE?
NOW: THE EXTRA CREDIT QUESTION...
IF YOU WERE BORN IN CUBA OR LIBYA, THE U.S. WOULD BE YOUR ENEMY.
DEATH TO AMERICA
IT'S ONLY A QUIRK OF FATE THAT YOU'RE AMERICAN.
SO WHY GIVE A SHIT ABOUT ANY OF THIS STUFF? WHY NOT JUST DRINK AND WATCH TELEVISION?
WWW.TEDRALL.COM
PATRIOT
Z Z Z Z
©2002 TED RALL

STRIPES

© 2002

Peter Kuper

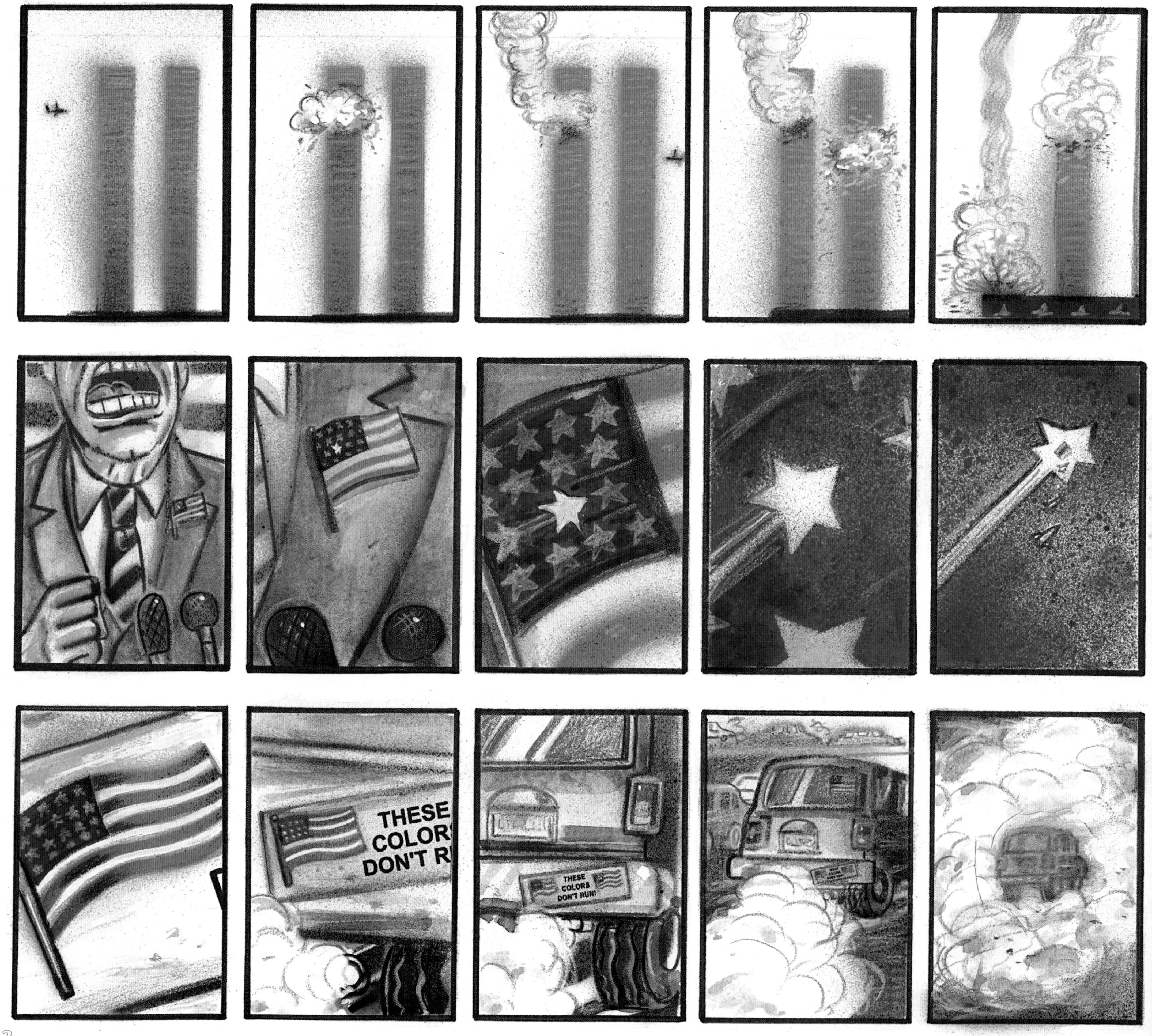
THESE
THESE COLORS DON'T RUN!

AND STARS ★★★

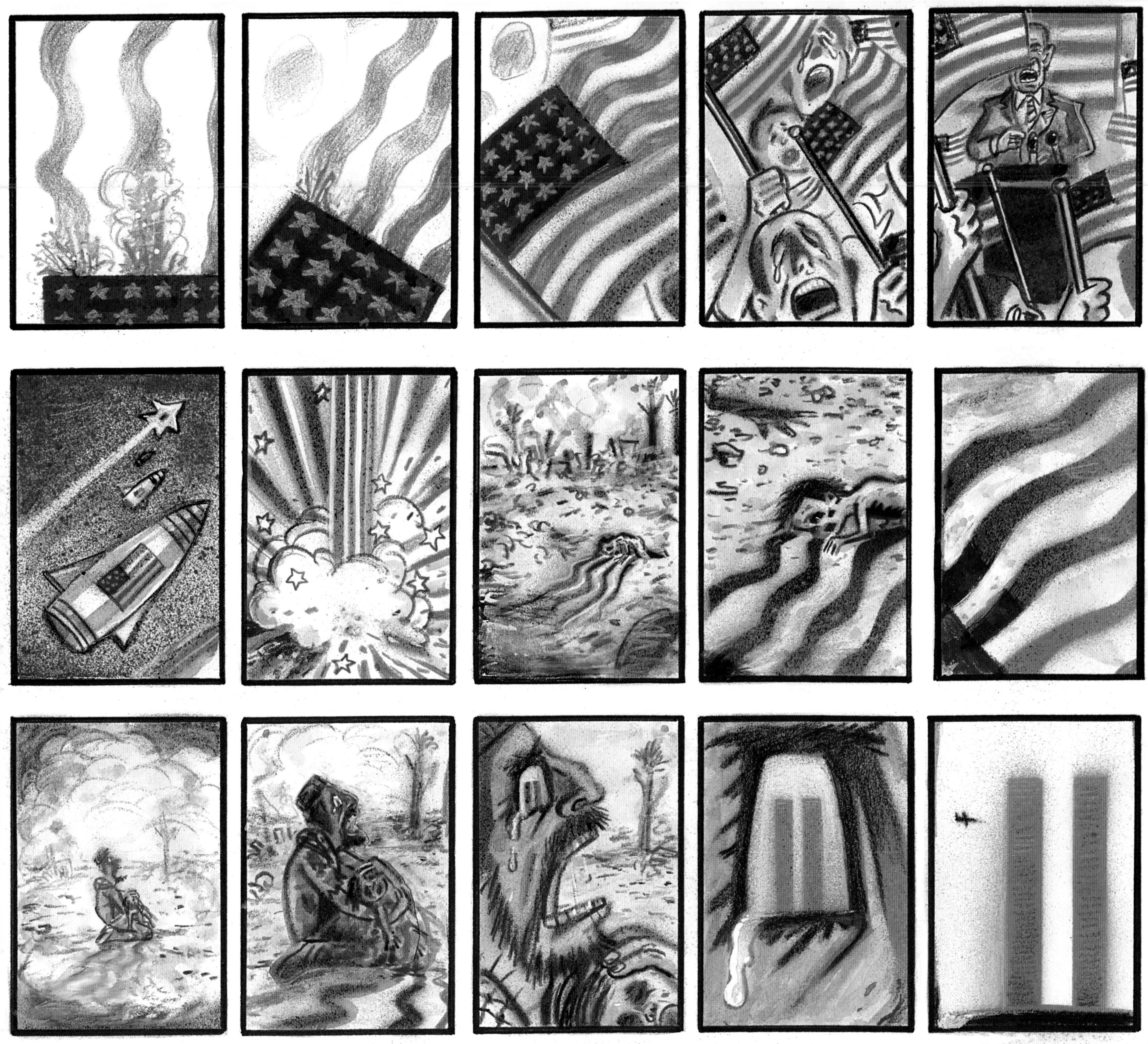

A Bird's-Eye VIEW of AMERICA

Penny Van Horn © 2002

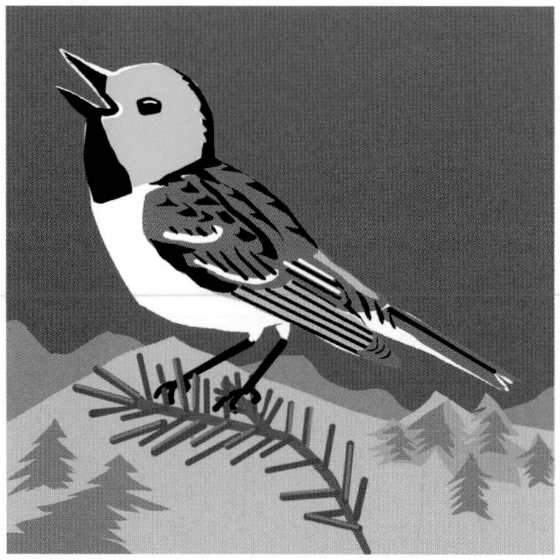

Hermit Warbler: threatened by logging/development

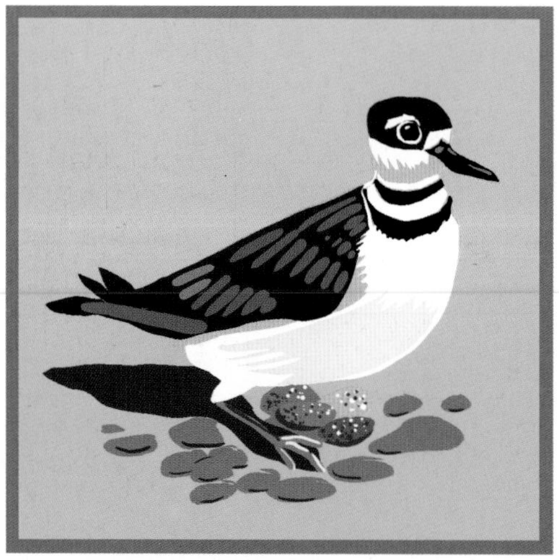

Killdeer: accidentally shot by President

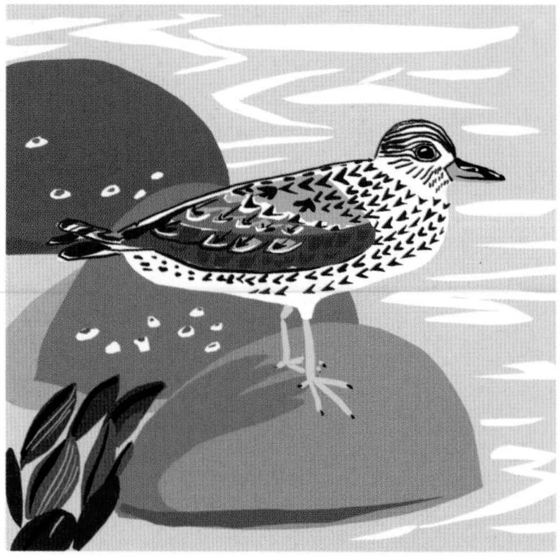

Surfbird: habitat coincides with oil tanker routes

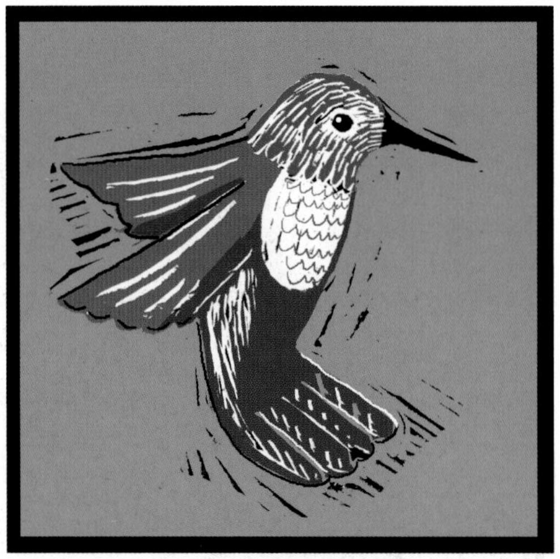

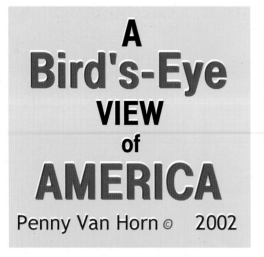

Hummingbird: encroaching development limits habitat

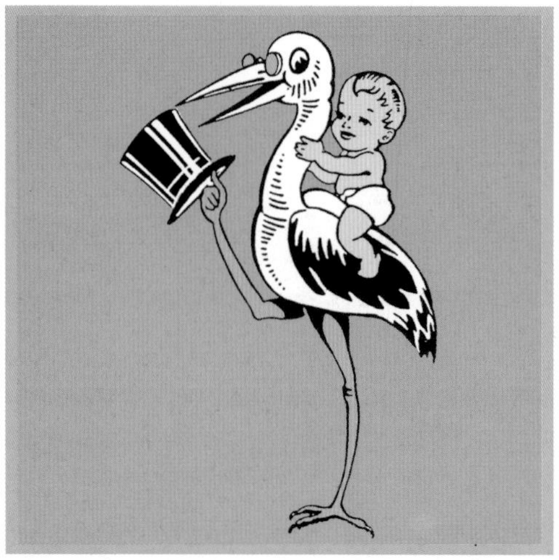

Wood Stork: declining due to loss of freshwater wetlands

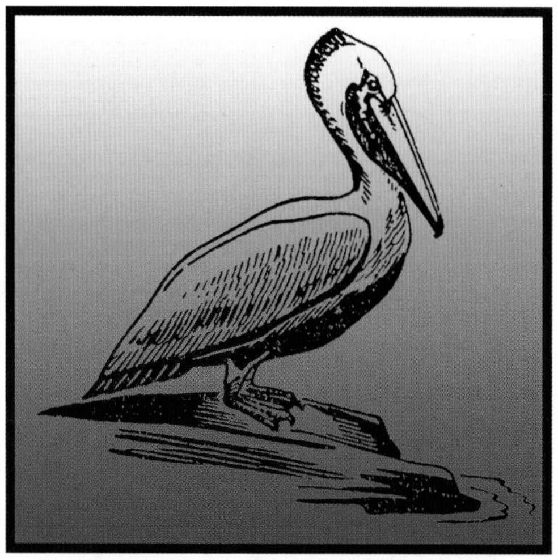

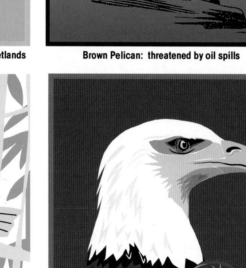

Brown Pelican: threatened by oil spills

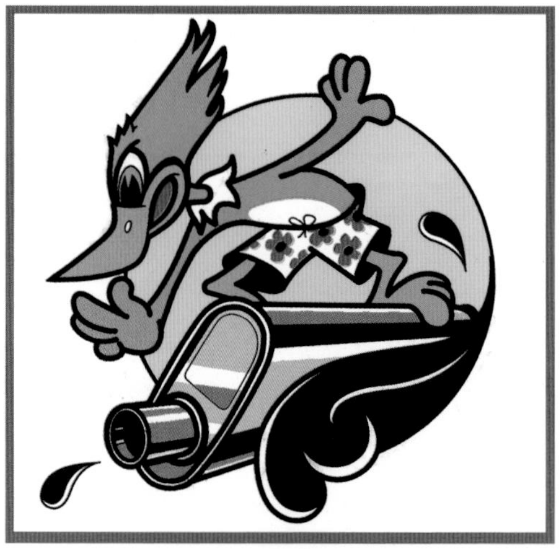

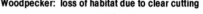

Woodpecker: loss of habitat due to clear cutting

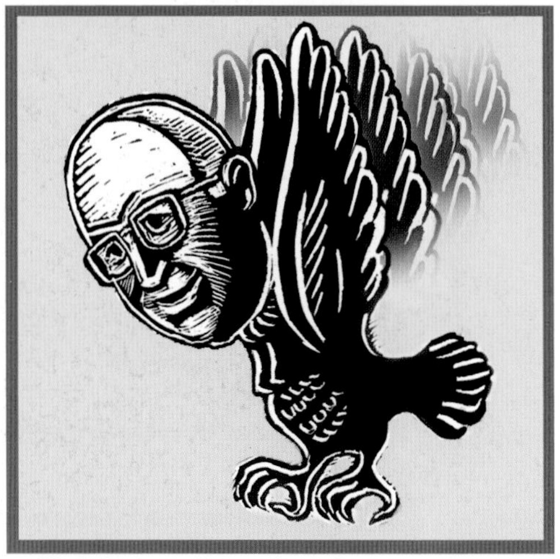

Black Hawk: declining w/loss of cottonwood groves

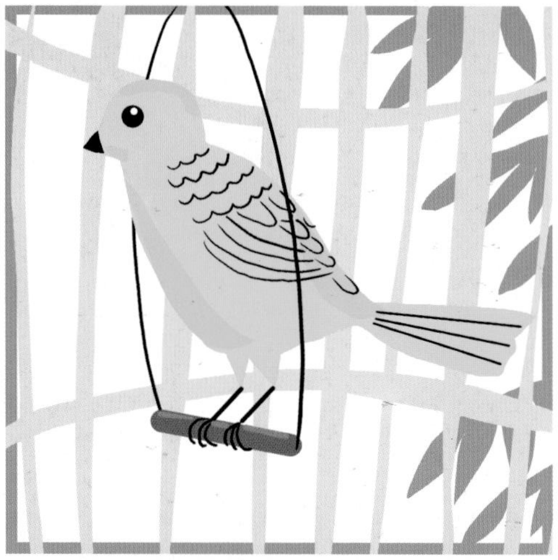

Canary: "captivity requires from us a song"

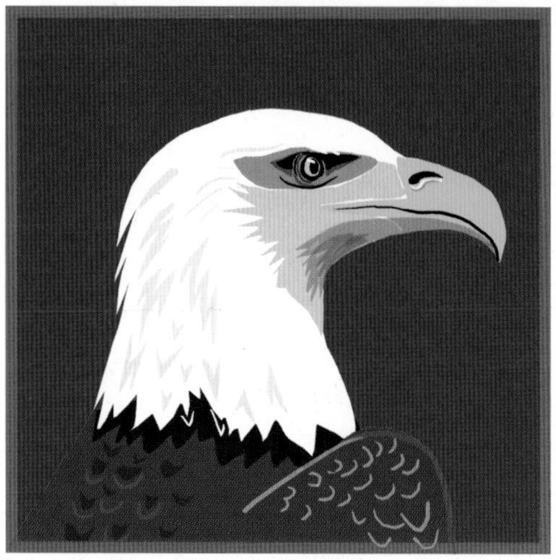

Bald Eagle: recovering from pesticides and shooting

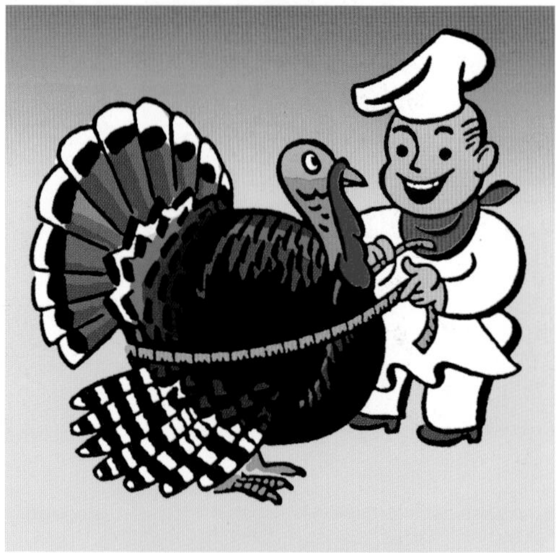

Wild Turkey: roosts in trees. Shy.

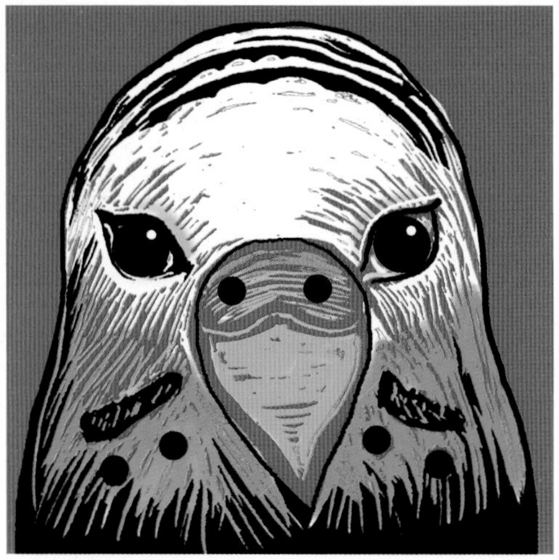

Budgerigar: bringing good feng shui to American prisons

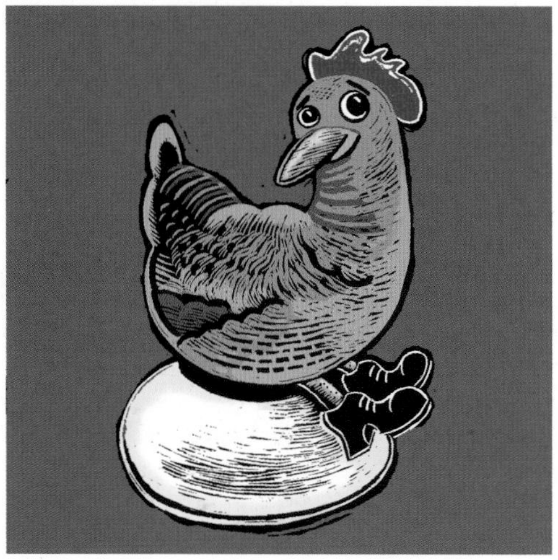

Chicken: 45 million "processed" weekly by 1 corp. alone

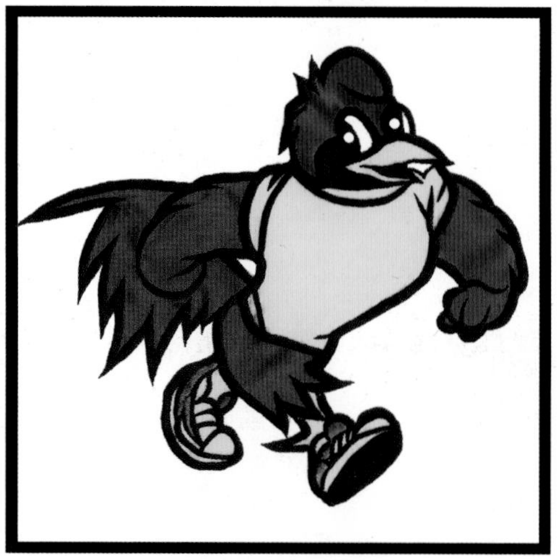

Bluebird: threatened by competition for nest holes

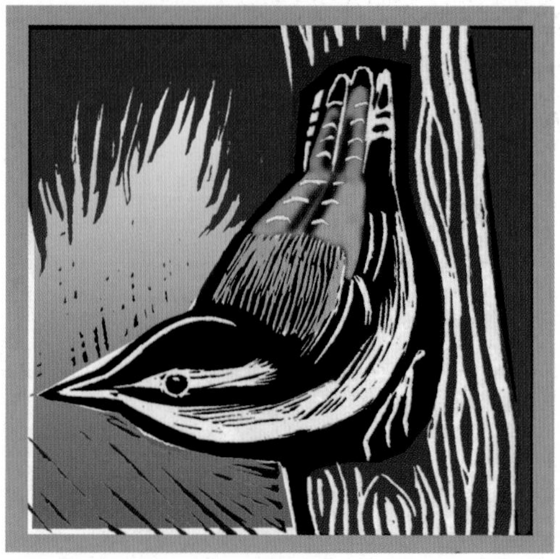

Nuthatch: loss of ancient forests has greatly affected birds

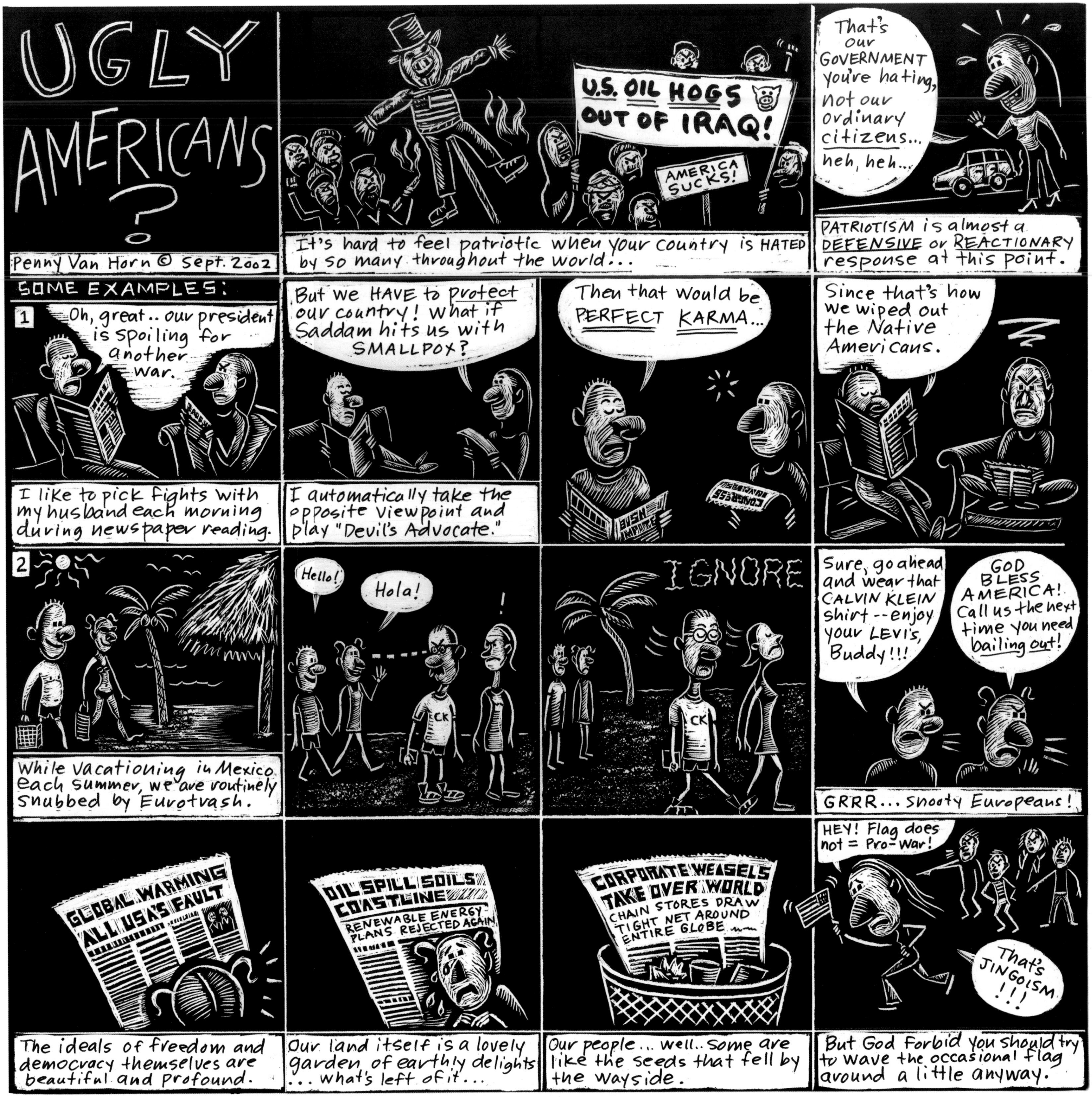
UGLY AMERICANS ?
Penny Van Horn © Sept. 2002
U.S. OIL HOGS OUT OF IRAQ!
AMERICA SUCKS!
It's hard to feel patriotic when your country is HATED by so many throughout the world...
That's our GOVERNMENT you're hating, not our ordinary citizens... heh, heh...
PATRIOTISM is almost a DEFENSIVE or REACTIONARY response at this point.
SOME EXAMPLES:
1
Oh, great.. our president is spoiling for another war.
I like to pick fights with my husband each morning during newspaper reading.
But we HAVE to protect our country! What if Saddam hits us with SMALLPOX?
I automatically take the opposite viewpoint and play "Devil's Advocate."
Then that would be PERFECT KARMA...
Since that's how we wiped out the Native Americans.
2
While vacationing in Mexico each summer, we are routinely snubbed by Eurotrash.
Hello!
Hola!
CK
IGNORE
CK
Sure, go ahead and wear that CALVIN KLEIN shirt -- enjoy your LEVI's, Buddy!!!
GOD BLESS AMERICA! Call us the next time you need bailing out!
GRRR... Snooty Europeans!
GLOBAL WARMING ALL USA'S FAULT
The ideals of freedom and democracy themselves are beautiful and profound.
OIL SPILL SOILS COASTLINE
RENEWABLE ENERGY PLANS REJECTED AGAIN
Our land itself is a lovely garden of earthly delights ... what's left of it...
CORPORATE WEASELS TAKE OVER WORLD
CHAIN STORES DRAW TIGHT NET AROUND ENTIRE GLOBE
Our people... well.. some are like the seeds that fell by the wayside.
HEY! Flag does not = Pro-War!
That's JINGOISM!!!
But God Forbid you should try to wave the occasional flag around a little anyway.

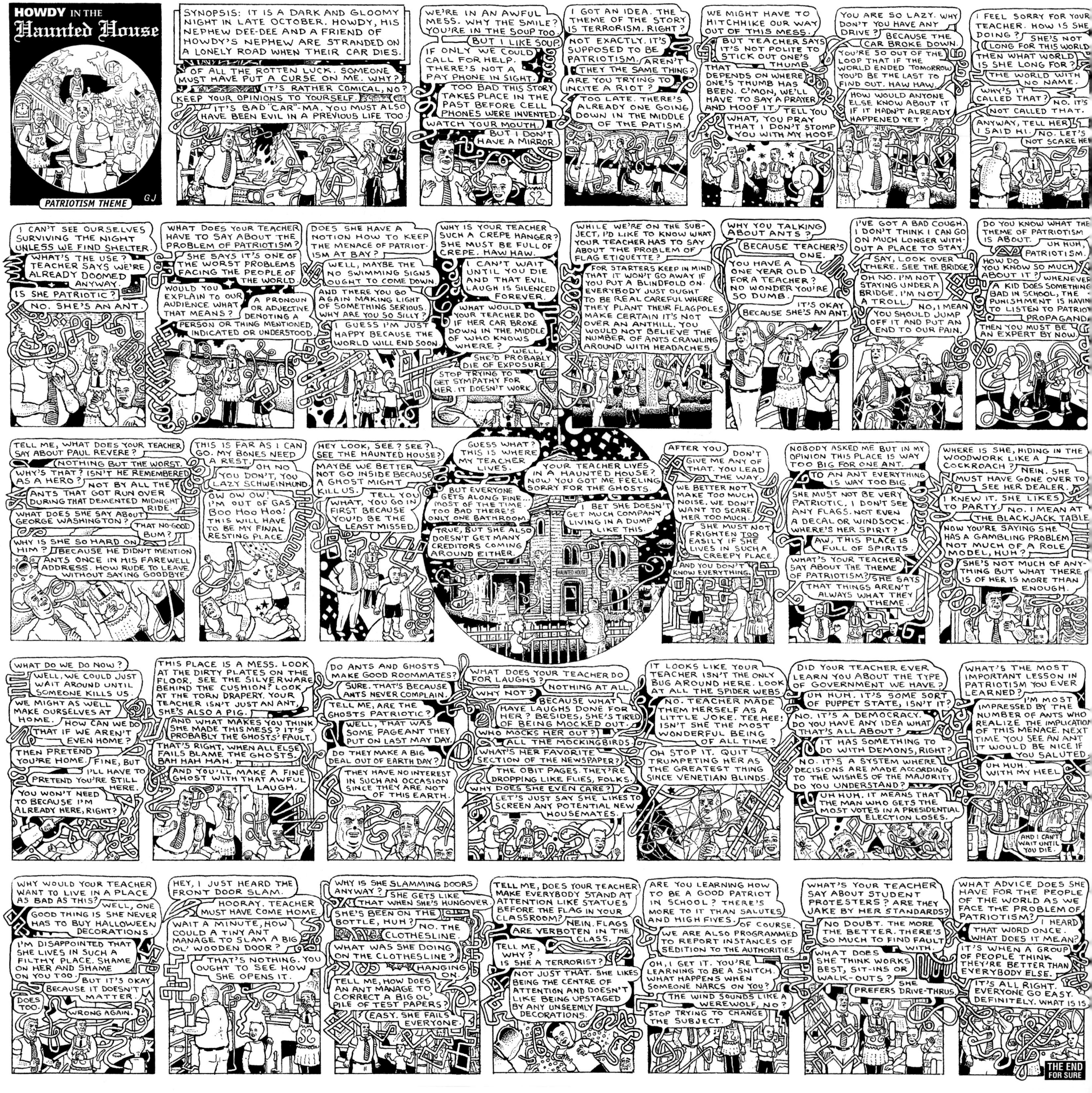
HOWDY IN THE
Haunted House
PATRIOTISM THEME
GJ
SYNOPSIS: IT IS A DARK AND GLOOMY NIGHT IN LATE OCTOBER. HOWDY, HIS NEPHEW DEE-DEE AND A FRIEND OF HOWDY'S NEPHEW ARE STRANDED ON A LONELY ROAD WHEN THEIR CAR DIES.
OF ALL THE ROTTEN LUCK. SOMEONE MUST HAVE PUT A CURSE ON ME. WHY?
IT'S RATHER COMICAL, NO?
KEEP YOUR OPINIONS TO YOURSELF.
IT'S BAD "CAR"-MA. YOU MUST ALSO HAVE BEEN EVIL IN A PREVIOUS LIFE TOO.
WE'RE IN AN AWFUL MESS. WHY THE SMILE? YOU'RE IN THE SOUP TOO.
BUT I LIKE SOUP.
IF ONLY WE COULD CALL FOR HELP. THERE'S NOT A PAY PHONE IN SIGHT.
TOO BAD THIS STORY TAKES PLACE IN THE PAST BEFORE CELL PHONES WERE INVENTED.
WATCH YOUR MOUTH.
BUT I DON'T HAVE A MIRROR.
I GOT AN IDEA. THE THEME OF THE STORY IS TERRORISM. RIGHT?
NOT EXACTLY. IT'S SUPPOSED TO BE PATRIOTISM.
AREN'T THEY THE SAME THING?
ARE YOU TRYING TO INCITE A RIOT?
TOO LATE. THERE'S ALREADY ONE GOING DOWN IN THE MIDDLE OF THE PATISM.
WE MIGHT HAVE TO HITCHHIKE OUR WAY OUT OF THIS MESS.
BUT TEACHER SAYS IT'S NOT POLITE TO STICK OUT ONE'S THUMB.
THAT DEPENDS ON WHERE ONE'S THUMB HAS BEEN. C'MON, WE'LL HAVE TO SAY A PRAYER AND HOOF IT.
TELL YOU WHAT, YOU PRAY THAT I DON'T STOMP YOU WITH MY HOOF.
YOU ARE SO LAZY. WHY DON'T YOU HAVE ANY DRIVE?
BECAUSE THE CAR BROKE DOWN.
YOU'RE SO OUT OF THE LOOP THAT IF THE WORLD ENDED TOMORROW YOU'D BE THE LAST TO FIND OUT. HAW HAW.
HOW WOULD ANYONE ELSE KNOW ABOUT IT IF IT HADN'T ALREADY HAPPENED YET?
I FEEL SORRY FOR YOUR TEACHER. HOW IS SHE DOING?
SHE'S NOT LONG FOR THIS WORLD.
THEN WHAT WORLD IS SHE LONG FOR?
THE WORLD WITH NO NAME.
WHY'S IT CALLED THAT?
NO. IT'S NOT CALLED THAT.
ANYWAY, TELL HER I SAID HI.
NO. LET'S NOT SCARE HE
I CAN'T SEE OURSELVES SURVIVING THE NIGHT UNLESS WE FIND SHELTER.
WHAT'S THE USE? TEACHER SAYS WE'RE ALREADY DOOMED ANYWAY.
IS SHE PATRIOTIC?
NO. SHE'S AN ANT.
WHAT DOES YOUR TEACHER HAVE TO SAY ABOUT THE PROBLEM OF PATRIOTISM?
SHE SAYS IT'S ONE OF THE WORST PROBLEMS FACING THE PEOPLE OF THE WORLD.
WOULD YOU EXPLAIN TO OUR AUDIENCE WHAT THAT MEANS?
A PRONOUN OR ADJECTIVE DENOTING A PERSON OR THING MENTIONED, INDICATED OR UNDERSTOOD.
DOES SHE HAVE A NOTION HOW TO KEEP THE MENACE OF PATRIOTISM AT BAY?
WELL, MAYBE THE NO SWIMMING SIGNS OUGHT TO COME DOWN.
AND THERE YOU GO AGAIN MAKING LIGHT OF SOMETHING SERIOUS. WHY ARE YOU SO SILLY?
I GUESS I'M JUST HAPPY BECAUSE THE WORLD WILL END SOON.
WHY IS YOUR TEACHER SUCH A CREPE HANGER? SHE MUST BE FULL OF CREPE. HAW HAW.
I CAN'T WAIT UNTIL YOU DIE AND THAT EVIL LAUGH IS SILENCED FOREVER.
WHAT WOULD YOUR TEACHER DO IF HER CAR BROKE DOWN IN THE MIDDLE OF WHO KNOWS WHERE?
WELL, SHE'D PROBABLY DIE OF EXPOSURE.
STOP TRYING TO GET SYMPATHY FOR HER. IT DOESN'T WORK.
WHILE WE'RE ON THE SUBJECT, I'D LIKE TO KNOW WHAT YOUR TEACHER HAS TO SAY ABOUT THE PROBLEM OF FLAG ETIQUETTE?
FOR STARTERS KEEP IN MIND THAT IT WON'T GO AWAY IF YOU PUT A BLINDFOLD ON. EVERYBODY JUST OUGHT TO BE REAL CAREFUL WHERE THEY PLANT THEIR FLAGPOLES. MAKE CERTAIN IT'S NOT OVER AN ANTHILL. YOU WOULD NOT BELIEVE THE NUMBER OF ANTS CRAWLING AROUND WITH HEADACHES.
WHY YOU TALKING ABOUT ANTS?
BECAUSE TEACHER'S ONE.
YOU HAVE A ONE YEAR OLD FOR A TEACHER? NO WONDER YOU'RE SO DUMB.
IT'S OKAY BECAUSE SHE'S AN ANT.
I'VE GOT A BAD COUGH. I DON'T THINK I CAN GO ON MUCH LONGER WITHOUT A PLACE TO STAY.
SAY, LOOK OVER THERE. SEE THE BRIDGE?
OH NO. I'M NOT STAYING UNDER A BRIDGE. I'M NOT A TROLL.
NO, I MEAN YOU SHOULD JUMP OFF IT AND PUT AN END TO OUR PAIN.
DO YOU KNOW WHAT THE THEME OF PATRIOTISM IS ABOUT.
UH HUH, PATRIOTISM.
HOW DO YOU KNOW SO MUCH ABOUT IT?
WHENEVER A KID DOES SOMETHING BAD IN SCHOOL, THE PUNISHMENT IS HAVIN TO LISTEN TO PATRIOT PROPAGAND
THEN YOU MUST BE AN EXPERT BY NOW.
TELL ME, WHAT DOES YOUR TEACHER SAY ABOUT PAUL REVERE?
NOTHING BUT THE WORST.
WHY'S THAT? ISN'T HE REMEMBERED AS A HERO?
NOT BY ALL THE ANTS THAT GOT RUN OVER DURING THAT DEMENTED MIDNIGHT RIDE.
WHAT DOES SHE SAY ABOUT GEORGE WASHINGTON?
THAT NO-GOOD BUM?
WHY IS SHE SO HARD ON HIM?
BECAUSE HE DIDN'T MENTION ANTS ONCE IN HIS FAREWELL ADDRESS. HOW RUDE TO LEAVE WITHOUT SAYING GOODBYE.
THIS IS FAR AS I CAN GO. MY BONES NEED A REST.
OH NO YOU DON'T, YOU LAZY SCHWEINHUND.
OW OW OW! I'M OUT OF GAS. BOO HOO HOO! THIS WILL HAVE TO BE MY FINAL RESTING PLACE.
HEY LOOK, SEE? SEE? SEE THE HAUNTED HOUSE?
MAYBE WE BETTER NOT GO INSIDE BECAUSE A GHOST MIGHT KILL US.
TELL YOU WHAT, YOU GO IN FIRST BECAUSE YOU'D BE THE LEAST MISSED.
GUESS WHAT? THIS IS WHERE MY TEACHER LIVES.
YOUR TEACHER LIVES IN A HAUNTED HOUSE? NOW YOU GOT ME FEELING SORRY FOR THE GHOSTS.
BUT EVERYONE GETS ALONG FINE... MOST OF THE TIME. TOO BAD THERE'S ONLY ONE BATHROOM.
I BET SHE DOESN'T GET MUCH COMPANY LIVING IN A DUMP LIKE THIS.
TRUE, BUT SHE ALSO DOESN'T GET MANY CREDITORS COMING AROUND EITHER.
HAUNTED HOUSE
AFTER YOU.
DON'T GIVE ME ANY OF THAT. YOU LEAD THE WAY.
WE BETTER NOT MAKE TOO MUCH NOISE. WE DON'T WANT TO SCARE HER TOO MUCH.
SHE MUST NOT FRIGHTEN TOO EASILY IF SHE LIVES IN SUCH A CREEPY PLACE.
AND YOU DON'T KNOW EVERYTHING.
NOBODY ASKED ME BUT IN MY OPINION THIS PLACE IS WAY TOO BIG FOR ONE ANT.
TO AN ANT EVERYTHING IS WAY TOO BIG.
SHE MUST NOT BE VERY PATRIOTIC. I DON'T SEE ANY FLAGS. NOT EVEN A DECAL OR WINDSOCK. WHERE'S HER SPIRIT?
AW, THIS PLACE IS FULL OF SPIRITS.
WHAT'S YOUR TEACHER SAY ABOUT THE THEME OF PATRIOTISM?
SHE SAYS THAT THINGS AREN'T ALWAYS WHAT THEY THEME.
WHERE IS SHE, HIDING IN THE WOODWORK LIKE A COCKROACH?
NEIN. SHE MUST HAVE GONE OVER TO SEE HER DEALER.
I KNEW IT. SHE LIKES TO PARTY.
NO. I MEAN AT THE BLACKJACK TABLE.
NOW YOU'RE SAYING SHE HAS A GAMBLING PROBLEM. NOT MUCH OF A ROLE MODEL, HUH?
SHE'S NOT MUCH OF ANYTHING BUT WHAT THERE IS OF HER IS MORE THAN ENOUGH.
WHAT DO WE DO NOW?
WELL, WE COULD JUST WAIT AROUND UNTIL SOMEONE KILLS US.
WE MIGHT AS WELL MAKE OURSELVES AT HOME.
HOW CAN WE DO THAT IF WE AREN'T EVEN HOME?
THEN PRETEND YOU'RE HOME.
FINE, BUT I'LL HAVE TO PRETEND YOU'RE STILL HERE.
YOU WON'T NEED TO BECAUSE I'M ALREADY HERE, RIGHT?
THIS PLACE IS A MESS. LOOK AT THE DIRTY PLATES ON THE FLOOR. SEE THE SILVERWARE BEHIND THE CUSHION? LOOK AT THE TORN DRAPERY. YOUR TEACHER ISN'T JUST AN ANT, SHE'S ALSO A PIG.
AND WHAT MAKES YOU THINK SHE MADE THIS MESS? IT'S PROBABLY THE GHOSTS' FAULT.
THAT'S RIGHT, WHEN ALL ELSE FAILS BLAME THE GHOSTS. BAH HAH HAH.
AND YOU'LL MAKE A FINE GHOST WITH THAT AWFUL LAUGH.
DO ANTS AND GHOSTS MAKE GOOD ROOMMATES?
SURE. THAT'S BECAUSE ANTS NEVER COMPLAIN.
TELL ME, ARE THE GHOSTS PATRIOTIC?
WELL, THAT WAS SOME PAGEANT THEY PUT ON LAST MAY DAY.
DO THEY MAKE A BIG DEAL OUT OF EARTH DAY?
THEY HAVE NO INTEREST IN SUCH AN OCCASION SINCE THEY ARE NOT OF THIS EARTH.
WHAT DOES YOUR TEACHER DO FOR LAUGHS?
NOTHING AT ALL.
WHY NOT?
BECAUSE WHAT HAVE LAUGHS DONE FOR HER? BESIDES, SHE'S TIRED OF BEING MOCKED OUT.
WHO MOCKS HER OUT?
ALL THE MOCKINGBIRDS.
WHAT'S HER FAVORITE SECTION OF THE NEWSPAPER?
THE OBIT PAGES. THEY'RE DROPPING LIKE FLIES, FOLKS.
WHY DOES SHE EVEN CARE?
LET'S JUST SAY SHE LIKES TO SCREEN ANY POTENTIAL NEW HOUSEMATES.
IT LOOKS LIKE YOUR TEACHER ISN'T THE ONLY BUG AROUND HERE. LOOK AT ALL THE SPIDER WEBS.
NO. TEACHER MADE THEM HERSELF AS A LITTLE JOKE. TEE HEE! ISN'T SHE THE MOST WONDERFUL BEING OF ALL TIME?
OH STOP IT. QUIT TRUMPETING HER AS THE GREATEST THING SINCE VENETIAN BLINDS.
DID YOUR TEACHER EVER LEARN YOU ABOUT THE TYPE OF GOVERNMENT WE HAVE?
UH HUH. IT'S SOME SORT OF PUPPET STATE, ISN'T IT?
NO. IT'S A DEMOCRACY. DO YOU HAVE ANY IDEA WHAT THAT'S ALL ABOUT?
IT HAS SOMETHING TO DO WITH DEMONS, RIGHT?
NO. IT'S A SYSTEM WHERE DECISIONS ARE MADE ACCORDING TO THE WISHES OF THE MAJORITY. DO YOU UNDERSTAND?
UH HUH. IT MEANS THAT THE MAN WHO GETS THE MOST VOTES IN A PRESIDENTIAL ELECTION LOSES.
WHAT'S THE MOST IMPORTANT LESSON IN PATRIOTISM YOU EVER LEARNED?
I'M MOST IMPRESSED BY THE NUMBER OF ANTS WHO REALIZE THE IMPLICATION OF THIS MENACE. NEXT TIME YOU SEE AN ANT IT WOULD BE NICE IF YOU SALUTED.
UH HUH. WITH MY HEEL.
AND I CAN'T WAIT UNTIL YOU DIE.
WHY WOULD YOUR TEACHER WANT TO LIVE IN A PLACE AS BAD AS THIS?
WELL, ONE GOOD THING IS SHE NEVER HAS TO BUY HALLOWEEN DECORATIONS.
I'M DISAPPOINTED THAT SHE LIVES IN SUCH A FILTHY PLACE. SHAME ON HER AND SHAME ON YOU TOO.
BUT IT'S OKAY BECAUSE IT DOESN'T MATTER.
DOES TOO.
WRONG AGAIN.
HEY, I JUST HEARD THE FRONT DOOR SLAM.
HOORAY. TEACHER MUST HAVE COME HOME.
WAIT A MINUTE, HOW COULD A TINY ANT MANAGE TO SLAM A BIG OL' WOODEN DOOR?
THAT'S NOTHING. YOU OUGHT TO SEE HOW SHE OPENS IT.
WHY IS SHE SLAMMING DOORS ANYWAY?
SHE GETS LIKE THAT WHEN SHE'S HUNGOVER.
SHE'S BEEN ON THE BOTTLE, HUH?
NO. THE CLOTHESLINE.
WHAT WAS SHE DOING ON THE CLOTHESLINE?
HANGING ON.
TELL ME, HOW DOES AN ANT MANAGE TO CORRECT A BIG OL' PILE OF TEST PAPERS?
EASY. SHE FAILS EVERYONE.
TELL ME, DOES YOUR TEACHER MAKE EVERYBODY STAND AT ATTENTION LIKE STATUES BEFORE THE FLAG IN YOUR CLASSROOM?
NEIN. FLAGS ARE VERBOTEN IN THE CLASS.
TELL ME, WHY? IS SHE A TERRORIST?
NOT JUST THAT. SHE LIKES BEING THE CENTRE OF ATTENTION AND DOESN'T LIKE BEING UPSTAGED BY ANY UNSEEMLY DECORATIONS.
ARE YOU LEARNING HOW TO BE A GOOD PATRIOT IN SCHOOL? THERE'S MORE TO IT THAN SALUTES AND HIGH FIVES.
OF COURSE. WE ARE ALSO PROGRAMMED TO REPORT INSTANCES OF SEDITION TO THE AUTHORITIES.
OH, I GET IT. YOU'RE LEARNING TO BE A SNITCH. WHAT HAPPENS WHEN SOMEONE NARCS ON YOU?
THE WIND SOUNDS LIKE A WEREWOLF, NO?
STOP TRYING TO CHANGE THE SUBJECT.
WHAT'S YOUR TEACHER SAY ABOUT STUDENT PROTESTERS? ARE THEY JAKE BY HER STANDARDS?
NO DOUBT. THE MORE THE BETTER. THERE'S SO MUCH TO FIND FAULT WITH.
WHAT DOES SHE THINK WORKS BEST, SIT-INS OR WALK-OUTS?
SHE PREFERS DRIVE-THRUS.
WHAT ADVICE DOES SHE HAVE FOR THE PEOPLE OF THE WORLD AS WE FACE THE PROBLEM OF PATRIOTISM?
I HEARD THAT WORD ONCE. WHAT DOES IT MEAN?
IT'S WHEN A GROUP OF PEOPLE THINK THEY'RE BETTER THAN EVERYBODY ELSE.
IT'S ALL RIGHT. EVERYONE GO EASY. DEFINITELY. WHAT IS IS.
THE END FOR SURE

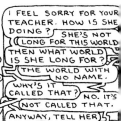

I AM OF NO COUNTRY

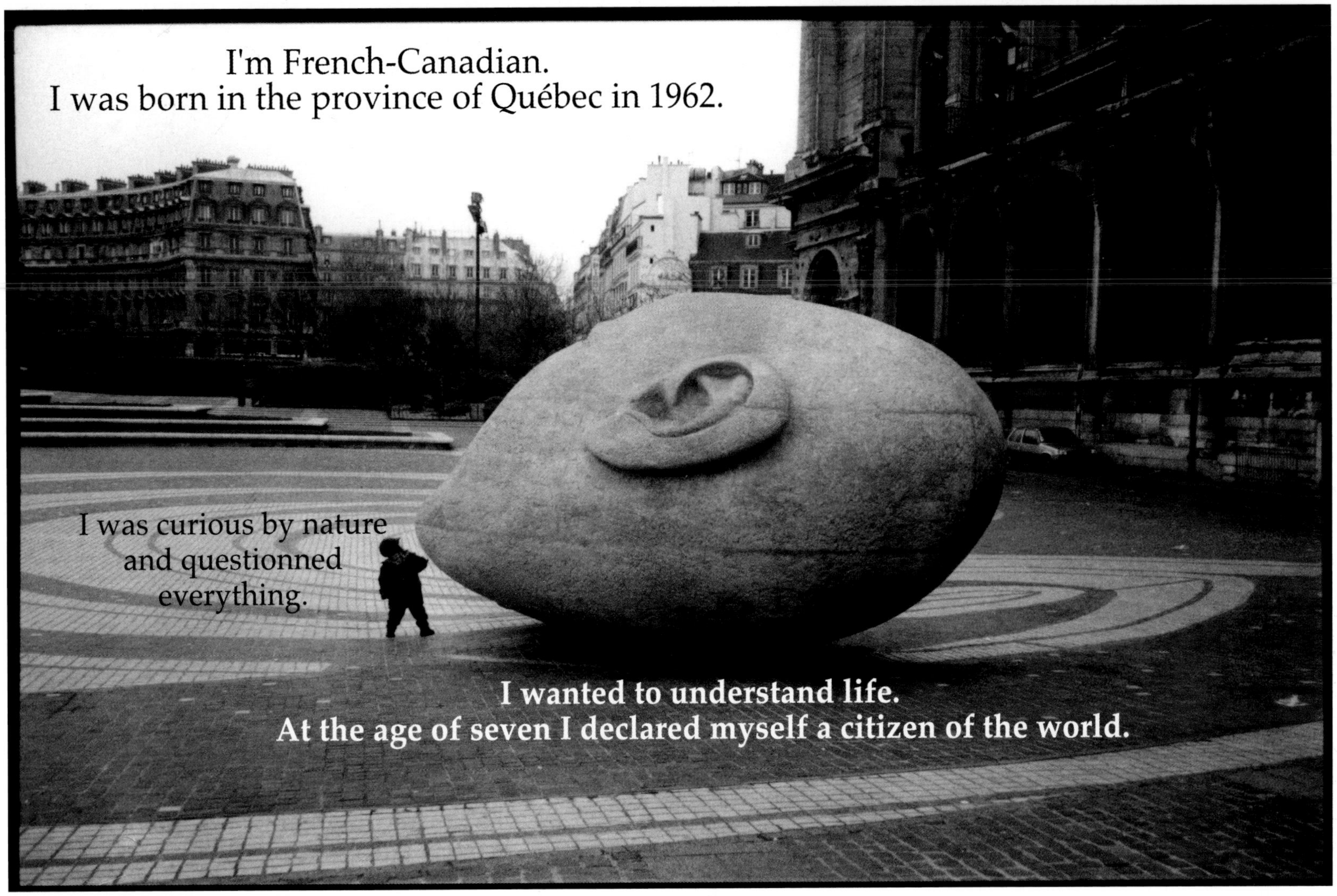
I'm French-Canadian.
I was born in the province of Québec in 1962.
I was curious by nature and questionned everything.
I wanted to understand life.
At the age of seven I declared myself a citizen of the world.

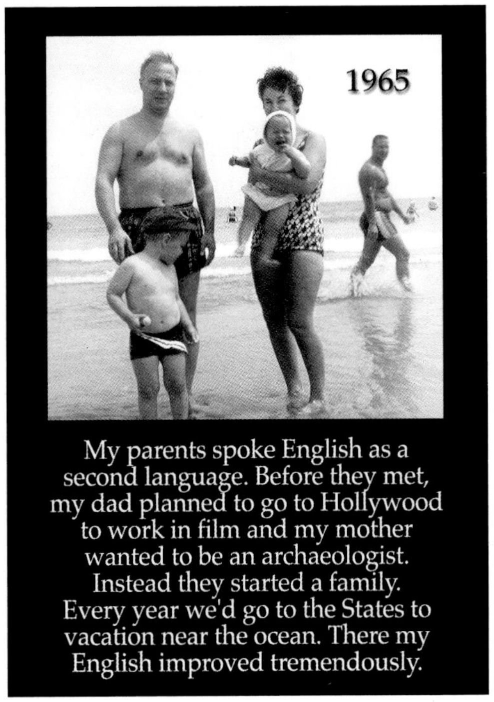
1965
My parents spoke English as a second language. Before they met, my dad planned to go to Hollywood to work in film and my mother wanted to be an archaeologist. Instead they started a family. Every year we'd go to the States to vacation near the ocean. There my English improved tremendously.

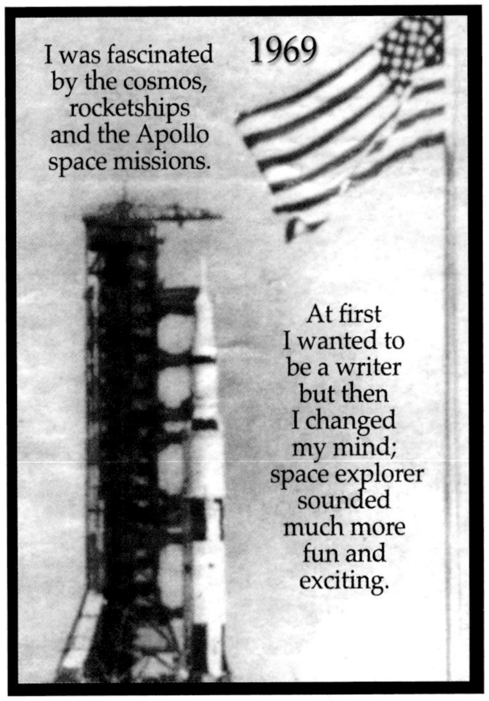
I was fascinated by the cosmos, rocketships and the Apollo space missions.
1969
At first I wanted to be a writer but then I changed my mind; space explorer sounded much more fun and exciting.

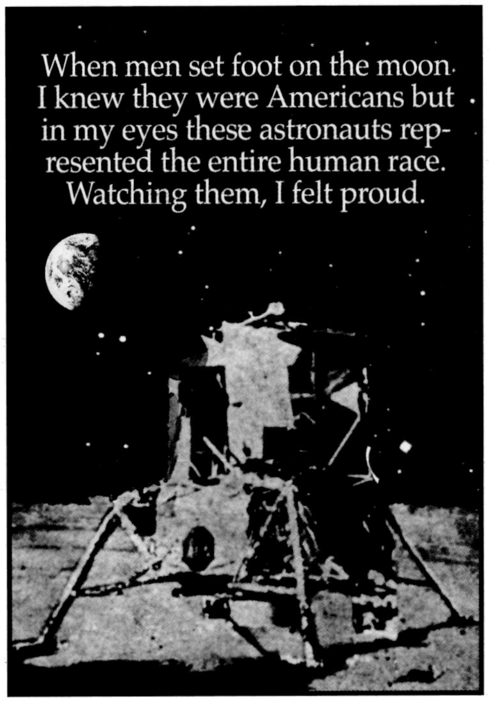
When men set foot on the moon. I knew they were Americans but in my eyes these astronauts represented the entire human race. Watching them, I felt proud.

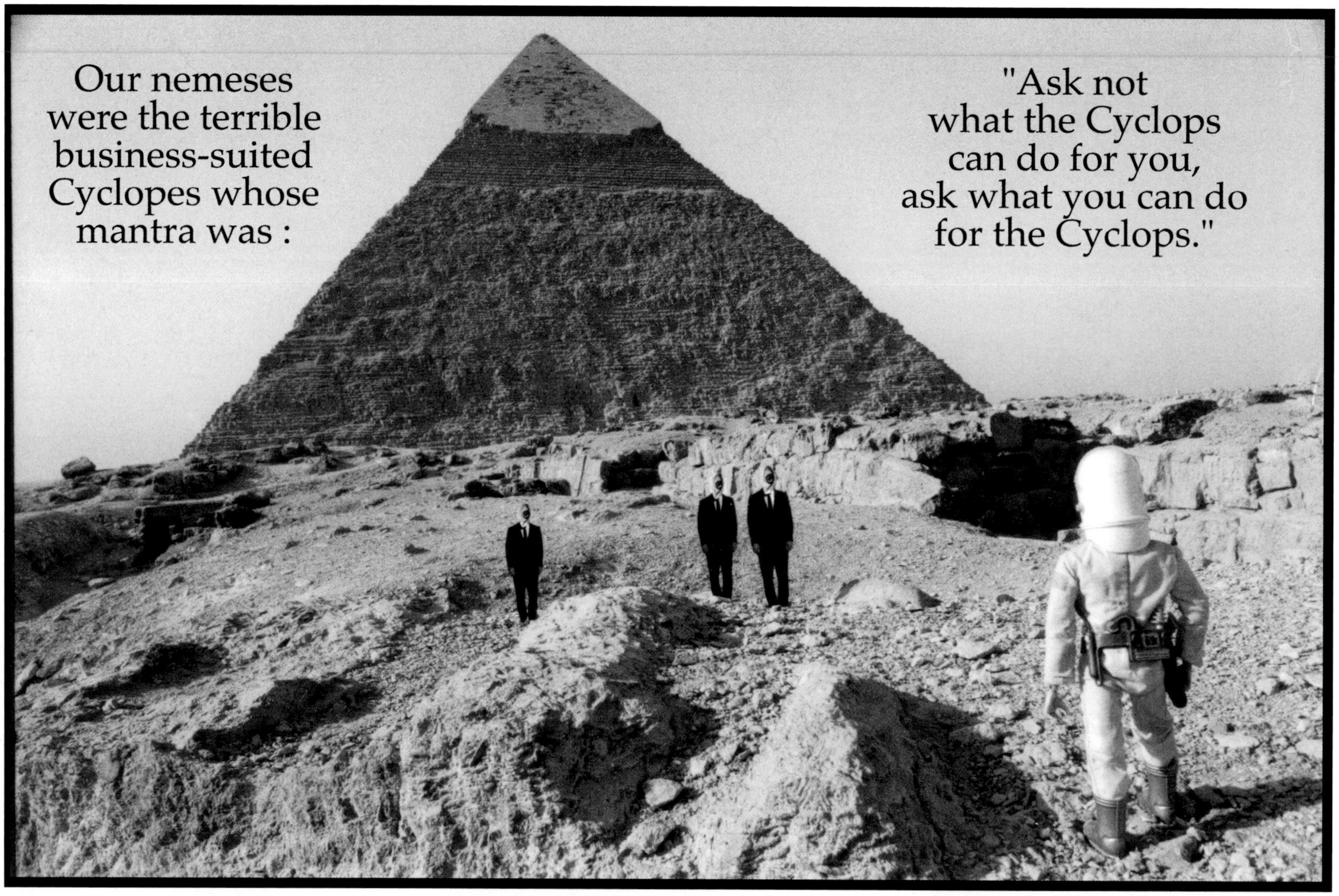
Our nemeses were the terrible business-suited Cyclopes whose mantra was :
"Ask not what the Cyclops can do for you, ask what you can do for the Cyclops."

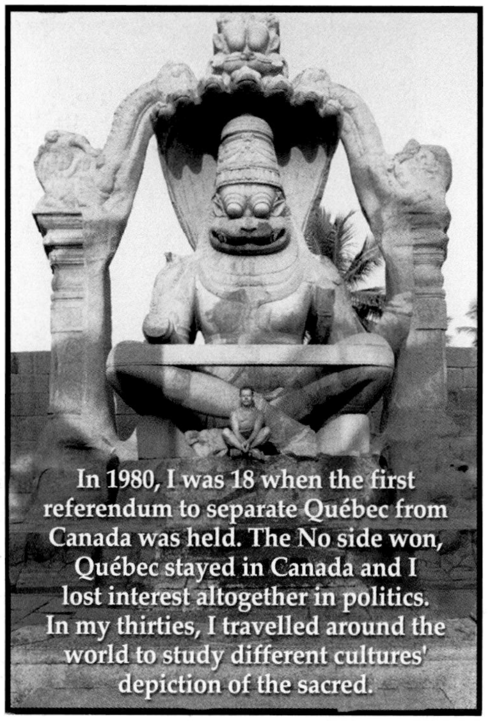
In 1980, I was 18 when the first referendum to separate Québec from Canada was held. The No side won, Québec stayed in Canada and I lost interest altogether in politics. In my thirties, I travelled around the world to study different cultures' depiction of the sacred.

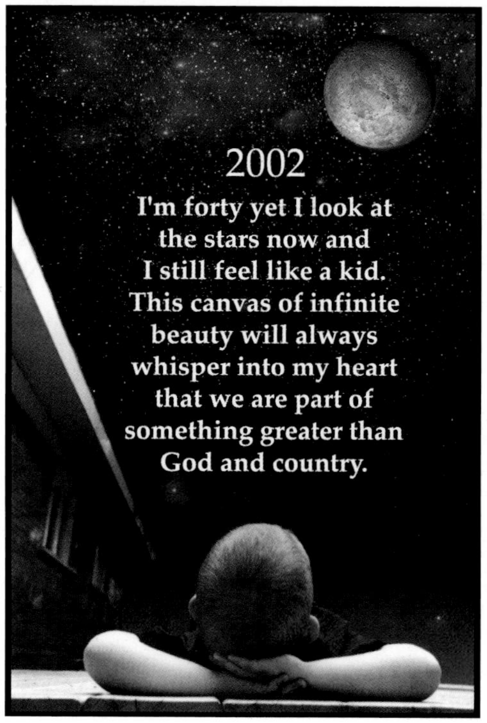
2002
I'm forty yet I look at the stars now and I still feel like a kid. This canvas of infinite beauty will always whisper into my heart that we are part of something greater than God and country.

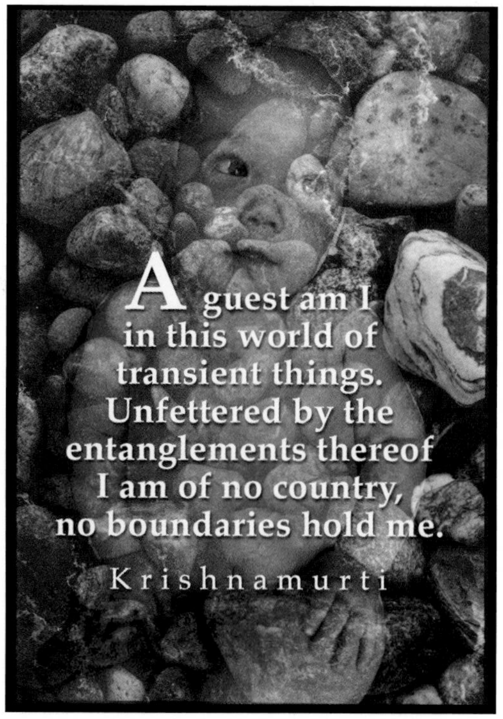
A guest am I in this world of transient things. Unfettered by the entanglements thereof I am of no country, no boundaries hold me.
Krishnamurti

Written, photographed and directed by Marc Tessier

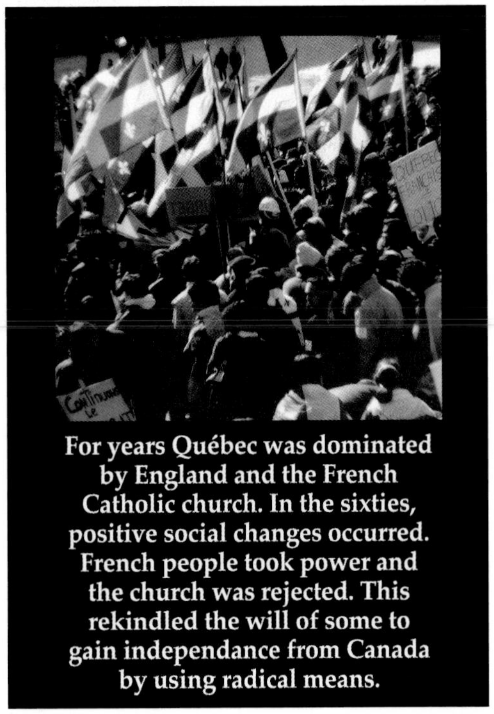
For years Québec was dominated by England and the French Catholic church. In the sixties, positive social changes occurred. French people took power and the church was rejected. This rekindled the will of some to gain independance from Canada by using radical means.

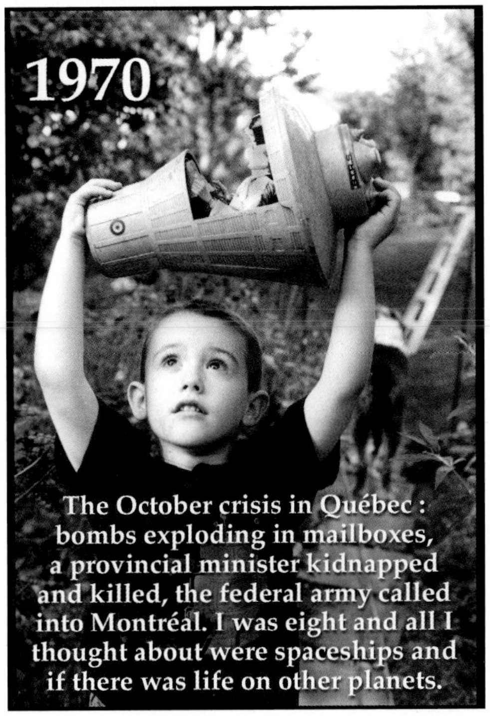
1970
The October crisis in Québec : bombs exploding in mailboxes, a provincial minister kidnapped and killed, the federal army called into Montréal. I was eight and all I thought about were spaceships and if there was life on other planets.

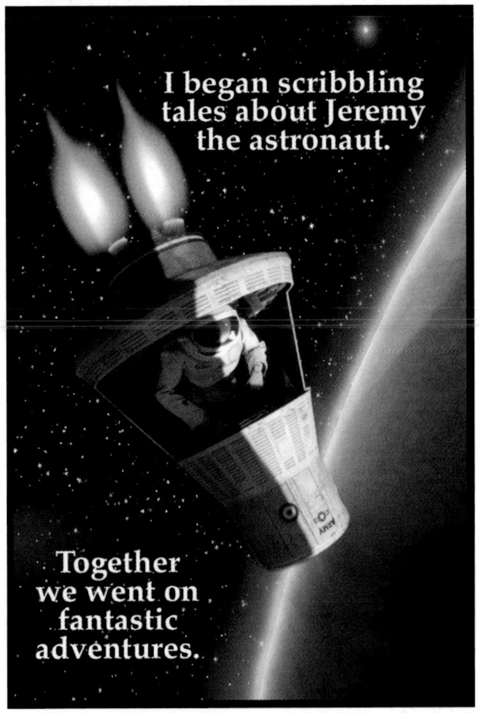
I began scribbling tales about Jeremy the astronaut.
Together we went on fantastic adventures.

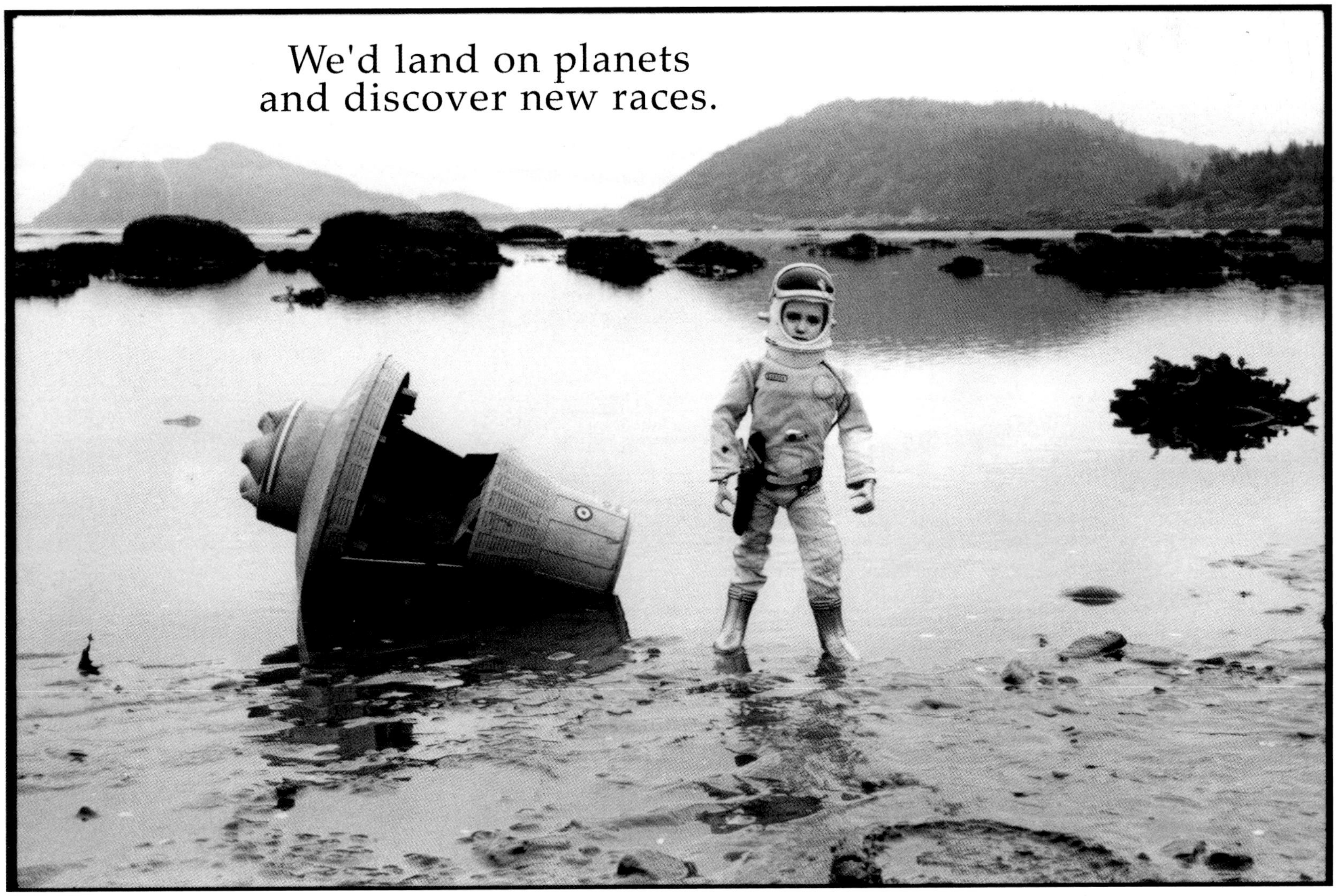
We'd land on planets and discover new races.

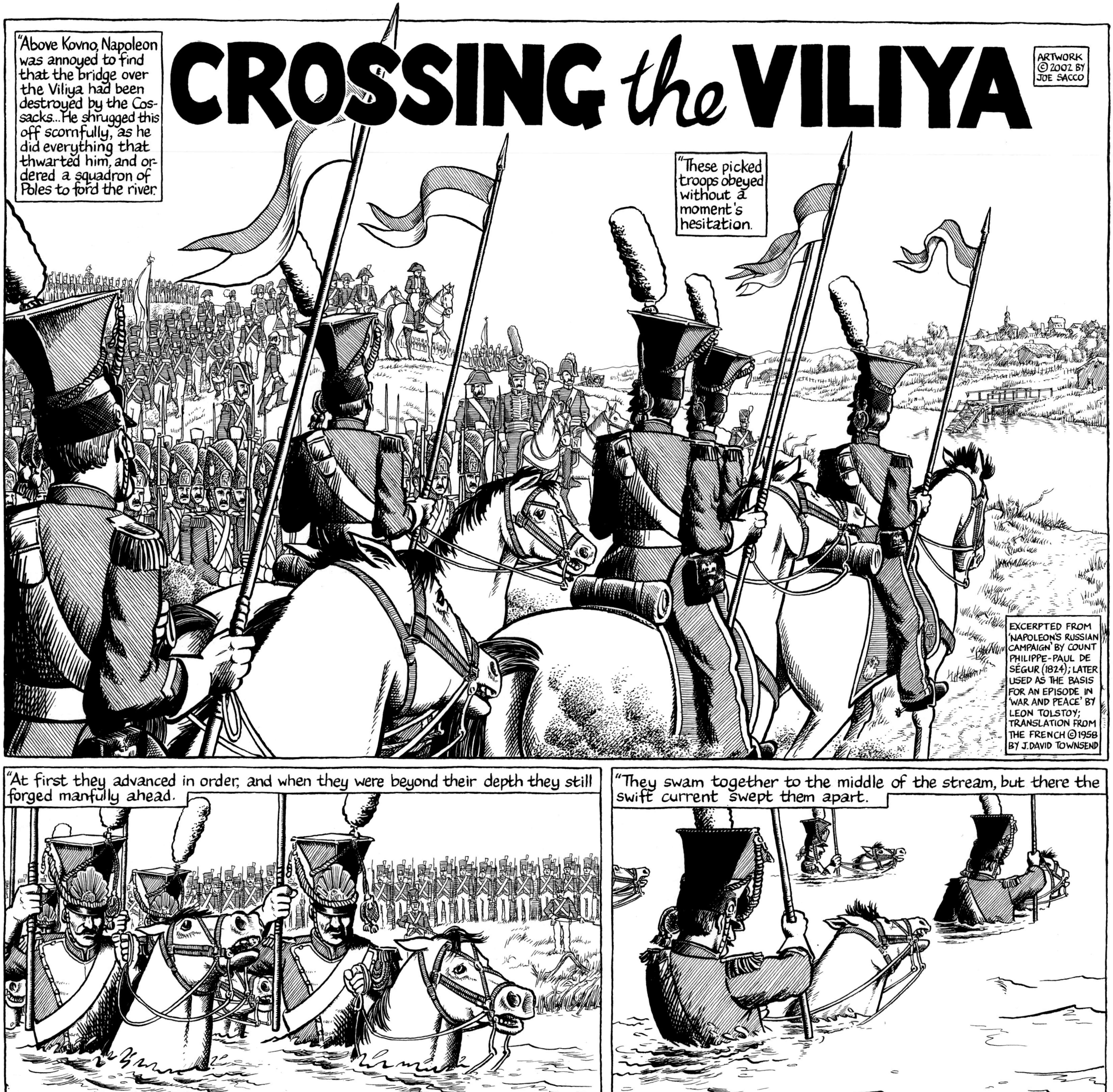
"Above Kovno, Napoleon was annoyed to find that the bridge over the Viliya had been destroyed by the Cossacks... He shrugged this off scornfully, as he did everything that thwarted him, and ordered a squadron of Poles to ford the river.
CROSSING the VILIYA
ARTWORK © 2002 BY JOE SACCO
"These picked troops obeyed without a moment's hesitation.
EXCERPTED FROM 'NAPOLEON'S RUSSIAN CAMPAIGN' BY COUNT PHILIPPE-PAUL DE SÉGUR (1824); LATER USED AS THE BASIS FOR AN EPISODE IN 'WAR AND PEACE' BY LEON TOLSTOY; TRANSLATION FROM THE FRENCH © 1958 BY J. DAVID TOWNSEND
"At first they advanced in order, and when they were beyond their depth they still forged manfully ahead.
"They swam together to the middle of the stream, but there the swift current swept them apart.
J. SACCO 8-02

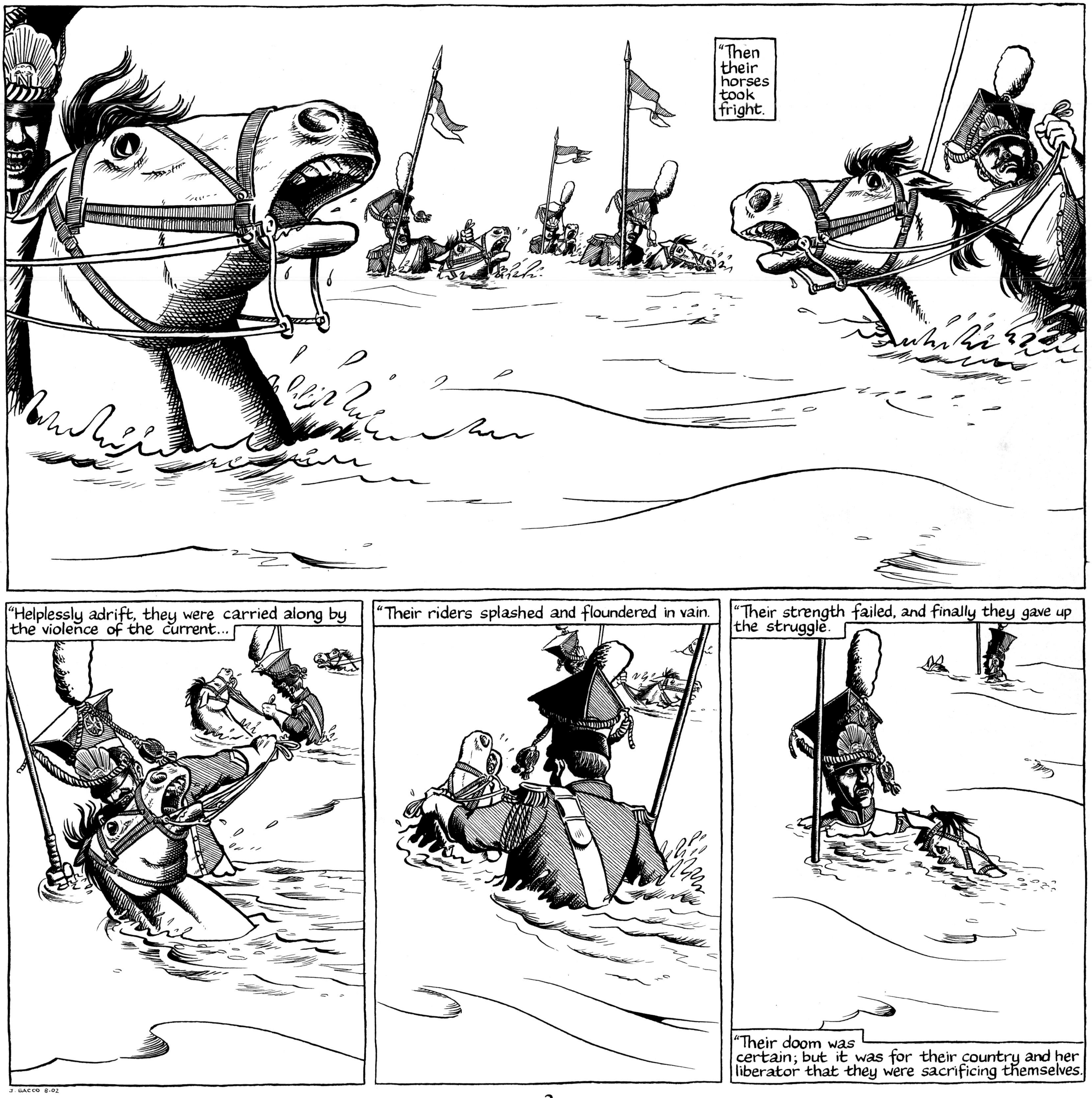
"Then their horses took fright.
"Helplessly adrift, they were carried along by the violence of the current...
"Their riders splashed and floundered in vain.
"Their strength failed, and finally they gave up the struggle.
"Their doom was certain; but it was for their country and her liberator that they were sacrificing themselves.
J. SACCO 8-02

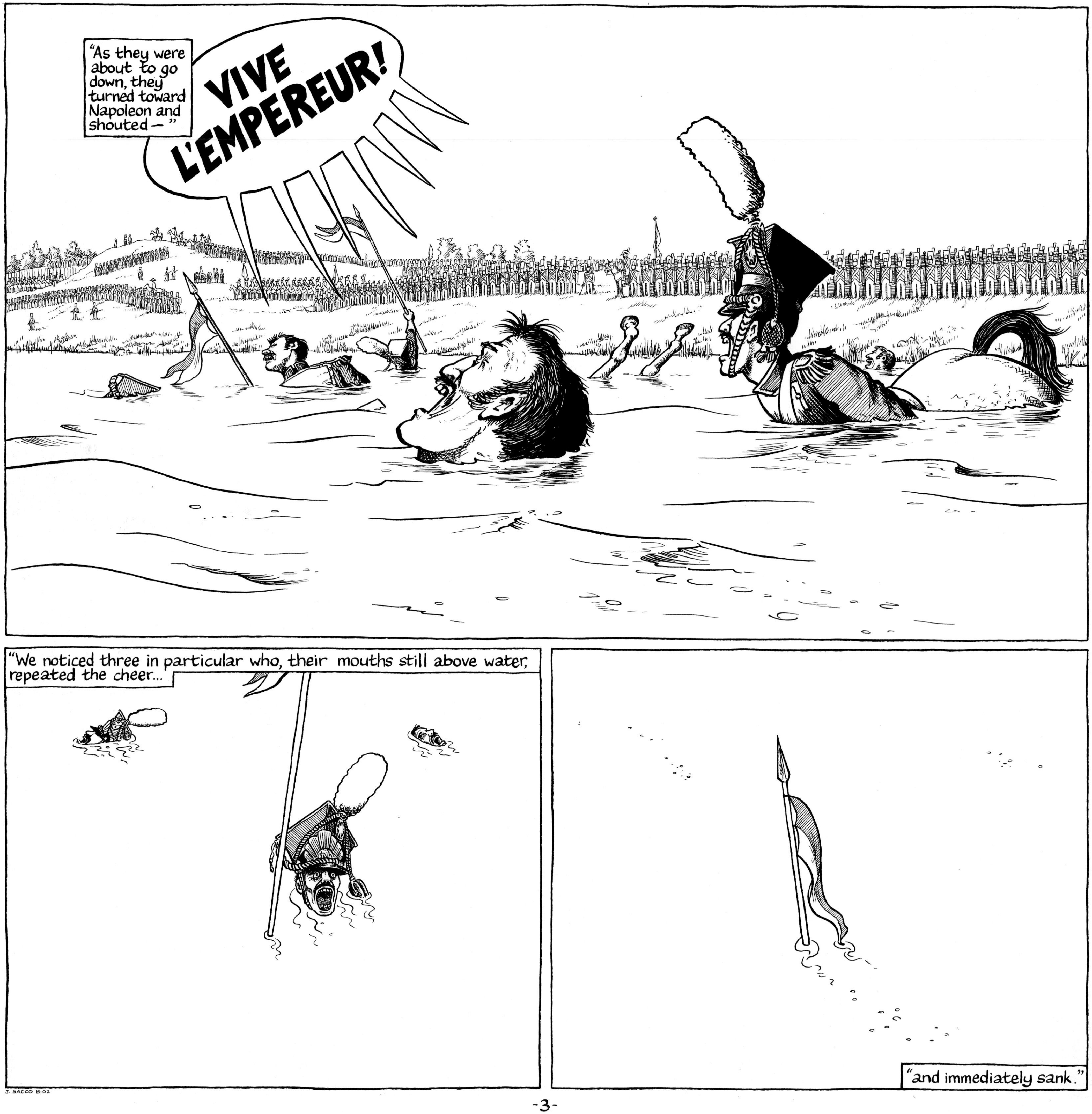
"As they were about to go down, they turned toward Napoleon and shouted— "
VIVE L'EMPEREUR!
"We noticed three in particular who, their mouths still above water, repeated the cheer...
"and immediately sank."
J. SACCO 8·02

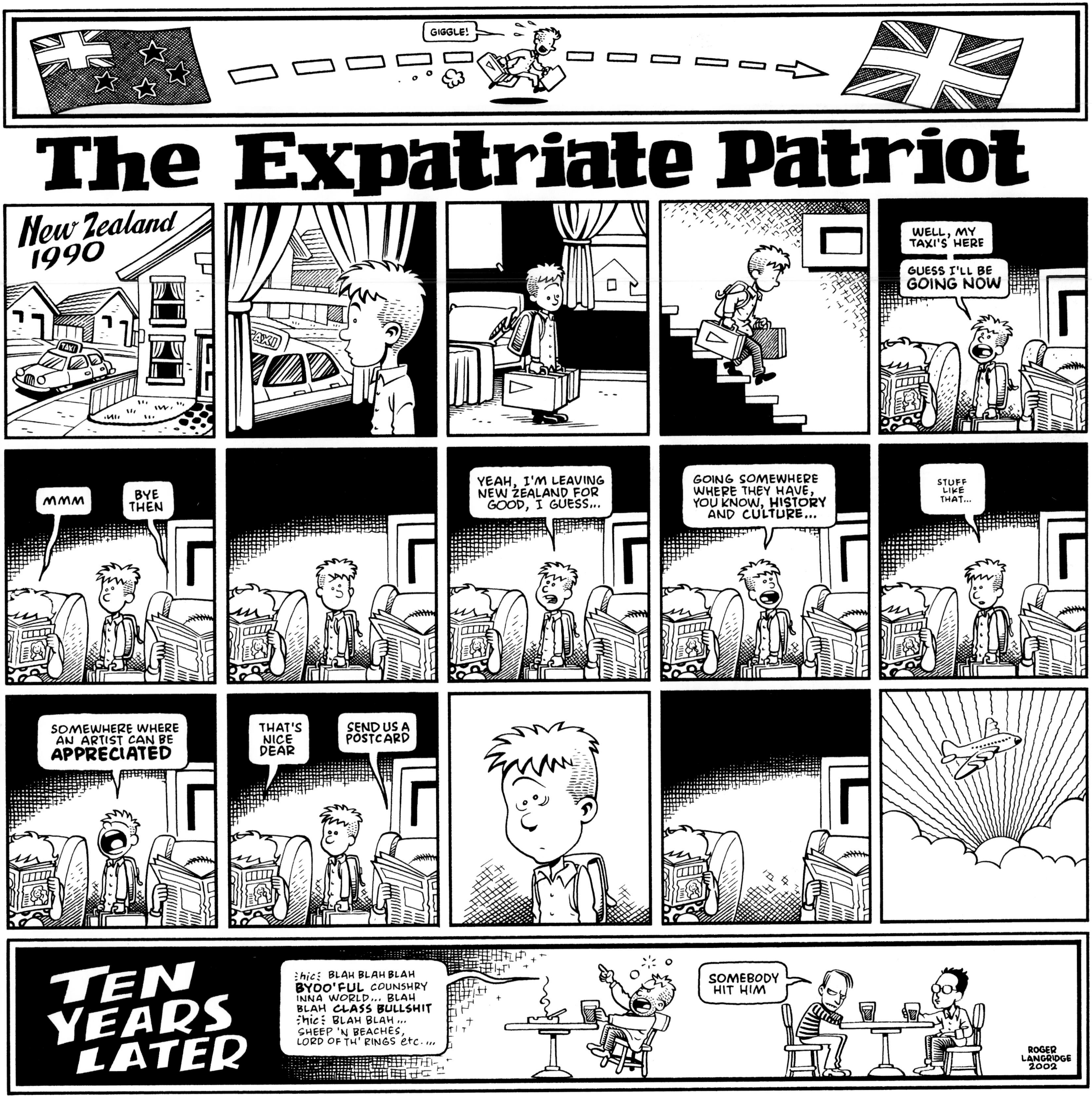
GIGGLE!
The Expatriate Patriot
New Zealand 1990
TAXI
TAXI
WELL, MY TAXI'S HERE
GUESS I'LL BE GOING NOW
MMM
BYE THEN
YEAH, I'M LEAVING NEW ZEALAND FOR GOOD, I GUESS...
GOING SOMEWHERE WHERE THEY HAVE, YOU KNOW, HISTORY AND CULTURE...
STUFF LIKE THAT...
SOMEWHERE WHERE AN ARTIST CAN BE APPRECIATED
THAT'S NICE DEAR
SEND US A POSTCARD
TEN YEARS LATER
hic BLAH BLAH BLAH BYOO'FUL COUNSHRY INNA WORLD... BLAH BLAH CLASS BULLSHIT hic BLAH BLAH... SHEEP 'N BEACHES, LORD OF TH' RINGS etc....
SOMEBODY HIT HIM
ROGER LANGRIDGE 2002

UNCLE BOB

BY MARK KALESNIKO © 2002

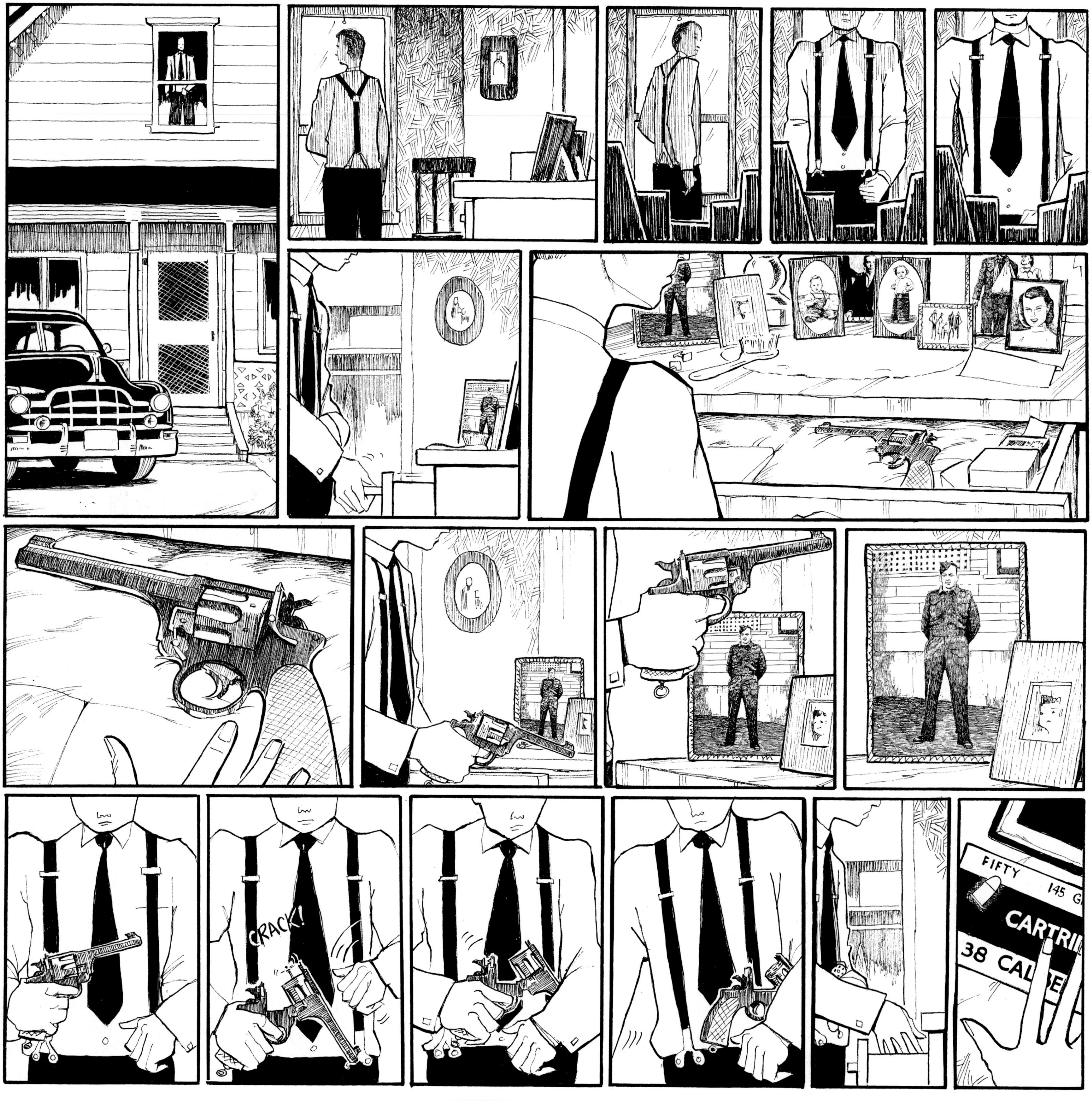
CRACK!
FIFTY
145 G
CARTRI
38 CAL

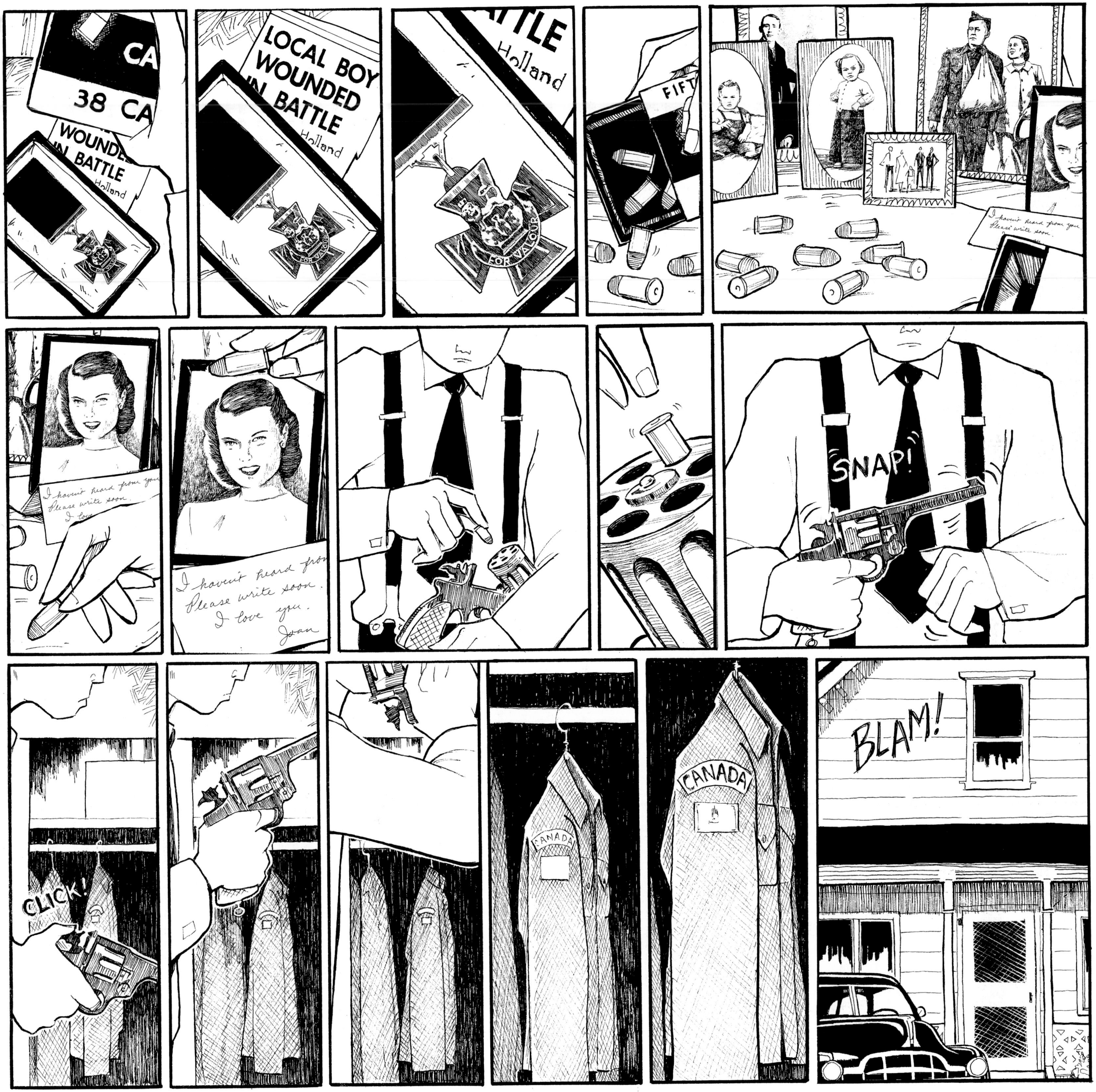
38 CA
WOUNDE
IN BATTLE
Holland
LOCAL BOY WOUNDED IN BATTLE
Holland
FOR VALOUR
TTLE
Holland
FOR VALOUR
FIFT
I haven't heard from you.
Please write soon.
I haven't heard from you
Please write soon.
I love
I haven't heard from
Please write soon.
I love you.
Joan
SNAP!
CLICK!
CANADA
CANADA
BLAM!

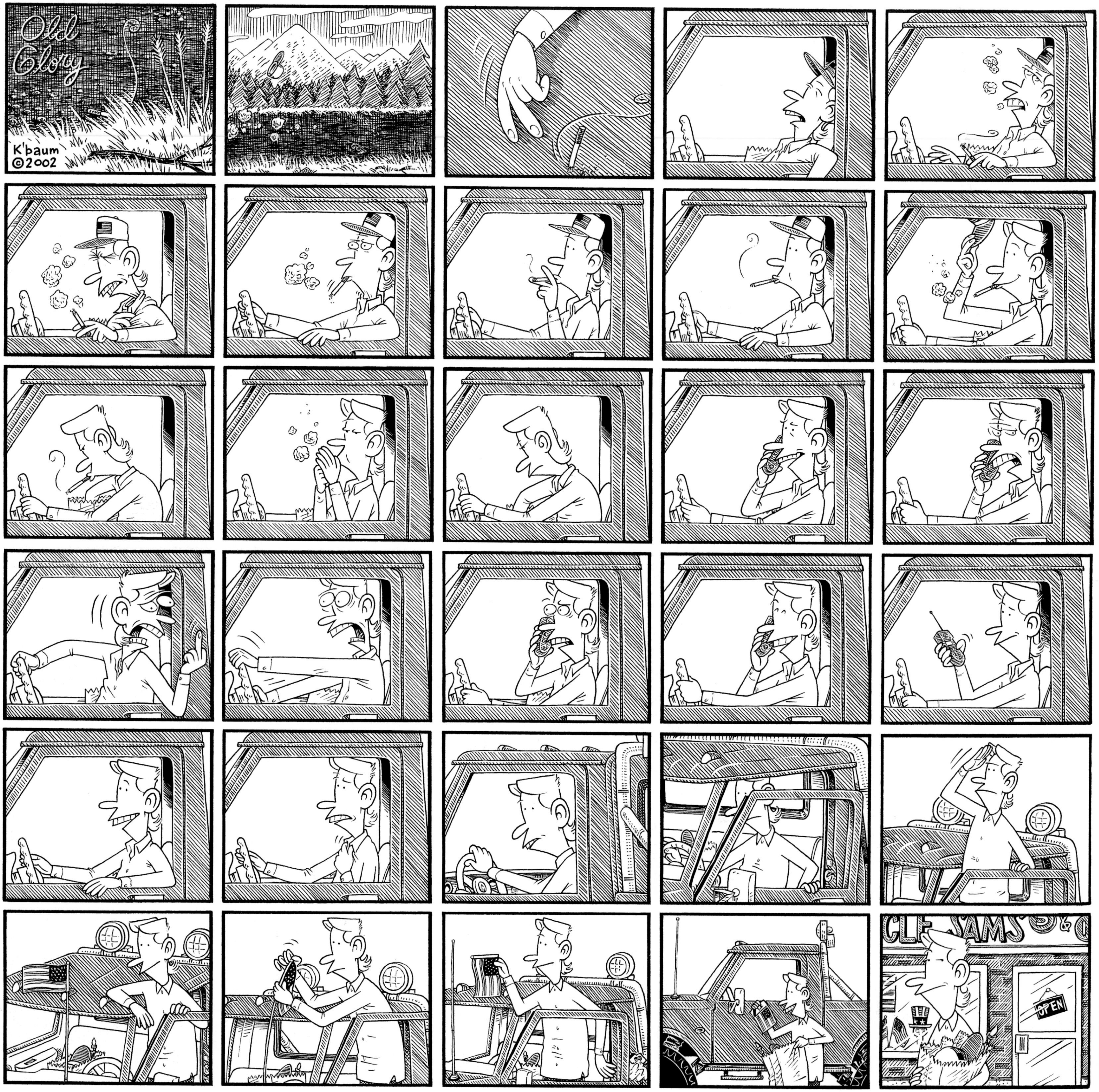
Old Glory
K'baum
©2002
CLE SAMS
OPEN

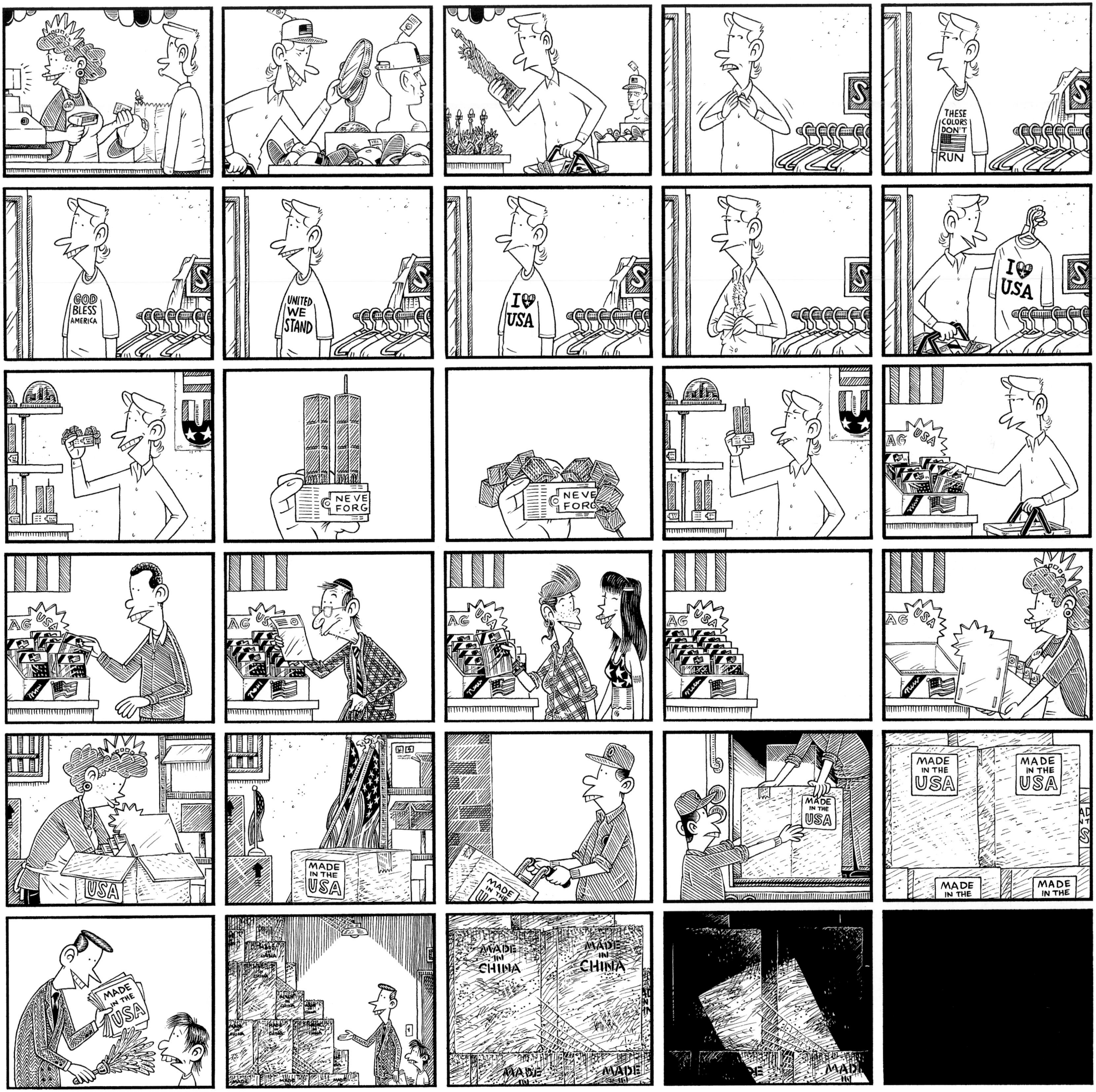
THESE COLORS DON'T RUN
GOD BLESS AMERICA
UNITED WE STAND
I ♥ USA
I ♥ USA
NEVE FORG
NEVE FORG
AG USA
AG USA
AG USA
AG USA
AG USA
AG USA
USA
MADE IN THE USA
MADE IN THE U
MADE IN THE USA
MADE IN THE USA
MADE IN THE USA
MADE IN THE
MADE IN THE
MADE IN THE USA
MADE IN CHINA
MADE IN CHINA
MADE IN
MADE IN
DE
MADE IN

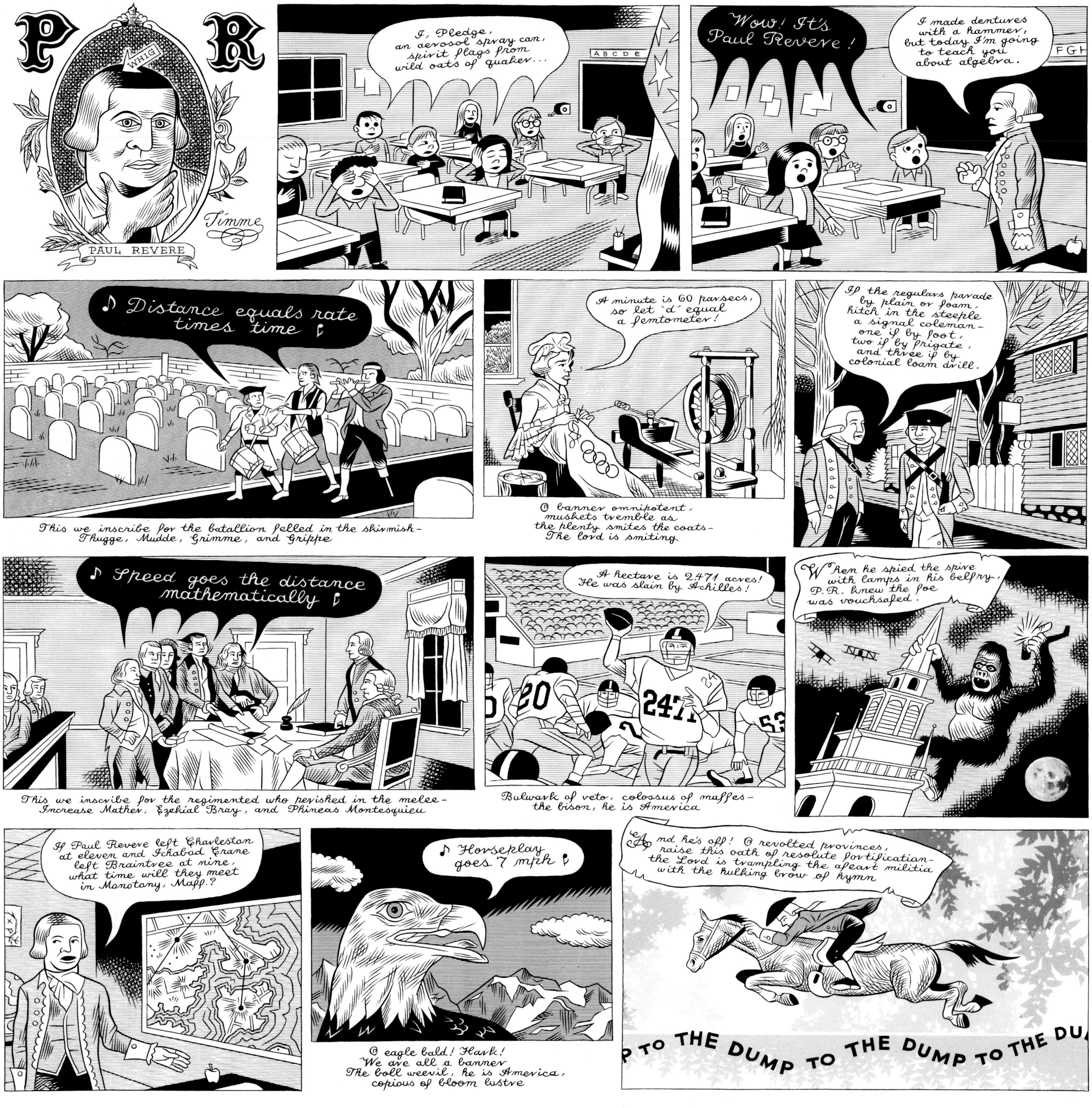
P R
WHIG
PAUL REVERE
Timme
I, Pledge, an aerosol spray can, spirit flags from wild oats of quaker...
ABCDE
Wow! It's Paul Revere!
I made dentures with a hammer, but today I'm going to teach you about algebra.
FGH
♪ Distance equals rate times time ♪
This we inscribe for the batallion felled in the skirmish-
Thugge, Mudde, Grimme, and Grippe
A minute is 60 parsecs, so let 'd' equal a femtometer!
O banner omnipotent, muskets tremble as the plenty smites the coats-
The lord is smiting
If the regulars parade by plain or foam, hitch in the steeple a signal coleman- one if by foot, two if by frigate, and three if by colonial loam drill.
♪ Speed goes the distance mathematically ♪
This we inscribe for the regimented who perished in the melee-
Increase Mather, Ezekial Bray, and Phineas Montesquieu
A hectare is 2471 acres! He was slain by Achilles!
20
2471
53
Bulwark of veto, colossus of maffes-
the bison, he is America
When he spied the spire with lamps in his belfry, P.R. knew the foe was vouchsafed.
If Paul Revere left Charleston at eleven and Ichabod Crane left Braintree at nine, what time will they meet in Monotony, Mass.?
♪ Horseplay goes 7 mph ♪
O eagle bald! Hark!
We are all a banner
The boll weevil, he is America,
copious of bloom lustre
And he's off! O revolted provinces, raise this oath of resolute fortification- the Lord is trampling the apart militia with the hulking brow of hymn
P TO THE DUMP TO THE DUMP TO THE DU

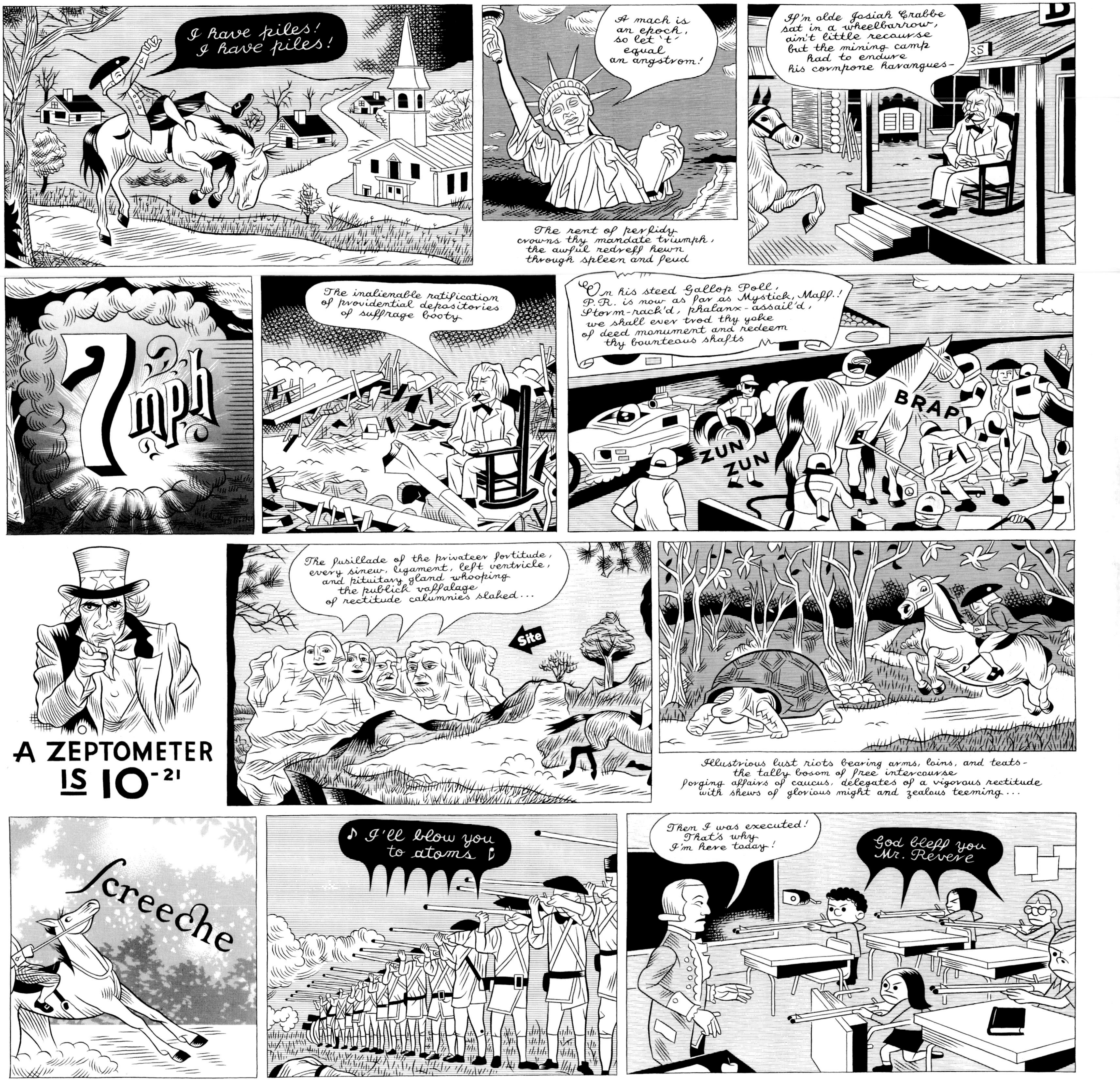
I have piles! I have piles!
A mach is an epoch, so let 't' equal an angstrom!
The rent of perfidy crowns thy mandate triumph, the awful redreff hewn through spleen and feud
If'n olde Josiah Crabbe sat in a wheelbarrow, ain't little recourse but the mining camp had to endure his cornpone harangues-
7 mph
The inalienable ratification of providential depositories of suffrage booty
On his steed Gallop Poll, P.R. is now as far as Mystick, Maff.! Storm-rack'd, phalanx-assail'd, we shall ever trod thy yoke of deed monument and redeem thy bounteous shafts
BRAP
ZUN ZUN
A ZEPTOMETER IS 10^{-21}
The fusillade of the privateer fortitude, every sinew, ligament, left ventricle, and pituitary gland whooping the publick vaffalage of rectitude calumnies slaked...
Site
Illustrious lust riots bearing arms, loins, and teats- the tally bosom of free intercourse forging affairs of caucus, delegates of a vigorous rectitude with shews of glorious might and zealous teeming...
Screeche
♪ I'll blow you to atoms ♪
Then I was executed! That's why I'm here today!
God bleff you Mr. Revere

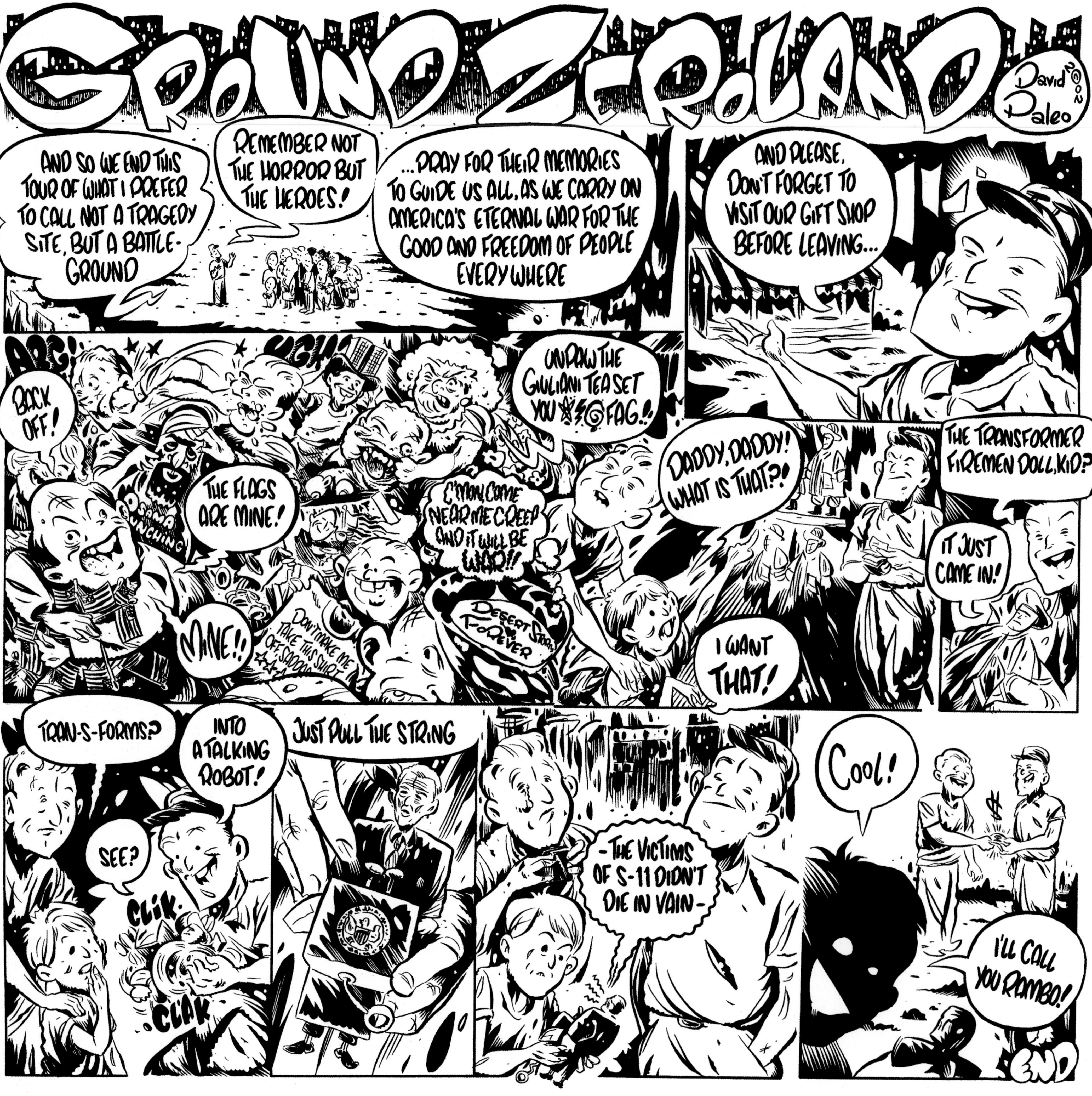
GROUND ZEROLAND
David Paleo 2002
AND SO WE END THIS TOUR OF WHAT I PREFER TO CALL NOT A TRAGEDY SITE, BUT A BATTLE-GROUND
REMEMBER NOT THE HORROR BUT THE HEROES!
...PRAY FOR THEIR MEMORIES TO GUIDE US ALL, AS WE CARRY ON AMERICA'S ETERNAL WAR FOR THE GOOD AND FREEDOM OF PEOPLE EVERYWHERE
AND PLEASE, DON'T FORGET TO VISIT OUR GIFT SHOP BEFORE LEAVING...
ARG!
UGH
BACK OFF!
UNPAW THE GIULIANI TEA SET YOU *#@ FAG!!
OSAMA PUNCHING
THE FLAGS ARE MINE!
C'MON, COME NEAR ME CREEP AND IT WILL BE WAR!!
MINE!!
DON'T MAKE ME TAKE THIS SHIRT OFF, SADDAM
DESERT STORM FOREVER
DADDY, DADDY! WHAT IS THAT?!
I WANT THAT!
THE TRANSFORMER FIREMEN DOLL, KID?
IT JUST CAME IN!
TRAN-S-FORMS?
INTO A TALKING ROBOT!
SEE?
CLIK
CLAK
JUST PULL THE STRING
-THE VICTIMS OF S-11 DIDN'T DIE IN VAIN-
COOL!
I'LL CALL YOU RAMBO!
END

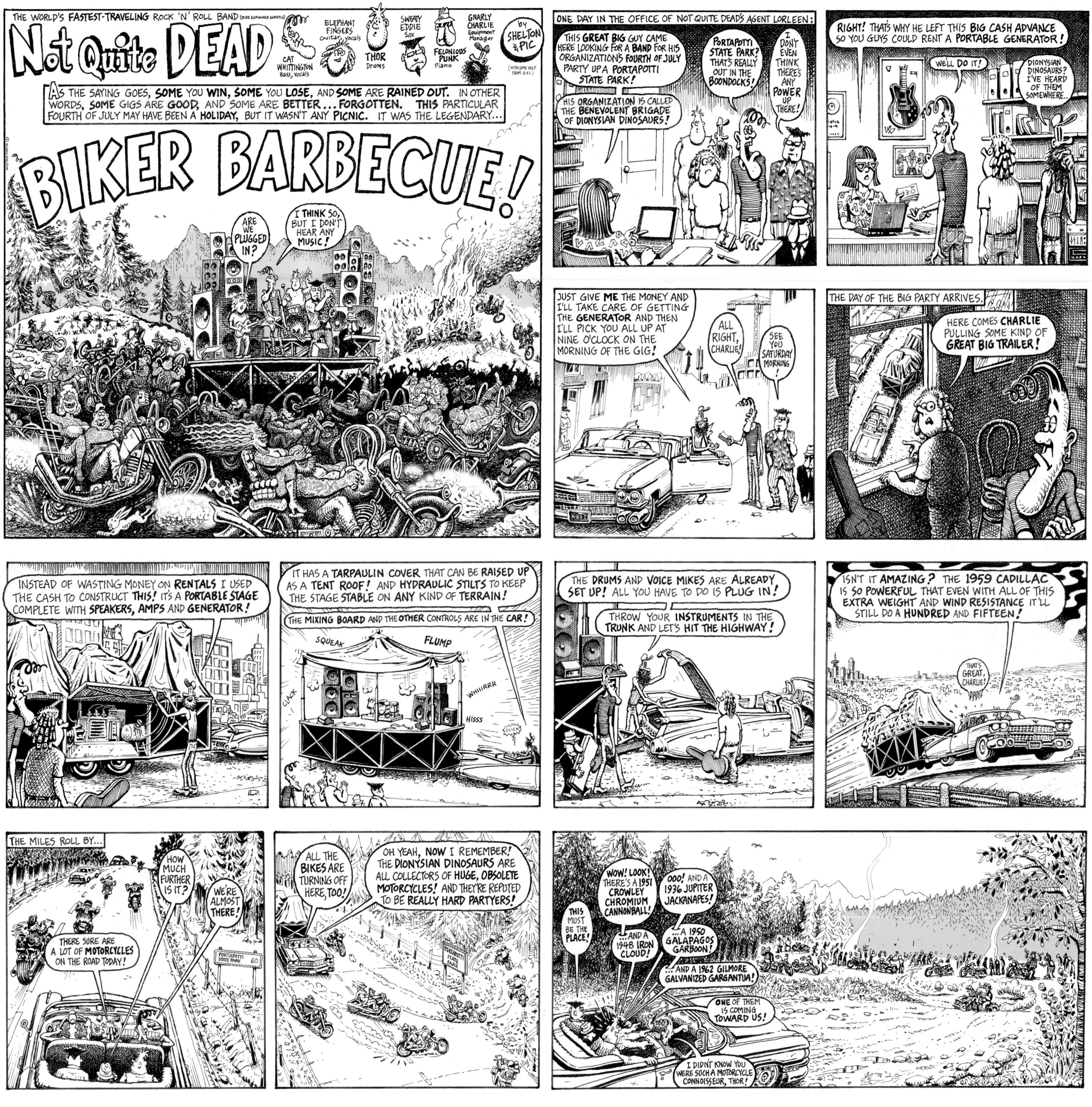

THE WORLD'S FASTEST-TRAVELING ROCK 'N' ROLL BAND (TO BE EXPLAINED SHORTLY)
Not Quite DEAD
CAT WHITTINGTON Bass, vocals
ELEPHANT FINGERS Guitar, vocals
THOR Drums
SWEATY EDDIE Sax
FELONIOUS PUNK Piano
GNARLY CHARLIE Equipment Manager
by SHELTON & PIC
(WITH SOME HELP FROM G.V.L.)
AS THE SAYING GOES, SOME YOU WIN, SOME YOU LOSE, AND SOME ARE RAINED OUT. IN OTHER WORDS, SOME GIGS ARE GOOD, AND SOME ARE BETTER ... FORGOTTEN. THIS PARTICULAR FOURTH OF JULY MAY HAVE BEEN A HOLIDAY, BUT IT WASN'T ANY PICNIC. IT WAS THE LEGENDARY...
© STUDIO SHELTON
BIKER BARBECUE!
ARE WE PLUGGED IN?
I THINK SO, BUT I DON'T HEAR ANY MUSIC!
ONE DAY IN THE OFFICE OF NOT QUITE DEAD'S AGENT LORLEEN:
THIS GREAT BIG GUY CAME HERE LOOKING FOR A BAND FOR HIS ORGANIZATION'S FOURTH OF JULY PARTY UP A PORTAPOTTI STATE PARK!
HIS ORGANIZATION IS CALLED THE BENEVOLENT BRIGADE OF DIONYSIAN DINOSAURS!
PORTAPOTTI STATE PARK? THAT'S REALLY OUT IN THE BOONDOCKS!
I DON'T EVEN THINK THERE'S ANY POWER UP THERE!
RIGHT! THAT'S WHY HE LEFT THIS BIG CASH ADVANCE SO YOU GUYS COULD RENT A PORTABLE GENERATOR!
WE'LL DO IT!
DIONYSIAN DINOSAURS? I'VE HEARD OF THEM SOMEWHERE...
JUST GIVE ME THE MONEY AND I'LL TAKE CARE OF GETTING THE GENERATOR AND THEN I'LL PICK YOU ALL UP AT NINE O'CLOCK ON THE MORNING OF THE GIG!
ALL RIGHT, CHARLIE!
SEE YOU SATURDAY MORNING!
THE DAY OF THE BIG PARTY ARRIVES.
HERE COMES CHARLIE PULLING SOME KIND OF GREAT BIG TRAILER!
INSTEAD OF WASTING MONEY ON RENTALS I USED THE CASH TO CONSTRUCT THIS! IT'S A PORTABLE STAGE COMPLETE WITH SPEAKERS, AMPS AND GENERATOR!
IT HAS A TARPAULIN COVER THAT CAN BE RAISED UP AS A TENT ROOF! AND HYDRAULIC STILTS TO KEEP THE STAGE STABLE ON ANY KIND OF TERRAIN!
THE MIXING BOARD AND THE OTHER CONTROLS ARE IN THE CAR!
SQUEAK
FLUMP
CLACK
WHIIIRRR
HISSS
CLICK
THE DRUMS AND VOICE MIKES ARE ALREADY SET UP! ALL YOU HAVE TO DO IS PLUG IN!
THROW YOUR INSTRUMENTS IN THE TRUNK AND LET'S HIT THE HIGHWAY!
ISN'T IT AMAZING? THE 1959 CADILLAC IS SO POWERFUL THAT EVEN WITH ALL OF THIS EXTRA WEIGHT AND WIND RESISTANCE IT'LL STILL DO A HUNDRED AND FIFTEEN!
THAT'S GREAT, CHARLIE!
THE MILES ROLL BY...
HOW MUCH FURTHER IS IT?
WE'RE ALMOST THERE!
THERE SURE ARE A LOT OF MOTORCYCLES ON THE ROAD TODAY!
PORTAPOTTI STATE PARK 60
ALL THE BIKES ARE TURNING OFF HERE, TOO!
OH YEAH, NOW I REMEMBER! THE DIONYSIAN DINOSAURS ARE ALL COLLECTORS OF HUGE, OBSOLETE MOTORCYCLES! AND THEY'RE REPUTED TO BE REALLY HARD PARTYERS!
PORTAPOTTI STATE PARK
THIS MUST BE THE PLACE!
WOW! LOOK! THERE'S A 1951 CROWLEY CHROMIUM CANNONBALL!
...AND A 1948 IRON CLOUD!
OOO! AND A 1936 JUPITER JACKANAPES!
...A 1950 GALAPAGOS GARBOON!
...AND A 1962 GILMORE GALVANIZED GARGANTUA!
ONE OF THEM IS COMING TOWARD US!
I DIDN'T KNOW YOU WERE SUCH A MOTORCYCLE CONNOISSEUR, THOR!

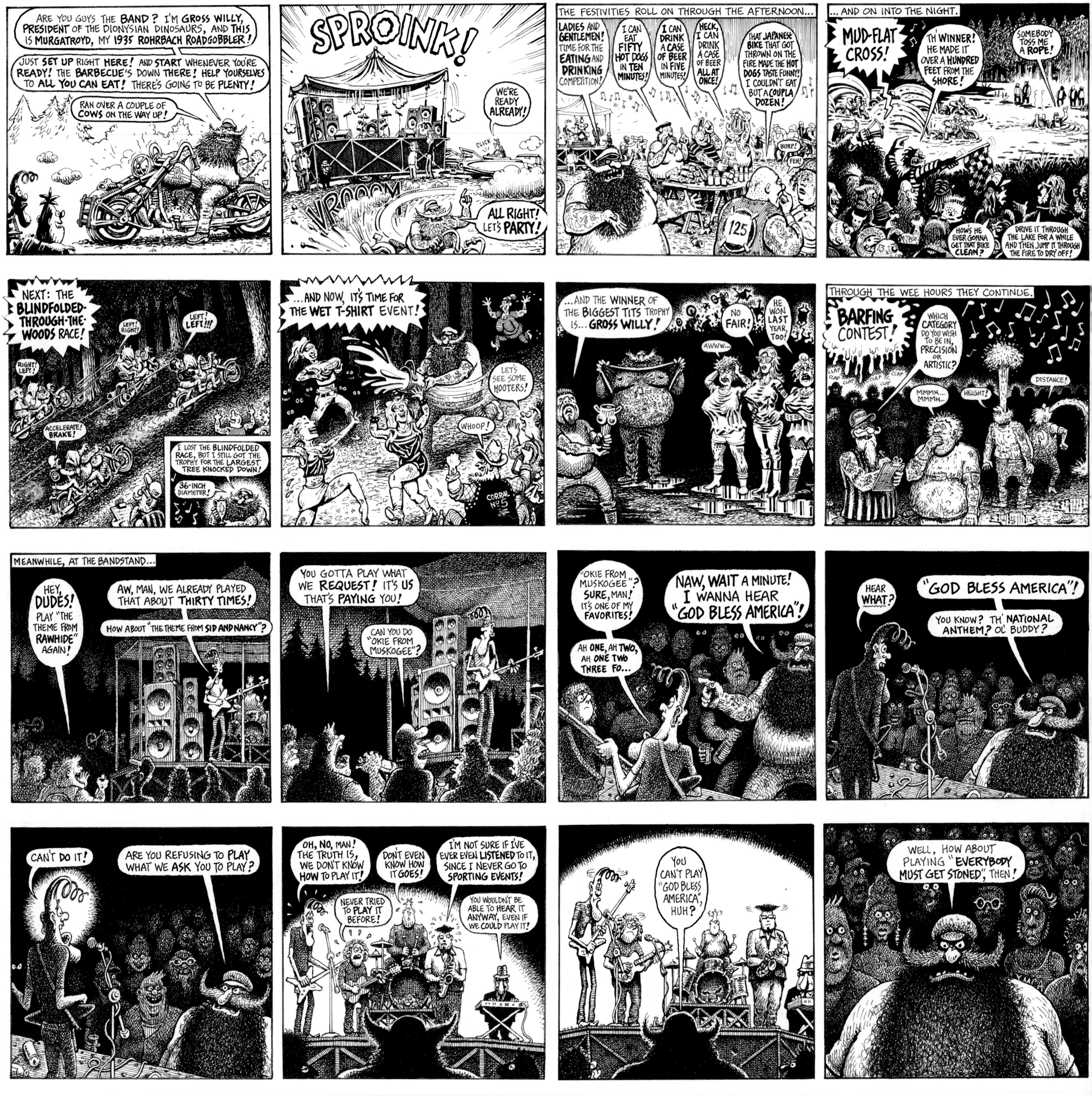
ARE YOU GUYS THE BAND? I'M GROSS WILLY, PRESIDENT OF THE DIONYSIAN DINOSAURS, AND THIS IS MURGATROYD, MY 1935 ROHRBACH ROADGOBBLER!
JUST SET UP RIGHT HERE! AND START WHENEVER YOU'RE READY! THE BARBECUE'S DOWN THERE! HELP YOURSELVES TO ALL YOU CAN EAT! THERE'S GOING TO BE PLENTY!
RAN OVER A COUPLE OF COWS ON THE WAY UP!
SPROINK!
WE'RE READY ALREADY!
CLICK
VROOOM
ALL RIGHT! LET'S PARTY!
THE FESTIVITIES ROLL ON THROUGH THE AFTERNOON...
LADIES AND GENTLEMEN! TIME FOR THE EATING AND DRINKING COMPETITION!
I CAN EAT FIFTY HOT DOGS IN TEN MINUTES!
I CAN DRINK A CASE OF BEER IN FIVE MINUTES!
HECK, I CAN DRINK A CASE OF BEER ALL AT ONCE!
THAT JAPANESE BIKE THAT GOT THROWN ON THE FIRE MADE THE HOT DOGS TASTE FUNNY! I COULDN'T EAT BUT A COUPLA DOZEN!
BURP!
FEH!
125
... AND ON INTO THE NIGHT.
MUD-FLAT CROSS!
TH' WINNER! HE MADE IT OVER A HUNDRED FEET FROM THE SHORE!
SOMEBODY TOSS ME A ROPE!
HOW'S HE EVER GONNA GET THAT BIKE CLEAN?
DRIVE IT THROUGH THE LAKE FOR A WHILE AND THEN JUMP IT THROUGH THE FIRE TO DRY OFF!
NEXT: THE BLINDFOLDED-THROUGH-THE-WOODS RACE!
LEFT! RIGHT!
LEFT! LEFT!!!
RIGHT! LEFT!
ACCELERATE! BRAKE!
I LOST THE BLINDFOLDED RACE, BUT I STILL GOT THE TROPHY FOR THE LARGEST TREE KNOCKED DOWN!
36-INCH DIAMETER!
...AND NOW, IT'S TIME FOR THE WET T-SHIRT EVENT!
LET'S SEE SOME HOOTERS!
WHOOP!
CORRAL Nº 5
...AND THE WINNER OF THE BIGGEST TITS TROPHY IS... GROSS WILLY!
NO FAIR!
HE WON LAST YEAR, TOO!
AWWW...
THROUGH THE WEE HOURS THEY CONTINUE.
BARFING CONTEST!
WHICH CATEGORY DO YOU WISH TO BE IN, PRECISION OR ARTISTIC?
CLAP CLAP CLAP CLAP CLAP CLAP
MMMH... MMMH...
HEIGHT!
DISTANCE!
JUDGE
MEANWHILE, AT THE BANDSTAND...
HEY, DUDES! PLAY "THE THEME FROM RAWHIDE" AGAIN!
AW, MAN, WE ALREADY PLAYED THAT ABOUT THIRTY TIMES!
HOW ABOUT "THE THEME FROM SID AND NANCY"?
YOU GOTTA PLAY WHAT WE REQUEST! IT'S US THAT'S PAYING YOU!
CAN YOU DO "OKIE FROM MUSKOGEE"?
"OKIE FROM MUSKOGEE"? SURE, MAN! IT'S ONE OF MY FAVORITES!
AH ONE, AH TWO, AH ONE TWO THREE FO...
NAW, WAIT A MINUTE! I WANNA HEAR "GOD BLESS AMERICA"!
HEAR WHAT?
"GOD BLESS AMERICA"!
YOU KNOW? TH' NATIONAL ANTHEM? OL' BUDDY?
CAN'T DO IT!
ARE YOU REFUSING TO PLAY WHAT WE ASK YOU TO PLAY?
OH, NO, MAN! THE TRUTH IS, WE DON'T KNOW HOW TO PLAY IT!
DON'T EVEN KNOW HOW IT GOES!
I'M NOT SURE IF I'VE EVER EVEN LISTENED TO IT, SINCE I NEVER GO TO SPORTING EVENTS!
NEVER TRIED TO PLAY IT BEFORE!
YOU WOULDN'T BE ABLE TO HEAR IT ANYWAY, EVEN IF WE COULD PLAY IT!
YOU CAN'T PLAY "GOD BLESS AMERICA", HUH?
WELL, HOW ABOUT PLAYING "EVERYBODY MUST GET STONED", THEN!

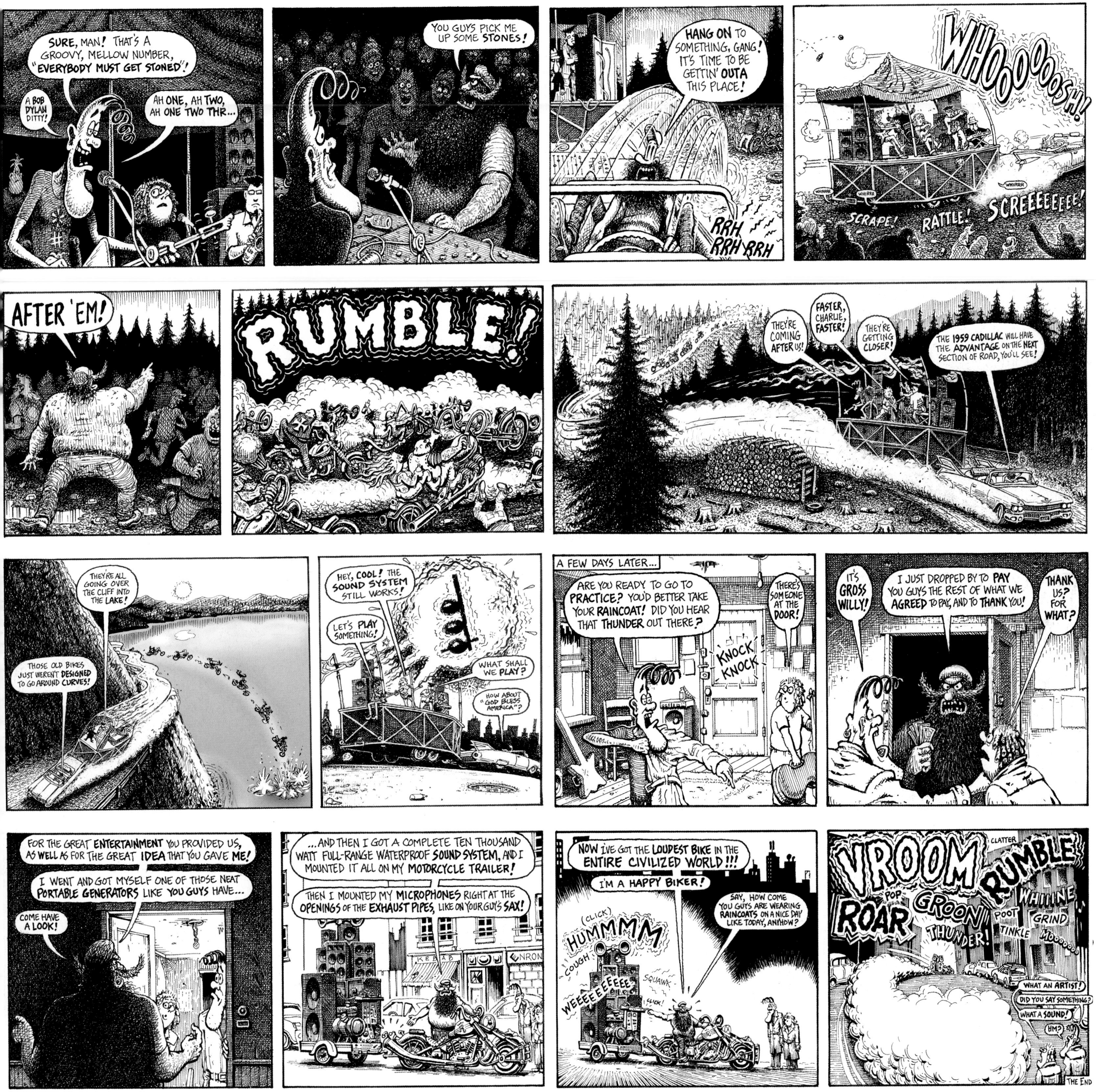
SURE, MAN! THAT'S A GROOVY, MELLOW NUMBER, "EVERYBODY MUST GET STONED"!
A BOB DYLAN DITTY!
AH ONE, AH TWO, AH ONE TWO THR...
YOU GUYS PICK ME UP SOME STONES!
HANG ON TO SOMETHING, GANG! IT'S TIME TO BE GETTIN' OUTA THIS PLACE!
RRH RRH RRH
WHOOOOOOSH!
SCRAPE!
RATTLE!
SCREEEEEEEE!
AFTER 'EM!
RUMBLE!
THEY'RE COMING AFTER US!
FASTER, CHARLIE, FASTER!
THEY'RE GETTING CLOSER!
THE 1959 CADILLAC WILL HAVE THE ADVANTAGE ON THE NEXT SECTION OF ROAD, YOU'LL SEE!
THEY'RE ALL GOING OVER THE CLIFF INTO THE LAKE!
THOSE OLD BIKES JUST WEREN'T DESIGNED TO GO AROUND CURVES!
HEY, COOL! THE SOUND SYSTEM STILL WORKS!
LET'S PLAY SOMETHING!
WHAT SHALL WE PLAY?
HOW ABOUT "GOD BLESS AMERICA"?
A FEW DAYS LATER...
ARE YOU READY TO GO TO PRACTICE? YOU'D BETTER TAKE YOUR RAINCOAT! DID YOU HEAR THAT THUNDER OUT THERE?
THERE'S SOMEONE AT THE DOOR!
KNOCK KNOCK
IT'S GROSS WILLY!
I JUST DROPPED BY TO PAY YOU GUYS THE REST OF WHAT WE AGREED TO PAY, AND TO THANK YOU!
THANK US? FOR WHAT?
FOR THE GREAT ENTERTAINMENT YOU PROVIDED US, AS WELL AS FOR THE GREAT IDEA THAT YOU GAVE ME!
I WENT AND GOT MYSELF ONE OF THOSE NEAT PORTABLE GENERATORS LIKE YOU GUYS HAVE...
COME HAVE A LOOK!
...AND THEN I GOT A COMPLETE TEN THOUSAND WATT FULL-RANGE WATERPROOF SOUND SYSTEM, AND I MOUNTED IT ALL ON MY MOTORCYCLE TRAILER!
THEN I MOUNTED MY MICROPHONES RIGHT AT THE OPENINGS OF THE EXHAUST PIPES, LIKE ON YOUR GUY'S SAX!
KEBAB
NOW I'VE GOT THE LOUDEST BIKE IN THE ENTIRE CIVILIZED WORLD!!!
I'M A HAPPY BIKER!
SAY, HOW COME YOU GUYS ARE WEARING RAINCOATS ON A NICE DAY LIKE TODAY, ANYHOW?
(CLICK)
HUMMMM
COUGH
WEEEEEEEEEE
SQUAWK
CLICK!
VROOM
CLATTER
RUMBLE!
POP
ROAR
GROON
WHIIINE
POOT
GRIND
THUNDER!
TINKLE
MOOOOOO
WHAT AN ARTIST!
DID YOU SAY SOMETHING?
WHAT A SOUND!
HM?
THE END

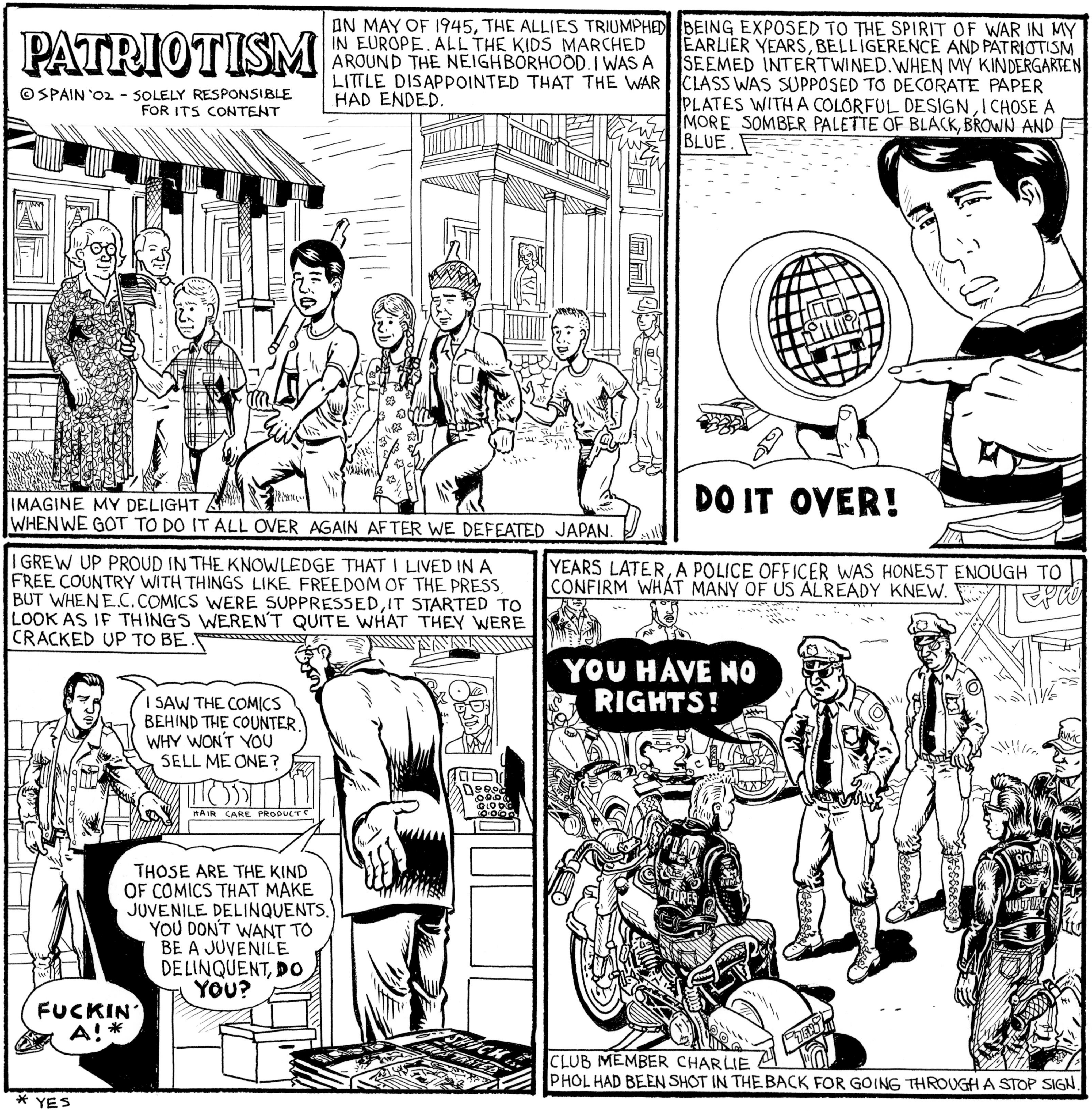
PATRIOTISM
© SPAIN '02 - SOLELY RESPONSIBLE FOR ITS CONTENT
IN MAY OF 1945, THE ALLIES TRIUMPHED IN EUROPE. ALL THE KIDS MARCHED AROUND THE NEIGHBORHOOD. I WAS A LITTLE DISAPPOINTED THAT THE WAR HAD ENDED.
IMAGINE MY DELIGHT WHEN WE GOT TO DO IT ALL OVER AGAIN AFTER WE DEFEATED JAPAN.
BEING EXPOSED TO THE SPIRIT OF WAR IN MY EARLIER YEARS, BELLIGERENCE AND PATRIOTISM SEEMED INTERTWINED. WHEN MY KINDERGARTEN CLASS WAS SUPPOSED TO DECORATE PAPER PLATES WITH A COLORFUL DESIGN, I CHOSE A MORE SOMBER PALETTE OF BLACK, BROWN AND BLUE.
DO IT OVER!
I GREW UP PROUD IN THE KNOWLEDGE THAT I LIVED IN A FREE COUNTRY WITH THINGS LIKE FREEDOM OF THE PRESS. BUT WHEN E.C. COMICS WERE SUPPRESSED, IT STARTED TO LOOK AS IF THINGS WEREN'T QUITE WHAT THEY WERE CRACKED UP TO BE.
I SAW THE COMICS BEHIND THE COUNTER. WHY WON'T YOU SELL ME ONE?
HAIR CARE PRODUCTS
THOSE ARE THE KIND OF COMICS THAT MAKE JUVENILE DELINQUENTS. YOU DON'T WANT TO BE A JUVENILE DELINQUENT, DO YOU?
FUCKIN' A!*
SHOCK
YEARS LATER, A POLICE OFFICER WAS HONEST ENOUGH TO CONFIRM WHAT MANY OF US ALREADY KNEW.
YOU HAVE NO RIGHTS!
ROAD VULTURES
CLUB MEMBER CHARLIE PHOL HAD BEEN SHOT IN THE BACK FOR GOING THROUGH A STOP SIGN.

* YES

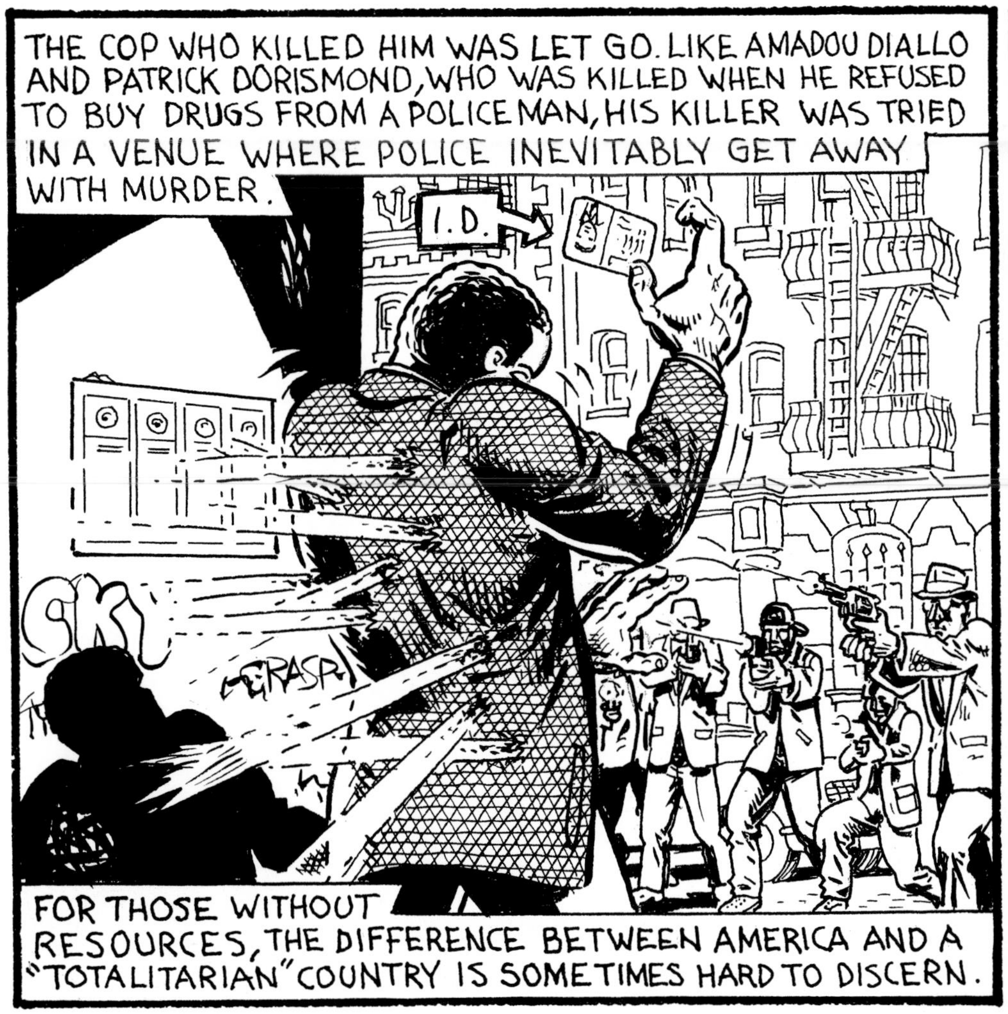
THE COP WHO KILLED HIM WAS LET GO. LIKE AMADOU DIALLO AND PATRICK DORISMOND, WHO WAS KILLED WHEN HE REFUSED TO BUY DRUGS FROM A POLICEMAN, HIS KILLER WAS TRIED IN A VENUE WHERE POLICE INEVITABLY GET AWAY WITH MURDER.
I.D.
FOR THOSE WITHOUT RESOURCES, THE DIFFERENCE BETWEEN AMERICA AND A "TOTALITARIAN" COUNTRY IS SOMETIMES HARD TO DISCERN.

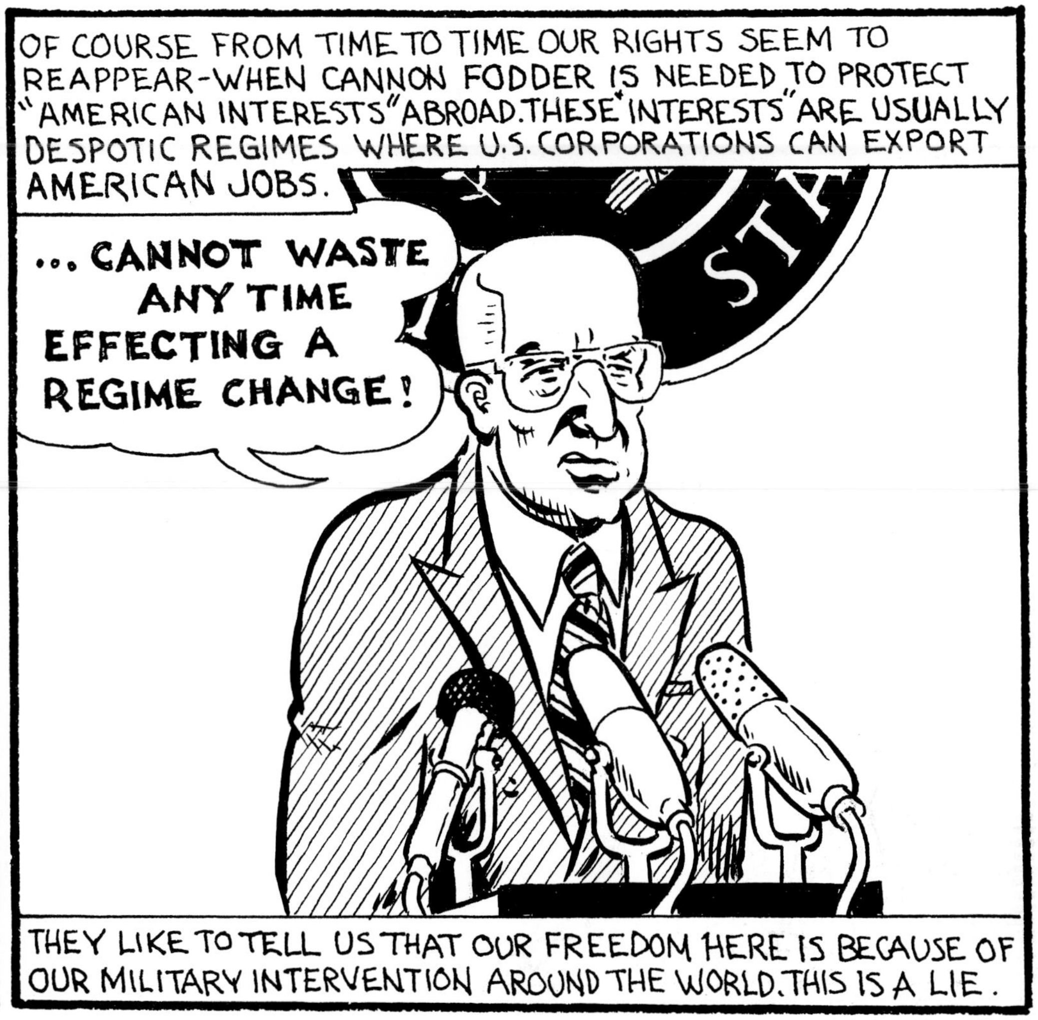
OF COURSE FROM TIME TO TIME OUR RIGHTS SEEM TO REAPPEAR-WHEN CANNON FODDER IS NEEDED TO PROTECT "AMERICAN INTERESTS" ABROAD. THESE "INTERESTS" ARE USUALLY DESPOTIC REGIMES WHERE U.S. CORPORATIONS CAN EXPORT AMERICAN JOBS.
...CANNOT WASTE ANY TIME EFFECTING A REGIME CHANGE!
THEY LIKE TO TELL US THAT OUR FREEDOM HERE IS BECAUSE OF OUR MILITARY INTERVENTION AROUND THE WORLD. THIS IS A LIE.

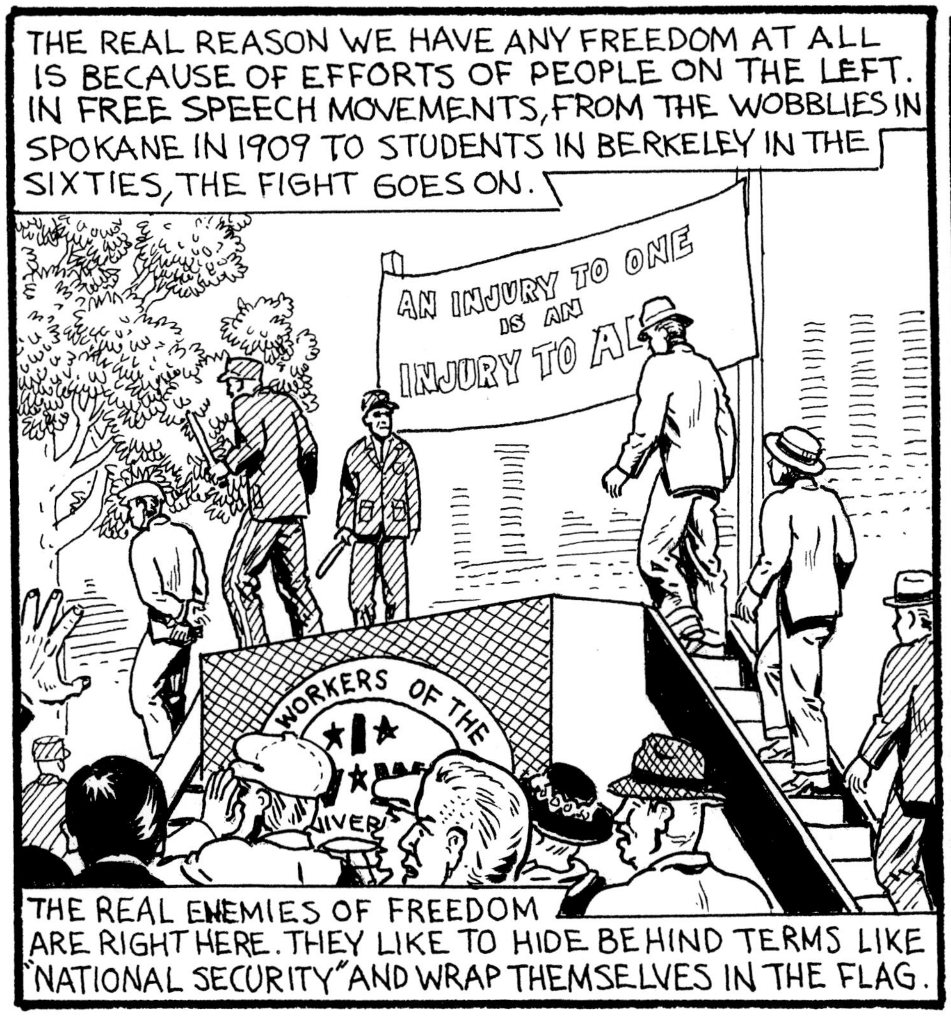
THE REAL REASON WE HAVE ANY FREEDOM AT ALL IS BECAUSE OF EFFORTS OF PEOPLE ON THE LEFT. IN FREE SPEECH MOVEMENTS, FROM THE WOBBLIES IN SPOKANE IN 1909 TO STUDENTS IN BERKELEY IN THE SIXTIES, THE FIGHT GOES ON.
AN INJURY TO ONE IS AN INJURY TO AL
WORKERS OF THE
THE REAL ENEMIES OF FREEDOM ARE RIGHT HERE. THEY LIKE TO HIDE BEHIND TERMS LIKE "NATIONAL SECURITY" AND WRAP THEMSELVES IN THE FLAG.

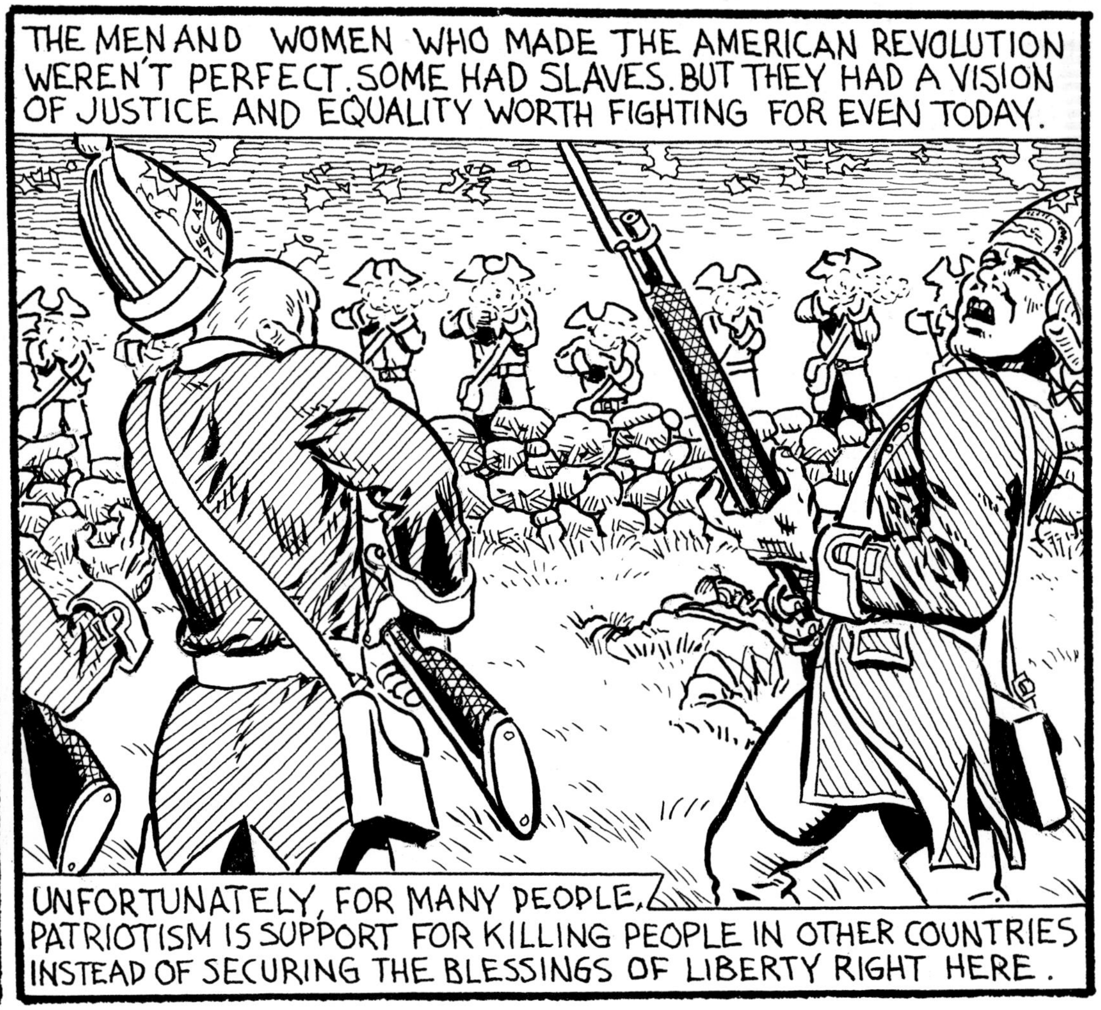
THE MEN AND WOMEN WHO MADE THE AMERICAN REVOLUTION WEREN'T PERFECT. SOME HAD SLAVES. BUT THEY HAD A VISION OF JUSTICE AND EQUALITY WORTH FIGHTING FOR EVEN TODAY.
UNFORTUNATELY, FOR MANY PEOPLE, PATRIOTISM IS SUPPORT FOR KILLING PEOPLE IN OTHER COUNTRIES INSTEAD OF SECURING THE BLESSINGS OF LIBERTY RIGHT HERE.

OPERATION NORTHWOODS

by
Mack White

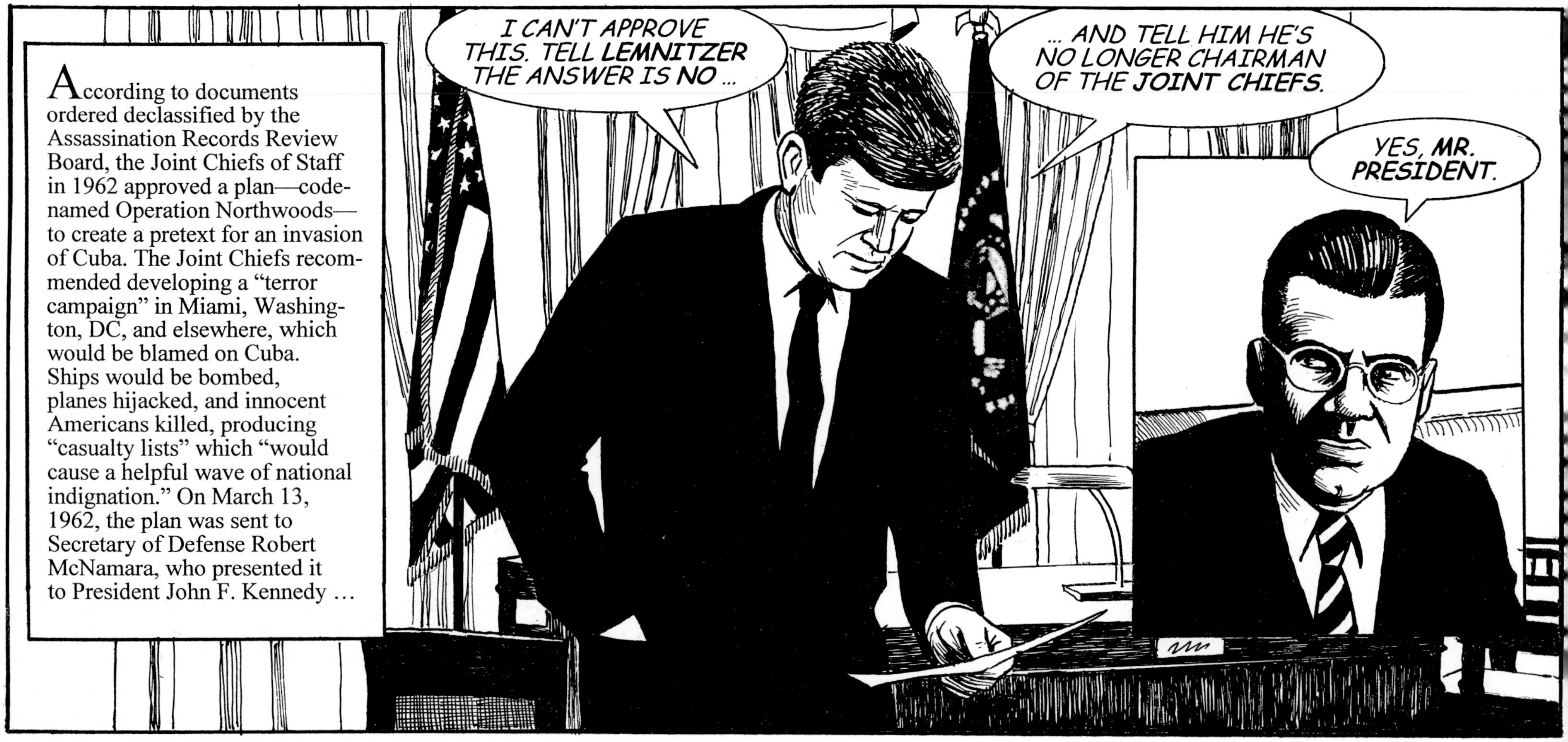
According to documents ordered declassified by the Assassination Records Review Board, the Joint Chiefs of Staff in 1962 approved a plan—code-named Operation Northwoods—to create a pretext for an invasion of Cuba. The Joint Chiefs recommended developing a "terror campaign" in Miami, Washington, DC, and elsewhere, which would be blamed on Cuba. Ships would be bombed, planes hijacked, and innocent Americans killed, producing "casualty lists" which "would cause a helpful wave of national indignation." On March 13, 1962, the plan was sent to Secretary of Defense Robert McNamara, who presented it to President John F. Kennedy …
I CAN'T APPROVE THIS. TELL LEMNITZER THE ANSWER IS NO …
… AND TELL HIM HE'S NO LONGER CHAIRMAN OF THE JOINT CHIEFS.
YES, MR. PRESIDENT.

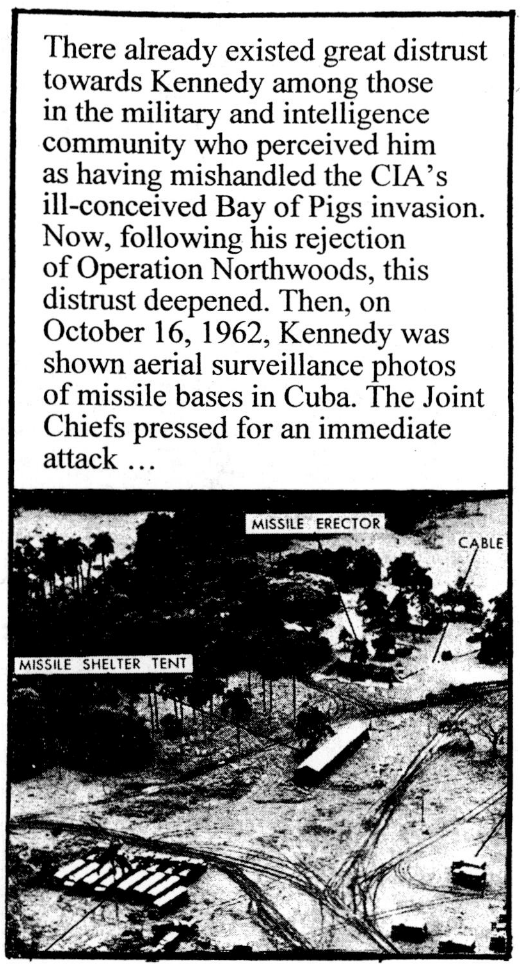
There already existed great distrust towards Kennedy among those in the military and intelligence community who perceived him as having mishandled the CIA's ill-conceived Bay of Pigs invasion. Now, following his rejection of Operation Northwoods, this distrust deepened. Then, on October 16, 1962, Kennedy was shown aerial surveillance photos of missile bases in Cuba. The Joint Chiefs pressed for an immediate attack …
MISSILE ERECTOR
CABLE
MISSILE SHELTER TENT

In the nuclear exchange with the Soviet Union that would have followed such an attack, more than 300 million human beings worldwide would have been killed. Fortunately, Kennedy resisted the pressure to attack and instead sent his brother, Attorney General Robert Kennedy, to meet with Soviet Ambassador Anatoly Dobrynin …

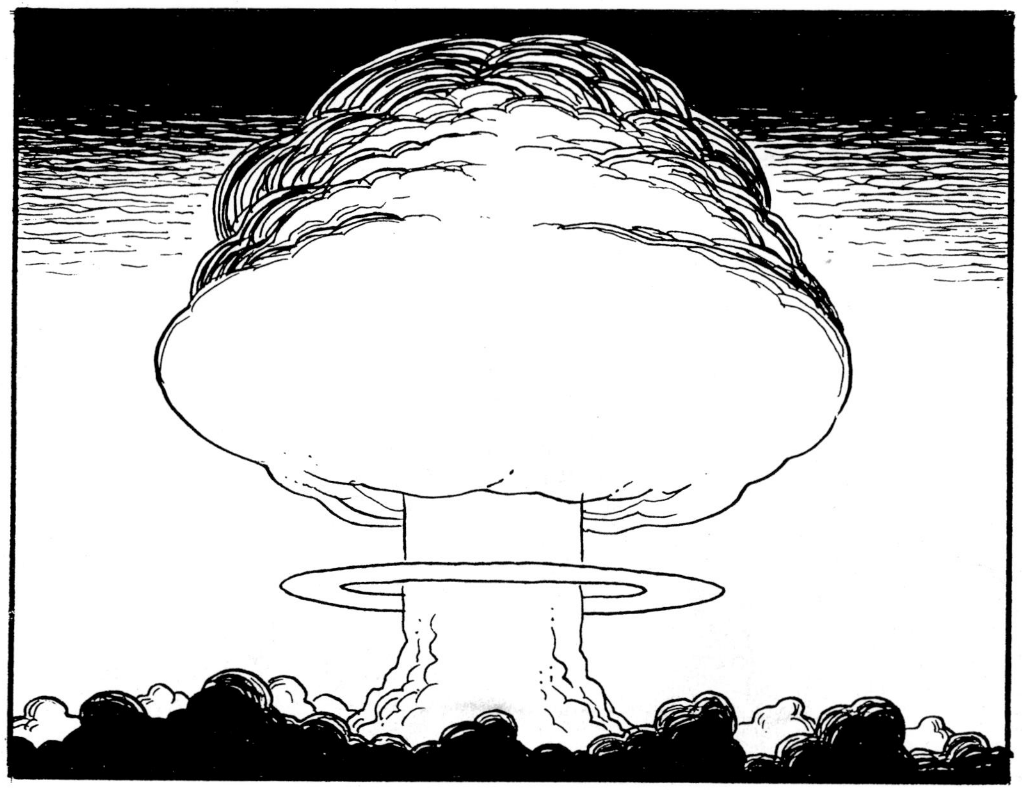

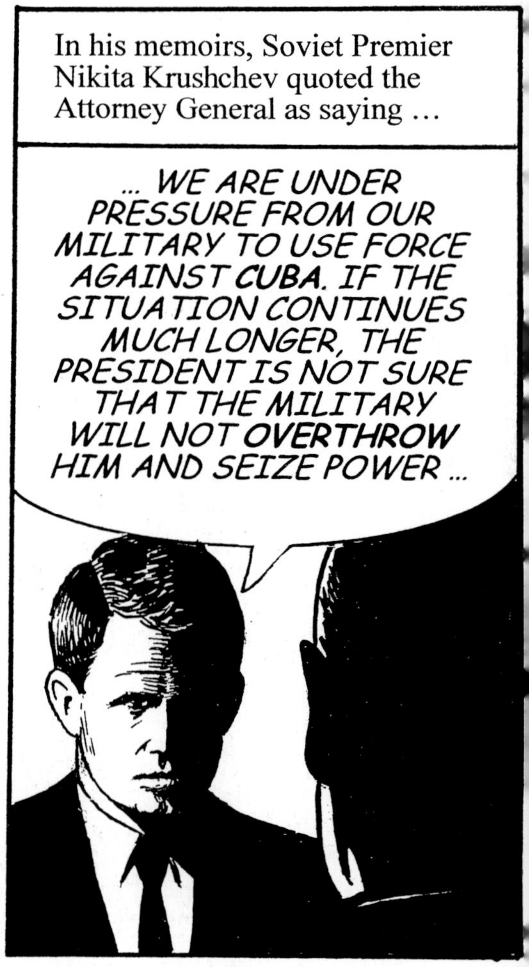
In his memoirs, Soviet Premier Nikita Krushchev quoted the Attorney General as saying …
… WE ARE UNDER PRESSURE FROM OUR MILITARY TO USE FORCE AGAINST CUBA. IF THE SITUATION CONTINUES MUCH LONGER, THE PRESIDENT IS NOT SURE THAT THE MILITARY WILL NOT OVERTHROW HIM AND SEIZE POWER …

Kennedy managed to avoid nuclear holocaust, but avoiding a military overthrow would prove more difficult. In exchange for Krushchev's commitment to remove the missiles from Cuba, Kennedy agreed not to invade Cuba. He also signed the Nuclear Test Ban Treaty. Many in the military-industrial complex were unhappy with these developments and feared that Kennedy would show the same "lack of resolve" with regard to Vietnam—a fear soon realized on October 2, 1963, when he announced the withdrawal of troops from Vietnam. Kennedy also eliminated the oil depletion allowance—a highly profitable tax dodge for oil companies—and in other ways was actively working to end the Cold War and the growing power of the military-industrial complex. At the same time, his brother was prosecuting organized crime figures such as Carlos Marcello, a business associate of Texas oil men. The Kennedys were making big changes—and powerful enemies in the process …

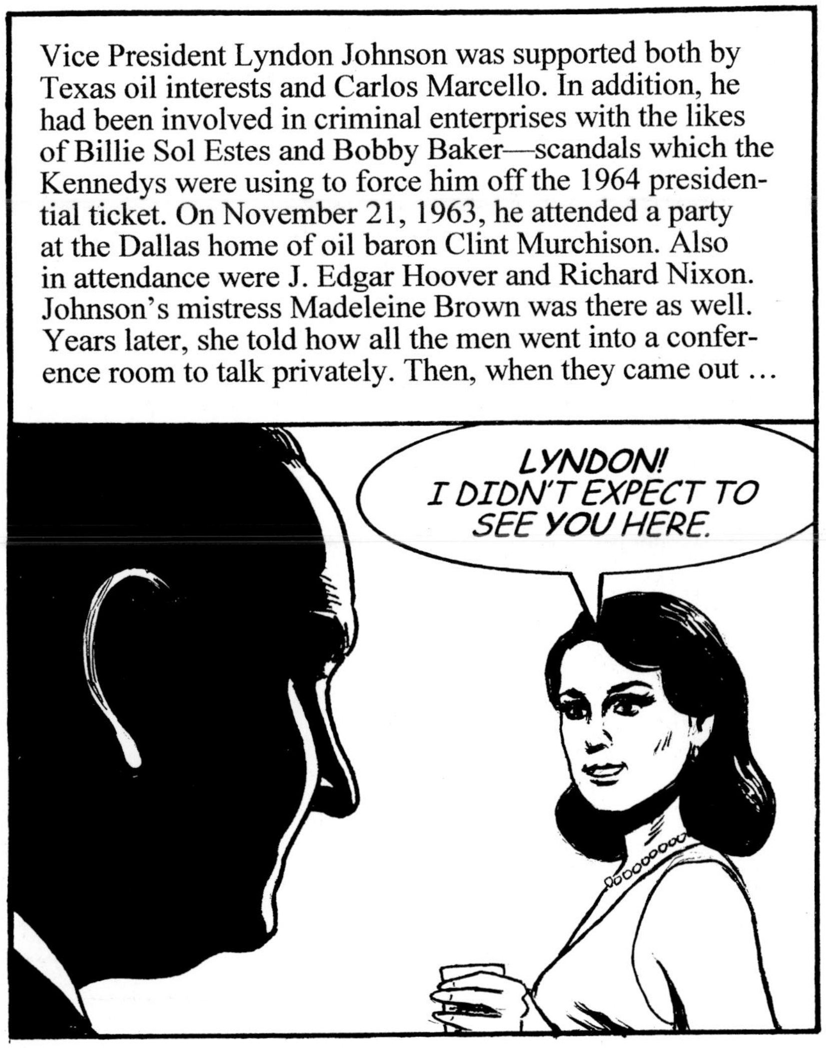
Vice President Lyndon Johnson was supported both by Texas oil interests and Carlos Marcello. In addition, he had been involved in criminal enterprises with the likes of Billie Sol Estes and Bobby Baker—scandals which the Kennedys were using to force him off the 1964 presidential ticket. On November 21, 1963, he attended a party at the Dallas home of oil baron Clint Murchison. Also in attendance were J. Edgar Hoover and Richard Nixon. Johnson's mistress Madeleine Brown was there as well. Years later, she told how all the men went into a conference room to talk privately. Then, when they came out …
LYNDON! I DIDN'T EXPECT TO SEE YOU HERE.

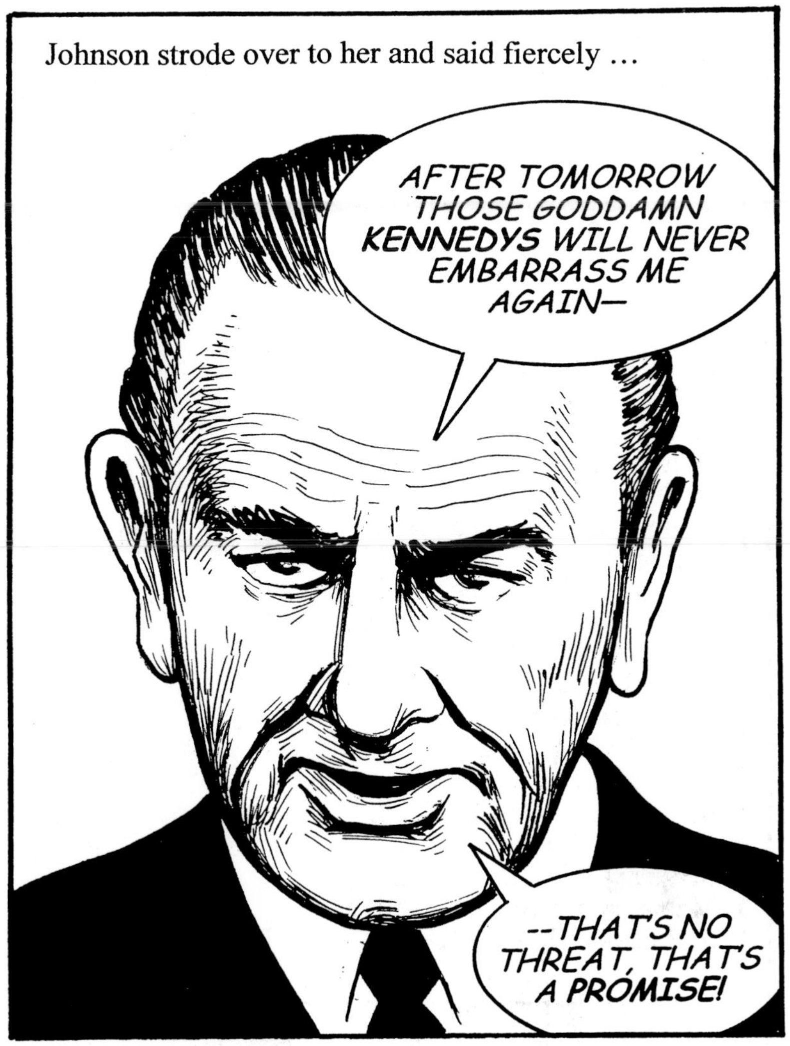
Johnson strode over to her and said fiercely …
AFTER TOMORROW THOSE GODDAMN KENNEDYS WILL NEVER EMBARRASS ME AGAIN—
--THAT'S NO THREAT, THAT'S A PROMISE!

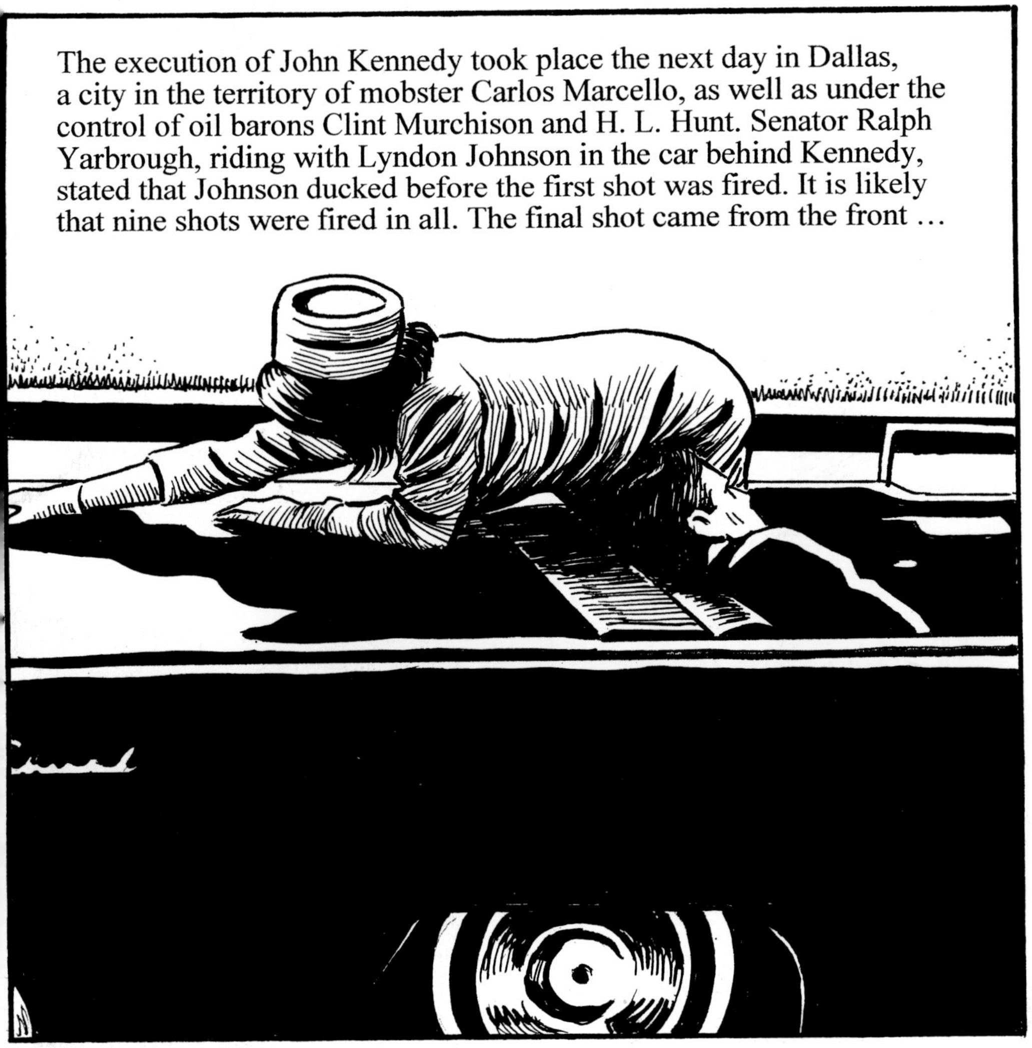
The execution of John Kennedy took place the next day in Dallas, a city in the territory of mobster Carlos Marcello, as well as under the control of oil barons Clint Murchison and H. L. Hunt. Senator Ralph Yarbrough, riding with Lyndon Johnson in the car behind Kennedy, stated that Johnson ducked before the first shot was fired. It is likely that nine shots were fired in all. The final shot came from the front …

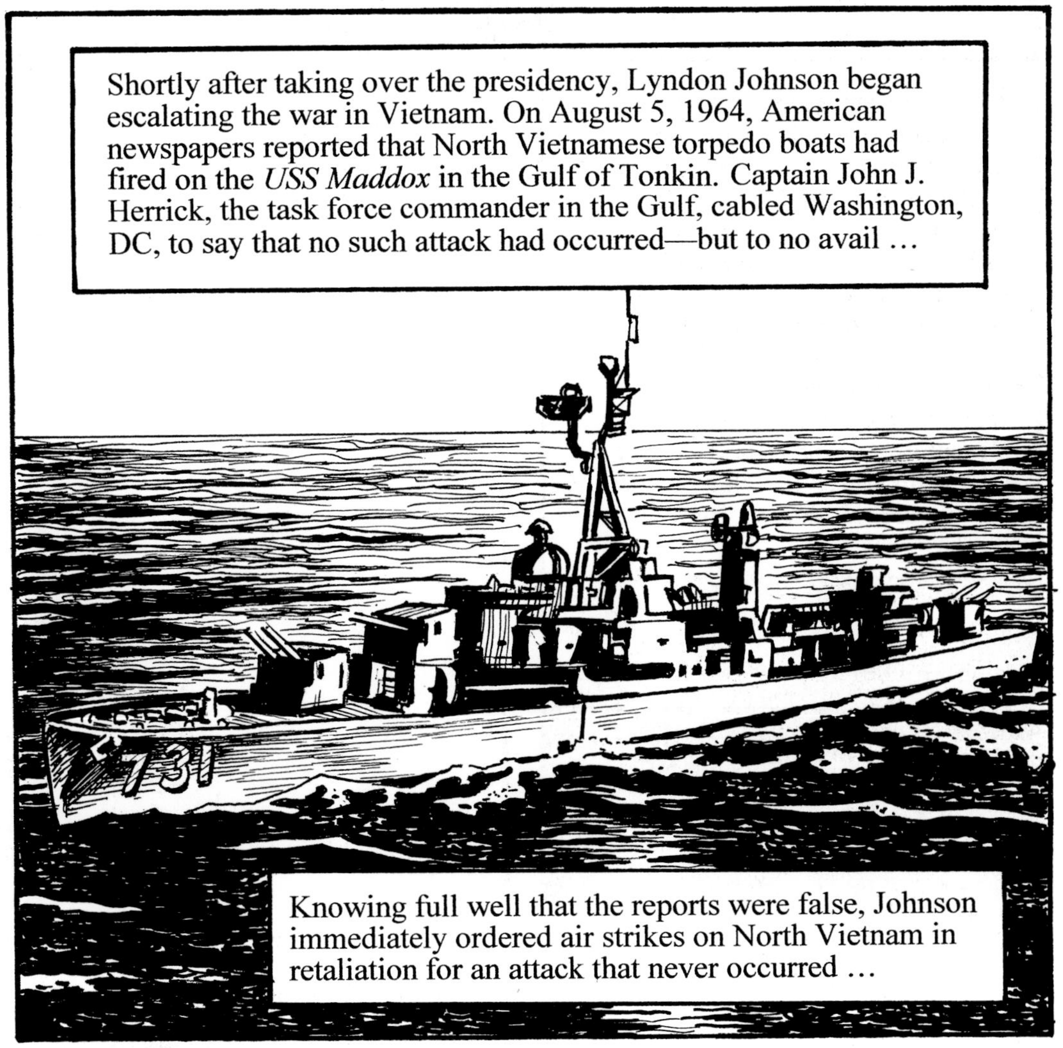
Shortly after taking over the presidency, Lyndon Johnson began escalating the war in Vietnam. On August 5, 1964, American newspapers reported that North Vietnamese torpedo boats had fired on the *USS Maddox* in the Gulf of Tonkin. Captain John J. Herrick, the task force commander in the Gulf, cabled Washington, DC, to say that no such attack had occurred—but to no avail …
Knowing full well that the reports were false, Johnson immediately ordered air strikes on North Vietnam in retaliation for an attack that never occurred …

By the end of the war in Southeast Asia, 58,000 Americans and 2 million Asians had been killed—and many billions of dollars had been made by defense contractors such as Brown and Root—Lyndon Johnson's largest supporter. To the men who make such great profits, the human cost of war is nothing …

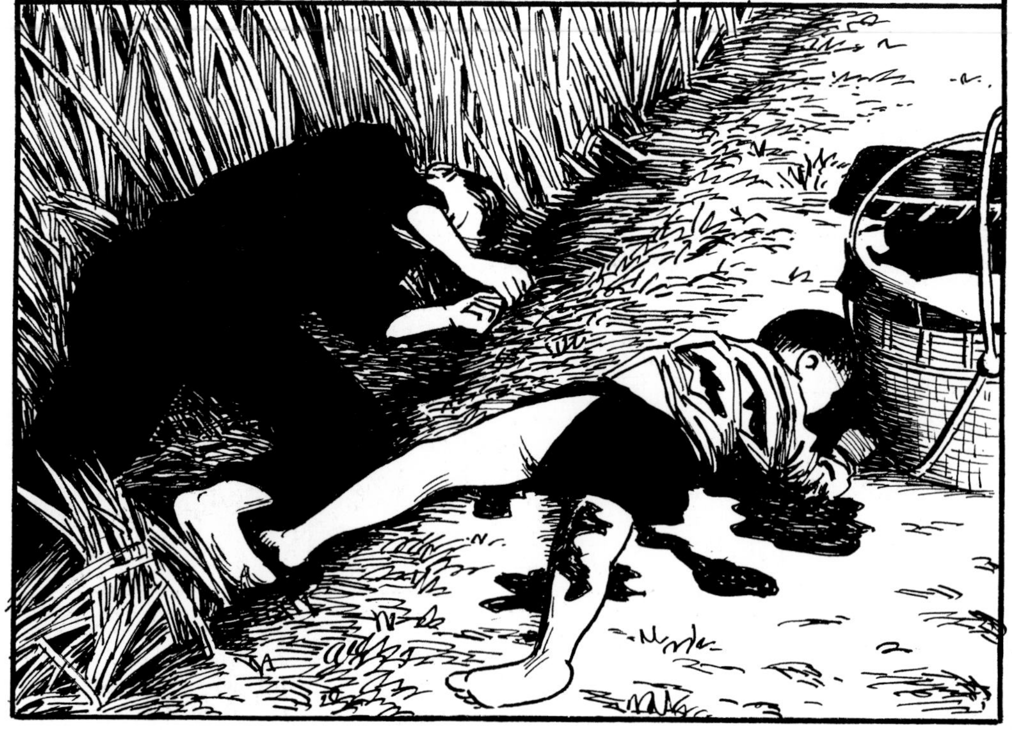

In addition to great profits, come the spoils of war—control of another nation's natural resources, mastery of its people. War also allows the government an excuse to exert more authority over its own people. Civil liberties are never more vulnerable than in wartime. The warmongers, then, have much to gain, and any means that advance their ends are considered justified. In the absence of a good reason to attack a nation, a reason can be invented—as shown by the Gulf of Tonkin Resolution and the Operation Northwoods documents. These are not isolated examples. The historical record shows, for instance, that the explosion of the *USS Maine* in 1898 was falsely blamed on the Spanish in order to ignite a patriotic outrage among the American people and herd them into the Spanish-American War—the motive being to seize Spain's territory in the Western Hemisphere …

It is in fact a very old trick, practiced throughout history by the world's worst tyrants …

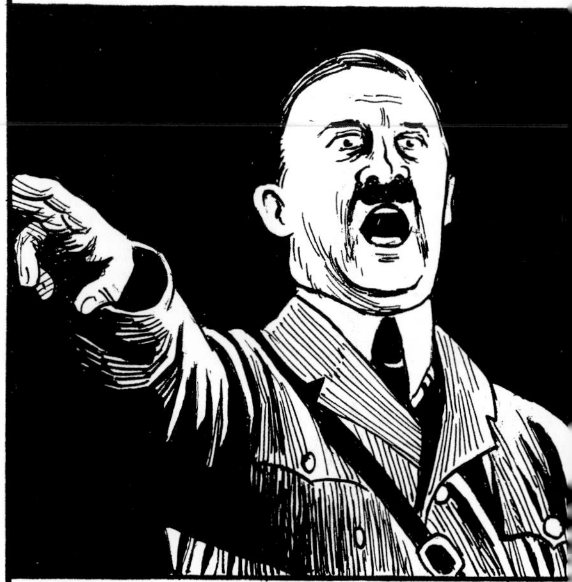

In 1933, the Nazis burned down the Reichstag and blamed their political enemies. The next day, Adolf Hitler was granted sweeping powers, thus setting the stage for the carnage of World War II …

The methods described in the Operation Northwoods documents, then, are not unique. What was unique was the president's refusal to carry out those plans. Since Kennedy's death, however, the military-industrial complex has encountered no more such obstacles. The Cold War has ended, but other excuses have been found to maintain a wartime economy—and always some hoax has been perpetrated to cause the American people to support wars which only serve corporate interests. One motivation for the Persian Gulf War, for instance, was to force Iraq to stop the "over-production" of oil which was driving down oil profits. In Senate testimony, April Glasspie, US Ambassador to Iraq, stated that, under orders from President George H. W. Bush, she informed Saddam Hussein that the U.S. would not intervene if Iraq invaded Kuwait. Saddam Hussein took the bait and invaded. Then, knowing that Americans would not support sending their sons and daughters to die for oil profits, the Bush administration hired public relations firm Hill & Knowlton to drum up war fever ...

In congressional testimony scripted by Hill & Knowlton, the Kuwaiti ambassador's daughter, pretending to be a nurse, described Iraqi soldiers looting incubators in a Kuwaiti hospital and throwing the babies on the floor to die—a completely false story. This resulted in a "helpful wave of national indignation," and so the war began …

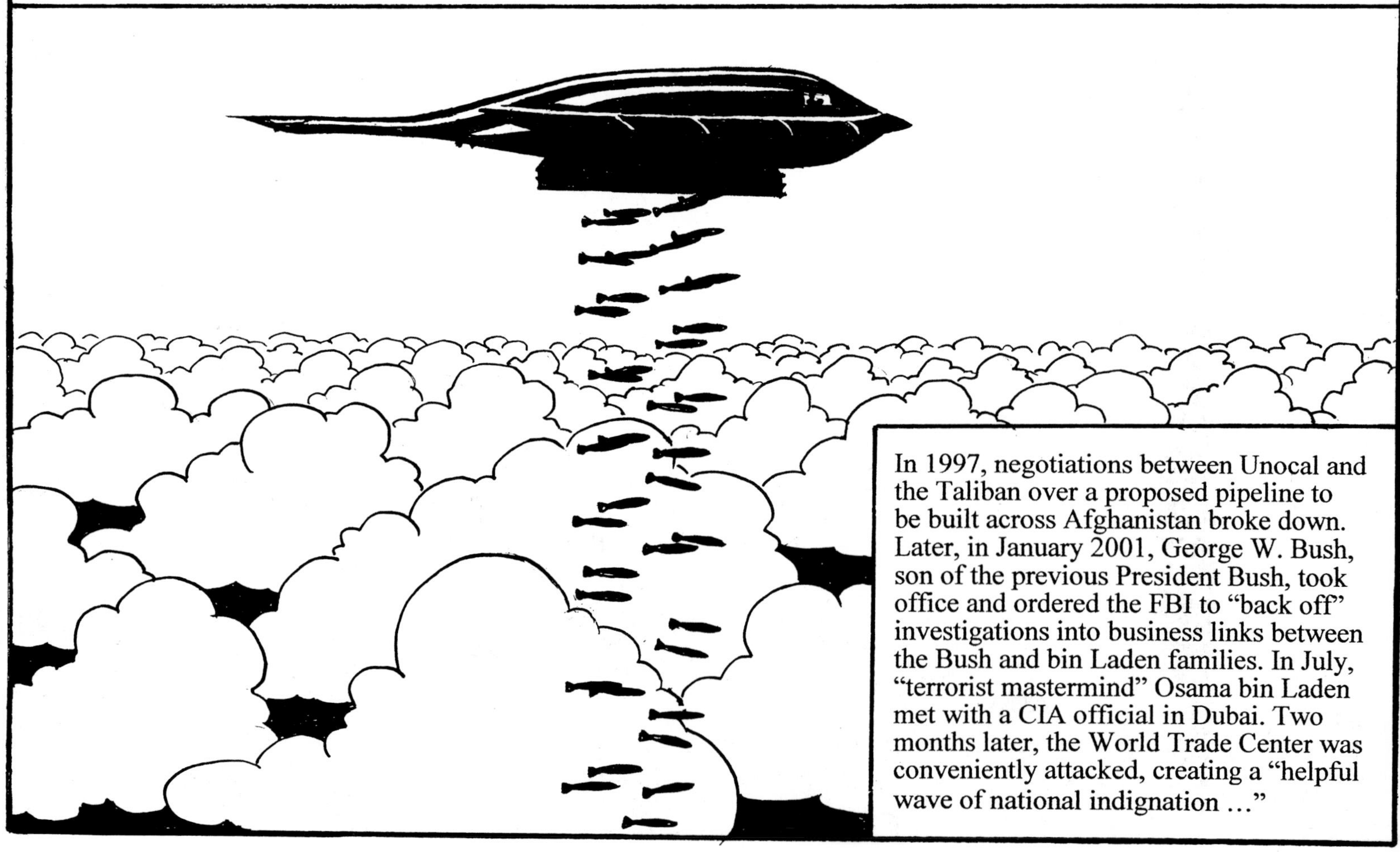

In 1997, negotiations between Unocal and the Taliban over a proposed pipeline to be built across Afghanistan broke down. Later, in January 2001, George W. Bush, son of the previous President Bush, took office and ordered the FBI to "back off" investigations into business links between the Bush and bin Laden families. In July, "terrorist mastermind" Osama bin Laden met with a CIA official in Dubai. Two months later, the World Trade Center was conveniently attacked, creating a "helpful wave of national indignation …"

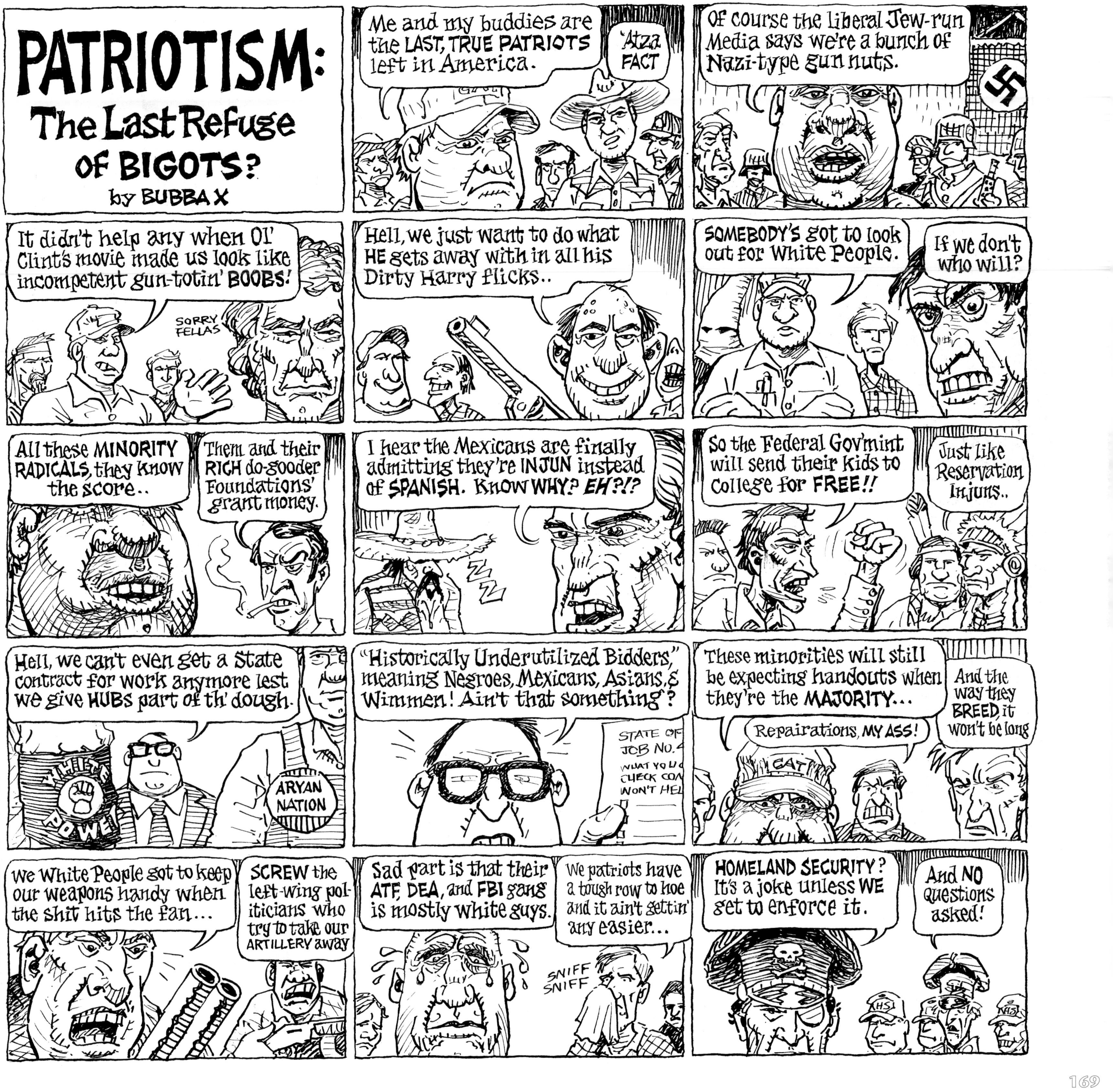
PATRIOTISM:
The Last Refuge
OF BIGOTS?
by BUBBA X
Me and my buddies are the LAST, TRUE PATRIOTS left in America.
'Atza FACT
Of course the liberal Jew-run Media says we're a bunch of Nazi-type gun nuts.
It didn't help any when Ol' Clint's movie made us look like incompetent gun-totin' BOOBS!
SORRY FELLAS
Hell, we just want to do what HE gets away with in all his Dirty Harry flicks..
SOMEBODY'S got to look out for White People.
If we don't who will?
All these MINORITY RADICALS, they know the score..
Them and their RICH do-gooder Foundations' grant money.
I hear the Mexicans are finally admitting they're INJUN instead of SPANISH. Know WHY? EH?!?
Z Z
So the Federal Gov'mint will send their kids to College for FREE!!
Just like Reservation Injuns..
Hell, we can't even get a State contract for work anymore lest we give HUBS part of th' dough.
ARYAN NATION
"Historically Underutilized Bidders," meaning Negroes, Mexicans, Asians, & Wimmen! Ain't that something?
These minorities will still be expecting handouts when they're the MAJORITY...
Repairations, MY ASS!
And the way they BREED, it won't be long
We White People got to keep our weapons handy when the shit hits the fan...
SCREW the left-wing politicians who try to take our ARTILLERY away
Sad part is that their ATF, DEA, and FBI gang is mostly white guys.
We patriots have a tough row to hoe and it ain't gettin' any easier...
SNIFF SNIFF
HOMELAND SECURITY? It's a joke unless WE get to enforce it.
And NO Questions asked!

WELL, SURE IT COULD BE REAL FUN TO GO OUT TO DINNER WITH YOU AND YOUR FAMILY.
CHRIS WARE
BLAH BLAH BLAH BLAH BLAH.
BLAH BLAH.
HEY! CAN WE HAVE A BREAK FROM ALL THIS "CHRIS TIME."
MY BROTHER PETE
I DON'T UNDERSTAND YOU! I WOULD NEVER SPEND SO MUCH TIME WITH SOMEONE JUST TO FURTHER MY CAREER!
NO, YOU DON'T UNDERSTAND! I GENUINELY LIKE HIM AND WANT TO BE HIS FRIEND!
GAK!
BUTTERKNIFE
NOW CHRIS HAS CHANGED INTO A WHITE SUIT WITH AN ART INSTITUTE LOGO ON IT WHICH IS FULL OF STAINS. I KNOW THAT HE GOT IT FOR FREE AT HIS GRADUATION, BUT IT IS STILL HIS ONLY SUIT.
SAIC
©2002 D. HEATLEY
SINCERE APOLOGIES TO C. WARE
HELLO! MY NAME IS DAVID HEATLEY AND I'M ASLEEP. I'M NAVIGATING THE MURKY WATERS OF MY UNCONSCIOUS MIND, STIRRING THE STEAMING CAULDRON FUELED BY INDIGESTION, AMBIENT NOISE, AND DAILY EXPERIENCE - ALL FOR YOUR VOYEURISTIC VIEWING PLEASURE.
I FOUND OUT THAT DAD WAS UNEMPLOYED AND WAS APPLYING FOR A JOB HE HAD DONE 20 YEARS AGO.
SOME MENIAL CLERK JOB.
SOB
TO ORDER DEADPAN DREAM COMICS #1
24 PAGES
FULL COLOR
SEND $5 concealed cash TO: 34-44 77TH ST. APT #4E Jackson Heights, NY 11372
OR GO TO: www.davidheatley.com
* THESE 2 DREAMS ARE BEING PRINTED HERE FOR THE FIRST TIME + ARE NOT IN DEADPAN #1.
** LOOK FOR A NEW 3-PAGE DREAM IN KRAMER'S ERGOT #4, OUT IN EARLY 2003.

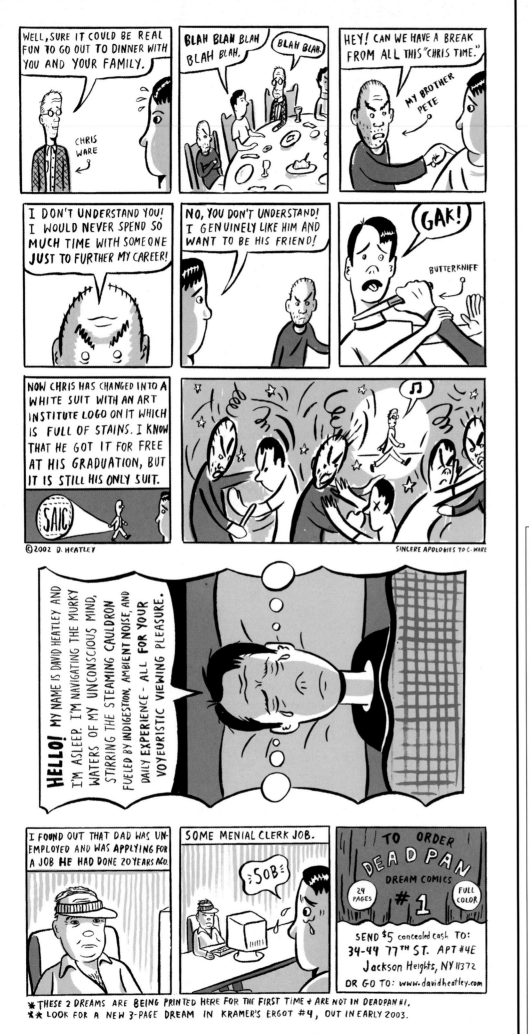

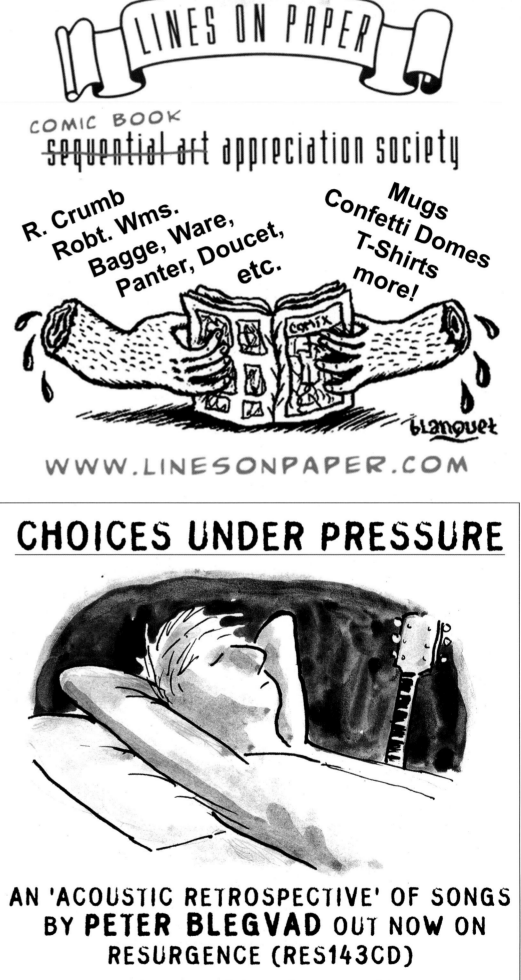

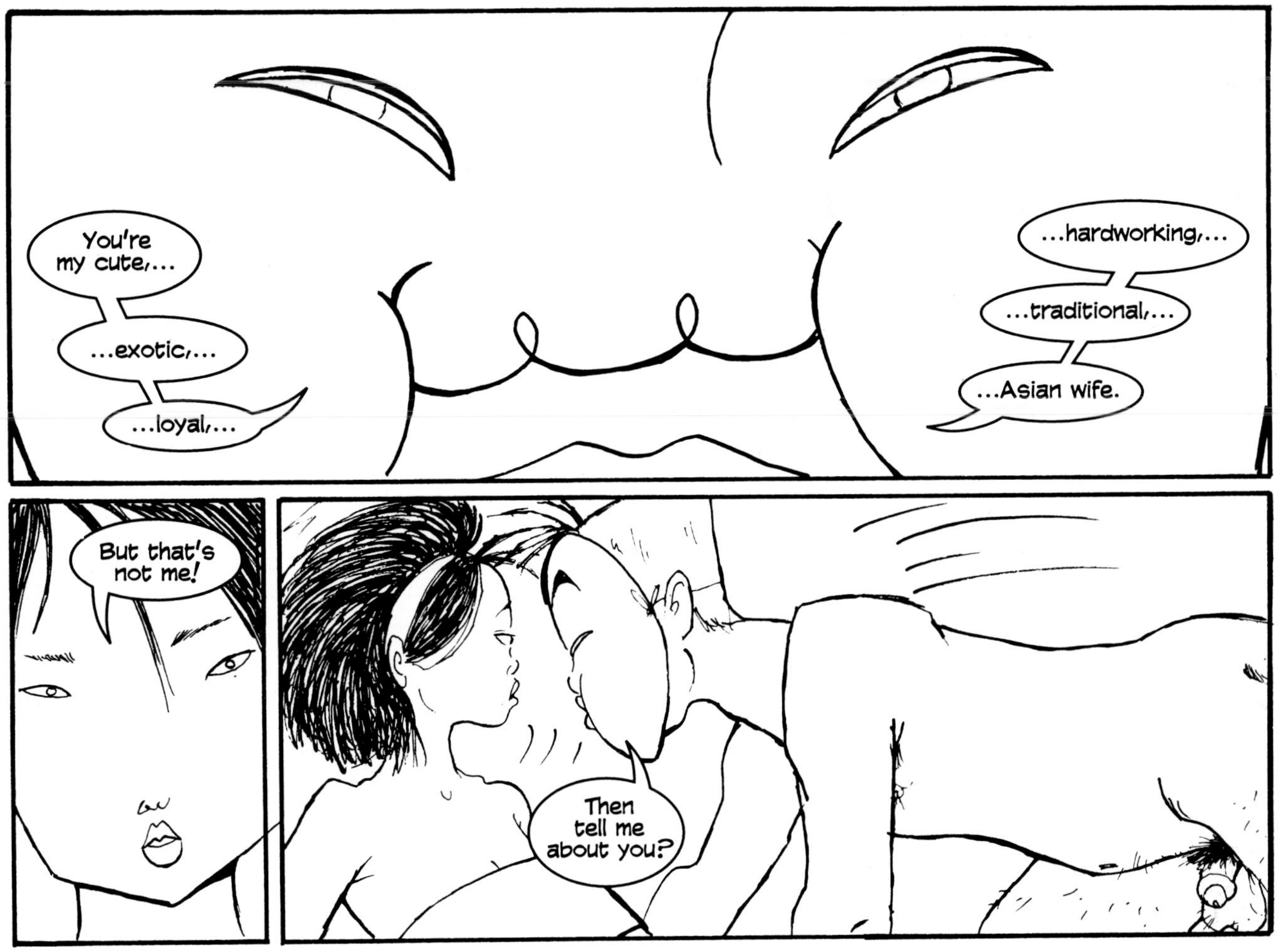
You're my cute,...
...exotic,...
...loyal,...
...hardworking,...
...traditional,...
...Asian wife.
But that's not me!
Then tell me about you?

Top: Panels from *Mail Order Bride.* © 2002 Mark Kalesniko.

ELEGANCE AND PAIN

The Art of Mark Kalesniko

by Mark David Nevins

Mark Kalesniko may well be the most under-appreciated "alternative" cartoonist currently working in North America. A professional animator who is rarely in comics' public eye, every few years this Canadian surfaces with another beautifully crafted graphical masterpiece; taken together, these pieces over the last decade or so comprise a collection of elegant, highly polished, and painfully honest comics.

Kalesniko's first published work was the short pantomime story "Adolph Hears a Who," which ran in the first volume of *Pictopia*, one of Fantagraphics' several short-run anthology series of the '80's and '90's. This eight-pager, the only color pages in the book, is an expressionist tour-de-force, marrying a lush, painterly style (a la Sienkiewicz and Steadman) with loose cartoony figures and a gifted sense of camera play. While the strip on its surface seems light and playful, there lurks below the surface a haunting seriousness — and that combination of the playful and the grave is a theme that runs throughout Kalesniko's work. In his early work, Kalesniko seems first and foremost interested in design and formalism — "Adolph" and the one-shot comic *S.O.S.* are infused with the lively experimentation of an animator discovering the possibilities of comics. *S.O.S.* is a sweet picture-poem about a young Asian woman lost at sea on a raft, her battles with a shark, and her growing discovery of feelings of freedom and independence. It's hard to say what this short comic is "about" — it's whimsical, funny, slightly erotic, and disorientingly dreamlike — but it's a virtuoso performance of energetic design, use of textures and patterns, and enrapturing movement.

As if to underscore his fascination with the juxtaposition of funny and serious, Kalesniko next presented us with *Alex*, a stunning and under-appreciated six-issue series that has been a cult favorite in spite of very little critical press; regrettably it has never been collected, and is not easy to find in the back-issue bins. *Alex* is a study of the slowly unraveling life of a cartoonist, told in a funny-animal style that serves to intensify the feelings of loneliness and despair which suffuse the story. A tale of psychological desolation told with deft, fluid drawings, *Alex* leaves its readers shaken, profoundly moved, and most of all hoping — for the sake of its creator — that the story is not in fact as autobiographical as it seems to be. Kalesniko followed *Alex* with the slim "graphic novel" *Why Did Pete Duel Kill Himself?*, which received a bit

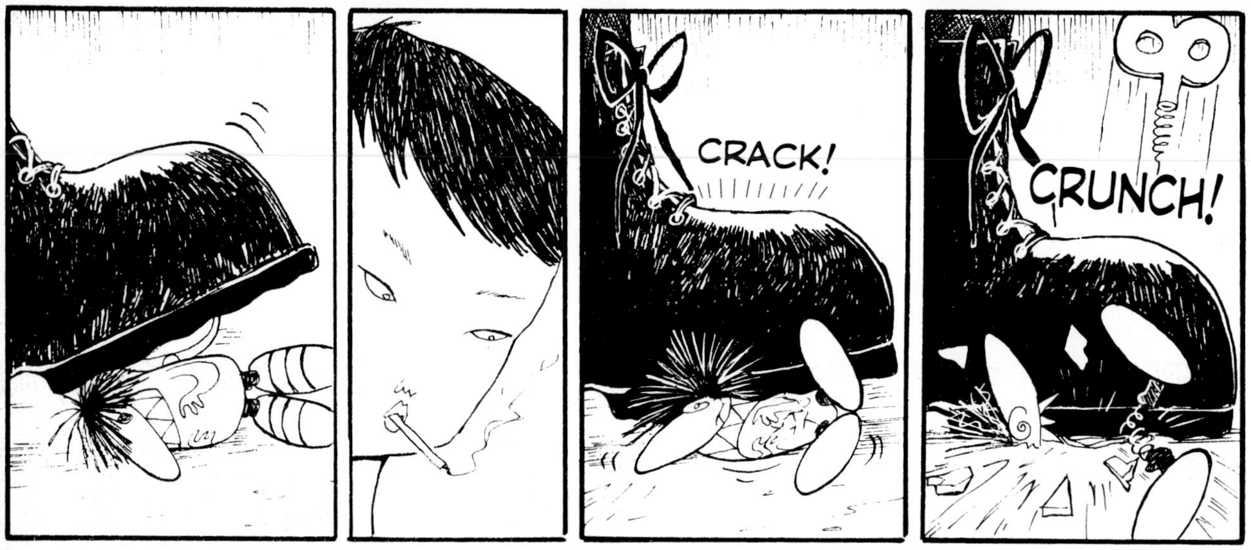
CRACK!
CRUNCH!

more acclaim. *Pete Duel* is another sobering apparent autobiography, again funny-animal style, this time examining a child's struggle to make sense of seemingly distant events that can nevertheless leave indelible lifelong traces. With *Pete Duel*, Kalesniko perfectly captures that the pain that all children must face as they grow up and realize that sometimes the world simply isn't fair.

* * * * * * * * * * *

As we enter the 21st Century, the still-maturing medium of comics seems, in America at least, to be gravitating toward "the big work." In the last few years, and almost always self-consciously in the shadow of *Maus*, a handful of efforts have seized the attention of comics aficionados as well as the mainstream press: *Safe Area Gorazde, Jimmy Corrigan, Cages, From Hell, David Boring*. Kalesniko's latest book, *Mail Order Bride*, stands taller and/or thicker on the bookshelf than most of those works, and yet, since its publication in early 2001, it has caused barely a ripple. That's a shame, because this book is ambitious, fresh, challenging, brilliantly drawn, and most importantly, an example of a developed and novelistic kind of storytelling far too rare in English-language comics.

An example of a developed and novelistic kind of storytelling far too rare in English-language comics.

Mail Order Bride is the story of Monty Wheeler and Kyung Seo; Monty is a comic-book and toy shop owner (this "easy" and obvious choice of occupation is one of the book's few weaknesses) and arrested adolescent living in a backwater Canadian town, and Kyung is the Korean woman whose immigration Monty enables by offering to marry her. However, soon after Kyung's arrival at the airport, it's clear she bears little resemblance to the "traditional" Asian wives the marriage service advertising brochure had promised. Worse, as time goes on Kyung rapidly adapts to her new environment, and poses a growing challenge to Monty when she refuses to be the stereotype he wants her to be ("obedient, domestic, hardworking, loyal"). To add further instability to this new relationship, Kyung

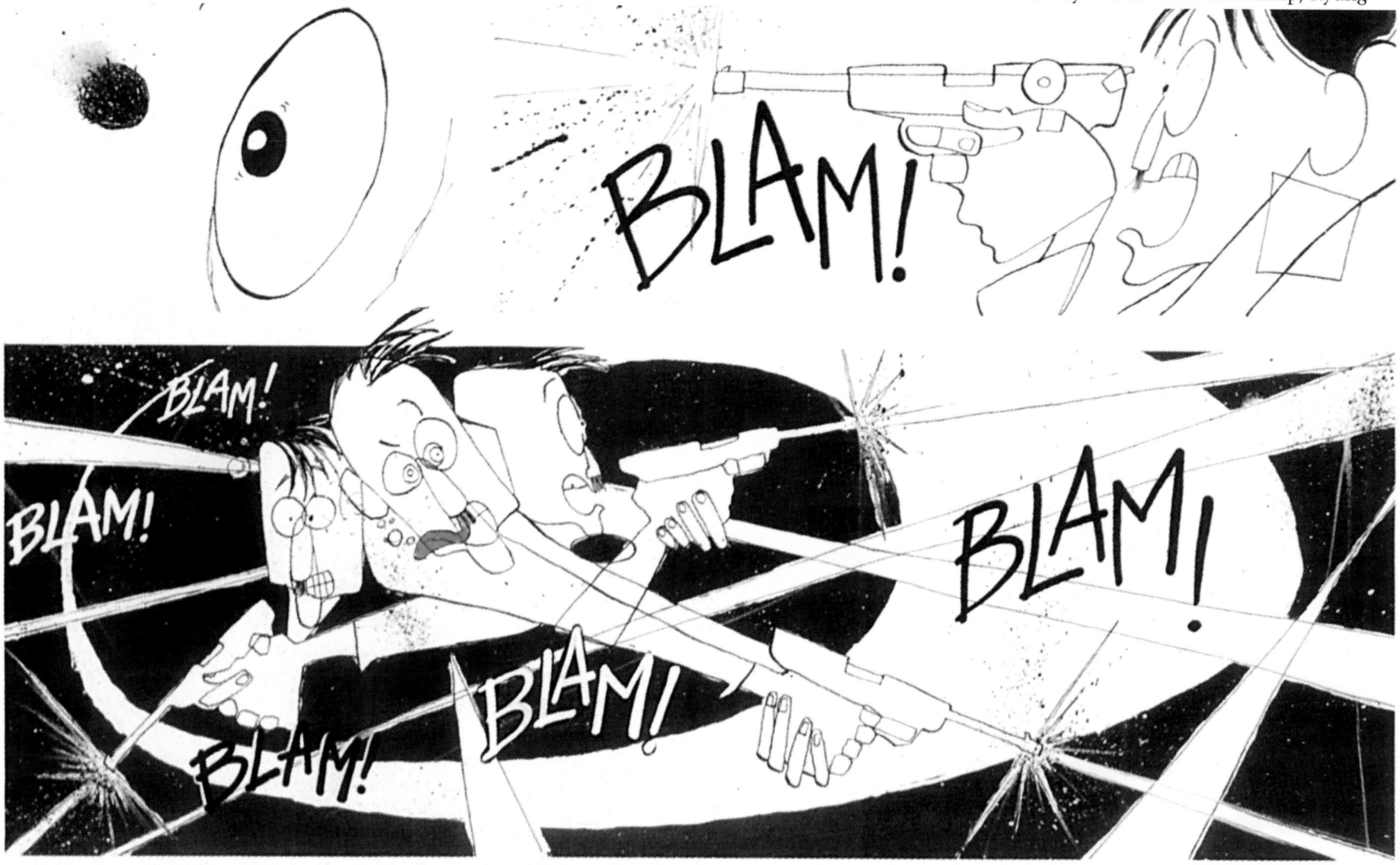
BLAM!
BLAM!
BLAM!
BLAM!
BLAM!
BLAM!

Top: Panels from *Mail Order Bride*. **Bottom:** Panel from "Adolf Hears a Who!" from *Pictopia* premiere issue. All © 2002 Mark Kalesniko.

begins to aspire to a life that is fuller and richer than the small and compulsively ordered one Monty has created for himself. There is an old saying that a woman falls in love with a man and immediately wants to change him, but that a man falls in love with a woman and wants her never to change from the way she was the day they met. *Mail Order Bride* deconstructs that idea, with the added twist that Monty cannot or will not accept or understand Kyung on her own terms because he's so trapped by what he *wants* her to be.

The author knows exactly where he wants to leave his reader: stunned, but struggling for meaning.

By means of repeated themes and motifs as well as a handful of vivid characters who act as foils to Monty and Kyung, *Mail Order Bride* offers a piercing exploration of race and identity, but it is also, more subtly, an ambitious study of how humans fashion themselves and how they make sense of others. This domestic story of considerable psychological depth is told via breathlessly graceful and fluid cartooning. Kalesniko's training as an animator is obvious — he is not afraid to draw, and the book's 270 deftly laid-out pages pull the reader through the story almost too quickly for him or her to enjoy Kalesniko's accomplished drawings. Every panel is a perfect illustration, but the pace is almost cinematic or manga-like. Unlike many talented comics artists, Kalesniko is not just an accomplished draftsman but is also such a good cartoonist that the reader is not trapped in the beauty of the individual panels; what remains in mind after closing the book are not distinct images but rather the broad narrative movements, the verbal repartee between characters, and the powerful emotions captured through Kalesniko's simple but expressive faces.

This graphic novel arrives at a somewhat unexpected conclusion when Kyung refuses to play her role as either a passive object in Monty's toy collection or one of the exotic playmates from his pornography collection. Kalesniko has been criticized as a cartoonist who doesn't know how to end his stories, and I've spoken with a number of readers who fault *Mail Order Bride* for an abrupt ending: that the tone of the book changes too radically, and that the ending is not "realistic." I disagree strongly with that assessment: while the comic does surge toward a violent ending, that ending is far more "realistic" than "melodramatic," and after several re-readings I can't imagine a better ending for this book. Visually and thematically the story comes full circle, and the author knows exactly where he wants to leave his reader: stunned, but struggling for meaning. Because in the end, the points Kalesniko wants to make are in fact not about race or stunted emotional development — rather, his points are about the concessions that everyone who is in a relationship must make; about the compromises people sometimes agree to in exchange for security; and about how the most essential reality of the human condition may well be loneliness. Thoreau famously claimed that "the mass of men lead lives of quiet desperation"; *Mail Order Bride* is a sensitive and unforgettable portrait of one couple who are doing just that.

Works discussed in this essay — all by Mark Kalesniko, all published by Fantagraphics Books:

"Adolf Hears a Who," in ***Pictopia*** Volume 1, Winter 1991
S.O.S. (single issue comic, 1992)
Alex (6-issue comic series, uncollected, 1994)
Why Did Pete Duel Kill Himself? (1997)
Mail Order Bride (2001) ★★★

Top: Panels from *Mail Order Bride*. © 2002 Mark Kalesniko.

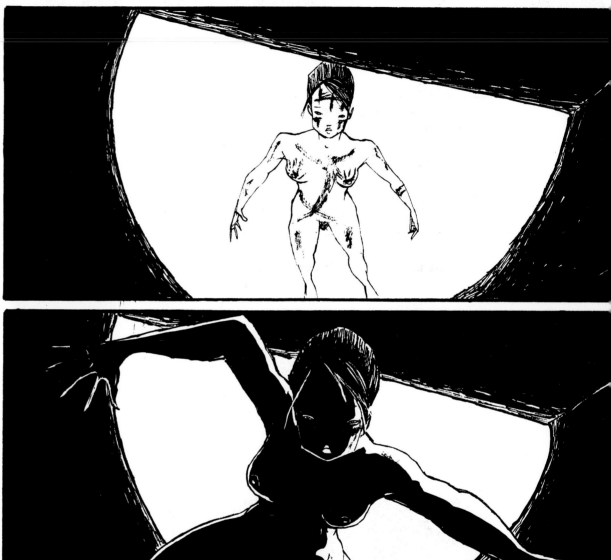

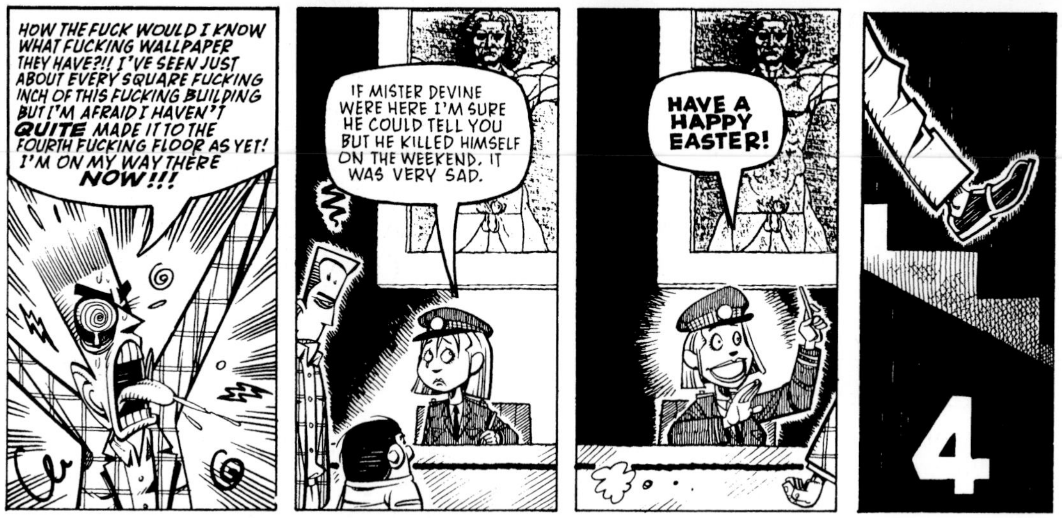
HOW THE FUCK WOULD I KNOW WHAT FUCKING WALLPAPER THEY HAVE?!! I'VE SEEN JUST ABOUT EVERY SQUARE FUCKING INCH OF THIS FUCKING BUILDING BUT I'M AFRAID I HAVEN'T QUITE MADE IT TO THE FOURTH FUCKING FLOOR AS YET! I'M ON MY WAY THERE NOW!!!
IF MISTER DEVINE WERE HERE I'M SURE HE COULD TELL YOU BUT HE KILLED HIMSELF ON THE WEEKEND. IT WAS VERY SAD.
HAVE A HAPPY EASTER!
4

Top: Crucifixion imagery from Andrew and Roger Langridge's *Zoot Suite*. © 2002 Andrew and Roger Langridge.

THE CIRCUS OF FOOLS HAS NO EGRESS

An Appreciation of Roger Langridge's Comics

by Milo George

One of the keystones of humor is that the fool never learns from his mistakes — at least, he never learns enough to escape his imbecility; there is no redemption for clowns. Artist/cartoonist Roger Langridge (b. 1967 in Auckland, New Zealand) has this simple premise down to a science. His fools are trapped on treadmills, unable to escape their fate, but what makes Langridge's work remarkable is how versatile it is, how he seems capable of blowing out a never-ending number of variations on the theme, often using the most limited of characters as his protagonist.

His comics, normally written by his brother Andrew or Cornelius Stone until recently, are always very smart, very smart-assed, but rarely didactic — Vladimir Nabokov once said that "Satire is a lesson; Parody is a game," and the bulk of Langridge's work is unapologetically parody, a steady stream of pure cartooning and humor for humor's sake, usually constructed in a marvelous narrative maze with blind alleys of non-sequiturs that baffle as much as they amuse. References to literature, high art, world history and the sciences abound throughout Langridge's work, but they're inevitably used as fodder for a joke. As such, there are some Will Elder-esque throwaway gags in some panels more richly clever than entire funnybooks by other humor cartoonists; one of my favorites is near the end of the first chapter of the Langridge brothers' brilliant novella *The Journey Halfway*: A well-known Leonardo drawing (the anatomy sketch of a male nude that illustrates the symmetry of the human body) is used as a poster behind the fifth-floor receptionist, cropped in a way that implies crucifixion, mirroring the same pose that Mr. Bodkin struck on the opposite page — in fact, a pose he strikes repeatedly in frustration while trudging up and down the stairs of the Council Building in a doomed attempt to recover his presumably impounded car before the office closes for the weekend.

A thread running through his work is that the conflict in any given narrative is fueled by violations of politesse: how a given protagonist deals with his antagonist's breach of etiquette, or how the protagonist is stuck in a system but is too polite to raise the ruckus needed to escape his situation. An example of the former would be the obnoxious can-throwing clods in "Short Story (Isolated Panel)" (*Zoot!* #4, 1993) where our hero demands an apology from the ne'er-do-well who hit his friend with a can of soda — Man: "Well, if they're arsehole enough to hurl cans of soft drink at a perfect stranger, there's probably no point demanding an apology from them ... [*to Jerk*] Did you throw that can?" Jerk: "Yeah, so?" Man: "Well, that was a pretty *stupid* thing to do." — needless to say, he doesn't get that apology by reason, so he beats it out of the Jerk.

The only difference between examples of the latter is that some of the prisoners are intelligent enough to know they're trapped and some aren't: The narrator in the (sadly unfinished) serial *The Derek Seals Story* repeatedly finds himself in a social situation, like a gallery party or an author's reading, where he's awkward and unsure what to do when Derek is confronted by a rather rude woman, but he's usually "saved" by Derek Seals himself; and Mr. Bodkin, from *The Journey Halfway*, stamps his feet, runs himself ragged and raises as much of a ruckus as he can, but still gets no closer than halfway to finding his missing car.

Kim, in the *Redoubtable Tarquin* series of short pieces, is repeatedly put-upon by Tarquin but is too polite to tell him to leave her alone — in fact, in the final Tarquin story from *Zoot!* (#5, December 1993) Tarquin imposes himself on Kim and her boyfriend Sam's hospitality, hijacking their dinner date to celebrate his birthday, which turns out to be an irritating ordeal for everyone except Tarquin. He orders an absurdly expensive meal, makes a complete ass of himself in the restaurant and skips out on Kim, Sam and the check he offered to pay, until he saw how much it was. The last we see of Kim, she and Sam are still sitting at the table, waiting for Tarquin to return from the bathroom, in the darkened restaurant, surrounded by shadowy restaurant workers, one of whom is politely clearing his throat to encourage the couple to pay and leave — without actually coming out and saying it, which would be rather rude. It's easy to imagine that, should the Brothers Langridge ever create another *Redoubtable Tarquin* episode, Kim may be angry with Tarquin, but she would still put up with his obnoxious behavior rather than be "rude" to him.

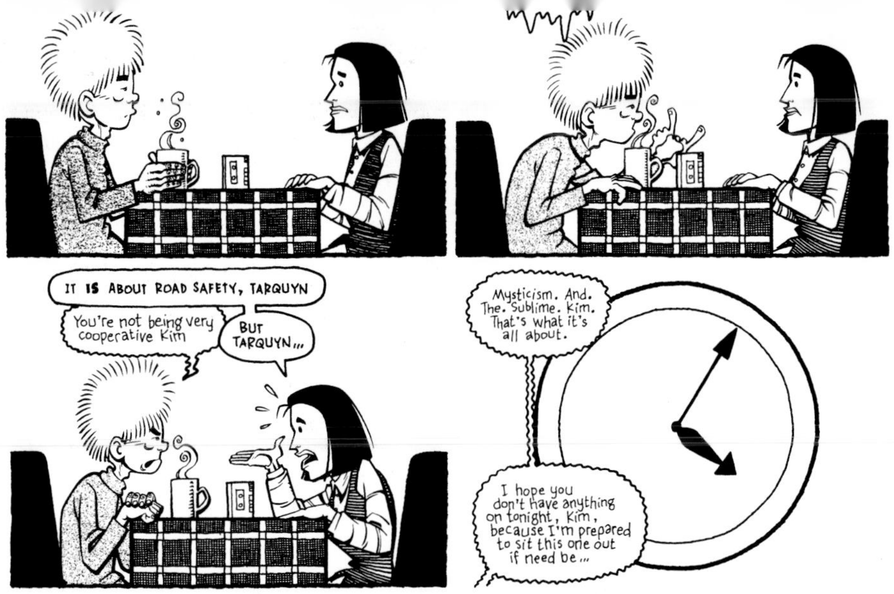

IT IS ABOUT ROAD SAFETY, TARQUYN
You're not being very cooperative Kim
BUT TARQUYN,,,
Mysticism. And. The. Sublime. Kim. That's what it's all about.
I hope you don't have anything on tonight, Kim, because I'm prepared to sit this one out if need be...

But it's Fred The Clown who's most chained by his politeness; he is bereft of almost any redeeming social trait, save his politeness; he's polite to the point of chivalry, an out-of-date attitude even in the slightly out-of-date world he inhabits. Most of Fred's problems are caused by his utter imbecility, but his outmoded sense of honor often leaves him with the shitty end of the stick; his notions of how to woo the opposite sex were old-hat when people stopped drinking phosphates and the market for buggy whips bottomed out, yet Fred continues to offer every woman he sees a flower in the hopes of the gesture winning her affection, usually getting a thrashing of some sort for his effort. The four issues of the self-published *Fred The Clown* comic-book series, Langridge's first solo work, present an interesting new wrinkle; Fred, as a character and a series, is monomaniacally focused on romance and love, something curiously absent from Langridge's collaborative work: Knuckles will fuck anything in sight, but there's no love involved, and the closest thing to a romantic relationship in the Brothers' oeuvre was the previously mentioned Kim and Sam relationship which is utterly disrupted by Tarquin. The other women in their work are curiously desexualized, usually peripheral figures in the narrative who act as the relative voice of reason, like "Em" in *Art D'Ecco* and Andrea in *The Journey Halfway* whose chats with Mr. Bodkin are oddly elided, making it difficult to determine if Bodkin is keen to chat with Andrea because he wants to see if she has more information about his missing car or because he's infatuated with her.[1]

Romances are never consummated and friendships are never quite cemented.

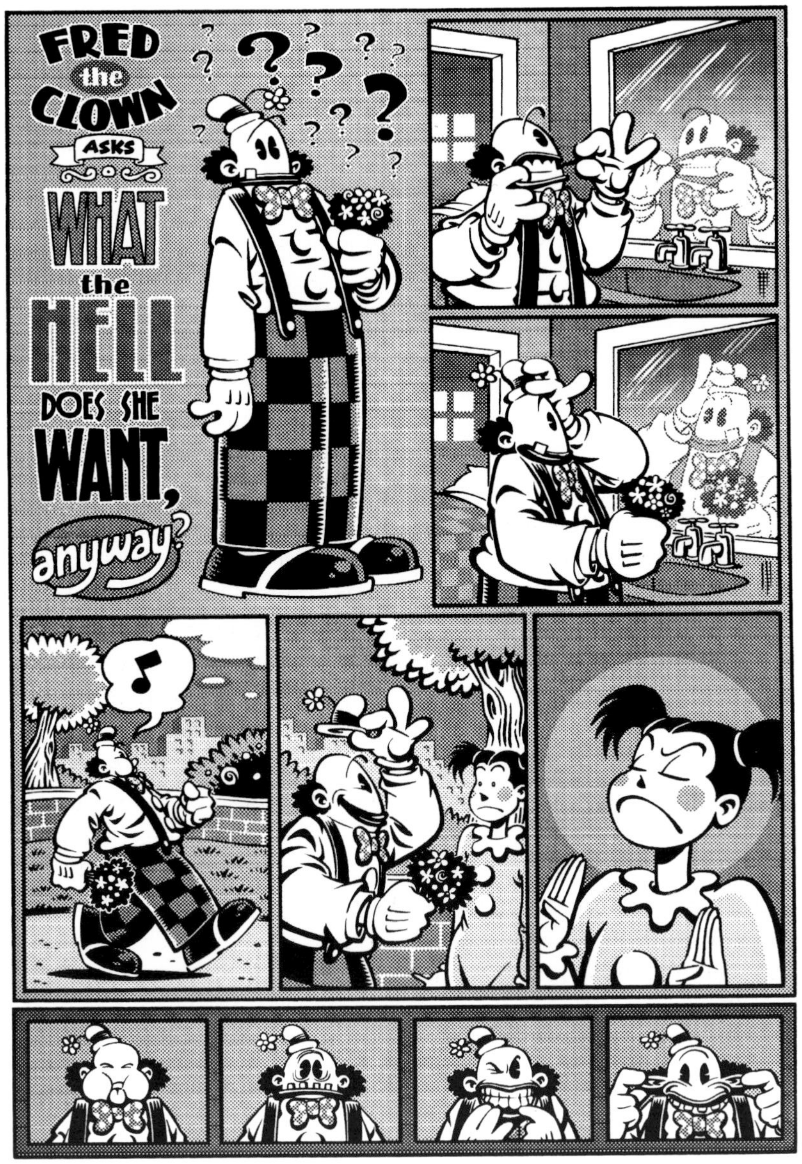

FRED the CLOWN ASKS WHAT the HELL DOES SHE WANT, anyway?

No one in Langridge's work ever quite makes a personal connection to another character; romances are never consummated and friendships are never quite cemented. Art D'Ecco would permanently get rid of the Gump in a heartbeat if he could; unfortunately, the Gump bounces back, completely unfazed, from every misfortune he suffers — especially those engineered by D'Ecco. Knuckles is somewhat fond of Spunky, but no one in Langridge's world is cruel enough to not love their pets. Bodkin and his little friend are surprisingly loyal to each other, the little guy accompanying Bodkin through his entire search and Bodkin staying at the little guy's hospital bedside after he's hit by a car while chasing after what he thinks is Bodkin's car. Fred The Clown has no friends to speak of; he has a pet dog in an early story (#1) and in a piece in the second issue, actually wins the girl, though it's the Fleischer-esque silent animated-film Fred, not the normal streamlined *Auguste*-clown Fred.

One recurring motif in Langridge's work is that almost all of his comic duos — Mr. Bodkin and his little friend, Art D'Ecco and the Gump, Mister Fussy and Mr. Coffee, God and Jesus, to a certain extent, in the Knuckles comics — are classic Whiteface-to-*Auguste* relationships: The big guy is inevitably "the boss," the straight man, the one who keeps the *Auguste* in line, and the little guy is a "red-nose"; the subordinate who is bossed around, the fool, an innocent id to the whiteface clown's knowing superego. An inversion of this dynamic is the Frankenstein-Shirley Temple relationship, where the big guy is somewhat more innocent and whimsical than the little girl, which is the also-classic comedy team of foolish-man and sensible-woman.

Standard *Auguste* clowns ("*auguste*" is German for "fool," and the story for how the *Auguste* got his name reads like something out of *Fred The Clown*) have orangey Caucasian-flesh tone color faces with only black-and-white paint (sometimes color) around their eyes and mouth.

Bottom left: From *Fred the Clown* #2. © 2002 Roger Langridge. **Top right:** "The Redoubtable Tarquyn" from *Zoot Suite*. © 2002 Andrew and Roger Langridge.

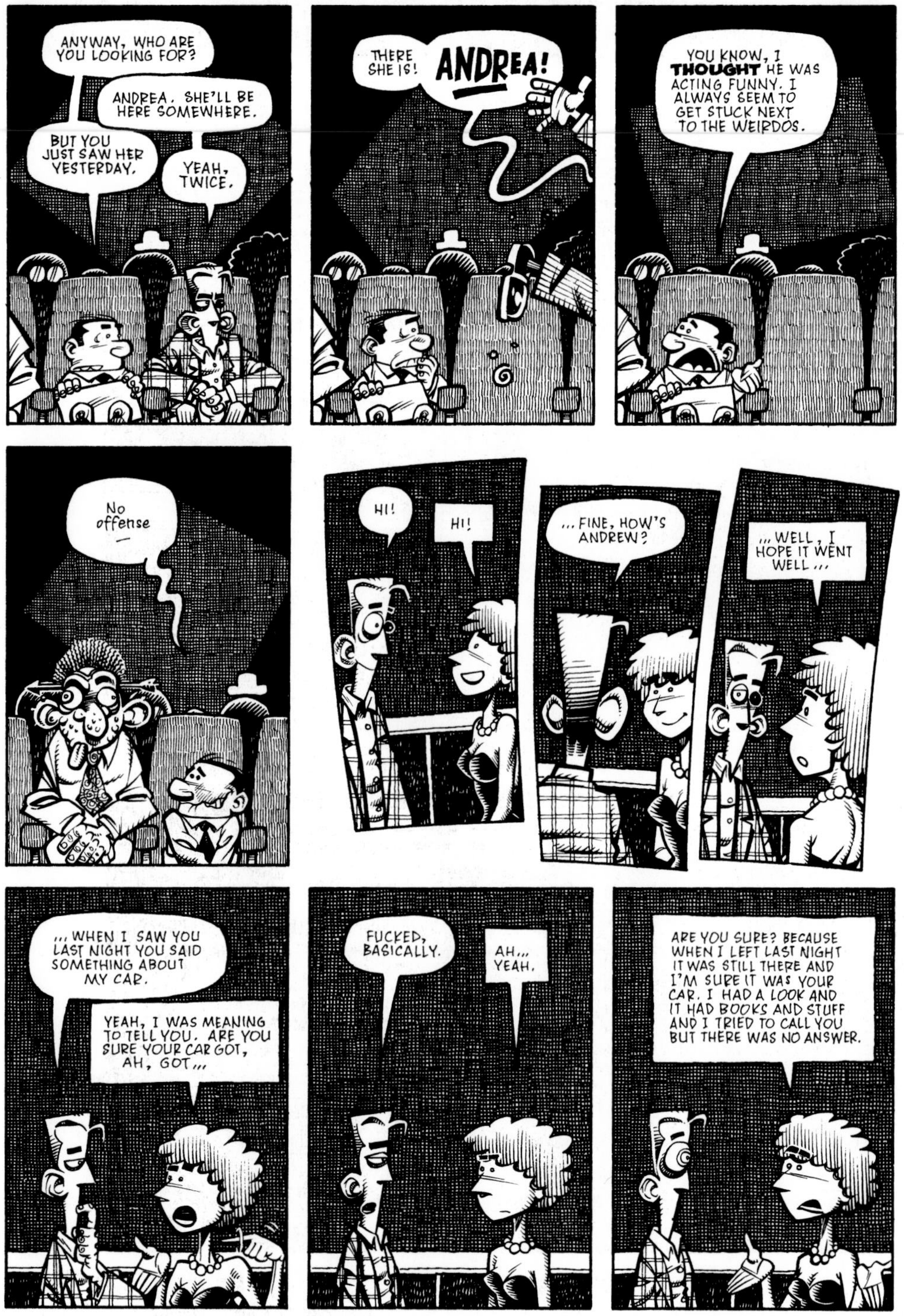
ANYWAY, WHO ARE YOU LOOKING FOR?
ANDREA. SHE'LL BE HERE SOMEWHERE.
BUT YOU JUST SAW HER YESTERDAY.
YEAH, TWICE.
THERE SHE IS!
ANDREA!
YOU KNOW, I THOUGHT HE WAS ACTING FUNNY. I ALWAYS SEEM TO GET STUCK NEXT TO THE WEIRDOS.
No offense —
HI!
HI!
...FINE, HOW'S ANDREW?
...WELL, I HOPE IT WENT WELL...
...WHEN I SAW YOU LAST NIGHT YOU SAID SOMETHING ABOUT MY CAR.
YEAH, I WAS MEANING TO TELL YOU. ARE YOU SURE YOUR CAR GOT, AH, GOT...
FUCKED, BASICALLY.
AH... YEAH.
ARE YOU SURE? BECAUSE WHEN I LEFT LAST NIGHT IT WAS STILL THERE AND I'M SURE IT WAS YOUR CAR. I HAD A LOOK AND IT HAD BOOKS AND STUFF AND I TRIED TO CALL YOU BUT THERE WAS NO ANSWER.

Top: The lighter side of Zeno's Paradox, from "The Journey Halfway," *Zoot Suite.* © 2002 Andrew and Roger Langridge.

They usually wear big red prosthetic noses and oversized, colorful stylized versions of normal clothing. The dynamic is that the red-nose Auguste rebels against his high-handed whiteface boss, making fun of him behind his back and such, winning the crowd's sympathy and cheers. Fred the Clown is an Auguste trapped in Langridge's whiteface universe. I'm not sure if any of Langridge's Augustes win the crowd over, save Bodkins' little friend.

Langridge's sole excursion into satire can be found in *Leather Underwear* (September 1990), a funny, passionate, decidedly Kurtzman-esque, rather blasphemous screed that marked Langridge's first major excursion into writing and drawing his comics. In *Underwear*, named because Langridge felt that accurately described the "constricting and uncomfortable about organized religion," Langridge deploys some invigoratingly Juvenalian comedy to stick it to the perversity and hypocrisy found in organized religion. His Knuckles comics with Stone are less focused on satire than straight-ahead disgusting and blasphemous laffs, but even the two-issue *Stench of Bitch* serial in the two-issue continuing series *Knuckles the Malevolent Nun* (1991) has that odd politeness; Knuckles is unrepentantly rude and obnoxious, but the conflict — the Devil, out of boredom and desire, has brought Knuckles to Hell, despite her not being dead yet — so Spunky and Witchbite the angelic penguin convince Jesus to travel to Hell with them to rescue her. Jesus and the Devil have a bizarrely civil debate until Jesus is rude to the Devil, who then kills him. You just can't win when it comes to deciding whether or not one should be rude to someone on his birthday.

Unlike most of his collaborations, where the majority of the humor lies in the dialogue and the narrative, a large amount of Langridge's solo *Fred The Clown* work is wildly imaginative pantomime, expressed in fluent body language and with an almost metronomic sense of pacing and rhythm. Langridge has a sure hand with staging creating some of the clearest, funniest comics slapstick which, like Jack Cole's best humor comics, has a curiously frozen feel, as if there's no such thing as momentum or inertia in his world.

The versatility of Langridge's work is remarkable.

Speaking of which: Leave it to those ingenious Langridge boys to take a mathematical theorem like Zeno's Paradox and apply it the mechanics of humor and narrative. *The Journey Halfway* (collected with some short pieces from the *Zoot!* series as *Zoot Suite*, the best funnybook of 1998) was built off the premise that you can't reach point B from point A, since you'll have to go half the distance between A and B but, to reach the halfway point, you have to first the halfway point to the halfway point, etc., thus giving Langridge's characters a semi-scientific law governing their actions. (Langridge "dirties" his style up for his Knuckles work with Stone and the deconstructionist adventure romps *Dr. Spin* and *The Kabuki Kid*, the latter two written by Gordon Rennie and serialized in *Dark Horse Presents,* the former dirtied up to the point of nearly inducing nausea in the reader.)

One of the things I value the most in Langridge's recent solo work is its keen and astute understanding of comics history; he clearly has a broad and deep understanding of what has come before him, and his work creatively builds on that knowledge, mapping out new areas where the medium can go while coming to grips with its rich history. Clever references and ingenious homage to century-class cartoonists like Carl Barks, Winsor McCay and George Herriman abound in even his earliest work, but it is for *Fred The Clown* (Collection Lilliput, 1999) that this knowledge is brought to bear to create a full-blown masterpiece. Ostensibly a cleverly packaged collection of the sample strips Langridge drew to pitch a *(Bill) Fred The Clown* newspaper strip as well as various odds and ends, this small pamphlet wends it way through a deadpan-hilarious pseudo-*roman à clef* of 20th century comics history that does Michael Chabon one better; Langridge illustrates his essay on his mirror universe's history of comics with spot-on imitations of a century's worth of cartoonists — R.F. Outcault, Frederick B. Opper, McCay, Herriman, Jack Kirby, Chic Young, R. Crumb, et al.

Most recently, Langridge has been producing a weekly comic for his Web site www.hotelfred.com, which also boasts of an absurdly rich collection of rare and unseen comics — even without the archive of the webcomic (recently moved to www. Moderntales. com), the site features PDF files of his minicomics; various magazine comics, including the beautifully color-painted Diabolical Liberty from the UK magazine

Deadline; newspaper series and material created for unproduced projects. If that weren't enough, Langridge has been self-publishing quarterly *Fred The Clown* comic-book collections of the weekly Webcomic (not that you'd notice) though the most recent issue, #4, features a story drawn specifically for the issue.

The versatility of Langridge's work is remarkable; his work — in some cases, the same piece — smoothly and usually seamlessly adapts to the minicomic, Webcomic, comic-book and graphic-novel format, a rare feat. Langridge's control of his tools — from crowquill, technical pen and brush inking to Zipatone film shading to full-color painting to Photoshop coloring — is as accomplished as it is broad. But one thing is fairly certain — no matter how skilled his cartooning skills become, his fools probably still won't be able to find their way out of the circus tent. You can't get there from here.

Fred The Clown #1-4 $2.95 each, Hotel Fred Press
Fred The Clown: Lilliput Collection, $5.95, Les Cartoonistes Dangereux
Zoot Suite $9.95, Fantagraphics
Zoot! #1-6 $2.50 each, Fantagraphics
Art D'Ecco #1-2 $2.50 each, #3 $2.75, #4 $2.95, Fantagraphics
Knuckles The Malevolent Nun #One $2.25, #2 $2.00, Fantagraphics
Leather Underwear #1 $2.50 Fantagraphics
Gross Point #1-14, DC Comics

Anthology Appearances:
A1 Vol.1, # 5, Atomeka Press
A1 Vol.2 #1-4 $5.95 each, Marvel/Epic Comics
The Big Book of … series: volumes *Bad*, *Conspiracies*, *Grimm*, *Hoaxes*, *Little Criminals*, *Losers*, *Martyrs*, *the '70s*, *the Weird Wild West*, *Thugs*, *Urban Legends* and *Vice* $14.95 each, DC Comics
Bizarro Comics $29.95, DC Comics
Comix 2000 $75.00, L'Association
Dark Horse Presents #97-99 $2.50 each, #115-118 $2.95 each
Expo 2001 $6.95, Comic Book Legal Defense Fund
9-11: Artists Respond $9.95, Chaos! Dark Horse and Image Comics ★★★

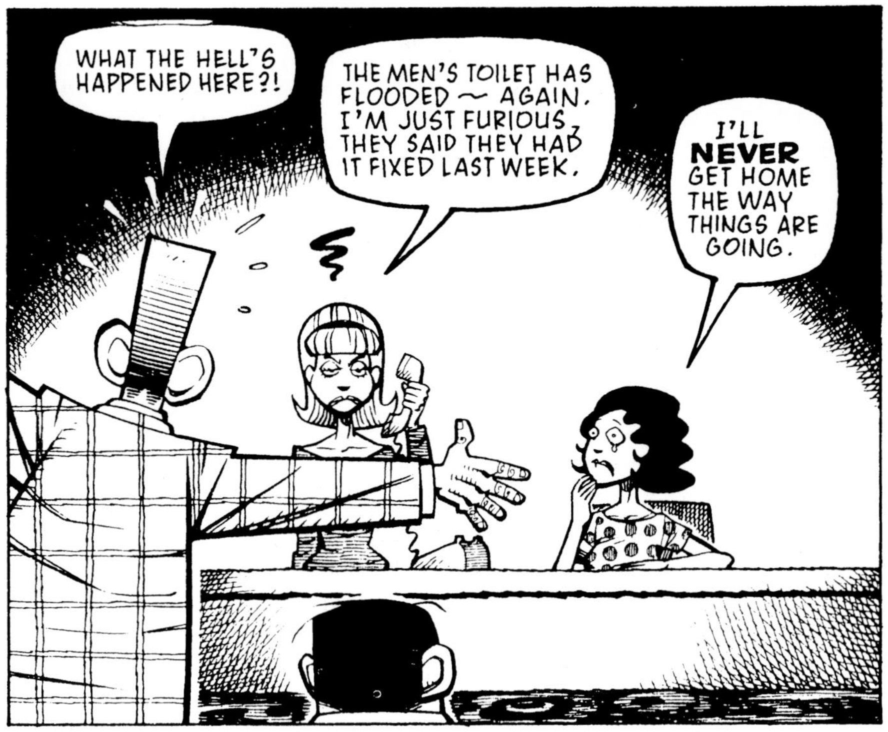
WHAT THE HELL'S HAPPENED HERE?!
THE MEN'S TOILET HAS FLOODED ~ AGAIN. I'M JUST FURIOUS. THEY SAID THEY HAD IT FIXED LAST WEEK.
I'LL NEVER GET HOME THE WAY THINGS ARE GOING.

Bottom left: Crucified again, from *Zoot Suite*. © 2002 Andrew and Roger Langridge. **Top right:** A keen understanding of comics history, from *Fred the Clown*. © 2002 Roger Langridge.

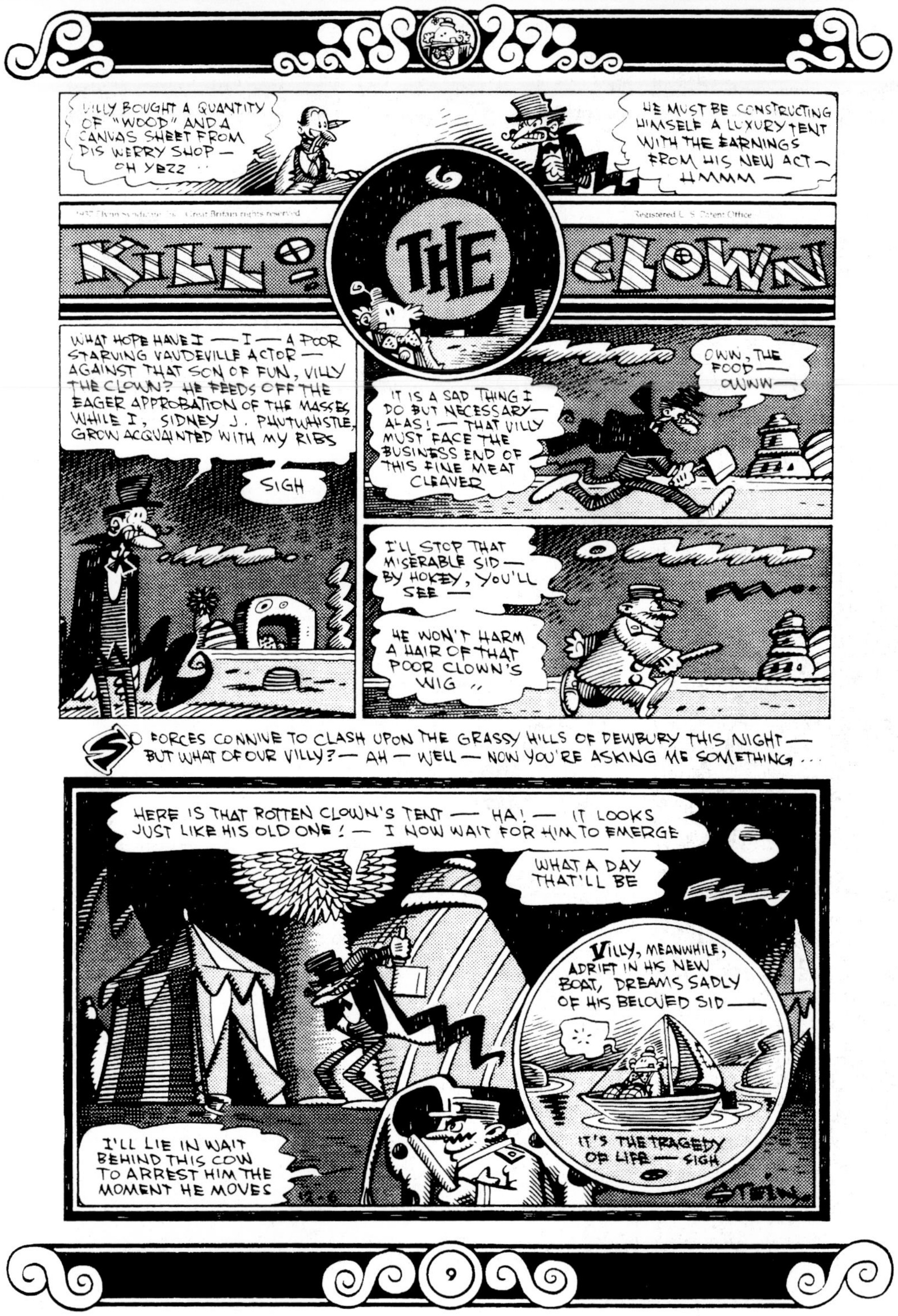
VILLY BOUGHT A QUANTITY OF "WOOD" AND A CANVAS SHEET FROM DIS WERRY SHOP — OH YEZZ ..
HE MUST BE CONSTRUCTING HIMSELF A LUXURY TENT WITH THE EARNINGS FROM HIS NEW ACT — HMMM —
Registered U.S. Patent Office
KILL THE CLOWN
WHAT HOPE HAVE I — I — A POOR STARVING VAUDEVILLE ACTOR — AGAINST THAT SON OF FUN, VILLY THE CLOWN? HE FEEDS OFF THE EAGER APPROBATION OF THE MASSES WHILE I, SIDNEY J. PHUTWHISTLE, GROW ACQUAINTED WITH MY RIBS
SIGH
IT IS A SAD THING I DO BUT NECESSARY — ALAS! — THAT VILLY MUST FACE THE BUSINESS END OF THIS FINE MEAT CLEAVER
OWW, THE FOOD — OWWW —
I'LL STOP THAT MISERABLE SID — BY HOKEY, YOU'LL SEE —
HE WON'T HARM A HAIR OF THAT POOR CLOWN'S WIG ..
SO FORCES CONNIVE TO CLASH UPON THE GRASSY HILLS OF DEWBURY THIS NIGHT — BUT WHAT OF OUR VILLY? — AH — WELL — NOW YOU'RE ASKING ME SOMETHING ...
HERE IS THAT ROTTEN CLOWN'S TENT — HA! — IT LOOKS JUST LIKE HIS OLD ONE! — I NOW WAIT FOR HIM TO EMERGE
WHAT A DAY THAT'LL BE
VILLY, MEANWHILE, ADRIFT IN HIS NEW BOAT, DREAMS SADLY OF HIS BELOVED SID —
I'LL LIE IN WAIT BEHIND THIS COW TO ARREST HIM THE MOMENT HE MOVES
IT'S THE TRAGEDY OF LIFE — SIGH
9

[1]I should mention here that, speaking of women in the Langridge brothers' work, the reason I don't discuss the remarkable "Short Story" from *Zoot!* #3 (a fairly brilliant comics-form essay on the Black Dahlia murder) here is because it was written *and* drawn by Andrew Langridge; from the looks of the piece, Roger merely lettered most of the story and inked some of Andrew's pencils. I don't want to start down that slippery slope, since Roger inked more of some otherwise dreadful *Captain America* comics than "Short Story."
I also don't discuss *Gross Point* here, since Langridge's work on the series is mostly as the inker of a monthly funnybook assembly line, not a true collaboration — and, even as such, Langridge inks far lesser artists' penciled art. The lead stories in issues #4, 5, 13 and 14, however, are small delights; all-Langridge art in full color, #5 featuring an assured parody of EC horror comics and #13-14 suggesting the best of Kurtzman's color-pamphlet *Mad* comics with nary a direct reference.

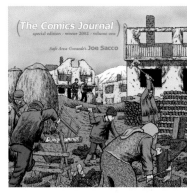

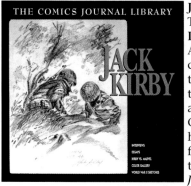

CONTRIBUTORS

Who are these deluded fanatics?

Ho Che Anderson, a resident of Toronto, is the author of the graphic novels *Young Hoods In Love* and *I Want To Be Your Dog* and the co-author of the mini-series *Pop Life*. *King* Volume 1, his controversial biography of the civil rights leader, earned him a 1995 Parents' Choice Award. *Publishers Weekly* listed *King* Volume 2 as a Best Book 2002 in the graphic novel category. *King* Volume 3, the concluding volume, is due out in the spring of 2003.

John Arcudi is a freelance writer. His work has appeared in numerous comics, a few online publications, and an occasional magazine.

John Bagnall studied painting and began self-publishing comics in Liverpool in 1984. His small-press titles included *Trashcan*, *Atlantic Garage*, *Goof Out*, *Corn Starch Primer* and *Ginchy Gazette*. At the same time his strips were regularly published in *Escape* and anthologies from the USA, Europe and Australia. During the 1990s he edited lowbrow-culture magazine *Hairy Hi-Fi* and settled in the ancient Norman city of Durham. *A Nation of Shopkeepers* was published by Corncob in 2000. A book of new strips, *Don't Tread on My Rosaries*, will be released in early 2003.

Peter Blegvad's *Book of Leviathan*, which originally ran in the *Independent* on Sunday, was collected and released by The Overlook Press in 2000 and was nominated for an Eisner Award. His recent musical work has included such releases as Choices Under Pressure, Hangman's Hill (with John Greaves & Chris Cutler) and Just Woke Up. He has recorded with Faust, Slapp Happy/Henry Cow, Kew.Rhone, The Lodge, Golden Palominos and the Peter Blegvad Trio.

Ivan Brunetti lives in Chicago, where he works as a web designer. His *Haw!*, a collection of hilarious and morally questionable gag panels, and three issues of *Schizo*, his autobiographical comic-book series, are all available from Fantagraphics. Brunetti is currently at work on a fourth *Schizo*, due out soon.

Jordan Crane currently lives in Los Angeles, and has published five issues of the acclaimed anthology *Non* and the comics novels, *The Last Lonely Saturday* and *Col-Dee*. His third book, *Keeping Two*, came out in 2002.

Glenn Dakin is a child of the '60s and from an early age fell under the influence of such people as Bingo, Fleagle Drooper and Snorky. In the 1970s he created Abe Rat. In the 1980s Glenn created many weird comics for the British Fast Fiction scene, including *Dakin Weekly* and *Paris the Man of Plaster*. In the 1990s he worked as an editor at Marvel Comics UK and carried his guitar around trying to impress girls.

Kim Deitch is one of the finest cartoonists of the underground generation. Two thousand-two was his year: His comic of all-new material, *The Stuff of Dreams* was published (Fantagraphics Books) and his big collection of previously published work, *The Boulevard of Broken Dreams* was released by Pantheon.

Phil Elliott is perhaps best known for his comic *Blite*. He is just now putting the finishing touches to some as yet untitled comic strips commissioned by the Agricultural Research Centre at Rothamsted, and 2003 should see the release of new work such as *Tupelo*, old work like *Illegal Alien*, and coloring Paul Grist's *Jack Staff*.

Hunt Emerson has drawn cartoons and comic strips since the early 1970s, mostly with Knockabout Comics (London), which include *Lady Chatterley's Lover*, *The Rime of the Ancient Mariner*, and *Casanova's Last Stand*. You can see more of his work on his website www.largecow.demon.co.uk.

Jesse Fuchs is a complicated man, and no one understands him but his woman. More of his work can be found at www.numbertwopencil.net, and his band Denver Zest frequently plays shows in Manhattan, Brooklyn, and the outlying provinces.

Rick Geary's work has appeared in *National Lampoon*, *Mad*, *Spy*, *Rolling Stone*, *The Old Farmer's Almanac*, *American Libraries*, *Pulse!*, *Wood & Steel*, *Computeredge*, *Roadstar*, *California Lawyer*, *Los Angeles Magazine*, *Heavy Metal* and *San Diego Magazine*. A collection of his short strips, *Housebound with Rick Geary*, has been published by Fantagraphics Books. NBM has published several volumes of his true crime tales of the last century, including *Treasuries of Victorian Murder*.

Milo George is the managing editor of *The Comics Journal* and claims to be a former "escape artist" (no relation to *Escape* magazine).

Phoebe Gloeckner's 1998 collection of short stories and illustrations, *A Child's Life*, earned the artist high praise for her hard-edged realism and a feature article in *The New York Times Magazine*. Her most recent book, a hybrid of the traditional novel and graphic novel forms called *Diary of a Teen-age Girl*, was released in November 2002.

Paul Gravett co-edited *Escape* from1983 to 1989 with Peter Stanbury and was the director of The Cartoon Art Trust in London from 1992-2001. He continues to curate comic art exhibitions and addresses the state of the comics medium through articles, lectures, broadcasts and publishing projects.

Bill Griffith co-edited the seminal comics anthology *Arcade*, *The Comics Revue* for its seven-issue run in the mid-1970s. He lives in Connecticut, where he writes and draws the syndicated *Zippy* strip. His most recent book is the *Zippy Annual 2002*, which is (almost) exactly what it sounds like.

Gary Groth is the esteemed founder of *The Comics Journal*, which has been raising the hackles of creators and fans alike for more than 25 years, Lord have mercy on our souls.

Sam Henderson is, quite possibly, the funniest cartoonist alive. His popular *Magic Whistle* series has recently hit issue #8 and his *Magic Whistle* collection *Humor Can Be Funny* will be reprinted by Alternative Comics in February 2003. Check out the publisher's website at www.Indyworld.com/whistle for more information about his work.

Tim Hensley's work recently appeared in *Dirty Stories* Volume 3 and *TCJ Summer Special 2002*.

Gerald Jablonski is the author of the comic book *Empty Skull*. He lives in Albany, New York. His Xeric Grant-awarded *Cryptic Wit* has just appeared.

Jack Jackson is generally credited with having created the first underground comic, *God Nose*, a collection of satirical strips he self-published in 1964. He co-founded Rip Off Press with Gilbert Shelton, Fred Todd and Dave Moriaty in the late '60s. He has two collections, *Optimism of Youth* and *God's Bosom*, available from Fantagraphics. He has just published his brilliant historical novel, *The Alamo*.

Ted Jouflas was born in Utah and raised in California. A contributor to the seminal 1980s anthology *Weirdo*, he's currently working on the follow-up to his earlier sociopolitical graphic novels, *Filthy* and *Scary*.

Mark Kalesniko is a former animator and author of the graphic novels *Alex* and *Why Did Pete Duel Kill Himself?*. The California resident's most recent work is *Mail Order Bride*, which earned him nominations for Eisner, Harvey and Firecracker Alternative Book awards.

Megan Kelso lives in Brooklyn, New York with her husband and cat. Her first collection of comics stories is *Queen of the Black Black* from Highwater Books. She's working on a graphic novel called *Artichoke Tales* that is being serialized on the Highwater Books website.

John Kerschbaum is, among other things, the cartoonist responsible for The *Wiggly Reader* and *Petey & Pussy*. His work has appeared in *The New York Times*, *The New Yorker*, *Nickolodeon Magazine*, *Newsday*, *Spy*, *National Lampoon* and *The Village Voice*. He is loosely based in New York City.

Michael Kupperman's 2000 HarperCollins release, *Snake 'n' Bacon's Cartoon Cabaret*, earned him instant cult status among comics fans. Cartoons from the book were adapted for Comedy Central's TV Funhouse. His comics and illustrations have appeared in *The New Yorker*, *Fortune*, *The New York Times* and *L.A. Weekly*. He lives and works in New York City.

Roger Langridge spent his New Zealand childhood drawing comic strips, both on his own and with his brother, Andrew. Fantagraphics Books picked up their first mini-comic and transformed it into the one-shot magazine-sized comic *Art d'Ecco*. *Zoot*, a six-issue series, appeared in the 1980s, followed by the graphic novel *Zoot Suite*, both from Fantagraphics. Langridge's most recent comic, *Fred the Clown*, marks his return to self-publishing and is available at ModernTales.com and in quality bookstores everywhere.

Mark Martin has appeared in *Tantalizing Stories* (in collaboration with Jim Woodring), and in the *Comics Buyers' Guide* (in his strip *20NudeDancers20*, which was collected into a book of the same name). Currently, he publishes an occasional strip in *Nickelodeon Magazine* and has contributed to the upcoming anthology *I Hate Cartoons* Volume 2.

Mark David Nevins is the New York correspondent for renowned Swiss comics periodical *STRAPAZIN*. He has served for the last seven years on the Executive Committee of the International Comic Arts Conference (ICAF) and sits on the Editorial Board of the International Journal of Comic Art.

Diane Noomin, the editor of the women-only anthologies *Twisted Sisters*, also created the always-ready-for-a-party DiDi Glitz.

David Paleo was born and lives in Argentina where he claims to be currently unemployed, friendless and lacking a high school diploma. His strip in this volume is his first published work, but he promises, not his last.

Savage Pencil was born in Leeds, West Yorkshire, England in 1951. He studied graphic design at Colchester School Of Art and the Royal College Of Art in London. While there, he started drawing *Rock 'N' Roll Zoo* strip for *Sounds* magazine, where he would go on to work as a designer, editor and illustrator. He worked for *Escape*, *NME*, *Kerrang!*, *Loaded*, *Top*, *Men's World*, *Frieze*, *Juxtapoz*, *Mojo*, *Bizarre* and is a regular contributor to *The Wire*. He currently lives in London.

Donald Phelps is a world-class critic, not just of comics, but also of fiction, film and poetry. He has been writing about the arts for over 40 years, published his own guerilla cultural magazine in the 1960s, *For Now*, and has appeared in various literary, political and film magazines including *Pulpsmith*, *The Nation* and *Film Comment*. His *Reading the Funnies* from Fantagraphics recently won the American Book Award. He writes regularly for *The Comics Journal*.

Woodrow Phoenix converts vast quantities of fizzy sugared water, cathode ray tube radiation, Trifle, old newsprint, curry goat, Pizzicato Five records, crêpes, and udon noodles into comics, book covers and magazine illustration. His comic The Sumo Family was a regular color strip in *The Independent on Sunday* and *Manga Mania* magazine. His other comics include a meta-fictional Sherlock Holmes tale with Gordon Rennie; *The Liberty Cat*, a short-lived series for Kodansha, Japan; and a contribution to *Grendel Black White & Red*. He is co-creator of the award-winning *Sugar Buzz!* from Slave Labor.

Ed Pinsent was born in Liverpool in 1960. Studied Fine Art and film theory 1979-1982. He wrote, drew and self-published his own comic strip stories 1982-1992, reckoned as part of the UK's "Fast Fiction" scene and appeared in *Escape* magazine. Now semi-retired from comics, he edits and writes a music magazine called *The Sound Projector*.

Gary and Warren Pleece started in comics with strips for *Escape* magazine and their own renowned rag, *Velocity*. They have also worked with magazines like *Crisis*, *Revolver* and at Dark Horse. Warren went on to draw various titles for DC Vertigo, including the recent series, *Deadenders*.

Ted Rall is a syndicated political cartoonist who appears in over 140 publications. His most recent books include *Attitude: The New Political Cartoonists*, a collection of alternative cartoonists, and *To Afghanistan and Back*, the first-ever instant graphic travelogue, chronicling Rall's experiences covering the war for the *Village Voice* and KFI Radio.

Spain Rodriguez was a founding member of the *Zap Comix* group, author of the classic *My True Story*, the politically charged *Trashman* and Last Gasp's collection of tales of sex and espionage, *She: Big Bitch Anthology*. His upcoming *Nightmare Alley*, an adaptation of William Lindsay Gresham's cult classic pulp novel, will appear in early 2003 from Fantagraphics Books. Spain resides in San Francisco.

Johnny Ryan is the creator of the uproariously funny *Angry Youth Comix*, nominated for an Ignatz Award in 2000. The fourth issue of *Angry Youth Comix* was released in October 2002 and his first book collection, *Portajohnny*, will appear in 2003 from Fantagraphics, as will a collection of his sketchbook work, *Shouldn't You Be Working?*

Joe Sacco is a Maltese citizen currently residing in Stockholm, where he makes his living as a cartoonist and journalist. In 1996 he received the American Book Award for *Palestine*. His *Safe Area Gorazde: The War In Eastern Bosnia 1992-1995*, based upon Sacco's travels to the war-torn region, has won widespread critical acclaim. His next release (in 2003, from Drawn and Quarterly) will be *The Fixer*, a sequel to *Soba*, featuring more stories from Bosnia.

Wilfred Santiago co-created *Pop Life* with frequent collaborator Ho Che Anderson. He has also co-written and drawn extensively for Eros Comix, including two graphic novels (*The Thorn Garden* and the recent release *Pink*) as well as the *Dirty Stories* series.

Gilbert Shelton is perhaps best known for *The Fabulous Furry Freak Brothers*, those hilarious hairy heroes of Haight-Ashbury and the Rip Off Press heydays. He still periodically releases new issues of *Not Quite Dead* (four to date) in collaboration with Pic.

Kenneth Smith is the author of *Phantasmagoria* and a regular contributor to *The Comics Journal*. He currently lives in Dallas, Texas.

Tom Spurgeon is a former editor of *The Comics Journal* and writer of the popular but short-lived *Wildwood* comic strip. He is the proud author of an upcoming book about breakfast culture in the USA.

Frank Stack has had a distinguished career as a Professor of Art at the University of Missouri, while continuing to work as a painter and printmaker. He has worked frequently with Harvey Pekar on his *American Splendor* series, most notably on Pekar and Joyce Brabner's *Our Cancer Year*. Other comics and books (occasionally published under the alias Foolbert Sturgeon) include *Dorman's Doggie*, *Amazons*, *Dr. Feelgood's Funnies* and *The Further Adventures of Jesus*.

Carol Swain was born London in 1962 and raised in rural Wales. Schooled there by mean Baptist hysterics, she sought a higher education, enrolling in art school for four long years. *Way Out Strips* was her first comic, and *Invasion of the Mind Sappers* her first graphic novel (both from Fantagraphics Books). A second, *Foodboy*, is due in 2003. She currently lives in London with her writer boyfriend and a whole heap of cats.

Marc Tessier is the co-author of The *Theatre of Cruelty* with Alexandre Lafleur (Fantagraphics Books, 1997) and is co-artistic director with Hélène Brosseau of the *Cyclops* comics anthologies (Zone Convective, 2002 and Conundrum Press, 2003). He is also an award winning photographer and book designer.

Carol Tyler lives in Cincinnati with her husband, the cartoonist Justin Green. Her work has appeared in the anthologies *Weirdo* and *Drawn & Quarterly*. Her first collection, *The Job Thing*, came out in 1993 from Fantagraphics Books. She is particularly proud of capturing the Grand Prize Best in Show in the 1996 California State Fair for "The Hannah Story." *C. Tyler's Ink Party*, a collection of her short black and white pieces, will appear from Fantagraphics in the spring of 2003.

Steven Weissman's charming and respectful portrayals of children have garnered him comparisons to Charles Schulz's *Peanuts* and Hal Roach's *Our Gang*. He is the proud author of *Champs* and *Don't Call Me Stupid*, and his most recent book, *White Flower Day*, an all-ages humor graphic novel, was released from Fantagraphics in 2002.

Carrie Whitney is an Art Director for Fantagraphics Books and The Comics Journal Special Editions. ★★★